Those Who Can, Teach

Fifteenth Edition

Those Who Can, Teach

Kevin Ryan
Boston University

James M. Cooper
University of Virginia

Cheryl Mason Bolick
University of North Carolina, Chapel Hill

Cory Callahan
University of Alabama

 Cengage

Australia • Brazil • Canada • Mexico • Singapore • United Kingdom • United States

Those Who Can, Teach, **Fifteenth Edition**
Kevin Ryan, James M. Cooper,
Cheryl Mason Bolick, and Cory Callahan

SVP, Higher Education & Skills Product: Erin Joyner

Product Director: Matt Seeley

Product Manager: Lauren Whalen

Product Assistant: Dallas Wilkes

Sr. Vendor Content Manager:
Charu Verma, MPS Limited

Sr. Digital Delivery Lead: Beth Ross

Director, Marketing: Neena Bali

Executive Marketing Manager: Mark Linton

IP Analyst: Ashley Maynard

IP Project Manager: Kelli Besse

Production Service: MPS Limited

Designer: Angela Sheehan

Cover Image Source: S292930121
Saowanee Jaroenratjaroon/Shutterstock.com;
1160305861 NooMUboN Photo/Shutterstock.com;
1279774151 iStock.com/ALENA DZIHILEVICH;
1089552638 iStock.com/Tinnakorn Jorruang;
666614312 iStock.com/alexkich

Interior image Source: karen roach/Shutterstock
.com; Picsfive/Shutterstock.com; Denis Ponkratov
/Shutterstock.com; Gunnar Pippel/Shutterstock
.com; Brian A Jackson/Shutterstock.com; Siede Preis
/Getty Images; Besim Bevrnja/Shutterstock.com

For product information and technology assistance, contact us at
**Cengage Customer & Sales Support, 1-800-354-9706
or support.cengage.com.**
For permission to use material from this text or product,
submit all requests online at **www.copyright.com.**

Library of Congress Control Number: 2020925720

ISBN: 978-0-357-51844-1

Cengage
200 Pier 4 Boulevard
Boston, MA 02210
USA

Cengage is a leading provider of customized learning solutions with employees residing in nearly 40 different countries and sales in more than 125 countries around the world. Find your local representative at **www.cengage.com.**

To learn more about Cengage platforms and services, register or access your online learning solution, or purchase materials for your course, visit **www.cengage.com.**.

Notice to the Reader

Publisher does not warrant or guarantee any of the products described herein or perform any independent analysis in connection with any of the product information contained herein. Publisher does not assume, and expressly disclaims, any obligation to obtain and include information other than that provided to it by the manufacturer. The reader is expressly warned to consider and adopt all safety precautions that might be indicated by the activities described herein and to avoid all potential hazards. By following the instructions contained herein, the reader willingly assumes all risks in connection with such instructions. The publisher makes no representations or warranties of any kind, including but not limited to, the warranties of fitness for particular purpose or merchantability, nor are any such representations implied with respect to the material set forth herein, and the publisher takes no responsibility with respect to such material. The publisher shall not be liable for any special, consequential, or exemplary damages resulting, in whole or part, from the readers' use of, or reliance upon, this material

Printed in the United Kingdom by Ashford Colour Press Ltd.
Print Number: 03   Print Year: 2022

Brief Contents

Contents

PART I: School and Students   1

PART II: Teachers   153

6 What Makes a Teacher Effective?   153

PART III: Foundations and the Future   269

9 What Are the Philosophical Foundations of American Education? 269

10 What Is the History of America's Struggle for Educational Opportunity? 300

11 How Are Schools Governed, Influenced, and Financed? 335

12 How Should Education Be Reformed? 359

15 What Does It Mean to Be a Professional?   446

Before we set out to write this text, we had taught in public schools and for many years taught aspiring teachers in their very first education course. Therefore, instructors teaching the introductory course in education were very much on our minds. As we saw it, instructors want to:

- **Help students examine their motives for teaching** so they can determine whether teaching is right for them.
- **Inspire these future teachers to form and sustain a commitment to teaching—** a commitment that is grounded in a realistic understanding of the teaching profession.
- **Offer instructional activities** that incorporate the way today's students learn, particularly with regard to their use of technology.
- **Prepare aspiring teachers to teach students whose cultural complexities—** such as race, socioeconomic status, and orientation to learning—may differ from their own.
- **Provide course experiences** that help prospective teachers bridge the "theory-to-practice" divide.
- **Make the history and philosophies of education relevant** to the lives and careers of future teachers.
- **Help prospective teachers develop the habits and skills of** reflective practitioners.
- **Prepare all students to do well on mandatory, high-stakes standardized tests** based on national, state, and local standards.
- **Provide honest information and context** for future teachers about the profession they are considering entering.

Another reality that we have kept in mind as we have revised this text is that today's college students are part of a fresh, new generation, which has grown up in this era of rapid technological and social change. For these students, **technology is a way of life**. They are both connected and insulated through technology, and are accustomed to processing information differently than the generations before them:

- They are **team oriented** due to the significant time spent on social networking sites and on instant messaging platforms.
- Many of today's students are **unaccustomed to academic difficulty**. Rather, they are used to rewards and accolades, and have high expectations for achievement and little tolerance for failure.
- The lives of today's students **are often quite programmed**. They suffer more stress and often feel more overwhelmed compared to those in past generations.

How Does *Those Who Can, Teach* Meet the Needs of Today's Learners?

How have we addressed the challenges of teaching today's students while meeting the goals of an introduction to education course in this 15th edition of *Those Who Can, Teach?*

We know that students who will use this text are facing many challenges. Many are at the beginning of their college experience and are still getting accustomed to their independence. There are almost certainly many activities—other courses, social events, and jobs, to name a few—competing for their time and attention. They, like all of us, struggle to balance all that is on their plate. Still, we believe that exploring what might be their life's work requires that they fully engage in the course and with the questions posed in this text. To help them do this, we have used a number of instructional tools, described as follows, to gain and keep the readers' attention and to inspire them to carefully consider all aspects of becoming one of Those Who *Can:*

- **Examining motives for teaching.** We begin and end the book with chapters that focus on examining "Why Teach?" Two or three times in each chapter, students are asked to **"Pause and Reflect"** on questions of self-examination and understanding. We have made a major commitment to help your future teachers become *reflective practitioners.* Thus, at the end of each chapter, we provide readers opportunities to consider and reflect in the sections entitled, **"Why Teach? Your Final Word."** In addition, two "bookend" sections, **"Let's Get Started"** and **"Before You Close This Book,"** offer important reflection questions before and after students read the text. **"Let's Get Started,"** in particular, was written to make clear to student-readers what we hope they get out of *Those Who Can, Teach,* and what we believe is the most productive way to engage the book.

- **Developing a realistic understanding of teaching.** A frequent complaint of beginning teachers is "that no one ever told us what it would *really* be like in the classroom." Although these complaints are sometimes unfair (people tried to tell them but they may not have been ready to listen), we have tried to capture the real world of schooling. Throughout the book, we have presented many case studies both within the text and in the **"Preservice to Practice"** boxes that portray the realities (both the good and bad) of teaching. The **"Voices from the Classroom"** feature is a reflection or comment on one of each chapter's key topics from actual classroom teachers. The classroom voices bring a fresh and realistic perspective to these topics and issues. The **"TeachSource Videos"** feature footage from in and out of the classroom to help students relate key chapter content to real-life scenarios. Critical-thinking questions, artifacts, and bonus videos help students reflect on the content in the video.

- **Learning through technology.** Because today's students learn so much through technology, we have integrated technology throughout the book. One whole chapter, "What Should Teachers Know about Technology and Its Impact on Teaching and Learning?" addresses the many uses of technology to increase and enhance learning for all students, including those with disabilities. The **"TeachSource Videos,"** mentioned previously, also provide multimedia ways of observing and studying teaching, and at the end of each chapter, there are three or four **websites** for students to explore in greater depth the topics and issues discussed in the chapter.

- **Understanding cultural complexities.** Women and whites predominate in both teacher education programs and in the teaching force, whereas over 50 percent of students in public schools are students of color. Many education students have had few interactions with students who differ from them in terms of race, ethnicity, and socioeconomic status. The chapter "Who Are Today's Students in a Diverse Society?" describes various diversities and implications for teachers. Throughout the book, we provide multiple examples of the diversities that teachers will encounter, and discuss implications for teachers and schools.

- **Bridging the "theory-to-practice" divide.** The book assists students to bridge this gap by providing realistic **case studies, "TeachSource Videos," Reflection Questions, "Voices from the Classroom" features, "Up Close" boxes,** and many **"Pause and Reflect"** questions throughout the book.

- **Bringing history and philosophy alive to students.** We try to enliven the history of American education through a lively writing style and by focusing on the people who have made or are making educational history. Our **"Leaders in Education"** feature presents biographical sketches of both historical (e.g., Horace Mann, John Dewey, and Anne Sullivan), as well as contemporary educational leaders (e.g., Robert Moses, Erin Gruwell, and Ron Berger). In discussing educational philosophies, we have developed statements by teachers who embrace each philosophy, so readers can see how those individual philosophies guide teachers' actions and behavior in classrooms. Chapter 9 includes **"Your Philosophy of Education Self-Inventory"** to help students bring their educational views to greater consciousness.

- **Reflective practice.** Throughout the book, we ask readers to stop and think: to reflect. We are convinced that our readers, like ourselves, live in a noisy world of words and pictures that is continually demanding and competing for our attention. We have tried to make a case for reflection but have also built into the text requests that readers stop and reflect what particular content means personally. Using a variety of devices throughout the book, such as cartoons and boxed inserts on research findings, we are unabashedly committed to helping students start on the road to become reflective practitioners. One such effort is our special feature, **"Truth or Fiction?"** which appears at the beginning each chapter. To quickly engage the readers in the chapter's subject, we present them with three or more statements having to do with the subject of the chapter and ask them to make a judgment as to whether each statement is true or false. Later in the chapter, they will encounter the subject of each statement (marked in yellow) and discover whether the statement was "truth" or "fiction."

- **Informal writing style.** Although there are many changes in this 15th edition, key qualities have been retained. Chief among them is the book's informal writing style. We have tried to communicate the seriousness surrounding professional topics and at the same time reflect the humor and humanity that is part of a teacher's professional life. We are helped in this "experiential" aspect of our book by the presence in the text of the actual words of practicing classroom teachers. We believe (and hope) that this writing style and heavy use of narrative give the text a greater sense of reality.

- **Standards testing for teachers.** Recognizing that virtually all prospective teachers must meet state and national standards to be licensed, *Those Who Can, Teach* tries to make the connection between standards and content crystal clear by including a correlation chart in the inside of the front and back covers of the book. The 10 core principles of InTASC are correlated to the chapters and pages in our 15th edition (see inside cover), and at the beginning of each chapter we identify the principles addressed in that chapter.

- **Educational currency.** The field of education is in a particularly dynamic state. The federal government has initiated the Every Student Succeeds Act (ESSA). Most of the states have embraced the idea and reality of Common Core State Standards. At the same time, state and local educational authorities are deeply involved in a variety of educational reform efforts. The policies of key players such as teachers' unions, as well as foundations such as the Gates Foundation, are changing. New groups and organizations are influencing the lives of teachers. All this and the ever-increasing research base in education need to be brought to the attention of those considering becoming teachers.

New and Improved for the 15th Edition

We have reviewed past editions of *Those Who Can, Teach*, and received some excellent suggestions from the teacher educators using the text with future teachers. As a result we have made a number of overall changes in this 15th edition. Among the major ones are the following:

1. **Learning Objectives:** The learning objectives correlated to the main sections in each chapter show students what they need to know to process and understand the information in the chapter. After completing the chapter, students should be able to demonstrate how they can use and apply their new knowledge and skills.

2. **Standards:** New and improved coverage of InTASC standards includes a chapter-opening list to help students identify where key standards are addressed in the chapter. These callouts and the standards correlation chart help students make connections between what they are learning in the textbook and the standards.

3. **Digital Downloads:** Downloadable and often customizable, these practical and professional resources allow students to immediately implement and apply this textbook's content in the field. The students download these tools and keep them forever, enabling preservice teachers to begin to build their library of practical, professional resources. Look for the TeachSource Digital Downloads label that identifies these items.

4. The **TeachSource videos** feature footage from the classroom to help students relate key chapter content to real-life scenarios. Critical-thinking questions provide opportunities for in-class or online discussion and reflection.

CHAPTER-BY-CHAPTER REVISIONS AND UPDATES

- Chapter 1 contains new survey findings from the Center for Educational Policy on the question of why teachers chose their profession and fresh research on what teachers find most satisfying about working with students. The section on vicarious ways readers can learn about teaching from the experiences of others has been greatly revised.

- Chapter 2's major section on the four basic purposes of school has been revised, especially Thomas Jefferson's views on the political and civic purpose, and the recasting of the social purposes drawing on the work of educational theorist Linda Darling Hammond. Also added is the new, tongue-in-cheek view that posits that the key value of schooling is for social "signaling." In addition, the chapter addresses educators' concern that school cultures are changing as a result of social media and how schools are responding.

- Chapter 3 contains new information that reflects the growing diversity of our nation. In particular, sections focused on immigration, religious diversity, and LGBTQ students and teachers have been included. The chapter includes a new "Voices from the Classroom."

- Chapter 4 has been revised to include updated data and statistics. Discussions centered on critical contemporary issues such as mental health, gun violence, and student activism have been added to the chapter, as well as a new "Voices from the Classroom."

- Chapter 5 contains updated information on the Common Core State Standards, as well as the newest development and trends in each subject matter area. The newest results of NAEP, TIMSS, and PISA assessments are also discussed, as well as implications for student learning as a result of the COVID-19 pandemic school shutdowns in spring 2020. Several popular instructional approaches are also covered.

- In Chapter 6, a model for effective teaching is discussed, including a new section on what research tells us about principles of effective instruction. Classroom management, questioning, and planning skills are reviewed.

- Chapter 7 includes new information about technology's impact in schools, degrees of its application in classrooms, and how schools tend to respond to concerns associated with technology (i.e., privacy, cyberbullying). It also includes many new specific examples of technological tasks and tools for classroom use and all new print resources.

- Chapter 8 has new material on the increase in teacher liability and legal vulnerability. A new feature is a list if eight practical steps to "keep teachers in their classrooms and out of the courtrooms." Specific attention is given to the need for teachers to document any and all activities what could possibly have legal consequences.

- Chapter 9's content, the major philosophical perspectives underlying American schools, is somewhat timeless. However, since the material is demanding, efforts have been made to clarify difficult concepts and their application to life in classrooms. In addition, new information on changes in policy in E. D. Hirsch Jr.'s Core Curriculum program making materials more available to teachers is reported.

- Chapter 10, the history of American education chapter, contains updated information on the education of African American, Hispanic American, Native American, and Asian American students.

- In Chapter 11, the profile of American administrators and school board members has been updated, along with local, state, and federal school spending data.

- Chapter 12 contains a thorough description of the Every Student Succeeds Act, the most recent national education reform initiative. The authors share key provisions in the legislation and discuss the various levels of responsibility from the federal, state, and local levels. It also includes updated information regarding forms of school choice, evaluation, and character in the curriculum.

- Chapter 13 contains updated information on the job markets in education, updated teacher salary data both nationally and by state, information on teaching in private schools, and suggestions on how to land a teaching job.

- Chapter 14 provides updated information regarding expectations novice teachers can have for entering the classroom as the instructional leader. There are also additional data about the trend for schools to provide induction and mentor programs to support new teachers. The authors also share new online and print resources.

- Chapter 15 contains updated information regarding the levels of professionalism that often characterize teachers. The chapter also contains new information about professional associations and professional development. The authors also share new resources for further exploration.

Accompanying Teaching and Learning Resources

The 15th edition of *Those Who Can, Teach* is accompanied by an extensive package of instructor and student resources.

POWERPOINT® LECTURE SLIDES

These vibrant Microsoft® PowerPoint lecture slides for each chapter assist you with your lecture by providing concept coverage using images, figures, and tables directly from the textbook!

ONLINE INSTRUCTOR'S MANUAL

An online Instructor's Manual accompanies this book. It contains information to assist instructors in designing the course, including sample syllabi, discussion questions, teaching and learning activities, field experiences, learning objectives, and additional online resources. Additional online resources and assessments include:

- TeachSource videos of teachers teaching and children learning in real classrooms, accompanied by case study questions to assess students' understanding of the video concepts.
- Case scenarios requiring students to analyze typical teaching and learning situations and create a reasoned response to the issue(s) presented in the scenario, reflecting about and justifying the choices they made within the teaching scenario problem.
- TeachSource Digital Download resources

COGNERO

Cengage Learning Testing Powered by Cognero is a flexible online system that allows you to author, edit, and manage test bank content from multiple Cengage Learning solutions; create multiple test versions in an instant; and deliver tests from your LMS, your classroom, or wherever you want. The updated test bank includes true/false, multiple-choice, matching, short-answer, and essay questions for each chapter.

Acknowledgments

Whenever any of us puts pen to paper or fingers to the keyboard, we stand on the shoulders of others. This is certainly true of this book. We are indebted to many people. In writing this book, we are especially appreciative of the help given by the following individuals, most notably, Matt Durant, for his revision of the chapter entitled "What Should Teachers Know about Technology and Its Impact on Teaching and Learning?" Special thanks go to our colleagues and students for their many good ideas and continuing support, in particular, the teacher contributors to the "Voices from the Classroom" feature. An advisory board of reviewers also made key contributions to the organization and content of this and the previous edition, most notably:

Elyse Adler, Liberty University

Jing Babb, Los Angeles Trade Technical College

Douglas Carothers, Florida Gulf Coast University

Erin Counihan, Washington College

Kathy Finkle, Black Hills State University

Kathleen Fite, Texas State University—San Marcos

Renee Funke, Jamestown Community College

Pam Green, Southwestern College

Sherry Green, Georgia Highlands College

Rhonda Gregory, Greenville College

Keicia Hawkins, Northwestern State University

Monique Henderson, Lone Star College, Montgomery

Kerbe Lee, Martin Methodist College

Frances Lowden, Medgar Evers College

Dianne Mark, Coastal Carolina University

Chelsea Martinez, Highland Community College, Freeport

Marsha Moody, Fort Hays State University

Lois Paretti, University of Nevada, Las Vegas

Kimberly Paul, Southeast Community College

Terrie Poehl, Northwestern State University

Karen Porfiri, Bakersfield College

Jessica Purvis, State University of New York at Buffalo

Carol Ramsay, Lake Erie College

Michelle Reiff, Walla Walla Community College

David Sloan, Brandman University

Melissa Szymczak, Joliet Junior College

Rita Verma, Adelphi University

Betsy Werre, Pensacola State College

Eleanor Wilson, University of Virginia

Joanne Yantz, Colorado Mountain College

A special acknowledgment is due to Marilyn Ryan for the substantial intellectual and psychological contributions she made to the several editions of this book. Writing and revising a textbook is a multifaceted process, particularly today with the addition of ancillary supports such as video cases and our website. Many people provide advice—some solicited and some not. We believe, however, that our best source of advice on this book has been the team we've worked with at Cengage Learning. We are appreciative of the support and leadership from our senior product manager, Jenny Zigler. She offered perspective and guidance from the inception of this work. Her enthusiastic commitment was significant in every aspect of this project. Our product manager, Lauren Whalen, has been a staunch advocate and supporter throughout the revision of this edition. We are grateful for her vision and encouragement surrounding all aspects of this project. Charu Verma, senior vendor content manager has meticulously managed the copyediting process and all of the final stages of production. Her attention to detail was essential in the final stages of the revision process. Finally, we acknowledge the thousands of students for whom this book is written. Your new learning as you become teachers is central to our work as authors.

Kevin Ryan
James M. Cooper
Cheryl Mason Bolick
Cory Callahan

So Let's Get Started . . .

And get to what this book is all about: students and teachers, schools and subject matter, ideas about learning, and the fascinating challenges of education today. If you take a look at the chapter titles, you can see that we have built the book around questions—questions you should try to answer if you are thinking about becoming a teacher. Questions such as, "What makes a teacher effective?" and "How should our schools be reformed?" The *most important question*, however, is the first chapter's question, "Why teach?" This question—and its potential answers—is the focus not only of the initial chapter, but it captures the purpose of the entire book.

One of life's most important questions is this: "What am I going to do with my life?" How you spend most of your time and energy—what *work* you decide to do—will determine, more than anything else, how content you are in life. Ideally, a career decision should be based on the best information available about the chosen field and on a deep understanding of *exactly who you are.*

Knowing Your Own Motives

Centuries ago, Francis Bacon told us, "Knowledge is power." Much earlier, Socrates (one of civilization's great teachers, whom we discuss in the chapter entitled "What Are the Philosophical Foundations of American Education?") recognized the enormous power of self-knowledge when he urged his students to "know thyself." Understanding yourself and your motives, especially in something as important as a career choice, is crucial to good decision making. Becoming a teacher without taking the time to carefully consider whether you're truly meant to teach, or without examining *the reasons you want to teach*, can lead to disappointment. For instance, let's say your fifth-grade teacher had an enormous influence on you. She took the time to get to know you, taught you new and interesting subjects, had loads of patience, and was just plain fun. In fact, you have considered becoming a teacher since fifth grade. You get to college and declare yourself an education major, without ever analyzing precisely why you want to teach or whether you have the ability, skills, attitudes, or drive to become a teacher.

Equally as important as knowing *who you are* is clarifying your motives for teaching. Why is knowing *why* you want to teach so important? Because understanding the reasons you want to teach will help you determine whether teaching is right for you. It will also help you uncover and plan for the unique challenges you may face as a teacher. Let's say your desire to teach stems from a passion for a particular subject. Someone whose desire to teach grows out of a passion for history, for example, will have to prepare for the reality that not all of his students will share that passion. How will such a teacher motivate students who would rather be learning math? Or playing basketball?

We have written this book to help you to uncover whether you have what it takes to become a successful, fulfilled teacher and to help you uncover the reasons you are considering teaching as a profession. We hope that you will use this book to gain a greater understanding of how you and a career in education might fit together.

The Habit of Reflection

As you will see throughout this book, we believe that effective teachers, indeed effective people in many areas of life, succeed in part because they are mindful of what they are doing. Always looking for ways to improve, they reflect on their performance and on what they are engaged in. Having acquired the habit of reflection, these people are called *reflective practitioners*. This is a fancy way of describing a person who is habitually thoughtful about what he or she does in life.

Everyone has experiences. We meet new people. Someone sends us a fascinating Web link. We encounter a truly wise person or a destitute, homeless person on the street. We have an unexpected and deeply personal conversation with a roommate. We all have special experiences. Truly effective people, however, *use* their experiences to understand their past and to chart their future. This very crucial practice of *reflection* is a habit you can start developing even now, as part of your career choice process. The way you use this book can help you on the path to be a reflective person. We think that recording what you think today, revisiting your thoughts throughout the term, and then noting what you think at the end of your course work will help solidify any choice you make about teaching.

Everyone can develop the habit of reflection. Begin right now by answering four questions. Take time to write your answers to these questions. By doing so, you will take your first steps to becoming a reflective practitioner, which, in turn, will help you in your life and in your career, whatever that may be.

Your Motives

The following questions will help you get in touch with your true motives for considering teaching as a career path and your personal thoughts about teaching. In this exercise, we ask you to think about four main questions:

Why do you want to become a teacher?

Which teachers have you admired most, and what made them so admirable?

What strengths or qualities do you have that will make you a successful teacher?

What concerns do you have about either becoming a teacher or about the teaching field itself?

First, list all of the reasons to become a teacher, and all of the reasons to choose another profession (or why *not* to become a teacher). Be sure to list not only the altruistic reasons you may want to teach—to help others or to inspire children, for example—but also the more selfish motives you may have, such as having the summers off to travel or finishing work at 3:00 in the afternoon. Do the same for choosing another profession in the second column. For this exercise to be valuable, you need to paint a full, complete picture of how you feel and what you think about teaching as well as possible other professions you may consider. As teacher Elida Laski asks in the "Voices from the Classroom" feature in Chapter 1, "Do you have to be born with that certain something in order to be a good teacher? If you are born with *it,* do you always know that teaching is the profession for you?"

(1) Why do you want to become a teacher?

Motives for becoming a teacher	*Motives for choosing another profession*
_____	_____
_____	_____
_____	_____
_____	_____
_____	_____
_____	_____
_____	_____

Now, think about some of the people—your teachers—who may have inspired you to consider teaching as a profession.

(2) Who are three teachers you had in your elementary and secondary education whom you admire most? What made them so admirable?

a. _____

_____

_____

_____

b. _____

_____

_____

_____

c. _____

_____

_____

_____

Next, take an initial look at yourself.

(3) What are your strengths? List at least five qualities you have that will make you a successful teacher.

a. _____

b. _____

c. _____

d. _____

e. _____

Lastly, think about what concerns you have. Do you see any blocks or barriers that might keep you from being a successful teacher?

(4) What concerns do you have about either becoming a teacher or the teaching field itself? List three questions about teaching and education that you want to know more about by reading this book.

a. _____

b. _____

c. _____

If you did not stop reading to think about your motives for becoming a teacher or if you failed to commit yourself in writing, please stop now and think about what kept you from seriously engaging one or more of the questions. Your answer may tell you a good deal about yourself as a learner, about the educational system of which you are a product, and possibly about how you will behave as a teacher. Have you been trained to devour pages and pages of textbook reading without really confronting the issues conveyed by the words? Have you learned to disregard your own views, even about issues quite central to you, such as how you are going to spend the bulk of your life? If your answers to these questions are *yes,* you are like many, many other students. But take heart. With practice, everyone can develop the habit of reflection.

We sincerely hope that this will be a different kind of book and a different kind of reading-questioning-thinking experience for you. Precisely because we are teachers, we want this book to have a very special impact on you. We want to help you make good decisions about whether you want to be a teacher and about what kind of teacher you want to become. For these reasons, you need to read this book in a different way. Take the book on fully. Encounter it. Fight with it! Improve it by adding yourself to it. The truism you probably heard from your parents, "You get out of things what you put into them," truly applies here.

Our hope is that by the end of the course, when you have finished reading this text, you will have acquired the habit of reflection and have developed a greater understanding of what it means to teach, of what teachers do, of how schools operate within their communities and society, and of several other issues you will need to consider as you think through the question, "Why teach?"

1

Why Teach?

Ariel Skelley/Getty Images

LEARNING OBJECTIVES

1-1 List your motives for becoming a teacher.

1-2 Explain the rewards that come with a career in teaching.

1-3 Describe several sources that expand your understanding of teaching.

1-4 Assess two case studies of teacher motivations.

1-5 Recount the views of others about teachers and teaching.

1-6 State the major reasons why teachers teach and the primary sources of satisfaction.

Truth OR Fiction?

T F American teens claim teachers contribute most to our society's well-being.

T F The majority of school superintendents and principals claim that the quality of new teachers entering the field has declined.

T F Of all the characteristics that contribute to teachers' satisfaction, new teachers rate highest "involves work you love to do."

People take education courses for many reasons, but three are particularly common: First, as citizens, people need to know how a major institution like the school system works so that they can make informed choices within their communities and at the voting booth. Second, as parents or potential parents, they need to know a great deal to be intelligent partners with the schools in their children's education. Third, those who consider a career in teaching need to understand the profession they may be entering.

This text is written with this third group in mind. And this chapter, more than any other, focuses on those people who are exploring the teaching profession. Its purpose is to help you answer a fundamental question: Why should you become a teacher? As you read about the following teachers, we hope you come to understand more fully your own motivations for teaching.

1-1 Examining Your Motives for Teaching

If you teach, it is quite likely that by the end of your second year of teaching, you will have had the following experiences:

1. Someone at a party or other social gathering will ask you what you do and how you like teaching. Soon the person will tell you that he or she has always wanted to be a teacher and regrets having become a stockbroker/bookkeeper/sales representative/flight attendant/disk jockey, and that he or she may still give it all up and become a teacher.

2. You will get to know an experienced teacher who confides that he or she deeply regrets having become a teacher. While in college, the person felt cut out for teaching and actually enjoyed it initially. But gradually, he or she became fed up with the whole thing—bratty kids, pushy administrators, the same old faces in the teachers' lounge, the instant expert parents, and the overemphasis on standards and high-stakes testing. Now the person feels trapped in teaching and sees no way out.

The purpose of this chapter is to keep you from becoming "the other person" in either of these situations. It is intended to help you make a well-thought-out decision about what to do with your life, particularly if you are still undecided about becoming a teacher.

1-1a COMPARING YOUR MOTIVES TO OTHERS

At this point, you have likely answered the question "What are my motives for wanting to become a teacher?" (and we surely hope you have). Here are a few motives you might check against your own list:

- I really like the idea of having a positive influence on 25 (or 150) kids every day.
- I can't think of anything else to do with my major.
- Teaching seems to be a fairly secure, low-risk occupation with many attractive benefits, including lots of vacation time and time to raise a family.
- I always loved history (or mathematics or science or literature), and teaching seems to be a career that will allow me to work with a subject matter that I love.
- I can't imagine anything more important to do with my life than helping children with disabilities learn to cope with, and even overcome, their barriers.

- The instruction I had in school was incredibly bad, and I want to correct that situation.
- My parents would really be pleased and proud if I were a teacher.
- Quite simply, I love children and love being around them.
- I enjoy being in charge and being a positive influence on students.
- I really don't know what else I could do. I know about teaching, and I think I could do it.
- I'm concerned that society is falling apart, and I want to look out for the kids.
- Education seems as if it's going to be the action field of the future, and I want to be part of it.
- One of my students might become a famous painter, or the president of a major foundation, or who knows what. It would be great to have a strong impact on just one significant life.
- I really want to become a principal/coach/guidance counselor/college professor/ educational researcher, and teaching seems to be the way to start.
- I have strong religious beliefs and see teaching as a good and useful way to live my life goals.
- Businesses are increasingly interested in training and educating their employees, and I want a career as a private-sector educator working in corporate America.
- I come from a family of teachers and teaching just seems to be the natural thing to do.
- I want to have fun in life, and as a teacher, I'll have fun and get paid for it!
- America's students of color often start out life with barriers and severe disadvantages. As a teacher I can do something about that.
- I have always felt I have a calling—a vocation—to be a teacher.[1]

You may be interested to see others' answers to the question "Why teach?" The data in Table 1.1 come from a recent study conducted by The Center on Education Policy. Notice how over two-thirds of respondents cite "to make a difference in students' lives" as a prime motivation. As we'll see, the rewards often match the desires of those who teach.

Pause *and* Reflect

1. Which three of the motives come closest to your thoughts about a career in teaching?
2. Thinking about these three motives, what does this tell you about yourself?

TABLE 1.1 Most Significant Reasons Why Teachers Joined the Profession

To make a difference in students' lives	68%
To help students reach their full potential	45%
A teacher inspired me when I was young	37%
To be a part of those "aha" moments when things just click for a student	32%
To share my enthusiasm for the subject I teach	31%
To make a difference in the larger community	24%
For the earning potential	1%

Source: Adapted from Figure 1-A (page 14) of *Listen to Us: Teacher Views and Voices*, a 2016 national survey from The Center on Education Policy (https://files.eric.ed.gov/fulltext/ED568172.pdf).
Note: Teachers could select three responses.

1-2 The Rewards of Teaching

As we have seen, responses to the question "Why teach?" run the gamut from "to help students reach their full potential" to I want "to make a difference in the larger community." Our individual motivations can change and may be quite different at different times and when we are in different moods. As social psychologist Peter Drucker quipped, "We know nothing about motivation. All we can do is write books about it."

> At twenty-two, I graduated Phi Beta Kappa. I had choices at my fingertips: law school, grad school . . . corporate America, here I come! Adults swelled their chests in pride. My peers practiced the "on my way to a Lexus" shuffle. Then the question: "And what are your plans after graduation?" Answer: "I'm moving to New York to teach elementary school in the South Bronx." As a twenty-three-year-old teacher with sore feet and twenty-eight incredible kids, my explanation reminds me of a song. I had a choice to sit it out or dance. I chose to dance.
>
> **—THALIA THEODORE,**
> *Washington Post* (December 2, 2001), p. F1

At the same time, the motivational *factors*—those qualities that reside within teaching—are clearer and relatively constant. Researchers have identified a set of occupational rewards that can help us sort out both the attractive and unattractive qualities of a teaching career.[2] These rewards are classified into two broad categories: extrinsic and intrinsic. **Extrinsic rewards** are the public, external attractions of an occupation, such as money, prestige, and power. The **intrinsic rewards** of an occupation are the internal psychic or spiritual satisfaction one receives from one's work, such as a personal sense of accomplishment or an enjoyment of the work itself. It will come as no surprise that, comparatively speaking, teaching is somewhat out of balance, receiving generally high marks on one set of rewards and low marks on the other.

1-2a EXTRINSIC REWARDS

Teaching has rarely been cited for its abundance of extrinsic rewards. Although it offers more extrinsic rewards than many other occupations, such as law enforcement and coal mining, when compared with other professions, teaching ranks low in extrinsic compensations.

Salaries and Benefits

Teachers' salaries and benefits, as you will see in Chapter 13, "What Are Your Job Options in Education?," is a complex and fluid issue. Relative to salaries in occupational fields with similar educational requirements (e.g., a college degree and specialized training), teachers' salaries do not compare favorably. On the other hand, teachers have benefits, such as health plans and retirement plans and job security that is lacking in those other fields.[3] Also, there is a growing specialization within teaching that is reflected in pay checks.

Further, the issue is clouded by the fact teachers' salaries vary significantly from one geographical location to the next, as you will also see in Chapter 13. Finally, the importance of salary, like the whole issue of monetary needs, varies enormously from one person to the next.

Status

Status refers to one's position in a group, that is, where one stands in relation to others. The status of a doctor or a beggar is rather clear, but the status of a teacher is more difficult to gauge. To young parents entrusting their child to school for the first time, the status of the teacher is quite high. To the same parents 12 or 15 years later, on hearing that their child wants to become a teacher, the status may be somewhat diminished . . . or not! The United States' current commitment to massively reform its educational system is, however, having a positive effect on the status of teaching.

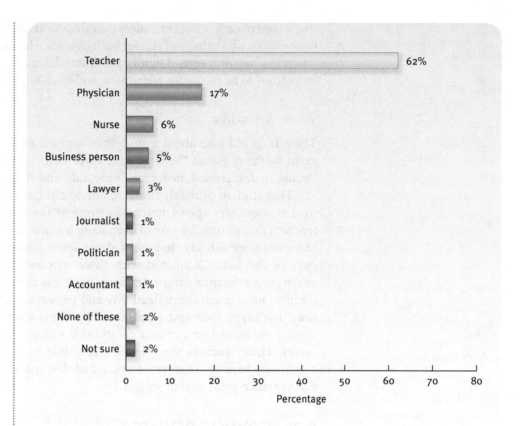

FIGURE 1.1 **Profession That Provides the Most Benefit to Society**

Source: David Haselkorn and Louis Harris, "The Essential Profession: A National Survey of Public Attitudes toward Teaching, Educational Opportunity, and School Reform." Reprinted with permission of Recruiting New Teachers, Inc., 1998.

Figure 1.1 shows the results of a turn-of-the-century public opinion survey that asked which of eight professions (including physician, lawyer, nurse, and journalist) "provides the most important benefit to society." Respondents put teaching first by close to a four-to-one margin over physicians (62% vs. 17%). This was a big improvement over a poll taken a decade earlier, in which only 35 percent of respondents put teaching first.[4] In more recent research looking at the public's attitude toward teachers, 71 percent reported that they had trust and confidence in the men and women who are teaching children in the public schools.

Power

Power is not usually seen as a reward of teaching, but it nevertheless is a quality that "resides in the office." Anyone who claims that teachers do not have power has forgotten what it was like to go to school without having done the homework and to sit in fear of being called on by Mrs. Gotcha. The power of the teacher is not a dollars-and-cents power, like that of a corporate chief executive officer, but any person who can make another's day or ruin another's year has power. Although, as sociologist Dan Lortie once observed, "Teachers are not supposed to *enjoy* exercising power per se,"[5] the public opinion survey discussed earlier clearly indicates that the public sees the quality of teachers as the greatest influence on student learning.[6]

A recent study by Harvard economists, coined by the press as "The $320,000 Kindergarten Teacher," should significantly boost the power and prestige of teachers. The study focused on the impact of early education on the lifetime earnings of people who attended and did not attend kindergarten. The cumulative financial impact on a single class of early school attendees over their working lives was a staggering $320,000! Compared with students of similar backgrounds who did not attend, the kindergarten "attendees" not only earned significantly more, but also were more likely to go to college, more likely to be saving for retirement, and less likely to become single parents.[7]

Work Schedule

There is an old joke about a student in an education course being stumped on an exam by the question "What are the three best things about a career in teaching?" Finally, in desperation, he writes, "June, July, and August."

That student probably flunked, but he did have a point. Compared with other workers, teachers spend much less time at their work sites. If we ignore what teachers do at home by way of preparing lessons, correcting papers, and checking homework, we can say they work six or seven hours a day for fewer than half the days of the year. Compared with those in power-and-status occupations, such as corporate finance or law, teachers have less demanding work schedules. Also, teachers have much more flexibility and personal control over how they use their time. For many men and women, family life is a top priority, and the time spent close to home and on summer vacations is a major plus associated with a teaching career. These teachers see sharing a schedule with their children or friends as a significant benefit. Teachers' work schedules, therefore, are one extrinsic reward that carries a great deal of weight.

1-2b INTRINSIC REWARDS

Extrinsic rewards, like company stock options or year-end bonuses, are tangible. Intrinsic rewards are, by their very nature, "in the eye of the beholder." What might be one person's intrinsic reward, such as taking a busload of students on an overnight field trip to the state capital, is another's living nightmare. However, the most satisfied teachers are usually those attracted to such intrinsic rewards.

Students

The attraction of working with students has long been one of the strongest rewards perceived by teachers. The daily contacts, the conversations and exchanges, and even the struggles to motivate students are a deep source of satisfaction for many teachers. Seeing children learn, grow, and develop—seeing them able to do things in May that they were unable to do at the beginning of the school year—is a genuinely fulfilling experience. Being important to others satisfies profound human needs, and teachers know about and appreciate this potential to affect the lives of others. And this does not go unnoticed. Nearly three out of five (58% of) teenagers surveyed mentioned teachers when asked by researchers who or what had influenced them to become the kinds of people they are.[8]

This reward is particularly meaningful to elementary school teachers, who spend so much time with the same group of 15 to 30 children. Secondary school teachers, who focus on a particular subject matter and may see as many as 150 students in a day, identify working with students as an important attraction, but not always to the same degree as their elementary school counterparts. On the other hand, middle and high school teachers are often heavily involved with their schools' clubs, intermural activities, and sports programs. As such they have deeply satisfying out-of-class experiences with maturing students.

> *To hear lessons and control restless children six hours a day through thirty-six weeks in a year is wretched drudgery, but to train and develop human minds and characters is the most inspiring work in the world.*
>
> —ELLEN HYDE,
> to the graduating class of the Framington Normal School, 1886

Performance of a Significant Social Service

In the award-winning film about early Renaissance England, *A Man for All Seasons,* Sir Thomas More says to Richard Rich, the man who eventually betrayed him but who at the time was seeking a cushy job at court, "Why not be a teacher, Rich? You'd be a fine teacher. Perhaps a great one." Disappointed, Rich replies, "And if I were, who would know it?" Thomas More then says, "You . . . your pupils . . . your friends . . . God—not a bad public, that."[9]

To many teachers, their greatest satisfaction is the sense that they are doing important work for the common good. This realization buoys them up and helps them tolerate the less attractive aspects of teaching. As we saw in Figure 1.1, the general public seems to agree that teaching provides valuable benefits for society. Whereas workers in government and business are aware in an abstract sense that they are contributing to the social good, teachers have daily flesh-and-blood testaments to the importance of their service right before them. Many college professors report that they see more college students not only seriously considering teaching as a career but also selecting teaching specifically because they see it as service to the nation and a way to pay back the country. For some students, the deeper motive behind this service for others is a religious one; that is, they see teaching as a way to serve God by serving the young.

Stimulation and Support from Fellow Teachers

When describing the work of teaching, researchers used to report on the sense of isolation many teachers reported they were experiencing.[10] As will be discussed in Chapter 15, "What Does It Mean to Be a Professional?," this is changing as more and more teachers are working in groups and sharing in-school leadership roles. This trend aside, for many teachers, their contacts and interactions with colleagues are an important intrinsic reward. Teachers enjoy the shoptalk and camaraderie that are a natural part of school life. Because teachers are not always rewarded for their individual job performance or for their individual expertise, feelings of competition are less prevalent than among such occupational groups as salespeople or lawyers who must compete for customers and grow their clientele. Teachers know they are part of a highly and increasingly cooperative venture. (The Video Case, *Teaching as a Profession: Collaboration with Colleagues,* provides a more in-depth look at how teachers can work together.)

The Work of Teaching

For many teachers, the process of teaching is a significant reward in itself. Whether they are explaining an idea, working with small groups, or designing instructional units, the actual work itself is highly gratifying. Like a pianist moving through a favorite sonata or a lawyer cross-examining a witness, teachers often draw their deepest satisfactions from the act of applying their craft. One teacher describes this feeling in this chapter's "Voices from the Classroom" feature. Of course, teachers vary in which activities they find rewarding. Some draw their rewards from establishing a nurturing, cooperative environment;

▶❚❚ TeachSource Video Case

© 2016 Cengage Learning®

Teaching as a Profession: Collaboration with Colleagues

Watch the video clips, study the artifacts in the case, and reflect on the following questions:

1. Were you aware that the collaborative process shown in this case goes on among teachers? In your own education, have you seen evidence of this collaborative planning process?

2. Does the planning process these teachers engaged in look like something you would enjoy as part of your career?

There is real joy when a student "gets it!"

Pause *and* Reflect

1. Which of the extrinsic rewards discussed in this section apply to you most? Which of the intrinsic rewards? Are there other rewards not mentioned here?
2. As you probe your own motives for considering teaching, what have you learned about yourself?

some from unraveling complicated problems for students; and some from seeing students work and learn independently. For many teachers, all else pales before their deep sense of fulfillment in simply doing the work of teaching.

As you continue reading and doing the work of this course, we urge you to keep in mind the issues of intrinsic and extrinsic rewards, personal satisfactions, and the "fit" between you and the work of a teacher. Begin now with some quiet reflection.

VOICES from the Classroom

Are You Born with It?

Elida Laski taught kindergarten for three years in Chula Vista, California, was a literacy coach in the Boston public school system, and is now an associate professor at Boston College School of Education.

In my second year of teaching, a colleague told me, "Good teachers are born, not made, and you were born with it." After four years of teaching, I still wonder about this comment. What is *it*?—That certain something that distinguishes excellent teachers? Do you have to be born with that certain something to be a good teacher? If you are born with it, do you always know that teaching is the profession for you? Is it true that some people are just not made for teaching, or can anyone learn what it takes? How do you know whether you are meant to be a teacher?

I never intended to be a teacher. In fact, it was not until my senior year of college that, as a frustrated premed student, I entertained the idea of teaching and took two education courses. Immediately, I knew that teaching was for me! I had done very well in the premed track, but I never felt invested in what I was studying. Education courses required just as much, if not more, time and thought, and they were

exciting in a way premed had never been. Education offered the academic rigor of the sciences but also appealed to my heart.

Teaching demands systematic thought and reflection to deliver instruction and analyze situations. It requires a solid understanding of content and pedagogy to be critical of new trends and develop curriculum. However, I believe it is instincts that humanize teaching—the gut feeling of what will work or not, the sense of how to connect with each child, and the ability to juggle 10 things at once and be fired up rather than stressed out, and so much more. Being in the classroom is still an adrenaline rush. I put in 12-hour days without thinking twice. I cannot go to a store, museum, or park without thinking how I might apply what I see to my classroom. The joy of teaching, itself, drives me. That, I think, is the *it*. Whether you can learn *it* or must be born with *it*, I still cannot say.

1-3 Sources of Useful Experience

One of the major educational insights applied to schooling in recent years concerns differentiating instruction to help each student maximize his or her potential.[11] There is a new appreciation for the unique learning preferences and learning problems of children and youth. As a result, the "one true way" approach to education is gradually slipping by the boards. The same insight about individual differences applies to making an intelligent career choice. Because people learn in such diverse ways and differ so much in what they already know and need to learn, we can offer only sketchy guidelines here. We consider four categories of experience, however, that may help you answer the question "Should I teach?" You should use the four sources in whatever combination best fits your present stage of life and career decision making.

1-3a REAL ENCOUNTERS

Students who aspire to be teachers should test their commitment by putting themselves in actual school situations. As much as possible, students of teaching should observe in schools and participate in various activities that give them **real encounters** with students. Some teaching candidates avoid contact with the young until they begin student teaching, only to find that young people are much different from the romantic images they have manufactured. "Those nasty little fifth-graders are so disgustingly . . . juvenile!" one shocked student teacher told us. Further, and all too frequently, teaching candidates limit their encounters to typical elementary and secondary school students. They do not consider teaching children with mental or physical disabilities or even becoming a specialist such as a reading teacher. As a result of limited experiences, they may have been exposed to only a narrow segment of the opportunities and challenges of teaching.

Increasingly, school districts are using college students as teacher aides and assistant teachers, both during the school year and in summer school. Also, a large number of teacher education programs have cooperative arrangements with schools that give college students opportunities to play various roles within the school, usually as part of their coursework in teacher education. In addition, we urge prospective teachers to explore opportunities to be substitute teachers in nearby schools. Although the work is demanding, much can be learned from it. Besides the valuable experience and the money earned, these substitute teaching stints often lead to regular teaching positions. School districts typically are more interested in hiring someone they have seen "in action" and who is a "known quantity" rather than strangers they only know from résumés and references. If your schedule doesn't permit substitute teaching, many schools will gratefully accept part-time volunteer help from education students.

Schools, however, do not exhaust the opportunities. There is much to be said for non-school contact with children, such as camp counseling, coaching sports, playground work, after-school recreation projects, work in orphanages and settlement houses, and youth-related church work. Other possibilities include coaching a team or sponsoring a youth club. The most important thing is to get your feet wet—to get the feel of working with young people in a helping relationship.

Vicarious Experiences

Not all learning has to take place in the school of hard knocks. In fact, civilization itself requires that we be able to capitalize on the experiences of others. Artists and other talented people can make others' experiences accessible to us for enjoyment, edification, or both.

One-to-one teaching is often the most satisfying.

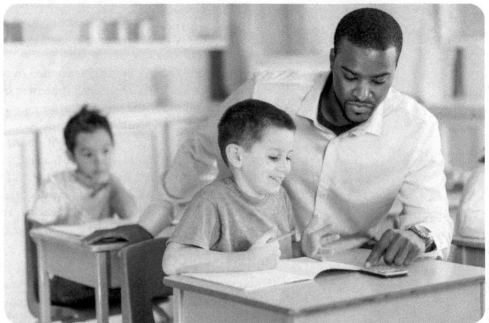

iStock.com/Christopher Futcher

Over the years, a number of films, documentaries, and television series have featured teachers and schools and can be sources of **vicarious experiences**. Among them are *Akeelah and the Bee, Boston Public, The Breakfast Club, Dangerous Minds, Dead Poets Society, Ferris Bueller's Day Off, Freedom Writers, Glee, Lean on Me, Pay It Forward, The Ron Clark Story, Stand and Deliver,* and *Waiting for Superman.* The sources cited above may help us both relive our own school experiences and see them in a different light. However, a caveat: We need to keep in mind that cinematic portrayals of teachers and classrooms often represent school life at its extremes, featuring heightened situations well beyond the typical experiences of most teachers. And there are other distortions. Many popular media representations of teachers and schools depict contexts that overrepresent men as teachers, secondary schools, teachers of color, and urban schools. Other distortions are that classes are small; teaching typically means the adult is talking (often with the skill and humor of Steve Harvey or Stephen Colbert!), and when the class finally gets around to it, learning is fun, fun, fun.[12]

Great fictional classics such as *Goodbye, Mr. Chips* by James Hilton and *The Corn Is Green* by Emlyn Williams portray teachers and schools well, as do somewhat more contemporary novels like Bel Kaufman's *Up the Down Staircase* and Evan Hunter's *The Blackboard Jungle.* (All four of these books have been made into films.) There have also been some fine nonfiction accounts of teaching; among the best are Rafe Esquith's *Teach Like Your Hair's on Fire,* Tracy Kidder's *Among Schoolchildren,* Samuel G. Freedman's *Small Victories,* Frank McCourt's *Teacher Man,* and Esmé Raji Codell's *Educating Esmé.*

Despite their occasional inaccuracies, a careful analysis of these works can prepare us for certain aspects of teaching and school life. Again, we must remember that books, films, and television often portray school life at its extremes.

1-3b GUIDANCE

Another aid in determining whether teaching is right for you is the advice and counsel gained from those who know you. Besides parents and friends (who may be too close to you to be completely objective), you can consult former teachers, career

Pause *and* Reflect

1. Are you really and truly using all the resources available to you to help you make a conscious, clearly thought-out decision about your future career? What can you do to enhance your chances of making a good decision?
2. Have you *really* acquired the mental habit of reflecting on your experiences?

placement counselors, and your college professors. The latter can be particularly helpful because, besides knowing you, they are familiar with the realities of teaching.

You should use caution when seeking guidance from others, however. First, choose people who know you well rather than those who have seen you just at your better moments. Second, do not expect a comprehensive computer printout of hard data with a firm decision at the bottom line. If you get a few glimpses of insight from the advice given, be satisfied. Third, be wary from whom you seek advice. Many people are simply compulsive advice givers. People often generalize on the basis of too little knowledge, and they are sometimes just plain wrong. To be open to advice may be quite useful, but follow it cautiously.

1-3c REFLECTION

The most important aspect of real school encounters, guidance, and vicarious experiences you collect is that they provide you with data for **reflection**. Indeed, the value of these experiences will be lost if you do not think hard about them. People are often so busy experiencing things that they fail to reflect on what they have done or heard to ensure that they get the most from the experience.

Reflection goes to the very heart of why we have written this book. We are convinced that many people make sloppy decisions about becoming teachers. Often, they have not asked fundamental or hard questions about themselves and about schools. This is precisely why we have organized this book around questions such as "Why teach?" and "What is a school and what is it for?"

As we wrote in the initial section, "So Let's Get Started," probably the greatest value of this text is to aid you in becoming a "reflective practitioner." If you didn't read or have forgotten this important idea, we urge you to go back to page xxii and capture it. (Okay. Your authors are nags, but we sincerely mean it!)

Getting Started as a Reflective Practitioner

All of us "reflect" in some way on what we experience. Typically, our reflections are brief and unsystematic. The *reflective practitioner* thinks more thoroughly and more systematically about experiences. The next time you visit a school or view a Video Case of classroom life, use these questions to stimulate your thinking:

1. What surprised you about what you observed? What was unexpected?
2. What were the teacher's goals? From what you could tell, were they achieved?
3. If you had the same goals, what would you have done?
4. How did the students appear to be responding during the class? Were they all involved? Most of them? Just a few? What could have been done to improve their involvement?
5. What, if anything, was different about these students from the way you and your classmates were at their age? Were there striking similarities?

1-4 Case Studies in the Motivation to Teach

This section offers two case studies illustrating common motives for going into teaching. Each case study is followed by a set of questions and a comment that raises important issues about the nature of teaching. The cases provide examples of how particular abstract motives take shape in teachers' lives. You may want to discuss the cases and the accompanying questions with other people. The shared experience of reading the cases and responding to the questions should help you probe and understand your own motivations.

1-4a CASE ONE: THE DESIRE TO TEACH A PARTICULAR SUBJECT

Julia Tucker had been a star science student since junior high school. She received a partial scholarship to study chemistry in college and earned high marks in everything connected with science. She also derived a good deal of personal satisfaction from quietly showing her mostly male teachers and fellow students that a female could excel at science.

When she graduated from college, Julia was heavily recruited by a chemical engineering firm and immediately fell in love with her job. It took a little longer—two years—but she fell even more in love with Nicholas, a chemist, who was working on the same project. They got married, and a year and a day later, Justin was born. Julia was back at work in six weeks. Both Nicholas and she hoped to have four children, but it didn't work out that way. There was no second pregnancy.

Julia was disappointed, but she took it philosophically. After all, she had a wonderful job, a loving husband, and a son who was the joy of her life. Everything was fine until Justin went off to middle school and began taking science courses. Julia couldn't wait to help him with his science homework. She stayed up late reading his science textbooks. She found all sorts of excuses to talk to Justin's teachers about science education. She found herself daydreaming at work about how to teach scientific concepts to children. Somewhere along the way, Julia also began losing interest in the highly specialized type of chemistry she was doing. So, after a great deal of soul searching and several late-night conversations with Nicholas, she quit her job and went back to school to get a teaching license in chemistry.

That was more than a year ago. Now Julia has a job—but it is hardly the job she fantasized about in her old lab or the teaching position for which she prepared. To her surprise, when she obtained her teaching license, the only available position (other than ones that would force her to move the family) was at the elementary level, as a fifth-grade teacher. The school superintendent realized that Julia would be a real asset to his school district but did not have an opening in the high school for two more years, when the chemistry teacher was scheduled to retire. So he presented Julia with a proposition: She could take some methods courses over the summer (at district expense), then teach fifth grade for two years, helping establish a new elementary science curriculum, and be the coordinator of the annual science fair.

At first, Julia was wary. She thought it would mean throwing away a good deal of her specialized knowledge and risking failure as an elementary school teacher, although the fifth-grade job would last only two years. But after talking it over with Nicholas and getting great support from her son, she reluctantly agreed.

A funny thing happened during the summer as Julia took the methods courses and prepared herself for her fifth-graders. She became more enthused about teaching children who she believed were "just becoming interested in the outer world." When Julia actually started working with her fifth-graders, she was hooked. They were so alive, responsive, and hungry to know about the world. What a challenge! Thoughts of ever becoming a chemistry teacher took a backseat to the elementary classroom.

By November, however, Julia had begun to have misgivings. A certain flatness in her class worries her. Much of the September curiosity has turned into an early case

There is no science-phobia in this classroom.

michaeljung/Shutterstock.com

of midwinter blahs. Her supervisor has conducted the first formal observation of her teaching, and Julia is curious about the supervisor's opinion.

"So, Suzanne," Julia says at their post-observation conference. "How did I do? You were writing up such a storm, I thought you would need another notebook!"

"Oh, I hope you didn't find that distracting. I probably should have warned you that I would be scribbling away."

"No, that's fine. I'm just curious to know how I did."

"I'd much rather hear what *you* think, Julia. How do you think the class went?"

"Well, I think pretty much as usual. They were a little quieter, perhaps because you were in there, but in general it was an average class."

"I did notice it being quiet, Julia. How do you feel about that?"

"As a matter of fact, I'm confused by it. Since September, the decibel level has been steadily falling in all my classes, but particularly when we are doing science. I couldn't get them to shut up in September. They ate up everything I presented, especially science. They just seem to have lost interest."

"From what I just saw, and from what I have observed passing by your door these weeks, I'd agree. Interest looks low."

"Suzanne, I've really worked to find topics that will interest them. I built a whole unit on pollution last month, with writing assignments and mathematics worked in. They said they were interested in heredity, so next month we're going to do family histories with interviews and collections of family facts and artifacts. They were all excited about this project in September, but now I'm stumped. What's the matter?"

"Quite honestly, Julia, I had a feeling this would happen."

"What do you mean?"

"When you came to interview last June, we were thrilled at the possibility of getting someone so knowledgeable and experienced, and particularly someone who loves science so much. But those same qualities made us hesitate too."

"I'm not getting you, Suzanne. I know we were all concerned that I didn't have traditional preparation for elementary teaching. You're not saying I know too much and I like science too much, are you?"

"Yes and no. No, you don't know too much. And yes, your love of science is a terrific asset. But at the same time, these qualities are keeping you from being the

Pause *and* Reflect

1. How would you characterize Julia's motivation to teach?
2. What do you think her students were thinking and feeling about her classes?
3. Julia is clearly an outstanding resource to the school. What are her liabilities?
4. Which clues should Julia have been picking up on?
5. What are some things Julia might do to stimulate romance for science in her students?

potentially fine teacher you can become. Julia, let me be honest. You are drowning these kids with information—and not just in science. You seem to be doing all the work. What worked so well for you during your student teaching with high school juniors and seniors just doesn't work with these elementary school wigglers."

"Honestly, Suzanne, I'm not giving them high school material. This work is within their range. I don't mean to sound defensive, but really . . ."

"Julia, think 'romance.'"

"Romance? I thought you told me to do health and human sexuality in the spring!"

"No, no. Romance. Like in 'the romance of science' and 'the romance of writing.' Do you remember telling us during your interview how you fell in love—your words, Julia—fell in love with science in the fifth grade when you had to do a project for the science fair? Well, I think you ought to do a little time traveling and think about what caused *your* romance with science. Was it a fascinating question? An unsolved problem? The excitement of maybe solving a problem the adults couldn't? Or was it a teacher pumping facts and theories into you?"

"Uh-oh. I think the dawn is breaking. I've been too busy talking at them and trying to teach them some basic information."

"Right. You've been so busy telling them about what you love that you forgot that romance is a two-way street. It's a classic mistake of rookie teachers, even ancient ones like you. Sometimes you can get away with it in high schools, but not in elementary schools."

"So what do I do now?"

"Well, let me put aside these notes, and let's see whether you and I can put a little romance into the rest of the week's lessons."

"A little pedagogical seduction! Suzanne, I think you found the key!"

Comment

All of us have had teachers whose excitement and enthusiasm for their subject were contagious. Love for a particular subject matter or content is an important and commendable motive for teaching. A major purpose of school is to pass on the best of society's knowledge. Another important purpose is to help young people develop basic skills and attitudes, especially a love for learning. A teacher who has a passion to convey the subject matter is effective at both of these goals. Such teachers may push students hard, but they are frequently the ones who have the greatest impact on students.

But carrying love for a particular subject to an extreme can cause trouble. Real learning is usually built on students' interest. Their interest in or love of learning can be blunted when the lover (the teacher) is too overpowering or insistent. The great teacher, like the great lover, knows how to draw out others' interests and help students "fall in love."

Another danger awaits the teacher who is "blinded" by love of a subject. This teacher may be so busy teaching what she or he enjoys that the rest of the curriculum gets shortchanged. For example, an English teacher who loves interpreting literature often finds it easy to avoid slugging it out with grammar, punctuation, and other essential writing skills. The elementary school teacher who loves science, like Julia, may fail to give the other subjects their due. Although this tendency to focus on what we know and love—and to avoid what we do not know or like—is understandable, it is also irresponsible. It is unfair to both the students and their later teachers, who will expect students to have a command over the avoided or neglected content.

Neither Julia's motive nor her problem is uncommon. Teachers who are strongly motivated by the desire to teach a particular subject matter have to be somewhat cross-eyed. While keeping one eye on what they want to teach, they need to keep the other eye on the students and their day-to-day progress and needs.

1-4b CASE TWO: THE DESIRE TO AID IN THE RENEWAL OF SOCIETY

Fred Harvey was in his late 30s. His disposition was so pleasant, and a smile came so readily to his face, that one of the other teachers in the large metropolitan high school referred to him as "everybody's uncle." Fred had a remarkable ability to remain relaxed when everyone else was tense, and he often broke up emotionally charged faculty-room situations and staff meetings with an appropriate quip or humorous question.

Each year, Fred asked to teach the Curriculum II freshman history class. Of course, his request was always granted because the Curriculum II classes were considered the dumping ground for slow students and students who had given up. Some of the other teachers regarded the Curriculum II classes as "punishment." Yet, year after year, Fred worked happily with students nobody else really wanted.

Fred's freshman history class was one of the most active in the school. He often took his students beyond the walls of the school on expeditions to day court, the police station, jail, and industrial plants in the area—and he also managed to sneak a baseball game into the field-trip lineup. Yet his classes were not characterized by fun and games: students worked hard to interpret sources, weigh contrastive evidence, make and support arguments answering persistent issues, and take informed action.

One year, Fred invited another teacher to speak to the class about shipbuilding in the eighteenth century. The talk went well, and after the session the other teacher, Todd Vincent, commented to Fred that the discussion following his talk had been very different from what he had anticipated: the questions were thoughtful and displayed observation of detail that the guest speaker had not expected from a "bunch of Curriculum IIs."

Fred laughed. "You know, Todd," he said, "they amaze me too sometimes. Most of these kids really have behavior problems, not intellectual ones. If you looked at their case histories, you'd find that the majority of them were 'dropped through the ranks.'"

"What do you mean?" asked Todd.

"They were in regular classes a good bit of their scholastic lives, but when they became problems in class, their teachers decided that the cause of their poor behavior was that the work was too hard for them. Most of the children in this class really represent the nonconformists, the 'antisocials'—the kids who some teachers claim 'won't go along with the system.' They're the kids about whom many teachers say, 'I don't care whether they learn history as long as they become good citizens.'"

"Yes, but you must admit that very few of them will go to college. Most Curriculum IIs just drop out," said Todd.

"Maybe you're missing my point," replied Fred. "I guess I'm saying that people can't be 'good citizens' unless they are contributing members of society, and that they should contribute something they think is worth contributing. If they can't get the basic tools that make a person productive, how can they be good citizens? It's a lot more than getting a job or making a decent living. In fact, I believe these kids are much more capable than so many of the kids we send to the university."

"In what sense?"

"In the sense that they are the least accepting of society as it exists now," replied Fred. "If you talked to some of them for an hour or so, you'd find that they really feel the school is hypocritical in many ways, and they aren't afraid to point out the hypocrisies. They'll tell you, for instance, that there are two sets of rules in the school, two sets of discipline procedures, two sets of privileges, and all the rest."

> *Those who educate children well are more to be honored than they who produce them; for these only gave them life, those the art of living well.*
>
> **—ARISTOTLE (384–322 BC),**
> Greek philosopher

"But I hear the same thing from my 'honors' classes," Todd protested. "Those kids know about the double standard too. They often tell me that an honors student here can get away with anything from cutting class to smoking weed in the parking lot."

"You've got me wrong again, Todd. What these kids are saying is not that we expect too much of them, but rather that we expect too little. For instance, if a kid dropped from an A to a C in your honors history course, what would happen?"

"The kid would probably get a 'request' to go in and see the counselor," Todd replied.

"That's right," Fred continued. "When a kid everyone believes is bound for college does poorly, bells go off and people get concerned. They try to help the kid take a look at what's wrong. If one of these students goes from a C to an F, though, everyone says, 'Well, what more do you expect? The kid's only a Curriculum II and doesn't have the ability to sustain a C.' And they get all the inexperienced teachers and martinets in the school. Oh, they know that if they become real problems, they'll get counseling and possibly even better teaching. But that isn't their complaint. They know that the system isn't out to punish them; they know the system would rather they just float along and not bother anyone. That's the double standard in this school: those who are cared about and those who aren't."

"You know," said Todd, "you're not just talking about the Curriculum II classes. I think the same thing is generally true of Curriculum I classes. It seems that a kid who's really bright gets a lot of attention, and so does the kid who is really slow, but it's that kid in the middle. . . ."

"Right," said Fred. "The kids in this class are the bottom of that middle group in terms of the concern they arouse from the system—and they know it. Yet, as you saw today, they are capable. We owe them a decent set of expectations. I've maintained high expectations for the kids. I would prefer to slightly overmatch them intellectually than undermatch them, because no development is possible when you're being undermatched constantly."

"Don't they complain about being pushed too hard?" asked Todd.

"Oh, sure! There's always a good deal of moaning, particularly in the early weeks, until they realize I don't dance to that tune. Pretty soon they settle in and decide to go along with the program. But then they realize that they are actually learning. At that point, they're hooked. They're mine, and I wouldn't trade teaching them for anything!"

"Well, Fred, this has been most instructive. I came to teach and I ended up learning."

"Me too. That's what keeps me going. And Todd, please come back next semester."

Pause *and* Reflect

1. How is Fred's commitment to social renewal specifically shown in his classroom teaching?
2. According to Fred, what is the criterion for assignment to Curriculum II classes in his school? Was this true of your high school?
3. What is the double standard Todd spoke of, and how do you explain it? What is the double standard Fred spoke of, and how do you explain it? Did either of these double standards exist in your school?
4. How do Fred's expectations for his students differ from those of most teachers you have known? In what other ways is he different from most of the teachers you have known?
5. What do you think were Todd's major misconceptions as a teacher?
6. What does Fred see as the role of academic disciplines in education? If you had to, how would you argue against his position?

Comment

In addition to the serious educational injustice of underchallenging many students, Fred was reacting against the perversion of an important idea: teaching good citizenship. In Fred's school, as in many others, the idea of teaching good citizenship has been badly distorted.

During the 1930s, in a reform started by U.S. educator and philosopher John Dewey, many schools adopted the policy of awarding a grade for citizenship. Dewey and many of his followers envisioned training for citizenship as a process of working out in class actual problems that arise in a democracy. They saw the schools as an appropriate place to teach students about democratic decisions and to give them low-risk but real practice in such decision making in a context where mistakes were not "for keeps."

As sometimes happens with reforms, educational and otherwise, the processes introduced to the classroom by these reformers gradually degenerated into empty forms. Good citizenship came to mean docility, doing what one is told. Students could earn "good citizenship" grades by "playing the game" and not bothering anyone. Citizenship became a code word among teachers. A teacher who was given a class of "low achievers" or "discipline problems" was sometimes told, "Don't worry about academic concerns with these children. Just make them good citizens." Parents were told that their child wasn't a very good student but was "an excellent citizen." This euphemism meant that even though he or she didn't learn anything, the child did without questioning everything that students were supposed to do.

The use of a citizenship grade as a conduct mark is an absolute travesty of the system Dewey and the reformers designed. As Fred noted, in reality, good citizens are not docile sheep who can be "conned" with impunity. The long-term effect of the misinterpretation of citizenship as conformity and docility has been to discredit it as an appropriate goal for schooling. Yet, in Fred we see a person consciously attempting to develop educated citizens. His class visits to courthouses, legislative sessions, and factories, as well as the classroom study of major social problems, are very much in keeping with what Dewey—and, indeed, Thomas Jefferson and James Madison—had in mind when they spoke of educating for freedom.

> *The role of the teacher remains the highest calling of a free people. To the teacher, America entrusts her most precious resource, her children.*
>
> **—SHIRLEY HUFSTEDLER,**
> former U.S. secretary of education

LEADERS in Education

Erin Gruwell (b. 1969)

Nothing could have prepared Erin Gruwell for her first day of teaching at Wilson High School in Long Beach, California. A recent college graduate, Erin landed her first job in Room 203, only to discover that many of her students had been written off by the education system and deemed "unteachable." As teenagers living in a racially divided urban community, they were already hardened by firsthand exposure to gang violence, juvenile detention, and drugs.

Courtesy of Erin Gruwell

Enter Erin Gruwell. By fostering an educational philosophy that valued and promoted diversity, she transformed her students' lives. She encouraged her students to rethink their rigidly held beliefs about themselves and others, reconsider their daily decisions, and rechart their futures. With Erin's steadfast support, her students shattered stereotypes to become critical thinkers, aspiring college students, and

(Continued)

citizens for change. They even dubbed themselves the "Freedom Writers"—in homage to the civil rights activists known as "Freedom Riders"—and published a book.

Inspired by Anne Frank and Zlata Filipovic (who lived through the chaos of war-torn Sarajevo), Erin and her students captured their collective journey in *The Freedom Writers Diary: How a Teacher and 150 Teens Used Writing to Change Themselves and the World Around Them*. Through poignant student entries and Erin's narrative text, the book chronicles their "eye-opening, spirit-raising odyssey against intolerance and misunderstanding."

Although Erin has been credited with giving her students a "second chance," it was perhaps she who changed the most during her tenure at Wilson High. Today, her impact as a "teacher" extends well beyond Room 203. Currently, Erin serves as president of the Freedom Writers Foundation (www .freedomwritersfoundation.org), and raises awareness by traveling across the United States to speak inside large corporations, government institutions, and community associations. But Erin's capacity to convert apathy into action matters most at schools and juvenile halls, where any observer can watch the expressions of troubled teens shift from guarded cynicism to unabashed hopefulness.

Erin and her students have appeared on numerous television shows, including *Oprah*, *The Rosie O'Donnell Show*, *PrimeTime Live with Connie Chung*, *The View*, *Good Morning America*, and CSPAN's *Book TV*. Her class has been featured on National Public Radio and in national newspapers and *People* magazine. In January 2007, Paramount Pictures released *Freedom Writers*, a film based on this remarkable story, featuring Hilary Swank as Erin. That same year, her personal account of becoming a teacher, *Teach with Your Heart: Lessons I Learned from the Freedom Writers*, was published.

Erin is a graduate of the University of California, Irvine, where she received the Lauds and Laurels Distinguished Alumni Award. She earned her master's degree and teaching credentials from California State University, Long Beach, where she was honored as Distinguished Alumna by the School of Education.

1-5 Opinions about Teachers and Teaching

The "Why teach?" question and the decision about whether teaching is the right career for you is intensely personal. Although what you think about teaching and whether it is a "good fit" for you is of primary importance, it may be useful to know what others think about teachers too. Here we'll consider the views of the general public, students, and administrators, and what teachers who are new to the field have to say about their work.

1-5a WHAT DOES THE PUBLIC SAY ABOUT TEACHERS AND TEACHING?

The education of America's children regularly tops the list of the public's social concerns. Particularly now, in the start of the third decade of the twenty-first century, our educational system is receiving major attention from social critics and politicians. Americans are relying on their teachers to instruct, guide, inspire, motivate, and occasionally prod their children to learn more than ever before.

The public—that is, the people whose taxes pay the salaries of public school teachers—overwhelmingly acknowledges and supports the nation's teachers. When asked to select which group provided "the most benefit to society," 62 percent selected teachers, whereas only 17 percent selected physicians (the second choice). Only 5 percent chose people in business, 3 percent chose lawyers, and only 1 percent chose journalists and politicians.[13] When asked to rate which factors have the greatest impact on student learning, 44 percent selected the qualifications of a teacher over other factors such as class size, socioeconomic status of the family, or the family's involvement and support.[14]

Finally, the public has a great deal of trust in teachers. According to the *National Credibility Index,* when asked which people were "the most believable when speaking out on public issues," teachers were rated the highest, above members of the armed forces, national experts, and community activists.[15]

1-5b WHAT DO STUDENTS THINK ABOUT TEACHERS?

The old ditty sung by generations of students, "No more pencils. No more books. No more teachers' dirty looks!" may be giving way to a new appreciation. As shown in Figure 1.2, in a 2010 survey of students ages 12 to 17, high school students, often thought to be somewhat cool toward their teachers, view them as the top contributors (32%) to society's well-being, ahead of the next two contributors, doctors (23%) and scientists (19%). Although many students may fail to show it in their daily dealings with their teachers, this survey shows the deep wellsprings of their appreciation for the work of teachers.

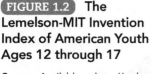
(T) F
American teens claim teachers contribute most to our society's well-being.

1-5c WHAT DO ADMINISTRATORS SAY ABOUT *NEW* TEACHERS?

The high regard the public and students have for teachers is encouraging. But what about new teachers, those who have recently entered the field? What do the administrators who work with new teachers and supervise them on a daily basis say about them?

Pause *and* Reflect

1. Does this information about students' high regard for teachers surprise you?
2. What are your personal reactions to this endorsement of teachers and does it fit with your experience?

FIGURE 1.2 The Lemelson-MIT Invention Index of American Youth Ages 12 through 17

Source: Available at http://web.mit.edu/invent/n-pressreleases/n-press-10index.html

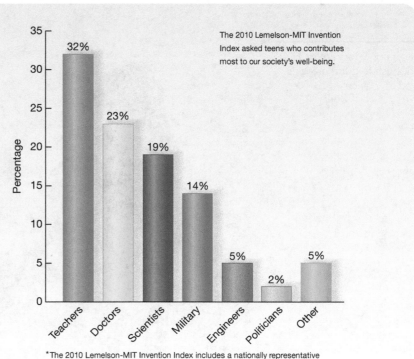

The 2010 Lemelson-MIT Invention Index asked teens who contributes most to our society's well-being.

*The 2010 Lemelson-MIT Invention Index includes a nationally representative survey sample size of 500 teens.

The opinions of principals and superintendents support those of the general public. A stunning 98 percent of superintendents and principals surveyed agreed with the descriptions of their new teachers as "motivated" and "energetic."[16]

T (F)

The majority of school superintendents and principals claim that the quality of new teachers entering the field has declined.

Rumors that the quality of new teachers has deteriorated are hardly borne out by those who do the hiring. A majority (52%) of these frontline administrators believe that the quality of those entering the profession has improved; only 9 percent of these educators believe it is declining.[17] We suspect that there are few professions or occupations where supervisors have such high regard for newcomers.

Pause *and* Reflect

1. Do the opinions of one of these groups—the public, students, administrators, other new teachers—matter more to you than the opinions of the others? Why?
2. How important is it to you to know what other people will think about you as a teacher?

1-5d WHAT DO NEW TEACHERS THINK ABOUT TEACHING?

An in-depth study, conducted at the beginning of the twenty-first century with 664 public school teachers and 250 private teachers who had all taught for five or fewer years, paints a picture of how today's newest teachers feel about their work. The researchers aptly titled their report *A Sense of Calling: Who Teaches and Why*, and they concluded that "most new teachers are highly motivated professionals who bring a strong sense of commitment and high morale to their work."[18] New teachers see themselves as talented and dedicated professionals.

Reflecting the title of the report, 86 percent of new teachers affirmed the notion that only those "with a true sense of calling" should teach.[19] Nine out of ten claimed that the teaching profession demands a high level of energy and effort, requiring more talent and hard work than many other professions. The teachers in this study continually commented on the need for enthusiasm to do the job well. An overwhelming 98 percent described other new teachers with whom they work as sharing in their sense of commitment and enthusiasm. This is hardly the portrait of a disappointed and disgruntled group of newcomers.

American educators are making a major push to get more girls involved in science.

Andersen Ross/Stockbyte/Getty Images

1-6 Why Teachers Teach

Let's get back to the question "Why teach?" by considering those already in the field. First, are teachers personally satisfied with their career choice, and second, why do they teach? The answer to the satisfaction question revealed what up until recently has been a dramatic and encouraging increase in teacher satisfaction in the last half century, going from a low in 1986 of 33 percent reporting being "very satisfied" to the most recent figure of 59 percent in 2009 (see Table 1.2).[20] However, the most recent version of this survey shows that teacher satisfaction has dropped precipitously in the last few years: from a high of 62 percent reporting "very satisfied" in 2008 to 39 percent in 2012. We need to consider, however, that this surprising 23 percentage point drop occurred during the difficult years of the 2007–2008 economic recession, a period that put particular stress on teachers' salaries and school budgets.[21]

Next, "*Why Teachers Teach*": *Attitudes about Teaching,* a somewhat dated 2003 study, reveals that nearly all new teachers (96%) reported that teaching is the work they love to do. Four out of five claimed that they would choose teaching again if starting over. Three out of four insisted that "teaching is a lifelong choice," and two out of three reported that they get a great deal of satisfaction out of teaching. Contrary to the rumor that many people simply drift into teaching, a mere 12 percent said that they "fell into teaching by chance." All but a handful had very altruistic attitudes about their work, telling the researchers that teaching offers them an opportunity for "contributing to society."

In another national survey of teachers, the 2016 *Listen to Us: Teacher Views and Voices,* teachers were asked about the most rewarding aspects of being a teacher. Table 1.3 shows that the response "making a difference in students' lives" was listed by 82 percent of teachers. Twenty-two percent of teachers cited "making a difference in my school community," while 17 percent responded with the "non-traditional work schedule."

TABLE 1.2	Teachers' Perceptions of Their School, Colleagues, and Job
Q. Teachers at this school like being here: I would describe us as a satisfied group.	
Strongly or somewhat agree	64%
Strongly or somewhat disagree	36%

Source: Adapted from Figure 1-C (page 19) of *Listen to Us: Teacher Views and Voices,* a 2016 national survey from The Center on Education Policy (https://files.eric.ed.gov/fulltext/ED568172.pdf)

TABLE 1.3	The Most Rewarding Aspects of Being a Teacher
Making a difference in students' lives	82%
Seeing my students succeed academically	69%
Making a difference in my school community	26%
Making a difference in the larger community	22%
Non-traditional work schedule	17%

Source: Adapted from Table 1-A (page 15) of *Listen to Us: Teacher Views and Voices,* a 2016 national survey from The Center on Education Policy (https://files.eric.ed.gov/fulltext/ED568172.pdf). Note: Teachers could select three responses.

For some teachers, teaching is clearly a short-term career. One in five respondents in the *A Sense of Calling* survey indicated that they would probably change careers at some point. Although this figure contrasts sharply with the 50 percent of young college graduates in other fields who say that they expect to change careers at least once,[22] the reference to teaching as a short-term career brings up an important point. The desire to teach for a few years and then to move on to another career or to raise a family is both common and to be respected. Also, our schools are filled with people who "dropped in" on teaching and stayed to make it their professional home.

Judging from this study, new teachers show a remarkable certainty that they made the right choice in pursuing a teaching career. It also appears that most of today's new teachers have taken the time to reflect on whether teaching is the right career choice for them.

The *Voices from the Classroom* study also asked early career teachers, "How valued do you personally feel as a teacher?" Table 1.4 summarizes the teachers' responses. An impressive 81 percent reported that they felt either "Somewhat valued" or "Very valued." Only 4 percent felt "Not valued at all." Clearly, today's new teachers, although not painting a perfect picture, seem personally valued in their work.

Teachers' widespread satisfaction and love for their work is largely unknown, even among teachers. This "good news" has been lost in the headlines focusing on students' cyberbullying, low test scores, and other educational problems. The reality is that most teachers love the job of teaching. Consider the following:

- Seventy-nine percent of teachers agree "strongly" with the following statement: "involves work you love to do."

- Seventy-four percent of teachers say that teaching is a lifelong career choice.

- Ninety-one percent of new teachers believe that teaching matches their skills and interests very well.[23]

1-6a A SPECIAL INTRINSIC REWARD

It is certainly encouraging news that others apparently are happy and satisfied as teachers. Nevertheless, it is your life—and your choice to enter the teaching field. Clearly, selecting a career is a personal decision and involves answering many questions: "Will I be happy?" "Will this career provide me with a satisfying lifestyle?"

> *Pleasure in the job puts perfection in the work.*
>
> —ARISTOTLE (384–322 BC),
> Greek philosopher

(T) F
Of all the characteristics that contribute to teachers' satisfaction, new teachers rate highest "involves work you love to do."

TABLE 1.4	Survey of America's Educators	
Q. How valued do you personally feel as a teacher?		
	Responses from all teachers	Responses from early career teachers
Very valued	27%	34%
Somewhat valued	46%	47%
Not very valued	23%	16%
Not valued at all	4%	3%

Source: Adapted from Question 65 from *Voices from the Classroom: A Survey of America's Educators,* a 2019 nationally representative survey conducted by Educators for Excellence. (https://e4e.org/sites /default/files/voices_from_the_classroom_2020.pdf)

"Will I be up to the challenge, and will I find the work satisfying?" "Will I grow in the experience?" People who are considering teaching as a life's work should grapple with these questions, which relate to the motives for their choice, but they must also scrutinize other, deeper motives.

vo.ca.tion n. 2. An inclination, as if in response to a summons, to undertake a certain kind of work.

—AMERICAN HERITAGE DICTIONARY

Teaching, like nursing, the ministry, and social work, is a service occupation. More correctly, teaching is a **vocation**. Built into teaching is the idea of contributing to the lives of others. For many people, the root of their decision to teach is deeper than a love of subject matter or an attraction to the life of a teacher. Many men and women select teaching for reasons that are, at heart, religious or humanitarian. They see themselves as *called* to the work.

OUR FINAL WORD

We have said much in this chapter about the extrinsic and intrinsic rewards that come with teaching. One of the intrinsic rewards mentioned was the knowledge that you as a teacher would be involved in crucially important work. This particular **psychic reward** is captured by the story of a U.S. television reporter who was filming a documentary on the work of the late Mother Teresa and her community of nuns in the slums of Calcutta, India. The reporter came upon a young American nun cleaning the running sores, filth, and infections covering the body of a dying beggar. After filming the young woman as she carefully cleansed the ruined body of this near-death man, the reporter looked down at the nun and declared, "Sister, I wouldn't do that for a million dollars!" Without taking her eyes off her dying patient, the young nun quietly replied, "Neither would I."

One of the great intrinsic benefits of a career in teaching—and one not shared by the vast number of other occupations—is the inner certainty that you are doing important work and that you are spending your life well. *Those who can, teach.*

WHY TEACH? YOUR FINAL WORD

1. As a result of reading this initial chapter and participating in the activities, you may be closer to clarifying your answer to the question "Why teach?" Describe what you discovered as you read this chapter and what you intend to do as a result.

2. Which of the intrinsic and extrinsic motivations cited in this chapter do you think most closely match your current motivations to teach?

3. This chapter includes several sources for experiences to gain greater understanding of teaching and its "fit" with your own motivations and values. Specifically, which of these do you think you will pursue?

KEY TERMS

extrinsic reward (4)
intrinsic reward (4)
psychic reward (23)
real encounter (9)

reflection (11)
vicarious experience (10)
vocation (23)

FOR FURTHER INFORMATION

Web Resources

Teaching Community: Where Teachers Meet and Learn

This site has multiple sources of information and support for teachers, from job openings to interviewing techniques, lessons plans, and disciplinary tips.

TeachersFirst

This all-purpose website is devoted to empowering and helping new teachers. It has multiple references to helpful and practical material from how to prepare for your first day of class to strategies for handling discipline problems.

Association for Supervision and Curriculum Development

This site of a major educational organization has many different features and supports for those exploring careers in education and for new teachers.

Print Resources

Rafe Esquith, *Teach Like Your Hair's on Fire* (New York: Viking Adult/Penguin Group USA, 2007).

The title captures the intensity and excitement of this inspired teacher's approach to teaching. Rafe Esquith's Los Angeles fifth-grade classroom is the scene of poor, immigrant children being exposed to Shakespeare, classical music, and the world of ideas—and loving it.

Erin Gruwell, *Teach with Your Heart: Lessons I Learned from the Freedom Writers* (New York: Broadway Books, 2008).

Erin Gruwell, featured in this chapter's "Leaders in Education" section, has written a personal, poignant account of her struggles as a beginning teacher and of finally reaching her goal of inspiring young students to become powerful writers.

Tracy Kidder, *Among Schoolchildren* (Boston: Houghton Mifflin, 1989).

The author spent an entire school year observing a fifth-grade teacher and produced a rich, fascinating account of a teacher's year that shows how one teacher shaped and moved the lives of her students.

Parker J. Palmer, *The Courage to Teach: Exploring the Inner Landscape of a Teacher's Life* (San Francisco: Jossey-Bass, 2007).

In this moving reflection on the teacher's life and work, Parker Palmer proves to be one of the wise voices reflecting on American schools.

Taylor Mali, *What Teachers Make: In Praise of the Greatest Job in the World* (Penguin Publishing, 2012).

This short book by slam poet, Taylor Mali, makes a powerful case for the work of teachers.

What Is a School and What Is It For?

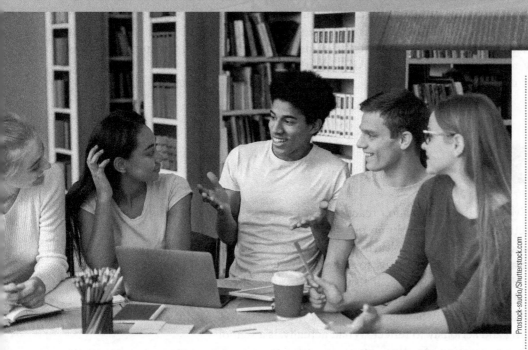

Prostock-studio/Shutterstock.com

LEARNING OBJECTIVES

2-1 Describe several different understandings of the concept "school."

2-2 Explain the important distinctions between "education" and "schooling."

2-3 Analyze the ideas of schools as distinctive cultures and the role of schools in socialization.

2-4 Compare the two different views of schools as transmitters or re-creators of culture.

2-5 Describe four basic purposes of school.

2-6 Identify at least two research findings about the nature of schools for each level: elementary, middle, and high schools.

2-7 Summarize what researchers claim is a "good school."

2-8 Describe the challenge of improving our schools.

Truth OR Fiction?

T   F   Although our schools have many purposes, all agree that developing intellectual skills is the clear, primary purpose.

T   F   Part of being a student in an elementary classroom is having to experience "denial of desire," which is frustrating, unnecessary, and detrimental.

T   F   Research shows that academically effective schools are good at remaining independent of parental involvement.

In this chapter, we explore with you two related and fundamental questions: What is a school? And what is it for? We pose and discuss these questions to aid you in forming your ideas about the underlying issues. It is unlikely that you can make a good career choice if you lack a fundamental understanding of the institution in which your career is centered. Also, if you hope to thrive and be happy within an institution, you have to know how it is put together and how it works. For example, you must know what the institution says it is doing and what, in fact, it actually does. If you are considering a job in a particular school, you need to know what the leadership of the school *really* expects of their teachers to know whether you want to work there. Finally, if you hope to improve the schools—that is, make them better because of your involvement with them, you must have a realistic view of what is going on in the schools now and develop your vision of what the schools can and should become in the future.

2-1 What Is a School?

We wouldn't blame you for reacting to the question, "What is a school?" with something like, "What a dumb question! I've spent a huge chunk of my life in and around schools. What's to learn?" Our answer is, "Yes, but..." Sometimes our most intimate experiences blind us to a lager reality. The late U.S. senator and linguist S. I. Hayakawa once wrote, "If fish were scientists, the last thing they would study would be water." Our point is that schools have been so much of your life that what they *actually* are may have become almost invisible to you. Again, we ask you to stop reading and seriously to reflect: What, actually, is a school?

Your reaction to this question reflects who you are and what your experience with school has been. Perhaps you responded in one of the following ways:

- A school is an agency that weans children from the protective warmth of the family and trains them for what society has decided is useful work.
- A school is a place where "they" fix your mind so you think like everyone else.
- A school is where children fall in love with learning.
- A school is a tax-supported babysitting agency.
- A school is a place where young savages have a chance to become civilized by engaging in the world's most precious wisdom.
- A school is a place where we explore who we really are and how we can become full, creative human beings.
- A school is an institution where the dead wisdom and worn-out skills of the past are force-fed to the young.
- A school is where *real* education takes place.

Each of these descriptions says a great deal about the school experience of the person who formulated it. Our conviction is that your definition of *school* is a crucial cognitive map that greatly affects how you put together information and impressions of schools. And, perhaps, how you will approach the work of a teacher.

Pause *and* Reflect

1. Before you read on, how would you answer the question "What is a school?"
2. Which of the previous descriptions best describes your understanding of schools? Which least describes your understanding? If none of them fit, write your own one-sentence description.

2-2 Education and Schooling

Before we burrow into schools, we need to clarify an important distinction—namely, the difference between *education* and *schooling*. In simpler, premodern societies, when a boy could learn to be a man by following his father around and imitating him and the other men of the village, and a girl could learn to be a woman by doing the same with her mother and the other women, schools were not necessary. Formal schooling became a social necessity when the home and the community were no longer effective or competent at preparing the young through informal contacts.

Most modern societies have realized for some time that education is too important to be left to chance. Whereas important things are sometimes learned on street corners, and grandparents often are excellent teachers, the informal educative process is simply too unreliable. Still, there are nagging and growing doubts about the way we are currently doing it in many communities. That is, is herding youngsters into school buildings for six or seven hours a day, five days a week, the most effective way to prepare our children for life in our modern world? More on that topic later.

It has been jokingly suggested that in today's society, children interrupt their education when they go to school. The distinction between schooling and education implied by this remark is important. Both schooling and education have myriad definitions. We have sprinkled a few such definitions here and there throughout the book for you to sample. Before we go further, though, we should look at these two related but distinct concepts in greater detail.

2-2a EDUCATION

For the moment, let us say that **education** is a process of human growth by which one gains greater understanding and control over oneself and one's world. It involves our minds, our bodies, and our relations with the people and the world around us. Ideally education is also characterized by continuous development and change.

> *All of us have two educations: one which we receive from others; another, and the most valuable, which we give ourselves.*
>
> —JOHN RANDOLPH (1773–1833),
> U.S. congressman

Education is much more open-ended and all-inclusive than schooling and knows few boundaries. It includes both the formal learning that takes place in schools and the entire universe of informal learning, from how to hook a worm on a line to how to burp a baby.

The agents of education can range from a revered grandparent to the guests on a late-night television talk show, from a child with a disability to a distinguished scientist. Whereas schooling follows a routine and has a certain predictability, education quite often takes us by surprise. We go to the movies to relax—and come home with a vivid sense of the human misery that results from warfare. We get into a casual conversation with a stranger and discover how little we know about other religions. Education is a lifelong process: it starts long before we begin school and should be ongoing our entire lives.

2-2b SCHOOLING

In contrast to education, **schooling** is a specific, formalized process, usually focused on the young. This general pattern has varied little from one setting to the next. Despite minor variations in teaching practices among schools, schooling remains a rather uniform practice throughout the United States. Children arrive at school at

Teachers come in many shapes and sizes—even as parents.

Fuse/Corbis

approximately the same time, take assigned seats, are taught by adults, use the same or similar textbooks, do homework, take exams, are given grades, and so on. The topics they learn—from fractions to the three branches of the U.S. government—have usually been mandated in advance by adults who are far from the school.

Schools are created for the express purpose of delivering a certain type of educational experience called the *curriculum*. Teachers receive preparation to fulfill the purposes of schooling as defined by the curriculum. The curriculum (discussed more fully in Chapter 5, "What Is Taught?") represents what a community believes young people need to know to develop into good and productive adults. In effect, what you were taught in elementary and high school represents society's wager—that is, its *social bet*, made by the older generation. The bet is on what they believe today's students will need to know to live well in the future. If the curriculum a society chooses turns out to be a losing bet, the individual and social consequences are indeed severe.

> I have never let my schooling interfere with my education.
>
> —MARK TWAIN (1835–1910),
> American author and humorist

Keeping the differences between education and schooling clearly in mind is often particularly difficult for the people who should be most sensitive to them—that is, teachers who *do* education *in* schools. Most people enter teaching because they wish to educate others. Consciously or unconsciously, they are committed to a particular educational philosophy. Over time, the everyday experiences of working in a school tend to cause their allegiances to shift from abstract educational ideals to the network of personalities and ideas surrounding the particular schools in which they teach. They become invested in schooling, in the way things are—that is, the routines of questioning, assigning homework, quizzes, and faculty meetings—and to varying degrees they tend to lose focus on the larger issues of education, that is, the growth of the human beings in front of them. For this reason alone, it is important for teachers to keep alive the questions "What is a school for?" and "What is my contribution to this child's and this class's education?" We will have more to say on this topic when we examine ideas about education in Chapter 9, "What Are the Philosophical Foundations of American Education?" In the meantime, we have tried to capture the distinctions between education and schooling in Table 2.1.

TABLE 2.1	Schooling versus Education
Schooling	**Education**
Rigid, structured	Life experiences, human relationships
Facts, information to be absorbed	Personal, individual interests
Time is its engine (minimum minutes, days)	Changing often, constantly
Stops and starts, finite	Applies to new situations
Redundant, scheduled, topics	Novel, random, and unplanned
Social requirements	Fewer social requirements
Works with others, large groups	Works with smaller groups, interactions with people
May not need all that is learned	Always going on
Success is determined by outside factors	Success is determined by factors within self
Can exist without education	Can exist without schooling
Often passive	Often active
Classrooms, subjects, curriculum	The world, everyday life

Source: Cory Callahan, Associate Professor of Secondary Social Studies Education, University of Alabama.

Pause *and* Reflect

1. Which have been the most important learnings in your life—those from your nonschool education or from your schooling?
2. Can you think of a time or two when you learned something in a classroom that was different from what you learned away from school? At home, with friends, at a place of worship? What may account for those differences?

2-3 Schools as Cultures

A **society** is a grouping of individuals bound together by a variety of connections. Some of these connections might be shared geographic space or similar racial features. What really connects people, however, is their shared **culture**, composed of beliefs about what is right and wrong, and what is good and bad. Culture also includes the dominant ideas, stories and myths, artistic works, social habits, and organizations of a group. Another of its key aspects is language and the ways people use it in relationship to one another. Every group of people who lives together in relative harmony can be said to share a culture, once defined as simply "just the way we are 'round here." Without a common culture, every time we walked into a room or passed someone on the street, we would grope for a way to respond. Our culture *tells* us what is "the correct" thing to do.

All sorts of cultures exist. A family possesses a culture, as does the U.S. Marine Corps. After a few weeks, a college dormitory assumes a distinctive culture, one that will vary from year to year, from class to class. So too with a school. Think about it: Each school you have attended has had its own culture—a set of beliefs, values, traditions, and ways of thinking and behaving toward one another—that distinguishes it from other social institutions and other schools.

Cultures, including **school cultures**, can be good or bad, leading to good human ends or poor ones. A strong, positive school culture engages the hearts and minds of children, stretching them intellectually, physically, morally, and socially. A school with a weak, negative culture may have the same type of facilities, student–teacher ratio, and curriculum as a neighboring good school, yet have a weak, negative effect on students, where everyone—students and teachers—goes through the motions, but with few of the positive effects that the strong-culture school provides.

The same can be said of classrooms. Even in a school with a positive cultures, the culture in individual classrooms may be one where students feel unsafe, afraid of bullies or a teacher that "doesn't like me."

2-3a SOCIALIZATION

Along with food, shelter, and loving care, adults pass their culture on to their young. A major part of any culture is the skills and attitudes necessary to function in that particular society. In our contemporary American society, we expect that most people will try to get along with one another, work cooperatively, and look after their families. The task of passing on a society's culture to the young is called **socialization**, defined as the general process of social learning whereby the child learns the many things necessary to become a well-functioning and acceptable member of a particular social environment.

Besides the family, the major socializing agencies in the life of a young person are schools, peer groups, youth organizations, the mass media, and in some cases work environments. Each of these agencies has its own values, norms, and mores that it attempts to teach so that children will know how to act and behave in a manner acceptable to other agency members. Some agencies, such as the school, are formally created and organized. Others, such as peer groups, are informally created and casually organized.

> *Our fundamental task as human beings is to seek out connections—to exercise our imaginations. It follows, then, that the basic task of education is the care and feeding of the imagination.*
>
> —KATHERINE PATERSON,
> American author

Schools, as one of the most common institutions in the United States, have a significant role in teaching young people how to be social in the American context. One of the core purposes of schools is to enrich students' understanding of their own culture—how and why people behave the way they do and think and believe as they do. The students who tend to succeed in school typically accept these values, whereas many of the less successful students reject the ways of thinking and behaving that the school tries to teach.

What are these values and how are they communicated to students? One value schools tend to encourage is compliant behavior as opposed to personal initiative. Students soon learn to give a teacher what is wanted or expected. Reward systems used by schools indirectly teach students to "read" both the teacher and the system to determine just what is expected of them to get the grade, the teacher's attention, or the sticker with the smiling face. Another value is competitiveness, learned through athletics, grading systems that compare students to one another, and ability grouping that separates students into classes according to their achievement levels. One social phenomenon the schools and our entire society have confronted in recent years is the importance of social media to the current generation. Social critics and classroom teachers report that the pull of screens and the attraction of social media are making students increasingly distracted from the work of schools and awkward in face-to-face situations. As a result, some schools are putting greater emphasis on students working in groups on problems and projects. The American culture is calling for more people who reach out and work creatively with others, including those with vastly different backgrounds and life experiences. As a future teacher, you should work to be able to *read school cultures*. What are the different messages the school's culture is sending out? Which rules of behavior, rituals and ceremonies, and accepted patterns of teacher–student interaction are communicated to students at a particular school? Does the "climate" of the classrooms and the school suggest warmth, support, and nurturing of individuals? Or do you observe a mood of disinterest, regimentation, and antipathy among staff and students?

2-4 Schools as Transmitters or Re-Creators of Culture

There are two views, or models, of how U.S. schools should socialize students: (1) the school as the social institution where the young receive from the older generation the very best of their culture and (2) the school as the social institution where the young learn skills and become agents of social change. Often an individual school is attempting to follow both models.

2-4a TRANSMITTING CULTURE

In the model of the school as acculturator, schools exist to advance society by ensuring that the young know and appreciate the dominant ideas and values of their society's culture. The goal of cultural transmission in U.S. public schools is to teach the American way of looking at the world and the American way of doing things.

This desire to ensure that the young share the common culture may explain why, in many U.S. school systems, we teach American history in the third, seventh, and eleventh grades. It can also explain why, for instance, we give little attention to the histories of China and India, even though they are among the most populous nations on earth and both have old, rich cultural heritages.

> *Education is simply the soul of a society as it passes from one generation to another.*
>
> **—GILBERT K. CHESTERTON (1874–1936),**
> British author

Technology may create learning opportunities for students.

Rubberball/Mike Kemp/Getty Images

Without even being conscious of it, our teachers instruct our young in our version of reality and our way of handling the real world. Of course, the schools of other countries do the same for their own young. Schools in Iran, for instance, differ markedly from schools in Ghana, and both differ dramatically from their counterparts in the United States. Even so, the schools of each country are attempting to perform a similar function: to transmit the unique culture of the country to its newest members, the young.

People who view schools as transmitting culture usually talk about society as an organism—that is, as a living thing that can thrive or deteriorate based on how well different elements of society function together. When a society is healthy, each of its various components (the government, schools, communities, families, and individuals) does what it ought to be doing and works in concert with all the other components. Conflict is viewed negatively, and society works toward finding consensus among different groups and eliminating any conflict. From this perspective, it is vitally important that the older generation, including parents and teachers, help the young find value and meaning in their own culture so that they will internalize its values and contribute to its smooth functioning. That may not seem particularly exciting, but it certainly beats social disorder.

Acculturation and Diversity

Several dangers lurk beneath the surface when schools adopt the position that they should concentrate on transmitting the dominant culture. If schools offer the young an understanding of only the prevailing culture, the result may be an attitude of smug cultural superiority, which often leads nations and individuals to commit foolish actions. In cultural terms, what we do not know we often do not respect, and without mutual respect people easily become enemies. In recent decades, instantaneous electronic communications, missile-delivered nuclear weapons, and interdependent national economies have increasingly made the world a "global village," and our students must learn how to function in this new world.

In recent decades, the United States has also experienced a surge of immigration from Central America, the Middle East, Southeast Asia, and elsewhere. These new Americans tend to be young, and both the newly arrived parents and their children are hungry for schooling. Although most are eager to learn American ways and American culture, teachers and students alike need to consider these students' native cultures. The majority of these immigrant children speak a language other than English at home. Sometimes schools, as part of acculturating children, unintentionally pull them away from their individual ethnic backgrounds. For example, one in five U.S. students goes home at night to a family in which English is a second language. As they become acculturated, using English becomes more important for these children, and their first languages become something private, rarely used in public.

Other school models try to acculturate the child while supporting his or her ethnic heritage. For example, elementary schools in Calexico, California, serve large populations of newly arrived Mexican children. Teachers design the classrooms so that American and Hispanic cultures are honored, and children learn to operate effectively in both languages.[1]

The presence of new Americans in a school can be a valuable resource in the effort to increase multicultural understanding and appreciation. Although U.S. schools need to transmit American culture, we must realize that what we call "American culture" has always embraced many cultures. Nevertheless, a primary responsibility of the schools is to assist foreign-born students in the acquisition of a high level of English proficiency. This can be a delicate and politically charged balancing act.

We will return to this thorny issue when we discuss multiculturalism and bilingual education in Chapter 3, "Who Are Today's Students in a Diverse Society?"

2-4b RECONSTRUCTING SOCIETY

The realization that the modern world is a dangerous place, faced with many complex issues, from international terrorists and nuclear weapons to widespread hunger and social injustice, has led some educators to posit that schools must become the tool of social reconstruction. Instead of seeing schools as places where past collective wisdom flows down to those who have the capacity and interest to make use of it, these educators assume a much more active, even assertive role for the school. According to this perspective, schools and teachers should work toward activating student interest and commitment to improving society. Unlike those who wish to transmit culture, educators who wish to reconstruct society accept the existence of conflicts among different groups and look at them as important tools to understand these groups' view of social problems.

> *The great aim of education is not knowledge but action.*
>
> —HERBERT SPENCER (1820–1903),
> British philosopher

Called **social reconstructionists**, these educators see the role of schools as forming the young into agents of change and participating in the decision about how society needs to change. Compared to those committed to cultural transmission, they have less reverence for the accumulated wisdom of the past and more concern for the world's problems and the necessity to create a new order. They reject the idea of schools being "sorting machines," separating students for different life roles, and see successful students not so much as cultivated people, but as autonomous citizens ready to join with others to tackle the world's ills and help in the reconstruction of society. Recently, the most influential advocate of this position is William Ayers.

Even among social reconstructionists, however, a wide range of emphases and views are evident. Social reconstructionists fall into two broad categories: *democratic reconstructionists* and *economic reconstructionists*.

Democratic Reconstructionists

Democratic reconstructionists see the solution to certain trends and current issues, such as racism, poverty, and the destruction of the ecosystem, as the responsibility of an aroused and skilled citizenry.[2] The school's mission, then, is to prepare students for vigorous participation in their government. The focus of schooling is on developing knowledge of democratic processes, critical thinking skills, and group process skills so the student can work fruitfully with others for social improvement. In more active programs, students select, study, and work on a community environmental problem, such as the polluting of landfills with unrecycled garbage. (We will return to this concept of democratic reconstructionism later in this chapter, in the discussion of Thomas Jefferson.)

Economic Reconstructionists

Economic reconstructionists tend to take a harsher view of the dominant culture and see schools as the pliant servants of those in power. The influence of corporate values is seen in many phases of school life, from the way textbooks are used to the widespread use of testing.[3] Moreover, economic reconstructionists often argue that schools *claim* to serve the needs of all but, in fact, serve the needs of the elites (i.e., the people with the most power), for whom the schools act as a convenient "social sorting-mechanism." Economic reconstructionists suggest that schools disguise this fact, either by their own naiveté or by their willing support of the existing system. Because of their deep suspicions of, and sometimes outright disgust with, capitalism, economic reconstructionists are often labeled *neo-Marxists*. Currently, two U.S. educators, Henry Giroux and Michael Apple, are major advocates for this economic reconstructionist view.

One noted economic reconstructionist was the Brazilian educator Paulo Freire. Freire's first book, *The Pedagogy of the Oppressed*, describes his work with poverty-stricken, illiterate peasants in his native Brazil.[4] As Freire tried to teach these adults to read, he saw they were trapped in an economic and social web over which they had little control. Likewise, the normal mechanisms of education, such as grading and control by the teacher, imposed on the peasants a passivity and subservience to authority. For Freire, the typical methods and routines of schooling are a form of oppression in that they keep people from becoming fully free and independent. To counter this tendency, Freire taught literacy by helping the peasants to (1) name their problem (a polluted water supply); (2) analyze the problem (sewage contamination of the springs); and (3) collectively take action (design and build a new sewage system) to solve the problem.

Although both democratic and economic reconstructionists focus on social problems and try to foster in students the attitudes and skills necessary to solve them, economic reconstructionists question more deeply the fundamental economic and social arrangements in a society. They see education as a necessary means for restructuring societal power structures. For them, money, power, and control of education are tightly bound together. Critics of the social reconstructionists' approach to education see it as naive and wrongheaded. They emphasize two points: (1) Our young need to acquire the basic skills and background before they become social activists, and (2) our current economic and social relations are too fragile and too serious to be toyed with by innocent and immature children.

Pause *and* Reflect

1. Which of these two broad educational approaches— transmitting the culture or recon- structing the culture—has more appeal to you? Why?
2. How open are you to seriously considering the other approach?

2-5 The Four Basic Purposes of School

Having most likely spent 12 or 13 years in school—the better part of your life—you are probably convinced you know the territory. Isn't it obvious what schools are and what they do? Perhaps. Yet most of us tend to think of schools in limited ways. Our own experiences within a relatively few schools influence what we think about all schools and what we understand of schools in general. Thus to gain a greater perspective, it is important to look at schools from different vantage points. The two missions we just examined, schools for "transmission of the culture" or for "reconstructing society," represent rather broad, general purposes for schools. Now we examine four purposes for schools that are closer to the everyday reality of teachers and students.

> To enable students to understand the world around them and the talents within them so that they can become fulfilled individuals and active, compassionate citizens.
>
> —SIR KEN ROBINSON,
> British author

What should our schools be trying to do? This fairly straightforward, almost innocent question is, however, also perennial and has stirred fierce arguments among different groups. If residents have strongly conflicting views about what their community's schools should do, the question can rip apart the often delicate fabric of a community. It taps into serious disagreements about what different people think of contemporary American culture and society and what they want the schools to do for their children.

To further illustrate that point, we have included several quotes about schools in this section. Some were written centuries ago, others more recently. As you read each, think about how the speaker

T (F)
Although our schools have many purposes, all agree that developing intellectual skills is the clear, primary purpose.

Students tend to learn more when instruction relates to their lives and concerns.

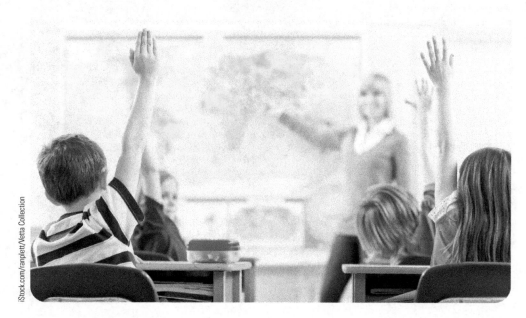

iStock.com/ranplett/Vetta Collection

characterizes the functions of schools and education. Also think about your own schooling and what you want to do as a teacher in today's schools.

2-5a INTELLECTUAL PURPOSES

Jacques Barzun was a cultural historian who until his recent death wrote frankly about the current state of schools in the United States:

> What do we really want from our schools? . . . Given the public's muddled feelings about brainwork (which is what "excellence" refers to) and the parental indifference up to now about what their children are being taught, the school has a double fight on its hands: against ignorance inside the walls and against cultural prejudice outside, the prejudice lying so deep that those who harbor it do not even know they do. . . . The difficulties of schooling . . . do not change. . . . Difficulties remain. It will always be difficult to teach well; to learn accurately; to read, write, and count readily and competently; to acquire a sense of history and develop a taste for literature and the arts. . . . For this purpose no school . . . is ever just right; it is only by the constant effort of its teachers that it can even be called satisfactory.[5]

> —JACQUES BARZUN

If you said that Barzun was emphasizing here the academic or *intellectual* purposes of schools, you would be right. One long-standing purpose of schools has been to foster the intellectual development of the young. Barzun was one of many observers who contend that promoting academic learning is the single most important purpose of schools.

Most people who highlight the intellectual purpose of schools believe that the development of reason, through intellectual pursuits, leads to individual enlightenment. Rationality—that is, the ability to know, to think, and to reason—is seen as an attribute distinct to humans and, more importantly, as the capacity that *makes us human*. Many of those who rank intellectual purposes as the highest priority see school as the one institution most available and most common to all people. They believe, therefore, that promoting intellectual development in schools is essential so that all children have the opportunity to become rational human beings.

Real materials help focus students' attention.

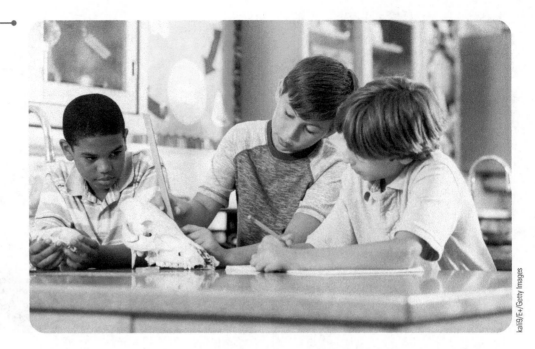

kali9/E+/Getty Images

The intellectual purpose of school is included in every school's mission. The way it is manifested, however, can look different from school to school. Some schools exist for the primary purpose of helping students develop their intellects. You may have heard about or even attended a secondary school that requires students to study "the great books" or one that has adopted the International Baccalaureate (IB) curriculum, currently taught in 1,725 U.S. schools and growing in popularity.[6]

2-5b POLITICAL AND CIVIC PURPOSES

Now, let's consider the views of Thomas Jefferson, our third president, who was a passionate advocate for establishing schools in order to assure the survival of the new republic he had helped establish. Historian Donald Kagan, a great student of Jefferson, summarizes his views here[7]: Jefferson was convinced that there needed to be an education for all citizens if they and their new kind of popular government were to flourish. He understood that schools must provide "to every citizen the information he needs for the transaction of his own business; to enable him to calculate for himself, and to express and preserve his ideas, his contracts, and accounts, in writing." For Jefferson, though, the most important goals of education were civic and moral. In his "Preamble to the 1779 Virginia Bill for the More General Diffusion of Knowledge" he addresses the need for all students to have a political education through the study of the "forms of government, political history, and foreign affairs. This was not meant to be a "value free" exercise; on the contrary, its purpose was to communicate the special virtues of republican representative democracy, the dangers that threatened it, and the responsibility of its citizens to esteem and protect it. This education was to be a common experience for all citizens, rich and poor, for every one of them had natural rights and powers, and every one had to understand and esteem the institutions, laws, and traditions of his country if it was to succeed.

You will read more about Jefferson's contributions to the American public schools in Chapter 10, "What Is the History of America's Struggle for Educational Opportunity?" For now, note that Jefferson hoped that American schooling would help establish and sustain the United States of America, an infant nation. One of the overriding concerns of the early political leaders was, in fact, how people would learn to be American citizens and *not* subjects of a foreign king.

Jefferson's views shared above underscore the *political and civic* purposes of schooling. Jefferson thought schools could help people learn how to govern themselves wisely and justly. The only sure way for any country to have a well-informed citizenry is through the systematic education that schooling can bring. He championed the concept of the "office of citizen," expressing his belief that American-style democracy obliges all who desire participation to become educated, engage their respective consciences, and act. Citizens' likeliest forays into political activity are voting for or against political representatives and legislation, joining or challenging civic organizations, and supporting or refuting societal reforms. Citizens may even abstain from public policy making entirely as a message, or pseudo-vote, of displeasure in their choices for governance.[8] That need may be more or less prominent at times, but the political purposes of schools have always been a primary reason why public schools exist.

In your own schools, you may have seen political and civic purposes emphasized through student government elections, voter registration drives, citizenship education programs, and even community service and outreach programs. Schools also promote these purposes by *how* they teach students to read, write, and discuss ideas rationally.

> *Never doubt that a small group of thoughtful, committed citizens can change the world. Indeed, it is the only thing that ever has.*
>
> —MARGARET MEAD (1901–1978), anthropologist

2-5c ECONOMIC PURPOSES

Let's now consider another fundamental purpose of education: the link between economics and schooling.

> An economy's ability to grow over time—its ability to innovate and raise both productivity and real incomes—is strongly tied to the quality of education provided to the vast majority of workers. Skills and intellectual capital are increasingly important in a modern economy, and schools play a central role in the development of valuable skills. We've seen this to be true in the United States as, over the past century, it expanded its economy in large part through expanding the number of people in society who received a strong, basic education.[9]

As this quote suggests, many Americans realize that schools primarily serve an *economic* purpose—that is, they believe that schools help students climb the economic ladder, obtaining the skills and knowledge required to attend college or to get a job. On the other hand, schools contribute to a nation by what economists call **"human capital,"** the stock of valuable knowledge, abilities, and other things possessed by an individual.[10] In essence, schools enhancing human capital is a win-win for both a nation and the individual.

Think about how you approach your own college education. If you and a good number of your fellow students were interviewed right now about why you are attending college, many of you would say that you attend college because you expect to earn a more comfortable living with a college degree than without one. Americans generally expect that more schooling will lead to greater personal wealth, and so far they are right. On the whole, high school graduates do obtain higher-paying jobs than those who didn't complete high school, and college graduates earn more than high school graduates.

Americans also expect that schools will prepare students for their future, regardless of whether that future includes a college education. High schools support that expectation by including courses of study that are *college preparatory* or *vocational* (more currently called CTE for career and technical education). Many Americans accept without question that schools guide students into curricular tracks that seem matched to their abilities and inclinations: Mathematically inclined students enroll in such courses as calculus and advanced placement (AP) physics, whereas labor-oriented students enroll in culinary arts or computer repair courses. The assumption underlying the economic purposes of schools is that well-schooled people and people *appropriately schooled* are vital to a strong national economy, regardless of whether they become business leaders or laborers. We will see later in the chapter that others question the practices that rest on this assumption, pointing out that curricular tracking and instructional practices are not always related so much to students' individual abilities as to their expected role in the work world.

The economic purposes of schooling have profound effects both on students and on society as a whole. You may have heard news accounts of the need for a "well-educated workforce" or the "new demands of working in 'green' industries." Pundits pronounce to one another what the new global economy will demand, and those predictions trickle down to schools. For instance, many school systems have placed emphasis on teaching computer skills and technology, with the goal of equipping graduates for the new realities of the workplace.

2-5d SOCIAL PURPOSES

We have identified intellectual, political, and economic purposes of schools. A fourth purpose is called the *umbrella purpose* because it is so all encompassing. Consider this last quote and think about what it means:

> A democracy that will survive and thrive in a world that demands a well-educated citizenry must build a system that can ensure all students the right to learn. . . . The [United States] can ill afford to maintain the structural inequalities in access to knowledge and resources that produce persistent and profound barriers to educational opportunity for large numbers of its citizens. Our future will be increasingly determined by our capacity and our will to educate all children well—a challenge we have very little time to meet if the United States is not to enact the modern equivalent of the fall of Rome.[11]

This quote draws attention to the *social purpose* of schools. At some point in your life, you may have heard that schools have a social responsibility and need to teach "social skills." What exactly does that mean to you?

Linda Darling-Hammond has been a major voice in American education for over 40 years. In the quote above, she has stressed the critical need to provide all our children with quality education not simply for their individual benefit, but for the very survival of our democracy. This means forming an educated citizenry with the intellectual skills to not only participate in our democracy but to preserve and improve it. But the social mission of our schools goes beyond just the intellectual realm. You may have heard the old adage, "It's good to be smart, but if you can't get along with people or don't know how to work with others, then it doesn't make much difference how much you know." Think of how many times elementary school teachers impress on pupils how important it is to *share*. Who decided that we needed to learn to share? Think of how frequently middle and high school teachers remind students to give their best effort on their homework or a project. What does "best effort" mean? Why not encourage students to "kick back and go with the flow"? Think also how schools and teachers emphasize punctuality and the importance of meeting commitments on time. These attributes are emphasized, in part, because they are characteristics prized by most employers. Further, the capacity to share, being sensitive to issues of time, and keeping commitments are habits that have wide value in marriage, family life, and community life. Sharing, concern for others, and promise keeping are three human qualities that illustrate how schooling helps children learn and adapt to social conventions. Because the social nature of schooling is so important, we will return to it later in the chapter.

Pause *and* Reflect

1. Thinking back on your high school experiences, how were these four purposes (intellectual, political and civic, economic, and social) evident in your schooling? Was one more dominant than the others? Which one? Why was this one purpose more dominant in your community?

2. Which of these four purposes of education do you believe ought to be given the greatest weight in the organization of schools?

Up CLOSE

Hold On! There's a New Entry. A Fifth Purpose for Schools: Signaling!

This brave new purpose rejects the other four and asserts that schools exist for employers, aiding them in deciding who they should and should not hire. Except for children learning their numbers and how to read, the curriculum—the content of schooling—has no real value to students. On the other hand, graduating from school "signals" to future employers that grads possess certain desirable characteristics: they can take orders, will conform to routines, have a certain level of intelligence, and will probably show up for work on time.

This theory of schooling is the work of economist Bryan Caplan, and his message is well captured in the title of his 2018 book, *The Case Against Education: Why the Educational System is a Waste of Time and Money*. Instead of spending their precious youth in classrooms learning things that they hate at the time and will never use in their adult lives (like trigonometry, crop rotation, colonial history, and cell biology),

young people should be out in the air and learning skills they will need in the workplace. Caplan is not shy about recommending that we relax child labor laws and begin feeding students into the workforce early on. He, also, dramatically recommends fewer colleges and universities enrolling a much-reduced percentage of students. While his signaling critique of schooling is attractive to the many who find schooling difficult or even punishing, it strikes your authors as simplistic and shallow. Caplan dismisses too easily the classic purpose of education to teach students "how to think:" evaluating evidence, reasoning logically, and formulating logical arguments. While this signaling theory may be attractive to those who believe we are spending too much on schools, for readers of this book it could make finding a teaching job a real challenge!

2-6 What Do Studies Reveal about the Nature of Schools?

What happens in schools, and how does the activity in a school contribute to or detract from its purpose? Researchers often look at the everyday events of human life and see patterns the rest of us may be only vaguely aware of. In the next several pages, we present a few of these studies and examine the patterns the researchers noticed, focusing first on elementary schools, then on middle schools and junior high schools, and finally on high schools.

2-6a LIFE IN ELEMENTARY SCHOOLS

One of the best perspectives on how time is usually spent in the elementary classroom is Philip W. Jackson's classic study *Life in Classrooms*.[12] Anthropologists have taught us that the humdrum aspects of human existence have cultural significance and that we must look at the most routine events in an elementary classroom if we are to understand what happens there. Are certain trivial acts repeated many times? How often do they occur? What is their cumulative effect on children? What do they teach children? Jackson's careful observations of elementary school classrooms show how revealing the answers to these questions can be.

Have you ever figured out how many hours a child spends in school? In most states, the school year is 180 days. The day typically begins at 8:30 A.M. and ends at 3 P.M., so it lasts a total of six and a half hours. If a child doesn't miss a day of school, he or she spends more than 1,000 hours in school each year. Including kindergarten,

VOICES from the Classroom

What Is a Good School?

Denis Gray is a law and justice teacher at Brighton High School in Boston, Massachusetts.

I teach in an urban high school, and it's a good school. For me, there are three criteria for what makes a good school:

1. The vast majority of its teachers want to have maximum impact on students through instruction.
2. Students have internalized the value of education and want to learn.
3. Most importantly, the educational and ancillary needs of all students are met.

To say the least, making this a reality in the lives of students does not go unchallenged. Students continually test us to determine whether we are "for real." Someone has said, "Students do not care what you know until they know that you care." Difficult students, in particular, test us. They test our patience, our self-control, our professionalism, our integrity, our faith, and our hope. Then, there are the self-doubt questions: "Am I a good teacher?," "Could my actions be interpreted as racist?," and "What could/should I be doing that I'm not?"

There are many models and methodologies for instructing and learning. Most of them assume that students *want* to learn. Yet the reality is that for many students, there is a profound disconnect between education and success. They see that high school students sign multimillion-dollar athletic contracts. Colleges that should know better are not interested in ensuring that their athletes graduate. Many parents shower their children with the latest designer clothes and sneakers. Many students have part-time jobs to ensure that they always have pocket money. In their minds is the question, "If I get what I want now, why do I need an education?" Then there are issues of alienation and mistrust. Many students view the education we are trying to give them as an attempt by the "establishment" to "mess with their heads."

Of the three criteria, I believe the last to be the most important. Today's urban school, as a matter of social conscience, must address the psychosocial needs of its students as never before. Today's teacher, as a matter of personal conscience, is required to assume many roles in students' lives, including parent, protector, counselor, and confidant. It is a tough and complex job, but it's a job I love.

the average child, by the end of sixth grade, will spend more than 7,000 hours in elementary school. How are those hours typically spent?

In pondering this question, you may think first of the curriculum, which specifies so many hours of reading, language arts, mathematics, science, play, social studies, music, art, and so on. But what do students really *do* when they are studying these subjects? They talk to each other or the teacher. They read silently and aloud. They yawn. They look out the window. They raise their hands. They line up. They stand up. They sit down. In short, they do a number of different things, many of them commonplace and trivial. To understand why some of these things happen, we must first look at what the teacher does.

The Teacher's Role

Jackson has observed that the elementary school teacher engages in as many as a thousand interpersonal interchanges each day.

The teaching–learning process consists, for the most part, of talking, and the teacher controls and directs discussion. The teacher acts as a *gatekeeper*, deciding who shall speak. (One may debate whether this *should* be the teacher's role, but clearly most teachers function this way.)

The teacher also acts as a *dispenser of supplies*. Because both space and resources are limited, and because the number of students wishing to use them at any one time is likely to be greater than the supply, the teacher must dole them out. A related function is as *granter of special privileges* to deserving students: passing out the milk, sharpening pencils, taking the roll, or spending free time at the computer. Although little teacher time is involved in awarding these special jobs, they are important. For better or worse, they help structure the classroom socially as a *system of rewards and punishments*.

Timekeeper is another teacher responsibility. It is the teacher who decides when a certain activity ends and another begins, when it is time to stop science and begin spelling, and when students go outside for recess. In some schools, the teacher is assisted in timekeeping by bells and buzzers that signal when a period is over. As Jackson observes, things happen because it is time for them to occur, not because students want them to happen.

All these teacher functions can be seen as responses to the crowded conditions in the classroom. If a teacher were dealing with one student at a time in a "one-on-one" tutorial situation, then gatekeeping, dispensing supplies, granting special privileges, and timekeeping would not be necessary. Given that a tutorial setting is not possible, much time and energy are spent *keeping order*. The resulting atmosphere has unavoidable effects on the students. What are some of the consequences for students in crowded classroom conditions?

What Students Experience

One inevitable outcome for students that results from the teacher's "traffic management" functions is *delay*. Because students' actions are limited by space, material resources, and the amount of teacher attention they can command, there are definite limits on their freedom in class. In addition, because the class ordinarily moves toward a goal as a group rather than as individuals, its slowest members often determine the pace of progress. *Waiting* is a familiar activity for elementary school children—that is, waiting in line to get a drink of water, waiting with arm propped at the elbow to be called on to answer a question, waiting to use the scissors, waiting until others have finished their work to go on to the next activity, waiting until four other students have finished reading aloud for a chance to do so, and on and on.

T (F)

Part of being a student in an elementary classroom is having to experience "denial of desire," which is frustrating, unnecessary, and detrimental.

Denial of desire is another common experience for elementary students. A question goes unanswered, a raised hand is ignored, talking out of turn is not permitted, relief of bodily functions is allowed only at specified times. Some denial is necessary and probably beneficial, but one thing is certain: Delayed gratification and denied desire are learned in school, and a certain amount of student frustration is bound to develop.

Students also experience frequent *interruptions* of many sorts, such as interruptions of seatwork by the teacher to give additional instructions or to clarify one student's question, interruptions when messages from the principal's office are read aloud to the class, interruptions for fire drills, interruptions when a teacher is working with one student and another student misbehaves, and so on. Students are expected either to ignore these intrusions or to quickly resume their activities. The emphasis on an inflexible schedule contributes to the sense of interruption by often making students begin activities before their interest has been aroused and stop at the height of their interest when the schedule dictates that they must begin another task.

A related phenomenon is *social distraction*. Students are often asked to behave as if they were alone, when they are actually surrounded by 20 to 30 other people.

It may be more effective for schooling to more closely resemble education.

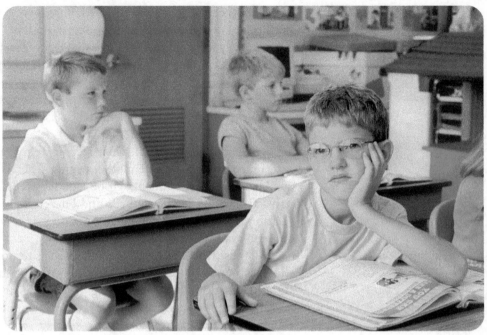

Butch Martin/Alamy Stock Photo

During assigned seatwork, for example, communication among students is often discouraged, if not forbidden. To be surrounded by friends, sometimes seated across from each other at a table, and not be allowed to talk is a difficult and tempting situation. As Jackson remarks, "These young people, if they are to become successful students, must learn how to be alone in a crowd."[13]

Delay, denial, interruption, and *social distraction*, then, are characteristic of life in elementary classrooms. Given these classroom conditions, it seems likely that students who either possess or quickly develop patience would find school more tolerable than students who lack it. The ability to control desires, delay rewards, and stifle impulses seems to be characteristic of successful students, whereas less successful students exhibit less patience and more impulsiveness.

2-6b LIFE IN MIDDLE AND JUNIOR HIGH SCHOOLS

In the "middle years," ages 11 to 13, students change in fundamental ways, becoming more independent, more social, and more involved in the world around them. It can be a stressful period for parents and teachers and, most especially, for the students themselves. Increasingly, these "middle years" are seen as a crucial time in an individual's formation. Early adolescence is characterized by a variety of developmental changes and needs that dramatically impact the school experience.

Among the major changes are:

- *Biological changes.* Early adolescence witnesses dramatic biological changes.[14] First, girls enter puberty an average of 18 months before boys during this stage. Second, even within gender the onset of puberty varies considerably, which complicates both genders' relationships with their classmates. Further, early-maturing girls, that is, the first to experience pubertal changes, often feel out of sync with their peers, resulting in emotional and adjustment issues.[15]

- *Cognitive changes.* Thinking also changes in significant ways during this period of development.[16] Students increasingly engage in abstract thinking and more sophisticated and elaborate information-processing strategies. They begin to use what Benjamin Bloom calls higher-order thinking.[17] Recent advances in cognitive research are revealing that the brain changes in significant ways during this period.[18] Continuing advances in this emerging field of brain structure and function will undoubtedly increase educators' understanding of adolescents' cognition and behavior.

- *Changes in self-concept, self-esteem, and identity development.* These three interrelated terms—self-concept, self-esteem, and identity development—all deal with slightly different aspects of an individual's *sense of self.* Early adolescence is a prime time for strong emergence of self-awareness. Children become vividly aware of their gender, race, and ethnicity during this period. Psychologists insist that integrating these experiences and characteristics into a coherent sense of self is fundamental to healthy development.[19]

- *Changes in achievement motivation.* Behavioral scientists have observed the somewhat obvious fact that some people have an intense desire to achieve something, whereas others may not seem that concerned about their achievements. They have labeled this phenomenon *achievement motivation,* the tendency to strive for success and to be goal oriented. Current criticism of middle schools frequently blames changes in achievement motivation as the direct cause of student disengagement.[20]

Although both younger and older students have these developmental needs, it is particularly important that schools serving children in the middle years meet these needs. Not meeting them often results in a young person's alienation from peers, loss of a sense of self-worth, and the onset of all sorts of destructive behavior, from fighting to escapism into drug use to promiscuity. As one specialist observed, "Every child wants to believe in himself or herself as a successful person; every youngster wants to be liked and respected; every youngster wants physical exercises and freedom to move; and youngsters want life to be just."[21] Easy to say, but enormously challenging for teachers in the modern school setting.

Types of Schools

Although many things in American schools remain constant, the way we educate young adolescents seems to be in constant flux. As will discuss more fully in Chapter 10, "What Is the History of America's Struggle for Educational Opportunity?," our knowledge about this topic is circumscribed somewhat by the plethora of grade-clustering patterns evident in U.S. schools. Up until the beginning of the nineteenth century, students went through eight grades of one-teacher-to-a-classroom elementary schools, and then some went on to multiple-teacher high schools. Reformers at the time thought the transition was too late and moved seventh, eighth, and ninth grade into what they called "junior" high school. This pattern was predominant until the 1960s, when theorists and reformers came to the conclusion that junior highs were becoming overly content focused and ignoring intellectual and development needs of young adolescents. Their answer was the "middle school," which stressed developmental goals in addition to more integration and exploration of subject matter. Since then, middle schools have become the dominant pattern, but with continuing debate about which particular pattern (grades 6–7, 5–7, 6–8, or 5–8) is most effective.[22] It is worth noting that most private and religious schools have traditionally resisted these changes and kept to the eight-grade elementary model.

While the middle school model is dominant in public education today, it is not without its critics. These middle school opponents site the information "drop-off" that is occurring between elementary and middle school. Recent test results in math and reading in all 50 states show that "between 1999 and 2004, elementary school students made solid gains in reading and math, while middle school students made

Schooling, instead of encouraging the asking of questions, too often discourages it.

—MADELEINE L'ENGLE (1918–2007), author

Pause *and* Reflect

1. What was the grade-clustering pattern in your junior high or middle school? Do you believe it was the best pattern for you?
2. Do you think that meeting the developmental goals cited previously is more crucial during middle school years than at other periods in students' lives? Why or why not?
3. Has your experience led you to agree or disagree with those who believe that academic achievement takes second place to personal growth in many of today's middle schools?

smaller gains in math and stagnated in reading."[23] Describing "the lost years of middle schooling" in the United States (grades 6, 7, and 8) as "an intellectual wasteland" and "the 'Bermuda Triangle' of American education," such critics call for a return to the K–8 pattern and a more rigorous, discipline-focused curriculum.[24] Supporters insist that the nature of the "middle years" requires a specially designed environment, but opponents characterize the curriculum as soft and disorganized, with the middle school's academic mission taking a backseat to addressing students' social and emotional needs. Urban school leaders in particular are moving back to the K–8 and 9–12 model.[25] They have been prompted by a New York City study, comparing the math and English achievement scores of students in middle schools and in K–8 schools. Not only did the middle schoolers do less well, but their disadvantage also grows larger over the course of the middle school years.[26]

Sometimes this is part of a reform agenda to "shake up" a failing status quo situation; sometimes to restore a more direct and rigorous academic focus; and sometimes for social and behavioral purposes. This last motive is supported by recent research that found that sixth-graders in middle schools got into significantly more discipline problems than those in K–8 schools, and further that this pattern of misbehavior and concomitant academic problems persisted.[27]

Developmental or Academic Purposes Foremost?

Is there one right way of educating students in the middle grades best? Probably not. No one pattern is superior for all students. Increasingly, the debate over middle schools versus junior high versus K–8 elementary school is being influenced by a greater focus on academic achievement, concerns over the earlier and earlier arrival of puberty in children, and even district financial and building issues affecting the configuration of grades. Like many issues in school, this one involves a series of trade-offs. However, what is consistently identified as important for educating students in the middle grades is that the developmental needs of early adolescents, such as self-esteem and interpersonal skills, must be acknowledged and considered in developing and organizing programs.

2-6c LIFE IN HIGH SCHOOLS

The role of the American high school has changed dramatically over the past century. A hundred years ago, it was still an institution designed to prepare the privileged few for college. Today, high schools are committed to provide a gateway for all students to either postsecondary education or the workplace. Although the intention is noble, many see our high schools as the soft spot in our entire—pre–K to graduate school—system of education.

Much criticism and censure of our nation's secondary schools tends to come from college professors and college students, both claiming incoming students had not received the necessary preparation to do college work. In a recent survey of nearly 1,500 recent graduates, "just 24 percent of graduates said they were significantly challenged during high school. Twenty percent of these high school graduates said that 'expectations were low and . . . it was easy to slide by.'"[28] The college instructors in this study claimed that 42 percent of college students are not adequately prepared by their high schools to meet college expectations.

On the other hand, the growing criticism is of a different nature: concern over what some see as our high schools' failure to prepare graduates for the world of work.

Technology can provide important educational opportunities

In 2012 testimony before Congress, a report revealed that nationally only three out of four students in a high school class graduate. In the past, when there were plentiful unskilled jobs, this was not a serious issue. However, we currently are turning out a million students a year lacking the skills and knowledge needed to find employment, and nearly three out of four high school dropouts in their 20s are not employed full time. In the new economics of the twenty-first century, this is a dangerous problem for individual students and the nation.[29]

A government website not long ago reported that "[n]ationwide, 7,000 students drop out every day and only about 70 percent of students graduate from high school with a regular high school diploma. Two thousand high schools in the United States produce more than half of all dropouts, and a recent study suggests that in the 50 largest cities, only 53 percent of students graduate on time. Research shows that poor and minority children attend these so-called 'dropout factories'— the 2,000 schools that produce more than 50 percent of our nation's dropouts—at significantly higher rates."[30]

Microsoft founder, Bill Gates, who has focused on the reform of U.S. secondary education as a primary target of his philanthropy, offered the following analysis of our high schools:

> America's high schools are obsolete. By "obsolete," I don't just mean that our high schools are broken, flawed, and underfunded—though a case could be made for every one of those points. By "obsolete," I mean that our high schools—even when they're working exactly as designed—cannot teach our kids what they need to know today. Training the workforce of tomorrow with the high schools of today is like trying to teach kids about today's computers on a fifty-year-old mainframe. It's the wrong tool for the times. Our high schools were designed fifty years ago to meet the needs of another age. Until we design them to meet the needs of the 21st century, we will keep limiting— even ruining—the lives of millions of Americans every year.[31]

Multiple Purposes

As the U.S. economy faces increasing competition from our trading partners around the globe, the intensity of criticism of our high schools has increased.

The Comprehensive High School. The high school years bring people to the front door of adulthood. They begin to think about and sense what their futures might become. In many developed countries, this is the moment when young people are separated into different schools, such as the European gymnasiums for those planning to go to college and onto the professions, and trade and technical schools for those who will take a more direct route into the work world. Americans, by and large, have chosen to educate young people in **comprehensive high schools**, multipurpose schools with different tracks. *Academic* tracks stress the traditional subjects of English, history, mathematics, science, and foreign languages as preparation for college. A *general* track usually allows a greater number of elective courses and less rigorous versions of the traditional subjects. *Vocational* tracks may include a combination of academic and job-related courses; students in these tracks are preparing for a job after graduation.

The comprehensive high school is part of our nation's democratic tradition, and like our focus on diversity, is meant to strengthen our democratic traditions. Nevertheless, because of the variations in courses required for these different tracks and the differing standards for student achievement among them, the reality of the term *high school education* takes on myriad meanings. Americans seem to want high schools to accomplish everything. The resulting confusion of goals is evident in the variety of goal statements adopted by states for their schools, in the written goals found in teachers' manuals or school district curriculum guides, and in teacher and student responses when asked about school goals. This is a major reason why our schools presently are making a fundamental shift: Graduation from high school will now mean the achievement of certain academic standards rather than 12 or 13 years of school attendance. Currently, the great majority of our states are in the process of adopting the Common Core, a set of curricular standards in mathematics and English language arts that students throughout the country may have to achieve for graduation.

> *Human history becomes more and more a race between education and catastrophe.*
>
> —H. G. WELLS (1866–1946),
> anthropologist

The Shopping-Mall High School

The important move toward standards-based education—which will be discussed more fully in Chapter 5, "What Is Taught?," and Chapter 12, "How Should Education Be Reformed?"—has been fueled from many sources. One of the most severe and therefore influential criticisms was that not only did our high schools have a confusion of goals, but also they had become quite lax. This goal confusion and laxity was brought to the attention of educators and the general public a few decades ago by a research study that compared our comprehensive high schools to shopping malls. The metaphor states that, like a shopping mall, our schools cater to a variety of student consumers, emphasizing variety and choice, trying to have something for everyone.[32] Schools have offered a diverse curriculum in an attempt to appeal to all comers. The student-customers, on the other hand, are expected to make their own course selections. The schools essentially maintain neutrality in regard to students' or parents' choices among the many alternatives offered. The customer has the final word.

Staying with the shopping mall metaphor, this study found that some customers (students) are serious about buying, others are just browsing and looking for ideas on what to buy, and still others are at the mall to meet their friends and "cruise." Faced with customers with such different levels of commitment, teachers reach accommodations, or treaties, that promote mutual goals or keep the peace. For example, some teachers make their deals crystal clear when they advise students, "Don't take my class if you don't want to work." If students don't want to play by these rules, they don't have to take the course. Another teacher in the study said, "Don't hassle me and I won't hassle you. I'll let you slide through if you don't interfere with the students who want to work."[33]

Within the "shopping-mall" high school can be found "specialty shops," the niches for students and families wanting more learning and school engagement. These venues include top-track programs, special education programs, vocational and technical education programs, and extracurricular programs, such as marching band or football. Because the students in these programs have been designated as special, they tend to receive special attention.

In contrast, the average or unspecial students (often called *general*, *normal*, or *regular*) are generally ignored by the specialty shops; they do not receive the additional commitment of time, personal relationships, and intensity of learning generally given to "specialty-shop" students. They have no important allies or advocates, and their treaties are characterized by avoidance of learning, not engagement. Schools may try to nurture these students' self-esteem, but they do not make academic demands of them at a crucial time in their lives for establishing important study and work habits. (Think Fred, the social studies teacher in Chapter 1.)

Since the shopping-mall high school metaphor was proposed a number of years ago, malls and their boutique retail shops have come under a great deal of pressure. Shopping tastes have changed, increasingly in the direction of the Amazon model of

Internet shopping from home. Does this new à la carte model where consumers can make individual selections as opposed to set combinations have any relevance for today's curriculum and schooling?

Typically, a career academy is a small learning community of students (30 to 60 per grade) and teachers dedicated to bridging the gap between the academic goals of secondary school and realistic preparation for work in a particular career, such as health care or computer technology. Besides their academic course work, students study vocational subjects that typically involve internships and other opportunities to gain work experience and earn money. Often, these career academies involve cooperative programs with nearby community colleges.

Nevertheless, criticisms of the *process* of our high schools (that is, ambiguous goals and laxity) and the *product* (graduates ill-prepared for the workplace) have propelled many of the standards-based reform efforts.

> *Expecting all children the same age to learn from the same materials is like expecting all children the same age to wear the same size clothing.*
>
> **—MADELINE HUNTER,**
> psychologist, principal, and
> assistant superintendent

Pause *and* Reflect

1. The high school years are often said to be "the best years of your life." Do you agree with this assertion? If so, why? If not, what could and should be done to change the high school experience?
2. Drawing on your experiences in school and in your teacher education program, how might you begin to balance the "process" and "product" of schools? Which, in your view, deserves priority? Why?

2-7 What Is a Good School?

First, the obvious: Not all schools are good schools. Second, good schools do not just happen—they are *made*. A school is the *product* of people's intellectual and physical energies. At any particular moment, the way a school *is* reflects the multiplicity of efforts that have gone into creating and maintaining it. Further, like towns and civilizations, schools rise and fall. They are human creations—dynamic and continually on the move.

No school, at least in the authors' experience, is "right" or "good" for all students. Nevertheless, some schools are strikingly better than others—that is, some schools provide a significantly better education for a much larger percentage of their students than do others. These schools, referred to in the educational literature as **effective schools**, are the focus of this section.

Defining an effective school has been a major concern of educators for several decades. A popular definition of an effective school is one in which learning for all students is maximized. Although this definition is certainly compelling, it is hardly precise. Besides the question of what constitutes learning, the meaning of *effective* is uncertain. Effective or good in what dimension? In academically engaged and happy students? In a teaching staff with high morale? In the percentage of students who are promoted or graduate? Those who go on to college? What kinds of colleges? How many students become skilled technicians and accomplished artisans? How many succeed in business or professional life? In athletics? Socially? Ethically?

Effective, as currently defined in most of the educational research literature, refers to students' achievement test scores in basic skills such as reading and mathematics. Although such tests measure skills that are not the only objectives of education, achievement in these academic areas is an important and widely acclaimed outcome of schooling. Also, achievement in reading and mathematics is easier to measure than character formation, artistic development, or passion for ideas.

2-7a CHARACTERISTICS OF AN EFFECTIVE SCHOOL

For many years now, some of our country's best scientific minds have been working to discover what makes some schools vastly better than others. These findings comprise effective schools research. The major focus of this research has been to discover the characteristics or qualities of effective schools.[34] Among the most significant characteristics that found to be correlated with high achievement in the basic skills were high expectations for student performance, communication among teachers, a task orientation among the staff, the ability to keep students on task, the expenditure of little time on behavior management, the principal's instructional leadership, the participation of parents, and the school environment.

The Teacher's Expectations

Through their attitude and regular encouragement, teachers in effective schools communicate to students their belief that the students will achieve the goals of instruction. In effect, the teachers get across to students a "can-do" attitude about learning. We discuss teacher expectations more in Chapter 6, "What Makes a Teacher Effective?"

Communication among Teachers

Teachers in effective schools do not operate in a vacuum, each in his or her isolated classroom. Instead, they talk among themselves about their work and converse about one another's students. They know the curricular materials and activities that go on in one another's classrooms, and they are helpful to one another. In short, effective schools have teachers who are good colleagues.

Task Orientation

The faculties of effective schools are highly task oriented. They begin instruction early in the class period and end instruction late in the period. The staff approaches its teaching responsibilities with a serious air and wastes little time in class. Whether the classes are formal or informal, underneath the surface of events lies a seriousness of purpose that is communicated to students.

Academic Engaged Time

Academic engaged time (or *academic learning time*) refers to the amount of time students are actually engaged in relevant content-related activities while experiencing a high rate of success. As we describe in Chapter 6, this characteristic involves the ability of a teacher to engage students in academic tasks, such as reading or solving math problems, and to keep their attention on these instructional activities. Research has demonstrated a tight link between the amount of time devoted to academic learning tasks and students' achievement.[35]

The teacher-parent-student triangle is a powerful educative force.

Digital Vision./Photodisc/Getty Images

© 2016 Cengage Learning®

▶❚❚ TeachSource Video Case

Parental Involvement in School Culture

Watch the video clips, study the artifacts in the case, and reflect on the following questions:

1. Which of the other aspects of an effective school and effective teaching can you see in the portrayals in this video case?

2. Were parents involved in the schools you have attended? How? How could their involvement have been improved?

3. Do you as a teacher feel comfortable about involving parents in your classroom? If not, what can you do now to address your concerns?

Behavior Management

We have all been in classrooms with teachers who spent huge chunks of time trying to quiet students to get them "on task" or who, in the course of correcting one student, disturbed all the rest, causing a ripple of distraction throughout the room. Teachers in effective schools have learned techniques to minimize the time devoted to managing students. They are efficient both in handling discipline problems and in implementing the learning activities. In addition, these teachers do not routinely resort to corporal punishment, because they use other techniques to deal with student behavior. (See Chapter 6, "What Makes a Teacher Effective?" for more on classroom management.)

The Principal

Principals play an important role in effective schools. Instead of being faceless bureaucrats aimlessly shuffling papers, the principals of effective schools are instructional leaders. They have strong views on the purposes of education and are vitally concerned about the quality of teaching and learning in their schools. Still, the principal is perceived as democratic in approach and cooperative in relationships with faculty. Effective principals gain teachers' confidence and clearly communicate to them a vision of what the school should accomplish and how each teacher can contribute toward this end.

Parents

An effective school reaches out and draws in parents instead of ignoring them or keeping them at arm's length. Parents are treated as key members of the learning team, as partners with the professional staff in helping their children achieve academic success. In addition to aiding in students' intellectual achievement, the involvement of parents can help improve their children's self-concepts, work habits, and attitudes toward school. The video case *Parental Involvement in School Culture* lets you view one example of how parents can contribute to an effective school.

T Ⓕ
Research shows that academically effective schools are good at remaining independent of parental involvement.

The School Environment

Attempts to answer the question "What is a good school?" are on-going. One of the newest factors to be identified as contributing to a school's effectiveness is trust. **Relational trust** refers to the network of trust among people. It is built on four factors: respect for the other, competence, personal regard for the other, and integrity. It involves all the players in a child's education and appreciates the contributions of each: fellow teachers, aides, administrators, parents, and the students . . . everyone in the school community. Schools vary greatly on this factor of trust, but where there are high levels of trust, there is a high probability of an effective school. A high trust school is where people feel cared for, where honesty among people is high, and where effort is appreciated. An environment of trust acts as a school's glue, keeping people together and moving forward.[36]

We strongly suspect that a number of qualities besides those mentioned here make major contributions to the establishment of an effective school. Among these are a pervasive sense of curiosity, a passion for excellence, a strong belief in students' capacity to grow, and an environment of kindness and support.

2-8 The Unfinished Work of the Schools

The question that we asked at the beginning of this chapter—What is a school?—has no single, satisfactory answer. Schools are human inventions. People bring schools into being for a variety of intellectual and social purposes. Ideally, the primary purposes of schools are to advance the common good and to help people live happy and successful lives. However, if schools are to serve a society, they must at least keep pace with that society. Many people who are concerned about our schools believe that the schools are moving very slowly, while the rest of society experiences dynamic change. They believe, in effect, the schools are out of step with society, usually being either too far ahead (a rarity) or lagging behind (the more common situation) the needs of the young people they exist to serve.

Schools, like every social institution, need to continually assess what they are *really doing*. They must first decide whether their purposes and goals are the right purposes and goals, and second to determine whether they are actually achieving those purposes. If you become an educator, you must have this commitment to continual re-examination and renewal of the schools.

The purposes for which schools are brought into being remain vital to our society. People—particularly parents—have a great desire for good schools for their children, and, as you will see later in this book, many excellent ideas are being generated and movements are underway for the renewal of our schools.

OUR FINAL WORD

Some readers may be uncomfortable with the idea that it is their job to renew the schools. Many may believe that becoming a good classroom teacher is sufficient. On the other hand, teachers are more than technicians in charge of their classrooms. As professional people, they and their teacher colleagues must have a forceful, clear voice in deciding how they render their services. It follows that teachers are not simply responsible for their own performance, but they also bear some responsibility for the total educational enterprise. To live up to this responsibility requires a deep understanding of the schools and much hard work. Indeed, it is the very critical nature of the problems confronting the schools that makes teaching such an exciting occupation today. In the immediate future, education is where the action will be. You have a chance to bring fresh new ideas and energy, and to complete this *unfinished work of the schools*.

WHY TEACH? YOUR FINAL WORD

1. Had you thought about your school being a "culture"? In what ways do you think the cultures in the schools you attended affected and changed you?
2. Review the four purposes of schooling described in the text. Which one appeals most to you as a potential educator? Why?
3. What do you see as "the unfinished work of the schools"? Specifically, what changes do you believe must take place for schools to serve the current generation of children?

KEY TERMS

comprehensive high school (45)
culture (29)
democratic reconstructionists (33)
economic reconstructionists (33)
education (27)
effective schools (47)
human capital (37)

relational trust (50)
school cultures (30)
schooling (27)
social reconstructionists (33)
socialization (30)
society (29)

FOR FURTHER INFORMATION

Web Resources

MiddleWeb: All About the Middle Grades

Middleweb.com is an all-purpose site developed for teachers of grades 4 through 8. It is an active resource for ideas and activities that offers a free newsletter.

Print Resources

Eric A. Hanushek, and Ludger Woessmann, *The Knowledge Capital of Nations: Education and the Economics of Growth* (Cambridge, MA: *MIT Press*, 2015).

This book lays out the authors' major theses about the link between quality schooling and a nation's economic progress, and the value of increasing an investment in enriching "human capital."

Ken Robinson and Lou Aronica, *Creative Schools: The Grassroots Revolution That's Transforming Education* (New York: Penguin Books, 2015).

Sir Ken Robinson is a fresh voice on the educational scene. His TED Talk on the subject is the most viewed in the organization's history. The theme in this book is how to transform the nation's troubled educational system through focusing on creativity and students' human potential.

Philip Jackson, *Life in Classrooms* (New York: Teachers College Press, 1990).

Philip Jackson's research is heavily relied on in this chapter. His careful observations of what is actually going on in classrooms has provided important insights into our schools' hidden curriculum.

Jacques Barzun, *Begin Here: The Forgotten Conditions of Teaching and Learning* (Chicago: University of Chicago Press, 1991).

Jacques Barzun, who was a leader in the movement to refresh schools' intellectual and academic mission, offers guidance for resolving the crisis in America's schools and colleges. The book offers an extraordinarily fresh, sensible, and practical program for better schools.

Who Are Today's Students in a Diverse Society?

InTASC Standards 1, 2, 3, 5, 7, and 10

LEARNING OBJECTIVES

3-1 Describe how the changes of the U.S. population are changing the demographic composition of school-aged children.

3-2 Give examples of ways schools seek to support English language learners' schooling experience.

3-3 List ways that teachers support students with disabilities.

3-4 Discuss how teachers provide enrichment experiences for gifted and talented students.

3-5 Discuss ways that gender issues affect the curriculum, classroom interactions, and achievement levels.

3-6 Identify strategies teachers and schools use to create a safe and supportive learning environment for all students, specifically lesbian, gay, bisexual, or transgendered students.

3-7 List effective instructional strategies to teach in a culturally relevant classroom.

Truth or Fiction?

T F   By 2060, the number of children who are two or more races will double.

T F   The majority of English language learners was born in the United States and are U.S. citizens.

T F   Most children receiving special education services do so in separate classrooms with special education teachers.

T F   After lagging men for many years, women now hold a similar number of jobs in STEM-related fields.

In some ways, children never change. The pictures of children in classic literature are as true today as when they were first written. Look at the overly curious Alice in Wonderland, the magical Harry Potter, or the courageous Scout Finch. These characters are endearing to us in part because we have all known children like them. Real children of today are also very much like the children of yesterday or the children of tomorrow. Yet, schools and society are more diverse now than ever. It will be important for you to consider how your students and your classroom are situated within our diverse society. As a teacher, you have the potential for engaging your students from a range of backgrounds in a way that will help students value their identity and respect diversity around them. Creating an inclusive learning environment is a careful balance of the teaching strategies you will employ and the curriculum you teach. There are many resources and supports to scaffold your journey to engaging students from diverse backgrounds. As a teacher, being prepared for diverse classrooms will help you work effectively and equitably with your students.

How schools approach issues of diversity have direct implications on student learning. Teachers hold the potential to bring about positive change not just for their students but for society. It is critical that we examine how to address our differences in developmentally appropriate ways. In this chapter, we hope to make you more aware of the diversity in our society and classrooms, the range of abilities among the students you will encounter, and schools' attempts to address these areas of diversity. We also hope to help you begin to consider strategies that will help you create an inclusive classroom for students of diverse backgrounds.

3-1 Sources of Student Diversity

You will see diversity in your students along a number of dimensions, including who they are, what they need, and what kinds of abilities they have:

- Students in your classroom are likely to come from a variety of *racial and ethnic backgrounds*, representing many different cultures and ways of looking at the world. Cultural differences among teachers and students can give rise to misunderstandings unless you learn more about your students' backgrounds and expectations. Culturally responsive teaching not only supports students in their academic learning, it also can push back against systemic inequities in schools and society.

- Some of your students may speak a primary *language other than English*. We will see that parents, educators, and policy makers have become divided, often bitterly so, over the best way to teach these English language learners in U.S. public schools.

- Another dimension of diversity will be seen in the *academic abilities and achievements* of your students. Some students will enter the school environment and immediately thrive. Others will appear not to respond to your teaching. It will be important for you to offer differentiated instruction for your students.

- Students in your classroom will develop at different rates and display *diverse needs*. Recognizing these needs will help you better understand some student behaviors and increase your insight into how to respond.

- *Boys and girls*, even when they come from the same socioeconomic, racial, or ethnic group, are different. They are raised differently even within the same families, and often society has different expectations of them. Treating boys and girls equitably as individuals and not as gender stereotypes is a constant challenge for both male and female teachers.

Students who enter your classroom may come from diverse racial or ethnic backgrounds, speak different languages, and have a variety of learning abilities.

iStock.com/monkeybusinessimages

- Regardless of your own beliefs on the subject of homosexuality, if you are going to teach in the public schools, you will likely teach lesbian, gay, bisexual, transgendered, or queer (LGBTQ) students, work with LGBTQ fellow educators, or interact with LGBTQ families. As a teacher, you are entrusted to establish and maintain a safe and supportive classroom environment for these and all of your students.

- Your students will come from families with varied *socioeconomic backgrounds*. The benefits of being a child from a family in a higher socioeconomic class often show up in school performance; children from such families typically do much better academically than students from families in lower socioeconomic classes. Teachers and schools are challenged to ensure all students have successful schooling experiences. This topic is discussed in more detail in Chapter 4, "How Do Social Issues Affect Students?"

Although American society has always been composed of various races, ethnicities, and cultures, today we are experiencing even greater cultural diversity. An analysis of demographic data reveals demographic trends that could have a significant impact on schools. These demographic shifts are:

- Generation Z will be the most diverse and educated generation. Almost half of this generation are racial or ethnic minorities.

- Hispanics are projected to become the largest racial or ethnic minority group in the United States.

- Twenty-five percent of parents are unmarried.

- Immigrants compose nearly 14 percent of the American population. This is the highest it has been since the 1890s.

- Household incomes are nearing record high, yet inequities across racial and ethnic groups continue to grow.[1]

Just as our American population is becoming more and more diverse, so are our classrooms. Given that schools are a microcosm of society, we must explore ways to create successful learning environments for the students who enter our classrooms. We know that schools that embrace diversity are richer learning environments. Students who attend schools that embrace diversity are better prepared to be engaged citizens.

The term *race* is a social construct that refers to people with common ancestry and biological characteristics, whereas the term *ethnicity* applies to people who may be racially similar or different but who share a common culture, usually including language, customs, and religion.

Public school classrooms include an even higher percentage of minorities than the population as a whole. Although about 40 percent of the total population are members of racial or ethnic minority groups, 50 percent of children born in the United States are minorities—a figure that will continue to increase in the coming years.[2] As shown in Table 3.1, birthrates among minority groups are higher than those of white Americans, and immigration patterns are contributing to the increasing size of the minority population.

These national averages disguise the fact that minority groups are unequally distributed across the country. For example, minority groups are in the majority in California, Texas, New Mexico, Hawaii, and the District of Columbia, whereas minorities constitute less than 10 percent of the population in Maine, New Hampshire, Vermont, Iowa, and West Virginia.[3] In the 47 urban school districts that constitute the "great city schools," including those in New York City, Los Angeles, and Chicago, an overwhelming majority of students are from minority groups.

As might be expected with increasing cultural diversity, teachers will encounter more students whose home language is not English and whose ethnic and cultural backgrounds reflect a different heritage. We discuss these English language learners later in this chapter.

Students from biracial or multiracial backgrounds represent a rapidly growing segment of the U.S. population. These students often face unique issues, such as being asked to declare a single racial identity, thereby denying the rest of their heritage. They may face challenges when considering their identity in school and society. Depending on their family, they may richly embrace identities of more than one race. Unfortunately, schools often categorize them as one of the other. Teachers need to be aware of the difficulties such children may face and be willing to accept whatever identities the students choose for themselves.

(T) F

By 2060, the number of children who are two or more races will double.

TABLE 3.1	Projections of the U.S. Population 2012–2060 (percentage of the population)	
	2016	**2060**
Youth		
White, non-Hispanic	72.5	62.9
Non-Hispanic, white	51.1	36.4
Black or African American	15.1	16.0
Native Americans and Alaska Native	1.6	1.4
Asian	5.2	8.1
Native Hawaiian and Other Pacific Islander	.3	.3
Two or More Races	5.3	11.3
Hispanic	24.9	31.9

Source: U.S. Bureau of the Census, *U.S. Population Projections,* released 2018. See https://www.census.gov/content/dam/Census/library/publications/2020/demo/p25-1144.pdf

With the development of a richer, more varied society, differences in values and family expectations are also more evident. For example, some families may place a premium on school and higher education, whereas other families may emphasize early entry into the workplace. Even though you will encounter a range of familial expectations for school achievement, be aware that all children deserve the best educational experience they can get while in school. Knowing your students and recognizing what they bring to the classroom can provide the understanding and insight needed for more effective instruction.

3-1a CULTURAL PLURALISM: NOT THERE YET

At one time, the United States was considered a "melting pot" of many different kinds of people. Immigrants were expected to give up the language and customs of their homelands and adopt the language and customs of their new country. During the nineteenth and early twentieth centuries, schools contributed to the melting-pot concept by socializing and acculturating immigrant children to American ways while discouraging them from maintaining the ways of their homelands. Some states even passed laws forbidding instruction in any language but English. The basic idea was to produce a society with one dominant culture. This process of incorporating an immigrant group into the mainstream culture is often referred to as *enculturation* or **assimilation**. Many European immigrant groups were easily assimilated into the dominant American culture, but people of color were often prevented from doing so.

In many ways, the U.S. population reflects individuals from nearly every part of the globe. As we have become more diverse, we have also shifted perspectives on how immigrants change or adapt to American society. The concept of the melting pot has generally been replaced by the notion of **cultural pluralism**, which calls for an understanding and appreciation of the cultural differences and languages among U.S. citizens. The goal is to create a sense of society's wholeness based on the unique strengths of each of its parts. Cultural pluralism rejects both assimilation and separatism, a philosophy that suggests each cultural group should maintain its own identity without trying to fit into an overall American culture. Instead, it seeks a healthy interaction among the diverse groups in our society—that is, each subculture maintains its own individuality while contributing to the society as a whole. As some commentators put it, cultural pluralism argues for replacing the melting-pot metaphor with that of a "mosaic," "kaleidoscope," or "salad bowl" in which the individual parts remain distinct yet combine to make a unique whole.

Many people have promulgated cultural pluralism as a desirable goal, but it does not currently exist in the United States. Although racial, ethnic, and cultural diversity do exist, equality among the various groups does not. In general, racial and ethnic minorities do not share equal political, economic, and educational opportunities with those of the dominant culture, even though our society espouses such equality. In addition, some people resist the notion of cultural pluralism as a desirable goal. Some opponents argue in favor of assimilation, contending that cultural pluralism will undermine the United States' common traditions, historically derived from western European cultures. Others favor separatism. Unfortunately, U.S. schools have often failed to support cultural pluralism. Traditionally, public schools have been run for the benefit of those in the dominant cultural group, thereby excluding minority groups from receiving the full range of benefits.

Schools that embrace cultural pluralism seek to promote diversity and to avoid the dominance of a single culture. Their faculty and administration provide minority role models for the students

> *While the school should reflect and perpetuate cultural diversity, it has a responsibility to teach a commitment to and respect for the core values, such as justice, equality, and human dignity, which are expressed in our major historical documents.*
>
> —JAMES BANKS,
> University of Washington professor

to interact with. Their curricula are infused with the histories and contributions of diverse groups. These schools attempt to use the cultural patterns of the students to provide instruction and promote learning. They may use the multicultural education approaches described next. The goal is for students to be comfortable operating within their own cultures and in other cultures as well. Students from all racial, ethnic, and cultural groups are urged to participate in the school's various social, athletic, and governmental activities. These schools seek to raise students from all racial, ethnic, and cultural groups to the highest academic standards. In short, the goal for schools that aim for cultural pluralism is that no particular cultural group either dominates or is excluded from those activities and accomplishments that schools value.

3-1b TEACHING FOR EQUITY

Multicultural education represents one approach to meeting the educational needs of an increasingly diverse student population. "Multicultural education is an idea, an educational reform movement, and a process whose major goal is to change the structure of educational institutions so that male and female students, exceptional students, and students who are members of diverse racial, ethnic, language, and cultural groups will have an equal chance to achieve academically in school."[4] Spurred by the civil rights movement of the 1960s, multicultural education is a response to economic inequality, racism, and sexism in American culture. At the heart of multicultural education is a celebration of diversity and the belief that all students deserve a quality schooling experience. Its goals include reducing prejudice and fostering tolerance, improving the academic achievement of all students, building commitment to the American ideals of pluralism and democracy, and incorporating diverse groups' perspectives into the curricula of our schools. Multicultural education provides opportunities for students of color to see themselves in the curriculum. Like the concept of cultural pluralism on which it is based, multicultural education rejects both the notion of the melting pot and separatist philosophies.

Central to multicultural education is that the education of all students is a shared public interest. Intending for multicultural education to go beyond content integration, James Banks identified five dimensions of multicultural education:

1. *Content Integration* is the work of broadening the curriculum beyond the dominant narrative.

2. *Knowledge construction* attempts to help students examine the values and assumptions within knowledge.

3. *Equity pedagogy* focus on teachers examining the teaching practice to engage all students in equitable ways.

4. *Prejudice reduction* calls upon teachers and students to examine their own biases and develop positive racial beliefs and attitudes.

5. *Empowering school culture and social structure* moves beyond the individual classroom to examine the wholistic school environment and structure.[5]

Multicultural education is not just for members of minority racial or ethnic groups, rather it is for all students. A major goal of multicultural education is to help students from diverse cultures learn to cross cultural borders and to participate in a diverse, democratic society. True multicultural education does not consist of only African American history or women's history months. Instead of simply adding information about particular groups to the curriculum and leaving the rest of it untouched, real multicultural education presents multiple perspectives and viewpoints to help students understand how various groups can interpret events and facts differently.

In addition to valuing cultural diversity, multicultural education is based on the concept of *social justice*, which seeks to do away with social and economic inequalities for those who in the past have been denied these benefits of a democratic society. African Americans, Native Americans, Asian Americans, Hispanic Americans, mixed-race individuals, women, individuals with disabilities, people with limited English proficiency, people with low incomes, members of particular religious groups, and individuals with different sexual orientations are among those groups that have at one time or another been denied social justice. Educators who support multicultural education see establishing social justice for all people—but particularly for those who have experienced discrimination—as a moral and ethical responsibility.

Culturally responsive teaching is another frame for considering how we acknowledge and embrace cultural diversity in the classroom. Culturally responsive instruction centers instruction around the cognitive development of students who have historically been marginalized in the classroom. Many educators have documented how cultural identity, communication styles, and social expectations of students from minority cultural groups often conflict with the values, beliefs, and cultural assumptions of teachers.[6] Culturally responsive teaching acknowledges students

Up CLOSE

Ethnic Studies Controversy in Arizona

Ethnic studies are courses that examine race or ethnicity through the perspective of underrepresented populations. Across the nation, ethnic studies classes offer students an opportunity to learn more about their ethnic identity. One of the most well-known cases of ethnic studies in the news originated over a decade ago, when the Arizona state legislature passed a law that banned all public schools across the state from offering courses designed for a particular ethnic group, that advocate ethnic solidarity or that promote resentment toward a race or group of people. At that time, the Tucson Unified School District (TUSD) offered Mexican American studies, Native American literature, and African American literature courses. However, the Mexican American studies course was the one that attracted the most controversy.

Supporters of the ban contend that the courses teach anti-American ideas and encourage Mexican Americans to think of themselves as victims. They argue that ethnic studies promote racism. Supporters of the Mexican American studies course argue that the course is culturally relevant to Latinx students. They contend that student achievement is higher for students who had the opportunity to take the courses. Students in the Mexican American studies program say that critics' claims that they're being taught to be victims is completely false. One student stated the difference between ethnic studies and regular high school courses: "We are more socially critical of a lot of things around us. We explore the other side of the story."

Following passage of the legislation, the Arizona department of education ordered the district to ban ethnic studies or the Arizona education department would withhold 10 percent of the district's funds. Teachers in the Mexican American studies department filed a constitutional challenge, arguing that it violates both the First and Fourteenth Amendments of the U.S. Constitution because it targets one school district and one group of people. In 2017, a judge found that the ban showed discrimination and overturned the original ruling. The controversy continued and sparked movements and counter-movements across the country for and against ethnic studies. Arizona, while garnering great notoriety over these issues, is only one example of the culture wars that affect the curriculum of the public schools.

Source: Mary Ann Zehr, "Tucson Students Aren't Deterred by Ethnic-Studies Controversy," *Education Week* 30 (September 22, 2010): 1, 16.

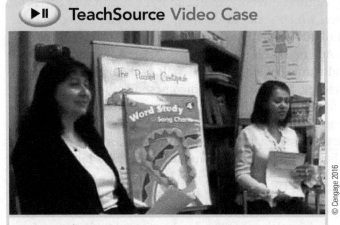

▶❚❚ **TeachSource** Video Case

© Cengage 2016

Culturally Responsive Teaching

Watch the video clips, study the artifacts in the case, and reflect on the following questions:

1. Which of the approaches to multicultural education listed in this chapter does the class shown in the Video Case represent?

2. How might teachers plan meaningful multicultural instruction for other grade levels or subjects?

funds of knowledge and seeks to strengthen students' academic achievement and lead to deeper learning. (Study the Video Case *Culturally Responsive Teaching* to see how one teacher helps students develop their writing skills.)

The school's dominant culture often places students from other cultures at a disadvantage in understanding the school's cultural codes and communication styles. Teachers who recognize this problem can implement an *equity pedagogy*, a style of teaching that uses instructional materials and practices that incorporate important aspects of their students' family and community culture.

Creating a welcoming and safe learning environment begins with awareness. Teachers and administrators must have an awareness of who their students are. Teachers should develop cultural knowledge and build an inclusive school climate. To develop a cultural awareness begins with exploring your own background and considering how it is like and different than others. Ask yourself some important questions:

- How do your race, ethnicity, culture, and other aspects of your identity influence your perspectives on school?

- How do you think these perspectives might be different for a student with a background different than your own?

- How are your notions of school and learning impacted by your cultural background?

- How might these perceptions be different for a student who is growing up in a family different than yours?

> *Culturally responsive teaching is defined as using the cultural characteristics, experiences, and perspectives of ethnically diverse students as conduits for teaching them more effectively.*
>
> —GENEVA GAY,
> University of Washington professor

Investing time into getting to know students and their backgrounds will help you better craft instruction for diverse learners in your classroom. To foster a cultural understanding of those different from you, attend a cultural event that is different than one you typically attend. Reflect on how it made you feel, what you learned, and how it makes you feel about teaching a diverse class of students.

Students often are forced to navigate dual worlds: their school world and their home world. Schools that honor diversity do not ask students to "check" their cultural backpacks at the front door of the school. Rather, they build on students' funds of knowledge or their culturally valued knowledge.

Teachers who teach in a culturally relevant classroom use student-centered stories and examples in their teaching. It is important for students to "see" themselves in the curriculum and curriculum materials. Selecting pieces of literature such as *All the Colors We Are* by Katie Kissinger, or *I Am Mixed* by Garcelle Beauvais is one strategy to help students begin to understand and have conversations around race. Another example is teaching World War II from the American-centric perspective and from the Japanese American perspective. Books such as *Sit-In: How Four Friends Stood Up by Sitting Down* by Andrea Davis Pinkney and *Malala's Magic Pencil* by Malala Yousafzai also introduce students to historical events through the lens of the counter narrative

Pushback

Many school districts are attempting to permeate their curricula and teaching strategies to support all students' learning and to combat the prejudice and divisiveness among the many different subcultures found in the United States. It counteracts what some call "subtractive schooling" or the notion that schools divest diverse students of their cultural resources leaving them destined for academic failure. By developing mutual respect for and appreciation of different lifestyles, languages, religious beliefs, and family structures, students may help shape a better future society for all its members.

However, parents and community members sometimes push back against schools working to bring about change. Some argue that by engaging with multicultural or culturally responsive teaching, common traditions, values, or purposes of privileged may be threatened. They may fear that their position of power may be lessened through the acts of teaching for social justice. Others argue that it shifts the purpose of schooling from the basic purpose of educating for civic, economic, and personal effectiveness. Similarly, this argument may stem from a worry about losing what is historically a position of power. Others may feel it could undermine a sense of a common morality because some advocates of multiculturalism claim there are no universal moral positions that the public schools can legitimately teach.

Clearly, the notion of multicultural education and culturally relevant teaching is not without controversy. This work has often been cast as a reform movement, designed to address inequities and discrimination resulting from the race, religion, socioeconomic status, gender, age, exceptionality, or language of students.[7] As with any attempt to solve social problems, excesses and overexuberance can occur. Nevertheless, schools do need to accommodate diverse populations in a way that removes barriers and enables those students to compete academically and economically while preserving the basic purposes of schooling. (See "Up Close: Ethnic Studies Controversy in Arizona" for more on these issues.)

Pause *and* Reflect

1. What are ways teachers can create successful learning experiences for students of diverse backgrounds?
2. In what ways do changing demographics of our society impact the ways we teach and learn in today's schools?
3. What are some specific strategies you could use to bring culturally relevant resources into your classroom?

3-2 English Language Learners

Just as schools must embrace multiculturalism, they must also embrace multilingualism. Ten percent of all students in schools are **English language learners (ELLs)**, meaning they have **limited English proficiency (LEP)**. Yet, the majority of classroom teachers are trained to teach these students. Nearly

400 different languages are spoken in U.S. homes. Spanish is the most common home language for ELLs. Arabic, Chinese, Vietnamese, Somali, Russian, Hmong, Haitian, and Portuguese are the next languages that ELLs most frequently speak at home.[8]

You might think that these non-English-speaking youngsters are new to the United States, and some of them are. However, nearly 90 percent of the children of immigrants were born in the United States, and approximately three-fourths of the ELLs were born in the United States, are U.S. citizens, and began school in kindergarten and first grade, the same as their English-speaking peers.[9] The remaining one-quarter of the ELLs included immigrant children and youth born in a country other than the United States. Some of these students are refugees from another country. Refugees are individuals who are permitted to enter the United States because they have fled their native country due to possible harm. The federal government determines how many refugees may enter the United States each year. It is important to note that about 40 percent of the refugees entering the United States are children who enter our schools.[10] These data indicate that the predominant need for English language development instruction in U.S. school systems is for a large native-born population that does not speak English proficiently.

Ⓣ F
The majority of English language learners was born in the United States and are U.S. citizens.

3-2a THE GOVERNMENT RESPONSE

Students whose native language is not English constitute one of the most conspicuous failure groups in the U.S. educational system. Historically, ELL students have faced challenges in school as they worked to navigate not only learning the academic content but also a new language and cultural norms. Many of these ELL students fall farther and farther behind in school, and overwhelming numbers drop out before finishing high school.

To address this problem, Congress passed the Bilingual Education Act in 1968, and subsequently amended it a number of times to provide federal funds to develop bilingual programs. Passage of the legislation signaled momentous changes for ELL students in our schools and signified changing perspectives about diversity in schools. Much of the expansion of bilingual programs in the 1970s can be attributed to a series of court cases that guided the legislation through different iterations. Perhaps most significant of these cases was the 1974 U.S. Supreme Court case of *Lau* v. *Nichols*, in which the court found that "where inability to speak and understand the English language excludes national origin–minority group children from effective participation in the educational program offered by a school district, the district must take affirmative steps to rectify the language deficiency in order to open its instructional program to these students."[11] Basing its ruling on the Civil Rights Act of 1964, the court held that the San Francisco school system unlawfully discriminated on the basis of national origin when it failed to cope with children's language problems.

As a result of the *Lau* case, the U.S. Office for Civil Rights suggested guidelines for school districts to follow, the so-called Lau Remedies. The guidelines specified "language minority students should be taught academics in their primary home language until they could effectively benefit from English language instruction."[12] The legislation continued to evolve in a way that reflected changing attitudes about diversity and immigration. In 1994, the Bilingual Education Act was further revised to advocate toward the goal of bilingualism for ELL students.

3-2b EVERY STUDENT SUCCEEDS ACT AND ENGLISH LANGUAGE LEARNERS

The Every Student Succeeds Act of 2015 recognizes the growing diversity of schools and the need to support linguistically diverse students. It provides for federal grant money to state education agencies for the purposes of helping to ensure that limited English proficient children develop high levels of academic attainment in English, and meet the same student academic achievement standards as all children are expected to meet. Title III provides more than $880 million a year to states, distributed proportionally, based on the number of ELLs in each state.[13]

The 2015 Every Students Succeeds Act legislation requires that schools provide education programs for students to gain English proficiency and high academic achievement. Further, the policy mandates that teachers and administrators are provided professional development to learn and develop strategies for teaching ELL students and the schools offer activities that support community and parent engagement for families of ELL students. The policy mandates that states measure the academic growth of ELL students on an annual basis. Additionally, within thirty days of newly enrolling in a school, students must be assessed for ELL status.

Although the policy doesn't specify what kind of instruction schools should use for ELL students, many school districts have discontinued bilingual education in such cases for three primary reasons: Accountability tests are typically in English, the heavy financial demands of the programs, and more time is needed for English instruction than for instruction in the student's native language. As might be expected, ELL students do not do as well on the tests as native-English-speaking students.

3-2c BILINGUAL EDUCATION MODELS

Students with a first language other than English have two goals in school: learning English and mastering content. Language programs for ELLs are of two types: (1) those that focus on developing literacy in two languages (**bilingual education**), and (2) those that focus on developing literacy in only English (English immersion). Among the models that focus on developing literacy in two languages are the *transitional* and *maintenance* or *developmental models*.

The *transitional model* provides intensive English language instruction, but students get some portion of their academic instruction in their first language. The goal is to prepare students for regular classes in English without letting them fall behind in subject areas. In theory, students should transition out of these programs within a few years.

Maintenance or *developmental* bilingual education aims to preserve and build on students' first-language skills as they continue to acquire English as a second language.

A recent trend in many schools has been to offer two-way dual-language education tracks for both ELL students and native English–speaking students. The two groups of students are combined in one class. Instruction is in English for part of the day and in another language (e.g., Spanish or Chinese) for at least half of the day. Often, these school programs are grounded in the philosophy that all students should be bilingual. Research on two-way dual-language programs reports that reading and math scores are higher for all students.[14]

In the *English immersion model*, students learn everything in English. Teachers using immersion programs generally strive to deliver lessons in simple and understandable language that allows

> *States have the opportunity to invest in … the fact that a child speaks a language other than English at home as an asset rather than as a deficit*
>
> —JOHN KING,
> former U.S. secretary of education

students to internalize English while learning academic subjects. The extreme case of immersion is called *submersion*, wherein students must "sink or swim" until they learn English. Sometimes students are pulled out for *English as a second language (ESL)* programs, which provide them with instruction in English geared toward language acquisition.

3-2d BILINGUAL EDUCATION CONTROVERSIES

Choosing the best method for educating students who need to learn English has become a divisive political battle. In the early 1970s, language-minority speakers and their advocates fought for bilingual education as their right. Decades later, however, many of them are expressing doubts about the effectiveness of bilingual programs. Civil rights and cultural issues are giving way to concerns that nonnative English speakers are just not sufficiently mastering the English language, which in turn is keeping them from fully participating in American life. Although many educators believe students who use English as a second language should be educated in their native language as well, critics insist such an approach doesn't work. The critics believe the best path to academic achievement for language-minority students in most cases is to learn English and learn it quickly. Too many bilingual programs, they say, place ELL students into slower learning tracks where they rarely learn sufficient English and from which they may never emerge. These critics basically support an immersion model of bilingual education, opposing the transitional and maintenance models.

In response, supporters of transitional and maintenance models argue that students can best keep up academically with their English-speaking peers if they are taught at least partly in their native languages while learning English. They also cite research indicating that instruction in the native language concurrent with English instruction actually enhances the acquisition of English. These advocates say it is not fair to blame bilingual education for the slow progress some students are making: The true problem is that becoming proficient in any second language takes longer than just one or two years. They also point out the shortage of well-qualified, fully bilingual teachers, which in many cases means that the problem with bilingual classes is not the curriculum, but rather the quality of the instruction. Some school systems have used paraeducators who speak the child's language to help connect the child and the school. The use of bilingual peer tutors may also help provide a greater sense of stability.

The transitional and maintenance models of bilingual education are in growing jeopardy. First California, Arizona, and Massachusetts gutted their bilingual programs, and now other states are threatening to follow suit. In 1998, California voters passed Proposition 227, which called for ELL students to be taught in a special English-immersion program in which nearly all instruction is in English, in most cases for no more than a year, before moving into mainstream English classrooms. Proposition 227 basically ended transitional and maintenance models of bilingual education in California, except when sufficient numbers of parents specifically request that their children continue in them. Many parents, administrators, and teachers are concerned that all children, not just ELL students, will be affected as mainstream teachers grapple with students who may be unprepared to deal with grade-level work in English after one year in immersion. The California Multilingual Education Act went into effect in 2017 and essentially rescinded the English-only requirement of Proposition 227. This law opened the door for students to learn English through a variety of programs, beyond English immersion programs. Schools are also required to seek parent and community input when designing and implementing new language acquisition programs. Although research on the effectiveness of bilingual education remains controversial, in a recent review of the research of bilingual education and overall school success presents evidence of the long term benefits of bilingual education.[15]

Despite the controversy over bilingual education, many school districts are in desperate need of bilingual teachers, particularly those who speak Spanish and Asian languages. If you speak a second language or still have time to include learning a language in your college program, you could help meet a serious educational need while greatly enhancing your employment opportunities. Speaking a foreign language, especially Spanish, is also an asset for regular classroom teachers who may have Spanish-speaking students in class.

Teaching Implications

The changing demographic trends in the United States make it quite likely you will teach students who speak more than one language. It is important to consider how schools are meeting their needs to ensure academic success. Teachers should consider ways to capitalize on students' linguistic strengths and build on the academic knowledge they possess in their first language. Many educators hold that central to teaching ELL students is to employ cultural relevant pedagogies to recognize and value the assets each child brings to the classroom. One of the first things you should do is get to know your students and develop an understanding of their cultural and language background. It will be helpful for you to know how long the students have been speaking English and what language is spoken in the home. From the beginning, you can assign a buddy student to partner with ELL students on classroom activities. Encourage the students to engage in authentic and meaningful communication.

As you consider your instruction, structure lessons that activate and build knowledge with pictures, videos, or graphic organizers. Engage students in cooperative learning activities so that they can support one another and learn together. When talking with students, be sure to give some extra time for them to respond, and be sure to model correct English usage. Other modifications or strategies you may incorporate in your classroom for ELL students include vocabulary notebooks, topical word walls, and dialogue journals. Among the modifications that have been shown not to work include asking another student to translate the assignments into the student's native language, providing extra time for an assignment with no added instruction or explanation, or excusing the student from doing an assignment.[16]

Pause *and* Reflect

1. How can you help prepare yourself for the diversity you are likely to encounter in the classroom?
2. What experiences with diversity will you bring to the classroom? How do you think these experiences will help you as a teacher?

3-3 Diverse Abilities

In some ways, many U.S. schools are not structured to address students' diverse abilities. In this section, we look at the theory that students may have many abilities and talents not tapped by traditional schooling. We also explore learning styles to see how different students learn; this exploration might broaden your views on approaches to teaching. Finally, we briefly examine characteristics of students along a range of differences. Schools and teachers must make special efforts to effectively educate all students who enter their classroom.

3-3a MULTIPLE INTELLIGENCES

Howard Gardner, a leading psychologist, proposes that we should move toward educating **multiple intelligences**, of which linguistic and analytic abilities are only two facets. In Gardner's books *Frames of Mind* and *Multiple Intelligences: The Theory in Practice*,[17] he explains that we all have strengths, weaknesses, and unique combinations of cognitive abilities. Gardner states that people have at least eight distinct intellectual capacities that they use to approach problems and create products:

1. *Verbal–linguistic intelligence* draws on an individual's language skills, oral and written, to express what's on the person's mind and to understand other people.
2. *Logical–mathematical intelligence* is a person's ability to understand principles of some kind of causal system, like a scientist does, or to manipulate numbers, quantities, and operations, like a mathematician does.
3. *Spatial intelligence* refers to the ability to represent the spatial world internally in the mind, like a chess player or sculptor does.
4. *Bodily–kinesthetic intelligence* is the capacity to use your whole body or parts of your body to solve a problem, make something, or put on some kind of production, like that of an athlete or a performing artist.
5. *Musical intelligence* is the capacity to "think" in music and to be able to hear patterns and recognize, remember, and manipulate them.
6. *Interpersonal intelligence* is the ability to understand other people—an ability that we all need but that is particularly important for teachers, salespeople, and politicians.
7. *Intrapersonal intelligence* refers to having an understanding of yourself and knowing your preferences, capabilities, and deficiencies.
8. *Naturalist intelligence* refers to the ability to discriminate among living things (plants and animals) and to have sensitivity toward features of the natural world, such as rock formations and clouds.[18]

An important distinction to note is that multiple intelligences are considered an individual's intellectual ability, while learning styles are the way one approaches a learning task.

Many of our schools tend to emphasize a curriculum that specifically targets the predominantly linguistic and logical–mathematical abilities students need to do well on commonly used standardized tests and to de-emphasize or exclude other possible intelligences. This constricted focus on a limited range of abilities results in an education system that teaches and reinforces only certain types of achievement. Children who are strong in linguistic and logical–mathematical tasks are likely to be successful in school and feel a great sense of achievement. Other children, even though they may be very competent or even gifted in nontraditional school tasks, may experience frustration or failure in school. In Gardner's theory, abilities in diverse areas would be valued as indicators of intelligence and be considered worthy of further nurturance and development in school.

Gardner's Five Minds

Howard Gardner's book, *Five Minds for the Future: Cultivating Thinking Skills,* argues that because the future is so unpredictable and changing, everyone needs to cultivate five different ways of thinking:

1. *The disciplined mind* has mastered at least one way of thinking—a distinctive mode of cognition that characterizes a specific scholarly discipline, craft, or profession.

2. *The synthesizing mind* takes information from disparate sources, understands and evaluates that information objectively, and puts it together in ways that make sense to the synthesizer and also to other people.

3. *The creating mind* breaks new ground. It puts forth new ideas, poses unfamiliar questions, conjures up fresh ways of thinking, and arrives at unexpected answers.

4. *The respectful mind* notes and welcomes differences among human individuals and groups, tries to understand these "others," and seeks to work effectively with them.

5. *The ethical mind* ponders the nature of one's work and the needs and desires of the society in which one lives. This mind conceptualizes how workers can serve purposes beyond self-interest and how citizens can work unselfishly to improve the lot of all.[19]

These five minds are different from the eight intelligences Gardner identified. He thinks of them as broad uses of the mind that can be cultivated in school, the workplace, or in professions. To be certain, Gardner asserts, these five minds make use of the intelligences. For instance, to cultivate the respectful mind, one would have to exercise interpersonal intelligence. Or to cultivate the disciplined mind, logical-mathematical intelligence would likely be used.

Teaching Implications

Acknowledging and fostering individual abilities in a variety of areas is one way teachers can help students. To address varied intelligences, Gardner emphasizes learning in context, particularly through apprenticeships. Student development in an area like music should be fostered through hands-on practice and experiences.

Even traditional subjects should be taught in a variety of ways, such as those listed in the Multiple Intelligences Menu in Table 3.2, to address the varied intelligences of both students and teachers. For example, history might be taught through a number of media and methods, ranging from art and architecture to biographies and dramatic reenactments of events. Assessments should also be tailored to different abilities and should take place in a learning context as much as possible.

Although the theory of multiple intelligences is very popular with many educators and resonates with their own experiences, it should be noted that a number of psychologists have criticized it based on the lack of scientific measures for Gardner's various intelligences. Some critics argue that what Gardner calls "intelligences" are merely talents, personality traits, or cognitive styles. Others worry that schools, in attempting to address a range of abilities, may not adequately stress the importance of verbal and mathematical abilities, which they say are critical to success in our society. Despite the critiques recent brain-based research supports this theory of learning.[20]

Nevertheless, multiple intelligences theory offers teachers some ideas for expanding instructional repertoires and infusing variety into lessons. It provides a framework for enhancing instruction and a language to describe the efforts. Gardner recommends that teachers be mindful of multiple intelligences as they craft their instruction. Using them as a framework can assist teachers in individualizing their instruction and "pluralizing" their teaching (teach content in multiple ways).[21]

TABLE 3.2   Multiple Intelligences Menu

Linguistic Menu

Use storytelling to explain ___.

Conduct a debate on ___.

Write a poem, myth, legend, short play, or news article about ___.

Create a talk-show radio program about ___.

Conduct an interview of ___ on ___.

Logical–Mathematical Menu

Translate a ___ into a mathematical formula ___.

Design and conduct an experiment on ___.

Make up syllogisms to demonstrate ___, ___, and ___.

Make up analogies to explain ___.

Describe the patterns of symmetry in ___.

Bodily–Kinesthetic Menu

Create a movement or sequence of movements to explain ___.

Make task or puzzle cards for ___.

Build or construct a ___.

Plan and attend a field trip that will ___.

Bring hands-on materials to demonstrate ___.

Visual Menu

Chart, map, cluster, or graph ___.

Create a slide show, videotape, or photo album of ___.

Create a piece of art that demonstrates ___.

Invent a board or card game to demonstrate ___.

Illustrate, draw, paint, sketch, or sculpt ___.

Musical Menu

Give a presentation with appropriate musical accompaniment on ___.

Sing a rap or song that explains ___.

Indicate the rhythmical patterns in ___.

Explain how the music of a song is similar to ___.

Make an instrument and use it to demonstrate ___.

Interpersonal Menu

Conduct a meeting to address ___.

Intentionally use ___ social skills to learn about ___.

Participate in a service project to ___.

Teach someone about ___.

Practice giving and receiving feedback on ___.

Use technology to ___.

Intrapersonal Menu

Describe qualities you possess that will help you to successfully complete ___.

Set and pursue a goal to ___.

Describe one of your personal values about ___.

Write a journal entry on ___.

Assess your own work in ___.

Naturalist Menu

Create observation notebooks of ___.

Describe changes in local or global environment ___.

Care for pets, wildlife, gardens, or parks ___.

Use binoculars, telescopes, microscopes, or magnifiers to ___.

Draw or photograph natural objects ___.

Source: Reprinted with permission from Linda Campbell, "How Teachers Interpret MI Theory," *Educational Leadership* 44 (September 1997): 18.

Pause *and* Reflect

1. Looking at Howard Gardner's list of intelligences, which are your strongest intelligences? How might you adapt instruction to meet different students' ways of learning?
2. Reflect back on your K–12 experiences. In what ways did your strengths support or challenge you as a student?

VOICES from the Classroom

Reflections on Individualizing Instruction

Anna Hinden was an elementary teacher in Durham, NC. She is now a Ph.D. student at the University of North Carolina at Chapel Hill.

With great power, comes great responsibility. I learned early on in my teaching career that I had a responsibility to my students to teach them in a way that I can help them learn the material, get to know them and their families, and provide them with a supportive and loving classroom environment. What I found out later was that while all of that is necessary, the responsibility we have to our students is much greater than that.

As teachers, we often find ourselves in classrooms full of students of different races and different religions, who speak different languages, and who have different home life experiences. It can be challenging to meet a diverse group of students, but we did not become teachers because we thought it would be easy, right? To build a positive and safe learning environment for a diverse classroom, we as teachers must foster an appreciation for the differences of others. Like many other concepts, students learn from watching how teachers interact with others. We must show our appreciation for the differences between all of us in order to teach our students how to appreciate and show appreciation for each other's differences.

Modeling appreciation for one another's differences can take many forms; however, it is important that we begin with analyzing our own internal appreciation for one another and identifying the implicit biases we may have in order to model positive appreciation for each other. I have had the experience of teaching many diverse groups of students, but one thing remained true for all of them—they were more engaged and invested in the learning environment when they knew that their classmates and their teachers appreciated them for who they are.

The following are suggestions and examples from my classroom that I have found to be helpful in creating a positive environment in which students appreciate each other's diversity:

- Model appreciation for the differences of all students (including even the smallest differences).
  - This took a lot of practice. In my lesson plans and everyday discussions with students, I aimed to provide students with examples of all different types of people who have become role models. It is important for students to see themselves in successful people as well as see others as having the ability to be successful. Students learning about the contributions of many different types of people increases their understanding that all types of people are valuable. I encourage teachers to think outside of the box when selecting role models and figures to teach about.

- Consistently correct students when they do not exhibit appreciation and acceptance of each other's differences.
  - Over the years I have had numerous students whose families were living in poverty and unable to provide their children with the necessary items to stay clean and wear clean clothes every day. At the first sign of students talking about one of these students, it was important for me to pull them aside and correct them by having a constructive conversation to help them better understand the circumstances and encourage them to be empathetic.
  This particularly is meaningful when students begin to correct each other!

- Allow students to take the lead in teaching the classroom and teachers about their culture, religion, language, home life, and learning abilities.
  - In my classroom, we had several students whose families were from Mexico. When Dia De Los Muertos came around, I encouraged the students to teach the rest of the class about the holiday and how their families celebrate. It is important to me that I allow the "experts" in the classroom to take on the teaching when appropriate. This can increase the meaningfulness of the learning as well as increase appreciation for others' differences.

- Use the Harvard Implicit Bias test to help you identify the implicit biases you may have in order to combat them: https://implicit.harvard.edu/implicit/takeatest.html.

3-3b STUDENTS WITH DISABILITIES

Within the range of diversity your students will display, there will be a range of learning differences. You may encounter many types of disabilities. For example, you may have students with intellectual disabilities, emotional disturbance, learning disabilities, attention deficit disorders, speech or language impairments, multiple handicaps, autism, traumatic brain injuries, orthopedic impairments, visual impairments or blindness, and hearing impairments or deafness. Unfortunately, disabilities can be stigmatizing. No matter the challenge a student may face, all students are deserved an inclusive classroom that supports their learning. As a teacher, you will need to consider how to use accommodations to differentiate instruction for your students.

Nearly 14 percent of all school-aged children are identified to have a specific disability. Table 3.3 shows the percentage of students in each of the officially recognized categories by race.

Special Education

The term **special education** is often used as a designation for services designed for students with disabilities. In 1975, the Education for All Handicapped Children Act

TABLE 3.3 Percentage of Students Ages 6 Through 21 Served Under IDEA, Part B, Within Racial/Ethnic Groups, by Disability Category: Fall 2017

Disability	Native Americans or Alaska Native	Asian	Black or African American	Hispanic/ Latino	Native Hawaiian or Other Pacific Islander	White	Two or more races
All disabilities	100.0	100.0	100.0	100.0	100.0	100.0	100.0
Autism	5.9	23.6	8.1	8.7	7.4	10.9	10.9
Deaf-blindness	#	#	#	#	#	#	#
Developmental delay*	6.4	2.6	2.9	1.9	3.6	2.7	3.7
Emotional disturbance	5.3	2.3	7.3	3.7	3.9	5.8	7.5
Hearing impairment	0.9	2.5	0.8	1.3	2.2	1.0	0.9
Intellectual disability	6.6	7.0	9.7	6.5	6.7	6.0	5.5
Multiple disability	2.3	2.9	1.9	1.5	3.0	2.2	1.8
Orthopedic impairment	0.4	1.2	0.4	0.6	0.7	0.6	0.5
Other health impairment	12.8	9.3	15.7	12.1	11.2	18.3	17.6
Specific learning disability	44.3	23.7	39.8	45.7	50.2	34.0	34.0
Speech or language impairment	14.2	23.7	12.5	17.3	9.9	17.6	17.0
Traumatic brain injury	0.4	0.4	0.4	0.3	0.3	0.5	0.4
Visual impairment	0.4	0.8	0.3	0.4	0.8	0.4	0.4

\# Percentage was non-zero but less than 0.05 or 5/100 of 1 percent.

*Percentages may not add up to 100 percent due to rounding.

Source: 41st Annual Report to Congress on the Implementation of the Individuals with Disabilities Education Act, 2019, (Washington, DC: U.S. Department of Education, 2019), Table 28.

(PL 94–142) established the right of all students with disabilities to a "free appropriate public education" (FAPE). The law specified that each such student must be provided with an **individualized education program (IEP)** outlining both long-range and short-range goals for the child. Since that time, a number of other federal laws have reinforced and extended the commitment to special education. The Council for Exceptional Children (CEP) recently conducted a survey of special education professionals. The results of the survey revealed:

- The IEP is critical in designing instruction for individual students.
- The majority of respondents feel prepared to accommodate their students' needs.
- Family engagement and involvement is essential to best support students.
- There is a need for systems-support for delivering special education.

Additionally, respondents report that the top supports needed to do their job are resources to meet IEP requirements, smaller ratio of teacher to student, and administrators who understand and support implementation of IEPs.[22]

Preschool Legislation

The Education of the Handicapped Act Amendments (PL 99–457), passed in 1986, provided for early intervention for children from birth to age 2 who are developmentally delayed. For states that choose to participate, programs must include a multidisciplinary assessment of the child's needs, a written **individualized family services plan (IFSP)**, and case management. Services may draw from a variety of areas, such as special education, speech and language pathology, occupational or physical therapy, or family training and counseling, depending on the developmental needs of the child.

PL 99–457 also stated that FAPE must be extended to children with disabilities ages 3 to 5 years. Although state and local education agencies administer these programs, they may contract with other programs, agencies, or providers to supply a range of services, such as programs that are home based for part of the day. Families play a particularly important role in preschool education, and instruction for parents is to be included in the IFSP whenever it is appropriate and the parents desire it. When students reach school age, they are covered by the provisions of the Individuals with Disabilities Education Act (IDEA), as discussed in the next section.

IDEA and ADA

In 1990, Congress passed two significant federal laws relating to people with disabilities: the Individuals with Disabilities Education Act (IDEA), subsequently reauthorized in 1997 and again in 2004, and the Americans with Disabilities Act (ADA). IDEA amended the Education for All Handicapped Children Act of 1975. ADA ensures the right of individuals with disabilities to nondiscriminatory treatment in aspects of their lives other than education.

Seven principles provide the framework of IDEA, around which education services are designed and provided to students with disabilities:

- Fair and appropriate education (FAPE)
- Appropriate evaluation
- An individualized education program (IEP)
- Least restrictive environment (LRE)
- Parent and student participation in decision making

- Procedural safeguards
- Response to Intervention (RTI)

Because of the wide variety of disabilities and infinite degrees of severity in which these conditions may be found in individual students, IDEA mandates that a "free appropriate public education" be defined on an individual basis, using the written IEP. The IEP identifies the child's current levels of educational performance, short-term objectives and annual goals, services to be provided, and criteria and schedules for evaluation of progress. In this way, it helps ensure that the educational goals designed for the child are appropriate to his or her individual learning needs and that these plans are actually delivered as intended. Provisions in the IEP must be reviewed and revised annually— or more often, if necessary. Teachers, parents or guardians, special educators, other professionals, and the child (whenever appropriate) are all involved in the development and approval of the IEP. IDEA also requires that all older students with a disability (usually ages 14 to 16) have an individualized plan for making the transition from school to work or additional education beyond high school through age 21.

Like the original act of 1975, IDEA further stipulates that services for students with disabilities be provided in a **least restrictive environment (LRE)**, meaning students with disabilities should be educated with children without disabilities to the greatest extent appropriate. Determination of what constitutes the LRE has been controversial. The social and academic benefits of the regular classroom must be weighed against the unique educational needs and individual circumstances for each child.

In the past, the term **mainstreaming** was used to describe the practice of placing special education students in general education classes for at least part of the school day, with additional services, programs, or classes being provided to these students as needed. More recently, the term **inclusion** has been used to mean the commitment to educate each child, to the maximum extent appropriate, in the regular school and classroom. Compared with mainstreaming, inclusion—and particularly *full inclusion*, as it is sometimes called—indicates an even greater commitment to keeping students with disabilities in regular classrooms. It usually involves bringing the support services to the child rather than moving the child to services located in separate rooms or buildings.

Controversy over Inclusion In recent years, full inclusion has become a civil rights issue. Advocates of full inclusion argue that segregated education for students with disabilities is inherently unequal (much like the earlier practice of racial segregation), and therefore violates the rights of these children. They also argue that traditional special education programs have resulted in a costly special education bureaucracy that has not shown the expected benefits in terms of academic, social, or vocational skills. Among the benefits of full inclusion for children with disabilities, they say, are higher expectations and better socialization, as well as greater acceptance of human differences by children without disabilities. The "Up Close" feature describes how one teacher has learned about the students with autism in his classroom.

Critics of full inclusion say that both teachers and students are being hurt in the rush to embrace this teaching approach:

- Parents of children without disabilities often worry that the curriculum standards will be lowered by the inclusion of students with learning disabilities and that those students with attention deficit/hyperactivity disorder (ADHD) or emotional problems can be a disruption to their classmates and teachers.
- Some special educators voice concerns that full inclusion may result in diminished or inadequate specialized services for students who have special needs. They point out that the regular classroom may not be the best setting for every child. Violent or emotionally disordered children, for example, may pose a threat

to themselves and to their classmates. These educators are wary of eliminating the range of service delivery options currently available in favor of a pure inclusion model. They argue that little evidence shows that inclusion programs strengthen students' academic achievement. (The same criticism could be made of many special education programs.)

- Classroom teachers have complained that they are given inadequate resources and training to deal with students with disabilities. Ideally, when students with disabilities are included in regular classrooms, their teachers receive special training and help from a special education teacher who serves as either a co-teacher or a consultant. In some cases, however, teachers have been given sole responsibility for a class of 30 students, with as many as 10 having disabilities. True collaboration between general education and special education teachers is essential for inclusion to work effectively.

The 2004 reauthorization of IDEA committed the federal government in principle to paying 40 percent of the average per-pupil cost of educating a special education student. A little over 13 percent of school-aged children are served by programs for students with disabilities. Unfortunately, this initiative is still not fully funded.[23] This is especially important because the Every Student Succeeds Act of 2015 requires that special education students take the same achievement tests that regular education students take, albeit sometimes with accommodations. Without additional funding or appropriate alternative assessments, many special education students will not pass these tests, and their schools will fail to meet the provisions of the law.

Despite the criticisms of the inclusion movement, one thing is certain: Inclusion of children with disabilities has become accepted practice in U.S. schools. The majority of students with disabilities are taking part in regular classroom and school life alongside their peers. Inclusion seems to thrive in schools that have a shared vision of the school's purposes; strong lines of communication among teachers, administrators, and parents; and a culture of innovation and reform. In many schools with successful inclusion programs, the presence of students with disabilities has sparked other reform initiatives such as cooperative learning, peer teaching, team teaching, authentic assessment, and interdisciplinary instruction.

T (F)
Most children receiving special education services do so in separate classrooms with special education teachers.

Special education laws aim to ensure all students, regardless of disability, receive a fair and appropriate education.

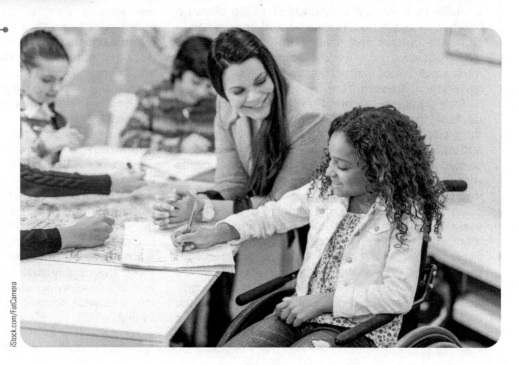

iStock.com/FatCamera

In addition to students receiving special education services, a number of children in elementary and secondary schools have "504 plans." The "504" in "504 plan" refers to Section 504 of the Rehabilitation Act and the Americans with Disabilities Act, which specifies that no one with a disability can be excluded from participating in federally funded programs or activities, including elementary, secondary, or postsecondary schooling. *Disability* in this context refers to a "physical or mental impairment which substantially limits one or more major life activities." This can include physical impairments; illnesses or injuries; communicable diseases; chronic conditions like asthma, allergies, and diabetes; and learning problems. A 504 plan spells out the accommodations that will be needed for these students to have an opportunity to perform at the same level as their peers, and might include such things as wheelchair ramps, blood sugar monitoring, an extra set of textbooks, a peanut-free lunch environment, home instruction, or an audio recorder or keyboard for taking notes.

Up CLOSE

Reaching Out: One Teacher's Journey to Support His Autistic Adolescents

Brian Dunlap is a Ph.D. student at the University of North Carolina at Chapel Hill. He formerly taught in Baltimore County, Maryland.

When your friends and family first hear that you work with children with autism, they usually come to the conclusion that you must be an uncommonly patient person. While patience certainly doesn't hurt in this line of work, it is a misconception that it is enough or even mandatory to be an effective special educator. What my classroom experience has taught me is that instead of patience, a special education teacher should strive to find understanding. While patience can help a teacher tolerate a student's behavior, only understanding allows a teacher to react humanely and authentically to a student's unique and valid experience. Likewise, while patience is a finite resource for even the most saint-like of instructors, understanding, in my experience, is evergreen.

As a first-year teacher, I remember being struck by how the amazing and celebrated diversity in the personalities and strengths of my students with autism smuggled with it a corresponding and unexpected challenge: that the needs of these students with identical diagnoses were incredibly diverse and mysterious as well. Furthermore, I found that compounding the challenge of beginning to understand these diverse and unsurfaced needs are the communication barriers, sensory irregularities, and unexpected behavioral manifestations associated with the disorder. One of the biggest pitfalls of teachers of children with autism is the failure to appreciate that from interactions on neurological, interpersonal, and cultural levels, the experiences of these learners

through this world can be fundamentally different from their own and that a near suspension of disbelief is required to begin to understand the true nature of their courage and the barriers they face.

One of the best pieces of advice that I received as a teacher was that students, with or without disabilities, regardless of how unexpected their behavior may be, rarely act irrationally. Whether engaging in violent self-injury, destroying their own property, or breaking down in the face of a seemingly innocuous sensory stimulus, children choose to engage in behavior because it has helped them meet their needs as human beings in the past. Appreciating the potential difference in these learners' experiences and taking a flexible, patient, and data-driven look at their behavior can go a long way toward bridging the gap to understanding these marginalized young people.

In an educational climate that has seen inclusion prioritized and the bar for the expected achievement of students with disabilities raised higher than ever, it is critical that all school professionals differentiate their understanding of their students and respond to their unique experiences. Fortunately, thanks to the efforts of groups of researchers and educators like the National Clearinghouse on Autism Evidence & Practice, we now have now have access to the most thoroughly researched, reliable, and effective information on understanding and supporting students with disabilities that has ever been made available.

Response to Intervention (RTI)

In the 2004 reauthorization of IDEA, a new term and concept, **Response to Intervention (RTI)**, was introduced. The purpose of RTI is to catch struggling children early, provide appropriate instruction, and prevent the need to refer the child for special education. The U.S. Department of Education permits school districts to use up to 15 percent of their IDEA funding for early intervention services in regular education.

RTI is a tiered process of instruction that permits schools to identify struggling students early and to provide appropriate instructional interventions. By intervening early, students will experience a greater chance for success and less need for special education services. Although there are several models of intervention, typically a child would move from Tier 1 general education (classwide intervention) to a Tier 2 (more targeted small-group interventions) and, if necessary, to Tier 3, where the student would receive additional support and individualized attention. RTI is designed to increase the percentage of children who can pass the NCLB state tests in reading and mathematics.

Assistive Technology

Just as many students use contact lenses or glasses to help them compensate for poor eyesight, so students with disabilities may rely on a variety of technology-based innovations to help them learn better. The term **assistive technology** refers to the array of devices and services that help people with disabilities perform better in their daily lives. Devices such as motorized chairs, remote control units to turn on appliances, voice recognition systems, ramps to enter and exit buildings, and computers or tablets can all assist people with severe disabilities. Computers are especially important in allowing many students with a range of disabilities to participate in normal classroom activities that would otherwise be impossible. For example, students with dyslexia may use assistive technologies such as text-to-speech and audiobooks to allow them to engage with text that matches their cognitive abilities. We discuss the use of technology more in Chapter 7, "What Should Teachers Know about Technology and Its Impact on Teaching and Learning?"

Congress incorporated definitions of assistive technology into IDEA, declaring that such technology must be provided whenever necessary as an element of free and appropriate public education. Assistive technology must be considered a potential component of the IEP for each student with disabilities.[24] As a new teacher, you should be prepared to encounter situations in which a child uses technology as a medium for interaction and engagement within your classroom.

Teaching Implications

If you are a regular education teacher, students with disabilities will likely be in your classroom for varying

© Cengage 2016

▶❙❙ TeachSource Video Case

Inclusion: Classroom Implications for General and Special Educators

Watch the video clips, study the artifacts in the case, and reflect on the following questions:

1. What are some of the strategies that general teachers and specialists use to keep the entire class functioning smoothly? Have you seen other successful strategies throughout your own education?

2. Do you find the work of general teachers or that of one or more of the specialists more interesting as a potential teaching position for you?

3. What information from this Video Case do you believe will be most helpful to you in your career as a teacher?

portions of the school day, depending on the types and amount of support services they are receiving. How will you approach meeting the different needs of these children?

It is most important that you do not stereotype these students. Certainly, different disabilities will have different implications for student learning. For example, a student with intellectual disabilities may require repetition and practice to master simple concepts, whereas a student who uses a wheelchair may learn even the most difficult material quickly. Even within the parameters of each type of disability, however, you will probably encounter a wide range of differences. Consider two students identified as having learning disabilities: One may display a low to average intelligence quotient (IQ) and have extreme difficulty in mathematics; the other may have an extremely high IQ and have difficulty in reading. Although both of these students have a learning disability, you would not provide the same instruction or have the same expectations for both children.

You should approach instruction for children with disabilities just as you would for other students in the classroom: Expect diversity, anticipate a range of abilities, and look for the particular strengths and learning profiles of each student. The special education teachers in your school will be helpful resources for recognizing student abilities and suggesting instructional strategies. The more you and a special education teacher can coordinate instruction and services for your students with disabilities, the better the students' educational experiences are likely to be. (The Video Case, *Inclusion: Classroom Implications for General and Special Educators*, introduces an elementary school teacher who has several special needs students in her classes, and shows some of the specialized adaptations that can help those students succeed in an inclusion setting.)

Here are a few other suggestions about how you as a regular education teacher can be effective in teaching children with disabilities in your classroom:

1. Be open to the idea of including students with disabilities in your classroom.
2. Learn about each child's limitations and potential and about available curriculum methodologies and technologies to help the child learn.
3. Insist that any needed services should be provided.
4. Use a variety of teaching strategies, including hands-on activities, peer tutoring, and cooperative learning strategies.
5. Avail yourself of opportunities for co-teaching with a special education teacher.[25]

Pause *and* Reflect

1. Have you had any contact with individuals with disabilities (e.g., a relative or neighbor)? What did you learn from this relationship that might be helpful in your teaching?
2. What is your position on "full inclusion"? What questions do you have about this strategy?
3. What do you think will be the most rewarding aspects of working with these students?

3-4 Gifted and Talented Students

The field of gifted education emerged in the 1970s. The term *talented* most often refers to an ability or skill (e.g., musical or artistic talent) that may not be matched by the child's more general abilities, whereas the term *gifted* usually includes intellectual ability. Gifted children are extremely bright, quickly grasping the ideas and concepts you are teaching and making interpretations or extrapolations that you may not even have considered. Gifted children may also have a creativity that shows itself in original thinking or artistic creations.

Students who are gifted and/or talented are sometimes overlooked when educators talk about students with special needs. Although special educational care and services for students with disabilities have long been recognized and accepted, American education has been slow to accept the notion that gifted children require special adaptations in both curricula and teaching methods. Because the idea of giftedness implies an elitism to many Americans, it seems undemocratic to provide special services to children who already enjoy an intellectual advantage.

When their special needs are neglected, gifted and talented students drop out of school at rates far exceeding the dropout rates for those not identified as gifted. Many of those students who stay in school feel unchallenged and become bored and apathetic. As a result, many of our brightest and most talented minds are being turned off or underdeveloped. However, many school districts have made serious efforts to identify gifted children and develop special programs for them.

3-4a IDENTIFYING GIFTED AND TALENTED STUDENTS

The areas in which states identify gifted and talented students can range from intellectual to psychomotor to artistic, with many variations. Through its evolution, the study of giftedness has moved increasingly toward more *inclusive* definitions and away from more *exclusive* ones. As we described earlier in the chapter, some people now think intelligence is composed of multiple factors. Consequently, in many schools, the definition of giftedness is shifting away from an emphasis on general intellectual ability (IQ) and toward the recognition that giftedness occurs in a variety of areas, such as mathematics, language, spatial ability, and kinesthetics.

In the past, school districts have tended to rely heavily on general intelligence and achievement tests in their assessment of students' intellectual abilities, as well as on teacher recommendations and grades earned in school. There is a danger of letting these assessment tools become synonymous with the *definition* of gifted and talented. To avoid this danger, teachers and administrators must study and interpret the data the tools provide rather than take the data at face value and use them for hard-and-fast cutoff points. Whether to recommend a child for a special program is a decision that should be made by responsible teachers and other professional educators on the basis of their objective and subjective appraisals of the student, the nature of the gifted program or activity, and the atmosphere in which the student lives and goes to school. Parents should be a significant part of these discussions. The point is that the complexity of the variables involved requires that professionals make individual decisions using their best judgments rather than according to arbitrary, predetermined cutoff points on tests.

A major concern in the identification of gifted and talented students centers on the underrepresentation of economically disadvantaged students, students with learning disabilities, and certain minority students. Asian American students are well represented in gifted and talented programs, whereas African American and Hispanic students are underrepresented in terms of their proportion in the total school population. Given this disparity, educators and parents are concerned that the measures being used to identify gifted and talented youngsters may work to the disadvantage of African Americans, Hispanics, and children from low-income families. Conversely, African American students are overrepresented in special education services, leading many educators and parents to wonder whether some form of cultural or racial bias is at work. The problem of identification is especially acute for bilingual children and children adjusting to a new culture.

3-4b PROGRAMS FOR GIFTED AND TALENTED STUDENTS

Programs for gifted and talented students exist in every state and in many school districts. The federal government reports that 3.3 million students were identified as gifted and talented in public elementary and secondary schools, representing about 6.5 percent of the total enrollment.[26] Yet, to this date there are not mandated federal funds to support gifted students.

The two main strategies for serving gifted children are **acceleration** and **enrichment**. With an accelerated curriculum, gifted children can learn at a pace commensurate with their abilities, allowing them to progress to advanced materials faster than their age norms or grade levels. By contrast, enrichment activities provide gifted students with opportunities to go beyond the regular curriculum in greater depth and breadth, to engage in independent or collaborative inquiry that develops their problem-solving abilities, research skills, and creativity.

Current educational programs for gifted and talented students are quite varied. Some programs establish special schools that are designated only for gifted or talented students and have special admission requirements. In such schools, stimulating courses can be devised and taught without concern for students who might be unable to keep pace, and teachers and students can be recruited on the basis of their talents.

Other programs adapt and enrich the regular school curriculum for gifted and talented children by grouping these students together for all or part of their instruction. This option normally is more flexible and practical than establishing special schools. Classes can be established on a continuing or short-term basis, in any subject area, with the intention of either enriching or accelerating the students.

In the United States, most gifted and talented students are likely to receive all, or nearly all, of their education in regular classrooms. In many school districts, in fact, separate programs for gifted students are being curtailed or phased out. The primary reasons for this trend are the spread of a philosophy that favors mixed-ability grouping, the cessation of tracking, and a lack of funds for separate gifted programs. In fact, the federal government does not fund gifted education programs or services. Some states, but not all, allocate funds to support gifted education. The trend toward meeting gifted students' needs within the regular classroom parallels the inclusion movement in special education. Some advocates for gifted education programs are disturbed by this trend and suggest that gifted students will be shortchanged in the regular classroom. They fear that teachers will concentrate their efforts on struggling students or that gifted students will be drafted to serve as tutors for these students rather than working to fulfill their own potential. Supporters of the current trend, however, believe that most gifted students' needs can be met in the regular classroom if teachers can differentiate curricula and instruction for them and increase the level of challenge.

Still others argue that it is important to keep a continuum of programs and services available for gifted students if for no other reason than that they represent a valuable resource to the United States. Along with instruction in the regular classroom, these educators argue, the options for such students should include pullout programs, special classes, grade skipping, and separate centers and schools. A range of giftedness exists, such that some students will do just fine in a regular classroom, whereas others can benefit from different programs.

Teaching Implications

If you want to focus on teaching gifted students, find out whether your state is one of the 20 or so that requires teachers to obtain a gifted endorsement to their teaching license. More likely, you will discover certain students in your regular education class to be gifted or talented and, lacking any special program, you will be responsible for teaching these students as part of your normal duties. If your school or school district has special programs for gifted and talented students, you may be expected to work with resource teachers to help prepare individualized education plans for these students. What do you need to know?

1. Recognize that gifted pupils generally learn the standard curricular skills and content quickly and easily. They need teaching that does not tie them to a limited range, that is not preoccupied with filling them with facts and information, but rather allows them to use the regular class as a forum for research, inquiry, and projects that are meaningful to them.

2. Realize that these students are persistently curious. They need teachers who encourage them to maintain confidence in their own ideas, even when those ideas differ from the norm.

3. Teach these pupils to be efficient and effective at independent study so that they can develop the skills required for self-directed learning and for analyzing and solving problems independently. Allow students of varying abilities to work together in areas of high interest, such as social action research projects.

4. Help students apply complex cognitive processes such as creative thinking, critiques, and pro and con analyses.

5. Expand your ideas concerning which instructional materials are available. Consider businesses, religious groups, national parks, and resource people as sources of potential instructional materials in addition to the textbooks and reference books available in the school. Be sure to investigate any technological resources that are available, including websites and other electronic links to information and knowledgeable people outside the school.

6. Use differentiated instructional strategies such as flexible grouping, "tiered" assignments (in which all students explore the same topic but the level of questions or products produced varies depending on students' abilities), learning centers, student contracts, and mentorships. (See Chapter 5, "What Is Taught?" for more on differentiated instruction.)

7. Implement *curriculum compacting*, in which teachers test students on what they already know on upcoming units. Students who demonstrate mastery in advance are allowed to accelerate through the material or pursue enrichment activities while the unit is being taught to the rest of the class.

8. Match students with mentors to help develop talent and engage students in relevant and applied problem solving. Mentoring programs encourage independent growth, increased self-confidence, and a willingness to reach out into new, untried areas.

If 2 + 3 is always going to be 5, why do they keep teaching it to us?

—A GIFTED FIRST-GRADE STUDENT

Individualizing instruction for students means not only supporting students with disabilities but also students who are identified as gifted and talented.

Dragon Images/Shutterstock.com

Pause *and* Reflect

1. What do you think will be the most challenging aspect of teaching gifted or talented students? How can you prepare for that challenge?
2. What will be the most rewarding aspect of teaching gifted or talented students?

3-5 Gender

Earlier in this chapter, we made the point that some racial and ethnic groups have been denied equal educational opportunities throughout our country's history. Another group, women, has also suffered discrimination and denial of equal educational opportunities; historically, women in our society have been denied educational and employment opportunities routinely extended to men. In recent years, considerable progress has been made to address these inequities. For example, women now constitute the majority of college students and have gained admittance into and success within many professions from which they were previously excluded. Teachers must be alert to avoid unfairness in their treatment of either girls or boys. (The Video Case, *Gender Equity in the Classroom: Girls and Science,* shows how one middle school science teacher tries to meet the needs of all his students: boys *and* girls.)

Fairness and equality may be difficult to achieve, however, because by the time they get to school, boys and girls are already used to being treated differently. From very young ages through adulthood, society holds different expectations for males and females. These expectations, in turn, generate different patterns of behavior toward boys

Gender Equity in the Classroom: Girls and Science

Watch the video clips, study the artifacts in the case, and reflect on the following questions:

1. This section of the chapter describes several ways in which boys and girls are treated differently in school. Which of these problems does this teacher avoid? How?

2. Did your own teachers treat male and female students differently? If so, give some examples. What do you think was the result of this differing treatment?

3. In addition to the strategies listed in this chapter, what are some ways that you, as a teacher, can be fair to boys and girls in your classes?

T (F)

After lagging men for many years, women now hold a similar number of jobs in STEM-related fields.

and girls. Whether it is pink or blue clothes, video games or drawing kits, or football helmets or ballet slippers, boys and girls get different messages from society about what is expected of them. Society tolerates aggressive behavior more in boys than in girls. Boys are encouraged to be independent, whereas girls often are expected to conform to accepted norms.

3-5a GENDER GAPS, SCHOOL ACHIEVEMENT, AND CAREER SELECTION

During the 1980s and 1990s, a number of research studies alleged that girls were being shortchanged in schools and classrooms. Researchers concluded that teachers often treated boys differently than girls, frequently to the girls' detriment, although teachers were generally unaware of their behaviors that favor boys.[27] These research studies suggested that in subtle and not-so-subtle ways, female students received the message that boys were more important than girls because teachers pay more attention to boys. Researchers also found there was considerable gender stereotyping in textbooks and other reading materials. Great strides have been made to level the playing field for girls and boys in the classroom.

Today, the majority of college graduates are women.[28] Girls have caught up with boys in terms of mathematics and science achievement. Yet, still fewer women than men tend to choose jobs in engineering and the sciences. In spite of comparable achievement levels in mathematics and science among boys and girls, recent studies on gender differences in **STEM (science, technology, engineering, and mathematics)** careers show that women lag men in choosing careers in those areas. Although the number of women in STEM-related fields has increased over the decades, they still make up just over a quarter of the STEM workforce. Yet, women who do work in a STEM occupation earn 33 percent more than women working in the non-STEM workforce. The gender gap concerns many experts who fear that the United States may be losing its competitive edge over the rest of the world in science and engineering fields. Because countries like China and India have so many more people in science and engineering fields, the United States needs women to enter STEM fields in order to expand its pipeline for math and science talent.

Multiple explanations for this gender gap in STEM fields exist. Some say that girls aren't exposed to career opportunities in STEM fields while in middle and senior high school, whereas others say that women look for careers where they can combine work and family, and that STEM fields seem less compatible with this goal. And, still another explanation is that girls may be choosing health-related and environmental-related fields because they see them as being more compassionate professions. In all probability, each of these explanations is valid for some portion of the female population.

Educational policy requires schools to provide STEM-focused experiences for girls.

Monkey Business Images/Shutterstock.com

If we're going to out-innovate and out-educate the rest of the world, we've got to open doors for everyone. We need all hands on deck, and that means clearing hurdles for women and girls as they navigate careers in science, technology, engineering, and math.

—FORMER FIRST LADY MICHELLE OBAMA

Some observers, while acknowledging the historic education discrimination and bias against girls, believe that schools are now failing boys more than girls. One clinical psychologist researcher at Harvard University argues that schools don't accommodate boys' learning styles and classroom needs. Boys perform best, he reports, when they have frequent recess breaks and are able to roam around the classroom. Boys are also more likely to enjoy argument and lively classroom debate, which is often discouraged.[29]

Researchers also cite the fact that the large gaps between the education levels of women and men that were evident in the early 1970s have essentially disappeared for the younger generation. High school females on average outperform males in reading and writing; take more credits in academic subjects; take more advanced placement (AP) courses in English, biology, and foreign languages; are more likely to be inducted into the National Honor Society; are more likely to attend college after high school; and are as likely to graduate with a postsecondary degree. Furthermore, two-thirds of all students receiving special education services are boys. Boys are much more likely to drop out of school than are girls.[30] If schools were really so biased against females, they argue, why are women doing so well academically?

Teaching Implications

What can you do to make sure that you are being fair to both male and female students in your classroom? To ensure sex-equitable learning environments in classrooms, teachers should consider the following steps:

- Have high expectations for all students.
- Examine instructional materials to be certain that sex role stereotyping or bias does not occur. If it does, try to find alternative materials.

- Examine and address, if needed, the frequency with which students are called on and the kind of responses that they provide the students to ensure that gender biases are not occurring. This can be done by audiotaping teacher–student interactions and listening to unintended patterns of interaction.

- Look at who uses or is encouraged to use computer technology in the classroom. Often, boys tend to monopolize computers and other technology.

- Eliminate the assignment of sex-stereotyped tasks.

- Organize classes so that students don't segregate themselves by sex.

- Model sex-equitable behavior.

- Choose your words carefully (e.g., *not* saying, "Boys will be boys"), and correct students' speech or actions when it borders on discrimination or bias.

- Pair learning with movement to increase brain activity and offset boredom.

Some school districts are attempting to address gender differences by offering single-gender schools or classrooms. Advocates of this approach argue that by separating the sexes, more attention can be given to the particular needs of boys or girls. Opponents argue that discrimination might still occur and suggest that keeping boys and girls together means that they learn to work with one another. At this point, insufficient research has been carried out to support either claim, but anecdotal reports claim successes for some single-sex classes. (See "Up Close: Urban Prep Academies" about a Chicago school for one such report.)

Up CLOSE

Urban Prep Academies: Single-Sex Education Success Story

Urban Prep Academies is one network of single-sex schools that report great success. Urban Prep Academies is a network of three charter high schools in Chicago, Illinois. Two thousand male African American students attend the schools. Eighty-five percent of the students qualify for free or reduced lunch. The school has graduated four classes of high school seniors. Each year, 100 percent of its African American seniors have been accepted to four-year colleges.

How do the Urban Prep Academies achieve this remarkable feat? And is it replicable elsewhere? The school operates on an extended school day, which provides an additional 1,200 hours of school time each year, and as part of that additional time, a double period of English and extracurricular activities and public service projects are required. The rigorous college prep curriculum is focused on language arts and mathematics. Parents are expected to be engaged with the school, and teachers participate in regular professional development.

More than this, the school's founder, Tim King, attributes success to the four R's: ritual, respect, responsibility, and relationships. Students are addressed formally, using their last names, and they wear coats and ties. Faculty members develop close, personal relationships with the students and are available by phone on evenings and weekends. For many of the young men, the teachers and administrators are the first positive male role models they've had. Every adult in the building knows and believes in the school's mission: to get students to college. They also know that admission to college is a milestone, and graduation from college is the real goal. Yet, King is quick to say there is not one secret recipe for a successful school. Rather, King believes the "recipe for success" is parents selecting the best type of school for their child.[31]

Are these results replicable at other schools? Urban Prep Academies started with one school. They have grown to three high schools. It is with purposeful intention that the results are replicable.

3-6 Sexual Orientation and Gender Identity

> People kept coming up to me and making fun of me. They would call me horrible names and I would cry all the time. Letters were put in my locker saying hateful things and how my parents shouldn't have had me and how I should just die. Kids would threaten me after school and follow me home yelling things at me. No one should have to go through what I went through in school.

This statement by a lesbian student reflects what many **lesbian, gay, bisexual, transgendered, and queer (LGBTQ)** students experience in school. According to GLSEN's 2017 school climate survey, the majority of LGBTQ students experience a hostile school climate. The survey defined a hostile school environment as one in which students hear biased remarks at school and feel unsafe at school because of their sexual orientation. A third of LGBTQ students skipped at least one day of school in the previous month because of safety concerns. LGBTQ students have lower academic achievement and poorer psychological well-being. An alarming study reports that 40 percent of LBGTQ youth and more than 50 percent of transgender and non-binary youth considered suicide in the past year.[32]

You are likely to have LGBTQ students in your classroom, and you are apt to meet LGBTQ parents of students. You will also likely teach with LGBTQ colleagues who may also experience similarly hostile school environments. Considerable evidence indicates that school is often a hostile environment for young LGBTQ students. Teenagers tend to ridicule differences in general and differences in sexual orientation in particular. LGBTQ students have often experienced taunting, harassment, and even violence because of their sexual orientation. Teachers and administrators who condone such name-calling, while prohibiting profanity or racial slurs, are also promoters of hostility toward homosexual youth. LGBTQ students have won lawsuits against school officials who failed to maintain a safe school environment and to discipline students who regularly tormented them.

The hostility that LGBTQ youth encounter in school is mirrored in the larger society, which bombards them with messages that they are outcasts. This hostility leaves many of them isolated, frightened, and uncertain about their own worth. As a result, gay students are a high-risk population. Many run away from home or are thrown out by parents, abuse drugs and alcohol, suffer from depression, or attempt suicide.

The National Education Association, the American Federation of Teachers, and other leading education associations have all passed resolutions calling on their members and school districts to acknowledge the special needs of LGBTQ students, provide supportive services such as counseling and support groups, and implement anti-harassment measures. Twenty-three states and the District of Columbia ban discriminatory acts based on sexual orientation or identity over and above the protection afforded by the U.S. Constitution and Title IX, and the U.S. Department of Education has issued guidelines spelling out that "gay or lesbian students" are covered by federal prohibitions against sexual harassment.

Many schools have taken initiatives to create a safe and inclusive school climate for all students, including LGBTQ students. Although all students stand the chance of becoming the victim of a bully, LGBTQ students are much more often the targets of bullying. Educating school staff and faculty also improves the environment for LGBTQ students. Often, teachers are unsure of how to discuss issues of bullying or gender roles with students. LGBTQ students report that they feel more accepted at school when they work with supportive teachers.

Nevertheless, the issue of sexual orientation and identity remains controversial, and actions urged by gay and lesbian organizations are certain to provoke opposition by some community members who believe such steps would signal that the schools are condoning homosexual behavior. Some people believe that while touting tolerance, LGBTQ organizations are actually seeking to promote homosexuality among students at a developmental period in their lives when the sexual identity of many is not fully developed. It will be important for you to be mindful of the community you teach within as you consider the steps you will take to ensure a supportive learning environment for your students.

All students—regardless of their sexual orientation—have the right to a safe and supportive learning environment. As educators, we also have the responsibility to promote and protect the emotional well-being of all of our students.

Teaching Implications

GLSEN (formerly the Gay, Lesbian & Straight Education Network) and the Trevor Project are organizations that provide resources to create safe and inclusive schools for all students. Their research suggests that school-based strategies that help make schools and classrooms safer spaces for all children include having supportive teachers, an LGBTQ inclusive curriculum, inclusive school policies, and supportive clubs such as Gender and Sexuality Alliances (GSAs). The organizations provide materials that can be used in the classroom and offer strategies and policies for school communities. Additionally, there are many things that schools and educators can do to make school safer for all students as well as those who are lesbian, gay, bisexual, or transgendered:

- Establish classroom guidelines about name-calling. Challenge homophobic remarks everywhere and all the time.
- Respect different points of view.
- Make no assumptions about students' families or their sexual orientations. Use inclusive language, such as *partner* or *spouse* instead of *husband* or *wife*.
- Be role models for how all students should be treated with respect and dignity.

Pause *and* Reflect

1. In your experience, did the school you attended treat boys and girls equally? What examples can you cite to support your response?
2. How are you prepared to support a student who is bullied at school based on their sexual orientation or identity? Consider specific strategies you might enact.

3-7 The Teacher's Response to Diversity

So far in this chapter, we have presented a great deal of information about the diversity of the children you will be teaching. Ultimately, how these children are educated will come down to you and your daily interactions with them in your classroom. How will you come to understand your students' differences and best support their learning and development?

3-7a TEACHER–STUDENT DISPARITY

Consider what we know about the typical teacher today. Women and whites predominate in the teacher force; 76 percent of all public school teachers are women, and 79 percent of those teaching in public schools are white.[33] Despite efforts to increase the number of minority teachers (see Chapter 13, "What Are Your Job Options in Education?"), this gap between teachers and students is likely to persist for some time. Profiles of preservice and beginning teachers show similar gender, racial, and ethnic patterns. Most of these teachers come from relatively stable family backgrounds. The majority of teachers and future teachers in our classrooms, then, come from very different backgrounds than many of the students they teach.

As we mentioned in Chapter 2, "What Is a School and What Is It For?," the more alike students and teachers are in social and cultural characteristics, the more they share tacit expectations about behavior and academic performance. As gaps in those social and cultural characteristics widen, teachers need to rely on solid pedagogical training to overcome these differences. Too often, white educators have been reluctant to recognize that their own backgrounds and the culture of the school have an effect on learning. As an incoming teacher, you will need to know about the commonalities and differences among students, and you will need to learn specific methods and techniques for addressing the plurality of culture and learning styles you will encounter.

3-7b DIVERSITY: A COMPLEX PHENOMENON

The school programs described in this chapter have been designed to address student diversity and create a more equal educational opportunity for children in our school systems. An inherent danger in these approaches to addressing diversity, however, is the tendency to label children and form stereotypic images of who they are. Student performance in school is affected by many factors, including social and cultural trends. The educational groupings we have been discussing are an administrative convenience, not a naturally occurring segmentation of children. Within each of these groups, each child will vary along a number of dimensions and have a very different learning profile of strengths and weaknesses.

Rather than thinking of minority students as having a culture that is valid—albeit different from theirs—teachers sometimes think of these students as deficient. We encourage you, as a teacher, to remember that we are talking about *differences* in students, not deficits. Teachers are challenged to recognize the diversity of cultures represented by their students and to address these cultures in their teaching.

Teaching Implications

Given this profile of the cultural discrepancy between students and teachers, and the complex diversity of today's student body, how can prospective teachers best prepare? Here are some steps you can take now:

- Seek out experiences and places to broaden your understanding of societal and cultural commonalities and differences (e.g., travel to other countries).
- Spend time in communities whose residents differ from you in terms of ethnicity, culture, or language.
- Volunteer in schools that differ from those you attended.

Once you have your own classroom, what can you do to address diversity there? Here are some guidelines:

- Learn about and appreciate the values and backgrounds of your students.
- Teach to your students' strengths rather than making them feel incapable or deficient.
- Provide a variety of educational experiences, and find ways for all students to achieve recognition from you and their peers for being good at something.
- Coordinate expertise and support with your students' parents or caregivers and other professional staff at the school so that students get a consistent message.
- Without lowering standards, recognize that the schools' traditional emphasis on middle-class values such as individual learning and competition may clash with the values represented by their students' cultures. Teachers can provide opportunities for students to learn ways to succeed in today's dominant culture, but they must also respect the value systems in students' home lives and help them, in positive ways, to bridge the gap between the two worlds.

OUR FINAL WORD

The purpose of schools has evolved as our society has changed over time. One of these changes is the growing range of diversity of the students who enter our schools each day. The increasing complexity and diversity of our students' lives requires other needs to be addressed and incorporated into the way schools are approaching education. A major goal of this chapter has been to highlight of the complexity of issues that directly affect many children's lives and their ability to get an inclusive and competent education.

You may be getting concerned about whether you can handle the breadth of diversities you may face in your classroom. Be assured that you do not face this challenge alone: Numerous assistance systems have been devised to help teachers respond to the range of student needs. Besides having other teachers and administrators to help you, most schools have specialists, such as nurses, school psychologists, and counselors, who often can give you valuable advice or partner with you to support your students. Families and parents are also essential partners in supporting the whole student. School volunteers may be community members who speak the language of ELL students in the schools. Interns or students from the local college may help as well, providing another adult in the classroom.

You will need to use all the resources available to you, including parents and other professionals. Some teachers may initially feel threatened by this involvement or have a sense that the classroom is their turf. As we have seen throughout this chapter, however, our students need the coordinated expertise and support of all school professionals and the crucial link with parents to be given a fair shot at acquiring the good education that is their due.

WHY TEACH? YOUR FINAL WORD

1. After reading this chapter, what questions or concerns do you have that you want to discuss with your colleagues or instructor?
2. What forms of diversity among students do you believe will present you with the greatest challenges? What ideas do you have for meeting these challenges?
3. Describe your ethnic heritage and the influence of ethnicity on your family's past and present. Share your family history with your classmates.

KEY TERMS

assimilation (p. 57)
cultural pluralism (p. 57)
multicultural education (p. 58)
culturally responsive teaching (p. 59)
English language learners (ELLs) (p. 61)
limited English proficiency (LEP) (p. 61)
bilingual education (p. 63)
multiple intelligences (p. 66)
special education (p. 71)
individualized education program (IEP) (p. 71)
individualized family services plan (IFSP) (p. 71)

least restrictive environment (LRE) (p. 72)
mainstreaming (p. 72)
inclusion (p. 72)
Response to Intervention (RTI) (p. 75)
assistive technology (p. 75)
acceleration (p. 78)
enrichment (p. 78)
STEM (science, technology, engineering, and
   mathematics) (p. 81)
lesbian, gay, bisexual, transgendered, and queer
   (LGBTQ) (p. 84)

FOR FURTHER INFORMATION

Web Resources

Teachers of English to Speakers of Other Languages
https://www.tesol.org

A professional organization that hosts conferences, publishes journals, and presents professional development sessions to support teachers.

Council for Exceptional Children (Special Education and Gifted Education) https://exceptionalchildren.org

This site contains many resources for teaching students with disabilities.

Center for Multicultural Education https://education.uw.edu/cme

The University of Washington's center that presents research and strategies to promote success for all students in schools.

Print Resources

James A. Banks and Cherry A. McGee Banks (eds.), *Multicultural Education: Issues and Perspectives*, 10th ed. (Somerset, NJ: John Wiley & Sons, 2019).

Various well-known educators explore the research, concepts, and debates about the education of students from both genders and from different cultural, racial, ethnic, and language groups.

Django Paris and H. Samy Alim (eds), *Culturally Sustaining Pedagogies: Teaching and Learning for Justice in a Changing World* (New York, NY: Teachers College Press, 2017).

This edited book examines culturally sustaining pedagogies as a way to embrace the diversity of all learners.

Samuel Kirk, James Gallagher, Mary Ruth Coleman, and Nick Anastaslow, *Educating Exceptional Children*, 14th ed. (Belmont, CA: Wadsworth Cengage Learning, 2015).

The authors present a comprehensive look at understanding children with exceptionalities and how to meet their classroom needs.

Daniel P. Hallahan, James M. Kauffman, and Paige Pullen, *Exceptional Learners: An Introduction to Special Education*, 14th ed. (Pearson, 2019).

An overview of a wide range of characteristics of exceptional learners with specific strategies and methods designed for the classroom.

Christine Sleeter and Miguel Zavala, *Transformative Ethnic Studies in Schools: Curriculum, Pedagogy and Research.* (New York, NY: Teachers College Press, 2020).

The authors present ethnic studies through a historical and contemporary lens with theory, research, and case studies.

How Do Social Issues Affect Students?

iStock.com/FatCamera

LEARNING OBJECTIVES

4-1 Identify critical social issues that directly influence the students' academic success in the classroom.

4-2 Discuss how changing American family patterns are impacting the demographics of the school population.

4-3 Describe the impact poverty has on a student's potential for success in schools.

4-4 Define the goals of sex education in schools.

4-5 Provide strategies schools are using to support students who live in dangerous family or community situations.

4-6 Identify signs of alcohol or drug abuse.

4-7 Discuss the critical need to address students' mental health.

4-8 List steps schools have taken to ensure schools are safe places for learning.

4-9 Discuss recent trends in student cheating in schools.

4-10 List risk factors associated with high school dropout rates.

Truth or Fiction?

T F One-third of today's children live with a single parent.

T F More than 10 percent of children today live in poverty.

T F Teenage mothers often live in poverty through their adult years.

T F Teachers who suspect that a student in his or her class has suffered child abuse must use discretion in deciding whether to file a report.

T F Although cheating in school has received much media attention, it only occurs with moderate frequency.

Rarely a day goes by when the American public is not assaulted by news of some heartbreaking event or newly revealed problem involving the nation's young. Because formal education is so much a part of their lives, many of the youth-related issues and problems spill over and affect our schools and classrooms. The nuances of the ways schools impact society and the ways society impacts schools are complex. This chapter explores some of the most sensitive and controversial issues in American education. In such a small space, we can treat each topic only briefly, but we urge you to pursue additional reading and resources on each issue.

As we discussed in the previous chapter, when students enter the classroom each morning, they carry with them experiences that impact their physical, social, emotional, and academic development. The paths our students take each morning before stepping foot in the school building may be different based on their race, class, gender, socioeconomic status, or other sources of diversity. For many students, the world in which they live outside of school is quite different than the world within the school building. It is unfortunate that the world many school-aged children experience outside of the school is tumultuous and even dangerous. It is difficult, if not impossible, for students to "turn off" their out of school experiences during the school day. We wish to make you more fully aware of and more deeply sensitive to the sorts of issues your students may bring to your classroom. As a teacher, you will need to consider many of these issues to best support student learning. It's important to recognize that schools and communities have trained specialists to support youth in distress. We want you to recognize the stabilizing power of education, which gives structure, purpose, and hope to youngsters whose daily lives often lack these stabilizing and motivating influences.

4-1 Recognizing Risk Factors

Chapter 3, "Who Are Today's Students in a Diverse Society?," profiled changes in our society that are resulting in increased diversity among today's students. These conditions affect many students' lives, but they do not necessarily negatively affect their academic achievement. Other changes or trends in society do pose a more direct threat to a student's opportunity to succeed in school. Many teachers may have difficulty recognizing and adapting to differences that contribute to the problems some children bring to the classroom, because—unlike many of their students— most teachers come from relatively risk-free backgrounds. Although a teacher's stable background can be a source of strength, it means that students often inhabit different worlds than their teachers. Often there are striking gaps between teachers' and students' social class and their personal exposure to major social problems.

In our discussion here, we deal with several difficult conditions and problems, including poverty, homelessness, child abuse, alcohol and drug use, teenage parenting, sexually transmitted diseases, mental health, violence, cheating, and school dropout rates. These pervasive societal problems do not occur in isolation, but rather tend to cluster or overlap. In real life, it is difficult to separate out discrete sources of social problems. The compounding of risk factors contributes to the incredible scope of these problems and places a number of students at risk for not completing or succeeding in school. Figure 4.1 illustrates the most prevalent risk factors for young children. For such **at-risk students**, as they are often called, the chances are great that they will have difficulty getting an adequate education.

FIGURE 4.1 **Children Under Age 9 Experiencing Poverty and Selected Risk Factors, 2018**

Source: http://www.nccp.org/tools/risk/?state=US&age-level=9&income-level=Poor&ids%5B%5D=77&ids%5B%5D=84&ids%5B%5D=76&ids%5B%5D=78&ids%5B%5D=74&ids%5B%5D=72&ids%5B%5D=83&submit=Calculate

There are 34,586,520 children under age 9 in the United States. Nineteen percent of them live in poverty. The graph below highlights the risk factors they face.

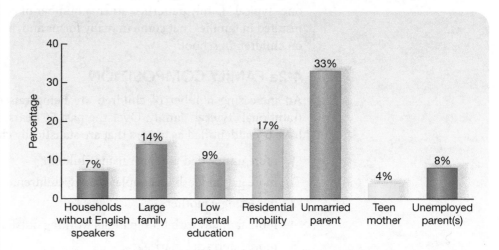

What are some of these risk factors? Here are seven major ones affecting students in today's schools:

1. A household without English-speaking adults
2. A family with more than four children
3. Parents without a high school degree
4. A change in residences one or more times in a year
5. Single-parenthood
6. A teen mother
7. Unemployed parents

We know that these risk factors do not necessarily predetermine students' success in school. Many children from families with these risks overcome the odds to succeed in school and in life. Recent research from the Center on the Developing Child at Harvard University suggests guidelines that schools can take to support students facing high-risk situations be more successful in schools.[1] These guidelines include: providing supportive adult-youth relationships that extend over time; implementing opportunities to develop social and emotional skills; and establishing clear routines for classroom procedures. Following these guidelines has been proven to offer students a higher rate of school success.

Let's examine some of these risk factors in more detail, starting with the changing patterns of the American family.

4-2 New American Family Patterns

In recent decades, our society has experienced dramatic changes in how families are structured. The once common image of the "breadwinner" father, a housewife mother, and two children of public school age now accurately describes only a very small percentage of households in the United States. So what is the typical family of our students like today? As we discussed in the previous chapter, there is no longer one "typical" family pattern. Rather, a number of economic and societal trends have resulted in families that come in many forms and, in turn, have a pervasive influence on children in school.

4-2a FAMILY COMPOSITION

An increasing number of children are being raised in families different that the traditional "typical" family. Over the past 50 years, the following five major trends have been identified as factors that are statistically changing family structures:

1. more unmarried parents raising children,
2. more gay and lesbian couples raising children,
3. more single mothers,
4. more families with both parents working outside the home, and
5. more interracial marriages.[2]

These trends are seen across the entire population. However, there are trends that are more prevalent for different demographic groups. Socioeconomic status is a stronger indicator of marital status than ever before. For example, marriage remains the status quo for adults with a college education. Race and ethnicity also are an indicator of marital status. Fifty-four percent of white adults are married, whereas 30 percent of African American adults are married, 61 percent of Asian Americans are married, and 46 percent of Hispanics are married.[3]

The changing demographics of families over the past 50 years is partly due to adults delaying marriages until an older age and partly our nation's high divorce rate. The divorce rate has tripled from the rate in the 1960s. In addition to divorce, factors such as births to single parents, separation, and death of a parent contribute to the number of children living in single-parent households or possibly with grandparents or aunts and uncles.

Being a child in a family in which the parents' marriage is conflict ridden and unhappy may be less preferable in some ways than living in a single-parent family. Nevertheless, single-parent families have one major disadvantage relative to two-parent households: lower incomes. One out of every three children is being raised by a single parent. These children are 4.5 times more likely to live in poverty. The risks are even higher for African American and Native Americans children.[4] Single-mother families have been called the *new poor*. It is not just the absence of one parent but also the loss of a two-parent income that puts a special burden on these families.

Another result of high divorce rates is the increasing number of children living in blended families with stepparents, stepsiblings, and/or half-siblings. In some cases, divorced parents share physical custody of the children, with the result that children must split their time between parental households. As we discussed in Chapter 3, "Who Are Today's Students in a Diverse Society?," you may also have students whose parents are of the same gender.

Changes in American family patterns will likely influence your interactions with students and their families in a number of ways. For example, in divorce situations, it may be difficult to keep both parents informed of their child's progress, or a single parent may have a very heavy workload and may be unable to

Ⓣ F
One-third of today's children live with a single parent.

"America's future will be determined by the home and the school. The child becomes largely what it is taught, hence we must watch what we teach it, how we live before it.

—JANE ADDAMS,
cofounder of Hull House and
Nobel Peace Prize winner

VOICES from the Classroom

Families and School

Whitney Allred Williams is an elementary teacher in Hillsborough, North Carolina.

I teach second grade in a semi-rural Title 1 Elementary School where 53 percent of students receive free or reduced lunch rates. About 25 percent of students are emergent bilinguals, all of whom come from Spanish-speaking homes. I feel it is imperative that all students feel comfortable in the classroom, especially students who are navigating a new language. Unfortunately, by the time many students reach second grade, they already feel unsuccessful at school. It is my job to reverse that thinking and provide opportunities for students that help them gain confidence and find success.

The first step in reversing this thinking is building a classroom culture that allows students to feel comfortable taking risks and making mistakes. Giving students ample time to think, guiding students to express their ideas, and teaching them how to listen and respond to their peers all contribute to a positive classroom culture. Knowing students' emotional needs is just as valuable as knowing their academic needs. Who puts too much pressure on themselves? Who will break down quickly? Who gives up easily? Understanding how students persevere and problem-solve is invaluable. Conferencing with students, asking questions about their work, and observing them during a productive struggle provide insight into their emotional needs.

The second step is providing student-centered, inquiry-based learning opportunities. Many students who do not find academic success in the classroom find success in our school's makerspace.

A makerspace is a space with equipment and supplies that students can use to engage in hands on learning to create and invent. This informal learning environment is vital to students who are learning how to fail and succeed. Tinkering and making is the perfect place for students to practice perseverance, problem-solving, and communication while also leveling the academic playing field. This type of learning is naturally engaging and interdisciplinary. These tasks require negotiation and collaboration that advance interpersonal skills. This can be something as simple as making a tower out of spaghetti and marshmallows or something more complicated like making a new piece of wheelchair accessible playground equipment. For "gifted" students, this may be the first time they experience failure. For struggling students, this may be the first time they experience success. Students see themselves and their peers in a different light when these roles shift and all students' talents are seen. To get inspired, visit pblworks.org or abdoakland.org.

As students gain confidence, the classroom becomes a trusting community where students can be vulnerable to ask questions and express ideas. When students are given the opportunity and support to navigate the emotional side of learning and failing, they will find success. Confident students who can persevere and problem-solve will thrive in the classroom and beyond.

attend parent–teacher conferences at the usual times. Varied family patterns will also require more sensitivity in daily interactions, such as avoiding asking students to bring a note from "your mother." It would perhaps be better to say "your parent" or "the adult who takes care of you."

Pause *and* Reflect

1. How does your own family background reflect traditional or emerging family patterns? How do you think your upbringing will affect your ability to teach students from different family situations?
2. How can you prepare to work effectively with diverse parents and caregivers?

4-2b SCHOOL AND TEACHER RESPONSES

In addition to limiting the amount of time children spend in close contact with their parents, the trend toward two-career and single-parent families has a direct impact on the schools. In the past, teachers could count on more support from families; now teachers often find it difficult to even get in contact with many parents. In the past, young people were actively involved outside of school in family and community. Today, however, the school is being urged to play a larger role in expanding and guiding the limited experiences of children and to connect with families of all students. As we discussed in Chapter 3, "Who Are Today's Students in a Diverse Society?," you will also want to be sure to be aware of what languages are spoken in your students' homes. Often, schools will provide translators to help you communicate with parents who speak a language other than English. It will be important for you to consider working schedules, language barriers, and other social issues as you attempt to build connections from the classroom to the home.

LEADERS in Education

James Comer

James Comer is a public health physician and psychiatrist who, through his work with low-income schools in New Haven, Connecticut, has shown that by fostering the social, emotional, and academic needs of children, it is possible for all students, especially low-income children, to achieve high academic success.

Over 50 years ago, James Comer, M.D. and his colleagues developed the Comer School Development Program in two of the poorest local schools. A team of educational and mental health professionals consisting of Comer, school administrators and teachers, a social worker, a psychologist, a special education teacher, and other support staff worked to involve parents in developing a social skills curriculum that integrated academic disciplines. The curriculum included four major areas: politics and government, business and economics, health and nutrition, and spiritual and leisure time—all areas in which the students would need proficiency to succeed in school and to lead productive lives. Through the curriculum, the students became more aware of their community and of how their involvement in it could make a difference.

By adopting the findings of child development and behavioral science research, the team concentrated on problem solving rather than blame fixing and made decisions based on consensus. This consensus process gave each team member a sense

Diana Walker/The LIFE Images Collection/Getty Images

of participation and ownership of decisions. The project was a great success: Students' standardized test scores rose dramatically, project schools had higher attendance rates than other New Haven schools, and students graduated to become school leaders in their later schooling.

Comer's model emphasizes the social context of teaching and learning. No academic learning is possible, Comer asserts, unless a positive environment exists at the school such that teachers, students, parents, and administrators like one another and work together for the good of all children. Built around three elements—a school governance team, a mental health team, and parental participation—Comer's model seeks to create schools that offer children stable support and positive role models. With the school and parents working successfully together, no conflict arises between home and school. The students learn desirable values, disruptions at school are reduced, and both teachers and students have more time and energy to focus on academic and social skills learning.

The Comer School Development Program has partnered with over 1,000 schools across the nation to implement the Comer program into the schools. They continue today to partner with schools to promote educating the whole child. They also partner with colleges and universities to integrate their program into teacher education programs.

The more dramatic social problems, such as poverty and homelessness, take on even greater urgency for the schools than work schedules. Schools are being asked to deal with the new problems that reflect the facts of modern family life and our changed economy. Many schools have responded to child care needs by offering both before-school and after-school programs. For example, schools may offer enrichment and recreational programs or on-site day care before and after school to address student and parental needs. Some schools even stagger their bus schedules to accommodate students who stay for after-school programs. Many schools provide both breakfast and lunch programs. We are also seeing a rise in programs that send weekend or evening meals home with students. In the "Voices from the Classroom" feature, Whitney Williams shares some of the ways she tries to build a positive classroom community for the students in her classroom.

Many schools today hire school social workers, sometimes called family specialists, to help support students' academic and social success. School-based social workers work with teaching teams to identify students who have family factors that may impact their success in school. They help to provide support within the school and identify referral services that will also support the child. A school social worker may help coordinate transportation for parents to attend school meetings or for a homeless student to come to school. The school social worker may coordinate a school supply donation or food donation and help distribute the supplies or food to students in need. The school social worker also works with outside agencies (i.e., Big Brothers/Big Sisters or Department of Social and Health Services) to make referrals and to maximize outside resources that can be used to support the "whole" child in the school. Unfortunately, thousands of students lost many of these services when school buildings closed in 2020 as a result of the COVID-19 pandemic. Schools, communities, and agencies scrambled to support students in ways that they were supported during the traditional school day. Consequently, much of the larger society began to realize the expanded role schools play in the lives of many students.

Some schools, such as those following the model developed by James Comer—described in the "Leaders in Education" feature—have responded in a very different way, by redesigning the whole school to make effective teamwork with families a priority.

Interagency Cooperation

In addition to developing their own responses, many schools work with other agencies to meet the changing needs of students and their families. These schools offer nontraditional programs that coordinate agencies dealing with health, social, and recreational services. The interagency programs enable the schools to deliver needed social and health services to students and their families, to promote success in school.

For example, the coordinated school health initiative responds to the risk factors that threaten children and youth by providing student health services. It assesses the health problems in particular school communities, builds consensus on which services should be provided, and puts together a comprehensive approach to improving children's health using agencies that address health, mental health, dental health, social services, recreation, and youth development. The guiding principle for the coordinated school health initiative is that schools and communities can do much more with their current resources if they work together in partnership rather than as separate, isolated agencies.

4-3 Poverty

The rich are getting richer and the poor are getting poorer. This aphorism describes the extremes of different socioeconomic levels in our society today. **Socioeconomic status (SES)** is the term used by the U.S. Census Bureau to classify economic conditions of people using a family's occupational status, income, and educational attainment as measures of status. Individuals high in income, occupational prestige, and amount of education are considered to be high in socioeconomic status and are usually seen by others to be upper-class people who are influential in their communities. In contrast, people low in socioeconomic status are seen as being lower-class people who have little prestige or power.

4-3a WHO ARE THE POOR?

In 2018, the number of impoverished Americans was estimated to be 38.1 million, or 11.8 percent of the total U.S. population.[5] In 2018, 16.2 percent of all children (11.9 million kids) lived in poverty in the United States—that's almost 1 in every 6 children. The coronavirus pandemic of 2020, which caused millions to suffer financial loss, will certainly result in increased rates of poverty across the United States.

Rates of poverty are not spread evenly across demographics. Native Americans have the higest poverty rate (25.4 perent). African Americans have the next highest poverty rate (20.8 percent). Over 10 percent of whites, 17.6 percent of Hispanic Americans, and 10.1 percent of Asian Americans live below the poverty line ($25,100/year for a family of four in 2018). Women are more likely to live in poverty than men. Single parents are also more likely to live in poverty. And, nearly a quarter of people with a disability live in poverty.[6]

Poverty rates declined over the past decade as the United States recovered from the 2007–2009 recession. However, it is anticipated the rates will climb in the wake of the 2020 COVID-19 pandemic. The problem of poverty is pervasive, and the prospects for breaking its grip on children are particularly bleak. As Figure 4.2 shows,

(T) F
More than 10 percent of children today live in poverty.

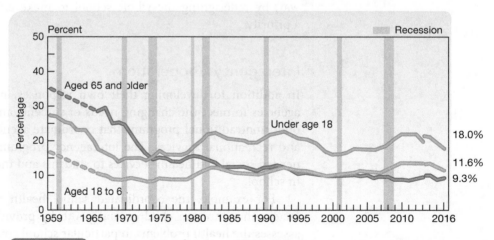

FIGURE 4.2   **Poverty Rates by Age: 1959–2016**

Note: The data for 2013 and beyond reflect the implementation of the redesigned income questions. The data points are placed at the midpoints of the respective years. Data for people aged 18 to 64 and aged 65 and older are not available from 1960 to 1965. For information on recessions, see Appendix A. For information on confidentiality protection, sampling error, nonsampling error, and definitions, see <www2.census.gov/programs-surveys/cps/techdocs/cpsmarl 7.pdf>.

Source: U.S. Census Bureau, Current Population Survey, 1960 to 2017 Annual Social and Economic Supplements.

17.5 percent of U.S. children live in poverty, the highest rate among all age groups and the highest rate in any industrialized country. Children make up about one-fourth of the total U.S. population, but they constitute over a third of the poor.

In the past, poverty was assumed to be the result of unemployment, and this remains true for many. Nearly one in three young people are growing up in families whose parents do not have secure employment.[7] Over 2.5 million children, or one in every 30, are living in poverty in a family in which at least one adult is employed full time.[8] This is the highest it has ever been in the United States. After World War II, many high school graduates could get manufacturing jobs that required minimal education but paid quite well. A high school graduate could support a family of four, buy a house, own two cars, and live comfortably. The U.S. job market has now changed. Many manufacturing jobs can now be done more efficiently and effectively by machines, and many of those jobs that are still done by people have been moved, or "outsourced," to countries with low-wage workers. The U.S. job market for unskilled workers today is found mostly in the service industry, specifically in food service that typically pay minimum wage and offer no benefits. Full-time employment at the current minimum wage is not enough to support a family above the poverty line.

4-3b HOMELESSNESS

For families in or close to poverty, the threat of homelessness is very real. Poor families often pay more than one-half of their annual incomes in rent. With such a large percentage of income consumed by rent payments, a single incident or emergency in the family can disrupt this tenuous equilibrium and jeopardize the family's ability to maintain a home. Imagine, for example, the domino effect that could occur from mechanical difficulties with the one family car. Even minor repairs costing $50 to $100 may be beyond the family's budget. Without a car, parents may be unable to get to work and the children unable to get to day care. It does not take long in such a situation to lose a job or a long-awaited slot in a child care center. If the main earner cannot work, paying rent can soon become impossible. It is easy to see why housing, which consumes so much of annual income, is a particular source of vulnerability for families in poverty.

> We have this morning, more people in poverty, in raw numbers, than at any moment in our long history; more, on a percentage basis, than at any time in a quarter century.
>
> —GENE NICHOL,
> Professor of Law,
> University of North Carolina at Chapel Hill

Approximately 1.5 million children and youth in the United States are homeless at some point each year.[9] The number of homeless school-aged children has increased over 70 percent since 2006.[10] Imagine the obstacles for homeless children trying to get an education. Uprooted from their homes, many live in shelters or other locations in distant parts of town. Attending school may require extensive transportation, which parents are not likely to be able to afford. Enrolling children in a school near a shelter may be a difficult and intimidating process for parents struggling with daily survival. Many parents, believing they will be homeless only for a short time, may not even try to transfer their child's enrollment. As days turn into weeks and months, the child may miss a great deal of school. If the child is fortunate enough to attend school, other difficulties may arise, such as poor health, hunger, emotional trauma, or simply being unable to stay awake in class.

Some homeless children are on their own, having run away from home or been thrown out by their families. Many of these chronically homeless youth have been physically or sexually abused, and many suffer from drug or alcohol abuse, poor nutrition, inadequate sleep, exposure to the elements, and lack of health care. School can be a stabilizing force in the lives of these children, but it can also exacerbate their problems.

Homelessness, an outcome of poverty, affects many families in the United States, with serious implications for the children's education.

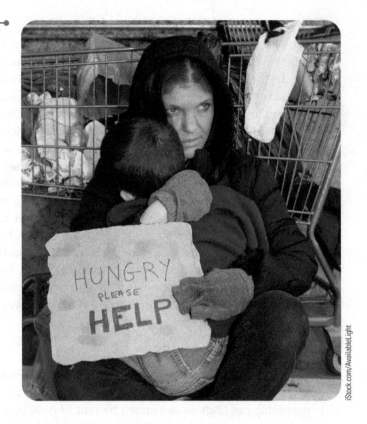

iStock.com/AvailableLight

In 1987, Congress passed the Stewart B. McKinney Homeless Assistance Act, which is intended to provide protection for the educational needs of homeless children and youth. Most importantly, this policy requires each school district to establish a liaison for homeless students. This legislation permits students to remain in one school even if they temporarily live in another school district. Under this act, schools must also allow students to enroll even if they don't have the typically required forms such as proof of residency. It also provides grants to states to make available money for the educational needs of homeless children. It also requires states to ensure that these children are educated with the rest of the youth in their area, and are not isolated and stigmatized.[11]

You may have homeless children in your classroom; if so, they are likely to require support and understanding from you. Your school social worker or homelessness liaison should be able to support your efforts to ensure these children are successful in school. Some may be malnourished or suffer from chronic health issues. They may show emotional needs. Other children may make fun of them. Your support and caring could provide these children with hope and be crucial in improving their chances for success.

More than anything else, homeless children need homes. As their teacher, you cannot be expected to provide the homes they need, but hundreds of local and federal programs serve runaway and homeless youth, and these agencies will help you work with these youngsters. Through them, some may find shelter.

4-3c SCHOOL AND TEACHER RESPONSES

Many people have thought that we could eliminate poverty through education and that, through schooling, it would be relatively easy to free people from the chains of impoverishment. The resulting efforts have been well intentioned but often too little, too late and, in retrospect, sometimes naïve. With poverty so prevalent, schools face a challenging problem, partly because they are not designed to serve poor children. The schools in the United States were created and continue to be supported by the middle class to perpetuate the middle-class way of life. There is nothing particularly startling about this bias. Middle-class people want their children to be like themselves or possibly somewhat better, so they have built and continue to pay for a school system that reflects their values and supports the way of life with which they feel comfortable.

Some critics see the middle-class bias of our schools in a more sinister light, as part of an enslavement system. They claim that schools do not help develop the individual talents and strengths of poor children, and that they make these children believe they are losers. After 8 to 11 years of schooling, many of these young people see themselves as unable to fit into the middle class and as people who, at best, will do society's menial work.

Although some of these critics see this system as a conscious plan of our society, we do not. Such a cynical view suggests that the teachers who are toiling in the poor urban and rural areas are either people of evil intentions or simply dupes. In our view, many of the most heroic teachers are those struggling to aid children trapped in and oppressed by poverty.

Our past and present inadequacies in educating the children of the poor have tempted some to turn away and devote their energies to more solvable problems. Our nation cannot follow this path. Ours is an evolving society; as a people, we are not finished with our own development. Eradicating the ravages of poverty and its withering effect on children should be at the top of our agenda as citizens of this nation and as educators. Although there are many important and solvable problems to work on, we cannot afford—in justice—to ignore this one.

> *We need to permanently abandon the belief that race and poverty determine how much students can and will learn.*
>
> —KATI HAYCOCK,
> founder and CEO of the Education Trust

As a teacher, you may go beyond considering homelessness just if you have homeless students. Rather, you may also consider ways that you can engage your students in learning about and better understanding homelessness. Organizations such as the National Coalition for Homelessness provides helpful resources for teaching about homelessness.

Pause *and* Reflect

1. What decisions of yours have been based on hidden rules related to your social class?
2. How can you prepare to adjust or reveal hidden rules to meet the expectations of students you teach?
3. Why do you think it is so difficult for schools to overcome the effects of poverty on the academic achievement for poor children?

4-4 Teenage Parenting

Each year approximately 200,000 American teenagers give birth—by far the highest teenage birthrate among the world's developed countries.[12] Since 1990, the birthrate among girls ages 15 to 19 declined from 60 to 18.8 births per 1,000, reaching a historic low.[13] This trend is due to fewer teens beng sexually active and more teens using birth control than in the past. Despite this trend, over 200,000 babies are born to teen mothers each year, and there is a wide discrepancy by race and ethnicity and region of the United States. Hispanic and African American teenagers are more than twice as likely to become teenage mothers. The lowest birthrates were reported in the Northeast and upper Midwest, while southern states had the highest teen birthrates.[14]

Teenage parenting is fraught with consequences for teens, children, and society. The consequences of early parenthood for teen girls are critical. Teens who give birth are less likely than their peers to graduate from high school. They are more likely to be stuck in a cycle of poverty as they enter adulthood. Perhaps most alarming is the statistics that tell us that the children they bear have a higher chance of having poor health and not succeeding in school.[15]

(T) F

Teenage mothers often live in poverty through their adult years.

Not only do teenage parents face the enormous task of juggling childrearing and employment or school, but also they must often care for a premature baby who is more likely to have health problems and possibly learning difficulties. Moreover, poverty often correlates with worse nutrition, less health care, more homelessness, and less education as compared to more advantaged families. To lessen this problem, many schools are working with local health officials to ensure that pregnant teenagers receive prenatal care and parenting advice. They are also encouraging these young women to stay in school and graduate. In many cases, the schools are permitting young mothers to bring their babies with them to school.

If you are planning on teaching in middle or secondary schools, you may work with some of these young parents and should keep in mind the challenges they face. You should also give some thought to what you would do if one of your female students informs you that she is pregnant or one of your male students tells you that he has gotten his girlfriend pregnant. Know both your legal and ethical responsibilities in these cases. If you plan to teach in an elementary school, be prepared to work with very young parents, including some who may be your own age.

To prevent teenage pregnancies, many schools have established sex education programs, and some operate clinics where students can obtain birth-control devices. Both of these steps, while increasingly common, remain controversial in some communities.

4-4a SEX EDUCATION

Issues and questions of sexual behavior and sexual attitudes cut deep into the heart of their spiritual and social views for most Americans. It is hardly surprising, then, that our schools' efforts to educate young people frequently stir up strong passions and inspire heated debates. In 2020, 29 states required that schools include sex education in the curriculum. Although most people agree that children should be given information about sex, the controversy centers on three issues:

- Is the school the appropriate institution to offer such instruction?
- If so, should it limit instruction to strictly factual information, or should the psychological, social, health, religious, and moral aspects of sex also be included in the curriculum?
- Should the school emphasize "abstinence-only" sex education programs, or offer "comprehensive" sex education programs?

Many people argue that because sex is such an intimate topic and is closely related to religious and moral beliefs, sex education is the responsibility of the home and the church and should take place there. In addition, they question the biases built

As pregnant teenagers struggle with the decision of whether to drop out of school, educators are finding ways to encourage these young women and mothers to stay in school and graduate.

Photofusion Picture Library/Alamy Stock Photo

into some of the popular sex education curricula. Advocates of sex education in the schools respond that they would agree with that position if parents did, in fact, provide adequate sex information for their children. In reality, they contend, the majority of parents fail to carry through on their responsibility to teach their children about sex. According to these advocates of sex education, the public school is the only institution that has access to most children over an extended period, and the responsibility must fall to the school because of the demonstrated failure of the home, church, library, and medical profession to provide effective sex education. Courts have also supported the right of state boards of education and local school boards to offer sex education in the curriculum.

Goals of Sex Education

Preventing teenage pregnancies and keeping teens mentally and physically healthy are the major goals of any sex education program. Besides endangering babies, early pregnancies place the future lives of great numbers of teenage girls in serious jeopardy, interrupting and often terminating their education. Despite the availability of special counseling and accommodations intended to help teenage mothers stay in school, the majority drop out, drastically diminishing their job and career opportunities as adults.

In addition to preventing pregnancies and STDs, sex education seeks to help teenagers become sexually healthy adults. Sexual health encompasses sexual development and reproductive health, and such characteristics as the ability to develop and maintain meaningful personal relationships, appreciation of one's own body, interaction with both genders in respectful and appropriate ways, and responsible decision-making skills. Recent trends in sex education in schools includes lessons around harassment and violence. Additionally, sex education curricula has expanded to include lessons that address sexual orientation and gender identity.

Students need not only scientific information about human sexuality and prevention of pregnancy and disease, but also help to gain the self-control and strength of character needed to avoid risky and irresponsible behavior. One important form of prevention—abstinence—depends on developing the necessary self-control to handle sexual situations and feelings. Likewise, developing true respect for one's partner is an important character-related aspect of sex education.

Pause *and* Reflect

1. What kinds of support do pregnant and parenting teenagers need from their teachers?
2. Do you think that you will be comfortable and well prepared to deal with your students' questions or remarks about sexuality? If not, how can you prepare now?

4-5 Abused and Neglected Children

The education of the young brings us into contact with humanity's best impulses. Occasionally, however, we see the wreckage of its darkest and most vicious urges. For many years, the phenomenon of child abuse was known only to a small percentage of social workers and law enforcement people. More recently, we have become aware of the magnitude of this problem and the variety of forms abuse can take, including physical or mental injury, sexual abuse, negligent treatment, and maltreatment.

Because of the hidden nature of much child abuse and neglect, reliable data on it are somewhat difficult to obtain. Professionals in the field strongly suspect that most cases go unreported. Nevertheless, more than 7.8 million incidents of child abuse or neglect were reported to U.S. child service agencies in 2018. Younger children are more susceptible to abuse than teenagers. Parental substance abuse was reported as a major contributing factor in child abuse cases. Classroom teachers, law enforcement officers, and social service workers were cited as the most frequent reporters of child maltreatment.[16]

The toll that abuse and neglect take on children's physical, emotional, and psychological development is difficult to assess. Children subjected to violent treatment may sustain injuries that cause serious learning problems in school. Abused children may be withdrawn or have trouble concentrating. They suffer enormous stress, and their self-esteem is low. They sometimes have excessive needs for control because they have experienced such helplessness. Also, they may be more likely to abuse their own children in the future.

T (F)
Teachers who suspect that a student in his or her class has suffered child abuse must use discretion in deciding whether to file a report.

Classroom teachers may not directly encounter the problem of abuse very often. However, in all 50 states, educators are legally responsible for reporting suspected cases of child abuse. Teachers must be aware of potential signs of abuse and know school policy and procedures for reporting suspected abuse. (See Chapter 8, "What Are the Ethical and Legal Issues Facing Teachers?" for a discussion of teachers' legal obligations regarding suspected child abuse.)

Teachers may recognize child abuse before other adults because of their frequent contact with students.

aldomurillo/iStock/Getty Images Plus/Getty Images

Teachers need to realize that even after an abusive situation has been reported and perhaps disclosed, these children's problems in school will not suddenly end. Children who have been abused have a continuing need for emotional safety and stability, including trustworthy praise, concrete rewards, and constructive ways to control their classroom environment. They need capable adult role models who can provide varied but predictable activities and measurable classroom achievement.

4-6 Alcohol, Tobacco, and Drug Abuse

Many of the trends mentioned in this chapter can severely stress the functioning of families, provoking self-destructive responses in children. Substance abuse—involving the use of alcohol or various other drugs—is a particularly destructive response. It may be the act of either parents or children. Unfortunately, when one family member becomes entangled in substance abuse, the entire family is usually a victim. Use of tobacco has declined over the years in adolescents; however, there has been a startling increase in the number of students who vape (or use e-cigarettes).

Alcohol is the most commonly abused substance, and the first use of alcohol may occur at a young age, sometimes in elementary school. Historically, the greatest number of teenagers with alcoholism has been male students, especially those with low grades, but the gap between males and females seems to be closing. The problem of alcohol abuse among high school students is widespread. Nearly 20 percent of teenagers report consuming alcohol in the past month. In one 2018 report, 14 percent of high school seniors participated in binge drinking (5 or more

▶❚❚ **TeachSource** Video Case

© Cengage 2016

Social and Emotional Development: The Influence of Peer Groups

Watch the video clips, study the artifacts in the case, and reflect on the following questions:

1. What kinds of peer pressure have you felt? How did you cope with the pressure?

2. What else can teachers do to help students resist pressure to try alcohol and other substances, become sexually active, or engage in other hazardous behaviors described in this chapter?

drinks in a row). Teenage boys living in rural areas and white teenagers had higher rates of binge drinking than their peers.[17]

The number of high school seniors who have used illicit drugs has declined over recent years.[18] Although these are lower than they were in earlier decades, student drug and alcohol abuse remain serious problems. As mentioned earlier, many child abuse and neglect cases involve parental substance abuse, which has devastating results for children. (Study the Video Case, *Social and Emotional Development: The Influence of Peer Groups*, to give you some ideas about how students experience peer pressure.)

Responding to the rapid spread of vaping, the U.S. Surgeon General declared youth vaping an epidemic. In 2017, 25 percent of high school seniors used e-cigarrates and 16 percent of eighth graders reportd vaping.[19] Curbing these numbers presents different challenges than cigarettes. The rapidly growing number of students who vape has prompted schools to consider how they can help curve the use of vaping among school-aged youth. Many schools developed tobacco-free school buildings and grounds, including vaping. Schools have embarked on educational strategies to teach school staff, students, and parents about the dangers of vaping.

Every public school in the United States is subject to the Safe and Drug Free Schools and Communities Act, which is part of the Every Student Succeeds Act of 2015. The basic purpose of these laws is to provide safe, disciplined, and drug-free environments conducive to learning by eliminating violence in and around schools and preventing illegal drug use on school property.

What should you do if you suspect one of your students is using drugs, vaping, or binge drinking? The most important step is to talk with the school counselor about the situation. He or she has been trained to deal with these problems and can offer you advice on both the legal aspects of the situation and ways to assist the students. Students want some level of consistency in actions, not just in words. It is quite distressing to students when educators do nothing to address drug or alcohol abuse. Schools need clear-cut policies about how to handle alcohol, e-cigarettes, and other drugs in the classroom and at school.

Pause *and* Reflect

1. Which elements of school culture serve to condone or even encourage student drinking and drug use? Which elements could be used to discourage substance abuse?

2. What can you, as a teacher, do to encourage responsible student substance use behavior?

4-7 Mental Health

The number of youth being diagnosed with mental illnesses has been growing. In particular, rates of anxiety, attention-deficit hyperactivity disorder (ADHD), and depression are climbing.[20] Over half of mental illnesses begins before the age of 14, and at least 10 million teenagers need professional support around mental health.[21] The U.S. Department of Heath and Human Services report that one in five of school-aged youth face mental health challenges during school years.[22] Of the students who do receive professional help, it is through school resources.

Unfortunately, these numbers continue to rise. Suicide is second only to unintentional injury accidents as a leading cause of adolescent death in the United States. Each year, almost 6,300 people ages 15 to 24 take their own lives. Studies of young people who have attempted suicide and those who have succeeded reveal several patterns. For every teenager who commits suicide, 100 more will try. Every year, 1 in 12 high school students attempts suicide, and one-fifth of all high school students report they have "seriously considered" suicide within the last 12 months. Female teens attempt suicide at a higher rate than male teens. However, male teens are more likely to die from suicide. LGBTQ adolescents are more likely to attempt suicide than heterosexual teens. The rate of suicide is higher for African American adolescents than other race or ethnic groups.[23]

Many schools turn to school counselors, school social workers, and school psychiatrists to address students' mental health. Schools often partner with community resources to best support students. Recent trends have seen efforts to educate teachers on how to recognize signs of mental health issues. Schools also have taken up teaching students about mental health and strategies to support health menthal heath.

Educators often have the opportunity to recognize children and youths who are at risk and to help them get the advice and support they need. As a teacher, it will be important for you to know warning signs for students who may be at risk. These warning signs may include one or more of the following:

- Feeling very sad or withdrawn for more than two weeks
- Seriously trying to harm oneself, or making plans to do so
- Sudden overwhelming fear for no reason, sometimes with a racing heart or fast breathing
- Involvement in many fights or desire to badly hurt others
- Severe out-of-control behavior that can hurt oneself or others
- Not eating, throwing up, or using laxatives to make oneself lose weight
- Intense worries or fears that get in the way of daily activities
- Extreme difficulty concentrating or staying still that puts the student in physical danger or causes problems in the classroom
- Repeated use of drugs or alcohol
- Severe mood swings that cause problems in relationships
- Drastic changes in the student's behavior or personality[24]

If you have concerns about a student, it will be important to know who to reach out to. Many schools have a support network made up of the guidance counselor, the school social worker, and/or the school psychologist. Recognizing symptoms

Up CLOSE

Whom You Will Teach

1. Percentage of children read to by a family member three or more times per week: 81
2. Percentage of high school seniors who report having used an illegal drug in the previous 30 days: 25
3. Percentage of children younger than age 18 living with two married parents: 69
4. Percentage of teens neither enrolled in school nor employed: 8
5. Percentage of births to unmarried women: 40

6. Parentage of children living in food insecure households: 17
7. Percentage of the teen population being treated by a medical professional for depression: 42
8. Percentage of children without usual source of health care: 4
9. Parental report of physical activity limitation: 11

Sources: Federal Interagency Forum on Child and Family Statistics. *America's Children: Key National Indicators of Well-Being, 2019.* Washington, DC: U.S. Government Printing Office.

and getting professional help for students who behave in this way help them develop effective coping skills so that they can deal with the situation.

4-8 School Violence and Vandalism

Massacre at Columbine High School in Littleton, Colorado—15 Die

Classes Cancelled After Teen Makes Social Media Threat

Girls Arrested for Planning "Attack a Teacher Day"

Mass Shooting at Marjory Stoneman Douglas High School

Teen Stabbed to Death in School Fight

These headlines suggest that U.S. schools have become a dangerous place for children. In urban areas, crime and violence from surrounding neighborhoods have spilled over into the schools, affecting children, staff, and teachers alike. In the suburbs, communities have seen some horrible examples of students killing other students.

How extensive is the problem of school violence and crime? Despite the ominous headlines, serious violent crime constitutes a small percentage of the total amount of school crime, and homicide is extremely rare. Single-victim homicide rates in schools have not significantly increased since the 1990s. However, multiple-victim homicide rates have significantly increased in the past decade. Although school-related deaths are relatively few and have declined since 2006, many students still fear going to school because of threatened violence. Factors such as weapon carrying, fights, the presence of gangs, and bullying create an atmosphere of fear for many students, such that many high school students report not going to school at some point because of safety concerns.

In 2016, 79 percent of schools reported one or more occurances of violence, theft, or other type of crime. For the same year, 10 percent of all teachers (elementary, middle, and high school) reported being threatened with injury by a student at their school, and 4 percent of teachers reported being physically attacked by a student at their school.[25]

4-8a GANGS

Criminal activity is often associated with gangs. Gang activity has been steadily increasing since the mid-1980s. Approximately 782,000 gang members and 33,000 gangs are estimated to have been active in the United States in 2019. The number of gangs increased 12 percent since 2006. The current estimates are the highest since 1997.[26] Forty percent of gang members are under the age of 18.

Although gang members are often stereotyped as belonging to the lower class, some are children of middle-class, suburban families who commit acts of vandalism, robbery, and drug dealing out of boredom or feelings of alienation from family and friends. Although most gang members are male, the number of females who are gang members, in either all-female or mixed-gender gangs, has grown in recent years. Gangs often display clothing, jewelry, tattoos, or graffiti that distinguish and identify their members.

Children and teenagers join gangs for a variety of reasons: the excitement of gang activity, peer pressure, physical protection, attention, financial gain, a sense of belonging, and sometimes because they feel ignored by the people they should be close to—usually one or both parents. In many cases, youths are not actively discouraged from gang involvement by their parents. Often, parents are unaware that their children are engaged in gang activity.

The character of gang activity has grown more violent as gangs have become increasingly more involved in drug dealing, sex trafficking, and other criminal activities. The easy accessibility and spread of guns and the greater tendency to use extreme violence to settle disputes or to avenge even the smallest acts of "disrespect" have also contributed to the trend toward increased violence.

How can educators minimize the negative influences of gangs? Useful actions include the following:

- Establishing and enforcing clear codes of school conduct that stress the unacceptability of gang behavior and the prohibition of weapons
- Establishing programs that stress positive youth involvement as alternatives to gang membership
- Assimilating gang-oriented students into the mainstream—academically, socially, and through extracurricular activities
- Creating school programs that focus on nonviolent conflict resolution and gang prevention
- Taking quick, decisive actions when instances of gang activity occur on school grounds
- Prohibiting gang "colors," insignia, and other signs of gang membership

4-8b BULLYING

Once dismissed as "kids will be kids" behavior, educators are now viewing chronic teasing and bullying as dangerous social acts. One in 5 high school students report being bullied while at school. One in 7 report being a victim of a cyberbullying event. Ninety-five percent of students who were victims of multiple bullying incidents were injured by firearms. Almost half of those inflicting school-based homicide gave some sort of warning or threat prior to the event.[27]

Nearly three-fourths of teens report they have witnessed bullying at school. Likewise, almost 50 percent of teachers indicate seeing bullying at least once a week. The Center for Disease Control's definition of bullying includes unwanted aggressive beahavior, power imbalance, and repetition of harmful behaviors. Bullying can be physical, verbal, relational, or include damage to property. Verbal and social bullying are the most prevalent forms of aggression. The highest rate of bullying occurs in middle schools. This is a growing area of education research as scholars seek to learn more about prevention.[28]

Cyberbullying is a newer form of bullying that is of growing concern. Cyberbullying refers to bullying conducted using electronic devices such as computers, cell phones, or tablets. It includes communication tools such as posts to social media sites, e-mail, and text messages. Cyberbullying is noticeably different than traditional bullying in a few ways. First, cyberbullying is ubiquitous. In other words, it can take place at any time and place as long as a student has access to electronic communication. Second, through social media sites, cyberbullying potentially can be disseminated to a much wider audience than classmates in one school. Third, victims of cyberbullying don't always know their bullies in person. More and more, cyberbullies are victimizing peers in disparate locations.

Preventing cyberbullying is primarily a matter of education and awareness. Parents and teachers need to understand the problem and the technologies involved. Becoming aware of the problem is the first step in the process of discussing with children the issues involved and bringing the problem out into the open.

Bullying takes a terrible toll on children. Their schoolwork suffers, as do their physical and mental health. Physical and psychological bullying is often reported to be a contributing cause in adolescent suicide attempts. Bullying is also bad for bullies, who rarely learn the consequences of their actions.

The federal government has created a home (stopbullying.gov) for data and resources for schools and families that highlights trends and suggestions for prevention. A nationwide program, Bully-Proofing Your School, teaches children to recognize bullying and to develop ways to protect themselves, such as humor and avoidance. As part of this program, teachers and other school workers also receive training. Civility training is another popular way to reduce bullying; it focuses on teaching children how to be kind and compassionate to all people. An evaluation of several anti-bullying programs found that reductions in bullying were associated with parent training, increased playground supervision, disciplinary methods, home–school communication, classroom rules, classroom management, and use of training

Students often feel there is no escape from cyber bullying.

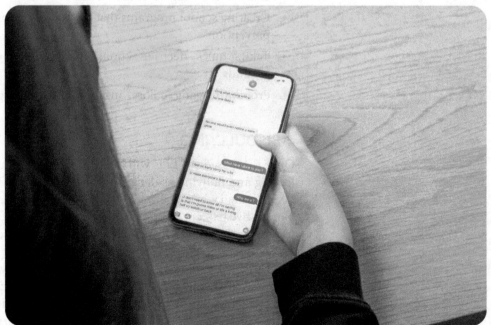

VOICES from the Field

The *Why* to the *What* of Teaching

Taylor Schmidt taught middle school in Durham, NC. He is now a Ph.D. student at the University of North Carolina at Chapel Hill.

In the summer before I first started teaching, I received packet after packet of formulas, flowcharts, and templates to plan out the entire year—weeks before I met a single student, family member, or colleague at the middle school, before I had even stepped foot in the community. I assigned state standards and catchy learning objectives to dates on the calendar; I revisited them so often that I nearly had them memorized by August. To my mind, most of what remained was simply strong execution—just follow the plan!

I would quickly discover that units and projects planned in the summer before teaching would either fizzle out or require a near-complete overhaul from the jump. They were met with increasing student detachment, disinterest, participation-by-obligation. This wasn't a classroom management problem; this was a planning problem. My students didn't see themselves in the learning; I didn't know my kids, and they intuitively understood that these generic projects were made for students whose lived experiences, whose lives weren't represented—weren't *planned for*. Those first predetermined months of learning did not, *could* not reflect students' stories, identities, strengths, passions, wisdom, family and community connections, history; my students rightly saw learning experiences that were made for *anyone*, and therefore *not for them*.

It wasn't until I learned about my students' unique lives that planning crossed over from a professional requirement to a daily reflection on the possibilities of these one-of-a-kind students and of the communities we inhabited. Centering students' lives and identities didn't distract from achieving high standards; it brought those standards to life, instilled purpose, gave *why* to the *what* of learning through experiencing.

Starting over and centering students in planning meant bringing cross-curricular standards into their lived realities; it called for building trust and teaching from vulnerable, authentic understanding of these middle school students by centering their voices and experiences with race, identity, power, and justice. Units and projects were messy, constantly adapting, unpredictable—and authentic. Shared, responsive planning opened the classroom up to the rich, complex, and rapidly changing context of our community, and students were hungry for a chance to wrestle with complicated realities such as redlining and rapid gentrification, immigration and healthcare, conflict and power. Students began voicing, then crafting their own learning outcomes. Students themselves took hold of the standards, cut them out and rearranged them, attached them to clipboards and sat on the curb outside the former Woolworths building whose past contributed to the standard's creation, where a towering new high rise embodied the forces they read about and lived.

Together, we planned new experiences that had them taking their learning to mayors and state senators; registering over one hundred new voters and approaching over a thousand different people about voting rights; evaluating, proposing, and demanding new school policies from our relationship with law enforcement to sexist dress code standards to LGBTQ+ inclusion and representation in curriculum and school culture. The buzzy terms from those early templates were naturally inhabited by learning *by* powerful individuals, *for* powerful individuals.

There's an innocence that comes with teaching by the template. In learning to shed this innocence layer by layer, I found planning to become an act of joy, of urgency, of driven purpose—of love. Effective planning is essential to effective teaching; but the summer before you launch, don't forget to first plan to see, to know, and to understand your students, their families, their communities—and yourself.

modules.[29] When a bullying problem persists, some schools have implemented **zero-tolerance policies** for aggressive behavior, under which they automatically suspend any student who harasses another student. By developing a heightened awareness of bullying and its negative consequences, teachers can take actions to make the school environment more hospitable and inviting for all students. In Voices from the Field,

TeachSource Video Case

© Cengage 2016

Social and Emotional Development: Understanding Adolescents

Watch the video clips, study the artifacts in the case, and reflect on the following questions:

1. What are your concerns, as a teacher, about violence in the schools?

2. Which of the strategies for teachers and schools listed in this chapter is represented in this case?

3. Can you think of additional techniques that you, as a teacher, could use to defuse potentially dangerous situations in school?

The Why *to the* What *of Teaching,* Taylor describes how he moved beyond template lesson plans to engage his students in learning in meaningful and inviting ways.

4-8c STEPS TO REDUCE SCHOOL VIOLENCE

Concern over school crime and violence has prompted many public schools to take measures to reduce and prevent violence and to ensure safety in schools. In particular, concerns about keeping schools secure from outsiders have increased since the 2018 deadly shooting at Marjory Stoneman Douglas High School in Parkland, FL. Schools have increasingly adopted safety measures including the following steps:

- Controlling building access during school hours
- Providing telephones in most classrooms
- Requiring faculty and staff to wear picture IDs
- Using one or more security cameras
- Requiring students to wear uniforms
- Requiring students to wear picture IDs

The Video Case, *Social and Emotional Development: Understanding Adolescents,* shows a group of middle school boys discussing productive ways to handle stress and anger.

The STOP School Violence Act of 2018 provides federal funding to schools and local organizations to make schools safe spaces. Several aspects of school organization can contribute to student aggression, including high numbers of students occupying a small space, imposition of routines and conformity that may anger some students, and poor building designs that may contribute to the commission of violent acts. Most incidents of violence occur during "transition times"—that is, at the start of school, during lunch periods, or at the end of the school day. Reducing crowding, increasing supervision, and instituting policies for handling disputes during these intervals can reduce the likelihood of conflicts and their resulting injuries. Students who enjoy positive interactions with faculty and staff, are academically successful, or participate productively in school activities are less likely to commit acts of violence. In most cases of school violence, warning signs are apparent—for example, notes, threats, journal entries, arguments, or physical fights. Teachers who are able to develop close relationships with students may be in a good position to spot these signals of impending violence. Developing mechanisms for reporting threats and other warning signs of potential violence can also help schools curb these incidents.

What else can schools—specifically, principals—do to reduce school violence?

- Establish common goals for the school and elicit commitment to these goals from teachers, students, and parents.
- Establish a firm, fair, and consistent system for running the school.
- Establish high expectations for the behavior and performance of students and staff.
- Create a curriculum that supports the values of honesty, integrity, kindness, and respect for others.

- Use a variety of security measures to keep intruders and weapons off school grounds.
- Establish the school as neutral territory for students, control rumors, and squelch loitering and tardiness.
- Create alternative schools for serious offenders.
- Provide students and teachers with training in effective communication.

What can teachers themselves do to prevent violence and vandalism?

- Establish a classroom environment centered on respect and kindness, where put-downs, ridicule, and sarcasm are not tolerated.
- Learn how to defuse conflict in ways that save face for both students and teachers.
- Develop intensive skills in classroom management.
- Use peer counseling or peer mediation to train students to handle problems before they become serious.
- Involve students in decision-making processes in areas such as finding methods to handle offenders.

Students have also taken action to reduce school violence. Across the nation, students planned the first National School Walkout in 2018. This was an organized school walk-out, protest, and action to halt gun violence in schools and society. High school students today have grown up in the shadows of high profile school violence that began with the 1999 Columbine High School shooting in Colorado. Student activists continue today by lobbying their elected officials and advocating for steps to further reduce school violence. The encouraging news is that although school violence and vandalism are serious problems, they affect a relatively small percentage of teachers and students in the public schools. Viewed from a broader perspective, this problem probably reflects as much a societal malaise as any particular flaw of schools. Boredom, frustration, alienation, despair, and low self-concept are characteristics that teenagers may experience in their homes and in society in general, as well as in school. As long as violence prevails in society, schools will likely be affected.

Pause *and* Reflect

1. Have you ever been afraid to go to school? Why?
2. What were the safety procedures in your high school? What suggestions do you have for school safety protocols?

4-9 Student Cheating

Cheating in schools has become an issue torn from the national headlines. A student watching the news in the evening may see a story about a superintendent indicted for pressuring teachers to change incorrect test scores from student exams or a news story about a Hollywood star bribing college admissions offices to accept their child. Gone are the days of a student passing a note to another student during a test or a student tucking a crib sheet up his or her sleeve with the test answers. It is as if cheating has become ubiquitous in our society. In fact, students may just tell you that. The number of high school students who represent someone else's work as their own has skyrocketed over recent decades. More than half of all high school students admit to cheating in the past year. With grades playing a high-stakes role in students' educational advancement, more and more students find it acceptable to cheat to earn a good grade. In the past, cheating students were most often low-achieving students. Today, high-achieving students are as likely to cheat in school as low-achieving students.[30]

T (F)
Although cheating in school has received much media attention, it only occurs with moderate frequency.

Unfortunately, more and more students report that cheating is acceptable in schools. They report that "everyone does it" or "I just got a little help." Cheating takes many forms, including text messaging test answers to another student, plagiarizing by downloading information or entire papers from the Internet, copying from another student, or getting test questions and answers from a student in a previous period. Cheating happens in isolation, such as when a student searches for answers to a test question on their phone. Cheating also happens in groups, such as when a group of students text answers to an assignment to others.

What can schools and teachers do to discourage cheating? Teachers can establish classroom norms that help combat cheating such as arranging the classroom so that students cannot physically cheat during independent work. There should be established rules for when it is acceptable to use electronic devices. For example:

- Ensure your assessment tools are clearly aligned with your instruction.
- Make sure your students understand what cheating (including plagiarism) is and why it is morally wrong and unacceptable.
- Talk with your students about the consequences for cheating.
- Establish an honor system using student input so that students will be invested in the system.
- Most importantly, institute character education programs that can help students to establish a moral compass.

4-10 High School Graduation and Dropout Rates

The dropout rate today is the lowest it has been since 1974. The high school graduating class of 2019 saw nearly 85 percent of their membership earn a diploma on time. The graduation rate is up across all ethnic groups, although there is still a gap across ethnic groups. Hispanic students have the highest dropout rate (6.5%) while white students have the lowest dropout rate (3.9%).[31]

What do these numbers mean to our society and to you as a classroom teacher? High school dropouts are more likely than their classmates who earn a high school degree to be incarcerated and will likely earn less money than their classmates. Yet, dropout rates are strongly related to income levels. Youth from low-income families are three times more likely to drop out than are students from high-income families.[32] Dropout rates are highest in schools with a larger proportion of students from low-income families.

Besides poverty, what contributes to high dropout rates? Students report poor grades, dislike for school, alienation from peers, marriage or pregnancy, and employment as common causes for leaving school. The role the family plays in monitoring students in school also plays a role in dropout rates. Students who live with both parents and the parents actively monitor the student's schoolwork are more likely to stay in school.[33] The most commonly reported factor is poor academic performance. Ninth grade serves as a bottleneck for many students who discover that their academic skills are lacking for high school–level work. Another cause of dropping out is unrealistic expectations about the world of work. Many students with high hopes for the imagined luxury of a regular income fail to realize that wages in the service sector of employment are low. Other teenagers may envision starting at the bottom of the work hierarchy and, through hard work, eventually climbing the ladder of success. Unfortunately, many of them lack job search skills and end up in

> *I am often asked whether I approve of compulsory education, and I usually reply that I do and that I wish we had it; we only have compulsory attendance.*
>
> **—JOHN BREMER,**
> former superintendent of Philadelphia Public Schools

jobs with limited potential for advancement. Despite this reality, the strong motivation to work often proves too powerful an incentive and results in a student leaving school. The immediate rewards of the workplace lure some students away from the more remote incentives of staying in school and attaining an education.

Students often give warning signs that they are at risk for dropping out—for example, increased absences, lethargy in completing work, and preoccupation with matters outside of school. Teachers can discourage students from dropping out by showing interest and care in their students and by talking to and encouraging them. Knowing your students well can help you detect changes in their attitudes and work habits. Across the country, initiatives such as dropout recovery programs, career academies, and early college high schools have been put in place to target at-risk students. Across these different initiatives, research shows that more individualized learning environments, supplemental academic support, and engaging instruction were instrumental in student retention.

Pause *and* Reflect

1. Can a secondary-level teacher, who may see 150 students each day, get to know them all well? What are strategies teachers can use to get to know their students?
2. What are strategies you could take the support a student who is at risk for dropping out of school?

OUR FINAL WORD

Given the range of social problems that we have discussed in this chapter and in the preceding chapter, it is not surprising to find that schools bear an ever-growing burden to guide young people's decision making. How well equipped are the schools to handle this task? Creating schools that are safe, healthy, and conducive to learning doesn't happen automatically. The climate in a school is a product of laws, rules, regulations, and, most importantly, attitudes and values held by those who work and study in school. When problems threaten the safety, health, or well-being of students, whether within the school or outside its boundaries, educators must intervene in productive ways to maintain a school climate that protects students and promotes learning.

WHY TEACH? YOUR FINAL WORD

1. Which of the social problems discussed in this chapter do you consider to have the biggest impact on student success in school?
2. What experiences have you had that would assist you in meeting the challenges of these issues in our schools and society?
3. How do you think technology contributes to, or alleviates some of the social issues discussed in this chapter?

KEY TERMS

at-risk students (90)
cyberbullying (108)

socioeconomic status (96)
zero-tolerance policies (109)

FOR FURTHER INFORMATION

Web Resources

Teaching Tolerance www.tolerance.org
A web resource from the Southern Poverty Law Center. The site offers articles and teaching resources related to teaching diverse populations of students.

Child Mind Institute www.childmind.org
This nonprofit is working to support students, educators, and families facing mental health challenges.

Stopbullying.gov
This website is hosted by the federal government to share facts and resources for youth and adults related to bullying.

Collaborative for Academic, Social, Emotional Learning casel.org
An organization that advocates for supporting academic, social, and emotional learning for children.

Print Resources

Karen Gross, *Trauma Doesn't Stop at the School Door:Strategies and Solutions for Educators, Pre-K- College* (New York, NY: Teachers College Press, 2020).

This book explores the concept of trauma and how it impacts students' schooling experiences.

Paul Gorski, *Reaching and Teaching Students in Poverty* (New York, NY: Teachers College Press, 2019).

The author shares tips and strategies that teachers can use to engage students living in poverty.

Jonathan Cohen and Dorothy Espelage, *Feeling Safe in School: Bullying and Violence Prevention Around the World* (Cambridge, MA, 2020).

This book offers a comprehensive perspective on issues of safety in schools.

What Is Taught?

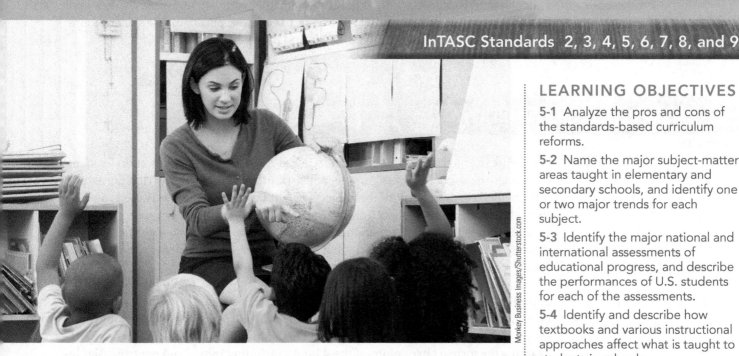

Monkey Business Images/Shutterstock.com

LEARNING OBJECTIVES

5-1 Analyze the pros and cons of the standards-based curriculum reforms.

5-2 Name the major subject-matter areas taught in elementary and secondary schools, and identify one or two major trends for each subject.

5-3 Identify the major national and international assessments of educational progress, and describe the performances of U.S. students for each of the assessments.

5-4 Identify and describe how textbooks and various instructional approaches affect what is taught to students in schools.

5-5 Explain the differences between a multicultural and a core curriculum, and describe how the practice of "tracking" affects what students learn.

5-6 Describe what changes in the elementary or secondary curriculum you would make to create greater relevance to today's world.

Truth OR Fiction?

T F   More than two-thirds of the states have adopted a common core of academic standards in mathematics and language arts.

T F   About two-thirds of American eighth-grade students score at the proficient or advanced level on the National Assessment of Educational Progress in reading.

T F   Compared to other industrialized countries, the United States scores below average in tests of mathematics and science.

T F   Differentiating instruction means assigning students of different abilities to classes with other students of comparable abilities.

T F   Research studies indicate that the practice of tracking students into different ability-level groups is detrimental to low-ability students.

What knowledge is most worth knowing? What should be taught in the schools? The answers to these questions take the form of curricula, and they are often a source of tension among teachers, school boards, education professors, textbook publishers, policy makers, and parents. Currently, these groups are seeking to raise academic standards through common curricular emphases while also accommodating various cultural and ethnic groups' demands for representation in the curriculum.

Baseball, debating, reading, and biology are all learned in school, along with love and tolerance, independence and frustration, mathematics and dramatics, values and ceramics, wood shop and poise, history and boredom, and computer science and leadership! Some are learned intentionally and others incidentally.

5-1 What Is a Curriculum?

We define the **curriculum** as all organized and intended experiences of the student for which the school accepts responsibility. In other words, the curriculum is not just the intellectual content of the subjects taught but also the methods used to teach them, the interactions that occur among people, and the school-sponsored activities that contribute to the "life experience." Educational theorists have identified several different kinds of curricula, including formal, extra, and hidden curricula. Let's briefly examine these different kinds of curricula.

The planned content and objectives of language arts, mathematics, science, and all other subject areas available to students constitute the *formal* or explicit curriculum. The states and the local school boards are responsible for determining the subjects that will be taught in this formal curriculum. Later in this chapter, we will examine the formal curriculum of the schools, including trends and controversies in each of the major content areas.

What students learn in the environment of the school extends beyond the planned curriculum of courses or subjects they will take, or the extracurricular activities in which they participate. That is, schools also teach a *hidden* or informal curriculum through which the classroom and school, as learning environments, socialize children to the values that are acceptable to the institution and society at large. The messages of the hidden curriculum are usually conveyed indirectly and deal with attitudes, values, beliefs, and behavior. These messages can either support or undermine the formal curriculum. When the hidden and formal curricula conflict, many observers believe the hidden curriculum carries more weight.

What are these attitudes and values, and how are they communicated to students? A major purpose of the hidden curriculum in schools has been to teach students the routines and values for getting along in school and in the larger society. Thus, it tends to have a conservative bent, focusing on preserving the status quo. In the eyes of some critics, the hidden curriculum of the schools works against diversity, equity, and social justice.[1]

One researcher suggests that schools value several specific ways of thinking and behaving.[2] For example, schools emphasize compliant behavior as opposed to personal initiative. Students soon learn to give the teacher what she or he wants or expects. Reward systems used by schools teach students to "read" both the teacher and the system to determine just what is expected to get the grade, the teacher's attention, or the sticker with the smiling face. Similarly, competitiveness is learned through the examples of athletics, grading systems that compare students to one another, and ability grouping to separate students into classes according to their achievement. The many ways in which students learn what a school values include how the school allocates time to subjects of study, the rules established for the school, and even the architecture and furnishings of the school.

As a future teacher, you should be able to identify which rules of behavior, rituals and ceremonies, and accepted patterns of teacher and student interaction are communicated to students at schools you visit. Does the "climate" of the classroom and the school suggest warmth, support for diversity, and nurturing of individuals, or does it convey a mood of disinterest, regimentation, and antipathy among staff and students? Most important, what is the school's deeper message about the stance its students should take toward the current society?

Pause *and* Reflect

1. How can you determine the hidden curriculum of a school? Which clues would you look for?
2. Thinking back on your own schooling, can you identify some of the messages that you received from the hidden curriculum?

5-1a STANDARDS-BASED REFORM MOVEMENT

In this chapter, we examine the formal curriculum—those subjects that are taught in schools and some of the forces and instructional approaches that influence how they are taught. The typical school curriculum is a **subject-matter curriculum**, organized according to subject-matter divisions, and most of the efforts that go into curriculum development are still concentrated around traditional subject matter.

> *All that is taught is a commitment to what is thought valuable.*
>
> —R. S. PETERS,
> expert on moral education

In Chapter 2, "What Is a School and What Is It For?," we discussed how the current curriculum is a *social bet* on which knowledge, skills, and attitudes the older generation thinks the young need to know to prosper, personally and economically, in the twenty-first century. There is, by no means, a consensus among the parties involved in placing this social bet. In fact, curriculum decision making can resemble a battlefield in which conservatives and liberals, religious groups and agnostics, whites and people of color, and many other groups grapple to ensure that their beliefs and perspectives are represented in the school's curriculum. These curriculum battles at both state and local levels can be heated because those engaged believe there is a lot at stake—in essence, the future of the United States.

The strongest influence on a subject-matter curriculum over the last few decades has been the *standards-based reform movement,* which is designed to promote academic excellence and equity. **Content standards** are statements of the subject-specific knowledge and skills that schools are expected to teach and that students are expected to learn.

In contrast to many other countries, the United States has traditionally had a decentralized system of state and local curricula. The national government has had little influence on what is taught in the nation's schools. During the 1980s and 1990s, however, spurred by concern about the U.S. ability to compete with other countries in economic terms, a strong movement emerged toward national curriculum standards, national testing and assessment, and the establishment of national goals. A 1994 law, the Goals 2000: Educate America Act, codified eight national goals to guide future educational initiatives and funded different academic groups to develop national standards in the various subject-matter fields. The National Council of Teachers of Mathematics led the way in 1989 by publishing its mathematics standards; a decade later, most subject-specific teacher organizations had followed suit.

By 1996, these centralization efforts had lost steam, giving way to a growing consensus that the setting of standards and curriculum should remain the prerogative of individual states. Interestingly, many states continued to use the national standards developed by different academic groups in formulating their own state standards. (For examples of current common core and state standards in different subject matter and grade levels, see Table 5.1.) By the beginning of the twenty-first century, every state had developed its own standards for student learning, and most states backed up their new standards with accountability measures for both students and educators. The national Every Student Succeeds Act of 2015 requires states to administer annual, statewide assessments in reading and mathematics to all students in grades 3 to 8, and in science (once each in elementary, middle, and high school). For more on this law, see Chapter 11, "How Are Schools Governed, Influenced, and Financed?" and Chapter 12, "How Should Education Be Reformed?"

The standards movement was immediately surrounded by controversy. Some critics objected to the attention and money lavished on the development and assessment of standards instead of other pressing educational needs, such as habitable school buildings. Other critics were concerned with the testing that accompanied the state standards. Many state legislatures linked student passage of standards-based tests with "high-stakes" outcomes, including graduation from high school or school accreditation. Some legislatures made educators accountable for students learning the standards and passing the assessment tests. Teachers' jobs and students' future education were suddenly at risk if students failed the tests, and educators and students alike felt much more pressure to succeed.

In spite of these criticisms, numerous polls show that the public overwhelmingly supports the idea of high standards. Chapter 12, "How Should Education Be Reformed?" discusses the current status of national education standards and assessment in more detail.

Common Core State Standards

In 2010, led by the National Governors Association and the Council of Chief State School Officers, a set of common core standards was developed in English language arts and mathematics. The **Common Core State Standards (CCSS)** define the knowledge and skills students should have within their K–12 education careers so that they will graduate high school able to succeed in entry-level, credit-bearing academic college courses and in workforce training programs. These standards addressed a weakness of the system of individual state standards, that is, the difficulty level of the standards and the tests used to assess them varied greatly. As a result, some states had high standards with lower pass rates, while other states had lower standards with higher pass rates. Many people believed that what students should learn in English language arts and mathematics shouldn't differ depending on the state they live in. As a result, these Common Core State Standards were developed, and as of 2019, 35 states and the District of Columbia had voluntarily adopted the standards. Most of these states also agreed to implement the tests that

(T) F
More than two-thirds of the states have adopted a common core of academic standards in mathematics and language arts.

TABLE 5.1	Examples of Content Standards

Language Arts

Grade Level	
3	Determine the main idea of a text; recount the key details and explain how they support the main idea. (CCSS-reading)
5	With some guidance and support from adults, use technology, including the Internet, to produce and publish writing as well as to interact and collaborate with others; demonstrate sufficient command of keyboarding skills to type a minimum of two pages in a single sitting. (CCSS-writing)
8	Analyze how particular lines of dialogue or incidents in a story or drama propel the action, reveal aspects of a character, or provoke a decision. (CCSS-literature)
11–12	Gather relevant information from multiple authoritative print and digital sources, using advanced searches effectively; assess the strengths and limitations of each source in terms of the task, purpose, and audience; integrate information into the text selectively to maintain the flow of ideas, avoiding plagiarism and overreliance on any one source and following a standard format for citation. (CCSS-writing)

Mathematics

Grade Level	
2	Solve word problems involving dollar bills, quarters, dimes, nickels, and pennies, using $ and ¢ symbols appropriately. For example, if you have 2 dimes and 3 pennies, how many cents do you have? (CCSS)
5	Find whole-number quotients of whole numbers with up to four-digit dividends and two-digit divisors, using strategies based on place value, the properties of operations, and/or the relationship between multiplication and division. Illustrate and explain the calculation by using equations, rectangular arrays, and/or area models. (CCSS)
7	Write verbal expressions as algebraic expressions and sentences as equations. (Virginia)
Algebra	Create equations in two or more variables to represent relationships between quantities; graph equations on coordinate axes with labels and scales. (CCSS)
9–11	Recognize the purposes of and differences among sample surveys, experiments, and observational studies; explain how randomization relates to each. (CCSS)

Science

Grade Level	
2	Construct an argument with evidence that some changes caused by heating or cooling can be reversed and some cannot. (NGSS)

(Continued)

Pause *and* Reflect

1. Study the standards for a discipline area in which you are interested. Do you believe they are appropriate for the level of students you would like to teach? Why or why not?
2. Do you support the use of high-stakes tests to determine graduation from high school? Why or why not?

TABLE 5.1	Examples of Content Standards (Continued)
6–8	Develop and use a model to describe how the total number of atoms does not change in a chemical reaction and thus mass is conserved. (NGSS)
9–12	Design, build, and refine a device that works within given constraints to convert one form of energy into another form of energy. (NGSS)
9–12	Evaluate the validity and reliability of claims in published materials of the effects that different frequencies of electromagnetic radiation have when absorbed by matter. (NGSS)

Social Studies

Grade Level

4	Use different types of maps to solve problems (i.e., road maps—distance; resource maps—products; historical maps—boundaries; thematic maps—climates). (Arizona)
7	Describe the money and banking systems in various countries in the contemporary world. (Maryland)
9–12	Compare and contrast the experiences of different ethnic, national, and religious groups, including Native Americans, in the United States, explaining their contributions to American society and culture. (New York)

Source: Common Core State Standards Initiative, Next Generation Science Standards, and Education World. Available at www.corestandards.org/; www.nextgenscience.org; and www.education-world.com/standards/.

are being developed to assess the standards. However, more recently policy makers in a number of these states are having second thoughts, as some opponents to the Core Curriculum and its assessments have challenged the plans for implementation. The first states to assess students using the new standards and tests have discovered that the failure rate has increased dramatically. In Kentucky and New York, for example, student scores fell dramatically as teachers and students struggled to teach and learn the higher standards and succeed with the more rigorous tests. Whether or not the majority of states that have signed onto the Common Core State Standards will stay the course remains to be seen.

5-2 What Is the Present Curriculum?

In looking at the courses of study prescribed by the 50 states, we will see that their similarities far outweigh their differences. Parts of this chapter discuss some reasons for this phenomenon, such as the influence of standards-based reform movements in the various states and the uniformity of available textbooks.

For now, we examine what is presently taught in elementary and secondary schools across the country. At both levels, the curriculum is organized into subject-matter areas, which ordinarily are English language arts, mathematics, science, social studies, foreign languages, the arts, physical education and health, electives, and career and technical education. Most of the national organizations representing teachers of these various subject areas have developed content standards describing what elementary and secondary students should know and be able to do in each content area. The websites for these organizations and their respective content standards can be found in the "For Further Information" section at the end of the chapter.

5-2a ENGLISH LANGUAGE ARTS

The *language arts* program seeks to develop in children the skills of reading, writing, speaking, and listening, as well as a knowledge of culture as represented in literature. The importance of language arts cannot be overemphasized because no subject can be successfully studied without adequate language skills. In elementary schools, most language arts programs focus on helping students develop written and oral communication skills, comprehension and problem-solving strategies, creativity, and appreciation for language and literature. At the secondary level, English courses focus on integration of the language arts using literature as the prime motivator.

Issues and Trends

Teachers today are selecting literature that is relevant to student interests yet representative of an accepted literary tradition; balancing classic literature selections with works by and about minority groups; instructing students in critical thinking; encouraging writing across the curriculum (discussed later in this chapter); integrating the various language arts by, for example, linking reading and writing together or speaking, listening, and reading; composing and creating in new media forms, such as video or online presentations; and maintaining a balance between composition and literature in the curriculum. Many English educators are chafing under the pressure to prepare students for the Common Core State Standards rigorous assessments that address topics and literature different from what they have been previously teaching. Adjusting the curriculum and use of standards for children from multiple language and cultural backgrounds constitutes a major challenge for language arts and English teachers.

Major disagreements exist in the field of reading education. The basic debate is whether reading instruction should

LITERATURE

BOOK

DaveCarpenter..

"JUST THINK OF IT AS IF YOU'RE READING A LONG TEXT-MESSAGE."

TeachSource Video Case

© Cengage 2016

Elementary Reading Instruction: A Balanced Literacy Program

Watch the video clips, study the artifacts in the case, and reflect on the following question:

1. Which aspects of the language arts curriculum, as discussed in this chapter, are most likely to apply to the grade levels or subjects you would like to teach?

2. What does a "balanced literacy program" mean to you?

emphasize the integration of language arts skills and knowledge in a literature-based approach, commonly known as the **whole language approach,** or whether it should focus on **phonics** instruction, an approach to reading that teaches the reader to "decode" words by sounding out letters and combinations of letters. The whole language approach to reading stresses that children should use language in ways that relate to their own lives and culture. Advocates of this approach tolerate the use of "invented spelling" by children because it is seen as part of a child's reading development and because it is feared that correcting a child's every spelling error will discourage the child from enjoying writing. Whole language teaching uses such common techniques as daily journal and letter writing, a great deal of silent and oral reading of real literature, and student cooperation. (The Video Case, *Elementary Reading Instruction: A Balanced Literacy Program,* provides a detailed example of a teacher who balances phonics and whole language approaches for teaching reading.)

During the 1970s and 1980s, whole language approaches to reading displaced the phonics approach in many schools. Eventually, discontent with declining reading scores in states that emphasized a whole language approach (notably California) spurred a renewed interest in phonics. In fact, the issue has become politically charged, with many conservatives supporting phonics and many liberals supporting whole language approaches. Although both the whole language and phonics camps have their strong believers, recent research concludes that it is important to teach explicit, systematic phonics within a context of meaningful literature.[3] *Phonemic awareness*—the understanding that sounds make up language—seems to be crucial in the development of good readers. Thus, a balanced use of both approaches, rather than abandonment of one approach in favor of the other, seems to be the key to reading instruction. Many major publishers are now including both approaches in their reading series.

The use of technology and video games to teach reading and increase motivation has also entered the reading literacy debate. The trick is to balance computer time and human interaction. Recent research shows that teaching children to read through educational sites like Reading Eggs can help improve U.S. literacy skills.[4]

5-2b MATHEMATICS

Before the 1950s, schools emphasized student mastery of basic computational skills. In the 1960s, a new type of mathematics curriculum, known as the *new math,* emerged. It saw mathematics as a language that both communicates ideas about numbers and describes the quantitative aspects of ideas and objects. As a result, the new math stressed *structure* rather than drill and computational skills. The new math tended to be abstract, and for the average student, its conceptual theories were of little practical use.

Today, the traditional approach featuring drill and practice, computation, and memorization tends to be used in courses for non-college-bound students. College-bound students, after studying algebra and geometry, often take optional fourth-year courses that place strong emphasis on structure, learning by discovery, definitions, properties, sets, rigor, statistics, calculus, trigonometry, and other abstract concepts.

Issues and Trends

A major educational debate focuses on whether children should be explicitly taught skills based on formulas or algorithms (fixed, step-by-step procedures for solving math problems), versus an inquiry approach in which students address real-world problems to develop fluency in number sense, reasoning, and problem-solving skills. In this latter approach, conceptual understanding is a primary goal, and algorithmic competence follows secondarily.

Mathematics at the elementary level emphasizes the use of hands-on manipulatives to aid students in learning about patterns in mathematics and the base-10 system. Mathematical reasoning and problem solving are emphasized. Experts in mathematics education are urging teachers to introduce multiple approaches for solving real-world problems. These emphases are consistent with the popular constructivist approach to learning, which is based on psychological theories suggesting that people must construct knowledge and meaning for themselves, rather than receiving knowledge passively from teachers or textbooks. (Constructivist approaches to learning are discussed further in Chapter 9, "What Are the Philosophical Foundations of American Education?," and Chapter 12, "How Should Education Be Reformed?"). Teachers are being urged to focus on conceptual mathematics understanding before introducing procedural rules. This ordering reflects the growing body of research that suggests if students learn procedural rules before they learn mathematical concepts, they will score significantly lower than do students who learn concepts first.[5]

Calculators and computers have become common in the classroom, even at the elementary level, as mathematics education focuses less on computational skills and more on developing concepts, relationships, structures, and problem-solving skills. Moreover, the use of computers and computer programming in mathematics classes enhances the practical utility of mathematics instruction for many students. Not only do computers create interest in the curriculum, but students also receive valuable experience that may prove useful as they seek jobs. As described in Chapter 7, "What Should Teachers Know about Technology and Its Impact on Teaching and Learning?," graphing calculators are seen as important tools to help students understand complex mathematical relationships.

In addition to using technology and emphasizing problem solving, mathematics programs have been moving away from the traditional compartmentalization of arithmetic, algebra, geometry, calculus, and so on. As newer topics such as probability, statistics, and computer science are emphasized, course designers have begun to integrate a variety of mathematics skills and topics in one course or across several courses. The blending of mathematics with other subject areas, including consumer economics and personal finance, will continue as part of the trend toward broadening students' applications of their mathematical understanding and skills.

Because of the relatively poor showing in mathematics assessments in the United States, compared to many other nations, the CCSS board urges that the mathematics curriculum be more focused and coherent. The U.S. mathematics and science curricula have been criticized as being "a mile wide and an inch deep." The new CCSS purport to be a step in making mathematics more like the mathematics taught in other high-performing countries.

Young children particularly benefit from the use of hands-on manipulatives to build basic understanding in mathematics.

BananaStock/Jupiter Images

5-2c SCIENCE

Science in the elementary grades takes advantage of children's natural curiosity about the world around them—plants, seasons, color, light, sound, and animals. In the upper elementary and middle school grades, the curriculum expands to include weather and climate, the solar system, electricity, and health-related topics. The secondary school science curriculum is still centered on yearlong courses—general science, biology, chemistry, and physics—despite the efforts of some science educators to foster an integrated approach in which each of these science subjects is taught each year.

Issues and Trends

Two major questions drive science education reform: "Where will the next generation of scientists come from?" and "How can all students be prepared to make informed judgments about such critical and science-based issues as environmental pollution, energy sources, and biotechnology?"

For reformers, there has been both good news and bad news concerning science education in the United States. The bad news is that American youth do not know much science. The good news is that the country is reaching consensus about how to remedy the problem. In 2013, a new set of science standards called the "Next Generation Science Standards" was published in an attempt to identify what science K–12 students should know. Concern that American students lag behind the science performance of students in other countries was a major impetus for the development of these standards. Developed by a coalition of science organizations, scientists, and 26 states, the standards are rich in content and practice, and arranged in a coherent manner across disciplines and grades. They are intended to overcome widespread scientific ignorance, to standardize teaching among states, and to raise the number of high school graduates who choose scientific and technical majors in college. It is still too early in the process to evaluate the standards' effectiveness, but those connected with the development of the standards are hopeful that when the standards are implemented, students will receive a science education comparable to that received by students in the highest-performing countries. The next steps will be for individual states to consider adopting the standards, and developing curricula and instructional practice to incorporate the standards.

Field trips to naturalist sites, such as aquariums, can both spur student interest in and enhance their knowledge of science.

Image Source/Jupiter images

5-2d SOCIALS STUDIES

Social studies—the study of people and their ideas, actions, and relationships—is not a discipline in the same sense as mathematics or physics, although it draws on the various social sciences disciplines (history, geography, political science, economics, psychology, sociology, and anthropology), as well as on religion, literature, and the arts, for its content and methods of inquiry. (A *discipline* has been defined as an area of inquiry containing a distinctive body of concepts and principles, with techniques for exploring the area and for correcting and expanding the body of knowledge.)[6]

History has traditionally been the leading discipline of social studies at both the elementary and secondary levels. Although other disciplines have made some inroads in recent years, history remains the dominant focus in these schools. Recently, efforts have been made to restore geography to the social studies curriculum, following assessments that pointed out students' inability to locate countries on maps. Government is also a staple of the social studies curriculum. Ultimately, the social studies curriculum at both the elementary and secondary levels encompasses a hodgepodge of approaches. In many elementary schools in particular, social studies has been neglected in favor of efforts to meet the reading and mathematics testing requirements set out by the Every Student Succeeds Act.

> *It is important for scientists to be aware of what our discoveries mean, socially and politically. It's a noble goal that science should be apolitical, acultural, and asocial, but it can't be, because it's done by people who are all those things.*
>
> **—MAE JEMISON,**
> former NASA astronaut

Issues and Trends

A major debate is raging over whether the social studies curriculum overemphasizes European history and culture at the expense of Asian, African, and Latin American history and culture. We discuss this issue later in the chapter.

Civic learning, or **civic education**, is another issue gaining the attention of social studies educators. Advocates of this focus call for courses that will acquaint a racially and culturally diverse student population with the heritage common to the American democratic tradition. These new courses would extend the basic study of American law and government to include trends in history, issues in contemporary society, and questions of character and values. Through critical study of case histories and current news reports, students would learn to apply principles of democracy to the everyday concerns they will face as citizens. Practical experiences in civic, cultural, and volunteer activities are also strongly recommended. The "new civics" courses may help unify educators who currently favor many different approaches to the teaching of social studies, including issues-centered, traditional, historical, critical thought, and character education approaches.

In 2013, the National Council for the Social Studies (NCSS) released social studies state standards, *College, Career, and Civic Life (C3) Framework for Social Studies State Standards*, which are designed to align with the CCSS in English language arts. These state standards offer guidance to states in formulating their standards in social studies, and relate to the 2010 set of content standards issued by NCSS. These latter standards articulate a framework that seeks to foster academic and civic competence by integrating the national standards across various social sciences. Ten themes are highlighted in the framework: (1) culture; (2) people, places, and environments; (3) individuals, groups, and institutions; (4) production, distribution, and consumption; (5) global connections; (6) time, continuity, and change; (7) individual development and identity; (8) power, authority, and governance; (9) science, technology, and society; and (10) civic ideals and practices.[7]

5-2e FOREIGN LANGUAGES

Compared with citizens in other nations, Americans are woefully unprepared to speak foreign languages. Approximately 20 percent of all students in U.S. public high schools are enrolled in a foreign language course, with Spanish and French being the most popular languages taken.[8] On the bright side, more elementary schools are offering foreign language programs in recognition of the ease with which young children learn foreign languages.

Issues and Trends

Foreign language departments in the public schools are trying to make the study of foreign languages more attractive by expanding their course offerings and integrating language study with concerns for international and multicultural education. Leaders in the field emphasize the cultural foundations of language, asserting that language study increases linguistic competence and cultural sensitivity. The Internet can assist students and teachers in gaining access to current materials from other countries and interacting with key-pals from other countries, thereby facilitating teaching and learning.

Early introduction of foreign languages continues to gain support, and concern about U.S. competitiveness in a global economy has led many business leaders and politicians to urge greater emphasis on foreign language instruction. For example, schools are seeing increased demand for instruction in Arabic and Chinese owing to U.S. involvement in the Middle East and the emergence of new trade opportunities in China.

Techniques used in elementary bilingual education—immersion, partial immersion, or the Foreign Languages in the Elementary Schools Program—have focused instruction on developing fluency in speaking, writing, and comprehension. Proficiency-oriented instruction, which focuses on what learners can do with the language (rather than what learners know about the language), marks modern-day language teaching.

Young children with musical interests typically receive instruction from private tutors and have opportunities to participate in recitals.

iStock.com/blackjake

5-2f THE ARTS

The arts include visual arts, music, dance, and theater. Art and music in elementary schools are ordinarily taught by regular classroom teachers, although some schools hire specialist teachers in one or both areas. Dance and theater are largely ignored in elementary schools, despite the fact that children of this age are less inhibited and seem to enjoy these activities more than do secondary school students. The small amount of instruction provided in the arts for elementary students contrasts with high school offerings such as drama clubs, orchestras, bands, and dance groups. In most instances, instruction in music or dance during a child's elementary school years takes the form of private instruction outside the public school.

Issues and Trends

Programs in the arts have traditionally tended to emphasize the creation of an art object or the development of a performance. More recently, newer programs have emphasized aesthetic education and art as a way of knowing and perceiving the world.

> *The arts are the rain forests of society. They produce the oxygen of freedom, and they are the early warning system when freedom is in danger.*
>
> —JUNE WAYNE,
> artist

Curriculum specialists have suggested integrating the arts with other subject matter to show the usefulness of the arts and to appeal to a broader range of intelligences. (See Chapter 3, "Who Are Today's Students in a Diverse Society?," for more on Howard Gardner's theory of multiple intelligences.) There is little doubt that the arts play a crucial role in the development of cultured, educated people, and that they respond to a deep instinct in humanity. Even so, the arts remain an "endangered species," subject to extinction whenever budget cuts occur and when high-stakes assessments of standards in language arts, mathematics, and science dictate what teachers should emphasize in their classrooms.

5-2g PHYSICAL EDUCATION AND HEALTH

Physical education—education by and through human movement—contributes to physical fitness, skill and knowledge development, and social and psychological development. Currently, physical education curricula are designed to respond

Given the obesity epidemic in the United States, physical education activity is more important than ever for America's youth.

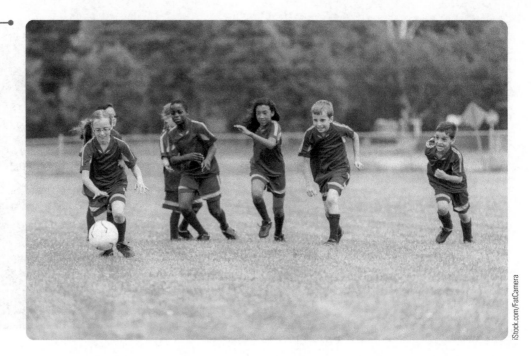

iStock.com/FatCamera

to four needs: (1) the need to develop aerobic capacity to maintain acceptable cardiorespiratory efficiency, (2) the need to achieve appropriate levels of body fat, (3) the need to acquire strength to perform expected tasks of living, and (4) the need to achieve flexibility and abdominal strength to avoid lower back injuries. To address these needs, sports skills are alternated with fitness development through such activities as swimming, jogging, bicycling, yoga, and cross-country skiing. Students are given information on exercise and nutrition so they can understand how to balance caloric intake and maintain an appropriate body fat level. Physical education teachers are typically licensed for both elementary and secondary school teaching, but teachers usually seek out the age levels in which they are most interested. Physical education teachers are also trained to adapt activities for children with disabilities.

The health curriculum addresses such topics as injury prevention and safety, prevention and control of disease (including acquired immune deficiency syndrome [AIDS]), substance abuse, nutrition, family life (sexuality), consumer health, and mental and emotional health. More than most academic subjects, health education strives to change students' attitudes and behaviors to get them to take fewer risks and use more preventive measures. Concerns over childhood obesity have focused renewed attention on the school's role in helping to prevent obesity. In spite of this recent attention, many health educators express frustration that health is not identified as a critical component of the K–12 curriculum, and that questions about health do not appear on high-stakes tests. Because health is not tested, it is not stressed in schools as much as health educators would like.

5-2h ELECTIVE COURSES

Most high schools today offer their students a number of options regarding the courses they take. However, the average high school student graduates with about 20 units (one year-long course represents one unit), and large high schools may offer as many as a hundred courses. The average student, then, will probably choose among optional courses according to individual interests and academic or career ambitions. Examples of elective courses might include personal finance, art history, introduction to computers and applications, psychology, and anthropology.

Issues and Trends

Although college preparation has been the major goal of many high schools, efforts have increased recently to provide comprehensive programs for students not planning to attend college. This trend is especially evident in rural areas, where small, local high schools have often been replaced by comprehensive regional high schools. Some of the courses involved—such as technology education, distributive education, home economics, business education, and agriculture—are specifically vocational. Others—such as consumer education—have been added to the curriculum because of an obvious societal need or in response to student interest.

> A liberal education is the only practical form of vocational education.
>
> —JOHN HENRY CARDINAL NEWMAN, (1801–1890), Roman Catholic cardinal

A disturbing trend for those who teach elective courses is the increase in requirements for graduation from high schools, which leaves less time for elective courses. Some argue that a common general education provides the best foundation for future work or academic study; others hope to maintain a large percentage of the curriculum as electives. These issues, when raised by teachers of elective courses, focus attention on the purpose of comprehensive schooling and on definitions of what is "basic."

5-2i CAREER AND TECHNICAL EDUCATION

The purpose of career and technical education (formerly called "vocational education") is to provide a foundation of skills that allow high school students to be gainfully employed after graduation. The subject areas most commonly associated with career and technical education are business, trade and industrial education, health occupations, agriculture, family and consumer sciences, marketing, and technology.

In recent decades, career and technical education has come under fire from those who note its inadequacy in preparing students for careers in high-technology fields or in the country's now-dominant service economy. Reformers urge teachers to help students see the relationships between the topics that they study and their applications in real-world contexts and to emphasize real-life problem solving.

Many School-to-Work programs, designed to help students develop skills and understandings that will prepare them to adapt to the changing needs of the workplace, have been developed. Such programs take many different forms, ranging from career academies that feature specialized career-oriented curricula in such areas as health professions, business, or law, to paid internships and co-op experiences. Schools work with local businesses to design courses and experiences that will prepare high school students for particular kinds of jobs that meet local business needs. Hundreds of thousands of businesses nationwide now participate in School-to-Work partnerships.

Issues and Trends

Approximately 8.3 million secondary students took at least one CTE course in 2017.[9] In fiscal year 2019, the federal government distributed $1.2 billion dollars to the states to promote secondary and postsecondary career and technical education.[10] Some educators and labor officials urge that the line between academic and career and technical education be blurred, and that all youngsters be provided with skills in traditionally "academic" subject areas, including mathematics, science, and English, as well as more applied learning experiences. Some states, such as Oregon, require all graduating high school students to have work experience and a career plan.

One form of work experience is apprenticeship programming, in which students receive on-the-job training with a company for four days a week and participate in classroom instruction on the fifth day. Such programs are designed to help youth make an easy transition from school to work.

Another promising trend is the development of "tech-prep" programs that link high school and postsecondary study. Tech-prep programs typically encompass the last two years of high school and the first two years of college (usually at a community college). They provide an attractive alternative for students who do not plan to attend a four-year college.

Pause *and* Reflect

1. What is your view of the issues and trends in your favorite subject field?
2. Are there any other developments or changes in the curriculum that you would like to see?

5-3 Assessing Student Academic Performance

Both supporters and critics of contemporary curricula often focus on the results—that is, what students actually learn from their studies of language arts, math, science, and so forth. The methods of assessing results are themselves highly controversial and will be discussed further in Chapter 12, "How Should Education Be Reformed?" In this section, we look at the results of both national and international studies that attempt to judge the academic performance of U.S. students.

5-3a NATIONAL ASSESSMENT OF EDUCATIONAL PROGRESS

Since their introduction 40 years ago, National Assessment of Educational Progress (NAEP) assessments have been conducted periodically in reading, mathematics, science, writing, history, geography, and other fields. Administered to a representative national sample of students, the NAEP assessments are the primary source on educational achievement in the United States, and they have become known as "the nation's report card." Although almost all the states assess their students' progress on content standards, they do not use the same standards or the same tests, so until the CCSS in English language arts and mathematics, discussed earlier in the chapter, become operational in many states, comparisons across states are mainly limited to the NAEP data. Assessment occurs at three grade levels: 4th, 8th, and 12th. Achievement levels are defined as *basic* (denoting partial mastery of knowledge and skills fundamental for proficient work), *proficient* (representing solid academic performance relative to challenging subject matter for the grade level), and *advanced* (signifying superior performance).

So how are American students doing? Figure 5.1 presents recent NAEP data on students' skills in mathematics, science, reading, writing, and U.S. history. Thirty-four percent of 4th graders, 32 percent of 8th graders, and 21 percent of 12th graders scored at or above the proficient level in science.

Over the past decade, student achievement on the NAEP mathematics tests has improved significantly for all ages and all racial and ethnic groups, representing improvements of as much as one year's worth of mathematics knowledge since 1990 for 4th, 8th, and 12th grades. Reading scores, by contrast, have increased only slightly since 1998. The 2019 reading assessment of 4th graders indicated that 66 percent of the students were at or above the basic

T Ⓕ

About two-thirds of American eighth-grade students score at the proficient or advanced level on the National Assessment of Educational Progress in reading.

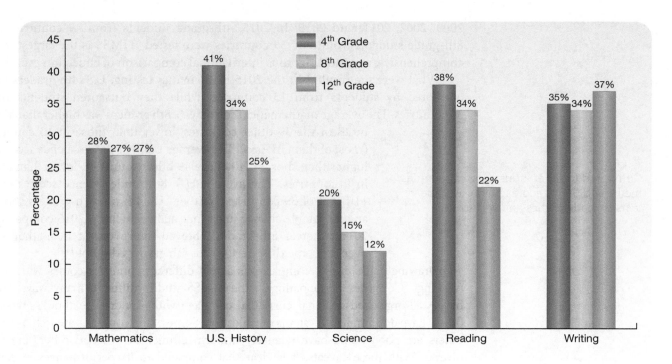

FIGURE 5.1 **Percentage of Students Scoring at the Proficient or Advanced Level on NAEP Assessments in Various Subject Fields**

Source: The National Assessment of Educational Progress, *The Nation's Report Card,* http:nces.ed.gov/nationsreportcard.

level, whereas 35 percent were at or above the proficient level. For 8th graders, the comparable figures were 73 percent and 34 percent.[11]

Further NAEP assessments reveal that despite improvements, U.S. students are still lacking in knowledge of history, geography, and civics. The 2014 and 2018 history assessments showed a slight improvement in the basic scores for 4th graders, but not much change in the percentage of students scoring at the proficient or advanced level. Seventy-three percent of 4th graders, 66 percent of 8th graders, and 45 percent of 12th graders achieved at the basic level or higher. By comparison, 20 percent of 4th graders, 15 percent of 8th graders, and 12 percent of 12th graders reached the proficient or advanced level.[12] In the most recent geography tests, 21 percent of 4th graders, 27 percent of 8th graders, and 20 percent of 12th graders reached the proficient or advanced level. As these data indicate, in every subject field, a large majority of American students are failing to achieve the proficient level in the NAEP assessments.

Many of those students are members of minority groups. African American, Hispanic, and Native American students continue to score significantly lower than white and Asian American students on the NAEP assessments, although the gap between African American and white students has been narrowing slightly. Males continue to outperform females to a slight extent on mathematics and science tests, although girls have made gains in recent years, whereas females significantly outperform males on the reading and writing tests.[13]

5-3b INTERNATIONAL COMPARISONS

Compared with the academic performances of students from other developed countries, U.S. students have tended to have average results. The **Trends in International Mathematics and Science Study (TIMSS)** tested the mathematics and science knowledge of students at two grade levels—4th and 8th—in 1995, 1999,

2003, 2007, 2011, and 2015. In 2015, 4th-grade students from 49 countries and 8th-grade students from over 39 countries were tested. TIMSS is the largest, most comprehensive, and most rigorous international comparison of education ever done.

What were the results? In the 2015 mathematics testing, U.S. 4th graders were outscored by students from 13 countries, while they outscored students from 34 countries. The average mathematics score of U.S. 8th graders was higher than those in 28 of the 39 other countries, lower than those in 10 countries (most of them in Asia). The average U.S. 4th-grade science score was higher than those in 40 of the 49 other countries, lower than those in 9 countries. The average U.S. 8th-grade science score ranked 11th out of 39 countries. Neither U.S. 4th nor 8th graders showed any detectable change in science achievement in 2015 compared to 2011, whereas 8th graders showed improvement in mathematics over the same time period, but 4th graders did not.[14]

T (F)

Compared to other industrialized countries, the United States scores below average in tests of mathematics and science.

Drawing achievement comparisons across different countries comes with many warnings. Countries participating in the TIMSS studies differ in many ways. Some have well-organized national curricula, complete with standard textbooks, whereas others have decentralized systems of education. Some of the countries are rich, whereas others are poor. Some have relatively uniform ethnicities, whereas others are very diverse. With these caveats, it is clear that compared to its performances in earlier TIMSS assessments, the United States has made some progress. Another international standardized assessment is the **Program for International Student Assessment (PISA)**, which is administered every three years to 15-year-old students and tests knowledge in mathematics, science, and reading literacy. The latest PISA assessment (2018) shows U.S. students scoring below average in mathematics and about average in reading and science literacy relative to their counterparts in other industrialized countries.[15]

A number of explanations have been proposed to explain the differences in mathematics achievement test scores between U.S. students and those from high-scoring countries, including cultural differences that result in greater value being placed on education in some countries than in the United States, lower expectations for U.S. students, and more U.S. students holding jobs. Moreover, the TIMSS studies revealed that the content of U.S. mathematics and science classes is not as challenging or focused as that of other countries. Many middle school students in the United States are still doing elementary arithmetic while their international counterparts are studying algebra and geometry. By the senior year of high school, many U.S. students have stopped taking math and science altogether. About 75 percent of students stop studying mathematics after algebra and geometry, while 25 percent of high school students never take chemistry and about 60 percent never study physics.[16]

Another factor may be the way that mathematics and science are taught in U.S. schools. TIMSS researchers note that the U.S. mathematics and science curricula cover many topics but devote little time to any one topic. The United States is number one in the world in one category—the size of the textbooks, which tend to be encyclopedic rather than focused! U.S. teachers, supported by the textbooks they use, teach more topics but in less detail than teachers from high-scoring countries. Furthermore, compared with Japanese teachers, they focus much more on procedures and skills and much less on concepts, deductive reasoning, and understanding. Perhaps surprisingly, U.S. teachers assign more homework and spend more class time discussing it than do teachers from Japan and Germany.[17]

National and international assessments show that by high school, students often fall behind in learning sciences and mathematics. Unfortunately, most standardized assessments don't measure actual performances, such as these students conducting a science experiment, which can foster a deep understanding of key scientific concepts and methods.

The total amount of time students spend on academic pursuits also likely has an effect on their performance. At the high school level, U.S. students spend much of their school day in such nonacademic activities as counseling, gym, homeroom, pep rallies, and education about personal safety, consumer affairs, and family life. An average of only 41 percent of secondary schooltime has to be devoted to core academic work to earn a high school diploma,[18] and that's probably the way most American parents want it. Although this study is 25 years old, there is little to indicate the situation has changed dramatically either way. Both parents and students disavow a "nerdish" emphasis on strong academics in favor of preparing "well-rounded" individuals, making it difficult for schools to strengthen their academic requirements beyond a certain point. As long as a majority of Americans feel this way, it seems unlikely that we will see a radical restructuring of schools to emphasize strong academics.

The coronavirus pandemic of 2020, which caused the closing of almost all public schools for the spring semester, will certainly result in less learning time for students. Many schools resorted to various distance learning strategies, but with mixed results. Many students lacked access to computers and schools' online networks, resulting in great disparities in learning outcomes. Educators fear that student achievement will drop dramatically until schools open again, jeopardizing future educational opportunities for many.

There are several lessons to be learned from TIMSS and PISA. First, we need to continue setting clear, high standards for what students should know and be able to do in mathematics and science. Second, we need to align everything else we do with those standards: initial preparation of teachers, selection of texts and other curriculum materials, design of assessments, and continuing professional development of teachers. The difficulty is that, unlike most of the other countries participating in the TIMSS, the

Unlike these students, many American high school students spend little time in science laboratories conducting experiments.

Monkey Business Images/Shutterstock.com

United States is highly decentralized in its educational decision making, which makes it extremely difficult to align the various educational components with the standards. Perhaps, the adoption of the CCSS in English language arts and mathematics by so many states, and the possible adoption of Next Generation Science Standards, will lead to a more unified approach to the teaching and study of these subjects.

Pause *and* Reflect

1. In your opinion, what would be the best ways to improve the performance of U.S. students in mathematics and science?
2. Do you think the United States should have a national curriculum, as do so many other industrialized nations? Why or why not?

5-4 Additional Influences on the Curriculum

Although we can examine what is taught in the schools in terms of the subjects offered, the curriculum as students experience it is affected by a number of other factors. The individual teacher, of course, is a major variable in what students actually learn. This whole book is about you as that teacher. The classroom and school context also affect the delivery of the curriculum, as does the academic track to which a student is assigned. In this section, we will focus on two other major influences on the curriculum that is actually delivered to students: textbooks and innovative instructional approaches.

5-4a TEXTBOOKS

Education in the United States is constitutionally the domain of the various individual states—that is, the states are empowered to establish curricula and to organize and finance school systems. Unlike in many other countries, there is no national curriculum established by the federal government and implemented throughout the country. Even so, some educational observers assert that we do have a national curriculum of sorts, called *textbooks*. Several studies have concluded that most of what teachers and students do in classrooms reflects the specific textbooks used in those settings. For example, the objectives and goals for student learning are defined by the textbook (even the text you are now reading); learning activities and materials are provided to teachers as part of the textbook package; and tests geared to the textbook's objectives are usually prepared by the textbook publisher for the teacher's use.

States do exert some influence on the content of textbooks. Put bluntly, they cast their votes on that content through their decisions on whether to use a particular book. Critics, however, have noted the shortcomings of many adoption systems that allow too little time and too little money to support the selection of excellent texts by qualified personnel.

More than 20 states (mainly in the Sunbelt) have a textbook adoption process that involves reviewing textbooks according to state guidelines and then mandating either specific books that schools must use or lists of approved textbooks from which schools must choose. As part of this process, citizens have the opportunity to examine textbooks being considered for statewide adoption and to express their objections to particular books. Because textbook adoption is a multimillion-dollar business, publishing companies must be careful not to include material that influential groups and factions might find offensive and that might jeopardize their books' chances of adoption.

With the implementation of content standards and the CCSS in 35 states, school boards and faculty responsible for adopting textbooks now examine how well textbooks address their state's standards. At one point in time, textbook publishers rarely customized their books for each state. Instead, they organized the books to meet the standards of those states that have a lot of children and that buy a lot of books. Publishers relied on the similarity of standards between states to assure that books geared toward the larger states' standards would meet at least some standards in nearly every state. As a consequence, standards set by large-population states such as Texas, California, and Florida greatly influenced the content of textbooks produced by commercial publishers. Today, however, textbook companies are more able to customize textbooks for each state. With the adoption of the CCSS in English language arts and mathematics by many states, a common set of textbooks is likely to be developed to address the standards in these two subject areas.

A wave of educational reform is directing attention to the quality of the textbooks that determine the curriculum. Some critics claim that texts are "dumbed down" to meet readability requirements; the writing style, designed to meet arbitrary criteria for lengths of words and sentences, can be awkward and stiff. Others believe that textbooks try to include too much material and so lack depth of coverage, a criticism certainly supported by findings from the TIMSS. Critics also complain about typical textbook emphases on skills development instead of stimulation of students' interest and intellect; these emphases, they say, create texts that are dry, barren of ideas, devoid of concepts, and lacking in the vigorous writing style that stirs students to comprehend and retain what they read. Many educational commentators suggest that teachers and curriculum developers rely too much on textbooks and not enough on primary sources.

Because what is taught in public schools touches people's hearts and minds, the content of the textbooks arouses political passions. One such controversy arose in Texas in 2010, when the elected Texas Board of Education voted (10–5 along Republican/Democratic lines) to make over 100 changes in the state's history and economic textbooks that put a conservative stamp on the textbooks. The changes stress the superiority of American capitalism, question the Founding Fathers' commitment to a purely secular government, and present Republican political philosophies in a more positive light. One of the changes included downgrading the role Thomas Jefferson played in our nation's founding, apparently because his secular views (he coined the phrase, "separation between church and state") conflicted with the more Christian-oriented views of a majority of the Texas board. Conservative members of the board believed that the history textbooks being used in Texas classrooms reflected a liberal bias by promoting multiculturalism, secular values, and a negative interpretation of American history, at the expense of Christian values, the importance of free enterprise, and a belief in the exceptionality of America. The actions by the board provoked much criticism and discussion around the United States. What is clear is that what states choose to include in their textbooks can be very controversial and influenced by political and religious perspectives.

A recent modification of the traditional textbook involves the use of electronic materials. For example, the University of California–Berkeley developed the Full Option Science System (FOSS) for K–8 science, which incorporates digital devices and online interactive activities both at school and at home. Several states have adopted this system as an option for school districts to use in their science curriculum. The online software is available in both Spanish and English. Besides keeping information current, the technology provides access to rich materials and interesting projects such as using interactive and video elements to engage in or observe scientific experiments that would be impractical to conduct in the classroom. The technology also provides alternative assessments by permitting students to answer questions and follow directions on the disk or online.

Some people have called for moving away from printed textbooks in favor of digital ones. The transition to digital involves much more than scanning books and uploading them to computers, tablet devices, or e-readers. Proponents describe a comprehensive shift to immersive, online learning experiences that engage students in a way textbooks never could. Florida has already passed legislation requiring districts to spend half of their instructional-materials budgets on digital content. Alabama, California, Indiana, Utah, and Washington State have all passed legislation promoting digital education content.[19]

Whether electronic media will make major inroads into textbook adoptions in other subjects remains to be seen. Conventional textbooks, although they lack technological pizzazz and become outdated more quickly, have some distinct advantages over their electronic rivals: Books are more portable, and they do not break down. Students also appear to prefer reading from print rather than on a screen. One thing appears certain: Textbooks, whether in paper or electronic form, are one of the major determinants of U.S. elementary and secondary school curricula, and that situation does not appear likely to change in the near future.

© Cengage 2016

Reading in the Content Areas: An Interdisciplinary Unit on the 1920s

Watch the video clips, study the artifacts in the case, and reflect on the following questions:

1. How do these teachers achieve the advantages associated with interdisciplinary instruction, such as making subject matter less fragmented? Do they succeed in making the students feel that learning about the 1920s is relevant to their lives?

2. For you as a teacher, what would be the advantages and challenges of planning and implementing an interdisciplinary curriculum or project?

3. Which kind of arrangements or support would help with implementing interdisciplinary curricula? For example, would you prefer working with another teacher or working alone to prepare interdisciplinary projects?

5-4b INNOVATIVE INSTRUCTIONAL APPROACHES

Curriculum and instruction are intimately related, and the instructional approaches that teachers use clearly shape how students experience the curriculum. Although these approaches have remained amazingly constant since the 1890s, especially at the secondary level, some alterations to traditional teacher-centered instruction have taken hold.[20] Educators are constantly searching for new ways to deliver the curriculum more effectively. All of the trends discussed here can be used in a variety of subject areas with students of many age and ability levels. We will look at six nontraditional instructional influences on the curriculum: interdisciplinary curriculum, cooperative learning, critical thinking and problem solving, writing across the curriculum, differentiated instruction, and flipped instruction.

Interdisciplinary Curriculum

Students—and particularly secondary students—are often critical of the traditional curriculum, which seems irrelevant to their lives outside of school. They often fail to see how English, history, mathematics, and science relate to them. The curriculum they experience is fragmented and isolated. In one language arts class, the teacher gave the dates of a famous author's birth and death, and asked the students to figure out how old the author was when she died. Silence fell over the room as students pondered the question. Finally, one student said, "It's hard to do math in English class." Students have learned to segment and separate their knowledge into compartments because of the way we teach content.

Many teachers agree. Noting that the real world is not organized by disciplines but contains situations and problems that cut across disciplinary boundaries, these teachers are returning to an old idea of organizing and teaching the curriculum in an integrated and interdisciplinary fashion. Although numerous definitions of **interdisciplinary curriculum**, or **integrated curriculum**, exist, both terms are often used synonymously to mean a curriculum that cuts across subject-matter lines to focus on comprehensive life problems or broad-based areas of study that bring together the various segments of the curriculum in meaningful association.

Many approaches to developing integrated, interdisciplinary curricula are possible. One of the simplest is for two or more teachers from different disciplinary backgrounds to plan and teach their respective subjects together, seeking different disciplinary perspectives on a particular unit of study. For example, an English teacher and a social studies teacher might team together to integrate the study of the nineteenth century by examining the history and literature of that period. (The Video Case, *Reading in the Content Areas: An Interdisciplinary Unit on the 1920s*, shows how two high school teachers combine social studies and literature instruction.)

Another approach is *thematic* in nature. In this case, a cross-departmental team chooses themes as overlays to the different subjects. "Inventions," for example, is a theme that could combine science and mathematics in the study of machines and their mechanics, reading and writing about inventors in language arts, and designing and building models in industrial arts. Another example, "health," would permit a number of different subjects to be addressed in an effort to better understand specific health topics (see Figure 5.2). Yet another thematic approach is to identify concepts that apply in different subjects, such as examining how symmetry, patterns, evidence, and proof apply in mathematics, art, science, social studies, and language arts.

FIGURE 5.2 Sample Interdisciplinary Approach

Source: Source: Joan Palmer, "Planning Wheels Turn Curriculum Around," *Educational Leadership* 49 (*October* 1991): 58. © 1991 by ASCD. Used with permission.

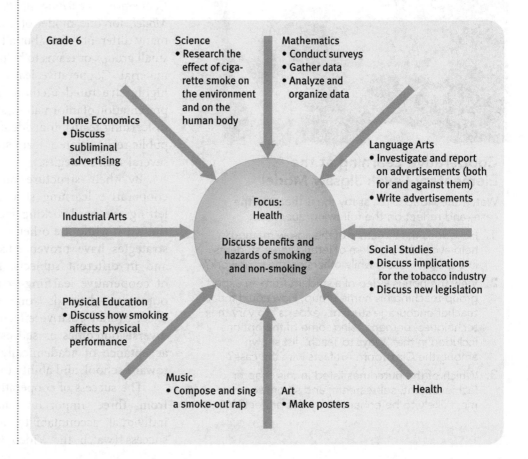

Proponents of the interdisciplinary curriculum argue that its merits far outweigh the extra expenditure of time and effort required to implement this approach. Students benefit by experiencing coherence in the curriculum and connections to real-world situations. Critical thinking and problem-solving skills are developed within specific contexts rather than in isolation. Teachers benefit by having students who enjoy learning and by working collaboratively with other teachers.

Although interdisciplinary teaching is enjoying a resurgence of popularity, particularly in middle schools, the disciplinary approach to curriculum in the secondary schools is well entrenched and is being reinforced by the development of national standards within each discipline rather than across disciplines. The tension between the disciplinary and interdisciplinary approaches to curriculum development will likely persist for some time. For more on interdisciplinary curricula, see the "For Further Information" section at the end of the chapter.

Cooperative Learning

Cooperative learning in classrooms is another trend influencing what is taught in the schools. Those who have analyzed the "hidden" curriculum (i.e., the implicit teachings that schools communicate to their students) have observed that U.S. schools tend to reward competitive or individual accomplishment more than cooperative effort.[21] Arguing for cooperative learning techniques, some educators maintain that such techniques can change the ways students learn, their attitudes toward what they are taught, and their perceptions of themselves and others.

What is cooperative learning? (See the Video Case, *Cooperative Learning at the Elementary Level: Jigsaw Model,* for one model of cooperative learning.) It takes many different forms, but all involve students working in small groups or teams to help one another learn academic material. Cooperative learning strategies are organized, highly structured methods that usually involve formal presentation of information, student practice and coaching in learning teams, individual assessment of mastery, and public recognition of team success. Table 5.2 summarizes several such strategies.

By their structure and individual assignments, cooperative learning strategies avoid the problem of letting the hardworking students in the group do all the work while the other students get a free ride. Such strategies have proven successful across grade levels and in different subjects. Although the effectiveness of cooperative learning—particularly for achievement outcomes—depends on the particular approach used, overall positive effects have been found on such diverse outcomes as self-esteem, intergroup relations, acceptance of academically slower students, attitudes toward school, and ability to work cooperatively.[22]

The success of cooperative learning strategies comes from three important characteristics: group goals, individual accountability, and equal opportunity for success (watch the Video Case, *Cooperative Learning:*

© Cengage 2016

▶❙❙ TeachSource Video Case

Cooperative Learning at the Elementary Level: Jigsaw Model

Watch the video clips, study the artifacts in the case, and reflect on the following questions:

1. How does the structure of the jigsaw method help avoid the problem of letting some students in a group "coast" while others do the hard work?

2. View the bonus video of a student from an expert group teaching his home group. How could the teacher encourage student "experts" to vary their techniques, perhaps using some of the options included in the "Ways to Teach" list shown among the Classroom Artifacts with the case?

3. Which of the outcomes listed in this chapter (achievement, self-esteem, and so on) seems most likely to be enhanced by this project? Why?

TABLE 5.2		Selected Cooperative Learning Strategies	
	Name	**Brief Description**	**Function**
1. Student team learning	a. Student Teams Achievement Divisions (STAD)	Four-member mixed-learning teams. Teacher presents lesson; students work within teams to make certain all team members have mastered the objectives. Students take individual quizzes. Points are awarded based on improvement over previous quizzes.	Four-member mixed-learning teams. Teacher presents lesson; students work within teams to make certain all team members have mastered the objectives. Students take individual quizzes. Points are awarded based on improvement over previous quizzes.
	b. Teams–Games–Tournament (TGT)	Uses same teacher presentations and teamwork as in STAD but replaces quizzes with weekly tournaments.	Same as STAD.
2. Jigsaw		Each student on a team becomes an "expert" on one topic by working with members from other teams assigned the same topic. Upon returning to the home team, each expert teaches the group, and students are all assessed on all aspects of the topic.	Acquisition and presentation of new material, review, informed debate; promotes interdependence, status equalization; used in social studies and other subjects where learning from text is important.
3. Jigsaw 2		Same as Jigsaw, except instead of each student being assigned a particular section of text, all students read a common narrative. Each student receives a topic on which to become expert.	Same as Jigsaw.

(Continued)

© Cengage Learning

TABLE 5.2	Selected Cooperative Learning Strategies (Continued)	
Name	**Brief Description**	**Function**
4. Group investigation	Students work in small groups using cooperative inquiry, group discussion, and projects. Students form two- to six-member groups. Groups choose subtopics from a unit, break subtopics into individual tasks, and prepare group reports.	Development of planning, investigating, and reporting skills.
5. Think–pair–share	Students think by themselves on a topic provided by the teacher, then pair with another student to discuss it, after which they share their thoughts with the class.	Generation and revision of hypotheses, inductive reasoning, deductive reasoning; fosters participation and involvement.

TeachSource Digital Download

High School History Lesson, on page 141 to see how a high school teacher uses an informal model of cooperative learning):

- *Group goals* usually take the form of rewards based on team success in academic tasks. To achieve team success, each member of the group must coordinate the completion of his or her assigned task with the work of the other group members; each team member is indispensable.

- *Individual accountability* involves assessing each student's mastery of the content, with the results usually given back to the group and the individual. Teammates practice together and support and coach one another, but people are assessed in the usual ways. The team's success is often judged by how much each team member improves relative to the earlier assessment. Even the lowest-achieving student can contribute to the team's success by improving over the first assessment.

- *Equal opportunities for success* are ensured by team scoring systems that are based on individual improvement over prior performance. This feature reinforces the perception that student effort—not just innate ability—counts.

Cooperative learning has been found to be a particularly effective instructional tool in teaching at-risk students who benefit from immediate feedback for their learning attempts. It works well because it offers students more involvement in and control over their learning activities. Because many schools attempt to do away with tracking (discussed later in this chapter) and to encourage heterogeneous grouping,

TeachSource Video Case

Cooperative Learning: High School History Lesson

Watch the video clips, study the artifacts in the case, and reflect on the following questions:

1. Three key characteristics of successful cooperative learning are listed in this chapter. How can teachers who use informal groups, like the teacher in the video, achieve those characteristics?

2. One of the students mentions the importance of careful grouping and placing students who can work together in groups with one another. What are some guidelines teachers might use for grouping their students?

cooperative learning provides a means to make all students feel they are essential to the classroom learning process. It enables students to recognize that all of them, when given a chance, have something to contribute to everyone's learning. Cooperative learning has quickly become a major instructional method in the United States, particularly in elementary and middle schools.

Critical Thinking and Problem Solving

A growing interest in helping students become better thinkers and problem solvers is evidenced by the multitude of publications, workshops, curriculum study institutes, journal articles, and course requirements addressing the topics of thinking and problem solving. Although many people favor teaching it, definitions of **critical thinking** vary widely. At the heart of all these definitions, however, is the intent to help students evaluate the worth of ideas, opinions, or evidence before making a decision or judgment.

Some educators favor approaches that help students detect bias or identify a wide range of propaganda strategies. The teaching of philosophy is also proposed as a way to provide criteria by which students can judge others' thinking. Still other approaches identify component skills (e.g., making inferences, testing hypotheses, and identifying assumptions) within the realm of critical thinking, and advocate direct instruction in each skill. Socratic questioning (a style of questioning that elicits a clear expression of truth that was implicitly known by the person being questioned) is also suggested as a way to teach the art of thinking.

Problem solving is an element of critical thinking that has attracted increased attention and seen increased use in recent decades. **Problem solving** generally refers to the process of either presenting students with a problem or helping them identify a problem and then observing and helping them become aware of the conditions, procedures, or steps needed to solve it. The problems may range from putting puzzles together, to solving simple science or mathematics problems, to solving more complex mental, logical, or social dilemmas. A problem may be presented as an individual activity, such as when independently predicting outcomes in a reading passage, or may be used with a group, such as when simulating wilderness "survival" activities that require group cooperation.

Despite the many possible ways of teaching problem solving, the emphasis in each case is on the *process* of reaching a solution. Proponents of problem-solving instruction point out that if students become more aware of their mental processes, they will be able to exercise greater control over their own learning and thinking in future situations. In group problem-solving activities, students may also benefit from interacting with one another and from being exposed to the variety of approaches used by peers in solving the same problem.

What is the role of critical thought in the curriculum? At one time, educators debated whether students could best learn effective thinking through separate courses or as an integrated part of every course. There is now widespread agreement that although students do benefit from stand-alone courses in critical thinking, they must also learn to think within the context of each discipline. The integration of critical thinking into subject areas appears to be the direction in which teaching is heading, especially given that the curricula of the schools are already so crowded. As the "Voices from the Classroom" feature suggests, most students, including those who do not speak English as a first language, can benefit from instruction that emphasizes critical thinking and problem solving.

Writing across the Curriculum

The **writing across the curriculum** movement has been a center of curricular interest for a growing number of educators since the 1960s. Also called *writing to learn* or *writing to learn in the content areas,* this instructional approach emphasizes writing as a tool for students' learning, not only in English classes but also in all other subject areas.

How can teachers use the act of writing as the medium through which subject-matter learning takes place? Students in social studies classes may be asked to take a written stand on school issues, moral questions, or political problems. Music students may write their own ballads. Students in science classes may work together to predict the future in story form or to write futuristic headlines and news features.

> *Many highly intelligent people are poor thinkers. Many people of average intelligence are skilled thinkers. The power of a car is separate from the way the car is driven.*
>
> —EDWARD DE BONO,
> British physician and author

VOICES from the Classroom

Triumphs and Setbacks

Judy Boch graduated from the University of Arizona and obtained a master's degree in educational leadership at Northern Arizona University. She has spent a total of 22 years as a classroom teacher and 13 years working as an instructional coach.

Up until the time he came to me as a second grader, Raul's content education had been conducted in Spanish. Only in the latter part of first grade did he begin to learn in English. My second-grade classroom was labeled "English as a Second Language" (ESL), but I spoke no Spanish. The only Spanish that Raul heard in the classroom was from a one-hour Spanish aide and from the other children.

I wondered how I was going to reach this obviously bright and talented boy. This was soon made clear during one of our first math lessons. Having been trained in cognitively guided instruction, I gave the children a story problem and asked them to solve it with their own invented strategies. Although Raul couldn't, at first, read the problem, another child translated for him. Raul came alive!

He drew pictures and used numbers to model his strategy to the problem. I knew I was taking a risk that day when I asked Raul to share his strategy with the other students. I wondered whether I had made a mistake when he grasped for words to explain. But explain he did! He drew his picture on the board, labeled it with numbers, and wrote a number sentence to match the problem. In short phrases, he shared his thinking sequentially.

Raul blossomed after that day. His English began to improve as he continually volunteered to share his thinking in mathematics. In his math journal, Raul wrote: "Math is my favrit becuz I get to be the techer. It makes me feel prowd."

Unfortunately, Raul's excitement has not continued. This year, as a lead teacher on my campus, I visit Raul's classroom once a week. He is learning math through more conventional methods using the traditional algorithms. It is painful to see him using traditional methods that he really doesn't understand and that take him so much longer than his invented strategies. His teacher says he is becoming unfocused and having discipline problems. Although his English has improved considerably, math is no longer his great equalizer or passion. My only hope is that Raul rediscovers his love and enthusiasm for mathematics. For if he does not, we have failed him.

I am now working with teachers and principals of second language learners. As teachers are becoming more proficient in their own understanding of mathematical content, and administrators are becoming instructional leaders, I see many "Rauls" who are being encouraged to learn math conceptually. Additionally, with the Common Core State Standards adopted in Arizona, I am hopeful that our students will find the love of mathematics that Raul had when he was my student.

Children in math classes can create their own word problems and keep records of what they have learned, their questions, and their observations. Art classes can write scripts for slide shows and cartoon strips, or create illustrated guides and storybooks. Teachers at many grade levels and in many subject areas can ask students to keep informal journals or "learning logs." In these journals, students record their responses to what they have read and studied, and can then interact both with text material and with the teacher's responses to their queries and remarks. These are just a few examples of the many ways teachers use writing as a thinking tool for students to use and apply their knowledge in the content areas.

T (F)

Differentiating instruction means assigning students of different abilities to classes with other students of comparable abilities.

Differentiated Instruction

The term **differentiated instruction** is relatively new on the educational scene, though its practice has been around for a long time. In its simplest form, differentiated instruction tries to respond to student variance rather than adopting a standardized approach to teaching that assumes all learners in a class are essentially alike. The academic diversity of students in today's classrooms is growing, and one instructional approach won't work for all students. (See Chapter 3, "Who Are Today's Students in a Diverse Society?," for more discussion of the various kinds of diversity found in modern-day U.S. schools.) As schools try to ensure that all students learn what is expected of them, teachers recognize that they need to customize their instruction techniques to meet individual student needs. That is, teachers are trying to tailor their instruction to provide appropriate challenges for gifted students, students who lag behind, and students who fall in between the two extremes. (See the Video Case, *Academic Diversity: Differentiated Instruction,* to see how one teacher adapts a writing workshop to the needs and interests of her students.)

> *Any subject can be taught effectively in some intellectually honest form to any child at any stage of development.*
>
> —JEROME BRUNER,
> psychologist

Differentiated instruction is a teaching philosophy based on the premise that teachers should adapt instruction to student differences in reading readiness, learning preferences, and interests. According to Carol Tomlinson, a national expert on differentiated instruction, teachers can differentiate three aspects of the curriculum—content, process, and products:

▶ ‖ **TeachSource** Video Case

© Cengage 2016

Academic Diversity: Differentiated Instruction

Watch the video clips, study the artifacts in the case, and reflect on the following questions:

1. As noted in the video and viewing questions, one key to differentiating instruction effectively is getting to know your students well. How will you, as a teacher, do this?

2. How do posters and handouts, like the artifacts included in this case, help provide "access points" to a lesson for students who need extra help?

3. In addition to those strategies listed in this chapter and shown in the Video Case, what might be some other strategies for differentiating instruction?

- *Content* refers to the concepts, principles, and skills that teachers want students to learn. All students should be given access to the same core content, but teachers can provide different means (e.g., texts, lectures, and demonstrations) to give students access to skills and knowledge.

- *Process* refers to the activities that help students make sense of and own the knowledge being taught. Teachers can vary the activities to provide some students with access to more complexity and others with more support, depending on their readiness levels, interests, or learning preferences.

- *Product* refers to culminating projects that students develop to demonstrate and extend what they have learned. The products assigned can vary depending on students' interests or learning preferences. For example, some students might prefer to work as members of a group while producing a play about the topic being studied, whereas others might prefer to work alone while writing a term paper.[23]

Differentiating content, process, and product for students requires teachers to know their students, their subject, and their materials. (See Table 5.3 for some strategies for differentiating instruction.) There is no formula for differentiation—no single best way to address all possible student differences. Rather, teachers must make a commitment to start with students and to make a match between learner and

TABLE 5.3	Strategies for Differentiating Instruction

Many teachers accept the desirability of differentiating instruction but don't know how to go about doing it. Here are some of the many strategies that teachers can use to avoid lockstep instruction:

Stations	The teacher sets up different spots in the classroom where students work on different tasks at the same time. This strategy encourages flexible grouping because not all students have to go to all stations all the time.
Compacting	The teacher assesses students before beginning a unit of study so they won't have to waste time learning something they already know.
Complex Instruction	This approach uses challenging materials, open-ended tasks, and small instructional groups. Teachers circulate among the groups as they work, asking questions and probing students' thinking.
Choice	The teacher writes work assignments on cards that are placed in hanging pockets. The teacher asks a student to select a card from a particular row of pockets, which gives the student some choice within circumscribed options. Each row represents work at different levels of complexity.
Problem-Based Learning	This approach places students in an active role of solving problems.
Entry Points	Using some of the multiple intelligences identified by Howard Gardner (see Chapter 3, "Who Are Today's Students in a Diverse Society?"), students explore a given topic through as many as five avenues: narrational (presenting a story), logical–quantitative (using numbers or deduction), foundational (examining philosophy and vocabulary), aesthetic (focusing on sensory features), and experiential (hands-on).
Orbital Studies	Students conduct independent investigations, generally lasting several weeks, around some aspect of the curriculum. Students select their own topics and work with the guidance of the teacher.
4MAT	Teachers plan some lessons for each of four learning preferences (mastery, understanding, personal involvement, and synthesis) over the course of several days on a given topic. Each learner can approach the topic through his or her preferred modes of learning. (See Chapter 3, "Who Are Today's Students in a Diverse Society?," for more information about learning preferences.)

Source: Carol Ann Tomlinson, *The Differentiated Classroom: Responding to the Needs of All Learners* (Alexandria, VA: Association for Supervision and Curriculum Development, 1999).

the material to be learned. The goal, however, is always the same: to maximize the capacities of each student.

One popular way of providing differentiation at the early childhood or elementary school level is through the **project approach**, which entails an in-depth investigation of a real-world topic worthy of children's attention and effort. The project approach uses a set of teaching strategies to guide children through their investigation. The project may involve a whole class or a subgroup of students.

Phase one of the project approach starts with an opening event (story, video, unusual object) designed to capture the students' attention. The teacher then gets the children to map out what they already know about the event and generate questions that they would like to investigate during the project.

In phase two, children participate in some type of field trip to investigate the topic and to try to answer their questions. A debriefing takes place after the field trip, and sometimes an outside expert is invited to share his or her knowledge about the topic.

In phase three, a culminating event takes place, to which parents, other classes, and other interested parties may be invited. Children also have the opportunity to personalize their knowledge through differentiated imaginative activities such as dramatic renditions or story writing.

Flipped Classroom

The **flipped classroom** is a model of teaching in which the typical lecture and the homework elements of a course are reversed. Students view short video lectures at home so in-class time can be spent in discussion, projects, and exercises. Teachers either prepare the video lecture themselves, or find online material that explains

Up CLOSE

Looping (Multiyear Teaching)

Suppose someone offered you an educational innovation with the following benefits: better teacher–student relationships, improved teacher job satisfaction, extra teaching time, a richer curriculum, increased student attendance, increased student development in social skills and a sense of community, and easy implementation at very little cost. Sound good? Proponents of an old but increasingly common practice called **looping** claim these outcomes as being among its benefits.

Looping (also known as "multiyear teaching") is a simple concept in which teachers are promoted with their students to the next grade level and stay with the group for several years, typically two years but sometimes as long as five years. Although not much quantitative research exists on the benefits of looping, qualitative research supports the benefits just mentioned. By keeping the same group of students together with the same teacher, everyone gets to know one another well and feel comfortable in the group. Teachers get to know their students' strengths, weaknesses, and interests. Forging bonds of trust and understanding between teachers

and students is at the heart of looping. Teachers who loop have fewer transitions to make at the beginning of the school year and can introduce curriculum topics right away at the start of the second year. They don't have to spend precious instructional time at the beginning of the new school year to establish classroom routines and expectations. Instead, teachers can spend the gained time exploring curriculum topics in greater detail.

Administrators argue that looping isn't for everyone, so implementation should be on a voluntary basis. Some administrators urge teaming teachers to implement looping. In that way, students can benefit from different teacher strengths, and if a student has a problem with one particular teacher, another teacher can compensate.

Source: "Looping—Discovering the Benefits of Multiyear Teaching," *Education Update* 40, (March 1998): 1, 3–4; *Looping: Supporting Student Learning through Long-Term Relationships*, Themes in Education (Brown University: LAB–Northeast and Islands Regional Educational Laboratory, 1997); Cheryl A. Franklin and Mary S. Holm, "Looping," in *Encyclopedia of Education*, James W. Guthrie, ed., 2nd ed. (New York: Macmillan Reference USA, 2003), 1520–1522.

the content and procedures that the teacher wants students to learn. After viewing the video, students come to class ready to talk about the concepts introduced in the lecture, prepared to ask questions to clarify ideas that they didn't understand, or test themselves in applying knowledge. In class, teachers then serve as advisers or coaches, encouraging students in individual inquiry or collaborative effort.

In the flipped classroom, teachers give up their traditional role as "sage on the stage," in favor of a more collaborative and cooperative role. Flipped classrooms require extra effort on the part of the teacher to record the short video lectures in advance. Students who may be used to a passive role as the teacher presents new material in class now find themselves bearing more responsibility for their own learning. The flipped classroom shifts priorities from merely covering the material to working toward mastery of it.

Pause *and* Reflect

Have you had personal experience with any of the instructional approaches described in this section? If so, were they positive or negative? What made them so?

5-5 Current Curriculum Controversies

Given the highly pluralistic society and many different educational philosophies represented in the United States today, it is little wonder that the questions of how and what schools should teach generate much controversy and debate. In this section, we briefly touch on two of the most highly charged curriculum issues: the question of whether the curriculum should strive to promote American unity or to recognize the diversity of the nation, and the issue of placing students in different "tracks" of study.

5-5a CORE VERSUS MULTICULTURAL CURRICULUM

American schools have traditionally played a central role in instilling the ideas and attitudes that maintain our pluralistic society as "one nation." They have helped weave the many ethnic and religious strands together to make a seamless national garment—at least that's the theory. Questions are now being raised about whether schools today provide a shared understanding of our culture, history, and traditions. Does the current curriculum of U.S. schools reflect our national diversity to the exclusion of our national unity? Or is the reverse true?

Proponents of a **multicultural curriculum** argue that minority students, whose representation in U.S. public schools exceeds 50 percent and is increasing every year, experience a Eurocentric (i.e., Europe-centered) curriculum that gives short shrift to the literary and historical contributions made by people from other parts of the world and to minorities within the United States. As a result, the proponents of multiculturalism argue, youngsters of color see the schools' curricula as being less relevant to them—and certainly not reflective of their own cultures or backgrounds. Some multicultural advocates take the position that the current school curriculum

> *Humanity's survival does not depend on reducing differences to a common identity, but on learning to live creatively with differences.*
>
> **—ANONYMOUS**

needs to be broadened to better reflect the contributions of people of color. Cultural pluralism, as a fact of our society, needs to be a fact of our school curriculum, they assert. (See Chapter 3, "Who Are Today's Students in a Diverse Society?," for more on multicultural education and cultural pluralism.)

A more extreme position is taken by those who demand that the whole curriculum be oriented to a particular ethnicity. For example, some advocates of an Afrocentric curriculum claim that African American schoolchildren can learn effectively only in an environment that recognizes and amplifies their African heritage. The theory is that if students learn of the accomplishments of those who share their ethnic identities, their self-esteem will improve, which will in turn promote learning. When schools emphasize the achievements of African cultures, especially ancient Egyptian culture, and of people of African descent, students will have a greater sense of pride and be more motivated to learn, thus raising their test scores. Although they were more popular in the 1990s, Afrocentric curricula are still being used in some large-city school districts.

In contrast, proponents of a **core curriculum**—that is, a course of study every student would be required to take—argue that ever since the 1970s, schools have focused on celebrating national diversity and pluralism but have failed to help students develop a shared national identity and common cultural framework. As described in Chapter 9, "What Are the Philosophical Foundations of American Education?," some advocates of a core curriculum, such as Mortimer Adler,[24] have promoted the great literary works that have endured over the years as the basic elements of a core curriculum.

E. D. Hirsch, Jr., also endorses education based on the great literary works, but goes beyond them in his push for **cultural literacy** (now called **core knowledge**).[25] Hirsch sees a culturally literate person as someone who is aware of the central ideas, stories, scientific knowledge, events, and personalities of a culture. Cultural literacy is important, says Hirsch, because authors and speakers make allusions and references in their writing and speaking, assuming that the audience understands these references. If a person doesn't understand the reference, he or she will miss the point and not understand the message. If an author writes, for example, of the "Midas touch," and the reader doesn't know the story of King Midas, then the point is lost and the knowledge meaningless.

Hirsch does not restrict his idea of a core curriculum to the great works of "dead white males," a criticism leveled at many traditional core curricula; rather, he sees American culture as incorporating the contributions of many ethnicities and subcultures. Hirsch believes that privileged youth gain much of their cultural literacy at home. Unfortunately, many poor, minority, and immigrant children do not receive cultural literacy at home, so it is especially important that they receive it in school. If they do not, Hirsch argues, poor children and the increasing numbers of immigrant children will not learn those aspects of our common heritage that are necessary to succeed in American society. Hirsch and his colleagues, through the Core Knowledge Foundation, have developed grade-by-grade guidelines for a core knowledge sequence for grades K–8, as well as a series of books entitled *What Your First Grader Needs to Know* (or second grader, third grader, etc.). During the 2016–2017 school year, there were 770 schools (ranging from preschool through eighth grade) in 45 states and the District of Columbia using all or part of the *Core Knowledge Sequence.*[26]

In a society as large and pluralistic as the United States, many philosophies and notions of school purpose have committed supporters. How can the schools incorporate in their curricula such highly divergent ideas of what a school should do? If a certain philosophy is dominant within a given community, the curriculum of that community's schools is likely to reflect that set of beliefs, and those who don't agree will remain dissatisfied. Some communities are responding to the diverse philosophical conceptions of the curriculum by providing choices among alternative schools, each with a different curricular emphasis. The debate between those who advocate a common curriculum to ensure that all students learn what society has determined and those who favor state, local, and individual choice in what is learned will likely continue indefinitely. The adoption of the CCSS in English language arts and mathematics would seem to indicate that the pendulum is swinging toward a common curriculum.

5-5b TRACKING

The curriculum that a student receives is influenced by many factors, including aspirations for further schooling, academic ability, motivation, and vocational interests. Based on these and other factors, students are often sorted by ability and placed into academic program *tracks* that determine what courses they take; this process is called **tracking**. The track in which a student is placed can open or close future academic and vocational options. The three most common tracks are academic (stressing the traditional subjects of English, science, mathematics, and foreign languages), general (allowing more electives and less rigorous versions of the traditional subjects), and career and technical (preparing students for the world of work with a combination of academic and job-related courses). Each track has variations in courses required and different standards for student achievement. Within the academic track, further options exist, including advanced placement (AP), International Baccalaureate, and honors courses.

(T) F

Research studies indicate that the practice of tracking students into different ability-level groups is detrimental to low-ability students.

During the 1970s and 1980s, tracking came under attack. Several prominent educational researchers produced studies showing that students placed in the lower tracks received an inferior curriculum and less stimulating instruction than students in the academic tracks. Studies also showed that poor and minority students were disproportionately placed in the lower tracks, where they had less qualified teachers, less rigorous curricula, and poorer instruction than students in the upper tracks.[27] *Tracking* became a dirty word, and detracking efforts ensued.

Other educational studies found conflicting evidence about the detracking movement itself. Although detracking does help the educational performance of low-achieving students, high-achieving students are hurt academically by elimination of tracking.[28] Parents of these high-achieving students often exert considerable pressure to ensure that their children have access to honors and AP classes, resisting efforts to detrack the schools. Tracking proponents argue that it is easier to teach relatively homogeneous classes, and unrealistic to expect everyone to master the same curriculum. They say students feel more comfortable and learn better when they're grouped with peers of similar abilities. And they say tracking enables teachers to tailor instruction to the needs of respective groups of students. One study of Massachusetts middle schools found that more top scorers in mathematics came from tracked schools than from detracked schools.[29] Furthermore, teachers who teach the high-track students often resist efforts to detrack because they enjoy the intellectual challenge and prestige that come from teaching these students. The general sense is that tracking benefits high-ability students but hurts low-ability students, whereas the reverse is true of detracking.

Pause *and* Reflect

1. Have the curricula you experienced tended to be more like the multicultural curriculum or the core curriculum described in this chapter? What were the strengths and weaknesses of the curricula you were taught?
2. Where do you stand on the tracking issue? Has your own educational background included tracking? How does your background affect where you stand on this issue?

5-6 Is the Existing Curriculum Relevant to Today's Society?

> *One looks back with appreciation to the brilliant teachers, but with gratitude to those who touched our human feeling. The curriculum is so much necessary raw material, but warmth is the vital element for the growing plant and for the soul of the child.*
>
> —CARL JUNG (1875–1961), psychologist

Today, the world community is confronted with staggering problems. There are over 7.8 billion people on our globe, and forecasters project that the world population will reach 10 billion by 2050. Those people will need food, shelter, and an education that will allow them to lead fulfilled lives. The twentieth century saw great advances in manufacturing, agriculture, technology, and the growth of information, but these advances did not come without costs. Acid rain, for example, polluted our vegetation, wildlife, and the very bodies of millions of people. Together, the United States and the rest of the world need to stop the systemic despoiling of our planet. Diseases such as AIDS and COVID-19 have weakened whole continents. Weaponry, such as nuclear devices and improvised explosive devices, daily threaten the world's peace and progress. Religious fanaticism, hunger, and poverty have bred a desperate terrorism in many corners of the world. It is no overstatement to say that we are in a race for global survival.

Schools and teachers will play a vital role in determining the outcome of this race. In Chapter 2, "What Is a School and What Is It For?," we described the curriculum as a social bet. The stakes of that bet are high. In fact, the most basic function of all education is to increase the survival chances of the human community.

Before anyone can determine whether a particular curriculum is relevant to today's urgent needs, some difficult issues must be addressed. In Chapter 2, "What Is a School and What Is It For?," we discuss the purposes of schools and different models of schooling, particularly the school as a transmitter of culture and the school as an agent of social reconstruction. In Chapter 9, "What Are the Philosophical Foundations of American Education?," we discuss four schools of educational philosophy: perennialism, progressivism, essentialism, and romanticism. In judging curriculum relevance, all of these matters come into play because the relevance of a curriculum strongly depends on one's basic beliefs about what people need and what is most worth knowing.

What you consider to be a relevant curriculum ultimately depends on your philosophical position. Conflicting trends have emerged in relation to the academic curriculum, each representing a different philosophy. For example, if

Pause *and* Reflect

1. In the current curricular controversies, who do you believe are the radicals and who the traditionalists? Why?
2. Which goals and knowledge do you believe are most relevant or important for schools to include in their curricula? Why?

one considers the school's primary objective to be the intellectual development of students, any curriculum that does not emphasize the mastery of certain subject matter and the training of the mind will be judged as irrelevant or wrongheaded. Conversely, if one believes the school should emphasize the development of the "whole child"—that is, the entirety of the child's emotional, social, and intellectual growth—a curriculum devoted exclusively to English, history, the sciences, mathematics, and foreign languages will be considered inappropriate for many students and thus inadequate. Those who take the view that education must equip students with necessary work and survival skills may consider a flexible curriculum that includes career and technical courses to be most relevant. "The Saber-Tooth Curriculum" (see the "Up Close" feature of that name) uses a humorous approach to demarcate the conflicts among different educational approaches.

Up CLOSE

The Saber-Tooth Curriculum

In his classic satire on curriculum irrelevance, Harold Benjamin (writing under the pseudonym J. Abner Peddiwell) describes how the first school curriculum was developed in the Stone Age. The earliest theorist, according to Benjamin's book, was a man named New-Fist, who hit on the idea of deliberate, systematic education.

Watching children at play, New-Fist wondered how he could get them to do the things that would gain them more and better food, shelter, clothing, and security. He analyzed the activities that adults engaged in to maintain life and came up with three subjects for his curriculum: (1) fish-grabbing-with-the-bare-hands, (2) woolly-horse-clubbing, and (3) saber-tooth-tiger-scaring-with-fire. Although the children trained in these subjects enjoyed obvious material benefits as a result, some conservative members of the tribe resisted the introduction of these new subjects on religious grounds. But in due time, many people began to train their children in New-Fist's curriculum, and the tribe grew increasingly prosperous and secure.

Then conditions changed. An ice age began, and a glacier crept down over the land. The glacier brought with it dirt and gravel that muddied the creeks, and the waters became so dirty that no one could see the fish well enough to grab them. The melting waters from the approaching ice sheet also made the country wetter, and the little woolly horses migrated to drier land. They were replaced by antelopes, which were so shy and speedy that no one could get close enough to club them. Finally, the new dampness in the air caused the saber-tooth tigers to catch pneumonia and die. And the ferocious glacial bears that came down with the advancing ice sheet were not afraid of fire.

The thinkers of the tribe, descendants of New-Fist, found a way out of the dilemma. One figured out how to catch fish with a net made from vines. Another invented traps for the antelopes, and a third discovered how to dig pits to catch the bears.

Some thoughtful people began to wonder why these new activities couldn't be taught in the schools. But the elders who controlled the schools claimed that the new skills did not qualify as *education*—they were merely a matter of *training*. Besides, the curriculum was too full of the standard cultural subjects—fish-grabbing, horse-clubbing, and tiger-scaring—to admit new ones. When some radicals argued that the traditional subjects were foolish, the elders said that they taught fish-grabbing not to catch fish but to develop agility, horse-clubbing to develop strength, and tiger-scaring to develop courage. "The essence of true education is timelessness," they announced. "It is something that endures through changing conditions like a solid rock standing squarely and firmly in the middle of a raging torrent. You must know that there are some eternal verities and the saber-tooth curriculum is one of them!" (pp. 43–44).

The Saber-Tooth Curriculum was written in 1939, but its continuing applicability seems to be one of the "eternal verities."

Source: J. Abner Peddiwell (Harold Benjamin), *The Saber-Tooth Curriculum.* (*Note:* One chapter of this book is reproduced in *Kaleidoscope: Readings in Education,* the companion volume to this text.)

OUR FINAL WORD

The rather innocuous word *curriculum* and the simple question "What is taught?" contain within them nothing less than the keys to our future. Inevitably, schools will have a curriculum and students will learn it, but the actual *stuff* of the curriculum and the ways in which students are encouraged to learn it constitute the key issue. Which knowledge from our past should be represented? Which deposits in our vast storehouse of scientific and cultural knowledge will they need? Which learnings from our moral heritage will they need to guide themselves and the nation to make the right choices? Which form of classroom and school life will encourage the habits of heart and mind that students will need to take up and meet the challenges they face in the world?

Our collective response will lead to either a prosperous and noble future or a future filled with disappointment and decline. What we select for students to learn in our schools will have a profound effect on their individual futures and on the future of our nation. Indeed, given the power and influence of the United States, the impact of our choices will be global.

What does this have to do with you as a future teacher? Plenty! What should be taught? What do students need to know? These questions are, and will continue to be, debated globally at the highest levels of governments, and here in the United States at national, state, and local school board levels. The people who bring the curriculum into the classroom—who make thousands of decisions every week about every detail of what and how to teach—are the teachers. Curriculum questions, for this reason, are the special responsibility of teachers, of those who have dedicated their lives to the education of the youth. No small responsibility!

WHY TEACH? YOUR FINAL WORD

1. In your opinion, has the standards movement improved or weakened the quality of education that most U.S. students receive? Why do you think so?

2. Are you decided or undecided as to the subject matter and/or grade levels that you want to teach? If undecided, what can you do to help make your decision?

3. After watching either the elementary or high school Video Cases on cooperative learning, what impressions are you left with regarding this teaching technique? Are you likely to use cooperative learning in your teaching? Why or why not?

KEY TERMS

civic learning (civic education) (125)
Common Core State Standards (118)
content standards (117)
cooperative learning (138)
core curriculum (147)
critical thinking (141)
cultural literacy (core knowledge) (147)
curriculum (116)
differentiated instruction (143)
flipped classroom (145)
interdisciplinary (integrated) curriculum (137)
looping (145)

multicultural curriculum (146)
phonics (122)
Program for International Student Assessment (PISA) (132)
problem solving (141)
project approach (145)
subject-matter curriculum (117)
Trends in International Mathematics and Science Study (TIMSS) (131)
tracking (148)
whole language approach (122)
writing across the curriculum (142)

FOR FURTHER INFORMATION

Web Resources

American Council on the Teaching of Foreign Languages

An executive summary of the national standards for foreign languages can be found at this website. Available at www.actfl.org/sites/default/files/publications/standards/World-ReadinessStandardsforLearningLanguages.pdf.

Council for Exceptional Children (Special Education and Gifted Education)

This site contains many resources for teaching students with disabilities. Available at www.cec.sped.org/.

Mid-Continent Research for Education and Learning

Originally one of 10 regional educational laboratories funded by the federal government, this lab has a great set of materials in different subject areas, as well as research reports on effective practice. The website also offers links to other useful sites.

The following journals and websites contain many interesting and helpful items for teachers in the respective subject-matter fields. To find both national and state-by-state content standards in the various subject-matter fields, go to *Education World* at **www.education-world.com/standards/**.

Art: *Art Education, Arts and Activities, School Arts;* ArtsEdge at the Kennedy Center website. **Career and technical education:** *Industrial Education, Journal of Home Economics; Business Education Forum; Business Education Review;* Association for Career and Technical Education.

Elementary and early childhood: *Young Children, Teaching Young Children;* National Association for the Education of Young Children.

English: *English Journal;* National Council of Teachers of English (includes national standards in English and language arts).

Foreign languages: *Modern Language Journal, Foreign Language Annals;* American Council on the Teaching of Foreign Languages.

Mathematics: *The Mathematics Teacher;* National Council of Teachers of Mathematics (includes national standards in mathematics); Math Forum website, particularly "Ask Dr. Math."

Music: *Music Educators' Journal;* MENC: The National Association for Music Education (includes a section for future teachers).

Physical education: *Journal of Health, Physical Education and Recreation;* American Alliance for Health, Physical Education, Recreation and Dance website (includes national standards in physical education).

Reading and language arts: *Language Arts, The Reading Teacher;* The Children's Literature Web Guide; and the International Reading Association.

Science: *The Science Teacher, School Science and Mathematics;* National Science Teachers Association; Next Generation Science Standards.

Social studies: *Social Studies, Social Education;* National Council for the Social Studies (includes national standards in social studies).

Print Resources

Carol Ann Tomlinson and Tonya Moon, *Assessment and Student Success in a Differentiated Classroom* (Alexandria, VA: ASCD, 2013).

A practical book that examines essential elements of differentiation, formative and summative assessment, and grading issues.

Robyn M. Gillies, *Cooperative Learning: Integrating Theory and Practice* (Thousand Oaks, CA: Sage, 2007).

This text highlights the strategies teachers can use to challenge student thinking and scaffold their learning, as well as the strategies students can be taught to promote discourse, problem solving, and learning during cooperative learning. It also situates cooperative learning within the climate of the No Child Left Behind legislation and high-stakes testing.

E. D. Hirsch, Jr., *The Knowledge Deficit: Closing the Shocking Education Gap for American Children* (Boston: Houghton Mifflin, 2007).

Hirsch proposes ways to close the knowledge gap between poor children and those from more privileged backgrounds by focusing on a content-rich curriculum. (See the Core Knowledge Foundation website at **www.coreknowledge.org**.)

Allan C. Ornstein, Edward F. Pajak, and Stacey B. Ornstein, *Contemporary Issues in Curriculum*, 6th ed. (New York: Pearson, 2015).

A compilation of articles, written by different authors, that addresses the emerging trends and controversial issues in elementary and secondary curricula.

What Makes a Teacher Effective?

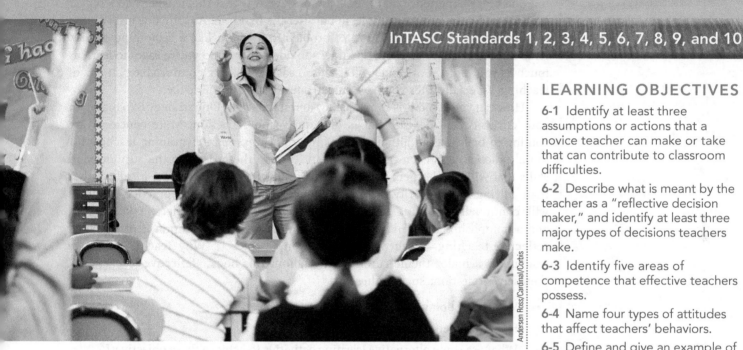

InTASC Standards 1, 2, 3, 4, 5, 6, 7, 8, 9, and 10

Andersen Ross/Cardinal/Corbis

LEARNING OBJECTIVES

6-1 Identify at least three assumptions or actions that a novice teacher can make or take that can contribute to classroom difficulties.

6-2 Describe what is meant by the teacher as a "reflective decision maker," and identify at least three major types of decisions teachers make.

6-3 Identify five areas of competence that effective teachers possess.

6-4 Name four types of attitudes that affect teachers' behaviors.

6-5 Define and give an example of "pedagogical content knowledge" in your own subject field.

6-6 Give an example of an educational theory that can be used to solve a practical problem in the classroom.

6-7 Define the term *personal practical knowledge*, and give an example.

6-8 Identify at least five classroom teaching skills that you believe essential for teaching effectiveness.

Truth or Fiction?

T F   The most important aspect of a teacher's effectiveness is his or her personality.

T F   A teacher's expectation that all students can succeed greatly affects students' achievement.

T F   Efficient teachers can provide students with as much as 180 hours a year more of engaged learning time than inefficient teachers.

T F   A primary difference between novice and expert teachers is the experts' ability to gather information in a short time and use it in multiple ways.

T F   Elementary and secondary school teachers plan their lessons in a similar fashion.

Effective teaching is much more than an intuitive process. Teachers must continually make decisions and act on those decisions. To do this effectively, teachers must have *knowledge*—both theoretical knowledge about learning and human behavior and specific knowledge about the subject matter to be taught. Teachers must also demonstrate a repertoire of teaching *skills* that are believed to facilitate student learning, and must display *attitudes* that foster learning and genuine human relationships.

We once knew a teacher who was described as having not 20 years of experience but one year's experience 20 times. The message was that this teacher had stopped growing and developing as a professional after the first year. As someone just starting in your teaching career, this kind of problem may seem like a remote possibility. After all, there's so much that you know you don't know, and you're eager to learn as much as you can. Unfortunately, it is all too easy to fall into comfortable patterns of teaching, especially after you have gained a few years of experience.

How can you avoid this complacency and stagnation? One strategy is to maintain your curiosity and develop habits of inquiry and reflection. More educators are coming to believe that, although it is important to prepare beginning teachers for initial practice, it is even more important to help them develop the attitudes and skills that will enable them to become lifelong students of teaching. Ideally, rather than relying on authority, impulse, or unexamined previous practice, teachers will continually examine and evaluate their attitudes, practices, effectiveness, and accomplishments. This process of examination and evaluation is often called **reflective teaching**, which was introduced in Chapter 1, "Why Teach?" Reflective teaching is a major theme running throughout this book. Reflective teachers ask themselves questions such as these:

- "What am I doing and why?"
- "How can I better meet my students' needs?"
- "What are some alternative learning activities to achieve these objectives?"
- "How could I have encouraged more involvement or learning on the part of the students?"

Even when lessons go well, reflective teachers analyze the lesson to determine what went well and why, and how else things might have been done.

Developing the habits of inquiry and reflection should begin now, in your teacher education program. Your experiences with schools, teachers, and students along this path will give you many opportunities to reflect on what has occurred. You can use journal writing, observation instruments, simulations, or video recording to help you examine teaching, learning, and the contexts in which they occur. Comparing your perspectives with those of classmates, professors, and school personnel will broaden your interpretations and give you new insights. As you reflect on your experiences, you will come to distrust simplistic answers and explanations. Nuances and subtleties will start to become clear, and situations that once seemed simple will reveal their complexities. Viewing the Video Cases associated with this textbook and considering carefully the actions of the teachers can bring you additional insights into what constitutes effective teaching.

As you reflect, you are likely to encounter and think about moral and ethical issues. Teachers make moral and ethical decisions every day when they decide how they will treat students and others, and when they elect to create a classroom climate that fosters trust, safety, and cooperation. When they select certain examples from history or literature for study, teachers also make ethical decisions. Clearly, you cannot teach without making ethical decisions. Chapter 8, "What Are the Ethical

The rapport that effective teachers establish with their students often goes beyond the classroom learning environment.

Tom Stewart/Corbis/Getty Images

The mediocre teacher tells. The good teacher explains. The superior teacher demonstrates. The great teacher inspires.

—WILLIAM ARTHUR WARD (1921–1994),
American author, pastor, and teacher

and Legal Issues Facing Teachers?," discusses this topic in greater detail, but we hope you will study and reflect on the cases we present throughout this book, as well as the Video Cases, that deal with moral or ethical issues. By practicing reflective teaching, you will grow and develop as an effective, professional teacher.

In the following case study of a new teacher who faces problems that many classroom veterans will find familiar, we take a critical look at the many teaching decisions that she had to make.

6-1 Carol Landis: A Case of Classroom Decision Making

As an example of how ordinary teaching situations can lead to useful reflection about effective teaching, consider the case of Carol Landis. Carol is beginning her first year of teaching. She prepared to be a high school social studies teacher, graduated, and accepted a job in her own community, a small city in the Northwest. Most of her students come from solidly blue-collar, working-class backgrounds.

Carol has been assigned three periods of world geography and two periods of American history. We join her as she prepares the first lesson of a new unit in world geography.

Carol plans to require her ninth graders to work in groups to prepare panel discussions about a country of their choice. She wants the groups to research the relationships among the geography, political history, and culture of a country and share what they find in panel discussions with the rest of the class. Carol sets two goals for her students: that they work together in groups and that they make effective oral presentations of their research.

When planning how to present the assignment to her classes, Carol has many questions. Do these students know how to use the library? If not, will she need to provide directions for using reference materials? Maybe the librarian has already taken care of this step, and Carol's students will just need a review. Do these students know what "culture" means or understand general concepts that will help them look for relationships among culture, history, and geography? What background information do they need before they start researching a specific country? Also, do these students know how to work in groups? Have they ever participated in a panel discussion? In planning how to help her students complete this assignment, Carol bases her decisions on what she thinks she knows about them as learners.

Although Carol has already planned this assignment to meet her state's curriculum standards in social studies, she is concerned about whether the books in her room and the library will provide the information her students need. Which other resources are available? Carol knows that other teachers have back issues of *National Geographic*, for example. Maybe she could help students use the Internet in ways that tie together the geography, political history, and culture for their respective countries.

In addition to the panel discussions, Carol has considered having each student submit a written report. For this first research assignment, however, she decides that an oral presentation by the group is appropriate. Later, she will work with the classes on report writing. In the beginning, she wants her students to enjoy her classes, feel a part of a group, and get to know one another. Carol prefers listening to her students over grading written reports anyway, so this assignment fits her style of teaching.

Despite her planning, when Carol reflects on her second-period class after the first day of library research, she wonders what went wrong. One group argued the whole period and never did select a country. Maybe she should have assigned groups and not let students choose their own partners. She tried to ignore this group, believing they should work out their own differences and come to a group decision. But what if they never work together? She noticed that another group was completely dominated by one of the top students. He decided which country they would research, assigned the topics, and told the others where to look for information. When Carol urged the other members to share equally in the group decisions, they asserted, "Tom always gets A's. We don't mind if he tells us what to do." Carol didn't know how to respond to their concern for grades without insulting Tom, so she said nothing.

Later in the period, Tom asked her which religion predominated in Indonesia. Carol wasn't sure but was afraid to admit her lack of information, so she told him, "Just look it up." Tom responded, "So you don't know either?" Carol testily told Tom that she was not his personal encyclopedia. Now she wonders if she overreacted. Maybe she should have admitted she didn't know. Was Tom challenging her authority, or was he just reacting to the sharp tone in her order to look it up? Did she turn Tom and his group against her?

Carol also wonders whether the other groups worked productively. She spent so much time watching the arguing group and Tom's group that she didn't have time to notice whether the chatter from the other groups was work or play. Maybe it didn't hurt to let the other groups have some fun today, anyway. She can direct her attention to them tomorrow.

There is so much to watch and monitor when students work in groups, Carol realizes. Many questions arise, such as "Where do I find this?" "Mr. Shaw won't lend me his magazines—what do I do now?" "This library stinks. Why do we have to do this assignment anyway?" and even "Miss Landis, what did you do this weekend?" Carol wonders if she will ever learn to field all her students' questions and comments and to distinguish the words on the surface from the real messages. She also worries about what to do about Ron, who has started reading a novel about life in Siberian concentration camps. Carol thinks it is the only book she has ever seen him read—but it won't help his group do their project on Kenya.

Maybe this assignment wasn't such a good idea in the first place, Carol thinks, or maybe she just wasn't up to working with her classes in groups. The stares from the librarian and the study hall teacher indicated that they didn't think she could handle her classes, and Carol hasn't even thought about how she will grade her students' panel discussions. Just thinking about it all exhausts her. How will she ever get through another day with that second-period class?

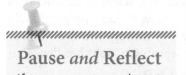

Pause *and* Reflect

If you were to teach the lesson Carol had planned, what changes would you make and why?

6-2 Teachers as Reflective Decision Makers

Indecision becomes decision with time.

—AUTHOR UNKNOWN

We present Carol's case to illustrate that a teacher's role can be described as one of a *reflective decision maker*. Indeed, some educational researchers have identified skill in decision making as the most important teaching skill. Some decisions are made as teachers quietly deliberate curricular and instructional goals; many more must be made almost instantaneously as teachers and students interact. Let's look at some of the particular decisions that Carol made or will make, dividing them into three basic stages: planning, implementing, and evaluating.

6-2a PLANNING DECISIONS

Carol wants her students to understand the relationships among geography, history, and culture. But what exactly does she want them to know about these relationships? She must decide the particular kinds of understanding she wants her students to achieve, and this decision affects her choice of teaching techniques.

From a variety of possible techniques, she has chosen independent group work and has also decided that a panel discussion will provide evidence of her students' learning. These decisions reflect Carol's personal preferences, her goals for her students' learning, and her skills in methods of evaluating their learning. In addition, her decisions are based on a series of judgments about her students' ability to do research, work in groups, and present panel discussions, as well as on judgments about how long they will need to work together and which resources they will need. Carol might have also made some plans for what to do in case her judgments turned out to be wrong and she needed to adapt her lesson.

6-2b IMPLEMENTING DECISIONS

Carol, like most teachers, must make many of her decisions almost instantly, as she adapts her teaching to changing classroom conditions. As Carol teaches this lesson or series of lessons, she has to decide when and how to intervene with some of her groups, whether to allow Ron to continue reading a novel, and how to respond to students' questions.

6-2c EVALUATING DECISIONS

After the first day's library work, Carol reflects on her interactions with the students, facing decisions about how she has to adjust her strategies for the next day. As the groups continue to work, she will also face decisions about how to evaluate the impact of her planning and instruction on her students' learning.

In each of these planning, implementing, and evaluating stages of instructional decision making, Carol chooses among alternative concepts her students could learn, approaches to help them learn the concepts, ways to manage the classroom to encourage their learning, and ways to measure their learning. Could her decisions improve with more adequate knowledge, skills, and attitudes?

Factors Influencing Instructional Decisions

Teachers do not make instructional decisions in a vacuum; many factors influence the process. First and foremost are the students. Knowing and understanding your students and their backgrounds is imperative if your decisions are to be effective. Students differ in many ways, all of which affect how they learn:

Poverty. Some students come from poverty backgrounds, which can influence their readiness to learn. Many students from poverty backgrounds are more likely to suffer from the effects of poor nutrition and inadequate health care, which can affect their abilities to attend school regularly, concentrate on learning, and do homework. School also tends to be oriented more toward serving middle-class children. Making the curriculum and instructional experiences germane to poor children constitutes a major challenge that our schools and teachers must meet.

Racial, ethnic, and cultural diversity. As our schools become more diverse— currently, 51 percent of school-age children are minorities—many students' native language will not be English, presenting a serious challenge to schools and teachers. (See Chapter 3, "Who Are Today's Students in a Diverse Society?," for more on this issue.)

Gender. Students' gender influences how we think of them and what we expect of them. Treating boys and girls equitably as individuals rather than as stereotypes is a challenge for both male and female teachers.

Special needs. You will undoubtedly have children with special needs in your classroom. Differentiating instruction to meet both their needs and the needs of your other students will be a challenge. (See Chapter 3, "Who Are Today's Students in a Diverse Society?," for more on this issue.)

Other factors. Students differ in terms of their needs for belonging, safety, and self-esteem. Children coming from secure home situations will likely have different needs than children who have not had this kind of stability. Your students will all have different abilities, achievements, and learning styles, and your challenge will be to provide a variety of learning experiences to accommodate the diversity that your students will bring to your classroom.

6-3 Competencies Needed for Effective Decision Making

Next, we explore the areas of competence that help teachers make more effective decisions. Many educators believe that to be effective decision makers, elementary and secondary school teachers must have attitudes, knowledge, and skills essential to the teaching profession. Teachers should ask themselves not only, "What am I going to teach?," but also "What should my students be learning?," "How can I help them learn it?," and "Why is it important?" To answer these questions, teachers must be familiar with children and their developmental stages. They must know something about events occurring outside the classroom and the expectations that the society has for its young. In addition, teachers must have enough command of the subject

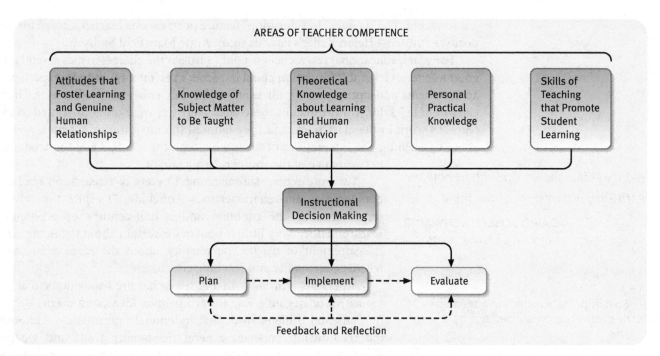

FIGURE 6.1 Relationship of Teacher-Competence Areas to Process of Instructional Decision Making

Source: James M. Cooper, ed., "The Teacher as a Reflective Decision Maker," in *Classroom Teaching Skills,* 10th ed. Copyright © 2014 by Wadsworth Cengage Learning Company. Adapted and reprinted with permission.

they teach to be able to distinguish what is peripheral from what is central. They must have a philosophy of education that guides them in their role as teacher, and they must know how human beings learn and how to create environments that promote learning.

What are the specialized skills and attributes of the effective instructional decision maker? We consider five areas of competence to be essential for teachers:

1. Attitudes that foster learning and genuine human relationships
2. Knowledge of the subject matter to be taught
3. Theoretical knowledge about learning and human behavior
4. Personal practical knowledge
5. Skills of teaching that promote student learning

Teachers draw on their competence in these five areas to inform the many decisions they make both as they plan instruction and as they spontaneously interact with the students in their classes. Figure 6.1 indicates the relationship of these areas of competence to the process of instructional decision making. Next, we examine these areas of competence, now and then referring to the instructional decisions that Carol made and the attitudes, knowledge, and skills influencing her decisions.

6-4 What Attitudes Do Effective Teachers Possess?

Many people believe that a teacher's personality is the most critical factor in successful teaching. If teachers have warmth, empathy, sensitivity, enthusiasm, and humor, they are much more likely to be successful than if they lack these characteristics. In fact, many people argue that without these attributes, an individual is unlikely to be a good teacher. The "Leaders in Education" feature portrays one teacher known for her positive attitude—Helen Keller's famous tutor, Anne Mansfield Sullivan.

For years, educational researchers sought to isolate the characteristics essential to good teachers. General information about a teacher's personality, attitude, experience, achievement, and aptitude were all examined in an effort to predict a teacher's classroom behavior. Unfortunately, these characteristics were often unrelated to the teacher's work in the classroom, and they ignored the most important measures of effective teaching: the interactions of the teacher with the learners and the academic performance of the students being taught.

> *How we think shows through in how we act. Attitudes are mirrors of the mind.*
>
> **—DAVID JOSEPH SCHWARTZ,**
> authority on human motivation

Two researchers, summarizing 50 years of research on teachers' personalities and characteristics, conclude, "Despite the critical importance of the problem and a half-century of prodigious research effort, very little is known for certain about the nature and measurement of teacher personality, about the relation between teacher personality and teaching effectiveness."[1]

T (F)
The most important aspect of a teacher's effectiveness is his or her personality.

A person's *attitudes*—that is, his or her predispositions to act in a positive or negative way toward people, ideas, and events—are a fundamental dimension of that individual's personality. Although the relationship between general personality traits and teacher effectiveness has proven elusive, almost all educators are convinced of the importance of teacher attitudes in the teaching process. Attitudes have a direct but often unrecognized effect on our behavior in that they determine the ways we view ourselves and interact with others.

We believe four major categories of attitudes affect teaching behavior: (1) the teacher's attitude toward self, (2) the teacher's attitude toward children and the relationship between self and children, (3) the teacher's attitudes toward peers and pupils' parents, and (4) the teacher's attitude toward the subject matter.

6-4a TEACHERS' ATTITUDES TOWARD THEMSELVES: SELF-UNDERSTANDING

There is evidence from psychology that people who deny or cannot cope with their own emotions are likely to be incapable of respecting and coping with the feelings of others. If teachers are to understand and sympathize with their students' feelings, they must recognize and understand their own feelings. Many colleges are responding to this need by including counseling sessions, reflective thinking, and awareness experiences as part of their teacher education programs. These experiences emphasize introspection, self-evaluation, and feedback from other participants. The goal is to help prospective teachers learn more about themselves, their attitudes, and how other people perceive them.

6-4b TEACHERS' ATTITUDES TOWARD CHILDREN

In general, a teacher's expectation that *all* students can succeed seems to make a difference in students' achievement. As a teacher, you need to believe that all of your students are capable of high academic achievement, and adjust your beliefs and behavior based on the needs, abilities, and aspirations of each individual student.

(T) F
A teacher's expectation that all students can succeed greatly affects students' achievement.

Most teachers occasionally harbor attitudes or feelings toward some of their students that are detrimental to being an effective teacher. Strong likes and dislikes of particular pupils, biases toward or against particular ethnic groups, low learning expectations for

LEADERS in Education

Anne Mansfield Sullivan (1866–1936)

The proof is in the pupil. In this case, Helen Keller, a blind and deaf pupil, was a terror. Wily and mean, Helen was also animallike. Nevertheless, her teacher, Anne Sullivan, enabled her to become an international celebrity.

Sullivan pioneered the teaching of individuals without sight and without hearing. Today we speak of a *deaf culture*, but this term was not used in the era of Anne Sullivan. "Teacher," as Helen always called her, is credited with making it possible to reach students who were thought to have mental retardation.

The daughter of Irish immigrants, Sullivan was born in Feeding Hills, Massachusetts, on April 14, 1866, and entered the almshouse at age 8 when her mother died and her father abandoned her and her brother. Half blind herself, she went to the Perkins School for the Blind in Boston at age 14, without a toothbrush, hat, or coat; her only possessions were a shirt and stockings tied in a bundle.

At age 21, Sullivan took a job offered by the Keller family in Tuscumbia, Alabama, to teach the Kellers' daughter, Helen. Helen Keller was an angry and frustrated child, but she was not stupid. Sullivan quickly realized this fact and began her assault on Helen's locked mind. Within a month, she had made contact with Helen in the now-famous pump story, immortalized in the drama *The Miracle Worker*. Sullivan finger-spelled words into Helen's hand, each word suiting an action. Finally, Helen, feeling water over her hand, realized the connection between word and object. She had broken the code and realized that everything had a name.

Sullivan's methods were practical. She taught Helen to play through games and exercises, stimulating her to ask the names of the motions. She kept a menagerie of animals for Helen to help her understand movement. She progressed to abstractions like peace and God as soon as her pupil was ready.

Walter Sanders/The LIFE Picture Collection/Getty Images

Sullivan wanted to make Helen as normal as possible, giving her every experience she could. She worked at teaching her to sit, stand, and walk properly. As soon as Helen could distinguish between right and wrong, "Teacher" sent her to bed for misdeeds. Laziness, carelessness, untidiness, and procrastination were dealt with by ingenuity, humor, and light sarcasm.

Helen used the manual alphabet for three years before she began to speak. When Helen was 9, Sullivan was rewarded with the words "I am not dumb now." It was one of the most dramatic achievements in the history of teaching.

Sullivan's great discovery was that a child should not be taught each word separately by a separate definition but instead should be given endless repetition of language he or she does not understand all day long. Sullivan continually spelled words into Helen's hand to mimic the way a hearing child in the cradle absorbs words. This method had never before been put into practice in the education of a deaf child, especially a deaf-blind one.

When Helen attended a school for deaf pupils in New York, Anne Sullivan went along. At Cambridge School and Radcliffe College, Sullivan attended classes, interpreting instruction and looking up words for Helen. She made herself into Helen's eyes and ears, and supplied knowledge to a starving mind as she fired her pupil's drive to study hard. After college, Sullivan accompanied Helen on worldwide lecture tours as Helen became a famous author and personality.

Extraordinarily close, teacher and pupil spent much of their lives together. The name "Teacher" has been enriched by Anne Sullivan's dedicated life, persistent high standards, and creative instruction.

Source: Marilyn Ryan.

children from poverty backgrounds, and biases in favor of or against certain kinds of student behavior—all can reduce teaching effectiveness. Self-awareness of such attitudes toward individual pupils or classes of children is necessary if teachers are to cope with their own feelings and beliefs. If teachers possess empathy for their students and value them as unique individuals, these teachers will be more effective and will derive more satisfaction from their teaching.

If a teacher expects a student or group of students to behave in a certain way, the teacher's attitude may serve as a **self-fulfilling prophecy**[2]—that is, the students may conform to the teacher's low expectations, thus confirming the teacher's original expectations. On the other hand, when teachers hold high expectations for students and communicate these high expectations, students will often act in ways to live up to the teacher's expectations. A teacher's attitude toward and expectation of students are powerful influences on whether or not students learn.

> " *High expectations are the key to everything.*
>
> —SAM WALTON,
> founder of Walmart

6-4c TEACHERS' ATTITUDES TOWARD PEERS AND PUPILS' PARENTS

Teachers do not exist in isolated classrooms. They interact with fellow teachers and administrators and often have sensitive dealings with parents. Sometimes teachers can be effective in dealing with children, but not work well with fellow educators and their students' parents. For example, some teachers may resent people in authority and resist their suggestions for improvement. Other teachers may yield too easily to suggestions from people in authority, only to later feel guilty about complying instead of sticking up for their own convictions. Or some teachers may feel the need to compete with other teachers for administrative or student approval. Many of the comments already made regarding teachers' attitudes toward themselves and children also apply to their attitudes toward peers and parents. Some teachers may harbor feelings of superiority or prejudice toward students' parents. Others simply have little tolerance for people who differ from them in values, cultural background, or economic status, and, as a result, they treat parents with disdain and contempt rather than patience and respect. By contrast, effective teachers—those who work well with colleagues and parents to empower children to achieve—show attitudes of acceptance. In their dealings with other teachers and parents, teachers should be real and genuine, value other people as worthy in their own right, and show empathy.

> " *Treat people as if they were what they ought to be and you help them to become what they are capable of being.*
>
> —JOHANN W. VON GOETHE (1749–1832),
> German poet and philosopher

When parents and teachers respect one another and work together, children are certain to benefit.

iStock.com/SDI Productions

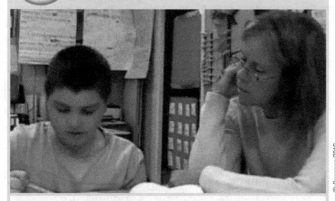

TeachSource Video Case

Elementary Writing Instruction: Process Writing

Watch the video clips, study the artifacts in the case, and reflect on the following questions:

1. In this chapter, we advise teachers to focus on subjects about which they have the most enthusiasm. How have these teachers applied that advice to themselves? How have they applied it to the students they teach?

2. What expectations do these teachers seem to hold for their students?

3. What are some ways that you, as a teacher, can generate similar enthusiasm and high expectations for your students?

6-4d TEACHERS' ATTITUDES TOWARD THE SUBJECT MATTER

The message, in one word, is ENTHUSIASM! Just as students are perceptive in discovering a teacher's attitude toward them, they are also sensitive to a teacher's attitude toward the subject matter. Teachers who are not enthusiastic about what they teach can hardly hope to instill enthusiasm in their pupils. After all, if you don't care about the subject matter, how can you ever hope to motivate your students into learning about it? (The Video Case, *Elementary Writing Instruction: Process Writing,* shows a teacher and a literary specialist who both demonstrate their enthusiasm for writing and their respect for their students.)

Some teachers find it difficult to feel enthusiasm for a curriculum they haven't constructed themselves, don't identify with, or don't want to teach. Unfortunately, as states have adopted learning standards geared toward mandatory testing for students, the latitude that teachers once had to choose content is being greatly curtailed. States expect teachers to teach to the standards, and the high-stakes assessment tests given to students exert considerable pressure on teachers to be certain they "cover the content" contained on the assessments.

If you have to teach something you would rather not, try to develop a positive attitude toward the subject. Enthusiasm is key to teaching success: If a teacher has it, life in the classroom can be exciting; if it is missing, there is little hope that students will learn much of significance.

A good sense of humor goes a long way in establishing teacher–student rapport.

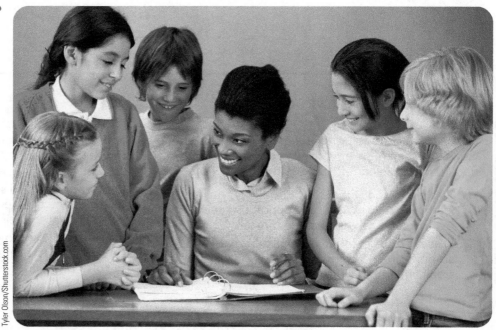

© Cengage 2016

Tyler Olson/Shutterstock.com

Up CLOSE

What Would You Do?

1. You are a woman, a beginning teacher in a ninth-grade English course. As the first semester proceeds, you realize that one of your students, Fred, has a crush on you. He is always volunteering to help you pass out papers, and he lingers after class each day to talk to you. He finds out your home address and comes to visit you one Saturday morning. His actions are becoming obvious to the other students, who are starting to kid him about his infatuation. *What would you do?*

2. You are generally recognized as one of the most popular teachers in your high school. The students look on you as a friend who can be trusted, and you have told them that if they ever have problems, whether school related or personal, they should feel free to come to you. One day, Maryanne, a junior in one of your classes, seeks you out. Close to hysteria, she tells you she is 10 weeks pregnant. You are the first person she has told. She begs you for advice but insists that you not tell her parents. *What would you do?*

3. You are a fourth-grade teacher. Until recently, you have been quite comfortable in your class of 23 children. About three weeks ago,

you had to speak to Debbie. Although she is your brightest student, she was continually talking when you were trying to address the class. Since your conversation, Debbie has been as cool as ice to you, and you recently discovered a nasty drawing in your desk drawer that was supposed to be you. *What would you do?*

4. You are a white teacher in a somewhat racially tense school. There are seven African American students in one of your classes. Because you worry about alienating the African American students and being accused of prejudice, you make special efforts to treat them fairly. One day, three of your white students come to see you and accuse you of coddling the African American students and discriminating against whites. *What would you do?*

5. You teach in a school that uses a letter grading system. You have assigned your students a term paper. You know that one student has spent hours and hours on his report, but its quality is quite poor. The student has already expressed his hope that you will take effort into account when grading the reports. *What would you do?*

Up CLOSE

Principles of Effective Instruction

Educational psychologist, Barak Rosenshine, reviewed research on effective teaching and identified 10 principles of effective instruction.

1. Begin a lesson with a short review of previous learning: Daily review can strengthen previous learning and can lead to fluent recall.

2. Present new material in small steps with student practice after each step: Only present small amounts of new material at any time,

and then assist students as they practice this material.

3. Ask a large amount of questions and check the responses of all students: Questions help students practice new information and connect new material to their prior learning.

4. Provide models: Providing students with models and worked examples can help them learn to solve problems faster.

(Continued)

5. Guide student practice: Successful teachers spend more time guiding students' practice of new material.

6. Check for student understanding: Checking for student understanding at each point can help students learn the material with fewer errors.

7. Obtain a high success rate: It is important for students to achieve a high success rate during classroom instruction.

8. Provide scaffolds for difficult tasks: The teacher provides students with temporary supports and scaffolds to assist them when they learn difficult tasks.

9. Require and monitor independent practice: Students need extensive, successful, independent practice in order for skills and knowledge to become automatic.

10. Engage students in weekly and monthly review: Students need to be involved in extensive practice in order to develop well-connected and automatic knowledge.

Source: Barak Rosenshine, "Principles of Instruction," *American Educator* (Spring 2012): 12–19.

Pause *and* Reflect

1. Can you think of any examples of where a teacher's expectations of you or another student led to a self-fulfilling prophecy? Describe the circumstances.
2. Do you have negative feelings or expectations about any group or type of people? Can you identify the basis of those feelings? Do you want to change them? If so, how might you try?
3. Do you have any concerns about your attitudes toward students' parents, school administrators, or other teachers? If you do, what can you do now to improve your attitudes?
4. Can you think of any ways that you, as a teacher, might be able to work up more enthusiasm for a topic that does not at first seem very interesting?

Enthusiasm is contagious. Be a carrier.

—SUSAN RABIN,
author and communications consultant

6-5 What Subject-Matter Knowledge Do Effective Teachers Need?

Very simply, prospective teachers need to understand the content of the subjects they teach as well as the methods of teaching the specific content. Three important components contribute to a teacher's content knowledge.

First, teachers need to understand the subjects they teach well enough to analyze and convey their elements, logic, possible uses, and social biases—that is, teachers need to understand the structure of the subjects they teach. Second, teachers must understand the content of the school curriculum that pupils are expected to know. Unfortunately, most college courses in the specific disciplines don't prepare prospective teachers to actually teach the knowledge that students are expected to learn. Much of what prospective teachers learn from their study of the academic disciplines is not taught to children and so is not directly applicable to teaching. This is particularly true for elementary school teachers, who are called on to teach content that is rarely taught in universities. For example, a mathematics major who is preparing to teach elementary school may never have occasion to use differential equations or calculus in the content she or he teaches to elementary-age children. Thus, although studying and understanding specific disciplines is crucial, it is not sufficient for effective teaching. Teachers must also study the actual curriculum taught in their school, as well as either the Common Core or state learning standards for the particular grade. Carol Landis, for example, designed her group project so that it would contribute to her students' ability to meet their district's standards in social studies.

A third type of knowledge shown by effective teachers is **pedagogical content knowledge**, the knowledge that bridges content knowledge and pedagogy. Pedagogical content knowledge represents the "blending of content and pedagogy into an understanding of how particular topics, problems, or issues are organized, represented, and adapted to the diverse interests and abilities of learners, and presented for instruction."[3] Skilled teachers draw on the most powerful analogies, illustrations, examples, explanations, and demonstrations to represent and transform the subject so that students can understand it. For example, a physics teacher who possesses pedagogical content knowledge might use the analogy of water flowing through a pipe to explain how electricity flows through a circuit, but he or she would also know the limitations of such an analogy. Pedagogical content knowledge enables teachers to recognize common misunderstandings that students may make in learning new concepts and to know how to overcome those errors in thinking.

Three types of knowledge—discipline content (including the structure of the discipline), curriculum content, and pedagogical content—are, we believe, essential for effective teachers. Did Carol Landis have such knowledge? We suspect not, at least not to the degree that she could communicate information and concepts to her class with the authority and expertise required for effective teaching. In the next section, we examine more closely another area of effective teachers' knowledge: theoretical knowledge about learning and human behavior.

Pause *and* Reflect

1. Which parts of the discipline content you are learning in college do you expect to teach to your own students? Which parts are you likely not to teach to them?
2. Do you recall any teachers from your own schooling who demonstrated especially strong or weak content knowledge? How did they demonstrate their level of knowledge?

6-6 What Theoretical Knowledge Do Effective Teachers Need?

Theoretical knowledge about learning and human behavior equips teachers to draw on concepts from psychology, anthropology, sociology, and related disciplines to interpret the complex reality of the classroom. Teachers who lack a theoretical background will have to interpret classroom events according to commonly held beliefs or common sense—much of which is based on erroneous notions of human behavior.

6-6a THEORIES-IN-USE

Carol Landis operated on the basis of certain ideas that are called *theories-in-use*, which differ from theories in important ways.[4] A theory is an unproved explanation of why something happens the way it does. In its simplest form, a theory is a hypothesis designed to bring generalizable facts, concepts, or scientific laws into systematic connection. By contrast, a theory-in-use is something people have in their heads and apply in their dealings with people and the world. Theories-in-use are often unexamined.

We all have our own theories-in-use, which guide us as we make our way through our daily lives. For example, you may eat certain foods because you have an idea that they have a healthy effect on the body. You may also decide to take a summer job in a public playground, believing that you will get to know children better and that future prospective employers might be pleased or impressed when they discover your experience.

Carol Landis has several theories-in-use. For example, she has the theory-in-use that groups should operate democratically and not be dominated by one student. She also has a theory-in-use that some children will perform better in school than others; as a result, Carol expects certain behavior from certain kinds of students. She also has a classroom management theory-in-use that she should give students some leeway before she resorts to firm discipline when they exceed her level of tolerance. Some of Carol's theories-in-use are clearly questionable. A few may have contributed to her problems that day in the library, and some may cause her more problems further down the line. Carol was not worried about her theories-in-use, however; she was worried about what she did and what she will do. In other words, Carol didn't question some of her conceptions. Theories-in-use were the last things she had in mind, even though they actually caused some of her problems.

6-6b WHY STUDY EDUCATIONAL THEORY?

The fact that Carol did not reflect on the validity of her theories-in-use or try to recall some theories she had learned during her teacher education is not unusual. Indeed, many teachers question the basic usefulness of theory. Many beginning teachers have been told by a senior colleague, "Forget all that theory they've been giving you in college. Here's what works in the real world." Further, preservice teachers often complain that courses are too theoretical. They want to get out to schools, where the real action is. This desire (perhaps it is your own desire) for things that work and ways to cope with real situations is vital, and we certainly do not want to diminish it. As a teacher, you will need practical techniques and solutions to real problems. Even so, it does not make educational theory any less important.

> *I touch the future. I teach.*
>
> —CHRISTA MCAULIFFE (1948–1986),
> first teacher in space

Pause *and* Reflect

Has reading about Carol Landis and her theories-in-use helped you identify any of your own theories-in-use or those of teachers you have known? If so, what are some of those theories-in-use?

The case of Carol Landis illustrates how a lack of theoretical knowledge of classroom management can lead to inappropriate behavior on the teacher's part. Both theory and empirical research support the notion of being consistent in your expectations of student behavior. Carol, however, thought it was acceptable to let students behave as they wished until they crossed her tolerance threshold, at which point she came down hard on them. Carol probably would not have encountered such trouble if more of her theories-in-use had been challenged and adjusted.

Like Carol, you may have your own theories-in-use, and they need to be challenged and tested. The best way to do so is to pit them against other theories and ideas. We believe that theoretical information *is* practical. The problem is not that theory is always wrong or unworkable, but rather that many teacher education programs offer students few opportunities to apply theory to practical situations. As the great American philosopher John Dewey said, "Nothing is so practical as a good theory."* By giving attention to theoretical knowledge now, we are also looking ahead to the future: At a later stage of your development, you will encounter theories that will undoubtedly enlighten and enrich your work with the young.

6-6c HOW CAN THEORETICAL KNOWLEDGE BE USED?

A teacher's theoretical knowledge can be used in two ways: to interpret new or ambiguous situations and to solve problems.[5] (Conversely, personal practical knowledge is more limited in applicability and is used primarily to respond to familiar situations; we discuss personal practical knowledge shortly.) As the "Up Close" feature, "Teaching: Art or Science?," describes, the "art" of teaching is knowing how and when to apply research and theory in the fast-paced classroom.

An Example of Using Theoretical Knowledge

Let's consider an example of how theoretical knowledge can help teachers interpret classroom events and solve the problems arising from them. Educational psychology includes the concept known as the **zone of proximal development**, meaning a range of tasks that a child cannot yet do alone but can accomplish when assisted by a more skilled partner. In other words, the child is on the verge of being able to solve a problem but just needs some structure, clues, help with remembering certain steps or procedures, or encouragement to try. (This assistance, called **scaffolding**, allows students to complete tasks they cannot complete independently.) This zone is where instruction can succeed and where real learning is possible. The concept of the zone of proximal development derives from the work of Russian psychologist Lev Vygotsky, who theorized that a child's culture shapes cognitive development by determining what and how the child will learn about the world.

Now suppose that a student, John, is experiencing difficulty doing some percentage problems in math. You, as the teacher, understand that the zone of proximal development is influenced by reasoning ability, background knowledge, and motivation. Armed with this theoretical background, you assess John's ability to understand the problems by watching him try to solve one of them. You ask him to explain to you what he is thinking as he attempts the solutions. Is he missing some important understanding, or is he making some procedural error? Are the problems too difficult, or should he be able to solve them with some assistance? If the latter, what kind of assistance does he need? Who should give him the assistance—you or another student?

*For the moment we downplay the fact that John Dewey was primarily an educational theorist.

Up CLOSE

Teaching: Art or Science?

One of the pioneers of research on teaching, the late N. L. Gage, of Stanford University, and Robert Marzano, a contemporary educational researcher, both believe teaching cannot be reduced to formulas or recipes for action, but see it as a blend of art and science. Teaching can be considered an art because teachers must improvise and spontaneously handle a tremendous number of factors that interact in often unpredictable and nonsystematic ways in classroom settings.

At the same time, both contend that teaching is also a science. Although science cannot offer absolute guidance for teachers as they plan and implement instructional strategies, research can provide a scientific basis for the art of teaching. For example, the research on academic engaged time has demonstrated the importance of keeping pupils on task

with intellectually challenging, but not too difficult, subject matter.

These two components of teaching—art and science—interact in exciting ways. Empirically derived knowledge of the relationships among teacher behavior, pupil behavior, material to be learned, and desired student learning can guide teachers as they make artistic decisions about their teaching—that is, teachers use their knowledge of the research on these relationships to accomplish the artistry of moving a unique classroom filled with unique students toward the intended learning.

Is teaching an art or a science? The answer is "yes."

Source: N. L. Gage, *Hard Gains in the Soft Sciences: The Case of Pedagogy* (Bloomington, IN: Phi Delta Kappa, 1985), 4–11; Robert J. Marzano, *The Art and Science of Teaching* (Alexandria, VA: Association for Supervision and Curriculum Development, 2007), 2, 4–5.

You decide that John is not lacking any fundamental knowledge and is very close to understanding the correct procedures. You ask Mary, a student who understands percentage problems pretty well, to come over and think aloud as she works on one of the problems. By thinking aloud and having John follow along, Mary provides John with insight into how she goes about solving the problem. You encourage John to ask Mary questions as she goes over her solution. You now ask John to work a similar problem, also thinking aloud as he tries to solve it. This time, he gets the problem correct. You ask him to do a couple more problems and to raise his hand when he finishes so you can check whether his understanding carried over to the new problems.

How did the theoretical knowledge about the zone of proximal development assist you in helping John? First, you had to determine whether John was close to understanding or was missing some fundamental knowledge. Was he in the zone of proximal development where additional coaching or assistance would help him, or would you have to reteach some important knowledge that he didn't have? Second, you had to decide which sort of scaffolding would benefit John. By having both Mary and John think aloud as they solved the problem, mistakes or errors could be easily determined and, if solved correctly, would provide a model for John. An understanding of the zone of proximal development and its related scaffolding strategies represents the kind of theoretical knowledge that can help you interpret and solve classroom problems.

This example helps show that teachers need much more than a commonsense understanding of human behavior. Capable and effective teachers use theoretical knowledge drawn from various education-related disciplines to formulate and test hypotheses about human behavior in the classroom. The translation of theory into practice cannot be left to chance; however, you must constantly take

> *Education must bring the practice as nearly as possible to the theory.*
>
> —HORACE MANN (1796–1859),
> nineteenth-century American educational reformer

advantage of opportunities that allow you to apply theoretical concepts to classroom situations and to receive guidance and feedback from your instructors about the application of these concepts. The field of cognitive psychology, in particular, has provided a treasure trove of research findings and theoretical concepts for teachers.

6-7 Personal Practical Knowledge

Personal practical knowledge is the set of understandings teachers have of the practical circumstances in which they work. Personal practical knowledge includes the beliefs, insights, and habits that allow teachers to do their jobs in schools. This type of knowledge tends to be time bound and situation specific, personally compelling, and oriented toward action. Teachers use their personal practical knowledge to solve dilemmas, resolve tensions, and simplify the complexities of their work. For example, the personal practical knowledge that Carol Landis must develop ranges from learning whether another teacher will loan his collection of *National Geographic* magazines to other classes, to clarifying her beliefs about whether assigning students to groups is better than letting them choose their own groups. Because teachers' personal practical knowledge is so intertwined with their identities as individuals, researchers have not been able to summarize this knowledge into a codified body of teaching knowledge. Case studies of teachers have, however, provided us with rich images of how teachers use their knowledge to make sense of the complex, ill-structured environment that characterizes most classrooms.

Teachers' personal practical knowledge definitely influences the decisions they make. Some researchers argue that a well-informed belief system is the most credible basis for rational teacher decisions. They assert that teachers should become aware of the assumptions that comprise their belief systems. Over time, as they develop attitudes and habits of practice, teachers should reflect on these beliefs to ensure that they conform to accepted educational principles.[6] Carol Landis, for example, is already reflecting on the educational soundness of her belief that students work well in groups with their friends. As you plan instruction, interact in classrooms, and evaluate instructional outcomes, continually testing your attitudes and habits of practice against sound educational principles can help protect you against poor educational decision making.

6-8 Which Teaching Skills Are Required of Effective Teachers?

Simply knowing something does not guarantee the ability to act on that knowledge. There is a profound difference between *knowing* and *doing*. Teachers may know, for example, that they should provide prompt feedback to their students on written assignments, but they are not always able to act on that knowledge. Teachers may also know that certain kinds of questions stimulate higher cognitive levels of thinking, but they may not be able to ask those types of questions during a discussion. No teacher education program can afford to focus only on theoretical knowledge at the expense of the practice—that is, the "doing"—dimension of teaching, just as no individual teacher can rely solely on knowledge of subject matter. All prospective teachers need to develop a repertoire of *teaching skills* to use as they see fit in varying classroom situations.

Among the skills that many educators believe are essential to effective teaching are the following:

- Asking different kinds of questions, each requiring different types of thought processes from students
- Providing effective feedback
- Planning instruction and student learning activities
- Diagnosing student needs and learning difficulties
- Varying the learning situation to keep students involved
- Recognizing when students are paying attention and using this information to vary behavior and, possibly, the direction of the lesson
- Using technological equipment, such as computers, to enhance student learning
- Assessing student learning
- Differentiating instruction based on students' experiences, interests, and academic abilities
- Using students' cultures to make learning experiences relevant and effective for them

Although far from complete, this list does suggest that teachers need a large repertoire of skills to work effectively with students who have varying backgrounds and different educational experiences. (Look at the list of InTASC standards on the inside cover of this book to see how many of these standards require particular teaching skills.) Using a variety of approaches is essential to meet the many different needs of students. As Figure 6.1 illustrates, effective use of teaching skills, along with appropriate attitudes, knowledge of subject matter, theoretical knowledge, and personal practical knowledge, leads to better instructional decision making.

Next, we focus on the skills preservice teachers need in three areas that are often of special concern: classroom management, effective questioning, and planning techniques. No other dimension of teaching causes more concern for beginning teachers than managing the classroom and maintaining discipline. "Will I be able to manage and control my class(es) so I can teach effectively?" is a question most beginning teachers ask themselves. Because this aspect of teaching generates so much anxiety, we have chosen to spend some time on this skill area first, before turning, somewhat more briefly, to questioning and planning skills.

6-8a CLASSROOM MANAGEMENT SKILLS

Classroom management refers to "the actions teachers take to create an environment that is respectful, caring, orderly, and productive. Classroom management supports and facilitates both academic and socioemotional learning."[7] Developing teacher–student rapport, arranging the physical environment, establishing rules and procedures, and maintaining students' attention to lessons and engagement in activities are examples of classroom managerial behavior. Managerial behavior also includes housekeeping duties such as record keeping, and managing time, facilities, and resources in the classroom. Effective classroom management focuses on how to prevent misbehavior, as well as how to handle misbehavior when it occurs.

A number of factors contribute to beginning teachers' concerns about classroom management. First, classrooms are complex, diverse, and crowded environments that challenge teachers to meet the different needs of each individual student. Second, classes are more culturally diverse than ever, and the norms of what constitutes acceptable and desirable behavior often vary among different cultures. Third, many children with disabilities are now educated in general education classrooms, presenting regular education teachers with considerable challenge to meet the needs of all the students. Fourth, many students come from circumstances (e.g., poverty, broken families, abuse) that create psychological and emotional problems with which teachers must cope. (See Chapter 3, "Who Are Today's Students in a Diverse Society?," and Chapter 4, "How Do Social Issues Affect Students?," for more on these topics.) And finally, beginning teachers often report that their teacher education programs did not adequately prepare them to address the factors mentioned previously.

The last 40 years or so have produced significant new knowledge about effective classroom management practices. The following sections describe some of those findings. See Table 6.1 for a summary of different approaches to classroom management.

TABLE 6.1	Different Approaches to Classroom Management

Name	Major Developers	Characteristics
Behavior modification	B. F. Skinner	Originates from behavioral psychology. Modify student behavior by consistently and systematically rewarding (reinforcing) appropriate student behavior and removing rewards for, or punishing, inappropriate student behavior.
Socioemotional climate	Carl Rogers William Glasser and Haim Ginott	Originates in counseling and clinical psychology. Emphasis on building positive interpersonal relationships between students and teachers.
Group process	Richard Schmuck and Patricia Schmuck Lois Johnson and Mary Bany	Originates in social psychology and group dynamics research. Emphasis on teacher establishing and maintaining effective, productive classroom group. Unity and cooperation, as well as group problem solving, are key elements.
Ecological	Jacob Kounin and Paul Gump	Emphasis is on *habitat*. Physical context has elements that must be established and managed to maintain order, such as planning and organizing lessons, monitoring activities, and explaining rules.
Authority	Lee Canter and Marlene Canter	Views classroom management as a process of controlling student behavior, primarily by using discipline. Emphasizes establishing and enforcing rules, using soft reprimands and orders to desist. *Assertive discipline* is a popular manifestation of this approach.

Academic Engaged Time

Research that focuses on student behaviors, such as academic engaged time, reveals some interesting insights into effective teaching skills.* **Academic engaged time**, also known as *engaged learning time,* is the time students spend being successfully engaged with academically relevant activities or materials. Several research studies indicate that academic engaged time is strongly related to achievement in those subjects.[8] Simply put, the more time elementary students spend working on reading or mathematics activities that provide them with successful experiences, the more likely they are to achieve in those areas. Although this finding may not seem very startling, observations indicate that tremendous differences exist in the amount of time individual students spend engaged in academic activities, both across classrooms and within the same classroom.

The research on academic engaged time clearly indicates that a primary goal of elementary teachers (and probably secondary teachers, although the research has been limited mostly to elementary schools) should be to keep students on task. Classes that are poorly managed usually have little academic learning time, so a major task of teachers is to learn how to manage their classes so that students are productively engaged.

Numerous studies indicate that the most efficient teachers are able to engage their students about 30 minutes a day longer than "average" teachers. If the most efficient teachers are compared with the least efficient, daily differences of one hour in academic engaged time appear. When this difference is extrapolated over 180 days, students of efficient teachers get 90 hours more of academic engaged time than students of average teachers and 180 hours more than students of inefficient teachers! Differences of this magnitude may help explain why students in some classes learn more than students in others.

(T) F
Efficient teachers can provide students with as much as 180 hours a year more of engaged learning time than inefficient teachers.

Designing the Physical Environment

How teachers set up the physical environment of the classroom directly affects the way teachers and students interact with one another. Deciding how the chairs, desks, computers and printers, tables, and books are arranged sends a message and affects the atmosphere of the classroom. By adding warm colors, plants, attractive and informative bulletin boards, teachers make the classroom a warmer and inviting atmosphere.

Weinstein and Weber offer some specific suggestions for designing classroom space:

- Place frequently used materials so that they are accessible to students.

- Organize shelves and storage areas so students know where materials and equipment belong.

- Reduce congestion and distraction by planning pathways through the room.

- Arrange seating so students have a clear view of instructional presentations.

- Decide how much interaction you want among students, and arrange desks/tables to reflect that interaction. For example, if you want interaction and collaboration among the students, don't put them in rows.

---

*On-task behavior, time on task, and academic engaged time are related concepts. *On-task behavior* is student activity that is appropriate to the teacher's goals. *Time on task* refers to the amount of time students spend engaged in on-task behavior. *Academic engaged time* adds the dimensions of a high success rate and academically relevant activities or materials to the concept of time on task.

Up CLOSE

Differences between Expert and Novice Teachers

A number of educational researchers have tried to identify expert and experienced teachers and compare them with novice teachers. But before you read what researchers have found out about expert teachers, stop and reflect on a teacher of your experience whom you consider to be truly an expert teacher. Not necessarily your favorite teacher, but the most skillful. What made this teacher so expert?

We can think of expert teachers as being similar to expert chess players. Expert chess players quickly spot trouble areas in any chessboard pattern; likewise, expert teachers quickly recognize trouble spots in a classroom setting. Experts in chess or teaching draw on their hours of experience to build a repertoire of recognizable patterns. In one experiment, expert and novice teachers were asked to look at a photograph of a classroom and identify the class activity. Experts were better able to "read" the classroom, making inferences about what was happening in the picture. When observed in action, expert teachers also show greater ability to gather information in a short time for multiple purposes. For example, an expert teacher may be able to accomplish many tasks in an opening review session: gather attendance information, identify who did or did not do the homework, and locate students needing help with the next lesson.

In comparison, novice teachers described the surface characteristics of the classroom pictures they saw. When presented with descriptions of student problems, they relied again on the literal features of the problems to suggest solutions. Their analyses did not correspond with the higher-order classifications expert teachers use.

Experts differed from novices in their approaches to planning as well. In a simulated task of planning, experts focused on learning what students already knew about the subject matter to be learned, whereas novices planned to ask students where they were in their textbooks and then present a review of important concepts. In other words, experts planned to gather information from the students, whereas novices planned to give information to them.

The research suggests that experts in any field demonstrate skill in planning and in classifying problems and formulating solutions. This is no less true for teachers: Expert teachers show problem-solving skills like those of other experts, whether in chess, bridge, or physics. The studies also indicate that the process of evolving from novice to expert teacher takes considerable time because extensive experience is necessary to develop enough episodic knowledge to interpret information about classrooms.

Source: David C. Berliner, "Expertise: The Wonder of Exemplary Performances," in *Creating Powerful Thinking in Teachers and Students,* J. N. Mangiere and C. C. Block, eds. (Fort Worth, TX: Harcourt Brace College Publishers, 1994), 161–186; Greta Morine-Dershimer, "Instructional Planning," in *Classroom Teaching Skills,* 10th ed., J. M. Cooper, ed. (Belmont, CA: Wadsworth, Cengage Learning, 2014), 63–70.

(T) F
A primary difference between novice and expert teachers is the experts' ability to gather information in a short time and use it in multiple ways.

- Personalize the classroom by including displays that reflect students' cultural backgrounds, interests, and accomplishments, as well as your own interests, goals, and values.
- Be certain the environment will accommodate students with special needs, such as wheelchairs.
- Locate computers so monitors are perpendicular to windows and away from magnets and water, out of major traffic paths, and in a space that will accommodate a small group of students.[9]

Building Positive Student–Teacher Relationships and a Sense of Community

A review of more than 100 studies concluded that positive teacher–student relationships are the key to effective classroom management, and such relationships can reduce behavior problems by over 30 percent.[10] Students who feel cared for and supported are more willing to accept a teacher's authority and to regulate their own behavior consistent with classroom norms. There is also evidence that caring, respectful teachers are particularly important to African American and Hispanic students, who often feel that many white teachers stereotype them and fail to honor their cultural backgrounds or understand their perspectives.[11]

All teachers want to have good relationships with their students, but how can they demonstrate this to students? Weinstein and Weber offer the following suggestions:

- Be welcoming. Standing by the door when students enter the classroom and greeting them sends a good message. Inquiring as to how they are doing, or commenting on a new look helps to build a connection. A brief inquiry at the beginning of the class (such as "You look really happy—what's new?") shows students you're concerned about their feelings.

- Learn about your students' lives. Try having your students complete a questionnaire about their favorite hobbies, music, pets, or after-school work. Attending their sporting events, concerts, or plays lets you see your students in a different context.

- Develop cultural literacy. Understanding your students' cultural background, values, and beliefs is essential for building good teacher–student relationships.

- Communicate high expectations. In interviews with inner-city students, many of them talk about the importance of having teachers who push them to do their schoolwork and who won't let them fail.

- Be a good listener. Be attentive and acknowledge students' feelings, and use "active listening" techniques (i.e., listen carefully and reflect back the message in your own words).[12]

To build a sense of community in your classroom, Weinstein and Weber offer the following suggestions:

- Provide opportunities for students to learn about each other.
- Use small-group work and cooperative learning activities.
- Hold group meetings to encourage open communication and group problem solving.
- Be alert for bullying and peer harassment.[13]

Other Research Findings

Many researchers have studied effective classroom management. Two key principles emerge from this research: (1) Good management is preventive rather than reactive, and (2) teachers create well-managed classrooms by teaching their students desired behavior.[14] Here are a few other important recommendations arising from the research:

1. *Establish clearly defined rules and routines.* Clear rules and routines decrease the complexity of the classroom, minimize confusion, and prevent loss of

instructional time. Having students help make the rules increases their commitment to abide by them.

2. *Ensure students' compliance with rules and demands.* To encourage students to comply willingly with the rules and routines, teachers must gain students' cooperation by establishing positive relationships, sharing responsibilities, and using rewards. This is accomplished more effectively by establishing and maintaining effective learning environments than by relying on authority or a teacher's role as a disciplinarian. Nevertheless, teachers must be willing to enforce the consequences for repeated misconduct and be able to administer those outcomes in a way that is not threatening, punitive, or perceived as unfair.

3. *Involve families.* When families understand what a teacher is trying to achieve, they can provide valuable support and assistance, including helping develop and carry out successful behavior management plans.

One school of thought rejects the notion of effective classroom management as a system of rewards and punishments, arguing that these outcomes are seen as instruments for controlling people. In this approach, instead of teachers seeing themselves as being in charge and taking steps to maintain that control, they should give up some of the control and help students work together to decide how to be respectful and fair; that is, teachers should help students develop an internal sense of how to work together in a community.[15] The approach may sometimes engender chaos and uncertainty, but advocates believe that students will learn ethics and democracy in action. One of your responsibilities as a teacher will be to develop a philosophy and ways of operating in the classroom that make sense to you and that accomplish what you value. Your attitude toward the use of rewards and punishments will be part of that development.

As a result of researchers' work, we are learning more about what constitutes effective classroom management behavior. Understanding the related theories and research and practicing the skills that this body of knowledge has identified as effective will help you establish and maintain the conditions that promote student learning. Effective classroom management is a skill that can be taught and learned. (See the "Up Close" feature, "Suggestions for Classroom Management Problems.")

Pause *and* Reflect

1. Do the research findings on academic engaged time surprise you, or do they seem obvious? If you think the findings reflect common sense, why do you suppose teachers vary so much in their ability to keep students engaged?
2. Are you concerned about your ability to establish and maintain a productive classroom environment? If so, what particularly concerns you?
3. We have included a number of suggestions for managing a classroom. Which seem most useful to you, and why? Which do you believe you would find most difficult to use, and why?

Up CLOSE

Suggestions for Classroom Management Problems

1. *When students misbehave, check your instruction.* Many behavior problems result from problems with instruction. Students may be bored or confused, in which case their response may be to get off task and into trouble.

2. *Take the time to ensure that students fully understand your classroom's rules and procedures.* As the old adage has it, "You have to keep school before you can teach school." At the beginning of the year, and again if and when things begin to break down, teachers need to fix in the minds of their students how the class is to be ordered.

3. *Regularly monitor the entire class.* Successful classroom managers frequently scan the class, noticing what each student is doing. Although teachers need not react to every sign of off-task behavior or deviation from the established procedure, students should know that what they are doing is being noted.

4. *Move in on repeated or flagrant breaches of conduct quickly and directly.* Do not let things drift. Students may think you are afraid to confront them, and they may end up confronting you!

5. *Correct in private.* As much as possible, deal with student misconduct in private. Don't disturb the rest of the students and get them off task simply to get one or two students back to work. Also, public reprimands may backfire and get you involved in a game of escalating remarks with a student.

6. *Don't make empty threats.* Do not say you are going to "do" something to a student or the class unless you have thought it over carefully and are really ready to do it. For instance, do not threaten to call the parents of every child in the room and tell them what rotten children they have unless you have a good deal of time—and alternative plans for next year.

7. *Don't put a hand on a student in anger or even annoyance.* Do not even think of striking a student, no matter how much you are tempted. When a situation is emotionally charged, even your well-intended gesture can be misinterpreted. If students are fighting, however, you may need to restrain them physically for their own good.

8. *Think through behavior problems.* When your class or an individual student is not behaving up to your expectations, treat the event as a problem-solving activity. Do not flail around or get panicky or discouraged. Coolly identify exactly what the problem is, consider possible causes, and test some possible solutions.

9. *Get help.* If management problems persist and you cannot solve them on your own, get help from a colleague or an administrator. Do not let things fester. Do not be shy about asking for help, particularly in relation to discipline problems, which are so common for many beginning teachers.

10. *Be sure there is a backup system.* If you need to remove a student from your room, you need to know that a system is in place to back you up.

11. *Be sure your rules are in accord with school-wide expectations.* For example, if the school has decided that chewing gum is tolerable and you crack down on it, you can expect to have more trouble than the issue is probably worth.

TeachSource Digital Download

6-8b QUESTIONING SKILLS

The questioning process is a central feature of most classrooms. Teachers ask questions not only to monitor student comprehension but also to stimulate students to engage with the content, relate it to their prior knowledge, and to think about its applications. Studies indicate that teachers may ask hundreds of questions in a day's lessons, but they often fail to ask questions that require students to process and analyze information, and many of their questions require only a rote response of memorized facts. Teachers also tend to rush students' responses, not giving them adequate time to provide varied and thoughtful answers. Some teachers do not direct as many questions to certain groups of students, such as minority students, girls or boys, or "slower" learners, thereby depriving them of the opportunity to be active participants in classroom learning.[16] Mastery of questioning skills contributes to students' learning and therefore is important for effective teaching.

Wait-Time

Good questioning behavior requires that teachers provide students with sufficient time to think about and respond to questions. What do you think is the average amount of time a teacher waits for a student to respond to a question she or he has asked? Mary Budd Rowe, a science educator, determined in a series of studies that the teachers she observed waited less than one second before calling on a student to respond. Furthermore, after calling on a student, they waited only about a second for the student to answer before calling on someone else, rephrasing the question, giving a clue, or answering it themselves! How can students think carefully or deeply when they have only a second to respond to a teacher's question?

> *A prudent question is one-half of wisdom.*
>
> **—SIR FRANCIS BACON (1561–1626),** seventeenth-century English philosopher

Rowe followed up these observations with studies designed to train teachers to increase their **wait-time** after questions from 1 second to 3 to 5 seconds. She reported amazing results: (1) an increase in the average length of student responses, (2) an increase in unsolicited but appropriate student responses, (3) an increase in student-initiated questions, (4) a decrease in failures to respond, (5) an increase in student-to-student interaction, and (6) an increase in speculative responses. In short, she found that longer wait-times led to more active participation on the part of more students and an increase in the quality of their participation. Subsequent research by others replicated Rowe's findings. If questions require students to think about material or generate original responses, they need a longer time to think about their answers than if they are being asked only to recall information from memory.[17]

Effective Questioning Techniques

In addition to longer wait-times, those who have studied the relationship between questioning strategies and student achievement have identified a number of other techniques as signs of effective teaching. This research suggests that teachers use the following strategies:

1. Phrase questions clearly. Avoid vague questions.
2. Ask questions that are purposeful in achieving the lesson's intent.
3. Ask brief questions because long ones are often unclear.
4. Ask questions that are thought-provoking, and demand original and evaluative thinking.
5. Encourage students to respond in some way to each question asked.
6. Distribute questions to a range of students, and balance responses from volunteering and nonvolunteering students.
7. Avoid asking "yes/no" and "leading" questions.
8. To stimulate thinking, probe students' responses or demand support for their answers.
9. Provide students with feedback about their responses, both to motivate them and to let them know how they are doing.[18]

Through effective questioning techniques, teachers can encourage and promote students' attention and participation in discussions.

Blend Images/Corbis

With knowledge and practice, teachers can learn questioning strategies that engage all students in the verbal interaction that supports learning.

6-8c PLANNING SKILLS

Another skill related to a teacher's effectiveness is skill in planning. The plans teachers make for lessons influence the opportunities students have to learn because plans determine the content students will experience in a lesson and the focus of the teaching processes. Effective teachers base their plans on a rich store of perceptions of classroom events and of their students' progress toward educational objectives and content standards. This store of perceptions (ways of looking at students and classroom activities) also helps teachers make adjustments during instruction when plans must be adapted to the immediate situation.

Teachers do four basic types of planning—yearly, unit, weekly, and daily—and all are important for effective instruction.[19] Research shows that experienced teachers don't plan the way curriculum experts recommend—that is, by beginning with instructional objectives and then selecting instructional activities to meet those objectives. Instead, many elementary school teachers begin by considering the context in which teaching will occur (e.g., the materials and time available); then they think about activities that students will find interesting and that will involve them; finally, they ponder the purposes these activities will serve. Secondary school teachers, by comparison, focus almost entirely on the content and preparation of an interesting presentation.[20] This discrepancy from the recommended approach doesn't mean experienced teachers don't have goals, especially in these days of content standards; rather, it suggests that the interest and involvement of their students are paramount. Because research shows that student achievement is related to academic engaged time, planning should include consideration of how to involve students.

In this section, we have looked at three skill areas—classroom management, questioning, and planning—that researchers have identified as competencies demonstrated by effective teachers. (Another important skill relates to the use

> *Failing to plan is planning to fail.*
>
> **—AUTHOR UNCERTAIN**

T (F)

Elementary and secondary school teachers plan their lessons in a similar fashion.

of technology, to which we devote a whole chapter.) Principals and other school evaluators assess beginning teachers' competence in these and other skills areas as part of their observations of beginning teachers. Standards for new teachers, such as those created by InTASC, also emphasize these skills. As a consequence, developing classroom management, questioning, and planning skills should be an important concern for those preparing to teach.

OUR FINAL WORD

This chapter is an important one because it provides an overview of what truly effective teachers should know and be able to do. It may have been a frustrating chapter if you concluded that there is no way you can achieve the ideal we describe. We share that frustration because we have not attained this ideal in our own teaching, and we're not certain that we ever will. Nevertheless, we continue to aspire to be the type of teacher described here. If you can fix your sights on this conceptualization of effective teachers and continually work toward this ideal, you are certain to observe positive and rewarding results in your own classroom.

Although we can detail the various proficiencies teachers need, noted educational author Jonathan

Kozol cuts to the chase in his description of what he would look for in a teacher:

[O]bviously we want people who can teach [their subjects]. . . . But if I had to narrow it down to one characteristic, I would always hire teachers whom I wouldn't mind getting stuck with on a long plane flight to California. I would look for people who are capable of making the world seem joyful, people who are a delight to be with, people who are contagiously amusing human beings. To me, that's more important than almost anything else. I would put the emphasis on the capability to create contagious enthusiasm for life. There are a lot of teachers like that, but not enough.[21]

WHY TEACH? YOUR FINAL WORD

1. We have maintained that decision-making skills are important for teachers. What can you do to improve your ability to make good decisions as you plan and deliver instruction?
2. Can you think of any ways that you, as a new teacher, could speed up the process of gaining personal practical knowledge?
3. Which of the classroom skills listed in this chapter seem most important to you? Which skills would you add to the list? Which skills would you subtract from it?

KEY TERMS

academic engaged time (172)
classroom management (171)
pedagogical content knowledge (166)
personal practical knowledge (170)
reflective teaching (154)

scaffolding (168)
self-fulfilling prophecy (162)
wait-time (178)
zone of proximal development (168)

FOR FURTHER INFORMATION

Web Resources

Education World

Education World presents a range of information concerning classroom management, including many tips for how to handle certain management problems.

Interstate Teacher Assessment and Support Consortium (InTASC)

A consortium of state education agencies, higher education institutions, and national educational organizations dedicated to the reform of the education, licensing, and ongoing professional development of teachers.

The New York Times

This newspaper website has daily lesson plans for grades 6 to 8 and 9 to 12, as well as daily news "snapshot" activities that can be developed into lesson plans for grades 3 to 5 (www.nytimes.com/section/learning). Search under "Learning Network." This site can be a valuable resource for exemplary lessons and activities, especially by allowing users to access related academic standards for many individual states.

Teachers.Net

This excellent site has an online reference desk, an active chat board, and a lesson plan exchange.

Print Resources

James M. Cooper, ed., *Classroom Teaching Skills*, 10th ed. (Belmont, CA: Wadsworth, Cengage Learning, 2014).

This self-instructional book is designed to help teachers acquire basic teaching skills such as writing objectives, evaluation skills, classroom management skills, questioning skills, and differentiating instruction skills.

Charlotte Danielson, *Enhancing Professional Practice: A Framework for Teaching*, 2nd ed. (Alexandria, VA: ASCD, 2007).

This useful book, organized around a framework of professional practice, is based on the PRAXIS III criteria, including planning and preparation, classroom environment, instruction, and professional responsibilities.

Thomas L. Good and Jere E. Brophy, *Looking in Classrooms*, 10th ed. (Boston: Allyn and Bacon, 2008).

This excellent book provides teachers with concrete skills that will enable them to observe and interpret the classroom behavior of both teacher and students.

Robert J. Marzano, *The Art and Science of Teaching* (Alexandria, VA: ASCD, 2007).

This highly readable text presents a framework for effective teaching based on research findings.

Carol Simon Weinstein and Molly Romano, *Elementary Classroom Management: Lessons from Research and Practice*, 7th ed. (New York: McGraw-Hill, 2019).

This practical book, based on sound research findings, addresses the major issues in establishing and maintaining effective learning environments. Weinstein has a secondary school version entitled *Middle and Secondary Classroom Management* (2007), also published by McGraw-Hill.

Jay McTighe and Grant Wiggins. *Essential Questions* (Alexandria, VA: ASCD, 2013).

An excellent, short book on how to ask good questions.

7

What Should Teachers Know about Technology and Its Impact on Teaching and Learning?

InTASC Standards 1, 2, 3, 4, 5, 6, 7, 8, and 10

LEARNING OBJECTIVES

7-1 Explain how technology in the classroom has evolved over the years.

7-2 Describe the impact new technologies have on the way we use technology in our daily lives.

7-3 Define *technology pedagogical content knowledge*.

7-4 Discuss ways technology tools are used to enhance student learning.

7-5 Explain how technology can help teachers change their role from dispensers of information to facilitators of students' learning.

7-6 Describe the different ways technology can be arranged to support student learning.

7-7 Summarize why issues of equity, teacher education, and budgeting need careful consideration as more and more technology is being used in schools.

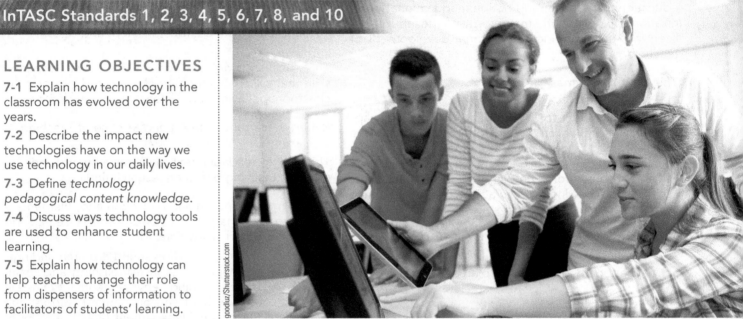

goodluz/Shutterstock.com

Truth OR Fiction?

T F Teenagers are the most prevalent technology users, spending up to 9 hours a day watching or interacting with screens

T F Drill-and-practice programs increase fluency of a skill.

T F Technology produces a generation of rote learners.

T F Students from lower socioeconomic families are more likely to use computers for drill and practice than children from the middle class.

The use of technology in the classroom has gained attention as an issue in education. As our society continues to embrace new technologies, our schools are scrambling to keep up. In this chapter, we explore what teachers should know about technology and its use in the educational setting, which roles technology may fulfill in education, and how those roles may change what students and teachers do in the classroom.

Patricia Gonzalez is one such teacher who uses technology to extend learning in the classroom. She challenges her eighth-grade class: "Where should the next landfill be built in our state?" The students are interested in this current, authentic, and engaging local issue. They hear their parents discuss this topic, read about it, watch news videos, and discuss it in class. They start their investigation by gathering background information as they read online newspaper stories that discuss the controversy. They hold video conferences with environmentalists and elected officials around the state to inform their research. Then, Patricia coaches them on the mechanics of using a geographic information system (GIS). A GIS, in simple terms, is a collection of tools that translate data into a digital map. The power of a GIS comes from its ability to display several layers of maps on the screen at a single time which allow students to deeply study an area by looking at several factors at once. For example, students can look at a map showing population density overlaid with another map that depicts the drainage basin of the surrounding rivers and lakes.

Students use mapping software to respond to authentic dilemmas.

They can then search the GIS database to make sure they will not disturb any known historic or archaeological sites or local nature preserves. In addition, students study photographs of the area, including street views, as they begin to narrow down their choices for the future site of the landfill.

After two weeks of investigation, Patricia's class divides into teams to present their choices. During their collaborative work, students learn from one another as they share their thinking in blog discussions and model their site choices while drawing together using online whiteboards. Through this process, each student contributes to their group's understanding as they organize their thinking into a cohesive argument. Three sites are offered, and a different group presents the case for each location. The culminating activity requires students to role-play a city council meeting, assuming such roles as city councilor, mayor, geologist, environmentalist, and angry citizen. Each side supports their oral arguments with a visual slideshow that includes map overlays and photographs of the area allowing students to illustrate their thinking and build upon their arguments.

Two years later, the same students are using the GIS to examine the landfill, that was actually built, to determine where the best place would be to gather water samples. Students meticulously record data into an app on their iPads. They will use this data along with environmental databases to monitor the safety of the landfill. These findings will help students understand how the local water quality is affected by the landfill and how water quality can affect their health.

Patricia Gonzalez's role in the classroom is far from the traditional view of the teacher as sole dispenser of information. Instead, Patricia functions as a facilitator. She allows her classroom to become an active laboratory where students take charge of their own learning path, pace, and space. Her students hypothesize, analyze, and evaluate possible solutions to authentic real-world problems. As she circulates around the room, she challenges her students to consider what evidence they will need to convince an area's citizens that their backyards are the best place for the future landfill. She asks lots of questions to help her students understand what they are reading and connect their new learning to prior knowledge. She guides her students to organize their thinking in ways that create coherent and persuasive arguments that are supported by evidence and reasoning. Importantly, Patricia is just one reference point that her students must consult, along with online resources, the GIS data, municipal officials, and other students.

As this example demonstrates, technology is not replacing teachers. In fact, teachers have an expanded role in this technologically enriched environment, though this role differs from the traditional one associated with teaching. Later in the chapter, we explore in more detail how teachers can use technology to change the roles of both students and teachers. To put contemporary changes in perspective, let's first look at the way technology has affected American schools in the past.

7-1 A Brief Look at Education's Technological Past

Today, people usually equate educational technology with computers, tablets, and smartphones. But technology in a more general sense is by no means new to education. In the early 1800s, a technological innovation was introduced to classrooms that had a profound impact on teaching. Although advocates called this new tool "invaluable" and it was installed in classrooms throughout the country, many teachers ignored it at first. Schools had to encourage use of this new technology by preparing training manuals with step-by-step instructions to help teachers integrate the device into their lessons. What was this technological wonder? The chalkboard!

In the old one-room schoolhouses, where students of different ages worked on their own individual lessons, the function of a chalkboard was not immediately apparent. During the nineteenth century, however, classroom structure began to evolve from a one-room orientation to the graded classrooms we know today. When innovative teachers began to teach the same lesson to an entire group of students, the chalkboard came into its own.[1]

The twentieth century brought a variety of technological devices into the classroom, including the filmstrip projector, the overhead projector, the motion picture, and educational television.[2] Such changes were viewed as so significant that, in 1913, technological proponent Thomas Edison stated, "Books will soon be obsolete in the schools. Scholars will soon be instructed through the eye. It is possible to teach every branch of human knowledge with the motion picture. Our school system will be completely changed in ten years."[3]

Similarly, when microcomputers became affordable in the 1980s, many software products were introduced to drill students on basic skills, and some educational visionaries predicted the end of classroom instruction and the end of the teaching profession as we know it. Of course, this forecast turned out to be no more correct than Edison's overstatement.

Today, educational technology is viewed as a powerful tool that teachers can use, rather than as something that can or should replace teachers. Technology supports and extends what teachers and students can do in the classroom whether it's a digital database enriching a research project or interactive GIS software allowing students to engage in real-world problem solving. Today's teachers continue to act as a gatekeeper, making decisions on which technology they will use in their classroom. There are a variety of forces at play as teachers appraise and decide to adopt technology including teacher and student comfort level with the technology, culture and mindset of their workplace, the sustainability of the technology, and how well the technology supports the classroom ideas, strategy, and pedagogy. The key idea is that, from the chalkboard to the computer, the needs of teachers and students shape the uses of technology in the classroom, not the other way around.

Once a technology enters the classroom, the uses to which it is put are affected by the level of comfort of the teacher who is using it. In education, the integration of new technologies tends to go through four degrees of application. Dr. Ruben Puentedura categorizes these four different degrees of classroom technology integration with his "SAMR" Model.[4] The letters in "SAMR" stand for Substitution, Augmentation, Modification, and Redefinition.

1. In the first stage, the technology is applied as a Substitution to things we already do with no functional change. For instance, when most teachers begin to use presentation software (such as *Slides* or *PowerPoint*), they initially use it to show text and pictures, which is exactly what previous technologies, such as slide projectors and overheads, have done in classrooms for decades.

2. In the second stage, the technology is used as an Augmentation to functionally improve upon existing tasks. To continue the previous example, many teachers use *Slides* or *PowerPoint* to link to websites, videos, or other slides as part of the presentation. Instead of delivering a linear march through information, these innovative teachers can branch out in different directions as the topic and the discussion suggest. Ambitious teachers can even use these tools to produce games, quizzes, tutorials, or branching narrative activities.[5]

3. In the Modification stage, the technology is used to do things that were not possible in the past, allowing for significant redesign. Teachers use presentation tools such as *Prezi* to present information in a nonlinear style that allow

Pause *and* Reflect

1. How have recent developments in technology affected how you learn as a student?
2. When you were in high school, which types of technology were your teachers using? At what stage of the SAMR model was the technology applied?

students to explore on their own path and pace. The Prezi presentation can be shared with or mutually developed by students in classrooms down the hall or across the globe.

4. In the Redefinition stage, the technology is used in ways that were previously not conceivable. In this example, teachers can use nonlinear presentation tools to share playlists and choice boards allowing their students to explore on their own, which can allow the teacher to act as a facilitator.

Put another way, teachers who are just beginning to use technology may start with integrating software or apps that are similar to something they already do. As they begin to learn about technology's possibilities, they will move on to applications, such as GIS, that allow them to innovate. In these ways, technologies open up new possibilities rather than just allowing teachers and students to do old things in new ways. As we examine different technologies, ask yourself at which stage they can be applied and at which stage you would feel comfortable using them.

7-2 How Is Technology Impacting Schools and Society?

(T)   F

Teenagers are the most prevalent technology users, spending up to 9 hours a day watching or interacting with screens.

▶︎❚❚ TeachSource Video Case

Twitter and First Graders

Watch the video clips, study the artifacts in the case, and reflect on the following questions:

1. How is technology enabling the students to learn in ways impossible before social media?
2. What role does the teacher play in creating this learning activity?
3. How might you adapt this activity to your classroom?

Technology has become an integral part of our daily life. Today, over 90 percent of American adults use a smartphone. Use among our youth is even higher as 95 percent of kids between ages 13 and 17 own a smartphone.[6] Clearly, the smartphone has become a rapidly adopted technology.[7] More people are accessing the Internet from their mobile devices, quickly growing from 23 percent in 2010 to 84 percent in 2018. All this technology use is leading to much more of our time being spent online. Today, the average American spends nearly 24 hours a week online (up from 9.3 hours a week a decade ago).[8] One way that people are using smartphones is to communicate via email. Over the past 10 years, the number of emails sent and received each day has increased from 12 billion to 306 billion.[9] School-aged children are also using technology at increasingly higher rates. Children ages 8 to 12 in the United States spend 4 to 6 hours a day in front of a screen. Teenagers are the most prevalent technology users, spending up to 9 hours a day watching or interacting with their screens.[10]

The rampant adoption of smartphones has had a transformative impact on society. Taking photos, recording videos, banking online, and looking up medical information are just a few of the most prevalent smartphone uses. The alarm clock app makes the smartphone one of the first things many people touch each day. Smartphone usage is so deeply embedded into our society that YouTube's news director purports that within one hour of a significant news story, live footage is uploaded to their site.[11] This is made possible because of the proliferation of smartphones that are capable of taking photos and videos and quickly uploading them

© Cengage 2016

FIGURE 7.1   **Percent of Teen and Adult Internet Users Who Use Social Networking Sites Is Drastically Increasing**

Source: The Common Sense Census: Media Use By Tweens and Teens (2019), https://www.commonsensemedia.org/sites/default/files/uploads/research/2019-census-8-to-18-full-report-updated.pdf.

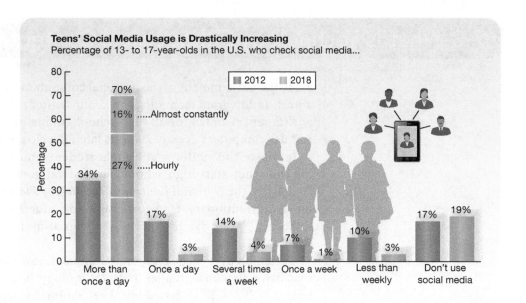

Teens' Social Media Usage is Drastically Increasing
Percentage of 13- to 17-year-olds in the U.S. who check social media...

Legend: ■ 2012 ■ 2018

- More than once a day: 34% (2012), 70% (2018); 16% .....Almost constantly; 27% .....Hourly
- Once a day: 17% (2012), 3% (2018)
- Several times a week: 14% (2012), 4% (2018)
- Once a week: 7% (2012), 1% (2018)
- Less than weekly: 10% (2012), 3% (2018)
- Don't use social media: 17% (2012), 19% (2018)

© Cengage 2016

▶❚❚ TeachSource Video Case

An Expanded Definition of Literacy: Meaningful Ways to Integrate Technology

Watch the video clips, study the artifacts in the case, and reflect on the following questions:

1. Which of the pressures to use technology described in this chapter are evident in the comments of the teachers in this case?

2. What roles do these teachers seem to take when their classes use technology?

3. Which advice from this case about integrating technology do you believe will be most useful to you as a teacher?

to social media sites. With the publication of his book, *App Generation,* Howard Gardner and co-author, Katie Davis, contend that youth today are immersed in apps so deeply that they perceive their existence as a menu of apps.[12]

In the Video Case, *Twitter and First Graders,* students tweet with pen pals from across the globe to expand the social-emotional growth of the students.

The ubiquitous nature of technology has contributed to a boom in social media usage, which allows users to create and participate in online communities. The vast majority of people, 90 percent, use at least one social media platform.[13] Teens are the largest consumers of social media—45 percent of teens reported being online "almost constantly."[14] Teachers are also accessing social media for professional learning opportunities. A recent study found that 65 percent of teachers use social media to connect with other educators to share and learn about new teaching ideas, strategies, and pedagogy.[15]

Figure 7.1 illustrates the exponential use of teenager and adult use of social media.

Most people agree that schools should prepare students for life in the twenty-first century. If pervasive use of technology is a fact of life, shouldn't our classrooms consistently and thoughtfully integrate technology? New opportunities are becoming available to teachers with skills in technology, which are seen as giving candidates an important competitive edge in the job market. In addition, the drive to incorporate new technologies into the classroom presents tremendous opportunities for students, as the next section describes.

In the Video Case, *An Expanded Definition of Literacy: Meaningful Ways to Integrate Technology*, three teachers talk about the importance of using technology as well as the benefits and challenges of doing so.

7-3 What Is Technology Pedagogical Content Knowledge?

Pause *and* Reflect

1. How do teachers of different disciplines use technology in different ways?
2. As a student, how do you use technology to support your learning?

Since the development of the personal computer in the early 1980s, there has been a push to integrate technology into our nation's classrooms. The 1983 *A Nation at Risk* report called for all high school graduates to be able to both understand and use computers. Nearly 20 years later, the No Child Left Behind Act continued to reinforce this notion stating that students must be technologically literate by the time they start high school. The federal government went a step further in 2010 when the *National Education Technology Plan* (NTEP) was published calling for a "revolutionary transformation [of education] rather than evolutionary tinkering."[16] Clearly, thoughtfully integrating technology into schools is no small task.

Technology Pedagogical and Content Knowledge (TPACK) is a framework that helps us conceptualize how technology is used to enhance teaching and learning. TPACK is based on Lee Shulman's work on pedagogical content knowledge (PCK).[17] As we discussed in the previous chapter (see Chapter 6, "What Makes a Teacher Effective?"), Shulman contends that PCK is a teacher's ability to translate disciplinary knowledge into forms that learners could master through pedagogical knowledge. TPACK extends PCK and attempts to make sense of the complex intersections of content, pedagogy, and technology. This framework (see Figure 7.2) contends that classroom teachers must not only know a content-specific technology tool but also understand how that technology should be used to best support their teaching and their students' learning. Thus, the TPACK framework presents a model for effective use of technology in the classroom by taking into account that instruction must encompass the nuances across content areas, pedagogy, and technology.[18]

FIGURE 7.2   **A Visualization of How Technology, Pedagogical, and Content Knowledge Components Interact.**

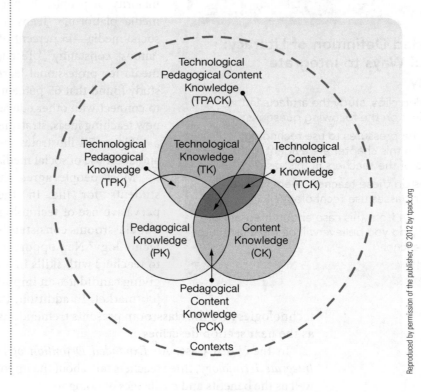

7-4 How Are Technologies Affecting Student Learning?

As the example of GIS software shows, many new technologies have been introduced into the educational setting. To discuss technologies for education, we must take several different approaches to this topic. First, we touch upon technologies you probably use in your personal life and how teachers seek to use those tools in the classroom. Second, we organize technologies around specific tasks that teachers and students might undertake (see Table 7.1). Third, we group technologies into content-specific categories.

TABLE 7.1 Tasks and Technology Tools for Teachers and Students

Task	Technology Tools	Example	Educational Benefits
Research and exploration	• Search engines • Databases • Online archives • Virtual Field Trips • Note-taking tools	Gale's U.S. History in Context database provides students quick-access to high-quality reference articles, audio and video files, primary sources, and more.	Online databases provide users with a tremendous variety of information.
Collaboration	• Blogs • Online composing software • Digital storytelling tools • Wikis	The *GLOBE* program provides students with opportunities to participate in data collection and sharing of findings.	Through participant driven databases, users can interact with other learners around the world or within the same classroom.
Communication (local to global)	• Email • Blogs • Video conferences • Chats • Podcasts • Online pen pals • Webinars • Wikis	Primary Source provides courses, face-to-face workshops, and online webinars to teachers to learn how to use primary sources to learn about global citizenship.	Participants in webinars can learn and ask questions, provide advice, share resources, and enrich one another's professional practice.
Composing	• Word processing • Image and video editors • Audio recorders • Screencasts • Infographics • Three-dimensional modeling tools	*WeVideo* provides a powerful, cloud-based video editor that allows users to import video, photos, and audio. Students can easily export their videos to share them.	Composing tools allow students to collaborate and take greater control of their learning path, pace, and place.

(Continued)

TABLE 7.1   Tasks and Technology Tools for Teachers and Students (Continued)

Task	Technology Tools	Example	Educational Benefits
Digital storytelling tools	• Slideshows • Video creation • e-book makers • Concept-mapping software • GIS tools	Teachers looking for alternatives to slideshows are turning to cloud-based products such as *Prezi. Prezi* uses one large canvas to display the whole presentation, and users can zoom in on certain parts.	Well-designed, media-rich presentations can stimulate student interest and enhance understanding.
Collecting data	• Probes and sensors • Digital cameras and video cameras	Students can combine *Adafruit sensors* with *Arduino Micro controllers* and coding to create inexpensive probes. They can use their probes to easily gather all kinds of data.	Data collection tools easily capture real-world phenomena. Now students can spend more time analyzing their data.
Analyzing data	• Spreadsheets • Data display programs • GIS • Graphing calculators	Students can use *Google Sheets* to view and analyze census data to determine demographic trends and forecast future population levels.	Spreadsheets and other analysis tools provide students with multiple ways to view and think about data: as individual entries, as aggregated categories, or as graphs.
Acquiring and practicing skills	• Self-contained tutorials • Drill-and-practice software • Quiz games • Educational games	*Type to Learn* allows individualized instruction in keyboarding. Students practice at school or at home, progress at their own pace, and receive immediate feedback.	These tools enable teachers to efficiently differentiate instruction. They often contain built-in automated assessments.

(Continued)

TABLE 7.1	Tasks and Technology Tools for Teachers and Students (Continued)		
Task	**Technology Tools**	**Example**	**Educational Benefits**
Formative assessments	• Online questions and surveys • Interactive games and quizzes	Cloud-based products like *Pear Deck* (an add-on for *Google Slides*) allow teachers to add interactive questions to their slideshow.	Formative assessment tools allow teachers to build high-quality feedback into their instruction.
Publishing	• Websites • Slideshows • ePub books • Specific-interest forums	*Google Sites (New)* is a drag and drop website developer. This website creator can be accessed from any device, collaborated on by multiple students, and shared widely with authentic audiences.	By sharing students' work to the web, teachers encourage students to engage with a wider audience. As a result, students may be more motivated to do their best work.
Annotating and questioning	• Edpuzzle • Actively Learn • ListenWise • Kami	*Actively Learn* allows teachers and students to annotate documents with text, audio, and video notes (for themselves or to share with the class).	Annotation and questioning tools can help students collaborate with one another and give the teachers an in-depth look into students' understanding.
Video conferencing	• Google Meet • Microsoft Zoom • WhatsApp	Teachers use *Zoom* to host online video discussions with their students. They can share their screen, have students work in small groups, and utilize the chat feature.	Using video conferencing can help teachers host online discussions while remotely learning.
Social media	• Twitter • Instagram • Snapchat • TikTok • Facebook	Teachers can use *Twitter* to reflect on the effectiveness of their teaching moves and how their teaching impacted student learning.	Teachers provide insights into their teaching and learning when they share through social media.

(Continued)

TABLE 7.1	**Tasks and Technology Tools for Teachers and Students (Continued)**		
Task	**Technology Tools**	**Example**	**Educational Benefits**
Learning management systems (LMS)	• Seesaw • Google Classroom • Canvas • Edmodo • Schoology	Students use *Canvas* to check new assignments, obtain directions, communicate with their teachers, and hand in their completed work.	Using their LMS, students can review assigned work, communicate with their teachers, and check teacher feedback.

Source: Adapted from Thomas C. Hammond, "A Task-Oriented Framework for Stand-Alone Technology Integration Classes," *Journal of Computing in Teacher Education* 23 (Summer 2007): 119–124.

You are probably familiar with many technology applications already. You use a cloud-based application to save your photos, social media sites to communicate with friends and colleagues, and your navigation app to provide real-time directions. These **productivity tools** let you accomplish tasks more efficiently. Teachers certainly use productivity tools, but teaching with technology encompasses far more.

Some technologies can be classified as **cognitive tools** when they are used to engage and enhance thinking.[19] Cognitive tools manage information in ways that allow users to think more clearly, creatively, and critically. Teachers can structure students' use of cognitive tools by providing scaffolds for their thinking. For example, a math student can use a spreadsheet to dynamically generate and manipulate graphs in order to understand concepts such as slope and y-intercept. In an English class, a teacher might provide students with a shared *Google Doc* and ask them to collaboratively write a response from the reading selection.

Cognitive tools are not necessarily meant to make learning easier. They do allow students to dig deeper into their learning as they organize information in new ways, evaluate their thinking, and to construct new, meaningful representations of the information. At the same time, using cognitive tools often requires students to think harder, more critically, or more creatively than they might without the tool.[20] Patricia Gonzalez's students, for example, were thinking hard and working collaboratively to solve the problem of where to locate the landfill.

Another useful way to think about technologies for education is to consider the tasks in which teachers and students will engage. This task-oriented approach helps teachers concentrate on how technology will improve their teaching and their students' learning rather than focus on the tool itself. Table 7.1 presents a partial list of these tasks and the tools that can help you undertake them. In some instances, tools may be used merely as productivity tools, whereas in other circumstances they are used as cognitive tools.

As a teacher, you also want to think about technologies in terms of how they apply to specific content areas. Some technologies, such as sensors and probes, are more appropriate for math or science than for English or social studies. Other technologies, such as social media platforms, can cross disciplines and interweave subjects, such as social studies and math. As you prepare instruction for a particular content area, you will want to consider both how certain technologies add depth to students' engagement with the content and how these technologies may engage students in multidisciplinary thinking.

7-4a ENGLISH LANGUAGE ARTS (ELA)

Teachers of many disciplines will find the tools for developing literacy useful. In this section, we examine digital tools being used to teach ELA through writing, reading, listening, and speaking lessons.

Writing with Digital Tools

Although technology has vastly broadened the avenues of expression available to students, writing ability is still highly valued in our culture. Today, many students write using online word processors such as *Google Docs*. Word processors offer many advantages over paper and pencil. For example, editing is less tedious when you don't have to laboriously erase several lines of text, or even start over. The result, students who learn to write using word processors tend to more frequently edit and revise their work and make substantial revisions.[21] Built-in tools like spelling and grammar checks help students focus on their ideas, and the keyboard itself avoids the handwriting obstacle many students face. Teachers are combining written text with multimedia tools such as *BookCreator, Google Sites (New),* and *Edublogs* to share students' work with authentic audiences, which in return motivates students to become more invested in the writing process.

A recent study reports that 96 percent of teachers believe that digital technologies such as the Internet, digital storytelling apps, and social media can aid educators in improving their teaching. Teachers also believe that digital tools broaden the audience for their students' work and encourage greater collaboration.[22] These aids are controversial, however, as some educators believe they are often used as a crutch. A National Writing Project survey found that the same teachers who reported great enthusiasm for teaching with writing technology tools also report concerns. They note that students are more likely to take shortcuts when writing and write in a careless fashion. The teachers express concerns over plagiarism and students' understanding and practicing of copyright and fair use guidelines. Nonetheless, the more students edit their writing, the more they learn about the writing process. In this respect, digital tools engage students and enhance thinking, making them cognitive tools.[23]

These cognitive tools can be used across all grade levels to teach writing:

- Take, for example, a first-grade teacher with a class set of tablets. The teacher can select a digital storytelling app such as *Tell About This* where the teacher provides a written and visual prompt. Then, the students create and record an oral story that can be saved and played back to them or shared with their parents.

- A middle school teacher may select a comic maker, such as *Pixton,* that allows her students to write and illustrate graphic novels. Students create their graphic novels in *Pixton* and share them online to reach a wider audience of readers.

- Take a glance into a high school, and you may find students creating their own e-books. Using *Book Creator,*

▶❚❚ **TeachSource** Video Case

© Cengage 2016

Multimedia Literacy: Integrating Technology into the Middle School Curriculum

Watch the video clips, study the artifacts in the case, and reflect on the following questions:

1. In what ways are the students using technology in this case? What is the role of the teacher?

2. This chapter mentions that the use of particular technological tools is not limited to specific disciplines. How could these students use their new ability to create slideshows in another subject area, such as mathematics or science?

3. What are some ways that teachers can balance content instruction with technology-skills instruction, a concern mentioned by the teacher in this case?

students can draft a story that incorporates text, audio, images, and video. Then, the stories can be shared online with a wider, authentic audience.

Communicating in Multimedia

The spread of technology has required an expanded definition of literacy. Students are now becoming literate not just in the written word but also in the spoken word using video, audio, and multimedia productions. In Chapter 3, "Who Are Today's Students in a Diverse Society?," when we discussed Howard Gardner's theory of multiple intelligences, we emphasized that different individuals learn best in different ways. Students who struggle with written expression may enjoy the chance to publish a web page or create a multimedia presentation instead of submitting a traditional five-page essay. Presentation tools, such as *Slides* and *Prezi,* combine text, graphics, audio, and video to communicate complex ideas. Students can use multimedia tools like *VoiceThread, Book Creator,* and *Explain Everything* to create and illustrate their own interactive stories. These multimedia tools can empower students to shift from the role of passive observer to active creator of digital media. Students can use their strengths in expressing themselves while they develop visual literacy, become familiar with valuable tools for the future, and strengthen their ability to analyze and synthesize information.

Digital Storytelling

Digital storytelling projects engage even the most reticent students. In digital storytelling, students combine their video, audio, and illustrations (photos or their own drawn images). For students who are having trouble beginning to write, the pictures they choose can serve as prompts to engage them in the writing. Because students have created or chosen the images to accompany the narrative, they have greater ownership and connection to their stories. With the introduction of smartphones, tablets, and increasingly user-friendly software, digital storytelling is being utilized more frequently.

Students can even research, direct, and produce their own digital documentaries. For example, a student might film a Native American elder telling an important story from his or her tribal culture and illustrate this interview with powerful digital images as the culminating project. It is relatively easy to publish student work on the Internet, and the knowledge that their work may be seen by a wider audience motivates students to care more about their creations.[24]

Learning to Read Drill-and-Practice Programs

Learning to read drill-and-practice programs were the earliest form of educational software and games. First used as interactive worksheets, the software provided feedback to users, usually by labeling an answer as right or wrong, and then presented the next task. Now, many programs monitor the students' progress so they may not move on until they have mastered the current concept. Drill-and-practice programs are most often used to increase the fluency of a skill rather than actually teaching it.[25]

(T) F
Drill-and-practice programs increase fluency of a skill.

Many of today's drill-and-practice programs also feature a motivational, game-like design. One interesting tool for integrating individualized and whole-class drill-and-practice is *Kahoot.* This game allows teachers to create fun and challenging quiz games. Students can play live in the classroom or participate in *Kahoot* challenges, which allow students to work in their own place and at their own pace.

Making Mind Maps and Webs

Students and teachers often create graphical representations, known as **mind maps** or **webs,** to demonstrate their understanding of a story or concept. Online applications such as *Coggle* use these visual learning techniques to support students as they clarify, organize, and prioritize their thoughts. Mind maps are often used as a pre-writing activity to help students brainstorm, draft, and revise their writing ideas. They can also serve as a formative assessment tool for teachers, who can examine the thinking patterns, interrelationships, and even misconceptions revealed by students' diagrams.

Combining Technology and Crossing Disciplines

Technology can facilitate interdisciplinary connections in a powerful way. Multimedia tools are used across the disciplines—from a presentation on the Depression that includes music of the era and clips from President Franklin D. Roosevelt's "fireside chats" to a hurricane project with graphs, images, video clips, and links to the National Weather Service website.

A specific example combining several types of technologies and crossing content areas is the *Flat Stanley project*.[26] Based on the *Flat Stanley* book series, elementary-aged students from around the world use digital tools to share their own experiences and learn about the experiences of others. Students design their own cutout copy of "Flat Stanley," take a photo of their cut-out in an interesting place, and write about Flat Stanley's experience there. Then, they digitally send their Flat Stanley to students in other locations. The recipients are asked to write about the experiences Flat Stanley has while visiting with them. The stories can be emailed back or uploaded to the Flat Stanley website. Using these rich and diverse stories, teachers develop interdisciplinary activities. For example, students study maps to locate the countries where Flat Stanley has traveled. Students can also be connected with other children live, using videoconferencing programs such as *Zoom, Meet,* or *Whatsapp* to ask their "Flat Stanley e-pals" about the weather and local heroes of their regions. Students can use drawing software to illustrate their Flat Stanley stories. They can use their math skills, and perhaps graphing software, to chart the miles he travels. In this project, technology is functioning at the second stage we described as Augmentation: facilitating and enhancing what teachers can do.

7-4b SCIENCE EDUCATION

As the case study at the beginning of this chapter showed, technology can allow students to do legitimate scientific investigations on a scale that would otherwise be impossible. Technology enabled Patricia Gonzalez to use a constructivist approach to education that encouraged her students to build their own knowledge on the basis of their experiences. (See the "Up Close: Cognitive Tools and Constructivist Teaching" feature in this chapter. See also "The Influence of Two Psychological Theories" in Chapter 9, "What Are the Philosophical Foundations of American Education?", and "What Ought to Be the Elements of Educational Reform?" in Chapter 12, "How Should Education Be Reformed?") Students can use an app on their smartphone to see what the sky above them looks like at night to learn about constellations or monitor the regularity of Old Faithful's eruptions through a live web camera. Putting these technologies in students' hands allows learning to become an active process in which they do experiments, draw conclusions, and engage in problem solving, rather than merely reading about an investigation and memorizing the results.

Although the equipment to conduct many of these experiments is costly, there are ways around these financial obstacles. For example, many city governments are interested in partnering with a local school to share their expertise and sophisticated GIS software as government workers did with Patricia Gonzalez's class. Many organizations support collaboration between scientists and schools; for a reasonable membership fee, schools receive the technical support they need and an opportunity

Up CLOSE

Cognitive Tools and Constructivist Teaching

In the constructivist approach to teaching, learning is recognized as an active process. Students engage in constructing their own knowledge on the basis of their previous experiences instead of passively absorbing knowledge as presented by the teacher. This approach to instruction celebrates the differences among students instead of continually emphasizing their similarities.

Constructivist teachers find the flexibility of cognitive technology tools especially helpful in supporting their teaching and their students' learning. The student must bring the goals—and the content to achieve them—to the tool, and then the tool will help facilitate the student's discovery of knowledge and construction of meaning. One good example that demonstrates this is when students use *Screencastify* to narrate the design process they used for their hands-on STEAM (Science, Technology, Engineering, Art, and Math) project. As they organize their thinking, write their scripts, and record their screencast, students are reflecting on their learning process and making their learning visible.

Note that it is *how* the tool is used that makes it constructivist, rather than what tool is used. Although cognitive tools are excellent matches for constructivist methods, many other applications can be used in a similar manner. As so often is true in teaching, only the students' and teachers' ingenuity, creativity, and experience set the limits for a tool's educational use, not the tool itself.

---

to work with experts. Such partnerships let students see how people in the "real world" do their jobs, as well as allow them to participate in interesting projects.

This section discusses some of these opportunities, ranging from conducting sophisticated local research that contributes to an organized database to collaborating with NASA scientists via conferencing technology.

▶❚❚ TeachSource Video Case

Integrating Technology to Improve Student Learning: A High School Science Simulation

Watch the video clips, study the artifacts in the case, and reflect on the following questions:

1. Does the technology that the students are using in this case fit this chapter's description of a cognitive tool? Why or why not?

2. What is the role of the teacher in this case? How do you feel about taking this role as a teacher?

© Cengage 2016

Scientific Hardware

Imagine conducting class beside a stream behind your classroom and having the technology to test your water sample; instantly and accurately find the pH, temperature, and amount of dissolved oxygen in it; and graph the data on the spot. Revolutionary technology in the form of probes, thermometers, and sensors allow this scenario to become reality. No longer are teachers forced to demonstrate stale experiments in the sterile environment of a lab. Instead, schools are moving toward **1:1 computing**, where each student has access to a mobile computing device to use inside the classroom, in the field, and at home. Students can use technology to access rich data sets, perform calculations, and test their hypotheses themselves. Science students today do things like measure carbon and sulfur dioxide levels from the air near their schools. One example of how technology is being used to aid science education is *CSI: Community Science Investigators* (http://web.mit.edu/mitstep/projects/csi-community-science-investigators.html). This program utilizes augmented reality games to aid students in their exploration of local environmental problems. Students use GIS and other mapping tools to collect and visualize real data. They use this data to understand environmental challenges like local food production or invasive species.

When used effectively, technology can enable students to learn in ways not possible before the advent of computers.

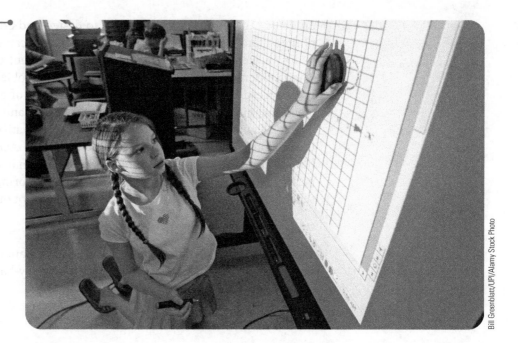

Bill Greenblatt/UPI/Alamy Stock Photo

Their observations inspire them to build their own narrative games tailored to their school or neighborhood so that others can learn from their work.

Digital Imagery

Much of science education is based on the skill of observation, and resources that allow students to visualize abstract concepts lead to greater understanding. The use of images and video in the science classroom has been greatly enhanced by digital tools. Teachers and students can go online to view images or video clips that illustrate processes such as amoeba reproduction or a lunar eclipse. Processes that are too fast to observe, such as dropping a ball, can be slowed down, and students can use time-lapse capabilities to capture processes that are too slow to see, such as the growth of a plant.[27] Or a teacher can use a document camera to capture real-time images that they share using a digital projector providing an opportunity for all the students to get a close view of an experiment without having to all fit around a small table.

Tools for Analysis

Students can collect data with a wide variety of scientific probes (e.g., collecting temperature, CO_2, pH scale, etc.) that connect directly to their computer or wirelessly to their smartphone. The collected data can then be organized and analyzed utilizing **spreadsheets**. *Excel* and *Sheets* are great tools to help students organize data sets, conduct numerical analyses, perform multiple calculations, and create graphs. Users can see all the numbers and formulas at once, and any change is immediately reflected in the entire sheet. Teachers can also project the charts they create from the collected data to visually represent the information and help their students to make meaning from the data.

Enhancing Learning Experience

Technology tools can augment learning by providing creative learning spaces. Elementary teachers are doing just this when they use NASA's Global Precipitation Measurement Mission. NASA uses precipitation data (collected by satellites) to create high-quality animations documenting rainfall during tropical storms. These animations provide students with in-depth information about the water cycle.

Students can then use a creation app to design and create their own representation of the water cycle. Middle school science teachers can enhance learning experiences using *Vernier* motion detectors to collect movement data from objects of all sizes. Their students are able to gather data on a falling objects' acceleration and velocity, use a spreadsheet to better understand principles of gravity forces on motion, and create meaningful charts that help students understand how gravity affects the falling object. High school science teachers create innovative learning spaces when they use anatomy apps such as the *Visible Body Human Anatomy Atlas* to investigate the human body. Students can not only rotate and zoom in on the body, but they can also perform dissections. Anatomy tools such as these bring the research lab to the high school classroom. These tools transform the concept of hands-on learning.

7-4c SOCIAL STUDIES EDUCATION

Digital resources, including online archives, simulations, and virtual field trips, can be used to promote historical thinking and inquiry-based learning in social studies classrooms.

Accessing Information

Research skills are an integral part of social studies education. Prior to the advent of the Internet, curriculum resources were limited primarily to textbooks or books from the library, and conducting research with primary resources was reserved for scholars, genealogists, or those who had access to archives. Today, teachers and students have access to a plethora of high-quality sources through digital databases and online archives. Some researchers claim that these digital resources have "democratized" the act of "doing history."

For example, the *Valley of the Shadow* is a detailed database of Civil War–era primary sources including census results, church records, newspaper articles, military records, and letters about two communities, one Southern and one Northern. Users can investigate the answers to questions such as "What was the average number of slaves people held?" or "How did occupations differ in the North and South?" The role of the teacher changes from dispenser of knowledge to that of a guide through the archives, helping students learn to ask the right questions and examine the sources critically. In this way, students and teachers construct their understanding of history together.

Students can research using the Internet to access other types of information in addition to primary sources. Imagine you are teaching a civics lesson and you want to discuss the impact of a new federal policy. Take, for example, national health care policy. Your classroom textbook would not have current information about the policy or its impact. But students can go online to get current information from multiple sources about the policy. They can read about the policy from the federal government website to learn the basic facts. Then, students can read about the impact of the policy from different perspectives. Evaluating the reliability of their web sources and corroborating information across multiple sources permits students to understand multiple facets of the policy. It also illustrates to students how the same news story can be biased and can be reported differently by different news sources.

Even the youngest of our school-aged children access information from the Internet in the social studies classroom. The proliferation of videos stored in different online databases make readily available resources to augment learning. Gale's U.S. History in Context is one such database that has been created to support classroom learning. For example, a teacher developing a unit on the first

Thanksgiving can find an assortment of readings, primary source materials, and videos from Native American songs to reenactors describing life for children in colonial Massachusetts.

There is so much information available on the Internet that teachers' worries have shifted from finding resources beyond the textbook to how to structure online learning. It is essential that teachers *carefully* design lessons that scaffold students' learning when they are using online resources.

Project-Based Learning (PBL)

PBL activities are one example of how teachers can carefully guide students through the process of constructing knowledge. Students research by finding and evaluating their sources to ensure that the information is reliable, gathering important information (note taking), and synthesizing the new information they found to answer their research question(s). Students apply the information from their research to create a project that will teach others (an authentic audience). For example, a middle-school adaptation of *A History of the World in 100 Objects* (BBC) could help students study ancient Rome. After some initial browsing, students choose an ancient Roman topic they are interested in learning more about. Students' choices can include ancient Roman gods, aqueducts, gladiators, weapons, and more. Students develop a research question, research their topic, and synthesize their findings. Next, students design and create an artifact that will teach others about their topic in the school's makerspace to apply and solidify their learning. Finally, students create a webpage to add more written and visual details to accompany the oral presentation of their artifact. In the example above, students constructed their own knowledge through research, application, and teaching others.

Simulations

A **simulation**, a representation of an activity or environment, is a time-honored and effective teaching technique. A simulation can be a fun way to explore an environment or a concept that would be too expensive, or possibly dangerous, to handle in reality. For this reason, a large variety of computerized simulations are available for classroom use in practically every field.

One collection of simulation games is *iCivics,* in which users assume different roles to explore different aspects of civics education. Sandra Day O'Connor, retired justice of the U.S. Supreme Court, founded iCivics. iCivics provides many online simulations that are organized by topical units so that they build upon one another. One game, *Do I Have a Right?*, puts students in the role of running their own law firm. Clients come to the firm with cases that may violate rights protected in the Bill of Rights. Assuming the role of an attorney, students work together to strategize the best way to help their "clients." Like many video games, these simulations have a learning curve and most students get better at engaging and learning from them as they progress.

Virtual and Augmented-Reality Tours

Virtual tours provide a wealth of opportunities to extend learning. Not limited to social studies, virtual field trips can be used to provide information about a site that students are unable to visit.[28] It is unlikely you will manage a class outing to the Amazon rainforest, for example, but National Geographic's *Jason Project* can send students there on a virtual field trip. Teachers, agencies, governments, and students themselves have produced hundreds of such sites.

No longer are students and teachers limited to resources in the textbook or school library.

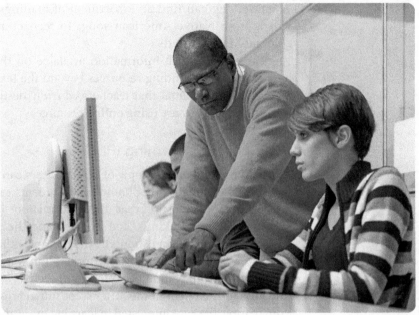

Diego Cervo/Shutterstock.com

Teachers can use programs like *Google Tour Creator* to make their own virtual-reality (VR) tours for use with their students. One such tour, *Shackleton's Journey: Exploring the Geography and Climate of Antarctica* (https://poly.google.com/view /eiQLjqk-TEw), has students don VR goggles to follow Sir Ernest Shackleton and the crew of the Endurance as they race to become the first to reach the south pole. Students follow Shackleton's harrowing journey in 3-D as they interact with embedded images and gain further information from written and audio details. *Google Tour Creator* can also be used by students to produce their own VR trips in connection with local history. They may conduct interviews, take pictures, and create videos of important sites and people in their community. Students can combine the information from their interviews with *Google Tour Creator* to create a VR tour that can be shared with an authentic audience. In this way, students act as historians who are contributing to the preservation of their community's story.

7-4d MATHEMATICS EDUCATION

From slide rules to calculators, math teachers have relied on technology for years. This section deals with some of the newer uses of technology in math education.

Tutorial Software

Tutorials are educational software applications designed to provide the initial instruction on a given topic. They are used in most disciplines. Unlike drill-and-practice exercises, tutorials present the skill or concept, check for understanding throughout the process, and evaluate the learner's grasp of the topic once the program is completed. More narrative in nature, supported by video, and more choice-based than the drill-and-practice programs, tutorial software allows for individualized learning where students can choose their own path, work in their own place, and proceed at their own pace.

The self-contained and self-paced nature of tutorial software supports students and allows the teacher to act more as a facilitator. Scaffolded chunks of information are delivered to learners in a careful sequence of instruction designed to adjust to students' needs, allowing them to achieve success. One such tutorial program is

Khan Academy. With this online software, users move through concepts such as fractions and decimals at their own pace; topics are explained, reinforced, and tested. The learners' progress through the material is saved from one session to the next. Generally more flexible than drill-and-practice applications, tutorials give teachers a powerful tool for individualizing instruction and monitoring student progress.

Other Math Software

Certain mathematics-specific software enhances what teachers can do. For example, *The Geometer's Sketchpad* allows students to explore the relationships among points, lines, planes, and angles in an environment conducive to experimentation. Users are offered a palette of tools for drawing and deriving geometric concepts. Tablets enable students to access powerful apps when learning math. *GeoGebra* is one app that lets students interact with geometric shapes to allow them to explore points, lines, angles, surfaces, and solids. These cognitive tools enable users to explore, question, learn, theorize, fail, succeed, and grow.[29]

One technology tool that is letting teachers teach in ways impossible before are 3-D design software and printers. Users build on their mathematical thinking to engineer and design anything from a prosthetic hand to a piece of jewelry on a flat screen, using design software like *Tinkercad*. The printer then generates layers to produce a 3-D object. Math teachers are challenging students to apply what they have learned about mathematical modeling or geometric functions to design and build all sorts of innovative creations.

Calculators and Graphing Calculators

Schools are trying to heed the message inherent in the National Council of Teachers of Mathematics' statement that "It is essential that teachers and students have regular access to technologies that support and advance mathematical sense making, reasoning, problem solving, and communication."[30] Many students find it difficult to make connections among the graphical, numerical, and algebraic representations of mathematical functions, for example, but the speed and ease with which graphs can be generated and manipulated using graphing calculators can help students to better understand those relationships.

Experts state that once students have mastered the basic computation of a problem, they can use calculators to bypass this to move on to higher-order concepts that they have not yet mastered.[31] Others point out that students who are struggling to develop the basic concepts of a math problem can compensate for these skills when they use technology to gain access to the higher-level skills.[32]

Technology also enhances what teachers and students are able to do. Students can use data collection devices connected to their calculators, such as various types of sensors or temperature probes, to gather their own data as the basis of their investigations into mathematical phenomena. Learning becomes more meaningful and authentic with these approaches, as students consult with both technology and the teacher.[33]

7-4e FOREIGN LANGUAGE AND ELL EDUCATION

The Internet and other communications tools open up vast opportunities in foreign language education. Years ago, foreign language teachers struggled to collect current materials in the target language. Now students can view authentic materials over the Internet or even use the Internet to communicate with students in other classrooms in a foreign country. Compare assigning a sterile textbook article about French food to connecting your students with *E-pals* in French-speaking Africa so they can ask about the cuisine themselves; the advantages of the latter approach are obvious.

Technology Supporting Instruction

Foreign language students and English language learners can use a number of technologies to develop their proficiency in English. Video provides low-stakes opportunities for students to record and hear themselves speak, make changes, and try it again. Audio podcasts are of great value as correct pronunciation can be modeled through teacher-created podcasts, and also practiced as the students create their own podcasts.[34] A number of free programs make it simple to create the audio recordings to use for your podcast. *Online Voice Recorder* is one such free program, providing a user-friendly interface with the option to convert to .mp3 files. This allows the recording to be played on other devices such as smartphones and implemented into a variety of websites, presentations tools, and storytelling sites. *VoiceThread* is another online program that allows students to combine recordings of their speaking with images and text. Students can invite their peers to have a "conversation" by replying with their own audio or video. *VoiceThread* provides a fun way for students to practice and gain confidence in the language they are learning so that they are more confident when they use it during class conversations.

Learning through the Home Language

As teachers are supporting their English language learners, they also need to follow the standard curriculum teaching math, science, and other subjects. This can be very difficult as the students are trying to decipher the language while perhaps learning a new mathematical formula. *Google Translate* is a powerful tool that helps students understand curriculum content in their home language. A number of apps and programs on the market enable students to learn concepts in their home language while they become more proficient in English. *BrainPOP ELL* is one such program. *BrainPOP ELL* provides fun and educational animated movies, interactive activities, quizzes, and games for students of all ages. Lessons are organized around a movie that introduces new vocabulary and grammar in ways that are differentiated for students at different levels of English proficiency and provide teachers ways to support standard curriculum content learning.

Connecting with People

As we discussed earlier in the chapter, social media tools provide many opportunities for students and teachers to connect with speakers of other languages. For example, teachers use *Padlet* for their students to post letters, images, and audio notes to their pen pal in another country. The pen pal can then reply with their own writing, images, audio, and video. These exchanges happen quickly and are a powerful way to hear others speak the language they are learning. Another example, Dickinson College hosts *Mixxer*, a language exchange community. *Mixxer* allows language learners to find one another; a classroom of English speakers learning Spanish can be connected with a classroom of Spanish speakers using English. Individuals or groups from these classes connect with tools that support text, voice, and video chat such as *WhatsApp*. As they participate in the discussion, students put their communication skills to the test. These engaging ways of learning foreign languages are changing the way we teach, and they encourage learners to be creative and flexible and to take risks—all of which are indispensable to learning any new language.

7-4f VIRTUAL SCHOOLS

School districts vary greatly in location, size, budget, composition of populations, and graduation requirements. Such differences often create educational inequities, particularly when a school district simply cannot afford to provide the quality and variety of courses offered by larger or more affluent districts. **Virtual schools,** or online schools, are a fast-growing alternative for schools that are trying to overcome such constraints.

Virtual schools are playing an ever-increasing role in the education of students. Twenty-five states offer online learning opportunities for students through virtual schools, and 2.7 million students take courses online.[35] The motivation for taking an online course for many students in rural areas is the opportunity to take a course otherwise unavailable. In Michigan, high school students must take an online course as a graduation requirement. Other states recommend taking an online course, but do not require it.

Full-time virtual schools are growing phenomena. Twenty-nine states operate a full-time virtual school. Across the nation, over 297,000 students are enrolled in a full-time online school.[36] Some students enrolled in these schools are home-schooled students. However, the majority of these students are enrolled in an online charter school. An emerging trend in virtual schooling is the growing number of private, for-profit charter virtual schools.

7-4g TECHNOLOGY FOR STUDENTS WITH SPECIAL NEEDS

Technology tools can also assist students with special needs. For students with learning disabilities, such tools can help level the playing field by presenting information in a manner best suited to the students' learning style and unique needs. Using the right software, a modified curriculum can support students with special needs and help ensure successful immersion in the mainstream classroom.

In addition to its direct instructional uses, assistive technology plays a second, very important role for students with special needs. Assistive technology describes the array of devices and services that help people with disabilities perform better in their daily lives and achieve successful inclusion in regular classrooms.[37] (See Chapter 3, "Who Are Today's Students in a Diverse Society?," for a further discussion of assistive technology and special education.)

There are a wide variety of technology tools to help students with special needs fully participate in school. Students with disabilities benefit from technology that helps with reading and writing using technology tools like *Actively Learn* where teachers can insert vocabulary definitions and provide additional video or audio sources to describe a difficult concept. These modifications can be assigned to the whole class or just to students with disabilities. Another option includes a word prediction software that facilitates keyboarding. After the student types a letter or two, the computer presents a list of likely words, and the student simply selects the correct word rather than typing it out completely. Other aids, such as speech-to-text software, which translates a student's spoken words into text on the computer screen, or programs that will read text aloud can make writing a satisfying experience for students who struggle in this area.[38]

Students who struggle with executive functions have difficulty organizing their time and materials and juggling multiple tasks. Software such as *Google Tasks* can help students scaffold large projects, follow a checklist (with due dates), and set alarms for reminders. Over time students can use these technology tools to assist them in becoming more organized and independent.

Computers are especially helpful in allowing students to participate in normal classroom activities that would otherwise be impossible. User-friendly keyboard enhancements simplify typing, and assistive technology can be used to control most basic computer applications. The Microsoft, Apple, and Chrome OS offer "access" features that enable users to select options such as visual prompts for the deaf or the ability to use a computer without a monitor for the blind.

Eye- and head-tracking software is a revolutionary technology that opens up opportunities for students with special needs. Students with special needs can use a number of different programs and even apps to operate a computer or handheld device without hand movements. The program tracks and records the users' eye or head movements and pupil dilation across a computer display, so that the system can be controlled with movement alone; this technology allows even extremely immobile students to communicate with teachers and classmates. Such applications allow users to do things like tilt their head to scroll through a web page or flip the pages of an e-book. Eye movements can be used to conduct more fine-tuned tasks such as drawing shapes. Blind students and their teachers can use Braille software, which provides easy-to-use, sophisticated print-to-Braille and Braille-to-print translations.

Tablets and smartphones offer even more ways that technology can support students with special needs. Take, for example, a student with cerebral palsy who has limited verbal skills and can only type with a modified keyboard. That student can now use an app to record information on the go with his or her tablet. The mobility features of handheld devices now enable technology to also support students with special needs such as attention deficit/hyperactivity disorder (ADHD). Apps are available that help students do things like set reminders, organize projects, or play concentration games.

As discussed in Chapter 3, "Who Are Today's Students in a Diverse Society?," assistive technology must be considered a potential component of the Individualized Education Program (IEP) required under law for each child with a disability. Regular classrooms now often include students with disabilities and other students with special needs, and you should be prepared to work with children who use assistive technology in your classroom. This process may be easier than you realize because many features developed for special needs users have been incorporated into general-use software.

From apps to mechanical devices, assistive technologies enable students with disabilities to become more independent and effective learners.

FatCamera/iStock/Getty Images Plus/Getty Images

Pause *and* Reflect

1. How can technologies help provide an equitable education for students with disabilities?
2. Pick the technology that most interests you in this section, and think about how you might use it in your classroom. Would the technology allow you to improve on something you already did? Would you be innovating with the technology?
3. Do you have any educational concerns about the use of these technologies in schools?

7-5 How Are Technologies Affecting Teaching?

As a teacher, you can expect that your students will have to meet standards relating to technology. Most states have standards exclusively for technology. In line with the current nationwide move toward standards-based learning (see "What Ought to Be the Elements of Educational Reform" in Chapter 12, "How Should Education Be Reformed?"), the International Society for Technology in Education (ISTE) has produced national technology standards.[39] ISTE encourages teachers to teach these skills within the context of their academic curriculum. To this end, ISTE provides resources for incorporating the ISTE technology standards into subject standards for the rest of the curriculum.

Although this trend is encouraging, for technology to be truly integrated as an important part of classroom instruction, current practices and attitudes must change in several other ways. The impact of technology on learning depends more on the ways in which teachers use the technology than on the characteristics of the technology itself.

7-5a A DIFFERENT ROLE FOR THE TEACHER

Integrating technology into your teaching can change the way you deliver content to your classes. Some schools and teachers have been slow to discover the true potential of new technologies, but some new trends are emerging. Technology can be more effective in a teaching environment where the technology helps facilitate instruction and foster a constructivist approach to learning, as discussed in "The Influence of Two Psychological Theories" in Chapter 9, "What Are the Philosophical Foundations of American Education?" As we have mentioned throughout this chapter, a constructivist approach to infusing technology is related to several other classroom characteristics, including:

- *Teacher as facilitator.* Think back to the scenario at the beginning of this chapter. Patricia Gonzalez was *facilitating* instruction as needed to bring a deeper understanding of the topics and their relevance to students. Because of the technology the students employed, she was no longer the sole source of information for her class. Teachers as facilitators become much more involved in higher-level evaluation of performance and can monitor students' projects; guiding their efforts, asking thought-provoking questions, and providing feedback.

- *Embedding technology in the curriculum.* With the encouragement of groups such as ISTE, the idea of teaching technology skills in isolation is giving way to a model of embedding technology skills within the context of the content.[40] For example, a social studies teacher might teach the mechanics of a program such as *VoiceThread* as part of a unit on the local community that asks students to create a virtual field trip. In this model, the subject matter drives the technology, rather than the reverse. In the words of one team of researchers, "We learn best 'with' technology rather than 'from' it."[41]

- *Small-group instruction.* To better use some technologies, teachers must move from whole-class instruction toward smaller group projects and activities that are more conducive to active, engaged learning and student collaboration. Classrooms that effectively collaborate are using technologies such as blogs and shared *Google docs* to discuss and collectively develop ideas or are using *Book Creator* or *WeVideo* to work collaboratively on a presentation may evolve into cooperative rather than competitive social structures, and student assessment should shift away from testing and toward the formative evaluation of products and progress.[42]

- *Importance of formative assessment.* When teaching with technology, educators use formative assessments to monitor both students' understanding of the technology tools and the content-learning goals of the lesson. Furthermore, because student use of technology often requires critical thinking skills, teacher feedback during the working process can be a catalyst for students to achieve a deeper level of understanding.

T (F)

Technology produces a generation of rote learners.

The connection between technology and constructivism is beginning to be understood more deeply. We know that teachers who have changed to a more constructivist approach in their classrooms are the same innovative teachers who have used technology consistently and in meaningful ways in their classrooms. These teachers are more willing to discuss subjects in which they are not experts and tend to assign longer, more complex projects that guide their students to think at a higher level. It appears that technology does not make teachers change; rather, technology facilitates changes that teachers already wanted to make.[43]

Of course, change in education is rarely swift. Even highly motivated teachers who regularly use technology take a while to become comfortable with new technology and fit it into their classroom goals. Given the increasing pressure on schools to incorporate up-to-date technology, and with other supporting factors present, such as sufficient funding and on-site technical support, we can expect to see changes in teachers' pedagogy as they become more comfortable with the power and teaching opportunities technology provides.

7-5b PROFESSIONAL COMMUNICATION

The teaching profession has long been known as an isolated profession. Often teachers enter the school building each morning, greet a few colleagues, walk into their classroom, and spend the rest of the day there with their students. One recent study found that only 31 percent of teachers reported having ample time scheduled to collaborate with other teachers. One encouraging statistic from this study found teachers who did have greater opportunities and time to meet with their colleagues reported higher levels of actual collaboration.[44] The surge of educational applications of social media are breaking down some of the isolating walls and providing teachers with creative ways of connecting with others outside of the classroom and even outside of their school.

Teachers can use social media, such as *Twitter,* to collaborate with colleagues. Over the short-term, when a teacher tweets about what their students are learning and why that learning is important, they are reflecting on the effectiveness of their teaching strategies and how those strategies impacted student learning. Over the long term, teachers can use hashtags to organize and use evidence from their tweets to notice patterns. These reflections can help teachers recognize and celebrate what ideas, strategies, or pedagogies are working well and calibrate their lessons to improve the quality of their teaching and student learning.

Teachers also use social media to collaborate with parents. Many teachers have replaced their weekly printed newsletter with digital forms of communicating with parents. Many teachers today use blogs or Twitter to share information with parents. There are many ways in which technology can now be used to keep parents connected with what is happening in the classroom. Texts, email, blogs, and websites, which are often welcomed by parents who do not have the time for many face-to-face meetings, are just a few of the technologies being used by parents to obtain information about their child's learning.[45] These have the added bonus that they are much more likely to get directly into the hands of parents; notes are often lost at the bottom of book bags, especially if there is bad news.

Many parents want to know what is happening at school, and websites provide a great way to post photographs, text, and even video to provide a window into your classroom community. Teachers can take advantage of the many good free website options available, such as *Google sites.* LMSs such as *Canvas* provide a secure place for posting homework, grades, school notices, and other resources that ensure parents can follow what is happening in the classroom.

Technology can be either a "hook" to get parents more involved or an obstacle between you and your students' parents. If you have a class website that gives pertinent information to parents, also ensure that you provide paper copies to those parents who do not have consistent access to the Internet.

Digital storytelling tools are also exciting cognitive tools that can support student learning. One of the most popular uses of these tools is to share student work. Teachers craft lessons that require students to upload assignments in a variety of digital formats such as movies or podcasts. When crafting such assignments, teachers should be aware that not all students will have access to technology with Internet access at home. When this is the case, teachers should be sure that students are able to complete their assignments at school, a public library, or a community center. Some schools will provide student access to technology before school hours or keep them open in the afternoon so that students can have supervised hands-on computer time to complete homework assignments.

Some teachers use the power of social media to share student work with a wider audience. As with all uses of social media, teachers should be mindful of their professional and personal uses of social media. Unfortunately, the headlines are reporting more and more stories of teachers being fired for inappropriate uses of social media.[46] Rather than avoid using social media, we suggest following guidelines for appropriate usage. A baseline guide is to only share information online that you would share in the classroom. Facebook suggests five tips for teachers using Facebook and other social media platforms:

1. Know your school's policy on using social media in the classroom, and comply.
2. Use public pages for your classes to post homework assignments and other updates.
3. Use groups to control membership and facilitate discussion.
4. Be a role model of a good online citizen.
5. Report inappropriate content to Facebook.[47]

Pause *and* Reflect

1. How can teachers use technology to improve communication with parents?
2. Do you envision yourself as a teacher who would be comfortable using technology in a constructivist way, such as Patricia Gonzalez did?
3. What do you see as the pros and cons of such an approach?

7-6 How Are Technologies Organized for Student Use?

Technologies generally operate in several different arrangements within the school setting, and it is useful to think of these arrangements as ranging across a continuum from concentrated to infused, as shown in Figure 7.3. When technology is *concentrated*, students are given intense exposure to computers from time to time. Technology that is integrated smoothly into the daily classroom experience is described as *infused*. Several common computer setups exist along this continuum.

7-6a COMPUTER LABS

Computer labs offer a concentrated arrangement in which all the students use computers at the same time. This setup is ideal for technology education—teaching about the computer or how to employ a particular application. In many labs, a digital projector displays important information while the teacher facilitates the demonstration of skills for more effective whole-class instruction.

Most computer labs do not lend themselves to interdisciplinary or cooperative group projects because of a lack of open table space, although some teachers foster collaboration by having two chairs around one computer. Access to computer labs is another key factor in their use by teachers. If many classrooms must share a single computer facility, there may be little lab time for each class, and visits to the lab must always be planned. For these reasons, computer labs tend to foster technology education rather than integration of technology into the curriculum.

7-6b SINGLE-COMPUTER CLASSROOMS

In a slightly more infused arrangement, the single-computer classroom might have the computer that is kept on the teacher's desk. Although a single computer makes it difficult to use the technology for active instructional tasks, using digital projectors, a teacher can make the rich resources of the Internet available for the entire class. For example, teachers

FIGURE 7.3

Arrangements for Computer Technologies

One way to think about the different ways of arranging computer technologies within a school is to consider where each arrangement fits along a continuum, from concentrated to infused. If the arrangement is concentrated, students are exposed to computers in an intense way from time to time, whereas technology that is integrated smoothly into the daily classroom experience is infused more consistently.

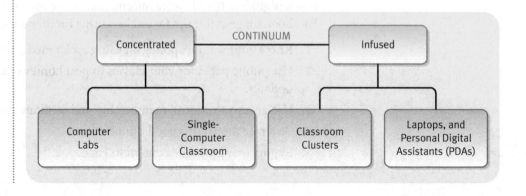

might use their one computer to demonstrate complex mathematical or scientific concepts by using dynamic visualization programs such as *The Geometer's Sketchpad* or *Starry Night*; when used properly, this strategy can support student learning and inquiry.[48] Unfortunately, projection systems are all too frequently misused, with students being subjected to endless and wordy *PowerPoint* slides in darkened rooms, where they become passive consumers of the digitally rendered information rather than active learners.

7-6c CLASSROOM CLUSTERS

In a more infused situation, a cluster is usually an area of a classroom where three to five desktop computers, laptops, Chromebooks, or tablets are available for use at any time. Clusters can allow teachers to plan collaborative group activities where small groups of students share these devices to engage in the research process. Students have discussions to decide what information is important, how to best paraphrase the information, and how to synthesize their learning to answer their research question(s). The teacher can act as a facilitator to help students gain a better understanding. This arrangement genuinely fosters integration of technology into the curriculum.

7-6d LAPTOPS, CHROMEBOOKS, AND TABLETS (SHARED CARTS AND 1:1 DEVICES)

1:1 technology programs provide one device for every student, providing equitable access throughout the school. Teachers who have had professional development in technology integration find 1:1 programs can facilitate deep, flexible use of technology by the students and encourages the teacher to assume the role of facilitator. For example, teachers can use *PearDeck* to create interactive slide shows that engage students in learning. The teacher asks students to work in small groups to discuss the prompts, but students respond individually with written responses, draggables, and drawings. The teacher can quickly check for understanding, ask questions to deepen their students' thinking, and share student responses to model a concept.

iPads and Chromebooks offer the benefit of achieving a 1:1 ratio at a fraction of the cost of laptops. iPad sales peaked in 2014, but with recently reduced pricing, sales have begun to increase once again.[49] In the meantime, Chromebooks have exploded onto the scene and have grabbed the greatest share of the education technology market. Cloud-based interactive websites, including *Google Apps For Education*, have improved, and schools have increased their high-speed Internet bandwidth making these inexpensive tools very appealing to school districts.[50]

More and more apps are being developed to support student learning with tablets.

©Irina Palei/Shutterstock.com

Pause *and* Reflect

1. Envision yourself teaching with each of these computer arrangements. What would you and your students be able to do in a computer lab?
2. How would that be different if each of your students were able to use a handheld device in school?
3. How would your instruction change if you were assigned to a classroom with a single computer?

7-7 How Do Issues of Equity, Teacher Education, and Budgeting Impact Technology in Schools?

To achieve the best use of available technology, schools must reach some consensus on several key issues, including questions about infrastructure, budgeting, teacher education, parent support, equity for students, and how to infuse technology into the curriculum.

7-7a EDUCATION OF TEACHERS

Because of the excitement and demands generated by new technology, there is increasing pressure to improve both the preparation of new teachers and the staff development options for in-service teachers.

Teacher Preparation

When you graduate, you can count on having to demonstrate your skills in technology. In addition to ISTE standards, most states have included technology components as part of their licensure requirements. Schools of education, much like elementary and secondary schools, are grappling with the challenge of developing competent teachers who will meet these goals.

Many instructors indicate that, even with the recent emphasis on computer literacy, instructional technology is not adequately modeled for future teachers.[51] Schools of education are continuing to rethink their programs and are gradually using modern technology to enhance what they offer. To this end, education students often develop digital portfolios of their work, create e-books to use with students, and use digital video to capture and reflect on their student teaching.

Staff Development

Some states are adding more stringent technology requirements that teachers must meet to renew their licenses. Teachers report, however, that one of the greatest obstacles to their use of technology is lack of professional development. Experts do not agree exactly how training should be offered. Some believe training should be an ongoing process that is accessed at the teacher's convenience, whereas others advocate for an intensive, off-site course with follow-up seminars to allow teachers a chance to learn with undivided attention. Many professional development courses are now offered online. Teachers who cannot be released during the school day can log on at night or during the summer to work through synchronous and asynchronous professional development.

VOICES from the Classroom

Technology

Samantha Shires is a middle school social studies teacher in Greensboro, North Carolina.

There is a common misconception that educational technology has to look a certain way in order to be successful. But what I have found is that the key to technology being successful in the classroom is that it is simple to use and that it benefits both teachers and students. One piece of technology, used correctly in a classroom setting, can completely transform how you teach and how your students learn.

I recently introduced my students to an interactive timeline tool called ChronoZoom. This timeline tool shows the history of the world starting with the creation of the universe, all the way up to modern day. The beauty of ChronoZoom is that it is able to show how vast and complex history actually is in a way that allows students to sift through information and see the depth and scope of history instantly.

As soon as my students started using it, I saw light bulbs going off over their heads as they started to understand how events of the past were shaped and influenced, and that more than one event can happen at a single time. They were able to instantly understand and see "big" history.

Such a magical tool must be complicated and require copious amounts of technology, right?

Wrong! My classroom has one computer that is hooked up to a digital projector. My students were introduced to ChronoZoom in the beginning of the year, as a way to show them the depth and scope of the history of the world. I told them they were going to become a part of the ChonoZoomer's Guild, and their main objective was going to be to find their own truths of the past using ChronoZoom as a way to gather and input information. I created timelines on ChronoZoom, inputting information, graphics, and videos of the unit we were studying at the time—the age of exploration. I also used ChronoZoom as an assessment piece, where students created their own timelines in order to show me that they understood what the age of exploration was and why it was a significant era.

ChronoZoom is an example of a technology tool transforming the way I teach and my students learn. Without this tool, timelines were a static line on a piece of paper. Now, they are complex and interactive. Watching my students become captivated by content was such a rewarding and beautiful feeling that has continued to transform and power my classroom forward.

Up CLOSE

Collections, Courses, Community: Primary Source

Primary Source is one example of how the Internet has transformed professional development and learning. The efforts of Primary Source educate global citizens by providing high-quality professional development, curriculum resources, and a robust professional learning community (PLC). Primary Source offers both asynchronous and synchronous courses, workshops, seminars, and webinars. Teachers from all around the globe participate in these courses. Typically, an expert will present on a topic and teachers learn from them and have the opportunity to ask questions. They also offer online curriculum resources providing a vast repository of audio, text, and multimedia for teachers. Primary Source goes beyond publishing resources and offering courses by building a robust PLC with a mission to educate global citizens. Using social media platforms and International Study Tours, Primary Source fosters a community of educators working collaboratively to share new ideas, strategies, and pedagogies to support their global teaching.

Pause *and* Reflect

1. Which skills in using media and technology do you think teachers should have?
2. How can you prepare yourself to use technology in your classroom?
3. What are your concerns about using technology in the classroom?
4. What kinds of support systems do the teachers you know have for using technology in instruction? Whom do they ask when they have questions?

7-7b EQUITY

Students who use technology at home have opportunities to develop skills and explore technology's potential that are not available to students without these resources. Students with Internet access from home, and particularly broadband access, may have opportunities that others do not. Although the divide is closing between those with Internet access and those without, there is still a large discrepancy between the two. In 2018, the FCC reported that 12 million children had no access to broadband or high-speed Internet services. In 2020, 14 percent of households with school-age children did not have Internet access.[52] Affordability remains the determining factor for whether households have high-speed connections.[53]

Some critics also argue that current patterns of technology use in schools contribute to disparities in educational quality. At school, data indicate that poorer students are at a disadvantage. Although the presence of computers in schools in wealthier and poorer areas has almost equalized, the digital divide still exists around how technology is creating opportunities as it is being integrated into the curriculum. Sociologist Paul Attewell describes the phenomena of a usage divide.[54] In his research, Attewell observed that underprivileged children are more likely to use computers in a rigid drill-and-practice format rather than in more flexible formats, such as doing online research, that build higher-level cognitive skills. The digital opportunity divide continues. In a 2020 interview, Patricia J. Brown, a technology specialist for the Ladue School District in Missouri said, "When I think about digital equity, I think about ensuring that everyone has equal access and opportunity. That they have knowledge about what technology resources are available to them and the possibilities that they can achieve through technology, whether it's creating or consuming. Access doesn't necessarily mean handing students devices. It is more about what they can create with that technology."[55]

There are models of teachers and community members using technology to break down the digital usage divide. One example is the URBAN TxT (https:// exploringtech.org/home) program based out of Los Angeles, California. This after-school program is designed to provide technology access to inner-city teenagers and to support their development as a community and technology leader. The program is geared not only to keep at-risk students from dropping out of school but also to equip them with skills that will help support their ability to become leaders in the field of technology. Students gain programming skills to develop websites and apps. One 15-year-old who participated in the program said that because of his experiences in the program, he sees himself as a "technology pioneer" and has set high academic goals for himself.[56]

T F
Students from lower socioeconomic families are more likely to use computers for drill and practice than children from the middle class.

Technology access divides along racial—as well as income—lines. A recent study found that Asian households are the most likely to use the Internet at home (88.8%). They are followed by white households (79.9%), Hispanic households (70.9%), and black households (64.9%).[57] As we discussed earlier in the chapter, smartphones are changing the landscape of communication and access to information. One good piece of news is that African Americans and English-speaking Latinos are as likely as whites to own and use a smartphone. In fact, they are more likely to use their phones for a greater variety of tasks than whites.[58]

Gender differences are also a factor in the effective use of technology in education. Researchers argue that certain types of technologies aggravate the differences (whether nature or nurture) between boys and girls. For example, many commonly used applications value speed, aggression, and efficiency[59]—qualities that boys tend to display. For girls, technology appears to be more interesting when it's used for a relevant problem-solving exercise or collaboration rather than as an end in itself.[60] The key to engaging girls in technology appears to be *how* technology is used in the classroom. Tasks that require versatility and collaboration and that move to an integrated approach are more inviting to girls. One organization, *Girls Who Code*, is having success engaging girls in learning coding skills and applying their new knowledge to collaboratively develop solutions to real-world issues. Technology need not become a wedge widening the gap between the "haves" and the "have-nots," along racial lines, or among genders, but without awareness of the problem and an investment to solve the problem, the potential for increased inequity is very real.

Pause *and* Reflect

1. Where do you see evidence of the digital divide in the world outside of the K–12 classroom?
2. How will the digital divide affect you and your classroom?

7-7c INTEGRATION INTO THE CURRICULUM

For technology to become a genuine part of school life, as it has in the business world, the tools of technology must be *integrated* into school behaviors. Integrating technology means bringing the tools of technology into daily learning and teaching activities, just as teachers already do with chalkboards and books. This is not an easy task. Much of this chapter has focused on how computer technologies can be used as tools for student learning, but we have also seen that many support systems must be in place.

Which conditions must be present in a school "to create learning environments conducive to powerful uses of technology"?[61] Among other conditions, schools must have the following:

- Student-centered approaches to learning
- Access to contemporary technologies, software, and communications networks
- Educators skilled in the use of the technology for learning

Up CLOSE

Teaching During a Pandemic

In 2020, our world was shut down due to the coronavirus pandemic. Schools closed their doors and educators and students moved to teaching and learning online. Educators found that there was no one-size-fits-all solution to remote teaching as every classroom, school, and district had unique challenges. The anecdotal evidence from respected educators (blogs, podcasts, Twitter, and more) have begun to uncover patterns that have led to successful teaching and learning. Educators who met with success during school closures had thoughtfully integrated technology before they had to move to remote learning. They combined a mix of synchronous teaching backed up by clearly defined and scaffolded asynchronous learning opportunities, focused on the social-emotional well-being of their students, and provided engaging learning opportunities that empowered their students to construct knowledge.

- Technical assistance for maintaining and using technology resources
- Ongoing financial support for sustained technology use
- Content standards and curriculum resources
- Community partners who provide expertise, support, and real-life interactions
- Vision with support and proactive leadership from the education system
- Assessment of the effectiveness of technology for learning

As this list indicates, real change in education and technology cannot be the job of a lone teacher who is a whiz on the Internet or a single school board member who votes for new software. It must be a systemic change coming from a critical mass of individuals who are committed to the integration of education *with* technology.

Teachers must be mindful of the conditions most conducive to integrating technology into the classroom.

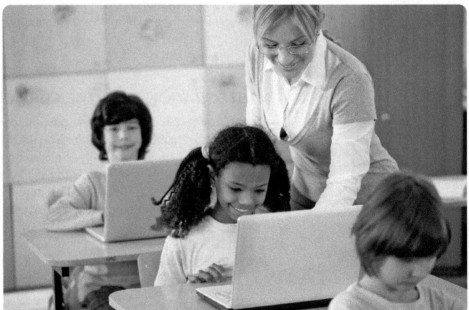

iStock.com/Vetta Collection/skynesher

OUR FINAL WORD

The final word on the role of technology in education must belong to the teacher. Are we spending billions of dollars on fancy hardware, remodeling schools to accommodate wireless networks, and asking veteran teachers to change their ways without reason? What do we lose when we incorporate technology into our teaching? With increased access to vast amounts of up-to-date information and powerful new technologies, are students learning "the basics" as well as they do in more traditional classrooms?

One view of the purposes of schools, as we discussed in Chapter 2, "What Is a School and What Is It For?," is economic: to prepare students for their future occupation. According to this view, equipping students with "twenty-first-century skills" includes preparing them to use technology.[62] Teachers, by comparison, tend to have a broader focus: They want to develop healthy bonds with their students that will lead to intellectual growth. Teachers hope to develop responsible, educated citizens who have every opportunity open to them. When teachers see the rapidly changing world of technology in which technology sometimes breaks, certain applications take a long time to learn, and some programs are not flexible enough to meet their needs, they hesitate to take part in it.[63] Although policy makers might rush to shove schools into the information age, teachers make up a crucial part of the integration question. To reach some consensus, the dialogue should begin not with the goals of technology, but rather with the goals of schooling. When agreement is found, educators should raise the question of how technology can help reach those goals.

Certainly new technologies are no panacea for classrooms. Districts around the country are grappling with concerns about excessive screen time, privacy and security, cyberbullying and hate speech, and news and media literacy. We suggest that instead of avoiding technology, you work with your district to use websites that have signed data privacy agreements and engage your students in being the best digital citizens that they can be.[64]

Thoughtful integration of technology can help change the classroom from a teacher-centered to a more cooperative and student-centered environment. Students can use technological devices as tools—not toys—in the same ways that they will likely use technology in their future lives. We believe that all teachers should have the opportunity to gain skill in educational technologies; in particular, it would behoove new teachers to develop these skills in the context of their preservice work. Most important, we want you to consider how technology will affect your future classroom. Ask yourself where technology can enhance what you do and where it can allow you to innovate. If it is not accomplishing these goals, ask yourself why you are using it.[65]

WHY TEACH? YOUR FINAL WORD

1. Do you think parents should be concerned about the role—or lack of it—that technological tools play in the education of their children? At what age do you think children should be taught to use computers?

2. Should governments spend billions of dollars on technology for schools, or should the money be spent differently?

3. What do you see as the goals of schooling? Are there ways you can use technology to reach those goals?

KEY TERMS

1:1 computing (196)
cognitive tools (189)
digital storytelling (194)
mind maps (194)
productivity tools (189)
simulation (199)

spreadsheet (197)
tutorials (200)
virtual schools (203)
virtual tours (199)
webs (194)

FOR FURTHER INFORMATION

Web Resources

International Society for Technology in Education (ISTE)

A superb list of resources that cover a wide range of issues related to teaching and learning with technology.

Edutopia

The George Lucas Educational Foundation's initiative to improve K–12 schools. The website shares a collection of videos, essays, lesson plans, and stories that highlight teachers using technology in innovative ways.

Print Resources

George Couros, *The Innovator's Mindset: Empower Learning, Unleash Talent, and Lead a Culture of Creativity* (Dave Burgess Consulting, Inc., 2015).

This book offers practical strategies to harness student excitement and engagement, asks thought-provoking questions, and fosters creativity in teaching.

Peter A. Hall and Alisa Simeral, *Creating a Culture of Reflective Practice: Capacity-Building for Schoolwide Success* (ASCD, 2017).

This book has many suggestions to help teachers be more reflective to improve their practice and pedagogy.

Liz Kolb, *Learning First, Technology Second In Practice: New Strategies, Research and Tools for Student Success* (ISTE, 2020).

This book is a great resource for teachers striving to thoughtfully integrate technology in ways that improve teaching and learning.

Jay McTighe and Harvey Silver, *Teaching For Deeper Learning; Tools To Engage Students In Meaning Making* (ASCD Assn Supervisory and Curriculum Development Dev, 2020).

Teachers can use the strategies suggested in this book to teach their students to think, question, and explore.

Catlin R. Tucker, et al. *Blended Learning in Action: a Practical Guide toward Sustainable Change* (Corwin, a SAGE Company, 2017).

The authors present their case for blended learning and teachers gain practical implementation strategies that can transform their teaching and empower student learning through choice of path, pace, and space.

Todd Whitaker and Jeffrey Zoul, *What Connected Educators Do Differently* (2015). Print.

The author suggests concrete ideas to use social media in a way that can allow teachers to reach beyond their classroom and school walls to collaborate with teachers from around the country and around the world.

What Are the Ethical and Legal Issues Facing Teachers?

Digital Vision./Photodisc/Getty Images

LEARNING OBJECTIVES

8-1 Distinguish between law and ethics, and state why these terms are important to teachers.

8-2 Elaborate on how ethics is involved in the professional activities of the teacher.

8-3 Report on the nature of the law and how it bears on the work of teachers.

8-4 Explain how a teacher's lifestyle is circumscribed by the law.

8-5 State the various legal issues surrounding religion and public education.

8-6 Describe how the law governs and protects the behavior of students.

Truth OR Fiction?

T F Unlike medical doctors who have the Hippocratic Oath, there is no single, universally accepted code of ethics for teachers.

T F It is legal in American public school classrooms to study religious books, such as the Bible, the Talmud, and the Koran.

T F After many years of delay, recently the Supreme Court has made corporal punishment in our schools unconstitutional and therefore illegal.

This chapter aims to sharpen your sense of the ethical dimension of teaching and your understanding of the legal underpinnings of many aspects of school life. We examine several common ethical problems faced by teachers, along with legal issues and recent court rulings that have affected them.

If each of us were the only person on the face of the Earth, we could behave exactly as we chose. We would not have to worry about the rights or feelings of anyone else. We would be free of the constraints and demands imposed by others as we went about doing our own will. Of course, this is simply not the case. Everyone who walks the Earth is bound by real—if unseen—connections with his or her fellow humans. The English poet John Donne said it most succinctly: "No man is an island."

Our systems of ethics and laws are a major part of these invisible connecting fibers. Together they make civilized society in a neighborhood and coexistence on a planet possible. Ethics, as we say in Chapter 9, "What Are the Philosophical Foundations of American Education?," brings us into the realm of what is the right way to act. **Ethics** refers to a system or a code of morality embraced by a particular person or group. Law is related to, but different from, ethics. An individual **law** is a written rule that members of a given community must follow. The law is the system of such rules that governs the general conduct of a particular community's citizens.

8-1 Laws, Ethics, and the Teacher's Responsibility

While one's ethics are a set of invisible obligations he or she is aware of, laws typically are statements that have been hammered out by the legitimate authority of a particular community, state, or nation, and are used in court as standards by which to judge, and often penalize, the actual behavior of individuals. What someone might refer to as an *unstated law* is not a law at all, however: It is an ethical statement.

Laws are concrete, made by people, and usually written down for the public to see; ethics, by contrast, consists of ideas that are less tangible and observable. Most of our laws are simply the codification of what we see as our moral or ethical obligations to one another. For example, we have laws against excessive speeding that follow from our ethical beliefs that we ought not endanger the lives of others. Sometimes, however, laws are unethical, such as the racial segregation laws that existed in this country a mere half century ago. Also, ethical obligations may not always be codified as laws, such as the ethical obligation we all have to help the weak, the poor, and the sick.

What does all this have to do with teachers? First, it is the responsibility of teachers to convey to the young the fundamental moral message that we are all legally and ethically bound to one another. Much of this moral message is incorporated into the content of our curricula, from our great stories to our history as a people. Second, as we explore in this chapter, a school is awash with ethical and legal issues. A unique set of ethical relationships and legal obligations is embedded in teachers' work. As a consequence, teachers carry a special ethical and legal burden. This second issue is the subject of this chapter.

At the heart of the teacher's unique ethical and legal relationship with students is *power*. Like it or not, power resides in the "office" of teacher. Compared with a corporate executive or a military officer, it may not appear that a teacher has a great deal of power. In reality, teachers have a special type of power. This power arises from the fact that teachers have an impact on people when they are still at a very malleable stage. Teachers are legally in command of a classroom insofar as they have the responsibility for what goes on. Teachers evaluate their students. They not only "mark" them with tangible symbols that become part of students' official records, but they also "mark" their minds and hearts. Many careers are open to you, but few offer such truly awe-inspiring power than that of a teacher.

If you wish to know what a man is, place him in authority.

—YUGOSLAV PROVERB

Because of the potential for abuse of this power, codes of ethics have been established to guide teachers, and a body of laws governs the work of teaching. Ignorance of the law (and ethics) is no excuse. We, therefore, urge you to take the material in this chapter quite seriously.

Pause *and* Reflect

1. When you think about some of your favorite teachers, can you recall ways in which they exhibited ethical habits or principles? Do you have memories of teachers behaving unethically? How?
2. How will you, as a teacher, act differently in similar situations?
3. What would you say is the greatest ethical obligation of a teacher? Why?

8-2 The Ethics of Teaching

Being an ethical teacher means having a special relationship with your students and the other people with whom you work. Consider the following case, as told to educator Kenneth Howe by a practicing teacher.[1]

8-2a THE SHOULD I SPY OR NOT SPY CASE

Marilyn Henderson is a fifth-grade language arts teacher at Willoughby Elementary in South Lake, a medium-size city with a population of roughly 150,000. Marilyn is troubled to learn that Connie Severns, a fifth-grade social studies teacher with whom Marilyn worked previously in another school in the South Lake system, will be transferred to Willoughby. Marilyn believes Connie to be incompetent and is uncomfortable with this knowledge, especially in light of the fact that her students will be moving through Connie's class. As Marilyn recalls, "Connie didn't teach anything; she couldn't teach anything." Others in the district share Marilyn's assessment of Connie as a teacher and apparently with good reason. Connie seems totally unable to motivate students and keep their attention. Children cry and complain about the chaos, some steal things from her purse, and on one occasion another teacher discovered a child chasing Connie around the room.

Pause *and* Reflect

1. As a colleague of Connie's, what should Marilyn do?
2. As a member of the teaching profession, what should Marilyn do?
3. If you were in this situation, what would you do?

Marilyn had previously tried to do something about Connie's incompetence, but met with little success. The teachers' union representatives advised her that they would have to stand behind a tenured teacher. The school administration claimed to have to follow procedures that could take years to build a case for dismissal. At this point in time (before Connie's transfer), the principal of Willoughby was unhappy with Connie coming to his school. He called the affected teachers together. He too was concerned about Connie's transfer and proposed that they discreetly and surreptitiously "write things down" to build a case that they could use to have Connie fired. Marilyn is asked to be a part of this effort.[2]

8-2b THE CHARACTERISTICS OF ETHICAL TEACHING

This story provides just a peek into the teachers' ethically complex world. Howe suggests that in dealing with issues involving ethical judgment, we as teachers need to exhibit six characteristics: appreciation for moral deliberation, empathy, knowledge, reasoning, courage, and interpersonal skills.[3]

Appreciation for Moral Deliberation

We need to see an ethical dilemma such as Marilyn's as a situation characterized by conflicting and competing moral interests—in this case, Connie's need for a job, the students' need for a competent teacher, and the other teachers' need to be fair in what they say to and about Connie. We must see the complex moral dimensions of the problem and appreciate that care must be taken to protect the rights of all parties.

Empathy

Empathy is the ability to mentally "get inside the skin" of another person. We need to feel what the others in an ethically troublesome situation are feeling. In the case described, we would need to empathize with everyone who is affected by the burden of a questionable teacher—the students and their parents, Connie, and Marilyn and the other teachers.

Knowledge

One of the most valuable tools of a teacher who is able to deal effectively with ethical issues is knowledge. We must remember the facts that will enable us to put an issue in context. What does Connie actually do in the classroom? Which formal procedures are in place to deal with ineffective or incompetent teachers? In Marilyn's case, she has to be able to think clearly about the alternatives—such as participating in the principal's questionable plan or perhaps directly confronting Connie—and she must think through, with some degree of accuracy, what the likely consequences of such actions would be. Knowledge of the situation allows Marilyn to move to the next step: reasoning.

Reasoning

To reason is to reflect systematically on an issue. We don't blur the decision with emotionality. When we reason about an issue, we move through it step by step and draw conclusions, or we compare a particular event or action with some moral principle and come to some conclusion. For instance, Marilyn may hold as moral principles the notions that people should not deceive others and that spying is deception. Through reasoning, she may come to the conclusion that what the principal has asked her to do is spying. Of course, this line of reasoning leaves Marilyn with another problem: how to tell her principal that his plan is unethical.

Courage

To feel, to know, and to reason are not enough. To be ethical, we must act—and action sometimes takes courage. To be ethically correct often requires the willpower to act in what we perceive to be the right way rather than in the comfortable way. Frequently, when confronted with a seemingly no-win dilemma like Marilyn's, we tend to ignore it in the hope that it will simply go away. However, as the theologian Harvey Cox sees it, "Not to decide is to decide." Among other things, Marilyn must find a way to tell her principal that she simply cannot be a part of his secret reporting network. Besides courage, this act will require tact.

Interpersonal Skills

Besides courage, acting on ethical principles demands sensitivity. In addition, teachers need the communications skills to deal sensitively with issues that demand great tact. They have to be able to call up the right words, with the right feeling and tone, and address the issue at hand openly and honestly.

8-2c NEEDED: A GUIDING CODE OF ETHICS

Behind this six-part process of dealing with ethical issues is something rather intangible, but nevertheless quite real: a personal code of ethics. Each of us has one, although some are beacons and others are dim lights in a dark room. For example, in Marilyn's response to her principal's request that she spy on Connie, what she does will be influenced by her personal code of ethics. That is, Marilyn's own answer to the question, "What is the right thing to do here?" is what will come into play.

When individuals enter the classroom as teachers, they are not always able to act in a manner that they find most satisfying. For instance, a student's rude remark to you may cry out for a sarcastic comeback, and you may have the perfect one on the tip of your tongue. The actions of a student—even a very small child—may provoke a rush of anger. An athletic coach, a good friend, may ask you to raise the grade of one of your students who has become ineligible to play on the coach's team. Whatever you would like to do or what you might have done before as a "civilian" is of little importance in these situations; you must respond as a professional, as a teacher. You need to be ready and act from a well-formed code of ethics.

As mentioned earlier, ethics deals with "the right thing to do." Everyone is expected to do the right thing, but teachers' *responsibility* and *power* ratchet up the demand for solid and sound ethical decisions on their part. In addition, teachers often must be able to make ethical decisions on the spot. Telling the athletic coach, "I'll think about it," won't do.

Our personal answers to questions about what is the right thing to do represent our code of ethics and whether we are immediately aware of it, we all have one. Unlike the formal codes of ethics that govern doctors (i.e., the Hippocratic Oath) and established teachers' organizations, such as the National Education Association, our personal codes are not written down. Nevertheless, they are quite real and serve as our daily guide in moral matters large and small.

Scholars often argue about whether humans are born with an imprinted sense of what is morally correct. Few would suggest that we are born with a full-blown, guiding moral philosophy of life. Instead, developing a strong, guiding code of ethics is one of our primary responsibilities as members of society. As part of this evolution, we can draw on a variety of sources, including human examples, spiritual and religious wisdom, secular guides, reason, and our moral compass.

Human Example

Humans are imitative creatures. First, we copy our parents and siblings, and then, as we move out into the world, we copy various people who cross our paths. Most of the important things we learn—such as language, physical skills, and ways to treat others—we learn from the example of others. Like Marilyn, when we are confronted with a "What should I do?" question, the human examples we admire play a strong role in helping us come up with an ethically sound response. We recall the vision of a revered grandfather, parent, or friend to guide us. "What would Grandpa do in a situation like this? What would he expect me to do?"

Many people regularly rely on the examples set by people they have never met, such as individuals from history or literature. For example, some people wear "WWJD" bracelets, standing for "What would Jesus do?" The bracelets are meant to be a regular reminder of how to respond to ethical situations. Others draw on the examples of staunchly moral Americans, such as George Washington, Abraham Lincoln, Martin Luther King, Jr., and Eleanor Roosevelt. This is one reason why these figures are studied in our schools.

Also, parents want their children to be taught by ethical people because they want their children to be influenced by good examples. Conversely, attentive parents often shield their children from "bad companions" and violent TV and movie characters out of concern that their children will acquire those behaviors.

Spiritual and Religious Codes

For many people, one of the primary sources of ethical guidance is the spiritual and religious domain. Sacred books, such as the Bible, the Torah, and the Koran, are rich in moral precepts and stories. Some of this ethical guidance is quite direct and pointed. For instance, the Old Testament's Ten Commandments are hardly the "Ten Suggestions to Christians and Jews," and the Eight Beatitudes of the New Testament are not simply a collection of nice ideas. Instead, these precepts are meant to be strong guides to practice and to become life habits. The ethical precepts of many other traditions, both religious and secular, serve much the same role.

Secular Guides

A large part of our ethical guidance comes from everyday life. A parent regularly repeats an aphorism, such as "the early bird gets the worm." We see a Nike commercial that urges us to "Just do it!" At a red light, we read a bumper sticker imploring us to "Question Authority." These everyday adages and maxims are guides to behavior. Many, in turn, are richly ethical, such as the message conveyed by the bumper sticker "Perform random acts of kindness."

In recent years, there has been an explosion of self-help books on topics ranging from how to succeed in business to how to be a good spouse. Much of this content is intended to provide ethical guidance to the readers. For instance, most of the self-help parenting books direct parents on issues such as how to raise "good" children— that is, children who will be considerate of others and know right from wrong. In reality, these books are helping parents instill a code of ethics in their children.

Reason

As we discuss in Chapter 9, "What Are the Philosophical Foundations of American Education?," ethics is a branch of the discipline of philosophy that aids us intellectually to examine issues of right and wrong. Through the use of our reasoning abilities, we can sort out whether an issue has an ethical component and think through the consequences of various courses of action. In the case of Marilyn, she can think through what might happen if she decides to help the principal build a case against her colleague, Connie. A significant aspect of being a *reflective practitioner*, as we urge throughout this book, is the capacity to bring reason to bear on the ethical issues you confront as a teacher.

Moral Compass

The factors that contribute to our personal codes of ethics do not operate in isolation from one another. Ideally, they work together to help us sort out a problem and act properly. As occurs with acquiring a good golf swing or achieving fluency in a foreign language, many small elements come together in a smooth, coordinated way. With our personal code of ethics, each factor contributes to our moral compass—the ethical "mental magnet" that quickly enlightens us about what we ought to do. The four elements that make up our code of ethics provide us with a moral North Pole. Someone with a strong moral compass doesn't have to tell the athletic coach that he or she will "get back to him"; instead, the teacher immediately rejects the proposal. When the principal makes an unethical request or the teacher sees a favorite student cheating, the teacher knows immediately what he or she must do.

8-2d ETHICAL DILEMMAS IN TEACHING

Again, as with golf or speaking a foreign language, the skillful application of a code of ethics takes practice. Throughout this book, we have sprinkled many teaching cases that are explicitly ethical in nature or have an ethical component. We urge you to take these opportunities to practice sharpening your ability to apply your personal code of ethics to professional situations. As you read each case, take time to reflect carefully on it. Keep in mind the six characteristics described by Kenneth Howe. Also, bring your own moral compass to bear on the cases. Discuss them with other people. We often see much more in a situation involving ethics and recognize many other possible courses of action once we have talked to other people about it.

8-2e THE BIG DEAL OR A LITTLE FUDGE CASE

Recently, drugs have plagued your community, and increasingly they are coming into the schools. You are a sixth-grade teacher, and there has been only sporadic evidence of drugs in your building. Your principal has been making what seems to you a big deal out of very little in his crusade to stamp out drugs in "his" school. He has threatened the student body, first-graders through sixth-graders, in a special assembly about what will happen to them if they are caught with drugs of any kind. Most of your in-service training time this year has been taken up with the subject of drugs. You are concerned about the misuse of drugs in our society, but, like most of the other teachers, you find the principal's preoccupation with drugs overzealous and slightly laughable—and you are afraid of what will happen to the first offender he catches.

Coming from lunch, you see Alan, one of your sixth-graders, showing two of his friends a plastic bag containing what appears to be three or four marijuana joints. You are startled, but unsure that you have actually seen what he has. Alan shoves the bag into his pants pocket, and you act as if nothing has happened and usher the boys into class. To gain time to think, you set the students to work on a composition.

Alan is a kid with a spotty record in the school. His family life is rumored to be rather chaotic, but he has behaved well in your class. You have never seen the slightest evidence that he has been high in school. Knowing Alan, you guess he got the dope from one of his brothers and brought it to school to impress his friends. But you could be wrong, and the situation could be much more serious. You are sure of one thing: If you report what you saw to the principal, as you are expected to, he will move in on Alan like a crazed SWAT team.

As you mull all this over, Alan and his friends are nervously watching you and anxiously looking back and forth at one another. Suddenly, Alan gets up, comes to your desk, and asks if he can go to the boys' room. What do you do?

8-2f THE YOUR ROLE IN RIGHTING WRONGS CASE

Donald Mitchell is a veteran history teacher in your high school, and he has "ruled the roost" in the department for the past 15 years. Many current and former advanced placement (AP) and honors students adore him. They find him exceedingly challenging, and they claim that his teaching prepares them for the rigors of college.

Apart from his senior AP classes, Mr. Mitchell teaches two sections of American government to tenth-grade students. A number of the students in those two classes have Individualized Education Programs (IEPs). Mr. Mitchell publicly claims skepticism about many of these students' learning disabilities, doing only grudgingly what he has to do to comply with the IEPs. (Learn more about learning disabilities and IEPs in Chapter 3, "Who Are Today's Students in a Diverse Society?")

You have often heard Mr. Mitchell complain about "lowering standards of educational excellence" when he sits with his cronies in the school lunchroom. He does not hesitate to announce to the others about what he sees as being wrong with the school administration, the student body, and on occasion even faculty from other departments. His latest pet peeve is the "laxness" with which the English department teaches writing, so he has designed a strict procedure for writing his history papers. You have often found Mr. Mitchell to be boorish, but you reasoned that his behavior and opinions are his own prerogative. After all, you think to yourself, his teaching approaches are really a matter of academic freedom.

One afternoon, one of your students comes to class visibly upset. Janelle is one of your more challenging students. She has had a few minor run-ins with the vice principal, and she does not demonstrate much interest in academics. You often have been frustrated by what you see as Janelle's lack of motivation and effort. Privately, you ask her what is wrong. She tells you that she has just left Mr. Mitchell's class, where she received a paper that was given a D–. You listen to her, reluctant to talk about the grading policies of another teacher.

After calming down, Janelle tells you that it wasn't the grade itself that made her so upset, but how the teacher returned the papers. She claims that Mr. Mitchell stood at the front of the class, stating that some of the students' papers followed the proper format. Others, he sneered, were so riddled with errors and so poorly written that the only use for any of them would be to line a kitty litter bin. He added that he designed his format so that some students would learn to write correctly, but that many of them apparently could not or would not even follow his simple format. With that statement, he tossed those papers on the floor. He passed the satisfactory papers to the rest of the students. When the rest of the students—all inclusion students—were left without their papers, he glanced at them and said, "Well, go on. They're right there if you want them." And he pointed to the floor.

Janelle tells you that she waited until class was dismissed to pick up her paper from the floor. You excuse Janelle so that she can go to the girls' room, and then you ask to speak to another student who is in that same class. When you ask him—again privately—if anything unusual happened in his history class, the student replies it was a regular class. You're still curious, so you ask him how Mr. Mitchell returned the papers. The student looks at you quizzically and says, "How'd he return the papers? The same way you do. He walked around the room and handed them back to us."

You're very disturbed by the story Janelle told you, and you want to do something to intervene. Yet, the other student's report makes you hesitate. What if nothing unusual did occur? Making an enemy of Mr. Mitchell would not be the politically savvy thing to do, and Janelle can certainly be difficult at times. Maybe she was just angry at the teacher for some reason and wanted to cause trouble, but what if that story were true? What should you do?

8-2g THE EVERYDAY ETHICS OF TEACHING

As we hope the preceding case studies make clear, serious ethical issues strongly influence the lives of teachers. Few teachers get very far into their careers without

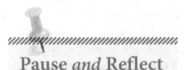

Pause *and* Reflect

1. What are the ethical issues in these two cases? Are there complexities that cause ethical conflicts? If so, what are they?
2. How did your moral compass react to these situations? To the case of Alan? To Janelle's situation?
3. In each case, what would you do? Who needs to be considered as you try to decide on your course of action?

having to deal with ethical dilemmas like these. Of course, these cases hardly exhaust the ethical responsibilities of teachers. A much larger area of ethical responsibility exists that we call the *everyday ethics of teaching*.

> *Living up to basic ethical standards in the classroom—discipline, tolerance, honesty—is one of the most important ways children learn how to function in society at large.*
>
> —ELOISE SALHOLZ,
> *Newsweek* senior writer and reporter

Although it is clear that parents have the primary responsibility for the ethical training of their children, schools do influence the character and moral lives of students. (We discuss character education in Chapter 12, "How Should Education Be Reformed?") Classrooms and schoolyards abound with issues of right and wrong: A student submits a report that is downloaded from an Internet site; two girls start a rumor that another girl is pregnant; a group of boys send lewd material to a girl's Facebook page; a teacher continually and harshly picks on the same student. Events like these send strong ethical messages to students. In particular, teachers ethically influence students in three ways: by their personal example, by the classroom climate they create, and by the dialogue they establish.

First, teachers can set a good *personal example*. An old adage states that "who you are speaks louder than what you say." The way in which teachers do their work, the care and seriousness of their teaching, and the manner with which they treat students are perhaps their most powerful ethical messages to students.

Second, teachers can establish a beneficial *classroom climate* by creating an environment of safety and trust where students are free from fear and ridicule, where a spirit of cooperation and friendly competition prevails, and where students are working hard and feeling the satisfaction of learning.

Third, teachers can establish an *ethical dialogue* in their classrooms by discussing with students the core ethical values, such as honesty, respect for others, and responsibility, that come into play not only in the study of literature and history but especially in the real-life events of the school.

The everyday ethics of teaching, then, means *doing the job as it ought to be done*. It means using ethical language and especially using carefully the precious minutes and hours that you spend with students and making sure they do not waste their time with you.

Pause *and* Reflect

1. Does that phrase, *doing the job as it ought to be done*, remind you of any teachers you have had in the past? What was their impact on you?
2. Do you recall any striking examples of the opposite? What can you learn from their example?

8-2h CODES OF PROFESSIONAL ETHICS

Teachers do not struggle alone when they face ethical issues. Besides their own understanding, reasoning, and moral compass, they have the support of a professional group. Professional groups, such as those composed of doctors, architects, and teachers, have special obligations to their clients.

(T) F
Unlike medical doctors who have the Hippocratic oath, there is no single, universally accepted code of ethics for teachers.

Whereas some entire professions have formulated their own universal code of ethics (like the Hippocratic Oath taken by all medical doctors), there is no single, universally accepted code of ethics for teachers. Nevertheless, several codes of ethics for teachers have been published. The best known is the code of the National Education Association (NEA). Another quite detailed one is the Code of Ethics of the Association of American Educators.[4] In recent years, a number of states' departments of education, such as those in Texas, California, and Alaska, have also developed codes of ethics to govern the work of their teachers. Alaska's "Code of Ethics and Teaching Standards" is particularly explicit with entries such as:

- Teachers may not expose a student to unnecessary embarrassment or disparagement.
- Teachers may not use professional relationships with students for private advantage or gain.
- Teachers shall accord just and equitable treatment to all students as they exercise their educational rights and responsibilities.[5]

Up CLOSE

Boston University Educator's Affirmation

I dedicate myself to the life of an educator, to laying the living foundations upon which successor generations must continue to build their lives.

I dedicate myself to the advancement of learning, for I know that without it our successors will lack both the vision and the power to build well.

I dedicate myself to the cultivation of character, for I know that humanity cannot flourish without courage, compassion, honesty, and trust.

I dedicate myself to the advancement of my own learning and to the cultivation of my own character, for I know that I must bear witness in my own life to the ideals that I have dedicated myself to promote in others.

In the presence of this gathering, I bind myself to this affirmation.[6]

Also, a number of teacher preparation programs have instituted a code of ethics for student teachers as they begin this intense field experience. Among them are teacher preparation programs at Northern Illinois University and Boston University. The Boston University Educator's Affirmation is taken voluntarily in a special and quite popular ceremony usually right before student teaching. Run by the education students, the ritual marks their commitment to the high ideals and standards of the profession. In this sense, this affirmation is similar to the Hippocratic oath that physicians take.

8-3 The Teacher and the Law

Once upon a time, teachers were like the kings and queens of small kingdoms. Their authority was wide, and their decisions were rarely questioned. Students who would not or could not do the work were "held back" or told not to "come back." Students who did not conform to the teacher's standards of behavior were expelled. Education was something of a scarce commodity, and students and their parents tended to view education as a special opportunity that put definite responsibilities on the student's shoulders. In fact, much of the legal authority of teachers was based on the principle of **in loco parentis**, meaning "in the place of parents." In other words, it was generally agreed that teachers acted as parental figures while students were in their care. For that reason, teachers' leeway in treating students was fairly broad, and they could make decisions about students based on what they believed was in the best interest of the student or students.

In the last few decades, however, the attitude toward schooling in the United States has changed. The authority of the adults in general, and of teachers in particular, has eroded noticeably, and many students are often more fixated on their rights than on their responsibilities. Many reasons for this change exist, but suffice it to say that today we are a very litigious society. The United States

© Cengage 2016

Legal and Ethical Dimensions of Teaching: Reflections from Today's Educators

Watch the video clips, study the artifacts in the case, and reflect on the following questions:

1. Which of the legal issues listed in this chapter and discussed in this case are you most concerned that you might face as a teacher?

2. How did this video help you feel more prepared to cope with the legal issues involved in teaching?

has more lawyers per capita than any other nation in the world—and our increasing tendency to use the courts to settle differences and conflicts has had its impact on the work of teachers. (The Video Case, *Legal and Ethical Dimensions of Teaching: Reflections from Today's Educators,* shows a roundtable discussion among real teachers about the legal situations they face.)

Our elementary and secondary schools have always been governed by school law. In recent years, however, the presence of the law in educational matters has grown dramatically. Like many societal changes, this trend has been a mixed bag. On the one hand, teachers are often cautioned to remember that students are autonomous, with individual rights that continue to exist even when students pass through schoolhouse doors and are under the supervision of teachers. As a result, teachers are required to be much more deliberate and cautious in their dealings with students to prevent an infringement of students' rights than they were in earlier decades. On the other hand, our new consciousness of the teachers' legal responsibilities and our heightened sense of students' rights have helped schools eliminate problems such as dictatorial practices by teachers and administrators, the thoughtless denial of certain rights to students, and the abusive use of corporal punishment.

Woodrow Wilson once said, "The law that will work is merely the summing up in legislative form of the moral judgment that the community has already reached." In other words, our laws represent our collective social judgments and decisions about what is fair and what is the right thing to do. Laws differ from codes of ethics, though, because they apply to all the people, not to a particular group like doctors or teachers. Laws are public, whereas ethics can reflect one's private standards. And laws have judicial teeth, whereas codes of ethics do not. Rarely is a teacher suspended, or expelled, or even sanctioned by the teaching profession for violating some code of ethics. Conversely, teachers are regularly affected by the law and are occasionally brought to court. The next sections examine some specific areas of law that can affect your work as a teacher.

One other issue complicates the legal front for teachers. The laws governing schools are part of a complex and overlapping system of federal, state, and local laws. Most of the cases discussed in this chapter started out as local school district disputes, only to travel to state courts, then to federal courts, and some, finally, to the U.S. Supreme Court. Some caused the Supreme Court to reinterpret past rulings, leading to new legal guidelines. Because of their broad impact, the majority of the cases we deal with in this chapter are Supreme Court cases and are a subset of the school law cases that deal directly with the work of teachers.

School law, like many other facets of our society, is dynamic and open to change. Although the Supreme Court justices are supposed to dispassionately interpret cases in light of the U.S. Constitution, it is said that "justices read the newspapers," meaning they are conscious of and sensitive to issues that are on peoples' minds, and this affects the cases they select to adjudicate. Therefore, cases involving contentious issues, such as school choice, are difficult for the court to avoid.

8-3a TEACHERS AND DUE PROCESS

- A young junior high teacher, on a lark, changes his "image." He comes to school one Monday morning sporting a shaved head and a diamond stud earring. He is fired on Tuesday.

- A teacher gives a speech at a meeting of the local LGBT alliance. The newspaper runs a story on the event, and the superintendent asks her to resign quietly.

- A business education teacher who has been teaching for three years has been visited by administrators only twice during that period. He loves teaching and was recently told by his principal that he was a "shoo-in for tenure." Instead of getting the expected letter from the superintendent outlining the upcoming tenure review process, he receives a dismissal notice in May, claiming that his teaching is not up to the district's standards.

All three of these examples represent violations of the teachers' rights to due process. Due process is one of the most important principles embedded in our nation's laws. The essential meaning of **due process** in education is that fairness should be rendered and teachers' rights as individuals should not be violated. Many of the most influential court decisions concerning education, teachers, and the law concern fundamental issues of due process.

Due process protections come directly from two amendments to the U.S. Constitution. The Fifth Amendment states, "No person shall . . . be deprived of life, liberty, or property, without due process of law." The Fourteenth Amendment adds, "Nor shall any State deprive any person of life, liberty, or property, without due process of law."

The Fourteenth Amendment goes on to stipulate that no person should be denied "the equal protection of the law." Legal rulings related to due process in education often reflect the requirement that individuals be treated equally in their education or by school officials.

Two Types of Due Process

When judging the fairness of an action, there are two due process concerns:

- *Substantive due process* has to do with the issue itself.
- *Procedural due process* concerns the fairness of the process followed.[7]

For example, if a teacher is fired because he wears a nose ring, it raises an issue of substantive due process. Is this matter substantive enough in this particular circumstance to deny a teacher employment? What is a fair decision in this matter? Procedural due process would involve how the case is handled. Suppose the teacher, after hearing several rumors that the nose ring is irking the superintendent, gets a curt letter saying his "services are no longer needed." Is this process fair? Has the teacher had a fair chance to defend himself?

The precise meaning of procedural due process varies from state to state, but the Supreme Court decision in *Goldberg* v. *Kelly* (1970) indicated that "the minimum procedural safeguards . . . demanded by rudimentary due process" would include the following:

- Procedural safeguards
- The opportunity to be heard at a reasonable time and place

- Timely and adequate notice, giving details of the reasons for the proposed suspension or dismissal
- An effective opportunity to defend oneself, including oral presentation of evidence and arguments
- An opportunity to confront and cross-examine witnesses
- The right to retain an attorney
- A decision resting solely on the legal rules and evidence adduced at the hearing
- A statement of the reasons for the determination and the evidence relied on
- An impartial decision maker[8]

Procedural due process exists so that individual teachers and students are protected from arbitrary actions against them. The principle of due process and these guidelines reach into many corners of a teacher's life, as will be discussed.

8-3b CONTRACTS, TENURE, AND DISMISSAL

Some of the most fundamental legal issues have to do with the legalities of employment. When, for instance, is a teacher actually hired? How does a teacher know he or she has an actual teaching position? What does having tenure really mean for a teacher?

Teachers are not self-employed; they are employees of a school board or, in the case of a private school, of a board of trustees. As employees of a governing body, teachers must be familiar with and abide by the stipulations of the contract issued to them by the school board. If teachers do not fulfill the requirements of the contract, they are at risk of losing their jobs.

Contracts to Teach

Imagine the following situation: You are a recent college graduate, newly licensed to teach, and you are actively interviewing for teaching positions. Your interview at the Long Meadow school district goes extremely well, and the superintendent tells you she would like you to join the faculty. She says that she plans to recommend your hiring to the school board, telling you that for all intents and purposes, you should consider that you have a teaching position, because the board usually votes to approve the superintendent's recommendations. You tell her that you would like to join the faculty, accepting her verbal offer.

Several weeks go by, and you hear nothing from the school district. In the meantime, you are invited to interview at the Centerville school district. When you interview there, you realize it is *the* ideal school district for you. The school administrators seem equally impressed with you, and in several days the superintendent calls and offers you a position. It's your dream job! Although you want to accept immediately, you ask the superintendent for a day to think over the offer. In fact, what you really want to do is find out your status at the Long Meadow school district. Do you really have a job there? If you accept the offer at Centerville, are you violating some legal obligations to the Long Meadow school district?

The answers to these questions depend on whether you have a legal contract for employment. A **contract** is a binding agreement between two or more people or parties. It indicates the rights and responsibilities of each party to the agreement, and all teachers, new or old, sign a contract with their board of education or trustees. Contracts differ from district to district and from state to state, but they generally specify the teacher's salary; course, teaching assignments, or instructional areas; the maximum class size, length of school day and school year; and grievance procedures. A **grievance** is the formal expression of a complaint

Teachers need to be aware of the fine points of their employment contracts.

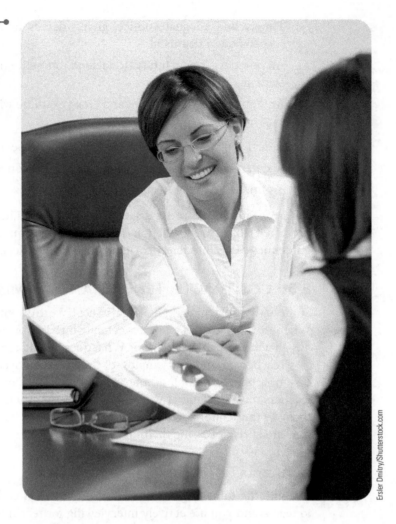

Ersler Dmitry/Shutterstock.com

about an unsatisfactory working condition. Grievances typically concern disputes over working conditions; when a person files a grievance, he or she usually argues that the working condition was in violation of the teacher's contract. Additionally, contracts generally indicate whether the local teachers' association or union is the official bargaining agent for teachers.

Contracts cover a set period of time. Most new teachers work on a contract that has to be renewed annually if the teacher is to stay employed by the school district. Even teachers on tenure (to be discussed shortly) sign a yearly contract stipulating the terms of employment. Occasionally teachers may work under a **continuing contract**, which states that its terms will remain in force until the teacher is given notice that the contract will be terminated on a particular date.

To be considered a legally enforceable document, a contract must do the following:

- Have a lawful subject matter
- Represent a meeting of the minds of both parties
- Include an exchange of something of value (called a *consideration*)
- Be entered into by parties who are competent to do so
- Be written in proper form (instead of in vague terms such as "pay the teacher what he or she is worth")

In addition, the school board must act officially to ratify a teacher's contract. Many people assume that contracts must be written. In fact, unless state law requires a written contract, an oral contract that includes all legal requirements can also be legally binding.[9]

In the previously described scenario, unless all of the conditions were included in your discussion with the Long Meadow superintendent and the school board acted upon, or *ratified*, the superintendent's recommendation to hire you, you did not have a legally binding offer. Therefore, you could accept the Centerville offer without hesitation.

Now suppose that scenario were altered slightly. What if you had signed a contract for the Long Meadow school district and then accepted the Centerville offer? In that instance, you could be held liable for **breach of contract**. A legal contract is binding on both sides—that is, on both the school district and the teacher. If either party violates conditions of the contract, the contract itself is said to have been breached, and the other party can sue for damages.

When an injured party successfully sues the other party for breach of contract, the court may order that the contract be fulfilled, that the injured party receive monetary damages, or both. For instance, the district may have to rehire a fired teacher and pay damages, or a teacher who walks away from a job may have to pay the district's cost of finding a replacement. In addition, whenever a teacher breaches a contract, his or her professional reputation is in danger of being tarnished.

Given these concerns, before you accept any position, you should study the contract carefully and ask about anything unclear to you. That contract will govern many of the important details of your life as a teacher.

Tenure

Imagine a few years have passed since you accepted the Centerville position. At what point are you granted **tenure** (or what some states call *continuing contract status*)? New teachers are hired on a probationary basis, with the **probationary period** often lasting three years, so the school district can ensure that a nontenured teacher can teach well enough to be granted permanent faculty status. State law determines when a teacher is eligible for tenure and outlines the requirements for earning tenure or continuing contract status. Some states require that the school board take some positive action to grant the teacher tenure status; in other states, the teacher is granted tenure automatically when he or she successfully completes the probationary period.

There are few concepts in education that are so often misunderstood than tenure. What does possessing tenure actually mean for a teacher? The word *tenure* comes from the Latin root meaning "to hold," as in "hold that job." Thus, if you become a tenured teacher in the Centerville school district, you are entitled to contract renewal every year. The general purpose of tenure was nicely stated by the Supreme Court of Pennsylvania in 1957: Tenure helps to maintain "an adequate and competent teaching staff, free from political or arbitrary interference." In addition, tenure allows "capable and competent teachers" to feel secure and to perform their duties efficiently.[10] It definitely does not mean a guaranteed lifetime job.

If your service is satisfactory, tenure guarantees your position as a teacher in the school district, but it does *not* mean that you are guaranteed to have the exact same teaching assignment every year. A teacher can be reassigned to teach second grade after being a fourth-grade teacher for years, or a school district can reassign a tenured teacher to another school in the district.

Tenure is an issue about which both the general public and teachers often hold strong views and, just as often, are greatly misinformed. Contrary to the views of many, poorly performing tenured teachers can be fired, and regularly are fired. There are clear sets of procedures administrators can follow to provide the evidence necessary for dismissal. Of course, following the procedures takes time and energy if a solid case is to be made. Recently, there has been a growing chorus of complaints about what many in the public believe is the failure of the nation's schools to get rid of ineffective teachers. The will to dismiss ineffective teachers appears to be growing. In 2010, the popular documentary film *Waiting for "Superman"* appeared to blame tenure for much of the ills of American public schools. One of the facts the film presented was that, in Illinois, 1 in 57 doctors loses his or her medical license; 1 in 97 lawyers loses his or her license to practice law; and 1 in 2,500 teachers loses his or her teaching credentials. This failure to dismiss poorly performing teachers is laid at the feet of administrators' not wanting to document a teacher's inadequacies, fear of heavy lawyers' fees, and the strong legal protections of teachers' unions.[11] For this reason, some education critics and school reformers advocate the elimination of tenure. In recent years, a number of states, such as Florida and North Carolina, have eliminated teacher tenure, others are considering this move, and several others have tightened their laws, making tenure more difficult to secure,[12] though it is doubtful that this will happen in the foreseeable future.

In fact, teacher tenure is no more than a guarantee of procedural due process. Nevertheless, a school district needs to follow a strict set of guidelines for disciplining or dismissing a teacher. These guidelines are somewhat different for tenured teachers than for teachers who have not yet earned tenure.

Dismissal

Sometimes teachers fail. Perhaps they simply cannot handle the job, or perhaps they make a big mistake, such as striking a child in anger. Occasionally, teachers have "philosophical differences" with administrators, sometimes further complicated by mild or severe cases of "personality conflict." These situations and many more may result in an attempt to dismiss a teacher. Dismissal procedures are covered by the laws in each state, and those procedures must follow due process.

If a school district decides in the middle of a school year (and therefore in the middle of a contract) to dismiss an untenured teacher, the teacher always has a right to a full hearing and due process. By contrast, if the district decides not to extend a second- or third-year contract to a new teacher, as in the example given earlier in this chapter, the situation is less clear. Although an untenured teacher who is not being rehired can demand a hearing in some states, in most states, a school district does not have to justify its reasons for not rehiring a teacher on probationary status.

For tenured teachers, the legal situation is different. Tenure is protected under the Fourteenth Amendment and is considered part of the teacher's "property." In effect, a teacher *owns* his or her tenure. It is like holding the title to your own car. Tenured teachers have the expectation that they will have continued employment, which is considered a "property interest." In a sense, tenured teachers have "earned" and "own" the job, and they can be separated from it only under very special circumstances. In light of that fact, teachers can call on the full protection of the law, just as they would if someone were trying to take away a home or a car. To justify dismissal, the school district must prove that a tenured teacher has violated some provision of the tenure law.

In most states, a tenured teacher can be dismissed only "for cause." States vary concerning what they consider due cause for dismissal, but most require a good reason that will withstand the scrutiny of the courts, such as sexually molesting a student, gross negligence, or clear incompetence. In some states, the law stipulates that tenured teachers cannot be dismissed without being given an opportunity to correct their deficiencies. In those instances, the courts usually determine what is "remediable," or faults that could be corrected by a teacher. For example, if a teacher demonstrates poor classroom management, that failure can be seen as something correctable, and most courts would not allow a tenured teacher to be dismissed before he or she was warned about the management problems and given a chance, and perhaps training, to correct them. Certain actions, however, are so unprofessional that the damage is "irremediable." Being convicted of a crime and engaging in sexual relations with a student are both considered irremediable.[13] In those instances, the school district is under no legal requirement to help a teacher correct his or her behavior, and dismissal procedures can begin immediately.

The most common reasons for dismissal include immorality, insubordination, incompetence, and "conduct unbecoming a teacher." The last reason is a fairly vague term that allows schools some leeway in dismissing a teacher whose behavior is unethical but may not be classified under the other, more specific causes such as insubordination or incompetence. For example, sometimes "conduct unbecoming" means a teacher has used the classroom for purposes other than teaching. One teacher was dismissed because he used class time to advocate that the students, their families, and their friends vote for a particular candidate running for superintendent of schools.[14] In another 2009 case, a pregnant teacher, Roberta Weisbecker, took maternity leave with several loose ends, including failing to leave her substitute teacher enough data to complete her students' final grades. The school board recommended Roberta be fired, but she resigned before the board acted. Later, she sued in federal court, claiming gender discrimination because of her pregnancy, but the court ruled against her, stating the evidence of gender bias was slim. This case has been cited as evidence that firing a teacher is getting easier.[15] It is the responsibility of the courts to weigh the individual situation, review the law on the subject, and determine whether the case justifies dismissal.

Reduction in Force

In most instances, a tenured teacher can only be dismissed for wrong behavior or incompetent teaching. The one exception to that occurs when the school district needs to eliminate some teaching positions for economic reasons. Sometimes the courts allow schools to dismiss teachers as a result of curricular reorganization. For example, a school board might decide to drop its classical languages department. Most commonly, however, reductions occur when the school district has a drop in student enrollment and does not need all the teachers that it employs or when it experiences a budgetary shortfall that requires teacher dismissals. Under those conditions, a school district can lay off tenured teachers, and the decision about which tenured teachers to dismiss is usually made on the basis of seniority. Called **reduction in force**, or "riffing" in slang, this practice was common in the 1970s and 1980s, when student enrollments were shrinking. More recently, as an effect of the economic recession of 2008 and 2009, school districts across the country resorted once again to riffing because of budget curtailments. For example, in the spring of 2009, more than 2,000 teachers in over half the districts in Washington State were riffed. Federal stimulus money was made available to many public-sector workers and in the case of Washington State, 87 percent of the "riffed" teachers regained their positions.[16]

8-3c TEACHER LIABILITY

The United States, for a variety of reasons, is the most litigious country in the world. One possible reason is there are 1.35 million lawyers in our country looking for business. Our country's 133,000 schools (not including nursery schools) are prime "business sites, filled with human activity often leading to accidents, physical assaults and hurt feelings and reputations." In each of these situations there is the potential for the "blame game." Enter: the law and lawyers.

Liability is the legal word for blame, as in "the teacher should accept liability for the injured student's dislocated shoulder" and other accidents and mishaps. Such a statement implies that the teacher behaved negligently or intentionally in a way that allowed an injury to happen. Put yourself into the shoes of Lori in the case below.

Lori Spinelli, a middle school Spanish teacher, often employed cooperative learning activities in her lessons so students would have more opportunities to practice speaking and listening to each other. Although the students worked together, Lori often circulated around the room to converse with each small group, using the week's vocabulary words in her brief conversations with them.

One afternoon, while she was working with a small group in the front of the classroom, Lori heard a scream from the back. One of her students, Jared, was writhing in pain on the floor. He had tried to show his group members a certain dance move and had dislocated his shoulder.

Later that afternoon, Lori replayed that class in her mind, feeling more and more dread, worrying and wondering about whether she would be held liable for Jared's injury. True, she had been in the classroom, but Lori realized that while she was talking to the group in the front of the room, her back had been turned to most of the students in the room, including Jared. What if Jared's parents held her and the school district liable for their son's injury?

Teachers are responsible for ensuring the safety and well-being of the students in their own classrooms and workspaces, and in the activities they oversee. This includes field trips and after-school clubs and activities, such as band, sports, and play rehearsals. Teachers are also liable if they do nothing when they observe a student in some potentially dangerous act that eventually turns out to be harmful. Turning one's back on misbehavior in no way lessens this responsibility. Teachers can be held liable for acts of omission.

Lori has good reason to be concerned. A court trying to determine whether her supervision was adequate would focus on whether Lori could have reasonably prevented Jared from getting injured or whether his injury was something that could not have been reasonably anticipated by her.

Two court cases help shed light on the extent of a teacher's liability. In one case (*Sheehan* v. *St. Peter's Catholic School*, 1971), an eighth grader was injured when her teacher took a group of students outside to watch a baseball game and then went back inside the school. In the teacher's absence, a group of students began throwing pebbles at the spectators, and Margaret Sheehan was hit in the eye with a pebble, sustaining a serious eye injury. In that case, the court ruled that the school did not take reasonable precaution to prevent student injury. It is impossible, after all, for a teacher to monitor students if the teacher is inside while the students are outside. The teacher should have anticipated that in leaving the group of students alone and unsupervised, a dangerous situation could develop.

Does that mean teachers need to be in a position of directly observing students at all times? Does it mean that a teacher like Lori would be considered liable for her student's dislocated shoulder? Maybe not.

In another case concerning liability, teachers took a group of junior high and high school students to visit Chicago's Field Museum of Natural History (*Mancha* v. *Field Museum of Natural History*, 1971). When the group arrived at the museum, the teachers allowed students to visit the exhibition halls on their own. One student, while in an exhibition hall apart from the teachers, was approached and beaten up by a group of teenagers who did not attend the same school. In this case, the court ruled that the risk of student injury in a museum usually would be "minimal," so it was an

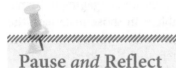

Pause *and* Reflect

1. What teaching mistake, if any, did Lori make?
2. In your judgment, is Lori liable for Jared's injury?

unreasonable expectation that teachers should have been able to foresee and prevent the student's beating. Furthermore, the court indicated that expecting teachers to directly supervise every student on the field trip would place such an unreasonable expectation on teachers that few would plan field trips or other educationally valuable activities for their students.[17]

To Lori Spinelli's great relief, no charges were brought against her. Lori had established an orderly classroom, and she was in the room when Jared was injured. Other students indicated that Ms. Spinelli had taught them rules of behavior and of courtesy, especially given that they would often be working in small groups. Jared was, in general, a well-behaved student, so there would be no reason for Lori to expect that he would decide to jump up and show a dance move to his group members. Finally, her lesson for the class, which covered presenting and practicing written dialogues for their partners, would not be considered a dangerous situation for students. The mere fact that her back was turned to Jared's group wouldn't be grounds to hold her liable—after all, no teacher can face all of the students all of the time. Lori's established good teaching practices and her sound judgment demonstrated her competence. In another situation, in which just a few of those factors were different, a teacher may have been held responsible.

Lori Spinelli's case demonstrates that even though teachers are required to exercise prudence and foresight in their supervision of students, the courts expect reasonable prudence and foresight. Some student injuries are accidents or unforeseen injuries, and in those cases the teacher is not held responsible.

Liability Precautions: Four Principles and Eight Useful Tips

The Principles: When teachers can demonstrate they have taken reasonable precautions to prevent student injury, courts have not found teachers liable for student injuries. To show that they have been "reasonably prudent," teachers need to be able to demonstrate that their actions met the following criteria:

- They made a reasonable attempt to anticipate dangerous situations.
- They provided proper supervision.
- They took precautions and gave a warning to minimize the chances of students getting hurt.
- They established rules.

A teacher is responsible for students' safety especially on field trips.

Image Source/Digital Vision/Getty Images

The eight tips to keep teachers in the classroom and out of the courtroom are:

- **Perform your duties, even when they seem boring or repetitive.** If you are assigned to monitor the hall during lunch, make sure you do it. The day you miss will be the day an injury occurs.

- **Observe safety precautions.** If any of your teaching involves your students' use of equipment or tools, check the equipment regularly and make sure you take the time to thoroughly review safety procedures. Make sure these procedures are written out and posted. Review the procedures often.

- **Rely on your school's rules—don't make up your own.** This is particularly true of discipline rules. If students are so unruly that they need harsh discipline, they should always be referred to the administrator.

- **Keep private information private.** Do not discuss the performance of a student with anyone other than the student, the student's family, or your supervisor/administrator.

- **Avoid "touchy" situations.** Use extraordinary caution when touching students in any fashion. What may seem to you as a "caring gesture" can be easily misinterpreted in today's climate.

- **Keep written discipline reports.** If you are having trouble with a student, start keeping a factual log of what is happening. It may turn out to be the important bit of evidence needed to defend your reputation if bogus charges are filed against you.

- **Punish in pairs.** Never discipline a student without having another school official present. But before that, discuss the nature of the conduct and reasoning for your discipline method with that other person before carrying out the discipline.

- **Do what is best for the student.** If you always act in the best interest of your students and make sure you do not let personal frustration or anger affect your decisions, liability is greatly diminished. (Adapted from John M. Drye, Esq., "Tort Liability101: When are Teachers Liable?" *Educator's Resources,* http://www.educator-resources.com/pdf/Teacher%20Tort%20Liability.pdf.)

Liability Insurance and Documentation

Because teachers are vulnerable to legal suits, it is important that they be covered by some form of liability insurance. In recent years, many teachers have been scared into buying more insurance than they need or, more commonly, into buying insurance when they are already covered by school district insurance policies. Every new teacher should check his or her on-the-job coverage with the district's personnel director before beginning work.

One area in which experts suggest teachers are particularly at risk is automobile liability. Often teachers volunteer to take students in their own cars to sports games or on field trips. Even if teachers have personal insurance, they often do not have enough to cover liability claims if a serious accident happens. Before taking students in a private car, teachers should be sure that the district's insurance policy covers such cases or that their own policy is adequate.

However, even though teachers are usually covered by liability insurance through their school district or professional organization (i.e., teachers' union), they still need to protect themselves through documentation. Simply stated, that means keeping one's principal or superintendent's office aware of a situation and keeping a personal record of events. For instance, if a particular student or parent is harassing you, keep a strictly factual log of what and when the events happen. If you are injured (for example, from being knocked over in the hallway while breaking up a fight), take pictures of your injury and save records of any medical costs. The best liability advice is three words: Document! Document! Document!

Finally, on all these issues of liability, it is important for teachers to use good judgment. Accidents often "just happen," and there may be no liability involved. If a school injury does result in a lawsuit, the courts will try to determine whether the teacher was providing reasonable care and, in general, was acting in a prudent and careful manner.

8-3d REPORTING CHILD ABUSE

In addition to preventing harm to students under their supervision, teachers have a legal responsibility to safeguard students from abuse and neglect at the hands of their parents and other adults. Teachers in every state are required by law to report suspected child abuse or neglect. The laws vary somewhat from state to state, but they all include two or more of the following elements in their definition of abuse and neglect: physical injury, mental or emotional injury, and sexual molestation or exploitation.[18] If teachers suspect that a student has experienced *any* of those injuries, they are legally obligated to report their suspicions of child abuse and neglect to the appropriate authorities. Schools typically have detailed instructions in their faculty handbooks about how to report such suspicions. Additionally, principals or other administrators will often remind teachers of those procedures so that all teachers understand explicitly the necessary reporting protocol.

A teacher does not have to be *certain* that a child is being abused before he or she makes a report to the principal. Child abuse is clearly one of those areas where it is better to act and be wrong. The true problem is failure to act. If a teacher has a reasonable cause to suspect that a child is being abused, that is sufficient grounds for making a report. To protect a teacher from reaction to an incorrect report or from the anger of an offending parent, the reporting is kept confidential. Further, teachers in all 50 states are granted immunity from accusations of slander or any possible libel suit.[19] Without such protection, many teachers would hesitate to report their suspicions. (For a more detailed discussion of child abuse, see Chapter 4, "How Do Social Issues Affect Students?")

8-3e SELF-DEFENSE

Schools are very crowded places, and they are crowded, by definition, with immature individuals. Thus it is not surprising that conflicts sometimes erupt and teachers find themselves encountering hostile behavior. For instance, a teacher may have to break up a playground fight or stop some students from vandalizing another student's locker, or a student may strike a teacher in anger. It is a myth, however, that teachers cannot touch a student. When a student or students are in danger of injury in a fight or a case of bullying, the law *requires* a teacher to act. What they do, however, must be *reasonable*.[20]

Self-defense is defined broadly here to take in all these situations. In the first two cases, fighting and vandalism, the teacher is expected to intercede in the interest of safety. In a fight, for instance, the teacher must act to stop the students from hurting one another. Strong and loud words usually are effective, but sometimes the teacher must become physically involved. The operating principle here is "reasonable force." If a teacher uses reasonable force and if, in the process of stopping the fight and separating the students, a student suffers an injury (say, a strained wrist or dislocated arm), the courts typically will find that the teacher is not liable. If the same injuries resulted from a fight the teacher did not act to stop, he or she may be held liable.

In more obvious cases of self-defense, a student threatens or actually strikes a teacher. The principle of reasonable force applies here too. What constitutes reasonable force is generally a matter of common sense, but the heat of the moment can make good judgment difficult. In one case, a male seventh-grader who weighed 110 pounds struck a 220-pound coach. The coach grabbed the boy, lifted him off the ground, and threw him against a wall, breaking the child's back. When the case was brought to court, the teacher-coach claimed self-defense. He lost—big time. In the court's view, the teacher's responsibility is to keep a level head.

Assault and Battery

A teacher's recourse against an abusive student is governed by assault and battery laws. In legal terms, *assault* has come to mean a threat to do harm. Threats should always be taken seriously and reported to the principal, but their legal status depends very much on the student's ability to carry through on a threat. An angry fourth-grader's threat to "do something terrible to you" does not have the same status as a high school junior's threat to blow up your classroom.

Battery means a willful attack on another person that results in harm. Being unintentionally knocked to the hall floor by a rushing student is not battery (although it may call for some disciplinary action by the school). Being intentionally pushed by a student or a parent is an entirely different matter, however, and makes the pusher immediately liable.

Incidents of assault and/or battery should be promptly reported, and disciplinary action demanded or legal charges filed. Often teachers, particularly new teachers, are hesitant about making a fuss or turning offending students in to the proper school authorities. They should not equivocate: Verbal abuse and physical violence have no place in our elementary and secondary schools.[21]

8-3f FREEDOM OF EXPRESSION

One of the most treasured rights of American citizens is the freedom of expression. Freedom of expression includes symbolic expression and verbal or written expression. For teachers, freedom of expression also subsumes **academic freedom**, the freedom of a teacher to select course materials and to teach in a way he or she thinks fit. Before we go on, take a moment to consider your ideas about freedom of expression.

Until about 50 years ago, teachers who publicly criticized administrators' decisions or school board policies received little sympathy from judges. The attitude of the courts was that judges had no business interfering in the legitimate affairs of the schools. Things changed, though, as a result of Marvin Pickering.

Pickering, a high school English teacher, wrote a long and sarcastic letter in the local newspaper about his superintendent and school board. He accused them of, among other things, taking the local taxpayers "to the cleaners," devoting excessive expenditures to athletics, and forcing teachers to live in an atmosphere of totalitarianism. It was later shown that Pickering's information on a number of issues was wrong.

Pickering was fired. He sued for his job, but the original court verdicts upheld the firing. Pickering's case was appealed before the U.S. Supreme Court in 1968. Because Pickering, an English teacher, made erroneous statements about athletic expenditures and those expenditures were matters of public record, the court indicated that Pickering did not speak with any greater authority on the matter than any other taxpayer. The court also found that his comments did not impede his proper

Pause *and* Reflect

1. Is the freedom of expression limitless? Can a teacher say anything or teach anything, claiming it is his or her right to free expression?
2. To what degree do you think that you, as a potential teacher, should have the right to select your own course materials or to provide information to students?
3. Are there any instances in which you think a teacher's freedom of expression should be limited? If so, what are they?

performance in the classroom or otherwise interfere with the regular operation of the schools, so the judges reversed the lower courts' ruling and ordered Pickering reinstated and compensated.[22] We suspect, however, that thereafter, Pickering did not receive a Valentine's greeting from the superintendent.

In effect, the court said in the *Pickering* decision that society needs to balance the interests of a teacher, as a citizen commenting on issues of public concern, and the interests of the state, as the teacher's employer trying to promote smoothly running schools. Although the court affirmed the teacher's right to free expression, it pointed out that this First Amendment protection is not an absolute right. A teacher cannot expect to say absolutely anything and then cry out for protection under "freedom of expression." As a U.S. Court of Appeals stated in the 1970s *Scoville* v. *Board of Education* case, "Freedom of speech includes the right to criticize and protest school policies in a nondisruptive manner, but it does not include the use of 'fighting' words or the abuse of superiors with profane and vulgar speech."[23] If teachers become disruptive forces in a school or make irresponsible statements, for example, the courts will not support the expression of their views. For instance, in 1981, the courts ruled against a teacher who had claimed that the racially derogatory comments he made to his principal and assistant principal were constitutionally protected.[24]

The Supreme Court also ruled against teacher John Stroman (*Stroman* v. *Colleton County School District,* 1992) after he circulated a letter harshly critical of school administration. In it, he urged fellow faculty members to stage a "sickout" to show the administrators just how unified the faculty was in their discontent. In its ruling, the court indicated that urging a "sickout" when individuals were healthy was an appeal for dishonest behavior and conduct unprofessional for teachers.[25]

Symbolic Expression

Personal expression is not limited to spoken and written words. Dress styles, armbands, tattoos, and buttons have been used in recent years to "make a statement." Typically, the courts support teachers (and students) in these cases of free symbolic expression. A key issue here involves the potential of this type of expression to lead to "substantial disruption" within the school. A school might forbid such symbolic clothing as a teacher's Ku Klux Klan button in a high school with many African American students or students' gang "colors" or jacket insignias if they provoke fighting. These judgments cannot, however, be a matter of a teacher's or an administrator's "taste." Bans on symbolic expression of one's views or preferences must be based on clear indications that the efficiency or safety of the school is endangered.

Cyberspace Expression

The popularity of the new electronic communication, particularly Facebook, Twitter, and email, has brought with it many benefits and some hazards. Used in schools, it can maximize communication among teachers, students, administrators, and parents in ways unimaginable just a decade ago. Among the hazards, however, is the fact that electronic messages, which a writer thought were personal and "deletable," can be retrieved and subpoenaed by the courts in legal conflicts.

Social networking can present a particular danger to teachers, especially young teachers who have grown up using it for personally revealing exchanges with friends. A 2008 federal court case in Connecticut illustrates the problem: A second-year teacher heard about MySpace from his students and soon opened his own MySpace account. So far, so good. The teacher, however, allowed students access to the account, and various exchanges ensued involving lewd inquires and responses about his sex life. Also, he posted the picture of a nude man, plus comments, on his site. Word got out, administrators investigated, and the young teacher was let go. Believing he had been badly treated, he filed suit in federal court, claiming the school system had violated his Fourteenth Amendment rights of procedural due process, substantive due process, equal protection, and his First Amendment freedoms of expression and association. The court made rather short work of his defense primarily because *he was a teacher,* and this type of communication was inappropriate. Commenting on the issues behind this case, education legal specialist, Perry A. Zirkel wrote (in a nicely titled piece, "MySpace?") that it is

> not surprising that teachers, like students, would get ensnared in the web of new technological issues. . . . However, at a time when the Supreme Court and the rest of the judiciary is leaning away from individual rights under the Constitution, including the cited First and Fourteenth Amendment decisions in the public employment context, the new technologies—including but not limited to e-mail, MySpace, Facebook, YouTube, and electronic surveillance tools—present traps for the unwary. The problem of establishing an effective relationship with students, close enough for internal trust but distant enough for external trust, is an age-old problem that is as tricky as distinguishing between the pertinent definitions of "confidence."[26]

Academic Freedom

A subcategory of freedom of expression, academic freedom deals largely with issues in the classroom and the teachers' (and students') rights to discuss ideas and read material of their choosing. Academic freedom allows teachers to speak freely about their subject matter, to select reading assignments, and to choose teaching methodologies based on their professional judgment. It is designed to allow experimentation with ideas and to foster an open spirit of inquiry.

Academic freedom can meet with opposition when teachers want to discuss controversial or unpopular ideas such as same-sexual marriage, gun control, or abortion. If such issues are a part of the school's curriculum, problems rarely arise. When a teacher "adds" them to the curriculum, however, he or she needs to make a reasonable case that they are relevant to the curriculum. Dismissal for teaching controversial issues may or may not be upheld by the courts. Teaching about volatile issues that may disrupt a particular school, such as homosexuality or the alleged characteristics of different races, is frowned on by the courts. So too is teaching controversial material considered unsuitable for the age of the students. In addition, courts have not allowed teachers to use controversial teaching methods that are unsupported by professional opinion or prohibited by reasonable school policy.

Political issues, both local and national, are also points of tension. In the classroom, teachers may discuss current political controversies, but they must deal with them neutrally and in a balanced way. Away from work, advocating a particular cause or political party is fine, but a teacher may not behave as a partisan supporter in the classroom.

Particular essays and books that contain sexually explicit material or even words that are offensive to certain members of a community have been a major source of legal controversy in schools. In one important case, *Keefe* v. *Geanakos* (1969), a Massachusetts English teacher, Robert Keefe, assigned his students an article from the well-respected *Atlantic Monthly* that contained offensive language. Keefe's assignment kicked up a firestorm of protest, and he was eventually fired for refusing to agree not to assign the article again. Subsequently, he was reinstated by a circuit court decision because the offending language existed in a number of books already in the school library; the school board had not notified him that such material was prohibited; and the court believed the word in question was not all that shocking to the students. As the decision stated, "With the greatest respect to such parents, their sensibilities are not the full measure of what is proper education."[27]

The court ruled similarly in another often-cited case concerning academic freedom (*Parducci* v. *Rutland,* 1970). Marilyn Parducci, a high school English teacher, had assigned *Welcome to the Monkey House,* by Kurt Vonnegut, to her 11th-grade English class. Ms. Parducci was called down to the principal's office the next morning and told not to teach that story in any of her classes. Parducci disagreed, contending that the short story had merit as a literary work, despite the principal's remark that it was "literary garbage." Parducci indicated to the principal and assistant superintendent that she would continue to teach her 11th-grade English class using whatever material she wanted and in whatever way she thought best. (Note: This happened prior to the initiation of state standards of learning.) Parducci was fired from her job, with the explanation that she was "insubordinate" and the course reading had a "disruptive" effect on students. The court found that the Vonnegut story was not inappropriate reading for 11th-graders. The finding added that the short story was met with "apathy" by most of the students, so the reading itself could not have created an undue distraction.[28]

Absolute academic freedom at the K–12 level does not exist, however, and some court decisions have limited teachers' perceived academic freedom. The decision in a later case (*Boring* v. *Buncombe County Board of Education,* 1998) stands in contrast to the rulings in the Keefe and Parducci cases. Margaret Boring chose *Independence,* a play containing mature subject matter, for her advanced acting class to perform in a statewide competition. After reading the script, the school principal informed Boring that the class would not be allowed to perform it at the state competition. Boring, along with parents of the actors, met the principal, requesting him not to cancel their performance. He agreed that they could perform the play, but only after certain portions were deleted. The students performed the play, with portions deleted, and won second place at the competition.

At the end of that school year, the principal requested the transfer of Boring from the high school, citing "personal conflicts resulting from actions she initiated during the course of the school year."[29] Boring argued that her transfer was in "retaliation" for expression of unpopular views through the production of the play and therefore violated her right to freedom of speech.

The Supreme Court ruled in the school board's favor. In its decision, the court stated that this was nothing more than an ordinary employment dispute, not a matter of public concern. For that reason, it found that the dispute did not constitute protected speech. The court also wrote that school administrators have a "legitimate pedagogical interest in the makeup of the curriculum of the school," and that the "school, not the teacher, has the right to fix the curriculum."[30]

Issues of academic freedom often generate a great deal of heat. When they reach the courts, the following considerations, among others, are brought to bear:

- The teacher's purpose
- The educational relevance of the controversial publication
- The age of the students involved
- The quality of the disputed teaching material and its effects on the class[31]

These considerations are critical guidelines to remember when one teaches.[32] Perhaps the most important point to remember is that academic freedom is limited: It cannot be used to protect incompetent teachers or indoctrinating zealots.

8-3g COPYRIGHT LAWS

Good teachers are always on the hunt for effective teaching materials: a story that carries a special message, a poem that captures an idea with beauty and economy, an article that contains the latest information about an issue students are studying. Having found the "perfect" piece, it is difficult to resist the temptation simply to copy it and share it with the class, and the wide availability of photocopying equipment makes this practice all too easy.

Printed matter is the product of someone's labor, the same way that a painting or a piece of furniture is. Under the law, it is considered **intellectual property**, and the creator or author has a legal right to receive a reward for his or her labor. Without such payment, few people could afford to write books, plays, or articles. For this reason, first in 1909 and more recently in 1976, the U.S. Congress passed copyright laws to protect writers and publishers from the unauthorized use of their material.

For teachers, the heart of the current copyright law is its **fair use** guidelines, which specify which printed materials teachers may photocopy and under which conditions they may do so. The general principle behind fair use is "not to impair the value of the owner's copyright by diminishing the demand for that work, thereby reducing potential income for the owner."[33] In other words, if people simply copy print materials whenever they want, they will not buy the books, and publishers and authors will suffer. Some copying is allowed, of course, and it is important for teachers to know what they may and may not do.

Teachers may copy materials under the following circumstances:

- If making a single copy for class preparation of a chapter from a book; a newspaper or magazine article, short story, essay, or poem; or a diagram, chart, picture, or cartoon from a book or magazine;
- If making a copy for each of their students of a poem if it is fewer than 250 words and printed on not more than two pages;
- If a complete article, story, or essay is less than 2,500 words or is an excerpt from any prose work of not more than 1,000 words or 10 percent of the work, whichever is less.

Teachers may not copy materials in the following situations:

- If making copies of a work for their classes if another teacher in the same building already has copied that same material for his or her class;
- If making copies of the same author's work more than once a semester or making copies from the same anthology, text, or periodical issue more than three times a semester;
- If creating a class anthology by copying material from several sources (a favorite trick of many teachers!);
- If making multiple copies of weekly newspapers or magazines specifically designed for classrooms, or of consumable materials, such as copyrighted games, exercises, and particularly worksheets from workbooks;
- If charging more for legally permissible copies than it cost to copy them.

These guidelines may seem overly restrictive and technical, but teachers actually have more liberal guidelines for copying than average citizens do.

Videos, Software, and the Internet

There is a great temptation for teachers to record or capture material "off the air" or from the Internet and to build personal libraries of material to use in instruction. Although this tactic may be effective pedagogy, it may not be legal. Commercially produced videos are intellectual property and, like printed materials, are covered by U.S. copyright laws. Copyrighted television programs (and most of them *are* copyrighted) can be kept for only 45 days, after which they must be erased . Also, during the first 10 days after the recording, the teacher may show the video only twice: once for initial presentation and once when "instructional reinforcement" is called for. Finally, schools cannot routinely record material for potential later use by a teacher; such recording can be done only at a teacher's request.

The personal computer has helped to revolutionize American life in general and American education in particular. Since 1976, a huge new source of intellectual property has burst on the scene and opened up a plethora of new opportunities—the Internet being the most dramatic example. Today, it is possible to copy information from government agencies, libraries, legal systems, commercial sites, and other schools with the click of a mouse.

Given the ready accessibility of websites, you may be tempted to copy a research report from an online news information service and make copies for all students in your class. However, contrary to what many believe, the Internet is *not* in the public domain. Most web pages—including the information on them and the code used to create them—are protected by copyright law. Because the Internet is global, it is regulated by an international treaty, the Berne Convention for the Protection of Literary and Artistic Works, to which the United States and most English-speaking nations are signatories. The law in this area is still evolving and until it settles, we suggest you follow the fair use guidelines cited earlier. Also, many teachers find that their school's media specialist can help them keep up with changes in copyright laws regarding digital, as well as print and video, materials.

Computer software programs are not treated in the same way as text, video clips, or still pictures. Commercially sold software differs from material "taken off" the Internet. Software should not be passed around and copied. In some cases, the software publisher may allow a purchaser to make one backup copy of the software, but making any other copies is a violation of the copyright laws.

Although all of this may seem like overkill, it is important for teachers to follow the rules—not simply because it is the law, but because students will follow their example.

8-4 Lifestyle and Teachers

Teachers bring into their classrooms more than their minds and their lesson plans; they bring their attitudes and values. Elementary and secondary teachers traditionally have been considered extensions of the family in passing on to the young the community's positive values. In past generations, teachers who behaved in ways counter to the community's values were dismissed out of hand. Teachers were summarily fired for homosexuality, being single and pregnant, living with someone of the opposite sex, using illegal drugs, being publicly drunk, or committing a crime. However, the late 1960s saw a shift in the balance between the community's right to require certain standards of behavior and the rights of individuals to pursue their own lifestyles and values. Although the law in some areas has not yet been settled, on many questions, judicial opinion (the way judges are tending to rule) is increasingly clear.

Pause *and* Reflect

1. To what degree do you believe that a teacher's personal life should be truly private? Should what teachers do in their own time always be off limits for school authorities and protected by the law? Are teachers completely free to live their life in whatever way they decide?
2. Were there teachers in your elementary or high school experience whose behaviors "pushed the envelope" and were in conflict with your community's standards? If so, how did the school district respond? Do you believe justice was served? Was the cause of education served?

8-4a PERSONAL APPEARANCE: HAIR, CLOTHES, AND WEIGHT

In the late 1960s and early 1970s, the courts tended to rule in favor of teachers' rights to do what they wished with their hair. More recently, the courts have often sided with school districts' rights to impose reasonable grooming codes for teachers. Teachers, according to the current view, do not have a *constitutional* right concerning their "style of plumage."[34]

The situation is similar for clothing. Courts have upheld districts' judgments on skirts that are considered too short, and requirements (in some districts) that male teachers wear neckties. Courts are asserting that the First Amendment does not extend to "sartorial choice."

For health reasons, obesity may be its own punishment. But does a school district have a right to fire a teacher because it decides she or he is too fat? A California school district released a 42-year-old female physical education teacher because, at 5 feet 7 inches and 225 pounds, the district felt she was "unfit for service." Her principal argued that she "did not serve as a model of health and vigor" and was restricted in her ability to perform on the trampoline, in gymnastics and modern dance, and in other aspects of the program.[35] In this case, the court sided with the teacher, claiming that the district had not proved that her girth had impaired her performance.

8-4b PRIVATE SEXUAL BEHAVIOR

In the past, sexual behavior was considered an area in which a community had a complete right to impose its standards on people selected to teach its children. More recently, the courts have increasingly viewed teachers' private sexual habits or preferences as separate from their public, professional lives as teachers.

One landmark case involved Marc Morrison, who was fired after his former lover, another male teacher, reported their brief relationship to the superintendent. The school district believed it was on solid ground in dismissing Morrison for several reasons. The district's representatives argued that California's law requiring teachers to be models of good conduct applied to the case that teachers are required to impress on their charges "principles of morality," and that homosexual behavior is contrary to the moral standards of the people of California.

In 1969, the California Supreme Court ruled in Morrison's favor. It acknowledged that homosexuality is, for many people, an uncertain or controversial area of morality. Nevertheless, the court made an important distinction between a teacher's private life and his or her professional performance. As there was no evidence that Morrison's sexual orientation had ever been part of his relationship with his students, or in any way affected the performance of his teaching duties, or affected his relationship with his fellow teachers, he was reinstated.[36] Although there are no new dramatic shifts in the law, what LGBT teachers can and cannot do in their professional status is being given substantial attention among activists and lawyers.[37]

Similarly, cases involving pregnancy out of wedlock and unmarried couples living together have been settled in favor of the individual teacher. To win such a case, however, the conditions just cited are required. Specifically, the behavior must not intrude into the classroom or seriously affect the teacher's professional performance.

A teacher would be misguided to think that his or her behavior after school hours is *always* protected under the law. For example, a tenured California teacher was fired after she was arrested by an undercover policeman for engaging in sexual activity at a swingers' club. California state courts ruled that her behavior at this semipublic party showed "a total lack of concern for . . . decorum or preservation of her dignity and reputation," and that she demonstrated a serious lack of "normal prudence and good common sense."[38] Flaunting one's deviation from the community's standard tends to increase the chances that the courts will uphold dismissal. In all these cases, however, circumstances play a crucial role in the courts' final opinion.

8-4c CONDUCT WITH STUDENTS

Whereas the courts have become increasingly lenient on issues of private sexual behavior, the line is being held firm with regard to socially unacceptable behavior that spills over into the classroom. One sure way to lose one's teaching position is to make a sexual advance or engage in any kind of sexual relationship with a student. Usually, even a single incident is enough to sustain a dismissal. The same goes for smoking marijuana for "recreational" purposes, taking other drugs, public drinking to the point of drunkenness, or even using excessively obscene language in the presence of students. In this area, teachers bear the full weight of the responsibility to be a role model.

Teachers should also realize that they can become "overinvolved" with students, even when no sexual impropriety has occurred. A fourth-grade teacher, Drew Kerin, was dismissed from his job when he became so involved with one of his students that he sued the boy's mother for custody. The child had been allowed to live with the teacher for nine months, but when the mother wanted her son to return home, Kerin filed suit for custody. The custody battle generated so much publicity that the district fired him. Kerin was found to have "exploited his position as a teacher," which provided "just cause for termination."[39]

In general, except in matters of personal appearance, the courts are allowing teachers a good degree of freedom in their private and personal lifestyles as long as their choices and their behavior do not adversely affect their performance as teachers. Table 8.1 summarizes the court cases and rulings discussed in this and the previous sections.

TABLE 8.1	Selected Court Cases Dealing with Teachers' Rights and Responsibilities	
Issue	**Case**	**Ruling**
A teacher's liability for student's injury	*Sheehan* v. *St. Peter's Catholic School* (1971)	A teacher is liable for student injuries (i.e., eye injury) if he or she leaves students unsupervised.

(Continued)

TABLE 8.1	Selected Court Cases Dealing with Teachers' Rights and Responsibilities (Continued)	
Issue	**Case**	**Ruling**
	Mancha v. *Field Museum of Natural History* (1971)	A teacher is not liable for student injuries under unusual circumstances (i.e., a fight in a museum) if he or she has taken appropriate precautions.
A teacher's right to free speech (such as criticizing the school authorities)	*Pickering* v. *Board of Education* (1968)	A teacher can criticize the operation of a school as long as his or her criticism does not interfere with the normal running of the school.
	Scoville v. *Board of Education* (1970)	Freedom of speech does not include the use of "fighting words" or the abuse of superiors with profane and vulgar speech.
A teacher and academic freedom	*Keefe* v. *Geanakos* (1969)	A teacher may not be dismissed only for selecting reading assignments with offensive words.
A teacher and his or her private life	*Morrison* v. *State Board of Education* (California, 1969)	A teacher's sexual orientation is not grounds for revocation of licensure, particularly when it in no way affects the performance of professional tasks.

8-5 Law, Religion, and the School

According to the First Amendment to the Constitution, "Congress shall make no law respecting an establishment of religion, or prohibiting the free exercise thereof." During the past two centuries, the U.S. judicial system has interpreted this amendment inconsistently with respect to the place of religion in public schools—a topic of high controversy and the cause of much public unrest in recent years. This controversy is not a new one: The role of religion has been a bone of contention since the beginning of public education in the United States.

Among the questions currently being asked are the following:

- Which religious observances, if any, are permitted in public school classrooms?
- Is all prayer, public and private, illegal in public schools?
- Are extracurricular religious clubs allowed in public schools?
- May parents insist that schools provide alternative textbooks consistent with their religious beliefs?

8-5a PRAYER AND SCRIPTURE IN THE SCHOOL

Until the mid-twentieth century, religious observances, including Bible reading and prayers, were common in the public schools. In fact, Bible reading and the recitation of the Lord's Prayer were required by constitutions or by statutes in a number of states. In *Abington School District* v. *Schempp* (1963), however, the Supreme Court ruled both to be unconstitutional.

In a 1962 decision (*Engel* v. *Vitale*), the court had already ruled against the recitation of a nondenominational prayer, holding that Bible reading and prayer violate both clauses of the First Amendment. The court recognized that the schools involved did not compel a child to join in religious activities if his or her parents objected; nevertheless, it held that the social pressures exerted on pupils to participate were excessive. In essence, no distinction was believed to exist between voluntary and compulsory participation in religious activities.

The court did note that the study of comparative religion, the history of religion, and the relationship of religion to civilization were not prohibited by this decision. It would also appear that, although the Bible may not be used to teach religion, it might, if objectively presented, be used in such areas of study as history, civics, and literature. Indeed, most thoughtful people would agree that failure to be conversant with the Old and New Testaments makes understanding of Western history and literature impossible. In the same way, if a student set out to learn about Chinese culture and was not permitted to read Confucius, he or she would be doomed to a very limited understanding.

The court has also affirmed the right of individual public school pupils who so desire to say prayers and read scriptures of their choice in the morning before school starts or after the regular school day has ended. As discussed in the next section, many students join clubs or groups for these activities. If prayers are said during lunch period, they must be silent. Many students who are religious continue to seek avenues for expressions of beliefs within the public school day, whereas other students and their families campaign to avoid mixing religious expression with school activities.

The daily recitation of the Pledge of Allegiance has been controversial in some quarters for several decades. Originally challenged on the ground that the compulsory recitation of the Pledge is unconstitutionally coerced allegiance to the country, courts allowed students to opt out of reciting it. This was not enough for a California atheist father who did not want his third-grade daughter to have to listen to the Pledge's phrase "under God." In an extremely controversial ruling in June 2002, the 9th U.S. Circuit Court of Appeals, which has the nine Western states under its jurisdiction, banned the teacher-led pledge for the nearly 10 million public schoolchildren. Two years later, in 2004, the Supreme Court rejected the father's case on a technicality. The ban imposed by the 9th Circuit Court has been lifted until the Supreme Court issues a final ruling. The Supreme Court has also determined that the recitation of prayers at a public school function is unconstitutional. In the *Lee* v. *Weisman* case (1992), the principal of a public middle school, Robert Lee, had invited a rabbi to say a benediction and invocation at the middle school graduation exercises, instructing the rabbi to offer nonsectarian prayers. Student Deborah Weisman and her father filed a suit in court seeking a permanent injunction against including prayers in graduation ceremonies. The court used the following facts to reach its decision: (1) Public school officials directed the performance of formal religious exercises at the graduation ceremonies, and (2) although such exercises do not require attendance, they are in a real sense obligatory for all students, even those who object. As a result, the court upheld the decision of the lower court, ruling that it is unconstitutional to include clergy members who offer prayers as part of school graduation ceremonies.[40]

Ⓣ F

It is legal in American public school classrooms to study religious books, such as the Bible, the Talmud, and the Koran.

"Teaching about religion is not the same as teaching someone to be religious. In our multicultural, multiethnic society, understanding another person's faith will foster tolerance and harmony, a goal common to all religions.

—MARGARET BARTLEY,
author and historian

Issues of religious freedom and the place of religion in the curriculum are tension points in many public schools.

ZUMA Press Inc/Alamy Stock Photo

What if the students themselves select the prayer or the person delivering the prayer at after-school events? In 2000, the court ruled that student-led, student-initiated prayer at football games violates the First Amendment, in part because attending school football games is mandatory for some students, such as athletes, cheerleaders, and band members, and other students who might object to the prayers feel social pressure and/or genuine desire to participate in high school football.[41]

8-5b RELIGIOUS CLUBS AND PRAYER GROUPS

Are extracurricular religious clubs legal in public schools? Court decisions provide no clear guidelines here. In at least one case, a district judge ruled in favor of such clubs based on students' right to free speech. A U.S. Circuit Court of Appeals later overturned the decision, maintaining that such clubs violate the First Amendment's "establishment of religion" clause. The U.S. Supreme Court did not clear the waters: The five-justice majority upheld the district court opinion on a technical point but declined to comment on the constitutional issues raised.[42]

In yet another case, *Board of Education of Westside Community Schools* v. *Mergens* (1990), the court ruled that extracurricular religious group meetings held on public school grounds do not necessarily violate the U.S. Constitution. The court stated that if the school provides a limited public access for other noncurriculum student groups, then, under the Equal Access Act, a student religious group may also use the school building for its meetings. Under these circumstances, a student religious group meeting in the cafeteria after school does not violate the constitutional separation of church and state.[43]

Subsequent court rulings have supported students' rights to use school facilities for religious club meetings, even if the club is directed by adults. The Supreme Court ruled that a school district could not prohibit the Good News Club, a private Christian organization for children 6 to 12 years old, from meeting in a school building after school hours. The court stated that the school district had already adopted a policy of broad community access to its schools and, in doing so, had created an open forum. Prohibiting the club from meeting violated the club's First Amendment right of free speech (*Good News Club* v. *Milford Central School District*, 2001). Although a key point in the *Good News Club* decision was that teachers do not participate in such meetings, the 8th Circuit Court of Appeals in St. Louis later ruled that a teacher may *on his or her own time* lead such religious meetings after school.[44]

8-5c RELIGION AND SECULAR HUMANISM

The many court cases dealing with prayer in school, extracurricular clubs, and the presence of the Bible in schools, as well as the publicity surrounding them, have had a chilling effect on teachers and administrators. Rather than get involved with what is clearly a controversial set of issues, many public educators have tended to discourage any expression or even mention of religious issues or topics. This, in turn, has caused a reaction from parents and others who think that by ignoring the religious dimension of life, the public schools create a distorted, and ultimately dangerous, view of humankind—a view labeled *secular humanism*. Secular humanism asserts the dignity of human beings, but ignores the idea of God and the spiritual.

Objecting to what they see as the prevailing secular humanism of the schools, some parents contend that such fundamental questions as "What is a person's true nature?" and "What is a well lived life?" can be treated in schools from every perspective except the religious view. They claim that this presentation is not only intellectually unbalanced, but also poses a danger to their children. Speaking to this issue, one legal scholar has written, "When government imposes the content of school, it becomes the same deadening agent of repression from which the framers of the Constitution sought to free themselves."[45] Many parents are voting not only with their pocketbooks, by turning down school budgets and tax requests for public schooling, but also with their feet, by walking away from the public school system. This trend has fueled a dramatic growth in religious schools and particularly in home schooling in recent years.

Specific objections to secular humanism in the schools have taken a number of forms. Two examples are the controversies over teaching about the origins of the human race and the debates over the use of certain textbooks.

The Creationism versus Evolution Controversy

Major concern over the teaching of evolution dates to the famous 1925 Scopes trial in Tennessee, in which a high school biology teacher, John Scopes, was accused of illegally teaching the theory of evolution. Scopes was found guilty and fined $100, but the verdict was later overturned on a technicality. Although the trial came to national attention at the time (and again decades later with the award-winning play and film, *Inherit the Wind,* based on that trial), it did not set any legal precedent.

The issue returned to the public eye later in the century, when citizens asked for equal time for the biblical account of creation. In 1982, the Louisiana legislature passed the Balanced Treatment for Creation-Science and Evolution-Science Act, which quickly came to be known as the Balanced Treatment Act. The act defined *scientific creationism* as "the belief that the origins of the elements, the galaxy, the solar system, of life, of all the species of plants and animals, the origin of man, and the origin of all things and their processes and relationships were created ex nihilo (from nothing) and fixed by God."[46] In addition to requiring that scientific creationism be taught whenever evolution was taught, the act required the development of curriculum guides and research services for teaching creationism. At the same time, the act provided none of these resources or protections for those teaching evolution.

After several challenges and lower court rulings, a case testing this act, *Edwards* v. *Aguillard,* reached the U.S. Supreme Court. In 1987, the justices ruled seven to two against the Balanced Treatment Act. According to the court, the Balanced Treatment

Act was, in fact, not balanced because its provisions favored the teaching of creationism over evolution. Further, the court asserted, the Balanced Treatment Act was motivated by the legislature's desire to promote a particular religious viewpoint, which violated the Constitution's provision against the establishment of a state-sponsored religion.

Despite the court's ruling, few observers think this controversy has been fully settled. For example, in 1999 and again in 2005, the Kansas Board of Education voted to drop the requirement in the state's academic standards that evolution be taught in public schools.[47] However, in 2013, the board voted to include the teaching of evolution in its standards. For several years, the creationism-versus-evolution clash has been the battleground between those who believe the public schools have become antireligious and are promoting secularism and those who are opposed to the schools teaching a religious point of view. Recently, this controversy has taken a somewhat different turn with the introduction of **intelligent design theory**. This theory suggests that some biological structures and other aspects of nature are so complex and so highly interdependent that they could not have developed through Darwinian evolution, or "undirected natural causes." Intelligent design theorists believe there is evidence that "an intelligence" either created or somehow guided their development.

Although this theory differs from creationism on several points, it is quite compatible with a belief in God and is frequently explicitly linked with such a belief. Some in the scientific community have criticized intelligent design as mere speculation and a violation of scientific principles because it relies on preexisting causes to explain natural phenomena. Whatever its merits, intelligent design theory has pumped new life into the arguments put forth by those who believe the public school curriculum, and science curriculum in particular, have been de facto antireligious.

The Textbook Controversy

Recent court cases have been launched by fundamentalist Christian parents who argue that texts used in their children's public school classes are anti-Christian and therefore a violation of their children's constitutional rights. In a 1986 Tennessee case, a U.S. district judge agreed that students' constitutional rights were violated when they were expelled after they refused to read certain texts. The following year, a U.S. Court of Appeals reversed the decision of the lower court, ruling that the texts in question did not promote or require a person to accept any religion.[48]

Shortly thereafter, another challenge to the public schools' choice of textbooks was made in Alabama by fundamentalist parents, students, and teachers. Forty-four textbooks used in history, social studies, and home economics courses were cited as advancing secular humanism. In this case (*Smith v. Board of School Commissioners of Mobile County*, 1987), the court rulings followed a pattern similar to that of the Tennessee case just described. Initially, the district court ruled that secular humanism is a religion and that some of the textbooks in question did discriminate against theistic religion. On appeal, this decision was reversed, and the court ruled that the textbooks promoted neither secularism nor any other religion.[49]

8-5d GUIDELINES FOR RELIGIOUS NEUTRALITY

Table 8.2 summarizes the court rulings on religion and the public schools. When all the cases are considered together, teachers may very well be confused about what they can and cannot do. Thank goodness, some attempts have been made to establish guidelines for teachers and schools.

TABLE 8.2	Selected U.S. Court Cases Dealing with Religion and the Schools	
Issue	**Case**	**Ruling**
Teaching evolution and/ or creationism		
Teaching evolution in public schools	*Scopes* v. *State of Tennessee* (1925)	The court upheld the state law disallowing the teaching of evolution as an explanation of the origins of the universe. The law was eventually struck down in 1996 by the state legislature.
Balancing the teaching of creationism and evolution in public school curricula	*Edwards* v. *Aguillard* (1987)	Schools teaching the biblical explanation of creation violate the Constitution's provision against teaching a particular religious viewpoint.
Public schooling, prayer, and the Bible		
The inclusion of Bible reading and prayer	*Engel* v. *Vitale* (1962)	Bible reading and teacher-led prayer in schools are violations of the First Amendment; because of the social pressures involved, there is no difference between voluntary and compulsory prayer in school. Private prayer and Bible reading are protected.
	Abington School District v. *Schempp* (1963)	Reading the Bible and reciting the Lord's Prayer in public schools are violations of the First and Fourteenth Amendments; however, the Bible may be studied for historical, cultural, or other general educational purposes.
Reciting nondenominational prayers at public school ceremonies	*Lee* v. *Weisman* (1992)	It is unconstitutional to include adult-led prayers at public school ceremonies because all students are virtually obligated to attend ceremonies such as graduations, including those students who object to the practice.

(Continued)

TABLE 8.2	Selected U.S. Court Cases Dealing with Religion and the Schools (Continued)	
Issue	**Case**	**Ruling**
Students reciting nondenominational prayer at extracurricular events	*Santa Fe Independent School District* v. *Doe* (2000)	Schools cannot allow student-led prayer at extracurricular events (e.g., sporting events) because attendance is not completely voluntary.
Public schools and extracurricular religious groups		
Extracurricular religious clubs meeting on public school property	*Board of Education of Westside Community Schools* v. *Mergens* (1990)	If a public school allows a limited public forum for other extracurricular groups, the Equal Access Act indicates that extracurricular religious groups may meet in public school buildings without violating the Constitution.

Thomas McDaniel recommends a *religious neutrality principle* in the classroom and offers four guidelines for putting it into practice:

1. Students may not be required to salute the flag or to stand for the flag salute if this behavior conflicts with their religious beliefs.
2. Bible reading, even without comment, may not be practiced in a public school when the intent is to promote worship.
3. Prayer is an act of worship and as such cannot be a regular part of opening exercises or other aspects of the regular school day.
4. Worship services, such as prayer and Bible reading, are not constitutional, even if voluntary rather than compulsory. Consensus, majority vote, or excusing objectors from class or participation does not make these practices legal.[50] This principle of religious neutrality does not mean that the public school must completely ignore religion. On the contrary, teachers in public schools are free to study the history and contributions (pro and con) of individual religions with their students, to have them read the Bible as literature, and in general to expose students to our culture's religious heritage. It is only when teachers cross the line by advocating a particular religion or involving students in prayer that they become vulnerable to legal action.

A few years ago, as debate over such issues continued, the White House asked the Department of Education to issue a directive on religion in the public schools. The resulting guidelines are an attempt to find a new common ground between religious expression and religious freedom and to correct the perception (or the fact) that schools are hostile to religion. Among the specific points listed in the guidelines are the following:

- Public schools should not interfere with or intrude on a family's religious beliefs.
- Public education should be respectful of religion, open to appropriate religious expression, and should teach about religion because it is so very much a part of our nation's history.
- Advocacy of a particular religion by teachers and administrators has no place in public education.
- Students' religious clubs and groups are entitled to hold meetings, to have common prayer, to read scriptures, and to have their meetings publicized through school bulletin boards, newspapers, and public address systems.
- Although school-sponsored prayer should not be permitted, it is appropriate to begin the school day with a moment of silence.[51]

A U.S. Department of Education directive gained teeth after the passage of the No Child Left Behind legislation; the directive contains a provision that federal funds will not be provided to a school district unless it stipulates in writing that "it has no policy that prevents or otherwise denies participation in constitutionally protected prayer in public schools." Although this directive and the federal legislative support have been well received by many parents and educators, they have yet to be tested in the courts, nor do they address all of the conflicting issues surrounding religion in public schools.

Pause *and* Reflect

1. Do you believe that the textbooks you used as a student or that you have seen in your fieldwork promote secular humanism? What can you do, as a teacher, if your assigned curriculum materials seem to you to promote or denigrate a particular religious viewpoint?
2. Do you believe that controversies about religion in the schools will have a chilling effect on your own willingness as a teacher to have students read religious literature or study the contributions of religions?

8-6 Students and the Law

Many of the most important legal issues that affect the lives of teachers relate directly to students and their rights. Students—and particularly public school students—have a special status under the law. In this section, we touch on a few of the more significant student-related issues that can affect teachers.

8-6a STUDENTS AND DUE PROCESS

As described earlier in this chapter, for many years the courts used the legal principle of in loco parentis in cases involving students. Teachers following this principle are expected to treat their students in a caring and informal manner instead of in the formal and legalistic manner that governs relationships "out in the world." By the same reasoning, because we do not require due process in the home, for a long time it was not valued in the schools.

Gradually, through decisions made in court cases such as *Tinker*[52] and others described in upcoming sections, the in loco parentis principle has been eroded, and the courts have come to appreciate that students often need to be protected from the arbitrary use of authority. As a direct result, many schools have developed clear statements governing procedures for expulsion, suspension, student privacy, freedom of speech and publication, and various breaches of discipline. Informing students of the rules, procedures, and consequences of violations in these areas is a major step toward providing due process rights. Even so, the most important aspect of due process remains the spirit of fair and evenhanded justice with which teachers respond to the daily events of the classroom.

In terms of disciplinary matters relating to students, schools can operate on a continuum with regard to student due process. For trivial matters or emergencies, schools may act without due process. For matters that may result in a short suspension (one or two days) or some entry on the student's record, schools must use some measure of due process; for disciplinary matters that may result in a long-term suspension or expulsion, they must demonstrate careful due process.[53]

8-6b SUSPENSION AND EXPULSION

Ever since schools came into existence, individual students have had difficulty following the rules and staying out of trouble. In recent decades, as schools have tried harder to keep older youth from dropping out, and as use of drugs and violence have increased in society as a whole, disciplinary problems within schools have escalated. Three of the most dramatic and horrible examples are the massacres that happened at Columbine High School in Colorado in 1999, at Virginia Tech (college) in 2007, and the Sandy Hook Elementary School in Newtown, Connecticut, in 2012.

Educators need to keep in mind that some students are severely troubled or deeply unhappy (or both). Some, having been compelled to stay in school, find little to capture their imaginations and to motivate them. For these students, school is a place of failure and frustration, and trouble is often close behind. Some of the more common forms of school infractions today are stealing; vandalizing school property or someone's private property; bringing a weapon to school; possessing, using, or selling drugs or alcohol; fighting (or encouraging others to fight); and repeatedly disobeying the reasonable directives of teachers and other school personnel.[54]

School districts are not powerless in the face of these kinds of disciplinary breaches. For maintaining a safe and effective academic environment, schools have three disciplinary alternatives at their disposal: in-school suspension, out-of-school suspension, and expulsion. Typically, in-school suspension is for minor offenses and is brief in duration. Out-of-school suspension and expulsion are more serious and last for longer periods, with expulsion meaning complete separation from the school. This school district power must be wielded in a manner that ensures that students' constitutional rights to due process are protected. Recently, the U.S. Department of Education sent to U.S. schools a useful publication, entitled *Early Warning, Timely Response: A Guide to Safe Schools*,[55] that not only stresses prevention but also offers helpful strategies for building good relationships with students. Nevertheless, it is in these areas—in the prevention of disruptions and violence and in the administration of suspension and expulsion—that school administrators have frequently become entangled in lawsuits.

Major Court Cases

One of the most important dismissal cases was *Goss v. Lopez,* a 1975 suspension case involving Dwight Lopez, a high school sophomore from Columbus, Ohio.[56] Lopez was suspended for 10 days for allegedly becoming involved in a cafeteria disturbance. This suspension occurred without a hearing and without any prior notification. Although a suspension of this length and without a hearing or prior notice was in accord with the Ohio statutes, a suit was filed stating that Lopez's constitutional rights had been violated because he was not given any notice or hearing. The case went to the U.S. Supreme Court, which ruled in favor of Lopez on the grounds that students facing suspension from a public school have property and liberty interests and therefore are protected by due process. In addition, the court stated that "longer suspensions (longer than 10 days) or expulsions for the remainder of the school term, or permanently, may require more formal procedures."

In a 1988 lawsuit with some similar elements, *Honig v. Doe,* the court ruled against California school officials.[57] In this case, a school district had indefinitely suspended two emotionally disturbed students on the grounds that they were dangerous. The court ruled that this suspension was a violation of PL 94-142 (later called the Individuals with Disabilities Education Act [IDEA]), which allows school authorities to suspend dangerous students with disabilities for a maximum of 10 days. Longer suspensions require either the permission of parents or the consent of a federal judge.

Because of the fear of school violence, which was exacerbated by the Columbine and Virginia Tech school tragedies, a number of school districts have adopted zero-tolerance policies toward weapons, drugs, and school fights, calling for automatic suspension or dismissal of student violators. Court cases involving "zero tolerance" have yet to be heard by the Supreme Court, although lower courts have already heard cases in which zero-tolerance policies have played a part. It would appear, however, from the 2008 federal court case, *Murakowski v. The University of Delaware,* that the law is shifting toward supporting the school's responsibility to maintaining a safe and constructive learning environment. The case involved a college student who built a website and posted his own essays, such as his personal "guide to sex" and a graphic piece on how to skin a cat. In addition, his essays were filled with racist, antigay, and anti-Semitic comments. Dorm mates, claiming to be frightened by his behavior, complained to university officials. After a hearing, he was banned from the campus and required to undergo a mental health assessment. Murakowski insisted that his writings were satire and humor and that the university was violating his constitutionally protected rights. He sued, hoping to receive $59,000 in damages. He won, but it was a Pyrrhic victory for Mr. Murakowski. The court, considering the university's action amid the recent killings at Columbine High School and Virginia Tech and the climate of fear on campuses, awarded him a mere $10.[58]

A 2000 court case in Illinois, *Fuller v. Decatur Public School Board of Education School District 61,* highlighted the zero-tolerance approach as well as the volatile issue of racial profiling.[59] This school district, in accordance with its zero-tolerance policy on fighting, expelled a group of students for two years for starting a fight in the bleachers at a home football game. The fight, from all accounts (including a videotape), was brief but violent; seven spectators were injured. The students argued that the expulsion was because of racial profiling;

they were unfairly singled out, they argued, because they were stereotyped as gang members. Further, they argued, because no guns, knives, or drugs were involved, their behavior did not merit an expulsion. The court ruled that the students failed to present any evidence that their expulsion was in any way based on their race.[60] Thus, although that court case found no evidence of racial profiling in the school's application of its zero-tolerance policy, it seems likely that future cases will involve both issues in school disciplinary actions.

School dress codes are another area where students' rights and strict (sometimes zero-tolerance) policies are clashing. In response to provocative and immodest student dress, these codes are being revised. Among the recent additions: no tank tops or tube tops; no low-riding, hip-hugging pants; no exposed midriffs; no capri pants; no overalls; no pajama tops or bottoms; no sweat pants; no shirts with slogans or offensive illustrations; no athletic jerseys; no hats; no hooded sweatshirts; belts are required unless the pants or skirt lack belt loops; shirts and blouses should be tucked in at all times—and should be long enough to stay tucked.[61] Although such a policy is difficult to enforce, as the "Voices from the Classroom" feature attests, educators are increasingly recognizing that there is a connection between edgy or over-the-line clothes and a school's poor learning environment.

Freedom of speech issues related to dress codes cut two ways. In response to the problems of students' overdressing and underdressing, some schools have gone

VOICES from the Classroom

Dress Codes

Rob Famularo, a former sixth-grade teacher, is now the principal of the Calvin Coolidge School in Wyckoff, New Jersey.

In my very first year as a teacher, I quickly realized the numerous and varied job responsibilities that undoubtedly come with the profession. On any given day, a teacher may be asked to be a coach, friend, counselor, helping hand, disciplinarian, or facilitator, to name just a few possible roles. What I did not realize quite so quickly, however, was the number of important decisions I would make on a regular basis. Many of these decisions carry moral, ethical, or legal implications. Consider, for example, the decisions involved in enforcing my public school's dress code.

Although the U.S. Supreme Court has stated that students relinquish some of their First Amendment rights in school, teachers nonetheless often struggle with the legal and ethical ramifications of controlling student dress and deeming what is "appropriate or inappropriate" attire for school. There are, of course, lots of theoretical, legal, and ethical questions surrounding dress codes, such as these: "Is it the responsibility of a public school to determine which attire is appropriate dress for school?"

"Can a school still make this determination even if a parent objects or disagrees?" "How can a teacher make an objective and consistent decision for every student?" These questions, which have deep moral, legal, and ethical significance, are worthy of thoughtful reflection and consideration by anyone entering the teaching profession.

The situation becomes quite real, however, when the administration sets a specific dress code that I am expected to enforce when students enter my classroom first period in the morning. Can (or should) I tell a female high school student that her skirt is too short or that her shorts are more appropriate for the beach than for school? Or should I simply turn a blind eye to the situation, saving both the girl and me the embarrassment? Am I really doing my job by ignoring the situation? This is when teachers get the chance to truly define their own personal meanings for what seem like abstract legal and ethical questions.

beyond dress codes and now require school uniforms. These policies are particularly popular in large cities. Currently, New York, Chicago, Houston, Philadelphia, Miami, and Los Angeles have uniform policies. Not surprisingly, many parents and students are suing their districts over these policies, claiming having to wear a uniform is an abridgement of their First Amendment rights to free expression.[62]

Zero-tolerance policies, though hailed by many as tools to bring greater order and discipline to schools, are not without their detractors. In recent years, there have been a number of highly publicized incidents, such as the suspension of a third-grader for bringing a butter knife to school, that have made this policy rather controversial. Collectively, these incidents have proved a key point: No school policy can substitute for an educator's common sense.

Teachers: Pregnancy, Parenthood, and Marriage

Not many years ago, unmarried teachers who became pregnant were routinely dismissed from their teaching positions. Similarly, once a student was discovered to be either married, pregnant, or both, she was dismissed. Pregnant students were considered to be morally corrupting influences on other students, and their presence in school was seen as legitimizing premature sexual activity and early marriage. Although many people still hold these views, the courts have tended in recent years to see such dismissals as discriminatory to young women and as a denial of their rights to an education. As a consequence, most school districts now make arrangements for the education of pregnant students. Nevertheless, vexing issues keep coming up, such as "Should an obviously pregnant cheerleader be allowed to continue cheering?"

Guidelines for Educators

Overall, the pendulum of judicial decisions seems to be moving away from an emphasis on student rights and back toward positions favoring the authority of the schools. Nevertheless, when dealing with matters that might lead to suspension or expulsion, teachers and administrators should follow these guidelines:

- *Documentation.* Before suspension and expulsion can take place, students must be notified (either in writing or orally) of the nature of their offense and the intended punishment.

- *Explanation.* The school must give students a clear explanation of the evidence on which the disciplinary charges rest.

- *Opportunity to defend oneself.* The school must give students an opportunity to refute the charges before a fair and impartial individual with decision-making authority.

8-6c CORPORAL PUNISHMENT

Although few educational theorists living today advocate it, corporal (i.e., physical) punishment is alive and well in American schools. The Supreme Court has regularly refused to rule on corporal punishment, leaving the issue up to the states. The trend among the states is clearly in favor of banning it. In 1979, only 2 states had banned corporal punishment in public schools, but currently 31 states prohibit it[63] (see Figure 8.1). A number of other states currently have legislation pending that would abolish corporal punishment. Still, many states leave the decision up to local school districts. In the 2013–2014 school year, 109,000 students were reported to have been subjected to corporal punishment in U.S. schools.[64]

T (F)
After many years of delay, recently the Supreme Court has made corporal punishment in our schools unconstitutional and therefore illegal.

FIGURE 8.1 **States Banning Corporal Punishment**

Source: The Center for Effective Discipline, "Discipline in Schools," www.stophitting.com/index .php?page=statesbanning.

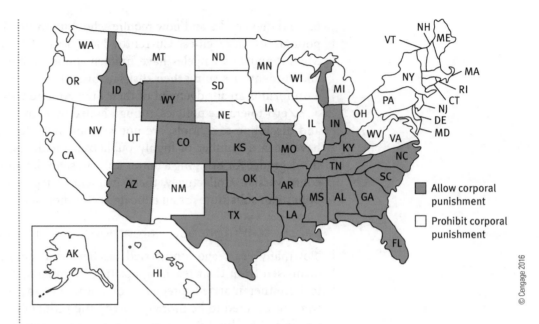

© Cengage 2016

What does this situation mean for teachers from a legal point of view, which is, of course different from a "best practice" point of view and a moral point of view? First, they must know the rules established by their state and school district. Second, they must be aware that the courts have ruled that corporal punishment can be administered only under certain conditions. Thus, teachers must be sure they use only "moderate" and "reasonable" corporal punishment and use it only to establish discipline. A teacher who severely punishes a child, especially if that punishment results in any permanent disability or disfigurement, is highly liable to a lawsuit. Also, punishment cannot be administered out of spite, revenge, or anger. In ruling on cases of excessive corporal punishment, the courts scrutinize the teacher's state of mind and motivation.

The instruments of corporal punishment and the locations on the body they can be administered are also matters of concern to the courts. Fists are totally inappropriate; so are switches and canes. Blows must not strike parts of the body where the risk of injury is high. Also, the punishment must be in scale with the crime—no horse whipping for whispering, for instance. Apparently, the days of the principal's dictum, "The beatings will continue until the morale improves," are over.

Although corporal punishment is administrated by administrators, teachers need to be aware of its important ethical implications. Is it better to paddle a schoolyard bully and keep him in school or to have legal hearings and separate him from the possibility of further education? One major problem with corporal punishment is that a ruler on the palm of the hand may provoke terror in one student, but it is essentially meaningless for the next student. Conversely, noncorporal punishment, such as the prolonged separation of an offending student from classmates, may cause true psychic pain for some children. The entire area of dealing with disruptive and offending students needs careful thought and even more careful actions. Until these issues are settled definitively, it is imperative for new teachers to become thoroughly conversant with their district's policies concerning punishment for student offenses.

8-6d SEARCH AND SEIZURE

Many students—even students of junior high and elementary ages—possess and sell illegal drugs. Schools have drug problems because American youth culture is inundated with images of drug use. Drugs are only one problem that poses questions relating to search and seizure in schools, however. Despite the risks of suspension or expulsion resulting from many schools' zero-tolerance policies, students also bring alcohol, pornography, and even dangerous weapons to school. As a result, school administrators may be urged to step up their searches of students for possession of drugs, alcohol, weapons, or other illegal items.

A student's locker may be searched by an appropriate school official, usually an administrator, *if there are reasonable grounds* to suspect that the locker contains something illegal or dangerous. The New York State courts have gone further in stating that "not only have the school authorities the right to inspect, but the right becomes a duty when suspicion arises that something of an illegal nature may be secreted there."[65] At the same time, courts have found that policies under which school personnel systematically spot-check lockers in hunts for drugs, weapons, or other illicit materials violate students' rights under the Fourth Amendment and therefore are illegal.

Reasonableness and Probable Cause

In the world outside school, authorities must have "probable cause"—that is, a substantial reason for believing that the person is in possession of something illegal—to conduct any kind of search of a person or possessions. Yet because schools are specifically designed for the education and supervision of minors, courts have often allowed schools to use greater latitude in their searches. These decisions have been in keeping with the principle of in loco parentis, the notion that schools act in place of the parents during the school day. Schools may merely need to demonstrate a "reasonable suspicion" that a student was in possession of an illegal substance to conduct a search of that student, rather than demonstrating the "probable cause" that law enforcement officials would need to demonstrate under similar circumstances in non–school settings.[66]

The importance of *reasonableness* in cases of search and seizure was shown by the 1985 U.S. Supreme Court ruling in *New Jersey* v. *T.L.O.*[67] In this case, a teacher found two high school girls smoking in the bathroom and immediately brought them to the assistant vice principal's office. One girl admitted to smoking, but the second denied not only smoking on this occasion, but also even being a smoker.

Many students are surprised to learn that their locker is not their private domain.

Robert Daemmrich Photography Inc/Corbis Historical/Getty Images

The administrator asked the second student to come to his office, where he opened her purse and discovered a pack of cigarettes, cigarette-rolling papers, marijuana, a pipe, empty plastic bags, a wad of bills, and a list of names entitled "People who owe me money." Enter the police. The student was turned over to the juvenile court, where she was judged to be delinquent. She appealed on the basis that the search of her purse had violated her constitutional rights, and therefore the evidence against her had been obtained illegally.

This case eventually made its way to the U.S. Supreme Court, where the student lost. The court stated, "The legality of a search of a student should depend simply on the reasonableness, under all the circumstances, of the search." Reasonableness appears to be determined, first, by whether the search has been initiated by a "reasonable" suspicion. In this case, having seen rolling papers, it was reasonable for the school administrator to look for marijuana, given that the two are so often closely related. The second criterion of reasonableness is that the search's scope and conduct must be "reasonably" related to the circumstances that gave rise to the search. Further, school officials must take into consideration the age and gender of the student and the nature of the offense.

The distinction between "reasonable suspicion" and "probable cause" is a fine line that is not always crystal clear. The prudent guideline for schools when conducting searches is that any invasive search (e.g., body searches) would require "probable cause," whereas less invasive searches (student lockers) would not require as rigorous a standard; in the latter cases, "reasonable suspicion" would suffice. Mistakes here, particularly in the case of unwarranted strip searches, can be not only painfully embarrassing to the students but also very expensive for the school district.

In 2009, the Supreme Court released a ruling in the rather sensational case of a 13-year-old middle school student who was strip-searched by school authorities. The girl, who was alleged to be selling prescription-strength Ibuprofen pills, first had her backpack and outer garments searched. Finding no pills, and even in the face of the girl's assertion of innocence, the school assistant principal was convinced she had pills hidden on her person, he therefore directed two female school employees to search her in the nurse's office. The search of her bra and her panties exposed her breasts and to some degree her pelvic area. No pills where found, and the girl sued. The court's ruling was a split decision. Yes, the girl's rights had been violated, not by the first searches, but by the intrusive body search. However, in this case, the school district received a pass. The school and the assistant principal were given immunity because their motives were impelled by a desire to protect students from the dangers of drugs.[68]

The police, on the other hand, do not have the same *custodial relationship*—the same kinds of responsibility toward students—that school officials do. Therefore, as a general rule, police need a warrant and the consent of school officials to search individual students or their lockers.

Drug Tests as Searches

Most people have heard of potential employees or Olympic athletes taking tests to see whether they have any illegal drugs in their systems. Can schools decide to administer such kinds of drug testing for those who go out for sports teams?

In the late 1980s, the Vernonia School District of Oregon noted a surge in students' use of drugs. Athletes, in particular, were leaders in this drug culture. In response, the school decided to institute random urinalysis to spot-check for drug use among the athletes. All students who signed up for a team were required to provide their own and their parents' written consent for testing.

In 1991, a seventh-grader, James Acton, signed up to play football, but was denied participation on the team because he and his parents refused to provide the test consent forms. The family sued, claiming that the drug testing was an invasion of student privacy and an illegal search. The case eventually was decided in the Supreme Court, which ruled in favor of the Vernonia School District. The justices took into consideration several of the district's arguments, including observations that athletes participate in any number of activities, from "suiting up" in the locker room to preseason physical exams, that reasonably decrease their expectations of privacy, and that the drug test was relatively unobtrusive. The court also considered the severity of the need, based on the widespread student drug use, and ruled that the policy was reasonable and constitutional. In its ruling, however, the court cautioned against assuming that suspicionless drug testing would be constitutional in all other situations. It indicated that in this case, the most salient factor was that the school district was enacting its governmental responsibilities in monitoring and supervising schoolchildren entrusted to its care.[69] In 2002, the court significantly broadened its ruling to include not just athletes, but all students engaged in "competitive" extracurricular activities, be they football or debating. The ruling reaffirmed and stressed the school's "custodial responsibility." Because search and seizure touches upon such fundamental American rights, schools will probably always need to be vigilant about how school policies and practices align with constitutional rights.

8-6e FREEDOM OF SPEECH

The right to say what we want, where we want, is the cornerstone of a free society, and as such it is near and dear to Americans. As Justice William O. Douglas stated, "Restriction of free thought and free speech is the most dangerous of all subversions. It is the one un-American act that could most easily defeat us."[70] Despite U.S. courts' vigilant protection of this right, however, it is not an *absolute* right. The great Supreme Court Justice Oliver Wendell Holmes wrote that freedom of speech does not give a person the right to yell "Fire!" in a crowded theater or to knowingly and maliciously say or write lies that damage the reputation of another. In schools, freedom of expression must be balanced with the school's responsibility to maintain a safe and orderly environment and to protect people's feelings and reputations.

Students' First Amendment Rights

During the 1960s and early 1970s, many social protests and antiwar demonstrations spilled over into the schools, and particularly into high schools. In one case, *Tinker v. Des Moines Independent Community School District* (1969), students who had been suspended for wearing antiwar armbands took the issue to court, claiming that the school had interfered with their right to freedom of expression. The Supreme Court ruled in favor of the students, stating that their black armbands were a form of symbolic speech in protest of the Vietnam War and should not be prohibited. A key point in this affirmation of students' First Amendment rights was the passive and nondisruptive nature of the students' protest. According to the court, there was no evidence wearing the armbands would "materially and substantially interfere with the requirements of appropriate discipline in the operation of the schools."[71]

A Shift in Legal Direction: Restricting Student Speech

During the 1970s and 1980s, the *Tinker* case was often cited, but the tide of court opinion in favor of students' right to free speech soon began to turn. In the 1986 case of *Bethel School District No. 403* v. *Fraser,*[72] Matthew Fraser, a high school student in Bethel, Washington, nominated another student for vice president of the student government in a formal speech at an assembly before 600 students. Despite the warning of two teachers, Fraser built his speech on an elaborate, graphic, and explicit sexual metaphor comparing the nominee to a sexual organ. The court records of this case fail to tell us the outcome of the election, but Fraser got the ax. He was suspended for three days and removed from the list of candidates to speak at graduation. Fraser sued and won initially, but when the case went to the Supreme Court, he lost by a seven-to-two decision. The court affirmed the school's right to "establish standards of civic and mature conduct" and to enforce them.

The definition of students' right to free speech was further refined in the 2007 Supreme Court ruling in *Morse* v. *Frederick* (No. 06-278). Joseph Frederick, a high school student in Juneau, Alaska, was suspended from school for 10 days when he unfurled a large banner ("Bong Hits 4 Jesus") across the street from the school when the Olympic torch parade went through Juneau en route to the 2002 Winter Games in Salt Lake City. Frederick claimed that it was a prank, a stunt to ensure that he and his mates got on television. As a public relations event, the act was a resounding success. The school principal, and eventually the majority of the Supreme Court, saw the banner as advocating—or at least celebrating—illegal drug use. Chief Justice John Roberts wrote, "The First Amendment does not require schools to tolerate at school events student expression that contributes to those dangers."[73] Although something of a worrisome ruling for high school pranksters across the land, this ruling reaffirmed the authority of school officials in these matters.

School Newspapers and Freedom of the Press

School newspapers have long been arenas for struggles over freedom of speech and freedom of the press. Often the very best efforts to make school papers "vital" and "relevant" draw newspaper staffs into controversies. That is what happened at Hazelwood East High School in the spring of 1983.[74] Attempting to make their paper, *The Spectrum,* speak more directly to the real issues confronting their fellow students, the staff submitted two controversial articles, one dealing with the personal accounts of three Hazelwood students who had become pregnant and one focusing on divorce and its effect on students.

In line with standard practice, the adviser and teacher of the journalism class that produced the paper passed the issue on to the principal for his approval. The principal eliminated the two pages containing the offending stories and sent the other four pages to the printer. In response, Kathy Kuhlmeier and the six other journalism students sued, contending that their freedom of speech rights had been violated. Eventually, in 1988, the Supreme Court ruled in favor of the school district. Although dissenting justices complained about the potential for "thought control" and the "denuding of high school students of much of the First Amendment protection that *Tinker* in itself prescribed," the majority supported the principal's actions as legal and responsible. As stated in the majority opinion: "A school may in its capacity as publisher of a school newspaper or producer of a school newspaper or producer of a school play disassociate itself not only from speech that would substantially interfere with its work or impinge on the rights of other students but also from speech that is, for example, ungrammatical, poorly written, inadequately researched, biased, prejudiced, vulgar or profane, or unsuitable for immature audiences. . . . A school need not tolerate student speech that is inconsistent with its basic educational mission even though the government could not censor similar speech outside the school."[75]

Implications of the Court Cases

Taken together, the three cases we have just discussed—*Tinker/Des Moines, Bethel/ Fraser,* and *Hazelwood/Kuhlmeier*—suggest that freedom of speech and expression in schools is hardly absolute. Students may be punished for offensive or disruptive speech or publications. Schools, then, are something like Justice Holmes's crowded theaters, and students' freedom of speech is somewhat limited. Students can and should express themselves, but in an orderly and nonviolent way. For its part, the school has the right and responsibility to ensure that language is not used to hurt or scandalize the students in its charge.

One cutting-edge freedom-of-speech issue involves the Internet. As discussed in Chapter 7, "What Should Teachers Know about Technology and Its Impact on Teaching and Learning?," the Internet can be a marvelous educational tool, opening up almost infinite intellectual resources to students. At the same time, it can expose students to written and visual pornography, obscenity through email, electronic bullying, and chat-room predators. Many school districts have been struggling to respond to these dangers without unduly restricting students' exploration of the electronic world beyond the school. Among the responses currently in place are orientation programs on appropriate use of the Internet, more careful supervision of computer stations, and special software designed to block forbidden sites. Many districts have **acceptable use policies** that provide rules of the road for students using this technology.

8-6f SEXUAL HARASSMENT

In a dated, but still landmark study entitled *Hostile Hallways,* the American Association of University Women (AAUW) initially reported in 1993 and reaffirmed in its 2000 update that 81 percent of U.S. students acknowledged that they were the subjects of sexual harassment at some time during their school lives. Only 11 percent reported the incident to a teacher. One-fourth of the girls and one-tenth of the boys reported being harassed by a school employee. Most harassment, however, was of the student-to-student variety. Teenage girls responded to the survey with stories of pervasive and overt sexual harassment. Girls described sexual jokes and taunts; attempts to snap their bras, lift their skirts, and grope their bodies; and other unwanted physical attention. Boys and girls get the message that girls are not worthy of respect and that it is okay for boys to exert power over girls. Spreading sexual rumors and calling a person "gay" or "lesbian" were often-reported verbal forms of harassment. Most of the harassment occurred in plain view of others—in hallways, lunchrooms, classrooms, assemblies, and playgrounds, and on school buses.[76]

Since the study first appeared, schools have attempted to address this abuse, focusing in particular on student-to-student harassment. The study's definition of **sexual harassment** is "unwanted and unwelcome sexual behavior which interferes with your life." Of course, what constitutes sexual harassment in a particular situation can be a thorny issue. For instance, in 1996, a North Carolina school suspended a *six-year-old* boy who had kissed a female classmate on the cheek, claiming that he committed sexual harassment. Conversely, many readers may know of truly serious and frightening harassment incidents from their own school experience. One such incident was the subject of a Supreme Court ruling in *Davis v. Monroe County Board of Education*.[77]

When LaShonda Davis was in fifth grade in Forsyth, Georgia, her harassment nightmare began. A fellow student began groping her, grinding up against her, and declaring that he was "going to get in bed with her." The girl and her parents made repeated complaints to her teacher and the school principal. After five months, the teacher finally agreed to move the boy's desk to the other side of the room. But the sexual taunting and lewd overtures continued until finally the family sought legal counsel. Six years after the initial incident, and with much legal work, the suit finally made its way to the Supreme Court. The court, in a controversial five-to-four decision, ruled for the Davises and against the school district.

What has made this case legally controversial is the perceived danger of our courts being flooded with cases ranging from innocuous flirtations to true, hardcore harassment. Further, judges worry that the budgets of school districts will be drained by the legal expenses involved in fighting frivolous suits. In the prevailing opinion, the *Davis* decision stresses that school districts are liable only if they were "deliberately indifferent" to information about "severe, pervasive, and objectively offensive" harassment among students.[78] It appears that although the court has come to the defense of harassed students, the criteria for what actually constitutes an offense have been set quite high.

Nevertheless, the problem of sexual harassment in our schools appears to be growing. In particular, whether it is a response to the new societal openness to same-gender sexuality or some other reason, the harassment of gay and lesbian students has increased significantly in recent years. Schools that formerly had taken this issue casually are now working to respond to it more seriously. Schools can work to avoid the problem by drafting a sexual harassment policy; requiring training programs for administrators, teachers, and students; acting quickly when confronted with sexual harassment; enlisting the support of parents; and instituting disciplinary actions against repeat harassers.

Many schools now have sexual harassment policies that they distribute to students and staff. However, as the AAUW study revealed, neither boys nor girls are likely to report actual incidents to adults for fear of being labeled a "snitch" or suffering repercussions. The challenge for educators is to change the culture of harassment in schools and to encourage the use of existing resources to address the problem. All our students—boys and girls—have the right to attend schools whose environments are free from such harassment. As a teacher, you cannot ignore such instances when you see them occur. Choose to make such times "teachable moments" by helping students learn to appreciate the dignity of others and ensuring that the classroom is a welcoming environment for all students.

Table 8.3 summarizes the *Davis* case, along with other major students' rights cases discussed in preceding sections.

8-6g RECORDS AND STUDENTS' RIGHT TO PRIVACY

In this information age, most of us probably have a digital history tucked away on some kind of computer discs or stored in "the cloud." For students, this history may consist of school records, various test scores, and ratings by teachers on everything from citizenship to punctuality. Teachers and other staff members judge a student's character and potential, and others use those judgments to

TABLE 8.3	Selected Court Cases Related to Students' Rights	
Issue	**Case**	**Ruling**
Students' right to free speech		
Students' right to make a symbolic protest	*Tinker* v. *Des Moines Independent Community School District* (1969)	Students have the right to symbolic protest, if that protest does not interfere with the school's operation.
Students' right to use lewd language for a school speech	*Bethel School District No. 403* v. *Fraser* (1986)	Schools have the right to establish and enforce standards of civic conduct.
Student newspapers and freedom of the press	*Hazelwood School District* v. *Kuhlmeier* (1988)	Because public schools are not public forums, school officials have the right not to publish student articles that may violate the sensibilities of other students.
Students' right to expression supporting drug use	*Morse* v. *Frederick, No. 06-278* (2007)	Schools have the right to discipline students even in cases involving playful expression of drug use.
Students' right to education		
Disabled students with behavior problems	*Honig* v. *Doe* (1988)	Dangerous students with disabilities may not be suspended for more than 10 days without parental consent or permission of a federal judge.
Students' school suspension for fighting at a game	*Fuller* v. *Decatur Public School Board of Education School District 61* (2000)	The school's policy of zero tolerance for fighting was upheld by courts.
Students' right to freedom from sexual harassment	*Davis* v. *Monroe County Board of Education* (1999)	The school can be held liable if it ignores excessive sexual harassment of one student by another student.
Students' right to due process		
Students' right to notification and hearing before a suspension	*Goss* v. *Lopez* (1975)	Schools violate students' constitutional right to due process if they suspend students without a hearing.
Students' rights regarding search and seizure		
Students' protection from school searches of personal items	*New Jersey* v. *T.L.O.* (1985)	Schools can search students' lockers and other private items if there is reasonable cause.

decide whether the student should go to this school or get that job. Certainly, we need some system for exchanging information about one another; otherwise, we would hire only our friends or attend only those schools where enough people knew us to vouch for us. Unfortunately, the kind of information in school records may be highly imperfect, and the danger that it will be misinterpreted or fall into the wrong hands is great.

In the early 1970s, a series of situations came to light in which information was poorly used or in which parents and students were denied access to records (e.g., when a diagnosis was used to justify sending a child to a class for students with mental retardation). In response, the U.S. Congress passed the Family Educational Rights and Privacy Act in 1974. The act, also known as the **Buckley Amendment**, outlines who may see a student's record and under what conditions. Parents, who previously were kept from many of the officially recorded judgments that affected their children's futures, are the clear winners as a result of this legislation. The Buckley Amendment states that federal funds will be denied to a school if it prevents parents from exercising the right to inspect and review their children's educational records. Parents must receive an explanation or interpretation of the records if they so request.

However, the Buckley Amendment does not give parents the right to see a teacher's or an administrator's unofficial records. For instance, a teacher's private diary of a class's progress or private notes about a particular child may not be inspected without the teacher's consent.

Although the Buckley Amendment has undoubtedly reduced the potential for abuse of information, it has had a somewhat chilling effect on teachers' and others' willingness to be candid in their judgments when writing student recommendations for jobs or colleges. Because students may elect to see a teacher's letter of recommendation, some teachers choose to play it safe and write a vague, general letter that lacks discriminating judgments, pro or con, about a student. In effect, some faculty members and other recommenders have adopted the attitude, "Well, if a student doesn't trust me enough to let me write a confidential recommendation, I'll simply write an adequate, safe recommendation."

Nevertheless, the Buckley Amendment's impact, in our view, has largely been positive. In the past, many students lost opportunities for higher education and desirable jobs because of inaccurate statements in recommendations or in their school records. One professor reported to us an incident that occurred in his school in 1975, shortly after the Buckley Amendment came into being:

> Our counselors at the junior high school where I taught were "purging" the records of subjective comments with black markers. In one student's permanent record folder, a *Playboy* magazine fell out. It seems a grade school teacher took it from Carl and included it in his permanent record because she wanted future teachers to know what kind of kid Carl really was.

Despite the fact that the Buckley Amendment is almost fifty years old, its implications for what constitutes a violation of students' right to privacy concerning his or her educational records are not always apparent. That fact was made all too clear in the fall of 2001, when the Supreme Court agreed to hear a case involving student rights to privacy.

An Oklahoma mother, Kristja Falvo, brought suit against the Owasso Independent School District for violating the Family Educational Rights and Privacy Act. Her son's classroom teacher asked the students to grade one another's quizzes and to call out the grades so the teacher could record them. The mother argued that such a practice violated her son's right to privacy because the practice publicly disclosed educational information about him. Ms. Falvo was especially concerned that this practice would have a detrimental effect on his learning. In a 2002 decision, the Supreme Court ruled in favor of the school district, stating that peer grading is not in violation of the Buckley Amendment.[79]

OUR FINAL WORD

This chapter marks the beginning of what we hope will be your ongoing probe of the important roles that two related issues, ethics and law, play in the life of a teacher. Together, these issues increasingly permeate the school environment. Whereas ethical issues may raise timeless questions, some laws continually change, and even now the courts may be giving a different complexion to some of the decisions cited in this chapter. Also, this chapter touched on many issues only briefly and omitted others entirely because of lack of space. We urge you to move on from this introduction to investigate further the work of the teacher in its larger ethical and legal framework.

WHY TEACH? YOUR FINAL WORD

1. Can you remember examples of the "everyday ethics" of teaching shown by the teachers you had in elementary and secondary schools? Can you remember examples in which your teachers' ethical behavior was clearly questionable?
2. What do you think about the current controversies over the place of religion in public schools? Of prayer? Of the Bible and other religious works?

   How would you solve the issues related to religion and public education?
3. Teachers are expected to be people of good character and to act as good role models to students. What are the limits of this expectation? What are some points at which the rights of the school district end and the rights of the teacher begin?

KEY TERMS

academic freedom (p. 238)
acceptable use policies (p. 263)
breach of contract (p. 231)
Buckley Amendment (p. 266)
continuing contract (p. 230)
contract (p. 229)
due process (p. 228)
ethics (p. 218)
fair use (p. 242)
grievance (p. 229)

in loco parentis (p. 226)
intellectual property (p. 242)
intelligent design theory (p. 250)
law (p. 218)
liability (234)
probationary period (231)
reduction in force (p. 233)
sexual harassment (p. 263)
tenure (p. 231)

FOR FURTHER INFORMATION

Web Resources

Internet Use Policy: Virginia Public Schools' Student Internet Use Policy Statement

This online resource is produced by the Virginia, Minnesota, Board of Education and is a rich source of information on using the Internet in schools and developing acceptable use policies. Available at http://www.vmps.org/technology-services/internet-use-policy/.

The Legal Information Institute Supreme Court Collection

This website gives you access to the most important Supreme Court school-related decisions. Available at https://www.law.cornell.edu/supremecourt/text.

Char Crusta, Kristyn Kirschenman, and Justin Lien, School Law

This PowerPoint presentation covers many of the cases discussed in this chapter and is a fine summary of the field. Available at https://www.slideshare.net/PseudonymIdaho/school-law-powerpoint11.

Print Resources

Nathan Essex, *School Law and the Public Schools: A Practical Guide for Educational Leaders,* 6th ed. (Boston: Addison Wesley, 2016).

This concise paperback provides contemporary and practical coverage of the relevant legal issues that affect teachers, prospective teachers, and policy makers at all educational levels.

David Schimmel, Louis Fischer, and Leslie R. Stellman, *School Law: What Every Educator Should Know, A User-Friendly Guide* (New York: Pearson Education, 2008).

This book, which was written by scholars who are lawyers and professors of education, bridges the worlds of the courts and the classroom with great detail and clarity.

Kenneth Strike and Jonas Soltis, *The Ethics of Teaching,* 5th ed. (New York: Teachers College Press, 2013).

This short book is an excellent source of ways to approach the topic of ethics in teaching. It contains a number of practice cases.

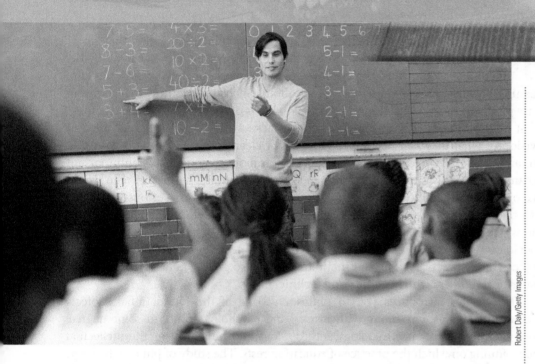

9

What Are the Philosophical Foundations of American Education?

InTASC Standards 2 and 9

LEARNING OBJECTIVES

9-1 Define, describe, and explain the nature of philosophical inquiry.

9-2 Identify the four branches of philosophy important to educators.

9-3 Explain the four schools of educational philosophy common in our schools.

9-4 Identify and outline two educational psychologies that influence our schools.

9-5 Describe your own emerging philosophy of education.

Robert Daly/Getty Images

Truth OR Fiction?

T F   A teacher's religious points should have no influence on his or her philosophy of education.

T F   Progressive educators view nature as being in flux, as ever changing. Therefore, teachers consider knowledge as something that must continually be redefined and rediscovered to keep up with that change.

T F   A late-night, college bull session is, by definition, non-philosophical.

- A medical student who wants intensely to be a surgeon, has marvelous hands, and displays a high level of technical skill, but does not know how the body functions or what constitutes health can hardly be called a doctor.

- An aspirant to the ministry who loves to work with people and possesses a marvelous gift of speaking, but has no opinion about humanity's relationship to God or about the purpose of religion, can hardly be suited for religious ministry.

- And a person who has a great desire to be with young people, wants to live the life of a teacher, and possesses great technical skill, but lacks a clear purpose and direction, is hardly a teacher.

These three individuals are like windup toys, moving along without a plan or an intellectual compass. Although this image may be somewhat dramatic, there are people who prepare for professions without delving into the core meaning of what those professions are all about. Such directionless behavior can cause problems in any occupation or profession but is particularly vexing in teaching. What kind of a teacher can someone be who lacks a view of what people are and a vision of what they can become? Who cannot clearly define right and wrong in human behavior? Who doesn't recognize what is important and what is unimportant or cannot distinguish clear thinking from sloppy thinking? The person who would take on the responsibility for educating the young without having seriously wrestled with these questions is, to say the least, dangerous because that individual is going against the very grain of what it means to be a teacher. In fact, it is safe to say that such a person is not a teacher, but a *technician*. The world needs good technicians, people who can apply practical skills and methods, it can also greatly benefit from creative and critical thinkers who become good technicians.

This chapter introduces you to philosophy, one of the foundational subjects in education. Philosophy, along with history and psychology (and, to some degree, economics, political science, sociology, anthropology, and the law), forms the intellectual underpinning on which the practice of education rests. The study of philosophy helps teachers systematically reflect on issues that are central to education, including such basic concepts as *learning, teaching, being educated, knowledge,* and *the good life.*

9-1 What Is Philosophy?

The word **philosophy** is made up of two root words: "love" (*philo*) and "wisdom" (*sophos*). In its most basic sense, then, philosophy is the *love of wisdom*. Although not all people love wisdom in the same way or to the same degree, all humans are questioning beings—that is, seekers of answers. As children, we are preoccupied with such lofty questions as "How do I get fewer veggies and more dessert?" Then we progress to such questions as "How does the teacher always know to call on me when I don't have the answers?" and "What do I need to do to get a decent grade in geometry?" Ultimately, we may move to more fundamental levels of questioning: "Who am I?," "What is the purpose of life, and what am I doing here?," and "What does it mean to be a truly good person?"

9-1a FUNDAMENTAL QUESTIONS OF EXISTENCE

Until approximately 100 years ago, most people relied on religion and philosophy for answers to such fundamental questions. Whereas religion is said to represent the revealed word of God, philosophy represents a human attempt to sort out by reason the fundamental questions of existence. Many of the great thinkers of Western civilization—Plato, Aristotle, Marcus Aurelius, St. Thomas Aquinas, René Descartes, Jean-Jacques Rousseau, Immanuel Kant, Friedrich Nietzsche, John Locke, John Stuart Mill, William James, Alfred North Whitehead, John Dewey, Jacques Maritain, John Rawls—have been philosophers.

Because education has always been a central human concern, philosophers have thought and written a great deal about education and the questions surrounding it. Twenty-three centuries ago in ancient Greece, Aristotle puzzled over how to educate the young:

> In modern times there are opposing views about the practice of education. There is no general agreement about what the young should learn either in relation to virtue or in relation to the best life: nor is it clear whether their education ought to be directed more towards the intellect than toward character of the soul. . . . And it is not certain whether training should be directed at things useful in life, or at those conducive to virtue, or at nonessentials. . . . And there is no agreement as to what, in fact, does tend towards virtue. Men do not all prize most highly the same virtue, so naturally they differ also about the proper training for it.[1]

Aristotle then went on to offer some of the most profound answers to these questions in human history. The questions about what and how the young should be educated are among society's most enduring preoccupations. Although there are few, if any, universally accepted answers, that in no way reduces the importance of the question and the issues that surround it.

9-1b THE NATURE OF PHILOSOPHY

Only a few people in our society are professional philosophers who earn their daily bread (usually a rather meager fare) by pursuing answers to the fundamental questions of life. However, all of us who wrestle with such questions as "Who am I?" and "What am I doing with my life?" are engaged in philosophical activity. The questions we ask and the answers we glean usually have a major influence on the practical affairs of our lives and determine how we choose to spend our life force. Or, at the very least, they should. For instance, whether or not a person knows it, the very practical decision of whether to become a teacher, a yoga instructor, a real estate broker, or a professional poker player has its roots in his or her philosophy of life.

In developing a philosophy, we draw on many influences: our home lives, our experience in the larger world, our religious views, our reading of literature, history, current events, and our culture. A major difference between professionals and amateurs, however, lies in the precision of their methods. Philosophy is an extremely pure and abstract science. Philosophers work with neither test tubes nor white rats, use neither telescopes nor microscopes, and do not fly off to remote societies to observe the natives. The method or process of philosophers is questioning and reasoning; their product is *thought*.

T (F)
A teacher's religious views should have no influence on his or her philosophy of education.

9-1c THE PHILOSOPHER'S METHOD AND LANGUAGE

Basically, philosophers are concerned with the meanings of things and the interpretation of those meanings. For example, they have an intense interest in the real meanings of words. Although some philosophical discussion and writing involves technical language, it generally uses "plain language," the ordinary language of people. At the same time, philosophers try to be extremely clear and careful about their use of terms. They do not want their ultimate goal (getting at the meaning of things) to become lost in a thicket of fuzzy language.

Although philosophy appears to deal with simple issues in simple language, behind the philosophers' questions are raging debates about profound issues that can have far-reaching implications. For example, the question "What is a human being?" leads to other questions, such as "Is a fetus human?" and "When, if ever, can a fetus be aborted?" or questions such as "What rights do severely disabled people have?" or "Should humans be allowed to clone humans?"

Pause *and* Reflect

Before you go much further in this chapter, you should clarify where you stand today. What are your answers to these philosophical questions?

1. What are the fundamental life questions to which you are seeking answers?
2. How might your answer to question #1 influence you as a teacher?
3. What are the ends or goals of the education you hope to provide students?
4. Should a school lay out what is to be learned, or should students have a larger say in what and how they learn? Why?

9-2 The Terrain of Philosophy

Philosophy covers a large amount of intellectual turf. The terrain of philosophy is divided into several areas, including four that are particularly important to teachers: metaphysics, epistemology, axiology, and logic. These four branches of philosophy are central to the educative process and speak directly to the work of teachers.

9-2a METAPHYSICS

Metaphysics involves the attempt to explain the nature of the real world or the nature of existence. It attempts to answer the question "What is real?" without relying on revealed religion, such as writings in the Bible. Most metaphysicians believe that it is not possible to address fundamental matters, such as the nature of a human being or of the universe, simply by collecting data and formulating statistically significant generalizations. From most metaphysical perspectives, the true nature of a person cannot be captured by measuring or counting alone—that is, a person is more than the sum of his or her height and weight, IQ and SAT scores, and other "vital" statistics.

In probing the nature of reality, the metaphysician asks a whole array of questions: "Does life have meaning?," "Are human beings free or totally determined?," "Is there a purpose to life?," "Is there a set of enduring principles that guide the operation of the universe?," "Can these principles be known?," and "Is there such a thing as stability, or is our world ever changing?"

Metaphysics and the Curriculum

The abstract questions addressed by metaphysicians are ones that educators cannot dismiss. Ultimately, the purpose of education is to help the young better understand reality. The curriculum—and the ways in which we teach and assess it—represents our statement of what that reality is and which part of that reality students should learn. In other words, the curriculum of a school represents what the community believes from the world's reservoir of knowledge is *most worth knowing*.

Although teachers may not actually be metaphysicians, they do take a stand on metaphysical questions. If a teacher decides to teach because he or she believes the most important thing in the universe is a human mind, that career decision is driven by a metaphysical view: the importance of an individual person. The people who serve on school boards also take stands on metaphysical issues. For example, whether a particular school system makes a major investment in educating individuals with severe mental disabilities or emphasizes vocational education depends very much on someone's metaphysical decision about the nature of the person and the place of work in a person's life.

9-2b EPISTEMOLOGY

Epistemology deals with questions regarding knowledge and knowing. Epistemologists, seeking the true nature of knowing, ask such questions as "What is true knowledge (as opposed to false ideas)?" and "What is justified belief as opposed to casual opinion?" and "Is truth elusive, always changing and always dependent on the truth seeker's particulars of time, place, and angle of vision?" Some people, whom we call *skeptics,* question our capacity to ever really know the truths of existence. Others, whom we call *agnostics,* are convinced that "truth" is unknowable and that seeking knowledge of ultimate realities is a wasted effort and an empty hope.

Epistemology deals not only with the nature of truth, but also with the ways in which we can know reality. Questions such as "How do we come to know the truth?" and "What are the sources for gaining knowledge?" are part of the conversation. We can know reality by a variety of ways, each of which has its advocates and detractors. Among the ways of knowing are by divine revelation, by authority, through personal intuition, from our own five senses, from our own powers of reasoning, and through trial-and-error experimentation.

Teaching and Ways of Knowing

Questions concerning knowledge and knowing are, almost by definition, of great concern to teachers. The epistemological question, "How do you know that?" goes to the heart of teaching methodology. If a teacher wants her students to have a concept of democracy, how does she proceed? Does she explain the characteristics of different forms of government, such as monarchy and oligarchy, and then the characteristics of democracy? Or does she take a more interactive approach and conduct a role-playing exercise during which students vote for a preferred activity? Students who have only read about democracy "know" it in an *epistemologically* different way than students who have experienced their votes determine a classroom outcome.

Individuals clearly differ in their preferred methods of learning. As discussed more fully in Chapter 3, "Who Are Today's Students in a Diverse Society?," much of the teachers' work focuses on helping students find the most effective way of gaining new knowledge. This important, breakthrough work on students' learning preferences grew essentially out of a philosophical quest—an epistemological question—"How do we know things?"[2]

Some people—for example, parents and community members—may have strong opinions regarding these epistemological questions. For instance, many people hold strong beliefs about what the true origin of humankind is and how one knows it. This issue, which is sometimes called the *creationist controversy,* reflects a sharp and fundamental argument over the questions "Who are we?" and "How did we get here?" One faction insists that the public schools should present the evidence of humans' origin that is given in the Book of Genesis, which we know by divine revelation. Others insist that the way to know the origin of the human race is through the scientific theory of evolution, grounded in the interpretation of artifactual evidence. Behind this ongoing educational controversy is a fundamental question of epistemology.

9-2c AXIOLOGY

Axiology focuses on the nature of what we value and how we value it. As human beings, we naturally search for the correct and most effective way to live. In doing so, we inevitably encounter questions of values. Of course, when different people look at life, they often come up with very different sets of values. For instance, *hedonists* believe in seeking pleasure and living for the moment. By contrast, *stoics* have an austere way of looking at life and seek to be unaffected by pleasure or pain. Many people regard values from a religious perspective, asserting that unless God originally created humanity and the rest of the natural world, existence as we know it is just the meaningless coming together of cosmic dust and debris. According to this view, the only genuine answer to how we should live and what we should value derive from God.

Most people would agree with Socrates (described in the "Leaders in Education" feature) that schools have a dual responsibility: to make people smart and to make them good. To the degree that teachers accept the second function—that is, to assist their students to become good people—they are grappling with an axiological issue. In fact, teachers are intimately involved with questions of moral values. Young people are seeking ways to live lives that are worthwhile, and teachers traditionally have been expected to help students establish moral values both as individuals and as contributing members of society. (See Chapter 12, "How Should Education Be Reformed?," and Chapter 8, "What Are the Ethical and Legal Issues Facing Teachers?,"

> *The function of education . . . is to teach one to think intensively and to think critically. Intelligence plus character—that is the goal of true education.*
>
> —MARTIN LUTHER KING, JR. (1929–1968),
> minister and civil rights leader

for more discussion of this issue.) Moral values such as honesty, respect for other people, and fairness are necessary if we are to live together in harmony. Although a majority of people agree on a substantial core of values, such as respecting others and avoiding violence in settling disputes, other value-related issues separate people. For example, certain sexual practices, capital punishment, gun control, and abortion are all contemporary social issues that evoke a wide range of viewpoints about the right or correct way for people to behave.

Ethics and Aesthetics

Axiology has two subtopics: ethics and aesthetics. Ethics takes us into the realm of values that relate to "good" and "bad" behavior, examining morality and rules of conduct. At one time, teaching children how to deal with issues of good/bad and right/wrong was the primary purpose of schooling. In recent decades, the pendulum has swung the other way, and schools have become more concerned with transmitting factual and scientifically verifiable knowledge and skills than with instilling ethical knowledge in students. There are signs indicating that schools are being called back to their earlier mission of helping children deal with ethical issues.[3]

The subject of ethics not only teaches us how we can intellectually ascertain the "right" thing to do, but also is often used to help us establish a particular set of standards, such as a code of ethics. Chapter 8, "What Are the Ethical and Legal Issues Facing Teachers?," devotes particular attention to the issue of how to develop your own code of ethics.

LEADERS in Education

Socrates (469–399 B.C.)

The ancient Greek philosopher Socrates was condemned to death for supposedly corrupting the youth of Athens. Today, we know him primarily through the written "dialogues" of his student Plato. How much Plato's portrayal resembled the actual man is open to debate. Nevertheless, the Socrates of Plato's dialogues has had a deep and lasting influence on both philosophy and education, as the source of terms such as *Socratic teaching, Socratic questioning*, and the *Socratic method*. The following paragraphs explain some of the basic tenets of Socrates' approach.

Socrates expressly denied that he was a teacher in the commonly accepted sense of that term. What he meant by this—at least in part—was that he was not a sophist, a professional pedagogue who, for a fee, would endeavor to transmit some knowledge that he possessed to someone who lacked it. Not only did Socrates charge no fees, he claimed not to have command of any such knowledge.

The learning that Socrates was concerned with simply didn't fit the information-transmission model of education implicit in the Athenian public mind and the teaching profession. Neither did his pioneering focus on virtue and wisdom square well with the popular attachment to honor, fame, and wealth. As he tries to explain at one point to Anytus in Plato's dialogue *Meno*, "[W]e are inquiring whether the good men of today and of the past knew how to pass on to another the virtue they themselves possessed, or whether a man cannot pass it on or

receive it from another." Because it was clear that wisdom and virtue could not simply be passed on from one person to another, Socrates sought an alternative way of conceptualizing how such excellences of mind and character were acquired. What was the teacher's role in that acquisition, if not simply being a supplier?

As an alternative to the receiving knowledge from another model, Socrates proposed that learning was "recollection"— that is, a process akin to dredging up knowledge from one's own resources. "Teaching" on this model he later compared to acting as a "midwife"— assisting in the birth of knowledge *in* another person rather than serving as a supplier of it *to* another person. This was to be accomplished in conversation, mostly by skillful questioning and cross-examination ("Socratic teaching," "Socratic questioning," and "Socratic method").

Socrates admitted to behaving like a "gadfly" in this dialectical pursuit of truth, goading people into serious thinking about human living. And he also confessed to acting like a benumbing "stingray" or "torpedo fish," referring to his ability to render people tongue-tied about matters that they thought they already knew perfectly well—but actually didn't. Not until people felt the sting of not really knowing about life's important matters could they be prompted to inquire into them seriously.

Source: Reprinted by permission of Steven S. Tigner.

The second subtopic of axiology, **aesthetics**, deals with questions of values regarding beauty and art. Many discussions about the value of a particular film, book, or work of art are attempts to reach some aesthetic judgment on the value of the work. Whether a person "has good taste" is an example of a common aesthetic judgment.

9-2d LOGIC

Logic is the branch of philosophy that deals with reasoning. One of the fundamental qualities that distinguishes human beings from animals is that humans can *think*. The pursuit of logic is an attempt to think clearly and avoid vagueness and contradictions. Certain rules of logic have been identified, and they constitute the core of this branch of philosophy. Logic focuses on reasoning and modes of arguing that bring us to valid conclusions. A primary task of the schools is to help children think clearly and communicate logically. Two types of reasoning are commonly taught in schools: deductive and inductive.

Deductive Reasoning

In **deductive reasoning**, teachers present a general proposition and then illustrate it with a series of particulars. The most highly developed form of this approach is the classic method of the syllogism. In a *syllogism,* one makes two statements, and then a third statement, a conclusion, is *deduced,* or drawn, from them. For instance:

> All human beings are mortal.
> I am a human being.
> Therefore, I am mortal.

In this kind of deductive reasoning, the general proposition—an abstract concept—is followed by a factual statement, which in turn leads to a new factual statement and the creation of new knowledge, at least for the learners.

As another example, imagine that in October, Mrs. Wells, a fifth-grade teacher, writes the following statement on the board:

> All trees that shed their leaves at the end of a growing season are deciduous trees.

As a two-week project, Mrs. Wells asks her class to observe and record data about the trees that surround their school. For two weeks, the students observe the three dozen maple trees shedding their leaves during the fall. The teacher then writes her earlier sentence on the board again:

> All trees that shed their leaves at the end of a growing season are deciduous trees.

Using their observational data (and with a little intellectual nudging from Mrs. Wells), the students complete the syllogism:

> Maple trees shed their leaves at the end of the growing season.
> Therefore, maple trees are deciduous.

Then the students try to identify other types of trees that fit the deciduous classification.

Much of what teachers do in school focuses on helping children both acquire the intellectual habits of deductive thinking and expand their storehouse of knowledge through this process.

Inductive Reasoning

Inductive reasoning works in the opposite fashion. With this type of reasoning, teachers set forth particulars, from which a general proposition is derived, or *induced.* For instance, a teacher may wish to lead students to the discovery that water is essential to plant growth. He gives each child two similar plants (a different type, from weeds to flowers, for each child) and then has each student daily feed one plant with water and leave the other plant without water. After 10 days, the teacher has the students report on the conditions of their plants. From all of these individual reports, he leads the students to generalize about the necessity of water to plant life. In fact, they have induced their answer.

Although the deductive and inductive forms of reasoning are opposites, both are essential to logical thought and therefore need to be developed in learners. Effective teachers design a variety of learning activities, some of which (like the tree example) help students think deductively, and others (like the plant example) that focus on inductive reasoning.

Pause *and* **Reflect**

1. Which of these four branches of philosophy do you think is of greatest importance to you as a future teacher?

2. Which of these four branches contains the questions and issues about which you are most comfortable? And least comfortable?

Logic is not confined to inductive and deductive reasoning. To think logically means to think clearly, in many different ways. Teachers need logic in many aspects of their work, from trying to understand the behavior of a child who seems to have an erratic learning pattern, to developing tests that accurately measure what has been taught in a course. Most of all, teachers need to model this clear, logical thinking for students.

Overall, the four branches of philosophy—metaphysics, epistemology, axiology, and logic—address some of the major concerns of teachers. We now consider the answers they suggest to teachers and the implications they have for actual classroom practice.

9-3 Schools of Educational Philosophy

skynesher/E+/Getty Images

Now that you know the philosophical "lay of the land," and before we explore the dominant philosophies of education that exist in our schools, it is time to pause and reflect. What are your deepest beliefs and attitudes about teaching, students, and what should be learned? This short inventory allows you to bring your current philosophy of education to the surface. We say "current philosophy of education" because the philosophies of many educators go through change—and sometimes quite dramatic change—as a result of study, classroom experience, or both.

Answers to the philosophical statements in the self-inventory and questions that pepper the preceding section have almost infinite variety. Over the years, however, certain answers by particular philosophers have received more attention and allegiance than others. These more enduring sets of answers or worldviews represent very different schools of philosophy. Some started with the early Greek philosophers and have grown and evolved through the centuries. Other schools of thought are more recent developments and offer fresh, new formulations to ultimate questions.

In this section, we describe four philosophies that have had a major influence on American education and demonstrate the variety of ways in which teaching and learning can be conceived. Be aware that many important philosophies relevant to education are not included here. Among them are neo-Thomism; existentialism; and classical Eastern thought, such as Zen Buddhism and Confucianism. In addition, some major educational ideas do not quite qualify as "philosophies," but are nevertheless having a major impact on schools.

The four philosophies discussed at length in this chapter are perennialism, essentialism, romanticism, and progressivism. Behind these rather daunting words are very different ideas of what people are, how we should live our lives, and how we should conduct the education of children. We elected to cover these four philosophies not because they form a "top philosophical playlist," but because each viewpoint has exerted a major influence on American educational thought and practice.

We have grouped these philosophies based on whether they are *subject centered* or *child centered*. For each philosophy, we present first a brief explanation of its origins and the core ideas it embodies, followed by its implications for teaching and learning, and then a "personal point of view" by a teacher (fictitious) who is committed to that particular philosophy. These positions are not just windy abstractions or the preoccupations of ivory tower thinkers; rather, they have practical implications for learning, shaping what people teach and how they teach it.

Up CLOSE

Your Philosophy of Education Self-Inventory

Following are 20 statements about teaching, students, schools, and the curriculum. Using a five-point scale (where 5 = strongly agree; 4 = agree; 3 = neutral; 2 = disagree; and 1 = strongly disagree), indicate your beliefs and feelings about each of the following statements. To gain the greatest insight from this survey, you should try to have your "average" ranking be a "3."

____1. Essentially, children learn by doing and by discovering things on their own.

____2. The goal of schooling should be to rigorously prepare children to be productive and engaged members of society.

____3. The teacher's role is to respond to learners' information needs, not to be a mere information dispenser.

____4. Teachers should be experts in content knowledge, ready to vigorously engage students in the culture's accumulated wisdom.

____5. Older students ought to be trained primarily to uncover key ideas and truths through Socratic questioning.

____6. The teachers' role is to stimulate students' interests and then to be effective facilitators of those interests.

____7. The true purpose of an education is to make us strong enough to overcome the evils of society.

____8. Students are in school primarily to acquire the knowledge that has lit the way for humankind from our earliest years.

____9. Because we live in a democracy, schools should be built around democratic principles, with a major focus on learning how to exist together in democratic harmony.

____10. Students are in school to listen and to learn the knowledge and skills that they will need to function and prosper in a modern economy.

____11. Education is serious business, so teachers should avoid methodological frills and focus on tried-and-true teaching strategies.

____12. Schools should aid students in becoming socially adept and politically literate so they can take up their responsibilities as democratic citizens.

____13. Instructionally, teachers must focus on creating an interesting and productive learning environment and, whenever possible, on individualizing instruction.

____14. Elementary schools should concentrate on teaching basic skills, whereas secondary schools should focus students' learning on disciplined knowledge and scholastic achievement.

____15. Students are naturally good, and their self-esteem must be protected and fostered.

____16. During the elementary school years, teachers should ensure that students master the basics, which will enable older students to study materials reflecting universal themes containing humanity's enduring knowledge.

____17. Teachers have to be skilled in group processing strategies and be able to get students to work together on projects.

____18. Teachers' primary concern should be teaching a common body of useful knowledge rather than focusing on cultivating the intellect, self-esteem, or democratic living.

____19. The curriculum should be fluid, based on the interests of learners, but students should not be forced to study.

____20. The schools should be devoted to a changeless vision of what is essential for human beings to know.

Find the answers to your self-inventory in the next section.

Interpreting Your Self-Inventory

Each of the 20 questions to which you have responded represents one of the four philosophies of education covered in depth in this chapter. The four philosophies and the five statements primarily associated with them are listed here. Fill in the score you gave each statement and then add up the topic score for each philosophy. The maximum score for any philosophy is 25, and the minimum is 5. These numbers will give you an indication of your philosophy of education preferences as you begin a closer analysis of this topic.

Perennialism	Essentialism	Romanticism	Progressivism
___ 4	___ 2	___ 3	___ 1
___ 5	___ 10	___ 7	___ 6
___ 8	___ 11	___ 13	___ 9
___ 16	___ 14	___ 15	___ 12
___ 20	___ 18	___ 19	___ 17

9-3a SUBJECT-CENTERED PHILOSOPHIES

The first two schools of philosophy, perennialism and essentialism, stress the importance of subject-matter knowledge in education. Both schools of thought show a strong allegiance to the curriculum, and both argue that well-educated students should possess a defined body of knowledge. Also, both often get a "bad name," being labeled as "teacher centered." The label "teacher centered" conjures up images of an authoritarian teacher turning himself or herself into the center of attention, making all the decisions, and attempting to control everything that goes on in a classroom. Clearly, authoritarianism and ego-tripping can hide behind each of the four philosophies we will explore. Although they are convinced of the importance of certain knowledge, subject-centered teachers can be passionately committed to student learning.

Perennialism

Perennialism, which is derived primarily from the writings of Plato, views truth and nature—in particular, human nature—as constant, objective, and unchanging. Beneath the superficial differences from one century or decade to the next, the rules that govern the world and the characteristics that make up human nature stay the same. The purpose of life, according to Plato, is the search for these constant and changeless truths, which reside in the nature of things. This search is achieved through the Socratic dialogue or dialectic, a process in which ideas are debated in a back-and-forth discussion until some recognizable clarity (the "light") is reached. Essential to undertaking such a pursuit is mental discipline and rational thought processes.

> *Never mistake knowledge for wisdom. One helps you make a living; the other helps you make a life.*
>
> —SANDRA CAREY,
> lawyer

Perennialists view education as crucial because it develops a person's mental discipline and rationality, which are necessary to the search for truths that will help humans avoid being dominated by the instinctual (i.e., animal-like) side of human nature.

Perennialism in the School

For perennialists, the purpose of education is to find the changeless "truth," which is best revealed in the enduring classics of Western culture. According to this perspective, schools should emphasize classical thought as their subject matter. Perennialists believe that schools should teach disciplined knowledge through the traditional subjects of history, language, mathematics, science, and the arts. They place particular emphasis on literature and the humanities, believing that these subjects provide the greatest insight into our human condition.

Although this view of the curriculum is evident in many areas of education, in its most complete form, it is known as the *Great Books approach,* as developed by Robert Maynard Hutchins, who was president and chancellor at the University of Chicago throughout the 1930s and 1940s, and the late Mortimer Adler, a professor at the University of Chicago during the same time period. The Great Books, which constitute a shelf of volumes stretching from Homer's *Iliad* to Albert Einstein's *On the Electrodynamics of Moving Bodies,* are perennialists' ideal curriculum. In perennialist-oriented high school curricula, a broader and more modern selection of works is included, though the emphasis remains on the intellectual richness of the material. (See the Video Case, *Middle School Reading Instruction: Integrating Technology,* for an example of how one middle school teacher makes use of an ancient book in a thoroughly modern setting.)

▶❚❚ TeachSource Video Case

Middle School Reading Instruction: Integrating Technology

Watch the video clips, study the artifacts in the case, and reflect on the following questions:

1. Does this teacher's approach represent perennialism as it is described in this chapter? Why or why not?

2. Which of the other philosophies mentioned in this chapter might be included in this teacher's approach?

3. How well would this teacher's approach fit with your own developing philosophy of teaching?

> ❝ *One glance at a book and you hear the voice of another person, perhaps someone dead for 1,000 years. To read is to voyage through time.*
>
> —CARL SAGAN (1934–1996),
> astronomer

> ❝ *The object of education is to prepare the young to educate themselves throughout their lives.*
>
> —ROBERT MAYNARD HUTCHINS (1899–1977),
> educational practitioner and theorist

For perennialists, in the early years of schooling the development of the intellect is best achieved through a teacher-directed instructional approach that develops the foundational skills needed for later learning. Socratic dialogue is then used to help mature learners question and examine their beliefs, enabling them to move closer to the truth.

Since the early 1990s, a controversy has arisen over the content of perennialist literature, history, and philosophy courses. Scholars and students have criticized colleges and high schools for promoting a "Eurocentric" view of knowledge and culture, one that ignores the contributions of everyone except "dead, white, male writers and thinkers." They urge adoption of a more inclusive curriculum—that is, one that gives greater attention to women, people of color, and members of African, Asian, Hispanic, and Islamic cultures. Although some perceive this movement to be a direct attack on the perennialist curriculum, others see it as a natural and useful extension of the perennialists' search for the best of the world's wisdom. One perennialist friend of ours, who welcomes this new approach, suggested, "Sure, students should know about Islamic literature and Eastern philosophy, but they should first get to know their own neighborhood, Western culture."

9-3b EDUCATION AS PREPARATION FOR ONE'S LIFE

Education is of great importance to perennialists, but it is an education that is rigorous and demanding. Perennialists insist that education is *preparation* for life and, therefore, believe that it should not attempt to imitate life or be lifelike. Students should engage in a rigorous examination of the classics—mostly ancient, but some modern—to discover the timeless wisdom embodied in this literature, rather than focusing on knowledge that might seem personally meaningful.

In summary, the perennialists' view is that through disciplined study of the great works, a person acquires reasoning skills and mastery of the important ideas of human history. This view leans heavily on the authority of the collected wisdom of the past and looks to traditional thought to guide us in the present. As such, the curriculum is structured and clearly defined. Perennialists also see education as protecting and conserving the best thought from the past. In this sense, they favor a very traditional or conservative ("conservative" as in *conserving* the best of the past) view of education. The following case study presents the point of view of a more or less typical perennialist teacher.

Essentialism

Essentialism is a uniquely American philosophy of education that began in the 1930s and 1940s as a reaction to what was seen as an overemphasis on a child-centered approach to education, and a concern that students were not gaining appropriate and adequate knowledge in schools.

PRESERVICE to PRACTICE

A Perennialist Teacher

I came into education 25 years ago for two reasons. First, I was bothered by what I thought was all the nonsense in the curriculum and by all the time my friends and I wasted in school. We were allowed to take whatever courses we wanted, the majority of which were electives that seemed to be little more than the teacher's hobby. There were so many discussions—discussions that seemed to go nowhere and seemed only vaguely to touch on the supposed content of the course. I often felt as if we were simply sharing our ignorance.

My second reason for becoming a teacher is a more positive one. I am convinced that our society, our culture, has great ideas, ideas that have been behind our progress in the last 2,500 years. We need to share these ideas, to vigorously teach these ideas to the young. Essentially, I see my job as passing on to the next generation, as effectively and forcefully as I can, the important truths—for instance, about human dignity and the capacity of people to do both good and evil.

That has always been the teacher's role until recent times, when we seem to have lost our way. I am convinced that a society that doesn't make the great ideas and the great thoughts the foundation of education is bound to fail. Nations and societies do falter and fall. The last 50 years have seen several formerly prominent nations slip to the wayside while other younger, more vigorous countries, like Singapore and South Korea and most recently China, have risen. I am convinced that most of those failed countries fell because of the inadequate education they provided. I am dedicated to the goal of not letting that happen here.

I think students are just great. In fact, I've given my life to working with them. But I don't think it is fair to them or to me or to our country to allow them to set the rules, to decide what they want to learn, or to tell me how to teach it. Sure, I listen to them and try to find out where they are, but I make the decisions. My job is to teach; theirs is to learn. And in my classroom, those functions are quite clear. Really, students are too young to know what are the important things to learn. They simply don't know what they need to know. As a teacher, as a representative of the larger culture and of society, that's my responsibility. Turning that responsibility over to students or giving them a huge say in what is taught just strikes me as silly. Worse, it's wrong.

I also believe that students should be pushed. School should be very demanding, because life is very demanding. I'm not worried about students' so-called self-esteem. Self-esteem is empty unless it is earned. It will come when students discipline themselves. All of us are lazy when we are young. We would much rather play than work. All of this "trying to make school like play" is just making it more difficult for students to acquire the self-discipline needed to take control of their lives. What schools are turning out right now—and it pains me to say this—are a lot of self-important, self-indulgent kids. And it's not their fault. It's our fault as teachers and parents.

And the answer is so simple! We just need to go back to the great ideas and achievements of the past and make them the focal point of education. When we achieve this goal, the students don't mind working. The students and the other teachers kid me about being too harsh. I don't really pay attention to that. But I do pay attention to the large number of students, both college-bound and non-college-bound, who come back two or three years out of high school and tell me how much they value having been pushed, how glad they are that I put them in contact with the very best!

Pause *and* Reflect

1. Have you seen elements of the perennialist view in your own educational background?
2. How much emphasis on classical enduring works do you hope to include in your own teaching?

Essentialism has its philosophical origins in two older philosophies and draws something from each. From Plato's *idealism*, it takes the view of the mind as the central tool for understanding an objective and unchanging reality, as well as for learning those *essential* ideas and knowledge that we need to live well. From Aristotle's *realism*, it takes the tenet that the mind learns through contact with the physical world; according to this view, to know reality, we must learn to observe and measure the physical world accurately. From our observations, we use our reasoning ability to gain new knowledge. This contrasts with the perennialist view that reasoning alone can lead to truth.

Essentialists believe that there exists a critical core of information and skills that an educated person must have. They are convinced that the overwhelming number of children can and should learn this body of essential material. Whether or not they embrace the label "essentialist," educators and others currently supporting the adoption of a nationwide Core Curriculum are promoting educational essentialism. (Refer to Chapter 5, "What Is Taught?," and Chapter 12, "How Should Education Be Reformed?," for more in-depth discussion of the Common Core.) According to this view, schools should be organized to transmit this knowledge and skill as effectively as possible. For essentialists, the methods used to transmit this knowledge and skill are not specifically prescribed. The focus is, instead, on the knowledge that students gain.

In many ways, essentialism sounds a good deal like perennialism. Although these two views have much in common, some important differences exist between them. For instance, essentialists do not focus as intently on "truths" as do perennialists. They are less concerned with the classics as being the primary repository of worthwhile knowledge. Instead, essentialists search for what will help a person live a productive life today. If the current economic realities strongly suggest that students need to graduate from high school with computer literacy, for example, essentialists will find a place for this training in the curriculum. In this regard, essentialists are very practical. Like perennialists, essentialists look upon the many elective courses in our high schools as "frills," distracting students from the core knowledge they will later need. At the same time, whereas perennialists will hold fast to the Great Books as the storehouse of critical knowledge, essentialists will make more room for scientific, technical, and even vocational emphases in the curriculum. Essentialists see themselves as valuing the past, but not being captured by it.

> " The ability to think straight, some knowledge of the past, some vision of the future, some skill to do useful service, some urge to fit that service into the well-being of the community—these are the most vital things education must try to produce.
>
> —VIRGINIA CROCHERON GILDERSLEEVE (1877–1965),
> stateswoman and scholar

The Core Knowledge program (discussed in Chapter 5, "What Is Taught?," and not to be confused with the Core Curriculum movement) is a curriculum which that sets out in detail what students from kindergarten to eighth grade should know. The educational philosophy behind it is probably best categorized as essentialist. Based on the book *Cultural Literacy*, by E. D. Hirsch, Jr., this content-rich curriculum stresses academics and learning of specific knowledge. Although its emphasis on important ideas and great works of the past makes it attractive to perennialists, the curriculum's focus on current literature and emphasis on science point more to its alignment with the essentialist movement. Until recently, the Core Knowledge curriculum was a "for sale" curricular package. However, today it is a downloadable package available free to schools, homeschools, and individuals.[4]

Essentialist Goals and Practices

For essentialists, the aim of education is to teach youth the essentials they need to live well in the modern world. To realize this goal, schools should focus on the

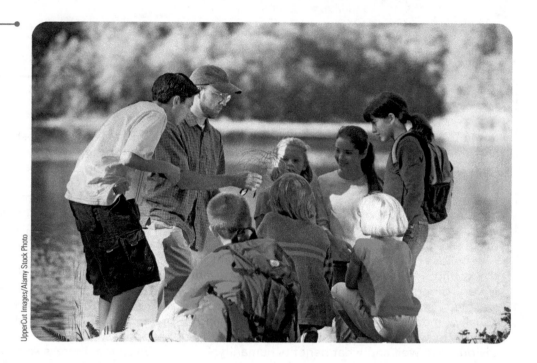

The great outdoors is a great environment for learning.

UpperCut Images/Alamy Stock Photo

Learning is not attained by chance; it must be sought for with ardor and attended to with diligence.

—ABIGAIL ADAMS (1744–1818)

established disciplines, which are the "containers" of organized knowledge. As captured in the educational slogan, "back to the basics," the elementary years should concentrate on the basics such as the "three R's." These and other foundational tools are needed to gain access to the disciplined knowledge with which one begins to come in contact in high school.

Although some debate persists about what is "essential" in the curriculum, essentialists believe this is not a debate to which children can contribute fruitfully. Instead, they see the role of students as simply that of learners; thus an individual child's interests, motivations, and psychological states are not given great attention in deciding what is to be taught. Nor do essentialists advocate a "romantic" view of children (discussed later in this chapter) as being naturally good. They see the students not as evil, but rather as deficient and needing discipline and pressure to keep learning. School is viewed as a place where children come to learn what they need to know. Teachers are not guides, but authorities. The students' job is to listen and learn. Given the imperfect state of the students, teachers must be ingenious in finding ways to engage their imaginations and minds.

One notable essentialist was James Bryan Conant, a Harvard professor and president for much of the first half of the twentieth century. Concerned about disparities in the knowledge and skills that high school students brought with them to college, Conant argued for standardization of college requirements for high school students. He was also influential in the establishment of the SAT as a measure of essential knowledge that a potential college student needs to possess. Although not purely "essentialist movements," much of the thought and energy behind the drive for state standards, standardized testing, the Every Student Succeeds Act, No Child Left Behind Act, the Race to the Top, and the Common Core have strong essentialist motivations.

The case study immediately above offers the perspective of a representative essentialist teacher.

PRESERVICE to PRACTICE

An Essentialist Teacher

In my view, the world is filled with real problems, and the young people who leave school have to be ready to take up the challenge of life and solve those problems. For me, the watchword in education is *usefulness*. I think everything that is taught has to pass the test of whether it is useful. My job as a teacher is to find out what is useful and then to make sure the students learn it.

I believe that school should be relevant to the young. However, my view of what is relevant is very different from the views of lots of other people. For me, relevance is not what is personally "meaningful" or a "do your own thing" approach; what is relevant is what helps the individual live well and what benefits humanity. For that, we need to look very carefully at the past and sort out the most valuable learning. That is what should be taught and what should be learned. I find the back to the classics approach quite valuable. However, most advocates go too far in concentrating on classics. They also stress the humanities and the arts a little too much and tend to underplay science and technology. If children are going to function in today's world, and if our world is going to solve all the problems it's confronted with, we have to give more attention to science and technology than we have in the

past. But clearly the past is the place to begin our search for the relevant curriculum.

It's not the most pleasing or satisfying image, but I think the concept of the student as an empty jug is the most accurate one. Certainly kids come to school with lots of knowledge and lots of interests. However, the job of school is to teach them what they don't know and to teach these things in a systematic and organized way. It's not to fill their minds with isolated fragments of information but to fill them with systematic knowledge. They need tools to learn, and, as they get older, they need human insights and skills that come from the disciplines.

Given that there is so much to learn, an emphasis on student "interests" and "projects" and "problem solving" is quite wasteful. There is plenty of time for that outside of school or when school is over. Inside the school, the teachers are the authorities, and the students are there to learn what they don't know. The environment should be task oriented and disciplined. It doesn't have to be oppressive or unjust or any of that. I tell my students that learning is not necessarily going to be fun, but that at the end of the year they will have a great sense of accomplishment. I'd take accomplishment over fun anytime. By and large, most students do too.

Pause *and* Reflect

1. What knowledge do you believe will be essential for the students you teach to learn if they are to be effective members of their society?
2. In what ways do perennialist teachers differ from essentialist teachers?

9-3c CHILD-CENTERED PHILOSOPHIES

In contrast to perennialism and essentialism, the next two schools of philosophy—romanticism and progressivism—look first to the learners rather than to the curriculum. Both consider the development of learners to be the main purpose of education. A well-educated person does not necessarily have a definite body of knowledge; rather, a well-educated person is able to function well in society and life.

Romanticism

Romanticism, also known as naturalism, is based on the writings of Jean-Jacques Rousseau, an eighteenth-century Swiss-French philosopher. In a condemnation of society and the educational system of the time, Rousseau wrote *Emile,* a novel that details Rousseau's ideas about education through the example of a fictional young boy, Emile. Rousseau believed that children are born good and pure. Once exposed to the evils of society, however, they become corrupted. To keep children good, they need to be isolated from society for as long as possible.

> *Our fundamental task as human beings is to seek out connections—to exercise our imaginations. It follows, then, that the basic task of education is the care and feeding of the imagination.*
>
> **—KATHERINE PATERSON,**
> American author

Rousseau describes a serene, yet well-controlled, bucolic environment for the ideal education of Emile; he is to be educated by a private tutor at the country manor where he lives. Emile's education begins with his exploration of the world of nature surrounding him. From his observations, he may ask questions about the natural world that the tutor answers. There are no formal lessons, no books to read or facts to memorize, no specific curriculum to learn. Emile decides what he learns about and when. As Emile matures, the tutor helps him develop rational thinking skills, but Emile continues to decide the topics of study. When Emile is around 15, he is slowly introduced to certain social situations until he is deemed "ready" by his tutor to resist the evils of society and live a productive life in the social world. By the time he is 20, Emile is ready to take a mate and make a life for himself.

Implications for Education

Unlike the perennialists and essentialists, who highlight the importance of educating the individual for society, the romantics consider the needs of the individual more important than the needs of society. For the romantics, the purpose of education is individual self-fulfillment—that is, education must help the students develop physically, intellectually, socially, and morally (usually in that order). Although clearly an unrealistic model for tax-supported education, the ideas embedded in Rousseau's *Emile* have had a strong impact on the thinking of many educators.

SolStock/E+/Getty Images

> *A sense of curiosity is nature's original school of education.*
>
> **—SMILEY BLANTON (1882–1966),**
> psychiatrist

Romantics believe that education is a natural process, which grows out of children's innate curiosity. This curiosity is most obvious during the "why?" phase of young childhood, when nearly every utterance out of the child's mouth is another question: "Why is the dog barking?," "Why is the boy sad?," or "Why is the bird blue?" (Exhausted parents often want to ask in return, "Why do you ask so many questions?") Romantics argue that we must let children's interests and curiosity drive their learning. The teachers' job is to respond to the children's questions as they arise and not to impose the learning of subjects that are not of interest to the child. The learners' responsibility is to maintain their natural curiosity and desire to learn. Because they perceive learning to be guided by student interests, romantics do not advocate the establishment of a set or common curriculum of study. Some students may be interested in kayaking, whereas others want to study photography, and still others may be fascinated by how an iPad can do all it can do. As students pursue their own areas of study, the approach to teaching and learning likewise becomes individualized. Much of the learning is self-directed and self-guided by the students, with teachers serving as sources of information or resources to help the students satisfy their curiosity rather than functioning as authorities on knowledge. On the other hand, the teacher may provoke student interest by asking a question ("Should we start a recycling club at our school?") or starting a discussion. ("I'm thinking about getting a new computer. Should I buy an Apple or a PC?")

Romanticism has been especially influential in the early childhood and elementary grades. Many early childhood educators, including such pioneers as

Maria Montessori, Friedrich Froebel, and Johann Pestalozzi, basically agreed with Rousseau's ideas about humans' innate curiosity and using a child's interests to define the curriculum. Although none proposed as radical a school setting as Rousseau's pastoral manor, they did adopt some of Rousseau's other ideas about education, such as providing young children with extensive opportunities to manipulate real things, such as wooden blocks, clay, and other materials. The purpose is to establish learning environments that provoke students' curiosity.

Today, schools such as Summerhill School in Suffolk, England, and the Sudbury Valley School in Framingham, Massachusetts, embody many of the beliefs of the romantics. At these schools, there are no set curricula, no formal classes, and no tests. Students decide what they want to study and, in some cases, are expected to take responsibility for their learning.

The following case study represents the views of a romantic teacher.

Pause *and* Reflect

1. How would teachers in public schools, who are held accountable for students' mastery of curriculum standards, be able to follow a romantic philosophy of letting student interest guide the curriculum?
2. Do you think you would be comfortable adopting the romantic approach? Why or why not?

PRESERVICE to PRACTICE

A Romantic Teacher

Have you ever seen the thrill on a young child's face when he or she figures out how to make something work? What about their wonder as they ask another question about why there are rainbows or thunder and lightning? I see these young children, and then I look at some of the students in school today. Their faces are filled with so much dread or disinterest or boredom that I get disheartened. What happened to that enthusiasm, that excitement for learning, I wonder? That schools, which should be places of learning, can turn students off to learning so strongly is the reason I became a teacher. I want my classroom to be a place where students can explore their interests and satisfy their curiosities. I cannot make them learn information if it's not something they're interested in.

In my classroom, students decide what they want to study, and I help them find the resources. Sometimes we get books from the library, or find websites on the Internet. The Internet has been a wonderful resource for my students. Some of them have been able to have online conversations with professionals in fields like aerospace engineering and bioengineering. Sometimes, I set up face-to-face meetings with professionals in a particular field. Last week, we had a computer programmer in to talk to a couple of students who were interested in learning more about writing code. It's so exciting to see students enthusiastic about what they are learning.

Other teachers and administrators really like objective tests and have trouble with my approach. Their view is that students have big holes in their knowledge; they don't learn "the hard stuff"; they cannot pass standardized tests. My students may not do very well on standardized tests (what do they *really* measure, anyway?), but they do learn the hard stuff! I mean, computer programming, aerospace engineering, and bioengineering? Those are not easy topics to understand. It may be that my students don't know a lot of facts in the standardized subjects, but they know well what they learn because they have selected these topics themselves. They want to learn about them, so they do.

Progressivism

Progressivism is a relatively young philosophy of education. It came to prominence in the 1920s, growing out of the progressive political and social movement of the time. This school of thought drew from some of the ideas of Rousseau and from the work of John Dewey, the most influential educational philosopher of the twentieth century (see the "Leaders in Education" feature in this section).

Progressivism views nature as being in flux, as ever changing. Consequently, knowledge must continually be redefined and rediscovered to keep up with that change. Whereas other philosophies see the mind as a jug to be filled with truth or as a muscle that needs to be exercised and conditioned, progressives view the mind as a marvelous mechanism for problem solving. Like the romantics, advocates of the progressive viewpoint believe that people are naturally exploring, inquiring entities. When faced with an obstacle, they will try to find a way to overcome it. When faced with a question, they will try to find an answer. For progressives, education aims to develop this problem-solving ability.

Ⓣ F
Progressive educators view nature as being in flux, as ever changing. Therefore, teachers consider knowledge as something that must continually be redefined and rediscovered to keep up with that change.

Progressive Education

Progressive educators believe that the place to begin an education is with the student rather than with the subject matter. When following this philosophy, teachers identify what each student's interests and concerns are and try to shape problems around them. Teachers then help the students develop strategies to solve the problems posed. Students' motivation to solve problems is the key to this educational model, and posing problems based on students' interests helps heighten their motivation.

Students should start with simple study projects and gradually learn more systematic ways to investigate until they finally master a variety of problem-solving strategies. Rather than being presenters of knowledge or taskmasters, teachers are intellectual guides, *facilitators* in the problem-solving process. Students are encouraged to be imaginative and resourceful in solving problems. They are directed to a variety of learning methods, from reading books and studying the traditional disciplines, to performing experiments and analyzing data. (The Video Case, *Middle School Science Instruction: Inquiry Learning*, shows how one middle school teacher guides students as they develop and test their hypotheses.)

Method is of great importance to advocates of the progressive philosophy. Conversely, knowledge—formal, traditional knowledge—is not given the same honored place. For progressives, there is really no special, sacrosanct knowledge or subject matter that all students must learn. Instead, the value of knowledge is seen as residing only in its ability to solve human problems.

Regarding the school curriculum, progressives believe that students can learn problem-solving skills from electronics just as easily as from Latin, from agronomy just as well as from geometry. The focus for progressive educators is teaching students *how* to think rather than *what* to think. The slogan "teacher as guide on the side rather

▶❚❚ **TeachSource** Video Case

© Cengage 2016

Middle School Science Instruction: Inquiry Learning

Watch the video clips, study the artifacts in the case, and reflect on the following questions:

1. Does this teacher's approach represent progressivism, as it is described in this chapter? Why or why not?

2. Which of the other philosophies or psychological influences mentioned in this chapter does this teacher's approach incorporate?

3. How well would this teacher's approach fit with your own developing philosophy of teaching?

than sage on the stage" captures the uniqueness of the progressive view and its special instructional process. Progressive teachers often introduce traditional subject matter, but they use it differently from the way it is used in a traditional classroom. Because the problems students are trying to solve are of paramount importance, the subjects contribute primarily through providing contexts for problems students must solve. Of course, subject-matter knowledge may also provide information that leads to solutions.

LEADERS in Education

John Dewey (1859–1952)

Hulton Archive/Archive Photos/Getty Images

John Dewey, the founder of instrumentalism, is widely considered the single most influential figure in the history of American educational thought. At the same time, his ideas and beliefs have been frequently misunderstood and misinterpreted, leading to the misapplication of his theories.

Dewey grew up in Vermont, where he attended public schools and the University of Vermont. As a graduate student in philosophy at Johns Hopkins University, he was deeply influenced by the ideas of Charles S. Peirce and William James, the founders of pragmatist philosophy. Dewey recognized the implications for education of Peirce's argument that ideas, or propositions, have worth only if they make a difference in future thoughts or actions. Calling his own philosophy *instrumentalism* to emphasize the principle that ideas are instruments, Dewey argued that philosophy and education both involve a practical, experimental attempt to improve the human condition.

Dewey denounced the public school's classical curriculum in the nineteenth century as totally unsuited to the demands of newly industrialized society of the United States. He claimed that the schools were divorced from life and that they failed to teach children how to *use* knowledge. Defining education as a "continuous reconstruction of experience," Dewey said that schools should teach children not what to think, but how to think. In his 1916 treatise *Democracy and Education,* he claimed that the schools offered students—as future citizens—no preparation for assuming the responsibility of citizenship in a democracy. Dewey called for schools to provide a concentrated study of democratic processes and to reflect those processes in the organization of school life, going as far as advocating that students be given the power to make decisions affecting life in the school in a democratic way. He considered participation in life, rather than preparation for it, the hallmark of an effective education.

In 1896, Dewey established the University Laboratory School, an elementary school at the University of Chicago. It was experimental in two senses: in its use of experiment and inquiry as the method by which the children learned and in its role as a laboratory for the transformation of the schools. The activities and occupations of adult life served as the core of the curriculum and the model teaching method. Children began by studying and imitating simple domestic and industrial tasks. In later years, they studied the historical development of industry, invention, group living, and nature. Dewey wrote that we must "make each one of our schools an embryonic community life, active with types of occupations that reflect the life of the larger society and permeated with the spirit of art, history, and science."

In the late 1920s to the early 1940s—the era of progressive education—a massive attempt to implement Dewey's ideas occurred, but the rigid (and often inaccurate) manner in which they were interpreted led to remarkable extravagances in some progressive schools. For instance, some educators considered it useless to teach geography because maps changed so rapidly. The role of subject matter was gradually played down in progressive schools, replaced by a stress on method and process. The rationale was that it was more important to produce a "good citizen" than a person who was "educated" in the classical sense. Until he was well into his 90s, Dewey fought vehemently against these corruptions of his views.

The centrality of John Dewey's thought to U.S. education has waxed and waned over the years. Traditionally more popular in universities than in actual classroom practice, Dewey's work is often invoked by people who are attempting to make the schools more humanistic and the curriculum more relevant to the current world. Whether in favor or out, John Dewey represents the United States' most distinctive contributor to educational thought.

With the progressive viewpoint, the process, that is, problem solving—not the product, that is content knowledge—is viewed as the critical concern. Although both romantic and progressive educators start with students' interests, progressives have more structure behind their teaching. They also have goals for their students, as discussed next.

The School as Training Ground for Democracy

Unlike romantic educators, who may see society as a negative influence on students, progressives see society as an integral aspect of the students' life. Progressives view schools as small societies in themselves, places where students are learning as they live life, not simply preparing for life. This gives progressive schools a unique atmosphere, different from that of perennialist storehouses of wisdom or places with the clearly defined roles and authority structures promoted by essentialists.

Progressive educators believe the school should be democratic in structure so that children can learn to live well in a democracy and become good citizens. They emphasize group activity and group problem solving so that students learn to work with others and help others.[5]

Education makes people easy to lead, but difficult to drive; easy to govern, but impossible to enslave.

—HENRY BROOKS ADAMS (1838–1918),
American novelist and historian

This is one reason many teachers who describe themselves as progressive educators are enthusiastic about cooperative learning strategies, such as those discussed in Chapter 5, "What Is Taught?"

Implicit in the progressive approach is the belief that children must not only learn to solve their own problems, but also help to solve the problems of their neighbors. For progressives, one of the main purposes of education is to make society better, which requires that people work together to solve problems. It is not uncommon for the problem-solving activities of the progressive school to spill out into the community and involve students in issues such as climate change and poverty. In this way, students learn an important principle of progressive education: Knowledge should be used to redesign or improve the world.

One notable progressive educator was William Heard Kilpatrick (1871–1965), who was a professor of philosophy of education at Columbia University in New York. He was a follower of many of Dewey's ideas about education, but differed on the importance of subject matter in a child's educational experience. Rejecting formal curriculum study, he developed the **project method** of education, in which students work in groups on a topic of interest to them. He believed that because students learn only what is of interest to them, they should be the ones to determine topics of study.

The main hope of a nation lies in the proper education of its youth.

—ERASMUS (1466–1536),
Renaissance philosopher

Both progressive and essentialist educators claim their particular approach is the true American philosophy of education. One can make a case that both match this description, but each reflects different aspects of the American personality. Progressivism represents our antiauthoritarian, experimental, and visionary side; essentialism speaks to our more practical, structured, and task-oriented side. In recent years, many of the tensions and public debates in U.S. education can be traced to struggles between these two philosophies of education. Clearly, essentialist educators gained ground on progressive educators in the 1980s and 1990s. Concerns over the country's global economic competitiveness and the perceived "softness" of our schools have created a receptive climate for essentialist views.

To judge your own sympathy for the progressive approach, see what you think of the following representative statement by a progressive educator.

PRESERVICE to PRACTICE

A Progressive Educator

I'm a progressive educator and proud of it. I'm not ducking that label just because it is unpopular in many quarters these days, usually among people who don't really understand what it is. Quite honestly, for the life of me I cannot understand how a teacher can be anything *but* a progressive educator.

I'm dedicated to a few simple and, I believe, obvious principles. For one thing, children come into the world with a very plastic nature, capable of being molded one way or another. We should therefore work to surround them with activities and opportunities that bring them in contact with good things. Also, by their nature, children are curious. Instead of rejecting their curiosities, I believe we should build on them. Schools should be exciting, involving places where students are caught up in interesting activities.

I think that I'm a progressive educator because I have looked at my own experiences. I know I learn best when I'm trying to solve a puzzle or a problem that really interests me. Somehow I've always been able to get much more interested in how we're going to solve the problems of our own society than in the affairs of the Athenians and Spartans. I can get much more involved in a research problem about which smartphone gives the best value for the dollar than about some dry economic problem presented to me by a teacher. And I really don't think I'm different from the overwhelming majority of students.

I see many of my fellow teachers spending all their energy damming up student curiosity and imposing work on their students. And then the teachers wonder why they themselves are so tired or burned out. I'm sure it's quite tiring to try to convert children into file cabinets and to stuff facts into their heads all day.

One of the things that sets me apart is that I'm not so hung up as others are on what I call the "talky" curriculum. I am convinced that students learn most effectively by *doing*, by experiencing events and then reflecting on and making meaning out of what they have experienced. I think more science is learned on a nature walk than from the same time spent reading a textbook or hearing teacher explanations. I think students learn more abstract principles, such as democracy, from trying to set up and maintain a democratic society in their classroom than from a lot of learned lectures and dusty prose on the subject. I'm trying to get to their hearts and their heads. The traditional approach gets to neither place.

To me, life is a matter of solving problems. New times have new problems and demand new knowledge. I don't want my students to be ready for life in the eighteenth century. I want them to be effective, functioning, curious citizens of the twenty-first century. They are going to need to be able to develop solutions to fit new and unique problems. Although much knowledge is important, they need to realize that knowledge is only today's tentative explanation of how things work. Much of what we know now is incorrect and will have to be replaced.

It's not that I think that ideas and content and the traditional subjects are worthless—far from it. I teach much of the same material as other teachers. I just get there by a different route. I let the issues and problems emerge and then give the students a chance to get answers and to solve problems. As they quickly learn, they have to know a great deal to solve some of the problems. Often they get themselves involved with some very advanced material. The only difference is that now they want to. Now they have the energy. And, boy, once they get going, do they have energy! No, it doesn't always work. I have students who coast, and I've had projects that failed. But I'd put my track record against those of my more traditional colleagues any day.

Pause *and* Reflect

1. Did any of your teachers take a progressive approach to teaching? If so, how did you, as a student, respond?
2. Do you believe your students would respond well if you chose to implement a progressive approach? What difficulties, if any, do you think you might encounter?

9-4 The Influence of Two Psychological Theories

Since early in the twentieth century, educational practice has been greatly influenced by the discipline of psychology. Psychology—the scientific study of the mind and human behavior— has been a major influence on the work of teachers, particularly given its focus on how we learn. Over the years, various schools of psychology have emerged, often having roots in particular philosophies. Some of these psychological theories have had a great deal to say to educators. Two in particular have strongly influenced our schools: behaviorism and cognitive psychology.

9-4a BEHAVIORISM: CONDITIONING STUDENTS OR SETTING THEM FREE?

The psychological theory of behavior modification, also known as **behaviorism**, is an educational approach that emerged directly from the pioneering research of B. F. Skinner (1904–1990), who himself was influenced by the social efficiency movement in education of the 1920s and 1930s. Skinner developed the theory called operant conditioning, which viewed learning as the learners' response to various stimuli (e.g., sounds, words, or the actions of people) present in one's environment. Subscribing to the view that humans learn to act in specific ways based on the response they receive for their actions (generally a reward or a punishment), behaviorist teachers believe that learners need incentives, both positive and negative, as motivators to learn.

In planning for teaching, behaviorists (1) use clear objectives, spelled out in terms of the specific behaviors to be learned; (2) establish a learning environment that will positively reinforce desired behaviors, such as staying on task, and eliminate undesirable behaviors; and (3) closely monitor and give learners feedback on progress until the goal is achieved. The curriculum is organized in sequenced, discrete segments. Because the same behaviors and knowledge are desirable for all students, standardization of the curriculum and of means to measure progress is important. Behaviorist teachers often use objective tests made up predominantly of multiple-choice questions to measure how well students have achieved the learning objectives and to give prompt feedback to students. In some behaviorist classrooms, students are expected to practice a specific skill until they show a certain level of mastery of the skill. At that point, they move on to the next skill or concept to be learned. Direct instruction (sometimes called "explicit direct instruction") is often identified as a behaviorist pedagogical approach.[6]

In the 1960s and 1970s, many educators made behaviorism their dominant, organizing educational theory. This educational movement has been criticized for being teacher dominated and causing teachers to treat students as passive objects to be conditioned and therefore manipulated. Nevertheless, behaviorism remains a dominant theoretical presence, particularly in the areas of special education and classroom discipline. The popular "assertive discipline," in which teachers are urged to "catch students doing good" and then reward that behavior, is based squarely on behaviorism.[7] Many teachers rely on behavior modification practices to get students to be quiet when they see or hear the teacher's signal or to get them to do their best work to receive a reward sticker.

Critics argue that behaviorist teachers exercise too much control over students' learning and focus on the learning of facts rather than deep conceptual knowledge. In response, behaviorist teachers insist that their goal is to eventually put control of learning in their students' hands once they have learned to respond appropriately to the teacher's prompts.

Klaus Vedfelt/DigitalVision/Getty Images

9-4b COGNITIVE PSYCHOLOGY: STUDENTS AS MAKERS OF MEANING?

Over the past 30 years, researchers in both medicine and psychology have been investigating the human brain to find out more about its role in human learning and memory. Cognitive psychologists, drawing heavily on the trailblazing research of Swiss psychologist Jean Piaget (1896–1980), the Russian psychologist Lev Vygotsky (1896–1934), and the American psychologist Jerome Bruner (b. 1915), have discovered a great deal about how people learn to think and solve problems. Their discoveries have led to the development of new theories about learning and cognition that have tremendous implications for how teachers teach. One increasingly popular theory derived from the research findings states that for new information to be internalized by learners, it must be integrated into the learners' preexisting knowledge base. This process of integration is referred to as **constructivism**.

> *What we want to see is the child in pursuit of knowledge, and not knowledge in pursuit of the child.*
>
> **—GEORGE BERNARD SHAW (1856–1950),**
> Irish playwright

According to this theory, knowledge cannot be *transmitted* directly from teachers to learners, but rather is *constructed by learners and later reconstructed* as new information becomes available. Instead of seeing students as partially full vessels waiting to be filled, as some essentialists do, constructivist teachers view them as actively engaged in *making meaning*. Teachers, therefore, need to create learning situations where students can build their own knowledge rather than having students sit and listen to the teachers' lectures. One constructivist technique for helping students "make meaning" of a concept is called scaffolding, whereby a teacher provides support as students attempt to understand that concept. (Scaffolding is also discussed in Chapter 6, "What Makes a Teacher Effective?")

Although not without its critics,[8] constructivism has become so influential in education in recent years that we give it particular attention here.

Constructivists view individuals as having an aversion to disorder. They believe that we are all continually trying to sort things out, to find clues and patterns amid our impressions that will help us to make sense of the world around us. When we encounter something new—say, a strange sound in the night—we immediately attempt to fit it into the patterns or structures we already possess (e.g., "Don't worry. That's the midnight whistle of the Ole Ninety-Eight headin' down to New Orleans."). But sometimes we encounter new information that leads (or forces) us to realize that our knowledge base as it is currently "constructed" is incorrect or outdated. ("Uh-oh! The railroad retired that train two years ago!") We may respond in a number of ways: We may search for new input from our senses, seeking either to reconstruct the knowledge base or develop different patterns and structures so that the information "fits." ("Maybe that noise was from the hot water boiler and it's about to explode," or "Maybe that creepy guy from the apartment down below is on my fire escape," or "Maybe I shouldn't read Stephen King novels before going to bed!") In some instances, we may be so convinced of our knowledge base that we refuse to make allowances for the new information. ("No, I'm sure that it was a train whistle. The railroad must have put that train back in service.") Students follow the same patterns as they try to make sense of new information they encounter in school.

TeachSource Video Case

© Cengage 2016

Constructivist Teaching in Action: A High School Classroom Debate

Watch the video clips, study the artifacts in the case, and reflect on the following questions:

1. Does this teacher's approach represent constructivism, as it is described in this chapter? Why or why not?

2. Which of the other philosophies in this chapter does this teacher's approach incorporate?

3. Is the approach used here with high school students adaptable to middle school students? Elementary students?

VOICES from the Classroom

Constructivist Philosophy

Susan Dougherty writes about her career as a fourth-grade teacher at Bayberry School in Watchung, New Jersey.

As I began my career in education, I held firm one belief about students: They must be active participants in the classroom. Twelve years later, I hold that same basic belief but have refined what it means for a learner to be active.

Early in my career, "active" meant that my students would not sit in rows and spend the day doing seatwork. My first position as a kindergarten teacher quickly revealed that I might strive for something greater than physical activity. Of course, kindergarten students are active—try and keep them from being anything but active! I came to recognize that although active bodies can be important, what I really wanted was to engage the minds of my students.

As I taught students at many elementary levels, I learned to ask probing questions that required my students to consider their learning carefully. How do you know to add these two numbers? What kind of person do you think the main character of this story is? How would you explain why oil floats on water to someone who didn't understand? Although my students were often physically active, acting out scenes from a novel we were reading, experimenting with magnets or prisms, or using pattern blocks to build models of math problems, they also spent time physically inert but inwardly engaged in active thought.

Soon, however, I was not satisfied with simply engaging the minds of my students. I wanted to reach their hearts. I wanted to awaken a passion for learning within each student. How might a teacher encourage the awakening of such passion? One key, I think, is to allow and encourage the students to ask and seek the answers to their own questions. In this way, students' minds and hearts become active, leading them on a lifelong journey of inquiry and self-motivated learning.

Cognitive psychologists also suggest that we organize our knowledge in ways that allow us easy access to knowledge we use regularly. These cognitive structures, which are called *schemas or schemata,* change constantly as new information is taken in, hypotheses are developed, and theories are tested. These processes of hypothesis development and testing can be done independently or in interaction with others. ("Maybe it is just my imagination and I should check with my neighbors if they are hearing that whistle.") Thus, real learning for constructivists involves moving from the *Trivial Pursuit* or *Jeopardy* type of factual or declarative knowledge to applicable knowledge—in other words, from "knowing what" to "knowing how." To achieve this transformation, learners must develop cognitive learning strategies for particular kinds of learning tasks; that is, they must learn how to think through or go about solving problems. One teacher describes how she puts her constructivist philosophy into action in the "Voices from the Classroom" feature.

9-5 Your Philosophy of Education

At this point, you may be a little confused and possibly discouraged by all this heavy vocabulary and lofty thought. To expect to be able to understand and evaluate critically every aspect of each philosophy is to expect of yourself what few professional philosophers are able to do. What you have just finished reading is a précis of some of the major ideas of Western civilization (see Table 9.1 for a summary). Some of these ideas have been around for centuries, and some are the fruits of thinkers who are still with us.

TABLE 9.1	Four Philosophies and Their Applications to Education			
	Perennialism	**Essentialism**	**Romanticism**	**Progressivism**
Metaphysics: What is real? Does it have meaning?	The meaning of life is the search for unchanging truth found in the collective wisdom of Western culture.	What is relevant is what helps an individual live well and what benefits humanity.	Reality is stable; the meaning of life is derived primarily through self-development away from society.	Reality is in flux and ever changing, so meaning is in the context of the individual, who is a "problem solver?"
Epistemology: Knowledge and knowing—what is truth?	Truth and knowledge are changeless, revealed through guided reflection and in classics of Western culture.	Truth exists in the classics *and* modern science. Students must learn process *and* content. Knowledge is gained through the interaction of experiences and rational thought.	Knowledge is gained through sensory experiences and interaction with one's environment.	Knowledge is gained via individual experience. Truth is individually defined so that emphasis is on learning how to learn.
Axiology: Values, ethics, aesthetics	Changeless. Determined by the very nature of reality.	Determined by the natural order of things. Values exist in the best of culture.	Determined by the individual.	Determined by each individual in interaction with his or her culture, based on the shared values of the community or culture.
Logic: How we think, deductive, and inductive	Rationality, especially deductive thought, is developed by studying classics and through the Socratic dialectic.	Rationality is best developed through interplay of deductive and inductive thinking.	Emphasis is primarily on inductive thought, because learning starts with experiences and moves to hypotheses.	Emphasis is on inductive thinking and problem solving.
Purpose of Education/Schooling	Educate the intellect; develop in learners rational thought and an understanding of the truths of humankind.	Prepare students to be productive, contributing members of society.	Make learners strong (physically, intellectually, morally) to resist the evils of society.	Help students become good citizens familiar with the workings of democracy and with good problem-solving skills.
Teachers	Teachers are experts of content knowledge, passing on the accumulated wisdom of the past to the next generation.	Teachers are experts of content knowledge, teaching essential knowledge and maintaining task-oriented focus.	Teachers respond to the learners' requests for knowledge, rather than initiating learning in the learners.	Teachers are facilitators of student learning, providing resources for students' problem-solving abilities; developing students' problem-solving abilities; and helping children do what they want to do.

(Continued)

TABLE 9.1	Four Philosophies and Their Applications to Education (Continued)			
	Perennialism	**Essentialism**	**Romanticism**	**Progressivism**
Teaching Strategies	This approach cultivates rational powers through contact with the culture's best and through imitation. For older students, Socratic dialogue is key to uncovering truths found in classics.	This approach avoids methodological frills and soft pedagogy and concentrates on sound, proven instructional methods.	This approach creates a productive learning environment for learners, and an individualized approach to learning, depending on students' interests.	This approach stimulates students to plan and carry out activities and research projects using group processes and democratic procedures.
The Children	Are there to learn what is taught.	Are there to listen and learn.	Are naturally good and must be protected from the evils of society.	Learn by doing and by discovering.
Curriculum	In younger grades, curriculum focuses on basic skills to develop mental discipline and rational thought processes. Older learners study materials reflecting universal and recurring themes through which the truths of humanity can be revealed.	Strong emphasis is on basic skills in elementary schools and on disciplined knowledge and scholastic achievement in secondary schools.	Curriculum depends on the interests of the learners. There is no set curriculum, no specific skills to be acquired.	This curriculum is centered on the students' interest in real problems and interdisciplinary solution seeking.

Source: Adapted from a table suggested by James Hotchkiss. Used by permission of James Hotchkiss.

Pause *and* Reflect

1. It is perhaps unfair of us to ask you so soon after having read descriptions of different philosophies and theories of education, but right now, which one holds the greatest intellectual appeal to you? Which one holds the least appeal? Why do you think so?
2. How has reading about these four philosophical alternatives changed your own philosophy of education? Consider retaking the "Philosophy of Education Self-Inventory" now that you have more knowledge about these philosophical underpinnings.

How can you use the summary in Table 9.1 to help you develop your own philosophy of education? First, recognize that selecting the philosophy by which you will live and by which you will guide your professional activities takes much more investment of time, thought, and energy than reading our short chapter. Second, realize that you have already begun to uncover your philosophy of education. You started when you filled out the "Philosophy of Education Self-Inventory." You can further your self-understanding by following the suggestions in the "Up Close" feature entitled "Identifying Your Own Philosophical Leanings." Third, realize that developing and refining one's philosophy of education is a lifelong endeavor, and commit yourself to making this journey.

Up CLOSE

Identifying Your Own Philosophical Leanings

Think of your favorite teacher from elementary or secondary school, or a teacher you have admired during your teacher education. On a separate piece of paper, list some of that teacher's practices that you admire most. Include instructional techniques, classroom management strategies, ways of relating to the students—anything you think helped that person be an effective teacher.

Now, on the same piece of paper, write the philosophical outlook that you think may underlie each practice you admire. This exercise will take some reflection, and you may well find that no single philosophy matches all the teaching characteristics you listed. Use whatever philosophical labels seem most appropriate.

After completing both tasks, what general conclusions can you draw about the philosophy of this teacher you admire? Does the teacher's practice reflect the tenets of a single educational philosophy discussed in this chapter? Or does he or she take an eclectic approach (described later), drawing on different philosophical traditions? Are there ways in which this teacher is too unique to fit any category?

As a final step, reflect on what your conclusion tells you about your own philosophical leanings. If you hold this teacher in high regard, presumably you share at least some of his or her philosophical convictions. Does anything surprise you about the philosophical beliefs you have deduced? Do they suggest that you are more traditional or more progressive than you supposed? More child centered or subject matter centered? More nicely balanced or just more muddled? Which aspects of your own philosophical base do you need to think about further and clarify?

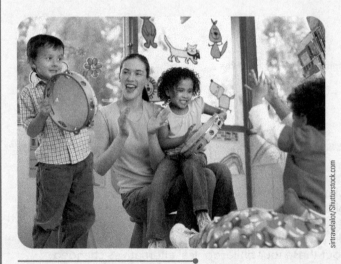

Using instruments to sound our syllables is fun for these students.

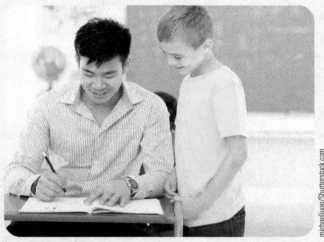

If done in the right spirit, even correcting a journal can be fun.

9-5a ECLECTICISM: NOT AN EXCUSE FOR SLOPPY THINKING

Some teachers, like the teacher-philosophers discussed in this chapter, settle on one philosophical view, and that view then serves to structure all of their work. Other teachers lean strongly toward a particular philosophy, even if they may not be fully conscious of their position or able to give it a proper philosophical label. Typically, they have a particular view of learners, including how learners should be approached and what is most worth knowing. Of course, few teachers are philosophical purists. Some teachers, recognizing that they draw ideas from various philosophies, label themselves *eclectics*. But what does it really mean to be an eclectic teacher in contemporary education? *Eclecticism* embodies the idea that truth can be found anywhere, and therefore people should select from various doctrines, systems, and sources. Eclectic teachers select what they believe to be the most attractive features of several philosophies. For example, a teacher might take from romanticism the innate curiosity of learners and from essentialism, a curricular viewpoint dominated by the criterion of usefulness.

Eclecticism is quite popular, but often for the wrong reasons. It sometimes appears as the easy way out of philosophical uncertainty, just taking what you please from the philosophical cafeteria of ideas. ("Let's see now: I think I'll begin with a light vinaigrette salad of romantic individuality and follow that up with a main course of progressive problem-solving projects, but with some hearty perennialist classics as side dishes. And, oh, yes—let's finish with a popular and tasty dessert of essentialist vocational training.") One problem with this approach is the probability of inconsistency. To take one's view of society from the romantic, who gives primacy to individual freedom, and one's teaching methodology from the progressive, who stresses group membership and democratic process, is liable to make everyone confused. Selecting eclecticism must not be an excuse for lazy thinking.

> " . . . it is our philosophy of life that dictates our philosophy of teaching, and that [it is] this "philosophical identity" (or lack of same) that we envelop ourselves in each day as we walk into our classroom that ultimately distinguishes those who find joy and passion in this profession from those who find drudgery and then just pick up a paycheck two weeks later.
>
> —JOHN PERRICONE,
> Author, *Zen and the Art of Public School Teaching*

Despite this warning, most teachers feel quite free and justified in borrowing teaching methodologies and strategies that are associated with various philosophies of education. An ardent perennialist teacher may choose to involve his or her sixth-grade students in a hands-on project that involves constructing a large topographical map of Odysseus's 10-year journey to his home after the fall of Troy. Conversely, a free-spirited romantic teacher may insist that each student memorize and be able to recite 50 lines of *The Odyssey*. Although this type of eclecticism may, in a narrow sense, seem philosophically inconsistent, at its heart is the recognition that no philosophy of education is able to dictate the ideal methodology or learning strategies for all situations or all students trying to learn all subject matter. Related to this notion is the growing realization (discussed in Chapter 3, "Who Are Today's Students in a Diverse Society?") that different students possess a great range of ways in which they learn and that what works with one student may flop with another. In sum, eclecticism can be a serious philosophical position, and eclecticism in the selection of teaching strategies is quite justified. But, to reinforce our earlier statement, the choice to be "eclectic" should not be a substitute for sloppy thought.

9-5b PHILOSOPHY AND LIBERAL EDUCATION

We are not suggesting that you sit yourself down with a cup of coffee, think through all these issues, and come up with a tight set of philosophical answers that will last the rest of your lifetime. Rather, we hope that we have focused—or refocused—your attention on some of life's most critical questions and on some issues that reside at the very core of teaching.

T (F)

A late-night, college bull session is, by definition, non-philosophical.

One purpose of the general education component of teacher education programs (i.e., the courses in the arts and sciences required of prospective teachers) is to provide a chance for future teachers to think through these fundamental questions of human nature and existence. A primary purpose of the college curriculum is to present students with a wide range of society's best thinkers and their attempts to understand their own existence. Of course, the infamous college bull sessions may be where the real philosophical inquiry occurs. These debates are frequently thinly veiled discussions of what really counts in life and what one should try to do with one's life.

In effect, then, both the formal apparatus of college and its curriculum and the informal opportunities to meet, talk, and test your ideas with a variety of people should help you discover where you stand on some of these essential human questions.

OUR FINAL WORD

The contemporary writer, Parker Palmer, has written about the need for teachers not merely to "understand" ideas, but to be ready to "stand under" certain ideas, letting them serve as the vital supports for what they do as educators.[9] This idea goes to the essence of this chapter. Teachers stand under a philosophy of education, a guide and support that has three components: (1) an expression of what teachers value—what they esteem and believe to be important; (2) an individual's moral compass—what the teacher relies on to make critical ethical decisions; and (3) an engine of ideas—the knowledge that teachers use to respond to new and changing situations that life presents.[10] As we said at the beginning of this chapter, teachers who will be more than mere technicians have an obligation to take philosophical issues and questions seriously. Teachers owe it to themselves and to their students to understand where they are going and to understand why they are going there.

As a wise teacher wrote, "A philosophy of education cannot be crammed down people's throats. They must feel it to be true in the marrow of their bones and look with trust and approval upon the leaders who attempt to give it expression. It must catch and reflect their temper, not arouse their distemper."[11] Teachers owe it to themselves to make sure that the schools in which they work are hospitable—and certainly not hostile—to their own philosophies of education. It is important that you be ready both to discuss your own philosophy of education with prospective employers and to inquire about the district's or school's philosophy of education. Do not, however, expect those interviewing you to be able to define their schools precisely according to the particular philosophies described in this chapter. Although educators live out a philosophy of education, we are not always able easily to capture it in words.

WHY TEACH? YOUR FINAL WORD

1. At the present time, which beliefs do you hold about the following: the role of a teacher, the nature of learners, the nature of the curriculum, and the ways in which people learn best? Explain your beliefs.

2. What role, if any, does religion or the spiritual realm play in your philosophy of education?

3. Why do you think that superintendents and principals often ask teaching candidates about their philosophy of education?

KEY TERMS

aesthetics (275)
axiology (274)
behaviorism (291)
constructivism (292)
deductive reasoning (276)
epistemology (273)
essentialism (280)
inductive reasoning (276)

logic (275)
metaphysics (272)
perennialism (279)
philosophy (270)
progressivism (287)
project method (289)
romanticism (285)

FOR FURTHER INFORMATION

Web Resources

Schoolmarm's Lil Red Schoolhouse

This site, constructed by classroom teachers, both expresses their teaching philosophy and also offers several resources to fellow teachers.

The Chancellor's Incentive Program

This website is a collection of research resources to help teachers clarify their understanding of the connection between their own philosophical leaning with what it means to know and to learn.

Society for Philosophical Inquiry (SPI)

SPI is a grassroots nonprofit organization devoted to supporting philosophical inquirers of all ages and walks of life. It offers a number of ways to get involved in the SPI's activities, such as its Socrates Café program and the Philosophers' Club.

Print Resources

Gary D. Fenstermacher and Jonas F. Soltis, *Approaches to Teaching*, 5th ed. (New York: Teachers College Press, 2009).

This slim volume shows how two philosophers can unpack the term *teaching* and explain what is behind several different approaches to instruction.

Gerald Gutek, *Historical and Philosophical Foundations of Education: A Biographical Introduction*, 5th ed. (Upper Saddle River, NJ: Prentice-Hall/Merrill, 2010).

This textbook is a comprehensive and up-to-date account of the competing schools of educational philosophy and their application to schooling. It provides thumbnail sketches of key figures and leads readers in investigating their thought.

John Perricone, *Zen and the Art of Public School Teaching* (Frederick, MD: PublishAmerica, 2005).

The author is a teacher and martial arts specialist who has written a witty, practical, and often inspiring book about how he puts his philosophy of education to work daily in his teaching.

Thomas W. Cathcart and Daniel M. Klein, *Plato and a Platypus Walk into a Bar: Understanding Philosophy through Jokes* (New York: Harry N. Abrams, 2009).

A book that proves that philosophy can be both funny and interesting. Although not directly related to teaching, the book contains amusing insights to human life.

What Is the History of America's Struggle for Educational Opportunity?

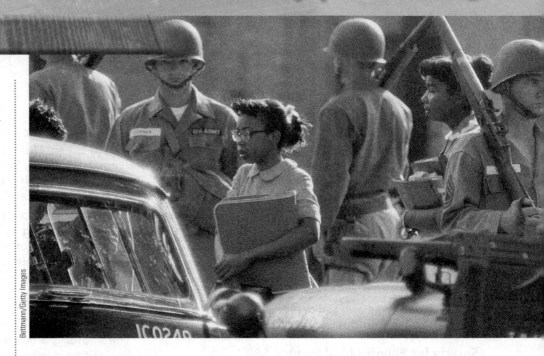

Bettmann/Getty Images

LEARNING OBJECTIVES

10-1 Identify a modern-day example for each of the seven major themes of American educational history discussed in this chapter.

10-2 Describe the major purpose of the common school during the nineteenth century and how it was financially supported.

10-3 Identify the two major purposes of the comprehensive high school during the latter part of the nineteenth century, and describe why this was unique to American education.

10-4 Describe the ways in which private education provides alternatives to the public schools.

10-5 Provide a brief overview of the historical struggles for equal educational opportunities for African Americans, Hispanic Americans, Native Americans, Asian Americans, and women in the United States.

Truth OR Fiction?

T F The Constitution of the United States guarantees a free system of public education to American children.

T F During colonial times, most students did not finish elementary school.

T F The great majority of private schools in the United States have a religious affiliation.

T F Efforts to desegregate the public schools from the 1960s through the 1980s came as a result of a Supreme Court ruling.

To understand the present U.S. educational system, its successes and failures, and the problems it still faces, we must look to our past. There we can identify the forces that have affected and continue to affect the development of American education. This chapter reviews the history of schooling and education in the United States, pointing out seven important themes and examining the contributions that significant men and women have made.

Rare are the college students who feel a burning urgency to answer the question, "What is the history of American education?" Unless you are a history buff, you will probably ask yourself, "Why do I need to know this stuff? How will it help me do a better job in the classroom?"

First, understanding American educational history will give you a sense of perspective. As educators, we are sometimes accused of being faddist, which implies that we blindly follow each new approach or idea, thinking it is the greatest thing since the Internet. At the other extreme, we are sometimes accused of reinventing the wheel, spending a great deal of energy discovering something that has been in the educational literature for years or was a significant part of the education program of a different culture.

> *The farther backward you can look, the farther forward you are likely to see.*
>
> **—WINSTON CHURCHILL (1874–1965),** prime minister of Great Britain during World War II

Second, studying the history of American education will enable you to better understand the culture and context in which you will work. It will help you see the "big picture"—that is, why things operate as they do in today's schools.

Finally, studying the history of education will help you appreciate its truly noble heritage. Schools have been a progressive instrument in the lives of most people who have attended them. They have freed people from superstition and false information and given them new skills, positive values, and world-expanding visions of what each individual, as well as what we as people, can become. Some of the greatest people who have walked the earth—Socrates, Jesus, and Gandhi, among others—saw themselves essentially as teachers. Teachers, then, are part of a long-lived, progressive, and inspirational human endeavor. Knowing our educational history and gaining a historical perspective will help you live up to and extend this tradition.

10-1 Themes in American Education

Kindergarten or nursery school led to elementary school, then to middle school or junior high school, then to high school, and now to college. You may have taken this progression for granted, assuming that's the way things have always been. In reality, you are presently enjoying a level of education that was available only to the elite of earlier generations. You are already close to the top of an educational pyramid for which the foundation was laid almost 350 years ago. The growth of the pyramid has been shaped and energized by seven major themes in American educational history:

1. *Local control.* Originating in New England during colonial times, the concept of local control of schools spread during the nineteenth century with the formation of the school district system. Because of their fear of a too-strong federal government, the framers of the U.S. Constitution made no reference to education. As a result, state governments assumed the role of educational authorities and then delegated substantial powers to local school boards. Not until the mid-twentieth century did the

T (F)
The Constitution of the United States guarantees a free system of public education to American children.

federal government become substantially involved in educational matters.

2. *Universal education.* Education for all children has been a developing theme in the United States. In the colonial period, education was reserved for a small minority—mainly white males. During the nineteenth and twentieth centuries, children from various groups previously omitted from educational opportunity (girls, minorities, immigrants, people with disabilities) gained access to elementary and secondary education. Today, a college education is generally available to all who actively seek it.

3. *Public education.* In the colonial period, education was generally private and primarily reserved for the middle and upper classes. Today, private education remains a small and important part of the overall educational system, but nationhood for the United States brought the expansion of publicly supported education. By the early twentieth century, not only was public education widespread, but education became compulsory as well.

4. *Comprehensive education.* The basic abilities to read, write, and do arithmetic were once sufficient to prepare most children for fulfilling their adult roles in society. Eventually, the growth of urban, industrial life in the United States during the nineteenth and early twentieth centuries demanded that people be educated for work. The result was the comprehensive public high school, which includes both training for trades and preparation for college.

5. *Secular education.* In the earliest colonial times, the purpose of education was religious training. Beginning in the eighteenth century and progressing through the twentieth century, the function of American education became increasingly secular, concerned with producing socially responsible citizens. Religious study has remained mainly in the private sector.

6. *Changing ideas of the basics.* Literacy and classical learning were the main goals of colonial education, whereas practical skills for a pragmatic, democratic society were the aims of nineteenth-century schools. Technical and scientific literacy were added to the basics in the computer age and space age of the late twentieth century. Today, preparing students to compete in a global marketplace seems to be the focus.

7. *Expanding definitions of educational access and equality.* In the nineteenth century, the goal for educational access was to build schools in places where children lived and to enroll as many of them as possible. Since then, the focus on **equality of educational opportunity** has expanded. By the beginning of the twentieth century, efforts to equalize education involved offering more curricular choices, including vocational training, to help prepare students for different economic and social roles. Throughout the middle of the twentieth century, the focus was on removing legal, racial, and economic barriers to schooling. From the 1960s through the 1970s, access and educational opportunity became redefined as they became increasingly tied to results. The removal of racial, linguistic, mental, and physical discrimination as the basis for expanded access was augmented by a focus on measuring learning outcomes among different groups as a test of whether improved access led to real educational opportunity. As one educational historian noted, "By the end of [the twentieth] century, . . . expectations had shifted to an emphasis on academic achievement."[1] During the first decade of the twenty-first century, the emphasis on academic achievement has continued.

Many contemporary educational issues have their roots in these seven themes, which continue to shape the character of American schooling and education. Consider these examples of current issues:

- *Local control.* What should be the role of the federal government regarding education? Should federal legislation, such as the Every Student Succeeds Act, require states to test students in particular grades and on particular subjects?

- *Universal education.* How can we ensure the quality of education regardless of whether students live in wealthy or poor school districts?

- *Public education.* Should private and religious schools receive public tax support?

- *Comprehensive education.* Should the schools require all students—vocational and college prep—to follow a common curriculum?

- *Secular education.* How should public schools treat the presence of religion in American society and world culture?

- *Changing ideas of the basics.* Is technological literacy a new "basic" of education? If so, how will schools finance the programs that train students to use new technologies?

- *Expanding definitions of equal access and opportunity.* What should schools do about "achievement gaps" between poor and minority students and students from white or wealthier families? Should states offer vouchers for students to attend other schools if their schools are not producing learning gains?

These are just a few of the issues facing today's policy makers. As you read the rest of this chapter, look for links between historical forces and the key topics and debates in contemporary education. This chapter's tour through history is not intended to be a dead-end journey into the past. What happened in earlier generations has greatly influenced the schooling you received and the system you will enter as a teacher.

Pause *and* Reflect

Why is it important for teachers to know the history of American education? How might you use such knowledge?

10-2 Elementary Education

Elementary education changed dramatically from the colonial period to today. Schooling became compulsory rather than optional. Schools went from being religiously oriented to having a secular focus. And, schools today are bright, colorful, and friendly environments, in contrast to the overly strict and punitive schools of the colonial era.

10-2a COLONIAL ORIGINS

In the 1600s, some girls received elementary instruction, but formal colonial education was intended mainly for boys, particularly those of the middle and upper classes. Both girls and boys might have had some preliminary training in the *four R's*—reading, 'riting, 'rithmetic, and religion—at home. Sometimes, for a small fee, a housewife offered to take in children to whom she would teach a little reading and writing, basic prayers, and religious beliefs. In these **dame schools**, girls also learned basic household skills such as cooking and sewing. The dame schools often provided all the formal education some children, especially girls, ever received.

Throughout the colonies, poor children were often apprenticed or indentured to local tradesmen or housewives. Apprenticeships lasted 3 to 10 years, generally ending around age 21 for boys and age 18 for girls. During that time, an apprentice would learn the basic skills of a trade and might also be taught basic reading and writing and perhaps arithmetic as part of the contractual agreement.

Although the lines were not drawn hard and fast, the three geographic regions of the colonies—New England, the South, and the Middle Colonies—developed different types of educational systems, which were shaped by each region's particular settlement patterns.

New England Town and District Schools

In New England, the Puritans believed it was important that everyone be able to read the Bible and interpret its teachings. As early as 1642, Massachusetts passed a law requiring parents to educate their children. That law was strengthened in 1647 by the famous **Old Deluder Satan Act**. Because Satan assuredly would try to keep people from understanding the Scriptures, it was deemed important that all children be taught how to read. Therefore, every town of 50 or more families was obligated to pay a man to teach reading and writing. With these schools, known as **town schools**, New England set the precedent that if parents would not or could not educate their children, the government was obligated to take on that responsibility.

When settlers spread out, seeking better farmland, the town schools began to disappear. What emerged in their place was the so-called **moving school**, in which a schoolmaster traveled from village to village, holding sessions in each place for several months before moving on.

Discontent with this system of education eventually led to the development of the **district school**. Under this scheme, a township was divided into districts, each having its own school and teacher and being funded by the town treasury. The theme of local control over schooling developed in these various kinds of schools. The district school system soon entrenched itself in New England because it was inexpensive to finance and gave some measure of schooling to every child. Laws made attendance compulsory, but they were not very rigorously enforced.

Some towns allowed girls to have one or two hours of instruction between 5:00 and 7:00 A.M., when boys were not using the school building. For the most part, however, girls had no access to the town elementary schools until after the American Revolution.[2] If few girls went to school in the towns, even fewer did so in the outlying districts. The theme of universal education, which would include girls, was not to develop until the next century.

Students entered school around age six or seven and stayed in school for only three or four years. They learned their ABCs, numerals, and the Lord's Prayer from a *hornbook*, which consisted of a page that was laminated with a transparent material made from boiled-down cows' horns and then attached to a flat piece of wood. Having learned the basics, students graduated to *The New England Primer*, an illustrated book composed of religious texts and other readings. Although other primers and catechisms existed, *The New England Primer* was the most famous and remained the basic school text for at least 100 years after the first edition was published in 1690.

The learning atmosphere of these colonial schools was repressive and grim. Students were under orders to keep quiet and do their work, and learning was characterized by an emphasis on memorization. If students did well, they were praised and given a new task. If they did poorly, they were criticized harshly and often given a rap across the knuckles or on the seat of the pants. If children did not pay attention, their lack of focus was taken as a

T F
During colonial times, most students did not finish elementary school.

Foolishness is bound up in the heart of a child; but the rod of correction shall drive it far from him.

—PROVERBS 22:15,
as found in *The New England Primer*

sign of how easily the devil could distract them from the path of righteousness. Such views continued to serve as a justification for severe classroom discipline throughout the first 250 years of American history.

Education in the South

Conditions in the South were quite different from those in New England. Many upper-class Englishmen emigrated to the South, where they established large estates. As opposed to the more centralized conditions in New England, the great distances between southern settlements encouraged plantation owners to educate their children with private tutors, who were often local ministers or itinerant scholars. As in England, education of the poor and orphans was often undertaken by the Anglican Church or by religious groups such as the Society for the Propagation of the Gospel in Foreign Parts. The society's main mission was to convert natives and slaves to Christianity.

Most southern settlers were members of the Anglican Church and did not share the Puritan belief that everyone had a religious obligation to learn to read. The lack of concern for general education of the entire community caused public education in the South to lag behind that of other regions of the country for many generations. Town governments established schools, but their administration was usually delegated to a group or corporation, which could collect tuition, own property, hire and fire teachers, and decide curriculum content.

Pause *and* Reflect

1. Why did the educational development of colonial America differ among the New England, Middle, and Southern colonies?
2. In what ways were the educational systems different?
3. Can you see similarities to any of the colonial systems in today's schools?

Discipline in colonial schools was often strict and harsh.

Roger Viollet Collection/Getty Images

Education in the Middle Colonies

Unlike Puritan New England and the Anglican Southern Colonies, the Middle Colonies were composed of various religious and ethnic groups. Quakers, Catholics, Mennonites, Huguenots, Baptists, and others each wished to train their children in their respective faiths; Dutch, German, and Swedish settlers also wanted a separate education for their children. As a result, **private venture schools**, which were licensed but not protected or financed by the civil government, flourished, and the use of public funds to educate everyone's children did not become customary.

In these private schools, parents paid the teacher directly on a contractual basis. Instructors managed the school and curriculum, accepting or rejecting students as desired. The denominational schools in the Middle Colonies shared the New England concern for proper religious training as a primary goal, but they also began early to offer, in addition to the basics, practical subjects such as bookkeeping or navigation.

10-2b THE COMMON SCHOOL

Before the American Revolution, the term **common school** referred to schools that provided education for the average person, albeit not necessarily at public expense or available to all. Even in colonial New England, parents had to pay for their children's schooling. In the first blush of the new republic, however, conditions began to favor **universal education**—the idea that some sort of elementary education should be provided free, at public expense and under public control, for everyone who could not afford or did not want private schooling.

Even though the Constitution had relegated control of education to the states, the impetus for such public schooling came from the federal government, in particular as a result of the enactment of the **Northwest Ordinances** of 1785 and 1787. Concerned with the sale of public lands in the Northwest Territory (which ranged from present-day Ohio to Minnesota), Congress passed the Northwest Ordinance of 1785. Every township was divided into 36 sections, of which one was set aside for the maintenance of public schools. In the ordinance of 1787, Congress reaffirmed that "religion, morality, and knowledge, being necessary to good government and the happiness of mankind, schools and the means of education shall forever be encouraged."[3]

> *If a nation expects to be ignorant and free, in a state of civilization, it expects what never was and will never be.*
>
> **—THOMAS JEFFERSON (1743–1826),**
> third U.S. president and author of the
> Declaration of Independence

Arguments for the Common School

After the American Revolution, it was recognized that a democratic government would be only as strong as the people's ability to make intelligent choices, which in turn depended on a basic education for all. It was also argued that education was a natural right, just like the very rights for which the revolution had been fought. During this period, Benjamin Franklin and Thomas Jefferson suggested educational plans, as did other leaders of the revolution.

This early period of independence also saw an increased concern with citizenship and nationhood. Leaders perceived that a system of common schooling would strengthen the new nation's unity. An influx of immigrants in the 1840s and 1850s, following a period of upheaval in Europe, further stimulated demand for an educational system that would serve to "Americanize" the waves of foreigners and keep U.S. society stable.

In contrast to European social structure, class membership in America was rather fluid: Wealth and social status in this country depended less on the social class into which a person was born. Universal education, one of the key themes of American education, was thus seen by the newly evolving working class as a means of equalizing economic and social opportunities. As a result, another reason given for spreading educational opportunity was that better-educated people would increase productivity and enhance everyone's prosperity while diminishing crime and reducing poverty.

In fact, school materials of the time reflected this argument. Whereas *The New England Primer* reflected the religious orientation of much colonial education, the textbooks of the nineteenth century began a trend toward secular education (another of the seven major themes in the history of American education), emphasizing morality and Americanism. No other book was more popular than the six-volume series of **McGuffey Readers**, which sold more than 100 million copies between 1836 and 1906. Besides training students in (American) English language and grammar, these texts introduced poetry and the writings of statesmen, politicians, moralists, and religious leaders.

Although universal education at this time was meant only for whites, the same arguments advanced by its advocates were used later to extend equal opportunities for education to include racial and ethnic minorities and children with disabilities, to name just a few groups that have been denied equal educational opportunities in the past. The desegregation efforts of the 1960s and 1970s, for example, were based on these very arguments.

Arguments against the Common School

As proper as these thoughts may sound to the modern ear, they often encountered opposition. The arguments against the public common school were based on economics as much as on educational or political principles: Why should one family pay for the education of another family's children? Many people believed that schooling, especially for the poor, should be the responsibility of religious groups. Still others thought that a free public school would gradually weaken or dilute the particular culture or religion that they had sought to establish in the United States. If ethnic groups mingled together, what would be the fate of each group's native culture and language? Similar concerns are reflected in the current controversies about multicultural and bilingual education, discussed in Chapter 3, "Who Are Today's Students in a Diverse Society?"

Educators also struggled with another question: What was to be done about religious study? The ability of different religious groups to exist together in one school, as in democracy itself, demanded that no one religious group be favored over another. Although many competing proposals were advanced, the common schools finally settled on the teaching of basic moral values such as honesty and sincerity, as a substitute for direct religious instruction. As described in Chapter 8, "What Are the Ethical and Legal Issues Facing Teachers?," the same issues continue to inspire controversy today.

Victory of the Common School

Between 1820 and 1920, the establishment of common schools made steady progress across the United States. By the middle of the nineteenth century and certainly by the end of the Civil War, thanks in large part to the efforts of Horace Mann (who is profiled in the "Leaders in Education" feature) and other advocates of the common school, the ideal of universal elementary education was generally acknowledged, if not universally practiced. By 1930, 11 states and the District of Columbia had passed compulsory attendance laws in addition to making common schools generally available.

As a result of these efforts, between the Civil War and World War I, the number of students in schools grew enormously. In 1870, 57 percent of children between 5 and 18 years old were enrolled in

> *The Common School is the greatest discovery ever made by man.*
>
> **—HORACE MANN (1796–1859),**
> nineteenth-century champion of the common school

Pause *and* Reflect

How are the arguments for and against common schools reflected in today's controversies about using vouchers to pay for private or religious schooling?

some form of schooling. By 1918, more than 75 percent of all U.S. children in that age range were enrolled.[4] In 1870, average attendance was 45 days per year; in 1918, it had grown to more than 90 days. Thus, in the hundred years between 1820 and 1920, people saw extraordinary growth in the commitment to free, publicly supported, universal education.

10-2c OTHER DEVELOPMENTS IN ELEMENTARY EDUCATION

Elementary education was influenced strongly by European educators, curricular changes, consolidation of school districts, and the ideas of progressive education.

European Influences

From Europe came new ideas about education. One of the most far-reaching experiments was the **kindergarten**, or "children's garden," where pleasant children's activities such as songs and stories were used to lay a foundation before formal education began. Friedrich Froebel of Germany developed the first kindergarten in 1837. The first U.S. experiments with this sort of education were actually made before the Civil War, but it was not until 1873 that a public school kindergarten was established in St. Louis, and the idea spread rapidly. Elizabeth Peabody brought Froebel's ideas to the United States and was influential in instituting early childhood education in our country.

European influence also resulted in greater emphasis on the interests of the children in elementary education. Johann Pestalozzi modeled his educational doctrines on a Swiss experimental school at the beginning of the nineteenth century. Pestalozzi attempted to educate the heads, hearts, and hands of his pupils, relying on attitudes of acceptance and love of individual students to reach large numbers of poor and handicapped children. Among his instructional techniques were *object lessons*, which focused on actual objects and pictures. Pestalozzi also emphasized learning through sense perceptions and sequencing of learning experiences from the known to the unknown. We can still see the influence of many of Pestalozzi's ideas in American education.

German educator Johann Friedrich Herbart, influenced by Pestalozzi's thinking, stressed that the primary purpose of education was moral development. Herbart also established a highly structured mode of teaching that strongly influenced American teachers during the early part of the twentieth century.

Many European thinkers, and American educators influenced by them, believed students could learn best by direct experience—that is, by using their senses and relating new learning to their previous knowledge. As a result, some schools incorporated more physical activity and manual training in their curricula. This innovation was designed not to train technical workers, but rather to complement and round out traditional intellectual instruction. Maria Montessori was particularly influential in developing a curriculum that emphasized learning through the senses for young children.

The theories espoused by Froebel, Pestalozzi, Herbart, and Montessori, among others, entered American education through their influence on issues of curriculum and instruction. The emphasis on the children's interest and experience, which was advocated by the progressive educators (described in this chapter and in Chapter 9, "What Are the Philosophical Foundations of American Education?") and remains a strong force in American elementary education, owes much to these European thinkers.

Curriculum Changes

The movement toward comprehensive education that occurred during this time period exemplifies one of the key themes of the history of American education.

LEADERS in Education

Horace Mann (1796–1859)

Hulton Archive/Archive Photos/Getty Images

Horace Mann was the radical educational reformer of his day. Born in Franklin, Massachusetts, Mann received only the most rudimentary schooling until he was 15. Most of his education was self-acquired, a fact that profoundly influenced his philosophy of education. He studied hard to be admitted to Brown University, where he became a brilliant student.

In 1827, Mann was elected to the Massachusetts House of Representatives. Although a luminous political career was clearly within his grasp, he became committed instead to education and to the use of political methods to bring about educational reform. Asked why he had exchanged the practice of law for education, Mann answered that "the interests of a client are small compared with the interests of the next generation."

Mann strongly believed in the ideals of the common school and championed its cause throughout his career. He saw education as a tool of liberation by which the poor could raise themselves, African Americans could become emancipated, and children with disabilities could adjust to their handicaps. After all, Mann reasoned, education had brought him fame and position. Thus, more than 150 years ago, the idea of social mobility through education was born in the United States.

For education to be as powerful a force as Mann envisioned it, he thought the school term must be lengthened and teachers' salaries raised. To make learning more relevant and enjoyable, he helped introduce new textbooks designed to illustrate the relationship between knowledge and the practical problems of society. Mann organized libraries in many schools, making books readily available to students. He believed less in the formal curriculum than in individual learning—undoubtedly because of his own self-education.

Mann was intensely interested in teacher preparation, and he believed teachers should serve as intellectual, moral, and cultural models for their communities. He was responsible for the establishment of the Massachusetts Board of Education and for the founding in 1839 of the first public *normal school* (a two-year school chiefly for training elementary teachers) in Lexington, Massachusetts. Although the normal school opened with only three students, the concept spread and was widely imitated throughout the country.

Another goal of Mann was to abolish the cruel floggings that were then routine in the public schools. Most schoolmasters of the day believed flogging was an aid to learning and that it was their duty to drive the "devil" out of their students. Many of them administered from 10 to 20 floggings a day.

Many of Mann's ideas were controversial, but he was most violently denounced for his position on religion in the schools. Although a religious man, he believed religious training belonged outside the schools, which should be run by the state. Because of his views, Mann was attacked from many Boston pulpits.

Mann was regarded as a dreamer and a visionary by many of his colleagues. When he took over the presidency of Antioch College in 1852, it opened its doors to members of all races and religious sects, and admitted women on an equal basis with men; some educators predicted that these measures would promote the collapse of higher education. Were he alive today, Mann might still be fighting for ideas he espoused more than a century ago, because many people have yet to accept these ideas.

During the colonial period, it was hardly necessary for people to know anything beyond the four R's unless they were wealthy and wanted to go on to college. In the early and mid-nineteenth century, the common school curriculum simply expanded on the colonial curriculum. The primary concern, however, was less with religious training and more with the task of obtaining functional knowledge for life after school. Subjects such as spelling, geography, history, and government were added because they were considered important for good citizenship. Instruction in the natural sciences, physical training, and mechanical drawing were also included to provide a complete, well-rounded education.

Consolidation

Although the one-room school had served well in the days of the frontier, in the twentieth century, it became clear that the smaller, poorer districts could not provide the educational opportunities available in larger, wealthier ones. As a result, people in the early 1900s saw a period of consolidation of smaller school districts into larger, unified systems. In 1910, more than half the states allowed such unification. By the 1920s, the growth of industry and the invention of the automobile (and the school bus) had helped consolidate the large number of one-room schools around the country into centrally located, modern facilities that could serve larger areas better than the old district schools did.

The Progressive Education Association

John Dewey (who is discussed more extensively in Chapter 9, "What Are the Philosophical Foundations of American Education?") and other educators tried to create new, experimental, child-centered schools in the early 1900s. In 1919, the Progressive Education Association was established in a formalized attempt to reform education according to the following principles:

1. The child should have freedom to develop naturally.
2. Natural interest is the best motive for work.
3. The teacher is a guide, not a taskmaster.
4. A student's development must be measured scientifically, not just by grades.
5. Students' general health and physical development require attention.
6. The school and the home must work together to meet children's needs.
7. The progressive school should be a leader in trying new educational ideas.[5]

The progressive school movement eventually went in several different directions. Some educators argued for letting children do whatever they wanted; others tried to turn the school into a community center for recreation, adult education, and even social reform. Critics ranged from traditionalist advocates of the subject-centered curriculum to some progressives, including Dewey himself, who argued that the ties between society and the child would be broken if children were granted total freedom to do whatever they wanted.

The 1940s brought a rather conservative reaction to the progressivism of the previous generation. Even so, many ideas we take for granted now—such as teaching through student projects, field trips, and nonlecture methods of instruction— were hotly debated innovations that were introduced by progressive educators and managed to survive the retrenchment of that era.

Since World War II

After World War II, the U.S. role in world affairs expanded dramatically, thus broadening the scope of educational objectives for the nation's schools. The use of the single textbook was supplemented by a great variety of learning resources. Other major developments in elementary education included the rapid growth of kindergartens and an emphasis on providing special educational programs for children with disabilities.

During the period of 1950s and 1960s, we were in what was called "the Cold War" with the Soviet Union. In response to the Soviet launch of the space satellite *Sputnik* in 1957, for example, national curriculum projects emphasizing mathematics, science, and social studies were developed and implemented in our elementary schools.

Also during this period, two types of students received major attention from elementary school educators: the gifted and the disadvantaged. (See Chapter 3, "Who Are Today's Students in a Diverse Society?," for more on gifted education and students from poverty backgrounds.) Gifted students received attention because of U.S. concern over the ongoing Cold War with the Soviet Union and the perceived need to produce scientific breakthroughs to ensure U.S. military superiority over the Soviets. As the movement for civil and human rights gained momentum, an increasing number of curriculum reform movements also focused on "culturally disadvantaged" children. In response to judicial decisions and protests by minority groups, the federal government advanced significant financial aid in an effort to change schools to better address the needs of these children. Compensatory education programs, such as Head Start and Title I of the Elementary and Secondary Education Act, improved the learning of disadvantaged children. (See Chapter 11, "How Are Schools Governed, Influenced, and Financed?," for more detail on compensatory education programs.)

As achievement test and Scholastic Aptitude Test (now known as the SAT) scores declined during the 1970s, many parents, politicians, and educators argued that the schools had tried to accomplish too much and had lost sight of their basic purposes. A return to the basics seemed to be the cry of the late 1970s and early 1980s. Today, academic rigor continues to be emphasized in the form of content standards, but more programs have been developed to meet the needs of students who are at risk of dropping out. (See Chapter 5, "What Is Taught?," and Chapter 12, "How Should Education Be Reformed?," for more discussion on standards.)

Although a public elementary school education is now available everywhere in the United States, the issues of what constitutes a proper education—how comprehensive it should be, how secular it should remain, and how basic learning should be defined—are far from finally settled. The changing nature of what constitutes the basics of education has been another key theme of the history of American education.

10-3 Secondary Education

Today's *public comprehensive high school* evolved from earlier forms of secondary education that included colonial *grammar schools*, which were designed to prepare students either for college or for particular careers, and private *academies*, which were popular throughout the nineteenth century.

10-3a EARLY FORMS

Secondary education changed considerably from the colonial period through the twentieth century, including different kinds of institutions with different purposes.

Latin Grammar Schools

In the colonial period, all secondary education—that is, all education beyond the elementary level—served the sole purpose of preparing for entrance to college. The earliest secondary institution was the **Latin grammar school**, whose name gradually came to mean "college preparatory school." The term *prep school* still carries that classical connotation today.

A boy entered a Latin grammar school around age seven or eight and spent the next seven years learning Latin and Greek from texts written by ancient Romans,

Greeks, or medieval scholars. Much work was memorized, and the student learned composition and writing of Latin verses over three or four years. He also might have given some attention to the study of the Hebrew language and the New Testament.

The first Latin grammar school in the colonies is generally considered to have been the one established in 1635 in Boston. It was public and open to boys of all social classes. The Old Deluder Satan Act of 1647, which required communities of 50 or more families to establish elementary schools, also required communities of 100 or more families to establish Latin schools. At first, Latin grammar schools were found primarily in New England; a bit later, they emerged in the Middle Colonies.

English Grammar Schools

The growth of middle-class businesses in the 1700s led to the demand for a secondary education that would provide practical instruction in everything from navigation and engineering to bookkeeping and foreign languages. To meet this demand, private **English grammar schools** were established. These schools catered to the growing number of students who needed more than elementary instruction but were not interested in preparing for college. Classes were offered at various times and places, sometimes to both girls and boys. Commercial rather than religious subjects were taught. Some subjects, such as music, art, and dancing, were actually not practical, but were meant to train students for socializing in polite company.

Secondary Education for Females

In the 1700s, private-venture English grammar schools were more flexible than the Latin grammar schools and, as a result, were the first secondary institutions to accept female students. Depending on the sophistication of the particular school and the preferences of its clientele, girls typically studied the three R's (reading, 'riting, and 'rithmetic), geography, and French, but they also sometimes learned English grammar, history, and Latin. Some practical vocational subjects, such as bookkeeping, were occasionally taught, along with such traditional and socially accepted skills as art and instrumental music.

Because of the somewhat larger number of private-venture schools in the Middle Colonies, girls who lived there probably had greater educational opportunities than girls elsewhere. Quaker leaders, including William Penn and French-born Anthony Benezet, were concerned with and supported the education of several deprived groups, such as African Americans and Native Americans—and women.

In the South, the daughters of wealthy landowners could receive traditional instruction in the various arts and letters, such as music, dancing, and French, which would give them the social skills appropriate for the lady of a household. By the end of the colonial period, separate class-based education tracks were developed for girls similar to those for boys in the English or Latin grammar schools.

10-3b THE ACADEMY

A new type of secondary school, known as an **academy**, emerged during the second half of the eighteenth century. The academy was an attempt to combine Latin and English grammar schools through separate Latin and English departments within one school. Academies were unlike the Latin grammar schools in that the primary language of the academy was English; they were unlike the English grammar schools in that they included classical subjects in the curriculum. Gradually, the academy took the place of both types of school.

> *The ability to secure an independent livelihood and honorable employ suited to her education and capacities is the only true foundation of the social elevation of woman.*
>
> **—CATHARINE BEECHER (1800–1878),**
> nineteenth-century champion of female academies

The availability of women teachers at low salaries during the late nineteenth century helped keep education costs down but, at the same time, contributed to the low-salary problem that persists even today.

Historical/Corbis Historical/Getty Images

Growth of Academies

The number of private academies grew rapidly after the American Revolution, in response to the growing need for practical business training. By 1850, approximately 6,000 academies were in operation.[6] Compared with the Latin grammar schools, the academies included instruction for a larger age range, which on the lower end overlapped the curriculum of the common schools and on the upper end sometimes provided instruction that was as extensive as that of colleges. Although academies first focused on practical, useful studies rather than on college preparatory courses, the emphasis over the years shifted back to the classical languages and curriculum. Because they were private institutions, the academies were also at greater liberty to accept girls.

Female Academies

The real surge of development in education for girls and young women came in the first half of the 1800s, with the growth of academies and seminaries that were established especially for young women. Female academies were established by Emma Willard in Troy, New York (1821); by Catharine Beecher in Hartford, Connecticut (1828); and by Mary Lyon in South Hadley, Massachusetts (1837).

A secondary education acquired at one of these institutions was often the highest level of education women would ever receive. Eventually, some of these academies themselves became colleges, such as Mount Holyoke College and Wheaton College.

The female academies had to buck the established norms against formal education for women, who in many quarters were still considered intellectually inferior to men. The schools compromised somewhat by offering courses related to home economics in addition to more classical subjects.

In practical terms, the leaders of the women's education movement were committed to two goals. First, they sought to produce women who could handle the domestic chores and challenges of wives and mothers intelligently and wisely so as to "become companions rather than satellites of their husbands."[7] To meet this goal, the curriculum of female academies was designed to include subjects similar,

> *The ladder was there, "from the gutter to the university," and for those stalwart enough to ascend it, the schools were a boon and a path out of poverty.*
>
> —DIANE RAVITCH,
> educational historian

but not identical, to those at men's institutions. Domestic skills were presented as practical applications of the more abstract traditional subjects. Second, women's education was intended to prepare women for life as teachers.

10-3c THE PUBLIC HIGH SCHOOL

Although the private academies reflected the democratic independence of the middle class, their tuition and fees effectively ruled out enrollment of members of the poorer working class. In the years following the American Revolution, the growing demand for free public elementary education understandably provided a basis on which to advocate for free secondary education. Such schooling at public expense was the educational system most appropriate for democracy, it was argued, and the only system that could maintain democracy.

Although by no means universally accepted, the argument for free public high schools was a logical one, based on the inequality of providing elementary schools for everyone but secondary schools only for those who could afford tuition. In 1821, Boston created the first public English high school; a second one, for girls, was established in 1826. Unlike the academies, high schools were governed by the public rather than by private school boards.

The number of public high schools throughout the states increased slowly but steadily as an extension of the common school system. Not everyone favored their spread. Opponents of the idea of public high schools did not dispute the need for common elementary schools, but did argue that secondary school was a luxury and was not within the domain of the taxing authorities. In 1874, in the famous **Kalamazoo case** (*Stuart and Others* v. *School District No. 1 of the Village of Kalamazoo and Others*), the Michigan courts finally ruled that the school district could tax the public to support both high schools and elementary schools. This court case set the precedent for financing public high schools.

Debate over the Secondary Curriculum

In the late nineteenth century, debate shifted from whether public secondary schools should be supported to what the content of the curriculum should be. As remains the case today, guidelines for the curriculum were derived largely from the goals expressed for the schools. One goal was to reduce social tensions and strengthen the democratic form of government by bringing together all social classes and ethnic groups.

Another goal was to provide better preparation for Americans to participate, on graduation, in the full range of industrial occupations. In addition, the high schools were to offer specialized vocational and technical training. At the beginning of the 1800s, the appeal of the academies had been to provide training in studies that prepared students for a practical livelihood and not necessarily for college. By the 1840s, the same goal was being applied to public high schools. Seen in retrospect, the academies were really a link between the earlier grammar school and the later high school. High schools were supposed to provide both a terminal educational experience for most students and a bridge to higher education for those who were capable and chose to pursue further studies.

The Comprehensive High School

To meet these varied purposes, the secondary curriculum underwent considerable revisions between the Civil War and World War I. The basic mathematics courses in arithmetic, geometry, and algebra tended to be taught in a more commercial and practical context. American literature began to compete with English literature, and commercial English was added to the study of literary English. The classical languages continued to give way to modern foreign languages. In the sciences, physiology, chemistry, physics, botany, and astronomy were joined by meteorology, zoology, forestry, agriculture, and geology. Physical education was added to the curriculum. In social studies, the number of courses in American history grew, although European history continued to be central. Civics and citizenship were added to history. Moral philosophy fell away completely and was replaced by purely commercial courses such as typing, stenography, commercial law, home economics, industrial arts, and manual training (wood and metal working).[8] The result was the institution known today as the **public comprehensive high school**, which embodies the notion of comprehensive education, another of the key themes of American education.

During the twentieth century, public comprehensive high schools continued to spread. Between 1890 and 2010, the number of students in public high schools increased as a percentage of all students attending public school, from 1.6 to 29 percent.[9]

10-3d GROWTH OF JUNIOR HIGH AND MIDDLE SCHOOLS

For some time, educators debated the best way to divide grade levels for elementary and secondary training. The main question was when to stop teaching basic skills and start teaching content: Should there be eight elementary grades and four secondary school grades, or six elementary grades and six secondary grades, or some other arrangement?

In an attempt to resolve these issues, educators began to experiment with various ways to reorganize the grades. Finally, in the school year 1909–10, in both Columbus, Ohio, and Berkeley, California, a separate program was established for the intermediate grades 7, 8, and 9. This new grouping was called **junior high school**. By 1926, more than 800 school systems had a six–three–three organization, and that pattern became the dominant one.[10]

Since the 1960s, the system of five elementary–three intermediate–four secondary grades has become increasingly popular, with a **middle school** being home to grades 6, 7, and 8 rather than a junior high school. Advocates argue that middle schools have significant advantages over junior high schools. For one thing, they offer a unique environment where 10- to 13-year-olds are free to grow up at their own rates and where attention is focused on the needs of this age group rather than on mimicking the high school's emphasis on academic and sports competition, as is often the case with junior high schools. Because of the earlier onset of puberty in today's children, sixth-graders may be better served in a school designed for early adolescents in grades 6, 7, and 8 than in an elementary school. Additionally, giving the ninth grade, which is still considered the first year in the college entrance sequence, to the high school frees middle schools to try new programs and new approaches without having to make them specifically applicable to college preparation.

Since the mid-1980s, the United States has made a deepening national commitment to improving the education of its early adolescents, with a strong emphasis on personal growth and development. To encourage this kind of personal growth, middle schools often use interdisciplinary team teaching, block scheduling, advisory homerooms, and exploratory activities and courses.

At least one report has questioned whether students of this age should be in separate schools.[11] A report from the RAND Corporation portrayed the middle school years as a time when American adolescents feel unsafe, socially isolated, and academically unchallenged, and it called for a reconsideration of stand-alone middle schools. The RAND report relied on research indicating that young teens

Pause *and* Reflect

1. What made the development of the American secondary school so unique in the history of the world?
2. How would you group the grade sequence from elementary to secondary school? Why?

do better in K–8 schools than in schools that require a transition to an intermediary school. Additionally, international comparison studies have revealed that the relative performance of U.S. students in mathematics and sciences declines from elementary school to middle school, and national tests of proficiency show that the majority of eighth-graders fail to reach proficiency in mathematics, reading, and science.

Teachers are the key to what goes on in the classroom. In the past, many states permitted teachers with either elementary or secondary teaching licenses to teach in middle school, but now more of them are upping the academic coursework required of elementary school teachers who want to teach in middle schools in an effort to refocus the middle school curriculum on academic subject matter. A number of states have broadened the licensure eligibility of secondary teachers to allow them to teach levels as low as the sixth grade. Thirty-three states also offer teacher licenses specifically for middle school that focus on both adolescent development and academic subject-matter preparation. The RAND study suggests that relatively few teachers obtain this type of licensure; only 12 to 25 percent of teachers have specialized training in middle-grades education.[12]

10-3e SECONDARY EDUCATION TODAY

Look at the pictures of the two secondary classrooms below, one taken in the late 1800s and the other today. In what ways are they similar? How are they different? The most remarkable observation made about secondary education today is how little it has changed over the last 100 years. There have been changes, of course, but they have been small relative to the dramatic changes that have occurred in American living patterns, values, technologies, and careers. The curriculum revolves around subjects that are taught by specialists and are not very different from the subjects offered in schools during World War I.

The reason for this consistency relates to the basic structure of the high school. Its organizing framework, which was initially developed in the nineteenth century, persists today across all regions of the United States. High schools are complicated organizations, requiring considerable orchestration to work efficiently. A change in one part of the system means that other parts must change in tandem. As a result, relatively little change occurs. (Chapter 12, "How Should Education Be Reformed?," examines recent efforts at structural or system-wide reform.)

Library of Congress, Prints & Photographs Division, Reproduction number LC-DIG-hec-20720 (digital file from original negative)

Martin Shields/Alamy Stock Photo

Compared to the changes that have occurred in most of society, the changes in high schools over the past 100 years have been small.

10-4 Private Education

Private schools have always been part of American education. For more than 150 years, until the growth of the common school movement in the early 1800s, most education in the United States was private. Historically, private schools have served three major purposes, providing (1) instruction for various religious denominations, (2) an exclusive education for the wealthy, and (3) an alternative for any group that finds the available forms of education unsatisfactory.

Since the middle of the nineteenth century, by far the largest private school enrollments have been in parochial schools run by the Roman Catholic Church. The earliest Catholic schools existed primarily in the Spanish-speaking Southwest and in French-speaking Louisiana. After 1840, however, Irish and Italian immigration increased the support of Catholic institutions in the North and East. The total number of Catholic schools grew from about 100 in 1840 to about 3,000 in the 1880s, to 8,000 in 1920, and to more than 13,000 in the early 1960s. From that point, however, many Catholic schools have closed. Today, the number of Catholic schools is slightly more than 6,180.[13]

(T) F
The great majority of private schools in the United States have a religious affiliation.

In terms of enrollment, Catholic schools now have a total student membership of about 1.73 million, compared with an estimated 1.93 million students in other religious schools and an estimated 1.07 million in nonsectarian private schools.[14] There are more than 34,500 private schools, with a total enrollment of about 4.9 million, or about 10 percent of all students in U.S. schools. About 67 percent of private schools, enrolling about 78 percent of private school students, have a religious orientation.[15]

Chapter 13, "What Are Your Job Options in Education?," offers more information about teaching opportunities in private schools.

The steady reduction in the percentage of private school students in the nineteenth and early twentieth centuries was not merely a sign of public school strength; it also reflected outright discrimination and pressure against those who wanted to be "different." In an extreme case following World War I, Nebraska passed a law prohibiting the teaching of German in either public or private schools. However, in 1922, the U.S. Supreme Court ruled that a state could not interfere with the prerogative of parents to educate their children as they see fit—in this case, at a private school that taught the German language—simply on the grounds of desiring to "foster a more homogeneous people with American ideals."[16]

When, in 1925, an Oregon law required all children to attend public school, a Roman Catholic school and another private school successfully challenged the law on the grounds that their Fourteenth Amendment rights were being threatened. In a landmark decision in *Pierce* v. *The Society of Sisters*, the Supreme Court overturned the Oregon law, holding that the act "unreasonably interferes with the liberty of parents and guardians to direct the upbringing and education of children under their control."[17] As a consequence of this decision, nonpublic schools survived efforts to eliminate them.

Public schools have clearly become the principal mode of education in the United States. Nevertheless, private education has remained an important alternative for about 10 percent of the population. This fact reflects a paradox. On the one hand, from the early days private schools have represented the freedom of immigrant groups to pursue life in America and to educate their children

Pause *and* Reflect

1. Do you believe the role of private education is likely to increase, decrease, or stay the same in the upcoming years? Why?
2. What are the advantages and disadvantages of private education versus public education?

as they choose. That privilege was essential to the young democracy and still represents a basic freedom of choice in America. On the other hand, some argue that private education supports a caste system that is, in principle, undemocratic. The very existence of private forms of education can be viewed as an implied criticism either of the quality of public education or of its availability on equal terms to all comers, irrespective of class, religion, or race. As discussed in detail in Chapter 12, "How Should Education Be Reformed?," this issue has become more prominent as school voucher plans expand to include private and religious school options.

The picture of American education that we have drawn up to now has been quite rosy because the educational achievements of this country over the past 350 years are clearly impressive. There is, however, a less pleasant side to the picture. The history of education provides insight into people's values in general, and the educational experience of minorities tends to reflect how a society relates to them. The somewhat idealized image of the melting pot begins to break down when we look at the experience of nonwhite groups.

10-5 Education of Minorities

The United States is a multiracial, multiethnic, and multiclass society. Indeed, many people consider it to be one of the most successful mixed societies the world has ever seen. Even so, it is far from perfect, and many children born into poor or minority-group families face severe disadvantages in their attempts to live decent lives and to climb the ladder of success. Schooling is intended to help individuals in this process. Traditionally, however, ethnic minorities such as African Americans, Hispanic Americans, Native Americans, and Asian Americans have not been given equal educational opportunity in the United States. Not until the late nineteenth century, for example, did the federal government make any serious effort to provide education for Native Americans. Many groups struggled throughout the nineteenth and twentieth centuries to claim their share of the growing access to education that was developed for the majority of white students. American society is still suffering today from the effects of educational neglect of various minority groups.

In our coverage of the education of minorities, we often discuss members of a minority group as though they were a homogeneous subgroup of Americans. In reality, the terms *African Americans, Asian Americans, Hispanic Americans,* and *Native Americans* encompass many ethnic, national, and linguistic groups. Although it is convenient to use these broader terms, we should not forget that great diversity exists within each subgroup.

10-5a EDUCATION OF AFRICAN AMERICANS

For African Americans, the struggle for equal access to schooling and education paralleled the growth of education for the majority, beginning with efforts to simply provide schools. Efforts throughout the twentieth century focused next on offering a broader variety of curriculum options to African American students, and then on removing legal obstacles to equality of education.

Before the Civil War

As is true of colonial education generally, the earliest motivation to educate African Americans was religious. In New England, Reverend Cotton Mather started an

> *Prejudices, it is well known, are most difficult to eradicate from the heart whose soil has never been loosened or fertilized by education; they grow there, firm as weeds among stones.*
>
> —CHARLOTTE BRONTË (1816–1855),
> nineteenth-century novelist (author of *Jane Eyre*)

evening school for slaves as early as 1717. In the South, the first attempts to educate African Americans were carried out by clergy, particularly English representatives of the Society for the Propagation of the Gospel in Foreign Parts. To dubious slave owners, ministers defended the education of slaves not only as a religious duty to save their souls but also because conversion to Christianity, it was believed, would make them more docile.[18]

In the North, schools were established for free African Americans. In 1731, Anthony Benezet, a French-born Quaker, started a school for slave and free African American children in Philadelphia. In 1774, another school was begun by Benjamin Franklin, as president of the Abolitionist Society. In 1787, an African Free School was established in New York City, with an enrollment of 40 students, which grew to more than 500 by 1820. The city provided funds in 1824 and took over the school in 1834, thus providing education for African Americans before many white children were receiving it.

Yet conditions were not all bright in the North. In 1833, Prudence Crandall, a white schoolmistress in Canterbury, Connecticut, began to take in African American girls. The villagers boycotted the school, threw manure into its well, and tried to burn it down. Finally, a mob broke the windows, and the school was closed.[19]

In the South, following slave rebellions in the early 1800s, states gradually prohibited altogether the teaching of African American children, whether slave or free. Some slaves were taught to read by favorably disposed masters. More generally, slave owners reasoned that reading would lead to thinking, and thinking would lead to the desire for freedom. As the Civil War approached, abolitionist agitation often emerged from the few liberal colleges that allowed the enrollment of African American students, such as Oberlin College in Ohio and Bowdoin College in Maine.

The Late Nineteenth Century

In the period following the Civil War, the seeds for the education of African Americans that had been sown before the war slowly began to sprout. During the period of Reconstruction, from 1865 into the 1870s, the federal government, through the Freedmen's Bureau and, in the former Confederacy, an occupying army, attempted to promote African American voting registration and schooling. Help also came from private and religious philanthropies in the North. Because it was hoped that whites also would benefit from these endeavors, schooling was advocated for the general public as well. Despite these efforts, the common school movement remained weakest in the South. At first, most whites there refused to participate not only in integrated schools but also in segregated schools, both of which they believed the northern carpetbaggers were forcing on them.

By the end of Reconstruction, southern whites began to allow the existence of separate schools for African Americans. African American enrollment in the schools, which had been only 2 percent of the school-age children in 1850, reached 10 percent by 1870 and 35 percent by 1890, although it dropped somewhat after that during a period of severe repression by the new "white state" governments.[20] During this period, "Jim Crow" laws were passed, separating African Americans from whites in all areas of life.

Into these conditions, a young African American teacher named Booker T. Washington (1856–1915) was called to start an African American normal school in Tuskegee, Alabama, in 1881. Originally named the Tuskegee Normal School for Colored Teachers, it was later renamed the Tuskegee Institute. In Tuskegee, Washington found only a few students, no buildings or classrooms, and a hostile white community.

Washington, who had been born a slave, thought that the traditional curriculum of the classics would neither prepare his students to help other African Americans learn nor help ameliorate the tensions with the white community. Believing strongly in the idea of learning by doing, Washington instructed his students to build the school themselves. In this process, they learned practical skills, grew produce that could be sold to the white community, and in general showed the whites that African Americans could be productive members of society. Washington gradually came to be considered the outstanding African American leader of the time by the white establishment.

Over time, a growing number of young African Americans who, unlike Washington, had not been born into slavery came to believe that Washington's conciliatory policy of training for menial positions in white society would not benefit African American people in the long run. They suggested that, although practical training was necessary, an intellectually sound and academically rich program of study must also be established for the "talented tenth" of the student body, who would form the African American intellectual leadership. This was the view of W. E. B. DuBois (1868–1963), an African American intellectual and scholar who held a doctorate from Harvard.

> *Education must not simply teach work—it must teach life.*
>
> —W. E. B. DUBOIS (1868–1963),
> African American civil rights activist

In 1862, the U.S. Congress passed the **Morrill Act**. This legislation granted each state a minimum of 30,000 acres of federal land with the proviso that the income from the rent or sale of these lands must be used to establish colleges for the study of agriculture and mechanical arts. A total of 6 million acres of federal land were donated to the states. The resulting land-grant institutions, such as the University of Illinois, Texas A&M, and Michigan State University, became the great multipurpose state universities that now enroll hundreds of thousands of students from all segments of society.

The Tuskegee Normal School was established in 1881 by Booker T. Washington.

Bettmann/Getty Images

In 1890, Congress enacted a second Morrill Act that increased the endowment of land to the original land-grant colleges but forbade the granting of money to a college with an admission policy that discriminated against nonwhites unless a separate facility for African Americans existed nearby. This second Morrill Act provided federal support to states to create "separate but equal" colleges for African Americans. As a result of this legislation, a number of so-called **1890 institutions** were created for the higher education of African Americans. Many of these historically African American colleges, such as Florida A&M and North Carolina A&T, still exist today, albeit now as integrated institutions.

In 1896, in the case of *Plessy* **v.** *Ferguson*, the U.S. Supreme Court upheld the constitutionality of "separate but equal" accommodations for African Americans. Although the ruling originally referred to seating in a railroad car, it was quickly extended to schools. The practical significance of this ruling was its federal sanction of the legal separation of African American schoolchildren from white children, most notably in the South—a condition that would persist for the next 58 years.

The Twentieth Century

The fact that southern schools for African Americans were not equal to those for whites is woefully clear from looking at financial expenditures alone. In 1912, the southern states, as a group, paid white teachers slightly more than $10 per white child in school but paid African American teachers less than $3 per African American child. In the 1930s, in 10 southern states, African American children accounted for 34 percent of the school population but received only 3 percent of the funds available for school transportation. Discrimination also existed in the distribution of federal funds, particularly in vocational education, the largest and most important educational program subsidized by the federal government.[21]

Most northern states did not have **de jure school segregation**—that is, segregation by law. Nevertheless, the crowding of African Americans into isolated neighborhoods often resulted in **de facto school segregation**—that is, segregation resulting primarily from residential patterns. Furthermore, large numbers of southern African American children who migrated with their parents to northern cities often had to be demoted because they had not mastered the same amount of material as their northern counterparts. Generally, even in the North, African American teachers taught African American children. For a vivid, firsthand description of one educator's experiences in segregated schools, read this chapter's "Voices from the Classroom" feature.

Although these conditions persisted in varying degrees through the 1940s, some gains were achieved. For example, the average daily attendance of African American children increased and approached that of white students. The salaries of African American teachers also increased, reducing the economic gap between African American and white teachers with equal training.

In the late 1940s, the National Association for the Advancement of Colored People (NAACP) began taking cases dealing with inequality in educational opportunities to the courts. Beginning with universities rather than elementary schools, the NAACP succeeded in having the courts rule that various law school facilities for African Americans were clearly unequal to those for whites.

The stage was then set for the precedent-shattering case of *Brown* **v.** *Board of Education of Topeka* (1954), in which the Supreme Court ruled that separate educational facilities are inherently unequal and that laws requiring white and

VOICES from the Classroom

Teaching in Segregated Schools

Mary Reese lived in Charlottesville, Virginia, until her death in 2014. She was an elementary school teacher for 11 years before becoming a principal. She later served as assistant superintendent of schools in Charlottesville, Virginia, and associate director of the American Association of School Administrators.

College diploma and job contract in hand, I headed to my first teaching job in a small, rural, segregated school. The advice, help, and insights provided by the experienced principal and teachers that first year convinced me that teaching was indeed a good career choice. It mattered not that the "new" books they were excited about receiving turned out to be the "used" books from the white school and that the children had to walk fairly long distances to get to school because there was no bus transportation provided for them. The belief that a new school year meant a new opportunity to help children created an unbelievable aura of new beginnings.

I later became a teacher in a segregated school in a large urban school district—a school serving students from three public housing units. Again, "new" books, except for newly adopted state textbooks, included used books from other schools. School repairs, if made at all, were taken care of after the needs of the white schools had been attended to.

One of the most powerful insights from both of these experiences was how important the teacher was to the life of the students and the community in which they lived. I taught more than the basic academic skills to students. I assumed the role of family social worker, financial adviser, and any other roles necessary to help students and their parents believe that the school was there for them. I had to convince the student and parent that getting a good education was the key to a better future. I took it as my responsibility to help them learn that segregation was only a barrier if we let it become one.

I became the principal of that urban school after 10 years of teaching in it. Shortly thereafter, the school was integrated, and we became a mix of low-income African American, and middle-class white students. It was bittersweet to see much of the maintenance work that had been requested, but never done, suddenly being taken care of without my having to submit work order requests. It was humiliating to have white parents come and give the woodwork and cafeteria equipment "the white-glove treatment." But it was as equally rewarding to know that their fears would be unfounded because of my belief that the school should be a clean and safe place for any student and staff member assigned there. Because we already had excellent teachers, a strong academic program, and a belief in and requirement of strong parental involvement, integration proceeded more smoothly than in some of the other schools.

nonwhite students to go to different schools were illegal. This decision held that segregated schools are inherently unequal because the effects of such schools are likely to differ. Thus a new component was introduced into the theme of educational opportunity: Equality of educational opportunity became defined in terms of the effects—rather than the provision—of schooling. Before *Brown*, the community and educational institutions were expected only to provide equal resources such as teachers, facilities, and materials. Responsibility for the best use of those resources lay with the child and the child's family. In the *Brown* decision, the Supreme Court found that even if the facilities and teacher salaries provided were identical, "equality of educational opportunity" would not exist in segregated schools. In the decades since then, many people have come to consider it the responsibility of the educational institution, not the child, to create achievement.

Ⓣ F
Efforts to desegregate the public schools from the 1960s through the 1980s came as a result of a Supreme Court ruling.

Desegregation Efforts

In *Brown* v. *The Board of Education,* the Supreme Court concluded that de jure school segregation violated the Fourteenth Amendment of the Constitution. Early desegregation efforts, therefore, were aimed at eliminating de jure segregation. Throughout the 1960s and into the 1970s, many school systems, often in response to specific court orders, also attempted to reduce or eliminate de facto school segregation. As a result, many school districts underwent desegregation efforts. What have been the results of these efforts? Several researchers have concluded that desegregated schools have accomplished more than mere educational reform—that is, African American students who attended integrated schools experienced desegregation in several aspects of adult life, including attending predominantly white colleges and universities, working in desegregated settings, and living in desegregated neighborhoods.[22]

Busing. Although these long-range findings are quite positive, desegregation efforts have produced some negative results. One major problem has concerned busing. Busing students to desegregated schools was one of the most inflammatory issues in education in the 1970s and 1980s. Emotions on the topic often ran very high—so high, in fact, that white parents sometimes slashed bus tires, burned buses, and physically prevented buses from running to avoid having their children bused to other schools.[23]

Busing to achieve desegregation has experienced mixed success. One of the most successful busing plans began in Berkeley, California, in 1968, without any disruptive incidents; standardized test scores subsequently indicated that white, African American, and Asian American students all made better progress after desegregation.[24] In many other communities, attempts to desegregate the schools by busing met with tremendous community resistance.

By the end of the 1980s, court-ordered busing was no longer the preferred method for integrating the schools. Busing, of course, was never an end in itself. It was merely one means of integrating society, and polls indicate that even opponents

Efforts to desegregate schools, especially busing white children to desegregated schools, met with stiff opposition from white parents in some communities, including those in the north.

Barney Sellers/ZUMA Press/Memphis/TN/U.S./Newscom

of involuntary busing agree that our society needs to be integrated. However, that goal remains elusive.

Big-city desegregation. A major obstacle to desegregating big-city public schools is that the minority percentage of inner-city populations has increased dramatically during the past several decades. In part, this trend has been the result of "white flight"—the exodus of white residents as parents have chosen to move to the suburbs or place their children in private schools. (This term is somewhat misleading, however, as not only whites are fleeing the city schools; middle-class African Americans are also leaving to give their children a chance to be educated in better schools.) Today, cities such as New York, Los Angeles, Chicago, Detroit, Atlanta, Houston, and Dallas have school minority enrollments over 90 percent.[25] How can schools in major cities be desegregated when the percentage of racial minority students is growing and the percentage of white students is decreasing?

In addition, several Supreme Court decisions during the 1990s dramatically reversed school desegregation plans ordered by lower courts, thereby eliminating much of the pressure to desegregate schools. In these rulings, the court essentially conceded that practical limits exist as to what a federal court can do to remedy prior discrimination; once school districts have corrected the initial racial imbalances, they are not required to remedy subsequent imbalances caused by demographic changes. In a 2007 ruling, the Supreme Court, by a five-to-four margin, further backed away from desegregation efforts by striking down plans in Seattle and Louisville that sought to maintain school-by-school diversity by identifying students by race and assigning them to schools based on that classification.

Recent developments. Increasingly segregated residential patterns and the slackening of legal pressures to desegregate during the 1980s and 1990s have led to a phenomenon known as **resegregation**, in which schools are becoming more segregated again. Evidence suggests that resegregation of African Americans has reached the levels seen before 1970. Fifty-eight percent of Black students attend schools whose minority enrollment is over 75 percent.[26]

Although many political and educational leaders remain committed to desegregated schools, others are questioning whether integration is an idea whose time has passed. In many communities, these leaders, who are typically members of minority groups, call for shifting the emphasis from integrating schools to improving the quality of one-race neighborhood schools. They have lost faith in the idea that desegregation is the answer to calls for better schools. These supporters of resegregation argue that it demeans African American children to believe that they can learn only when they sit next to white children in desegregated schools. Some also think that resegregation will protect African American culture from the gradual eradication that would occur in an integrated setting. Further, they argue, resegregation would relieve African Americans of the disproportionate burden they have carried under most desegregation arrangements.

Supporters of desegregation counter with the argument that most parents are mainly interested in good schools for their own children, not for the children of others. Accordingly, they say, whites will support only African American students who happen to be in school with their own children. Thus, if African American children are to benefit educationally, they need to attend school with white children. Otherwise, resegregation forces poor, largely African American school districts in cities with a low tax base to continue their losing struggle to find educational money that they don't have. As one advocate for desegregation says,

> *Segregation was wrong when it was forced by white people, and I believe it is still wrong when it is requested by black people.*
>
> **—CORETTA SCOTT KING (1927–2006),**
> wife of Martin Luther King, Jr. and civil rights leader

"[African Americans] who favor resegregation are doing whites the great favor of relieving both their guilty consciences and their pocketbooks."[27]

Desegregation versus integration. Another point must be made before we close this discussion—namely, desegregation does not necessarily lead to integration. True integration is a very human process that can occur only after desegregation has gone into effect. It happens when people from different racial and ethnic backgrounds learn to be comfortable with one another and to get along together. Integration means ending racial prejudice and respecting ethnic differences. Anyone who has spent time in racially mixed schools, especially high schools, knows that African American and white students who attend the same school can still be extremely distant from one another. Just bringing together students from different racial groups, social classes, and neighborhood backgrounds will not automatically lead to friendship, understanding, and appreciation of one another. As long as the larger society remains segregated, efforts to integrate our schools are likely to produce tension, at least in the short run. Integrating individuals with increasingly diverse racial, cultural, and linguistic backgrounds remains one of the key themes and challenges to schools and society.

10-5b EDUCATION OF NATIVE AMERICANS

As early as 1622, in an ominous foreshadowing of future policies, one colonist wrote back to England that it was easier to conquer the Indians than to civilize them.[28] The education of Native Americans traditionally received less public attention than that of African Americans because Native Americans were considered an impediment to westward expansion; they were far from major population centers; and their dealings were largely with the federal government.

Pause *and* Reflect

1. Where do you stand on the issue of de facto resegregation of urban schools? What, if anything, should be done about it?
2. In what ways did desegregation of American schools work, and in what ways has it failed?

Initially, the education of Native Americans, like that of African Americans, had a religious purpose. Once they had been put on reservations, Native Americans received schooling from missionaries, who attempted to "civilize" them through the three R's and, of course, the fourth R—religion. In the 1890s, these missionary schools were gradually replaced by government boarding schools, which tried to forcefully assimilate Native Americans into the mainstream culture by prohibiting them from speaking their native language and teaching them skills associated with white society, such as farming and mechanical skills for boys and domestic chores for girls. Little emphasis was placed on academics.

The people who had been living on the North American continent for 20,000 years finally became American citizens in 1924—but that did not mean they controlled their own education. The federal government, through the Bureau of Indian Affairs (BIA), directed the education of Native Americans until the

My son, Wind Wolf, is not an empty glass coming into your class to be filled. He is a full basket coming into a different environment and society with something special to share. Please let him share his knowledge, heritage, and culture with you and his peers.

—ROBERT LAKE-THOM,
author and native healer in the Seneca
and Cherokee tribes

mid-1970s. During this time, Native American participation was virtually ignored, as was acknowledgment of their own culture in their educational programs.

By 1965, Native Americans had begun to demand control of their schools, and a few demonstration sites for such tribal schools were funded. These schools were able to include much of the native culture in their curricula, but they remained financially dependent on the federal government, which meant limited instructional materials and lower-paid teachers than in many public schools.

Between 1972 and 1975, Congress enacted three bills that affected Native American education and self-determination. These bills encouraged the establishment of community-run schools, offered grants to develop culturally relevant and bilingual curriculum materials, and established an advisory council made up of Native Americans. The Department of the Interior's BIA is still actively involved in educational matters, though it now acts in a supportive rather than directive capacity. The federal government has shifted much responsibility for educating Native Americans from the BIA and tribal schools to public schools. The BIA oversees 183 schools across 23 states, primarily located in Arizona, New Mexico, North Dakota, and South Dakota. Approximately 70 percent of the schools are operated by Native American tribes or tribal organizations under grants or contracts with the BIA. The schools serve over 41,000 students—about 6 percent of all Native American students enrolled in K–12 schools in the United States.[29] The other 94 percent of Native American students in grades K–12 attend public schools.

This trend may have helped reduce the isolation of Native American students. However, because Native American community involvement in public education is slight, the move toward public schooling has resulted in a loss of the limited control Native Americans had begun to exercise over the education their children receive.

Today, the education of the Native American population in the United States, about 644,000 students or 1.2 percent of the school-age population, is still plagued by problems such as poverty, parental alcoholism, underachievement, absenteeism, overage students, and a high dropout rate. Indeed, Native American students drop out of school more often than members of any other racial group except Hispanics.[30] Many Native Americans believe that a culturally appropriate curriculum is needed to overcome these deficiencies and reduce the cultural discontinuities between home and school. Only a small percentage of Native American students have teachers from their same tribe; most of their teachers are white females. One evaluation of Native American schools concluded that they should integrate their programs into a whole-school, standards-based reform effort and increase the participation of the Native American community.

The **Every Student Succeeds Act** of 2015 (ESSA) promises unprecedented opportunities and funding for incorporating our nation's many indigenous cultures and languages into public schools serving Native American students. ESSA further solidifies the status of indigenous language and cultures in public schools through newly appropriated funds that support indigenous language immersion programs. It also allocates additional funds to promote indigenous languages and cultures, culturally responsive education, college and career preparation, dropout prevention, and mental health services. The success of ESSA with Native Americans depends on how well the programs are implemented and whether sufficient funding continues to be allocated.

At the beginning of the twenti-eth century, special schools for Native Americans, such as the Carlisle Indian School in Carlisle, Pennsylvania, taught basic skills, such as woodworking, to students.

Library of Congress, Prints & Photographs Division, Reproduction number LC-USZ62-26793 (b&w film copy neg.)

10-5c EDUCATION OF HISPANIC AMERICANS

As with Native Americans, the first contact Spanish-speaking people had with the United States was often a result of annexation and warfare. Although they have lived in the continental United States for more than 400 years, Hispanic Americans came into substantial contact with whites about 200 years ago, and almost from the beginning there was a cultural clash. Hispanic American children first attended religious mission schools, which were gradually replaced by secular public schools. In the process, the Spanish language and Hispanic American culture were subjected to a type of discrimination that was perhaps less blatant than that against African Americans, but just as pervasive. The common school of the nineteenth and twentieth centuries, although it opened educational and social opportunities for some minority students, often sealed off those opportunities for Hispanic Americans. Hispanic children tended to receive lower scores than white children on English-language intelligence quotient (IQ) tests, which not only were written in a language that was not their own, but also reflected white middle-class values. All of these factors combined to reinforce an image of Hispanic American children as intellectually inferior to their white counterparts.

There are about 5 million English Language Learners (ELLs) in public schools, and over 75 percent speak Spanish at home.[31] These students are likely to have parents who have less education than those who speak mostly English at home. Children whose parents have not completed high school, and who do not speak English, are less likely to receive at home the background skills and knowledge to begin school successfully. Schools need to develop programs to address the needs of these students, particularly those with limited English proficiency.

Because of increased tax burdens, some states enacted laws to deny a public education for children of illegal immigrants. However, in 1982, the U.S. Supreme Court in the case of *Plyler* v. *Doe*, struck down a Texas statute that denied free education funding for children of illegal immigrants. The court ruled that the Texas law was a violation of the Equal Protection Clause of the Fourteenth Amendment, which guarantees rights to people (not citizens), because undocumented immigrant

▶❚❚ TeachSource Video Case

Bilingual Education: An Elementary Two-Way Immersion Program

Watch the video clips, study the artifacts in the case, and reflect on the following questions:

1. How does the scenario depicted in this case compare with the historical treatment of Hispanic students described in this chapter?

2. How can you begin developing the skills you will need to work effectively with a diverse group of students?

children are people. The court majority found that the Texas law discriminated against children based on a legal characteristic over which the children had little control, namely, the fact of their having been brought illegally into the United States by their parents. The court's majority also observed that denying the children in question of a proper education would likely contribute to "the creation and perpetuation of a subclass of illiterates within our boundaries, surely adding to the problems and costs of unemployment, welfare, and crime." The majority refused to accept that any substantial state interest would be served by discrimination on this basis, and it struck down the Texas law.[32]

Since the 1940s, the courts have acknowledged that de facto segregation exists between white and Hispanic American schoolchildren, and have required corrective integration plans. The 1965 Elementary and Secondary Education Act provided new support to the education of Hispanic Americans, just as it did to the education of Native Americans. Another response has been the establishment of bilingual education programs to provide students with instruction in their native tongue at the same time they learn English. The goal of such bilingual education programs is for students to enter the English-language curriculum at the appropriate age levels for their grades. However, as mentioned in Chapter 3, "Who Are Today's Students in a Diverse Society?," bilingual education programs have fallen out of favor in recent years and have been replaced with English immersion programs in such states as California and Arizona. (The Video Case, *Bilingual Education: An Elementary Two-Way Immersion Program*, shows one current approach to teaching children whose first language is Spanish, known as two-way bilingual education.)

Although significant progress has been made, much concern remains about the education of Hispanics in the United States. For example, the high school completion rate for Hispanic Americans is 80 percent, compared with 88.6 and 77.8 percent for whites and African Americans, respectively.[33] Approximately 19 percent of Hispanic adults have earned bachelor's degrees, compared with 40 and 26 percent for whites and African Americans, respectively.[34] Furthermore, reading and mathematics proficiencies are significantly lower for the Hispanic American population in comparison with the white population. The public schools have not served these students well, and the cost of this failure in human and economic terms is enormous.

Hispanic American youth represent the fastest-growing segment of the U.S. population; about one in four children in the public schools is Hispanic. Demographers project that increasingly higher percentages of Hispanic American students will be enrolled in public schools in the twenty-first century, so the schools' responses to these students' needs will have important consequences for society. The problem is made even more acute by the estimated 11 million illegal immigrants living in the United States. Without increased educational attainment, Hispanic Americans, both legal and illegal, will be relegated to low-skill jobs and locked into the lowest socioeconomic brackets, with negative consequences for all Americans.

▶❚❚ **TeachSource** Video Case

© Cengage 2016

Diversity: Teaching in a Multiethnic Classroom

Watch the video clips, study the artifacts in the case, and reflect on the following questions:

1. How does the scenario depicted in this case stand in contrast to the historical treatment of Asian Americans, both in schools and in the larger U.S. society, that is described in this chapter?

2. In one of the bonus videos, the two teachers talk about how to make the best use of the limited number of students with strong Japanese language reading skills in the class. If a class had an even smaller percentage of students who shared a language other than English, could a teacher carry out a project like this one? How? In what other ways might a teacher incorporate the cultures of English language learners into the curriculum in a way that was useful for all students?

10-5d EDUCATION OF ASIAN AMERICANS

The diversity of Asian Americans is evident from the historical beginnings of different groups of Asian Americans in the United States, and it persists in educational issues today. The three largest groups of Asian Americans are individuals of Chinese, Filipino, and Japanese heritage.

Discrimination against early Asian Americans was rampant, especially in the West, where most Asian Americans originally settled. Although immigrants from China, the Philippines, and Japan often entered the United States to fill the need for hard-labor jobs, whites resented the competition for employment. Exclusionary laws limiting immigration of these groups were passed in the late 1800s and early 1900s.

School segregation of Chinese American children in California lasted until at least 1946. Japanese American children in California were forced to attend segregated schools up until World War II. With the outbreak of World War II, the "yellow peril," perceived as emanating from Japanese Americans, resulted in the imprisonment in detention camps of more than 110,000 Japanese Americans, most of whom were American-born citizens. With the end of World War II, discrimination against Asian Americans began to subside. Naturalization rights were eventually extended to resident Asian aliens. (The Video Case, *Diversity: Teaching in a Multiethnic Classroom*, shows how a teacher of an elementary school class with a large percentage of Japanese students works with the class today.)

Many Asian Americans benefited from greater job opportunities during the post–World War II expansion of the U.S. economy. Previously established immigration restrictions were lifted in 1965, and the influx of Asian immigrants greatly increased. Since the U.S. withdrawal from Vietnam in 1975, enormous numbers of Indochinese immigrants have also journeyed to the United States and entered our school systems.

Asians and Pacific Islanders currently account for approximately 5 percent of all students enrolled in public elementary and secondary schools, and this figure is expected to continue to rise for the foreseeable future. Current census estimates indicate that Asians and Pacific Islanders number roughly 18.2 million, or about 5.6 percent of the U.S. population.[35]

Owing to the higher educational achievement and income levels of some Asian Americans, this group has often been touted as a "model minority" that has overcome discrimination through hard work, perseverance, and industriousness. This rosy stereotype is misleading, however, and has sometimes contributed to misconceptions and complacency in meeting the educational needs and concerns of Asian American students. The success levels achieved by more recent Asian immigrants have varied because of the range of educational levels and previous socioeconomic circumstances associated with these new Americans.

Many recent Asian American immigrants to the United States have little or no knowledge of the English language. Slightly over 74 percent of Asian Americans spoke a language other than English at home.[36] This issue creates formidable language and cultural barriers for students entering the U.S. educational system, and it may lead to serious family–school discontinuities, alienation from school, and dropout problems. The Supreme Court established in *Lau v. Nichols* (1974) that schools must offer students sufficient special instruction to be afforded equal educational opportunity. (See Chapter 3, "Who Are Today's Students in a Diverse Society?," for more on *Lau* v. *Nichols.*)

Parental and community involvement of Asian Americans in the education process also should be fostered. In part because of the respect traditionally accorded to educators in their native countries, parents of Asian American students often hesitate to intervene when they are dissatisfied with their children's educational progress, instead deferring to the educational system's authority. Another deterrent to parental participation is the fact that a high proportion of Asian American families have two parents employed, a situation that makes attendance at traditional teacher conferences or parent–teacher organization (PTO) meetings difficult. Many communities are making efforts to organize and voice the needs of Asian American students.

As the number of Asian American students continues to grow, it will become increasingly important for teachers and administrators to be knowledgeable about and sensitive to the special problems and needs of Asian American students and their families. To serve these students adequately in our schools, educators must keep in mind that Asian Americans are a changing and complex group whose achievement, aspirations, and learning styles should not be relegated to a simplistic stereotype.

10-5e ACCESS AND EQUALITY OF EDUCATIONAL OPPORTUNITY

From our discussion of the education of minority students, it is clear that, even today, large numbers of minority-group students are leaving school without the academic and occupational skills necessary to function effectively in American society. The same is also true of poor students from all ethnic groups. Who—if anyone—is to blame for this situation? The schools? The students? The families? Teachers and administrators? Is the responsibility that of society as a whole, and are the schools merely being made a scapegoat? Talk to five different people, and you will probably hear five different opinions about where blame should be fixed.

At one extreme are those who think the problem resides in the so-called deficiencies of poor and minority children. Their impoverished home life, their particular cultural milieu, English language deficiencies, and even their mental capacities are cited as the sources of their unequal results in school.

At the other extreme are those who claim the problem lies with the schools. Some suggest that the problem is linked to the way schools are governed and financed. Numerous court cases have challenged the school finance systems in various states, charging that when educational spending in rich school districts exceeds that of poor districts by two or three times, students in the poor districts are not getting access to equal educational opportunities. In a number of cases, courts have ordered legislatures to redesign the school finance system. (See Chapter 11, "How Are Schools Governed, Influenced, and Financed?," for more on the topic of equitable school finance.)

Others believe that teaching must be improved, that teachers today neither stimulate nor instruct poor and minority children with the intensity that is needed. Teachers expect these children to do poorly, they claim, and this expectation becomes a self-fulfilling prophecy. As described in Chapter 3, "Who Are Today's Students in a Diverse Society?," this position assumes that it is the school's obligation to diagnose the learners' needs, concerns, and cognitive and affective styles and to adjust its program accordingly. In fact, the Every Student Succeeds Act of 2015, which requires schools to report the academic performance of students in various racial and ethnic groups, is intended to close the academic achievement gaps between white and Asian American students on the one hand, and on the other hand among African American, Hispanic American, and Native American students. Not everyone accepts this assertion, of course. In fact, many argue that the school should do its best to provide equal educational resources for all its students but cannot be held accountable for differences in student learning.

As with most controversies, the real answer probably lies somewhere in between these two extremes: Many poor and minority students do come to school with certain deficiencies, but the schools need to learn how to overcome them.

TABLE 10.1   Key Events and Curriculum Trends in American Education

Time Period	Key Educational and National Events	Educational Trends/Emphases and Characteristics of Curriculum	Dominant Educational Philosophies
1620–Revolutionary War	1635: Establishment of the Boston Latin grammar school 1647: Massachusetts Old Deluder Satan Act 1687–1690: First edition of The *New England Primer*	Education was limited by sex and socioeconomic class. Curricula emphasized religious training (Bible), moral development, reading, writing, and arithmetic basics.	Perennialism
1770s–1820s	1775–1783: Revolutionary War 1783: Noah Webster publishes *American Spelling Book* 1785, 1787: Northwest Ordinances 1788: U.S. Constitution ratified	Education emphasized literacy to make democracy work. Curriculum emphases included moral development and either practical education for a career or university education.	Perennialism
1820s–1880s	1821: First U.S. public high school 1821: Emma Willard establishes first school for women's higher education 1839: First U.S. public normal school, Lexington, Massachusetts 1860: First U.S. English-language kindergarten 1861–1865: Civil War 1862: First Morrill Act establishes land-grant institutions	Education was used to promote "melting pot" assimilation of immigrants and minorities. Curriculum emphases included basic tools of literacy, conservative moral values (McGuffey Readers), and cultivation of American identity.	Perennialism
1880s–1950s	1890: Second Morrill Act calls for nondiscrimination in college admissions or "separate but equal" institutions 1896: U.S. Supreme Court ruling in *Plessy* v. *Ferguson* establishes separate schools for whites and blacks 1914–1918: World War I 1930s: Great Depression 1939–1945: World War II 1944: GI Bill funds higher education for veterans	Child-centered curriculum became popular, emphasizing activities and experiences rather than verbal and literacy skills; cooperative rather than individual learning activities; citizenship; and self-adjustment.	Progressivism Romanticism

(Continued)

| TABLE 10.1 | Key Events and Curriculum Trends in American Education (Continued) |

Time Period	Key Educational and National Events	Educational Trends/Emphases and Characteristics of Curriculum	Dominant Educational Philosophies
1950s–1970s	1954: U.S. Supreme Court ruling in *Brown* v. *Board of Education of Topeka* requires desegregation of schools 1957: Soviet Union launches *Sputnik* 1965: Elementary and Secondary Education Act 1971: U.S. Supreme Court ruling in *Swann* v. *Charlotte–Mecklenburg County* states that busing may be used for desegregation 1972: Title IX 1975: Education for All Handicapped Children Act (Public Law 94–142) 1979: Department of Education established	Curriculum emphases in the 1950s and 1960s included structure of the discipline and the discovery method of teaching, and teaching gifted and talented students. Emphases in the 1970s were on mainstreaming, multicultural education, career education, and a flexible curriculum with many electives.	Essentialism
1980s	1983: *A Nation at Risk* published	Educational reform was introduced; reports were issued leading to back-to-basics movement, core curriculum, stronger academic requirements. Inclusion and multicultural education grew.	Essentialism Perennialism
1990s	1990: Americans with Disabilities Act (ADA) 1990: Individuals with Disabilities Education Act (IDEA)	The country experienced a growing teacher shortage. National Education Association (NEA) and American Federation of Teachers (AFT) merger talks failed. A growing standards movement led to high-stakes testing. There was a strong technology emphasis and growing rejection of bilingual education.	Essentialism
2000 and beyond	2001: No Child Left Behind Act (reauthorization of Elementary and Secondary Education Act) 2002: Supreme Court rules Cleveland's voucher plan does not violate U.S. Constitution 2004: Reauthorization of IDEA 2009: Race to the Top (federal program designed to spur reform in K–12 education) 2015: Every Student Succeeds Act replaces No Child Left Behind Act	Federal emphasis is on "scientifically based" instructional practices in schools and "highly qualified" teachers.	Essentialism

Pause *and* Reflect

1. In what ways were the histories of the education of minority groups and of women similar? In what ways were they different?
2. Limited English proficiency seems to be a major problem in increasing educational attainment for several minority groups. What ideas do you have about how this problem should be addressed?
3. Do you agree that equality of educational opportunity should be defined by its effects rather than by its provisions? Why or why not?

OUR FINAL WORD

At the beginning of this chapter, we identified seven major themes that have shaped the history of American education and schooling: local control, universal education, public education, comprehensive education, secular education, changing ideas of the basics, and expanding definitions of access and equal opportunity. If you think about the issues raised in earlier chapters of this text, you can see the effect of these themes on contemporary education. For example, the universal and public nature of the educational system strikes at the issue of equal educational opportunity and questions of school finance and governance. Current controversies over the content of education—questions about the secular or sacred nature of the curriculum, debate about the need for common core standards, and efforts to provide excellence in education without sacrificing equality of opportunity—relate to the concepts of secular, universal, and comprehensive education and the definition of what is "basic." Thus, these seven themes continue to play themselves out in our evolving educational system. Table 10.1 lists important dates and events in American education, many of which relate to these seven themes.

WHY TEACH? YOUR FINAL WORD

1. Which new piece of information about the history of education in the United States did you find most interesting or disturbing? Why?
2. Which educational legacies from the past are most likely to affect you in your teaching? In what ways?
3. Are you interested in teaching in an urban school district, as opposed to a suburban or rural school district? If you prefer one setting to another, why do you think that is?

KEY TERMS

1890 institutions (321)
academy (312)
Brown v. Board of Education of Topeka (321)
common school (306)
dame school (303)
de facto school segregation (321)
de jure school segregation (321)
district school (304)
English grammar school (312)
equality of educational opportunity (302)
Every Student Succeeds Act (326)
junior high school (315)
Kalamazoo case (314)
kindergarten (308)

Latin grammar school (311)
McGuffey Readers (307)
middle school (315)
Morrill Act (320)
moving school (304)
The New England Primer (304)
Northwest Ordinances (306)
Old Deluder Satan Act (304)
Plessy v. Ferguson (321)
private venture school (306)
public comprehensive high school (315)
resegregation (324)
town school (304)
universal education (306)

FOR FURTHER INFORMATION

Web Resources

Library of Congress

Users of this site will find easy access to THOMAS (legislative information), the Library of Congress catalog, and much more. Particularly relevant for the history of American education is the "Education Resources" heading, which provides information on using materials in the American Memory historical collections, as well as lesson plans and links to related web pages.

School: The Story of American Public Education

An interesting website, sponsored by PBS, which provides an excellent look at the history of the American public school.

Print Resources

K. Tsianina Lomawaima and Teresa L. McCarty, *To Remain an Indian: Lessons in Democracy from a Century of Native American Education* (New York: Teachers College Press, 2006).

The authors critically evaluate U.S. educational policies and practices—from early twentieth-century federal incarnations of colonial education through the contemporary standards movement—in this fascinating portrait of Native American education over the past century.

Vivian Gunn Morris and Curtis L. Morris, *The Price They Paid: Desegregation in an African American Community* (New York: Teachers College Press, 2007).

Focusing on an African American community in Alabama, the authors document not only the gains but also the significant losses experienced by students when their community school was closed and they were forced to attend a white desegregated school across town.

Erica Frankenberg and Gary Orfield, eds. *The Resegregation of Suburban Schools: A Hidden Crisis in American Education* (Harvard, MA: Harvard Education Press, 2012).

The editors demonstrate that the locus of racial and ethnic transformation is now clearly suburban, and illustrate patterns of demographic change in the suburbs with a series of rich case studies.

Joel Spring, *Deculturalization and the Struggle for Equality: A Brief History of the Education of Dominated Cultures in the United States*, 8th ed. (United Kingdom: Routledge, 2016.)

Spring interprets American history in terms of Anglo-American racism and school policies affecting dominated groups in the United States. In the process, he gives voice to the perspectives of African Americans, Asian Americans, Hispanic/Latino Americans, and Native Americans.

Abdin Noboa-Rios, *The Story of Latinos and Education in American History* (New York: Peter Lang Publishing, 2019).

A history of Latino education in the United States, and needed remedies to ensure students succeed academically.

James A. Banks, Marcelo M. Suárez-Orozco, Miriam Ben-Peretz, eds., *Global Migration, Diversity, and Civic Education* (New York: Teachers College Press, 2016).

Mass migration and globalization are creating challenges to educational systems across the globe to socialize diverse groups for citizenship and civic engagement.

How Are Schools Governed, Influenced, and Financed?

ZUMA Press, Inc./Alamy Stock Photo

LEARNING OBJECTIVES

11-1 Describe the typical state educational governance structure, including the relationships among the major governing bodies and offices.

11-2 Explain how professional organizations, parents, business, and the federal government influence public education, giving some specific examples of each.

11-3 Identify the major sources of revenue that support the public school systems in the United States.

Truth OR Fiction?

T F The administration and operation of public education are primarily the responsibility of each state.

T F Although women make up the vast majority of teachers, only one out of four school superintendents is a woman.

T F Approximately half of public school financing comes from the federal government, with the rest coming from state and local governments.

T F The United States spends about the same percentage of its resources on public schooling as the average of other industrialized nations.

Few beginning teachers are concerned about issues related to school governance and finance. The topic seems remote to them; it is something administrators and representatives of teacher organizations care about, but it does not seem particularly vital for beginning teachers, who are more concerned with learning how to survive in the classroom. We feel differently. We believe beginning teachers must have some understanding of the way schools and school systems operate because they will be affected personally by governance and financial decisions. Not understanding how these decisions are made and how they might affect you as a teacher will reduce your effectiveness as a professional.

How would you explain the following decisions?

- A very popular high school teacher was not given tenure.
- The sex education program being planned in your local school district was never implemented.
- A textbook with a fresh approach to the curriculum was removed from circulation after a year, even though the teachers favored its use.
- A coalition of superintendents from poor school districts in your state sued the state government for increased financial support.

It is quite possible that at least one of these decisions has been made in your local school district or state. All of them reflect the ongoing struggle for governance, control, and influence over the public schools. This chapter explores how the U.S. educational system is organized, governed, and financed. Although there are legal authorities for the schools and organizations established to exercise this authority, the educational system is strongly influenced by interest groups that do not appear on any organizational chart. We first examine the legal governing authority that exists in most states and then discuss special-interest groups that influence educational policy. Next, we look at how the U.S. educational system is financed and explore how disparities between rich and poor school districts are generating strong challenges to current financing policies. Finally, we examine the role of the federal government in education, particularly through the Every Student Succeeds legislation and the economic stimulus money sent to the states.

11-1 Who Legally Governs Public Education?

In most countries, the public schools are a branch of the central government, being federally financed and administered and highly uniform in curricula and procedures. In the United States, however, responsibility for the public schools evolved as a state function as a result of the Tenth Amendment to the U.S. Constitution, which reserves all powers to the states and the people that are not specifically designated to the federal government. Since education is not mentioned in the Constitution, each of the 50 states has legal responsibility for the operation and administration of the public schools within its own boundaries. In most aspects of public education (we discuss certain exceptions later), the authority of federal, county, and city educational agencies is subject to the will of the state authorities.

Although legal responsibility for school governance belongs to the states, policy decisions and administration have traditionally been delegated to local school boards (see Figure 11.1). These school boards exist largely because Americans have come to insist on control of schools at the local level. Recently, however, states have been reasserting their policymaking prerogatives.

Ⓣ F
The administration and operation of public education are primarily the responsibility of each state.

FIGURE 11.1
Organizational Structure of a Typical State School System

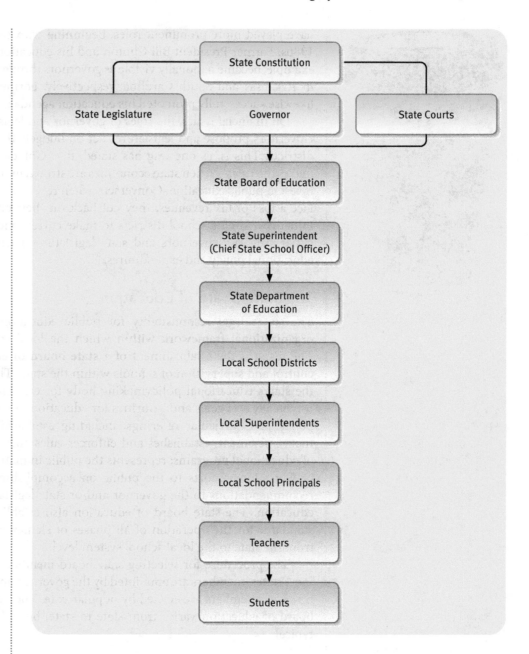

FIGURE 11.1
Organizational Structure of a Typical State School System

11-1a STATE OFFICES AND ADMINISTRATORS

At the state level, educational services can be influenced by a variety of actors, ranging from the governor to many employees of the state's department of education.

The Governor and the State Legislature

Policy analysts agree that the state legislatures are the most influential actors in establishing educational policy. Legislatures wield such power because they make the laws that govern and affect education within their states, and they appropriate the money needed to fund state government. In recent years, because of the high profile of educational issues, legislatures' interest in educational policy has increased, particularly in the areas of school finance and the establishment of standards for student academic achievement.

Like legislatures, the governor's office has the power to affect educational policy but often chooses to do so only on limited issues. Many governors, however, have played more prominent roles, beginning with the educational reforms of the 1980s. Former President Bill Clinton and his education secretary, Richard Riley, for example, became nationally visible as governors through their educational leadership in Arkansas and South Carolina, respectively. Former President George W. Bush likewise successfully promoted his education agenda as governor of Texas.

On financial issues, the roles of governor and legislature are especially obvious. Governors propose and legislatures act on budgets that contain funding for school districts. This is, as one wag has stated, the "Golden Rule: Whoever has the gold makes the rules." When state economies are strong, more tax revenues are available to invest in public education. Conversely, when recessions occur and state governments face a loss of tax revenues, they cut back on their educational commitments and initiatives, forcing school districts to make corresponding cuts in their budgets. In either scenario, governors and state legislatures have tremendous influence over educational policy and expenditures.

The State Board of Education

The state's legal responsibility for public education requires it to establish an organizational framework within which the local school districts can function. The result is the establishment of a **state board of education** to exercise general control and supervision of schools within the state. The state board of education is the state's educational policymaking body for elementary and secondary schools. It typically sets goals and priorities for education in the state; formulates education policy and curricular offerings, including establishing academic standards and their assessment; establishes and enforces rules and regulations for the operation of educational programs; represents the public in matters regarding the governance of education; reports to the public on accomplishments and needs; and makes recommendations to the governor and/or state legislature for the improvement of education. The state board of education also establishes and enforces minimum standards for the operation of all phases of elementary and secondary education from the state to the local school system level.

The procedure for selecting state board members varies from state to state. In most states, members are appointed by the governor; in about one-third of the states, however, members are elected by popular vote. The number of members on a state board of education varies from state to state, but a board of 9 to 15 members is typical.

The Chief State School Officer

The executive officer of the state board of education, the **chief state school officer**, usually is responsible for the administration of public education and reports to the state board of education. (The actual titles for this position, which vary from state to state, include *superintendent of education, commissioner of education, secretary of the state board of education,* and others.) The responsibilities normally involve serving as the chief administrator of the state department of education (discussed later in this chapter) and the state board of education; recommending improvements in educational legislation; arranging studies and creating task forces to identify problems and propose solutions; and reporting on the status of education within the state to the governor, legislature, state board of education, and the public. This officer exercises little direct administrative authority over local educational officials, but his or her indirect influence is widely felt at the local level. The officer is elected by voters in 14 states, appointed by the governor in 12 states, and appointed by the state board of education in the remaining 24 states.

The State Department of Education

The **state department of education** (sometimes called the *state department of public instruction*) usually operates under the direction of the state board of education and is administered by the chief state school officer. The state department of education is responsible for carrying out the policies of the state board of education and the laws passed by the state legislature. It consists of a large bureaucracy of officials, often numbering in the hundreds of employees.

Originally organized to provide statistical reports, state departments of education have grown in size, power, and influence over the years. Their primary responsibilities usually include administering and distributing state and federal funds, licensing teachers and other educational personnel, providing schools with technical assistance in improving curriculum and teaching, providing educational data and analyses, providing administration for special programs, accrediting college and university educational licensure programs, evaluating existing programs, and issuing reports. Most schools, school districts, and colleges of education are strongly affected by the policies and actions of these state departments. School and college personnel, including public school teachers, serve on advisory committees and task forces to assist the chief state school officer and the state department of education in their decision-making processes.

11-1b THE LOCAL SCHOOL DISTRICT

To facilitate local control of education, the state creates local school districts for the purpose of carrying out education in a manner that conforms to state policy. Thus, the school district is a unit of the state government and is usually distinct from the local municipal government.

> *In the first place, God made idiots. That was for practice. Then he made school boards.*
>
> —MARK TWAIN,
> nineteenth-century American author and humourist

The Local School Board

The policymaking body of the school district is the **local school board**, which represents the citizens of the district in setting up a school program, hiring personnel to operate the schools, determining organizational and administrative policy, and evaluating the results of the program and the performance of personnel. Many school boards are empowered to raise money through taxes. Although school board members are usually elected by the citizens of the local district, they are officially state officers (not simply local representatives), and they must follow the guidelines and policies established by the legislature, the state board of education, and the state department of education. The tension between states' efforts to regulate educational policy and local districts' desire to determine their own policies has increased in recent years as states have taken the initiative in the educational reform movement.

Methods of selecting school board members are usually prescribed by state law. Approximately 96 percent of all U.S. school boards are elected by popular vote, and the rest are appointed, often by the local mayor or city council.

What does the composite profile of school board members look like? The majority of today's school board members are almost evenly split between male and female, white, and between ages 40 and 59—demographic characteristics that have changed little in recent years.[1] The proportion of women serving on boards has increased from 12 to around 46 percent since 1972, but representation of minorities remains small. Seventy-eight percent of school board members are white, followed by African American (10%), Hispanic (3%), and Native American (1%). Almost half of school board members earned at least $100,000 per year. Three-fourths of them have at least bachelor's degrees. Most are professionals, managers, or business owners;

Local school boards often come under pressure from many groups, including parents, who want the schools to reflect their values and beliefs.

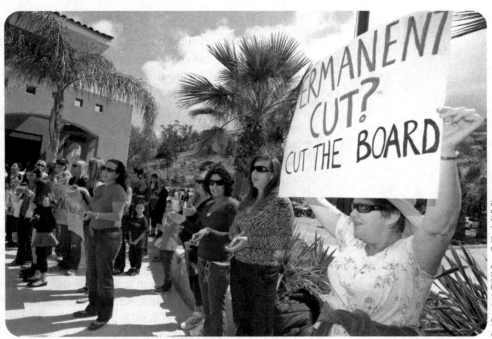

Paul Bersebach/ZUMA Press/California/U.S./Newscom

have children in the public schools; and consider themselves to be either moderates or conservatives. Thus, in many ways, school board members are not typical of the public they serve. Whether or how this difference influences their values and decisions is not known. Can you think of any ways in which it might?

The Superintendent of Schools

The **superintendent of schools** is typically a professional educator selected by the local school board to act as its executive officer and as the educational leader and administrator of the school district. In a few large urban areas, such as Chicago and Washington, DC, the mayor of the city chooses the superintendent, giving the mayor more power and accountability over the schools. The superintendent is undeniably the most powerful officer in the local school organization. Given that the school board consists of laypeople who are usually not education experts, it often delegates many of its responsibilities to the superintendent and his or her staff.

Ⓣ **F**

Although women make up the vast majority of teachers, only one out of four school superintendents is a woman.

One of the superintendent's most important functions is gathering and providing information to the local school board so its members can make informed decisions. Additionally, the superintendent must recruit, select, place, and promote personnel. Often, the superintendent plans the budget and supervises the maintenance, construction, and renovation of school buildings.

Decisions about how to improve educational opportunities, including all aspects of curriculum and instruction, may originate with the superintendent. The superintendent generally has responsibility for maintaining harmonious relations with the community by communicating the mission of the schools to the public and marshaling support for district programs.

Theoretically, the superintendent's role is administrative and executive—he or she (just 25 percent of the nation's superintendents are females) keeps the schools functioning, whereas the local school board of education retains policymaking responsibilities. In practice, the superintendent has become the major policy maker in the school district.

Superintendents versus Local School Boards

The way a school board and superintendent operate together to govern a school district depends on their relationship. According to independent observers, this relationship is often characterized by conflict.

One observer, Larry Cuban, asserts that "conflict is—and always has been—the essence of the superintendency."[2] One measure of conflict between superintendents and school boards is the turnover rate—that is, how often superintendents change their jobs. The average tenure for superintendents in urban districts is slightly less than five years, and the national average among all superintendents is five and a half years.[3]

Cuban describes the conflict between the superintendent and the school board, or between the superintendent and local private groups, as one of seeming competitors seeking to achieve their goals at the expense of the other participants. Cuban maintains that the issues over which boards and administrators disagree may change as a result of shifting political concerns, changes in school funding or demography, or constantly changing coalitions of teachers or local constituencies. Whatever the particular issues, however, the relationship often remains tempestuous. Although school boards hire and fire them, superintendents are expected to lead the board. If they fail to do so, board members are likely to act independently, often with poor consequences.

School boards and superintendents search constantly for local constituencies to provide the funding and support for school programs, and with every school board election new points of view may be brought to the governance of the district. Superintendents must weather these changes in points of view and the emerging coalitions resulting from board member turnover. Sympathies with the schools' mission may be in a constant state of flux, requiring superintendents to exercise coalition-building skills. Their survival as nonelected public officials rests on their ability to mobilize support and manage conflict.

The School Principal

For the schools within a school district, the superintendent and the local school board of education select professional educators to serve as principals. High schools and middle schools may have a staff of administrators to assist the principal, including assistant or vice principals with specific responsibilities for discipline or curriculum and instruction. At the elementary level, principals may be responsible for more than one school building or may serve part-time as teachers. Whatever the pattern of administrative assignments, those who act as principals are generally considered to be a part of the administrative organization, directly accountable to the superintendent and the local school board. (See Table 11.1 for a profile of school administrators.)

As administrators, principals usually interview prospective teachers and make teaching assignments, supervise and evaluate staff members, schedule students and classes, manage school budgets, administer district discipline policies, and procure and dispense supplies. Their tasks are many; to list them all would be almost impossible. Historically, the role of the principal has included management, supervision, and inspection duties. Most importantly, principals are expected to function as instructional leaders for their schools. In a number of states, principals and their teachers are being held accountable for increasing student learning on statewide assessments of achievement. However, as can be seen in the "Voices from the Classroom" feature, principals and teachers may not always be on the same page.

TABLE 11.1	Profile of School Administrators (in Percent)		
Characteristic	Superintendents	Secondary School Principals	Elementary School Principals
Sex			
Male	75	67	33
Female	25	33	67
Ethnic Background			
White	90.5	78.9	77
Black	3.8	10.6	10.8
Hispanic American	2.7	8.2	9.6
Other	2.0	2.4	2.9
Salary (12 Months)	$161,639	$104,600	$97,000

Note: Because of rounding, some totals may not add up to 100 percent.

Source: Characteristics of Public and Private Elementary and Secondary School Principals in the United States: Results From the 2017–2018 National Teacher and Principal Survey First Look (NCES 2019-142) (Washington, DC: National Center for Education Statistics, 2019), https://nces.ed.gov/pubs2019/2019141.pdf; "School Superintendent Salary in the United States," Salary.com, https://www.salary.com/research/salary/benchmark/school-superintendent-salary; Leslie Finnan and Robert S. McCord, *2017–2018 AASA Superintendent Salary & Benefits Study* (Alexandria, VA: American Association of School Superintendents, January, 2018), https://aasa.org/uploadedFiles/Policy_and_Advocacy/Final%20Report%202017-18%20 Non-Member.pdf.

Effective principals serve as instructional leaders by promoting a productive working and learning environment. They do so by understanding the mission of the school, communicating it to the staff and students, and rewarding excellent performance. They also represent the school to parents and the community. Involving parents and community members in the school's activities and securing their support for these activities are important functions of the principal.

Pause *and* Reflect

1. From what you have read about the role of the superintendent, what impressions have you formed about the power of the superintendent and the constraints on that power?
2. The authors of this textbook believe that the hardest job in public education is that of a high school principal. Do you agree or disagree with this position? For what reasons?
3. In your opinion, should chief state school officers be elected or appointed? What reasons do you have for your position? What arguments can you muster for the opposite opinion?

VOICES from the Classroom

Swimming against the Current

This testimonial is from an elementary school reading specialist in a small town in Virginia. The contributor wishes to remain anonymous.

Remember the cartoon where the "school" of fish swims along, sporting mortarboards? Well, I can carry the metaphor even further. Teaching with the support of the principal and local administration is like swimming downstream. When that support is missing, you're just bucking the current.

For several years, my colleagues and I taught an excellent comprehensive reading curriculum, with the support of principals and district administration. The curriculum's implementation produced dramatic effects among kindergartners and first-graders in the district's lowest-performing elementary school, Center City. This school was on its way, but it would take some time for the results to manifest themselves in the state tests, which were administered in third grade and later.

Then the current changed. Our superintendent retired, and shortly thereafter we lost our assistant superintendent in charge of curriculum and our literacy coordinator. The new superintendent mandated that Center City replace our successful reading program with a basal program. Some teachers scrambled to find time to supplement the basal program with instruction they knew worked, but it was difficult, and progress slowed among the primary-grade students. However, those early gains

in reading finally showed up on the spring state tests, and Center City made Annual Yearly Progress.

In the spring of the next year, Center City became eligible to apply for a federal Reading First grant. The district and a new principal, without consulting the school's reading specialists or classroom teachers, decided to apply, assigning the grant-writing job to an employee of the basal publisher. Despite their strenuous efforts, the faculty ended up with minimal input. The application was accepted and a reading coach hired. Although enjoying the principal's support, the coach made decisions that negatively affected student instruction and alienated the teachers. The following spring, after three years of inadequate reading instruction, Center City failed to make AYP.

What are the lessons to be learned from this experience? First, when new players enter the game, they want to make their own impact and will initiate changes that may not be as effective as instruction already in place. Second, the people closest to the action (the teachers and reading specialists) may not be consulted in decisions that greatly affect them. And third, although in our work as teachers the students should present our primary challenge, this isn't always the case. Still, we can never stop bucking the current on their behalf.

11-2 Who Influences American Public Education?

In this chapter, we do not intend to examine in detail the authority and power that enable various groups to influence certain aspects of public education. However, even a brief look at the interplay of influence exercised by professional education organizations, parents, business, the courts, and the federal government yields some fascinating insights into how decisions about public education are actually made.

11-2a PROFESSIONAL EDUCATION ORGANIZATIONS

Among the most influential forces on the schools are professional education organizations—in particular, the National Education Association (NEA) and the American Federation of Teachers (AFT).

In recent years, the role of teacher organizations in determining educational policy has greatly increased. At the national level, the NEA and the AFT exert considerable influence on educational policy and legislation. Moreover, the

> *Just as war is too important to be left to the generals, education is too important to be left to the educators.*
>
> —PAUL WOODRING,
> twentieth-century American education author and professor

state affiliates of both associations are among the most effective lobbying groups in their respective states. (See Chapter 15, "What Does It Mean to Be a Professional?," for more on these two teacher organizations.) State politicians pay attention to these organizations because of their power and influence. The NEA and AFT affiliates have well-articulated positions on selected issues, represent hundreds of thousands of teachers who can be mobilized to vote for or against particular legislators, and spend considerable amounts of money to make their positions known. At the local level—largely as a result of collective bargaining techniques, including work stoppages or the threat of them—teacher organizations have won more and more power over educational policy.

Today, many local teacher organizations, including NEA and AFT affiliates, have won recognition as the official bargaining representatives of their members. Such organizations are also demanding that issues previously considered the prerogatives of local school boards and superintendents be subject to collective bargaining. Among these areas of contention are teacher and paraprofessional salaries, clerical and secretarial assistance, curriculum development, fringe benefits, in-service training, class size, textbook selection, and even the appointment of department heads and other school administrators.

However, in some states, conservative legislatures and governors have implemented policies that were strongly opposed by teacher organizations. In both Florida and North Carolina, for example, teacher tenure was abolished, and in North Carolina, teacher salary increases for earning master's degrees were done away with. As a result, the influence of teacher organizations seems to be waning in some states.

11-2b PARENTS

Ask educators who has the most influence in determining whether children succeed in school, and almost all of them will have the same response: *parents*. Parents are their children's first and primary teachers and the only ones who follow a child's progress from year to year. As the two major forces for educating and socializing children in society, parents and teachers should be natural allies. Too often, however, a wide chasm separates them. Some teachers fear that parents will interfere in their classrooms; others feel pressed for time and don't want to spend the extra effort to communicate with and effectively involve parents. Some parents seem too consumed with the problems of work and raising a family to become involved in schools, whereas others actively participate in various school functions. Research is clear on this point: Without effective parental interest and involvement in the schools, most students will not succeed academically. In a national survey of public school teachers, 73 percent of teachers found engaging parents and the community in improving the education of students to be either challenging or very challenging.[4]

> *A parent is the most important teacher a child ever has.*
>
> —JOAN BECK,
> American author on child raising

The Parent Teacher Association (PTA) is a loosely knit national organization with over 5 million members and more than 26,000 local units. The local parent–teacher group, sometimes called the **parent–teacher organization (PTO)**, may or may not be affiliated with the national PTA. Local groups devise their own organizations and activities to fit the needs of the local school community. Generally, they serve as a communications link between parents and the formal school organization, with teachers usually acting as representatives of the schools.

Family support and emphasis on the value of education are extremely important influences on a child's success in school.

iofoto/Shutterstock.com

Most PTOs are comparatively impotent in achieving educational aims. This weakness of parent groups concerns educational reformers because they know that reforms will last only if parents become actively involved in the work of their schools. Some states have actually passed legislation mandating that schools involve parents in school governance and in the education of the students.

Many strategies can be implemented to increase parental involvement and improve the partnership between parents and teachers: frequent parent–teacher conferences; homework hotlines, websites, or emails through which parents can find out about homework assignments or communicate with teachers; workshops for parents that address a variety of topics; school volunteer programs; and school councils on which parents, teachers, and administrators discuss school policies and practices. Teachers and school administrators must be trained to overcome barriers to effective parental involvement and to create school environments where parents of all races, ethnicities, and social classes feel welcome.

11-2c BUSINESS

Throughout American history, concern about the quality of U.S. public education and its ability to produce workers with the knowledge and skills that business needs has prompted partnerships between educators and business executives. In particular, during the 1980s and 1990s and continuing into the twenty-first century, the business community has been at the forefront of efforts to restructure public education.

Business leaders have been substantially involved in almost every educational reform report. As a result, they have become both the strongest critics and the staunchest advocates for public education. More than 100,000 business–school partnerships have been formed since 1983, and business has donated hundreds of millions of dollars to improve elementary and secondary schools.

Why should the business community show such interest in the field of education? Its initiatives to improve the quality of American education go beyond altruistic impulses. One source estimates that children between the ages of 4 and 19 spend almost $200 billion per year, and children and teens influence the spending of up to $670 billion each year.[5] With that kind of money involved, businesses would certainly like to make their presence known in the schools, where these potential consumers are a captive audience. With many more children having access to smartphones, they are increasingly exposed to advertising that explicitly targets them and their preferences.

In addition, like the nation's governors, many business leaders are convinced that educational reform is essential to the health of the U.S. economy. Competition from Asian and European manufacturers in world markets, a massive U.S. trade deficit, and industry's perception that entry-level workers lack proper job skills have focused attention on educating the American workforce. In fact, U.S. companies spend billions of dollars annually on remedial education for their workers.

Purchasing Pressures?

Not everyone sees the greater business involvement in education as a totally positive trend. Some express concern that financial support from business will lead to business intrusion—that schools may be unduly shaped to meet business needs. Another concern centers on businesses' provision of free curriculum and instructional materials for teachers. Critics argue that corporate handouts are not simply supplementary gifts, but rather sophisticated marketing tools containing

Although they earn extra money from vending machine sales, more and more schools are trying to get rid of fattening or sugar products in favor of healthier snacks and drinks.

PAUL J.RICHARDS/Getty Images

subtle and not-so-subtle messages to support the corporations' biases and promote brand identification and product loyalty. For example, Clairol distributes free bags of shampoo to students as they leave school, along with surveys asking whether they had "a good or bad hair day." In another example, a Nike program asks young people to devote a week of classroom time to learning the life cycle of a Nike shoe. Other opponents of corporate involvement in the schools object to exclusive marketing contracts that schools sign with such companies as Coca-Cola or Pepsi, agreeing to sell only products produced by the particular company in exchange for funding from the firm. Some people cynically view businesses' push for the expanded use of technology in schools as an attempt to sell new products.

Pause *and* Reflect

1. Did the schools you attended work in partnership with business and industry?
2. What, in your opinion, is an appropriate relationship between business and schools?
3. Do you believe the local business community should be an influential decision maker regarding what goes on in the area schools? Why or why not?

Privatization Efforts

Another way business influences education is through the recent movement toward private management of public schools, known as educational management organizations (EMOs), that has occurred in some urban areas. Private corporations such as the Edison Learning, KIPP (Knowledge is Power Program), and Sylvan Learning, Inc., have contracted with some school districts to provide specific educational services, operate schools whose students have been performing poorly on academic tests, or begin new schools with promising designs. K12, Inc. partners with public and private schools to offer online learning for elementary and secondary students. Advocates of this **privatization** movement argue that private corporations can operate these schools more effectively and less expensively than can public entities. Opponents of this trend—especially teachers' unions—claim that schools operated under a profit motive may shortchange students' welfare in the private firm's drive to make money. They do so, the critics claim, by hiring inexperienced teachers, using unlicensed staff, and eliminating high-cost special education programs. To date, private management of public schools has often led to cleaner buildings, greater access to computers, and more individualized instruction, but the verdict is still out on whether they lead to academic improvement.

There is no question that the role of the business community in educational affairs has greatly expanded since the mid-1980s, and most people see this trend as a positive one. Businesses and corporations, which have a vested stake in the outcomes of public education, will undoubtedly continue to be major players in the reform of our educational system. The challenge for educators will be to walk the fine line between partnerships and cooperation on the one hand and exploitation for commercial purposes on the other.

The classroom is . . . a place in which the claims of various political, social, and economic interests are negotiated. The classroom is both a symbol and a product of deadly serious cultural bargaining

—NEIL POSTMAN (1931–2003),
American professor, media theorist,
and cultural critic

11-2d THE FEDERAL GOVERNMENT

Although the federal government does not have formal authority over education, all three branches of the government exercise considerable influence over schools in the country through legislation, court rulings, and the activities of the U.S. Department of Education.

The Federal Courts

The history of education has been shaped by important court decisions on the duties and responsibilities of school officials in such areas as school desegregation, religion in the schools, student rights, and, especially at the state level, school finance. The U.S. Supreme Court has played a particularly important role in changing educational policy in this country. (See Chapter 8, "What Are the Ethical and Legal Issues Facing Teachers?," for a more detailed discussion of the impact of Supreme Court decisions on U.S. education.) Because its rulings have altered or reduced the power of state and local educational authorities, some of the court's decisions have generated deep resentment among those who abhor this "federal intrusion" into states' rights. Other people applaud the court's decisions as steps intended to make American education more responsive to broad democratic principles. Over the years, the Supreme Court has issued key rulings affecting such important educational policies as desegregation, public aid to private schools, rights of people with disabilities, gender equity, voucher plans, and sexual harassment.

Even as powerful as they are, the courts cannot do everything by themselves. Often judicial rulings must be supported by federal administrative and legislative action before they can alter educational practice. In the famous 1954 case of *Brown* v. *Board of Education of Topeka* (discussed in more detail in Chapter 10, "What Is the History of America's Struggle for Educational Opportunity?"), for example, the U.S. Supreme Court ruled that the doctrine of "separate but equal" had no place in public education. But how was this momentous judgment to be implemented? The court declared that "all deliberate speed" should be employed to abolish the dual school system for African Americans and whites, but no judicial guidelines were developed to steer this process. As a result, almost no changes occurred for a decade, until a combination of new congressional laws on civil rights and education along with strong enforcement of desegregation by President Lyndon Johnson's administration took place in the 1960s.

The U.S. Department of Education

The Department of Education is a significant part of the federal government, with cabinet-level status and a budget of slightly more than $72 billion in fiscal year 2020.[6] The department administers a variety of programs passed by Congress, including programs concerned with elementary and secondary education, postsecondary education, educational research and development, vocational and adult education, special education, and civil rights. It also administers funds devoted to the collection of educational statistics. In addition, billions of additional federal dollars for education are administered by other federal agencies, such as the Department of Health and Human Services, the National Science Foundation, and the Department of Defense.

Pause *and* Reflect

Which other groups, besides those listed in this chapter, influence education?

Federal legislation and federal court decisions have significantly affected education, including the education of children with disabilities.

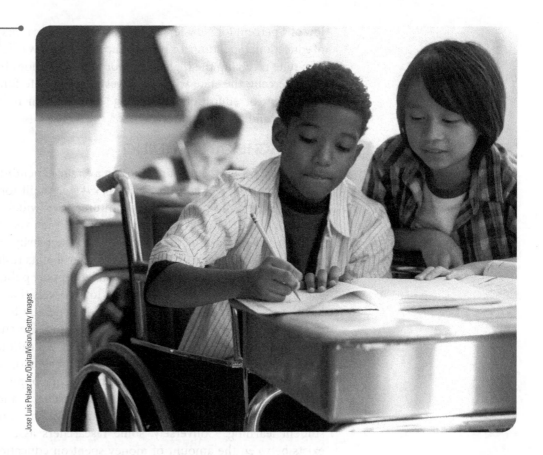

Jose Luis Pelaez Inc/DigitalVision/Getty Images

11-3 How Are Schools Financed?

T (F)

Approximately half of public school financing comes from the federal government, with the rest coming from state and local governments.

The federal government's level of involvement in education often fluctuates, depending on whether Republicans or Democrats control the White House and Congress, and on the particular ideology professed by the party in power. Republicans generally have sought to decrease the involvement of the federal government in education, even advocating abolition of the U.S. Department of Education, whereas Democrats tend to be more supportive of both the department and federal efforts to improve education. The federal government's share of K–12 spending is slightly over 7 percent.

The total amount of money available to a school district for education is the sum of locally raised revenues, state aid, federal aid, and miscellaneous revenues. During much of the country's history, most of the money used to support public elementary and secondary schools came from local revenue sources, primarily property taxes. Beginning in the late 1970s, for the first time in U.S. history the states' share of support for public education exceeded the local share, and this situation continues today. Increased state revenues have helped offset the decreases in local funding of the schools. Currently, state governments contribute about 47.5 percent; local governments provide approximately 45 percent; and the federal government provides slightly over 7.4 percent of the financing of public schools.[7]

The percentages of educational expenditures funded by federal, state, and local sources vary considerably from state to state. Federal contributions for public education range from a high of 14.6 percent of educational spending for Alaska, to a low of 4 percent for New Jersey. Local contributions range from a high of 64.7 percent of educational spending for New Hampshire, to a low of less than 2 percent for Hawaii. The state receiving the highest proportion of revenues from state sources is Hawaii, at 89 percent; the state with the lowest level of state funding is New Hampshire, at 30 percent of educational spending.[8] Let's look in more detail at state and local spending and funding patterns.

11-3a SCHOOL SPENDING

Figure 11.2 shows the upward trend in average expenditure per pupil in enrollment. The nationwide average stood at $13,384 per pupil for 2019–2020. From state to state, however, the per-pupil expenditures vary widely (see Figure 11.3), ranging from a high of $25,344 (New York) per pupil each year to a low of just over $6,700 (Idaho).[9] The reason for these differences is primarily economic. A state's ability to pay for education depends on the income level of its residents and corporations and the willingness of its citizens to financially support public education. In general, the southwestern states fund education at lower levels than do the northeastern states, but the cost of living in the Southwest is generally less than the cost of living in the Northeast. As a result of the lower funding, are students who live in some of the Sunbelt states being deprived of a quality education? The connection between funding and excellence of education is often disputed, but a thorough review of the research on this issue concluded that higher per-pupil expenditures, better teacher salaries, more educated and experienced teachers, and smaller class and school sizes—all directly a result of higher funding—are strongly related to improved student learning. Conversely, some researchers assert that no such relationship exists between the amount of money spent on education and the achievements of the students in that district.[10]

11-3b STATE AND LOCAL FUNDING

State governments use a combination of sales, personal income, corporate income, and excise taxes to generate revenues. Some states fund their schools partly with income from state-run lotteries. State revenue systems are as diverse as school

FIGURE 11.2 **Expenditures per Pupil**

Source: *Rankings and Estimates 2019-2020* (Washington, DC: National Education Association, 2020). 2020 Rankings and Estimates Report-2.pdf.

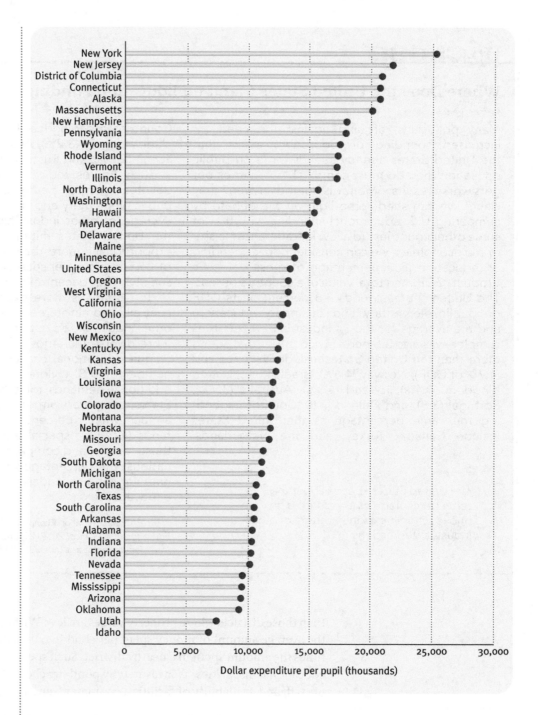

FIGURE 11.3 Average Expenditure per Pupil, by State, 2018–2019

Source: Rankings and Estimates 2019–2020 (Washington, DC: National Education Association, 2020), p. 60. 2020 Rankings and Estimates Report-2.pdf.

finance plans and reflect the socioeconomic makeup, the political climate, and the educational needs of each state.

Local governments, in contrast, rely primarily on property taxes for income. Most states require the citizens in a school district to vote either on the property tax rate to support education or on the school budget itself. Many states have begun to rely less on local property taxes to fund their schools.

Why would districts want to minimize their reliance on property taxes? Many knowledgeable educators and politicians argue that one of the major causes of unequal educational opportunities in this country is the method used to finance school systems. Because local districts rely heavily on property taxes, those districts where property values are high generate much more money to finance their schools

Up CLOSE

Where Does the United States Stand on Education Funding?

Many politicians, arguing against the need for increased spending on education, assert that the United States already spends more on public education than do most comparable countries but gets worse results. "Money is not the answer," they claim. We can shed some light on the debate by comparing U.S. educational spending with that of some other countries. To allow for differences in size of the economies, we can consider public spending on education as a percentage of gross domestic product (GDP), the total value of a country's output. The United States spends 3.5 percent of its GDP on public elementary and secondary education, and the average for the 34 industrialized countries sampled was also 3.5 percent. Countries that spend more than the United States include New Zealand (4.7% of GDP), Norway (4.6%), Israel (4.5%), United Kingdom (4.4%), Iceland (4.3%), Australia (3.9%), Portugal (3.8), and Finland (3.8). Countries spending the same percentage as the United States include Canada, Turkey, and the Netherlands.

Countries spending less than the United States include Hungary (3.2%), Austria (3.1%), Spain (3.1%), Japan (2.6%), and Russia (2.0%).

Such figures indicate that the United States devotes a similar percentage of its resources to public elementary and secondary education as the average of other industrialized nations. However, the United States might be expected to spend proportionally more than other countries because of certain characteristics of its school system and society. The decentralized school system in the United States is more expensive than the single, centrally administered system found in many other industrialized nations. The U.S. population is more diverse than most countries', which presents unique educational challenges, and the very high number of U.S. children living in poverty creates additional demands for schools. Also, the United States, compared with the other countries, spends a much greater percentage of its public education funds (17%) on special education services. Given these factors, and compared to other industrialized nations, the percentage of U.S. GDP spent on elementary and secondary education does not seem extravagant.

(T) F
The United States spends about the same percentage of its resources on public schooling as the average of other industrialized nations.

Source: Organization of Economic Cooperation and Development, *Education at a Glance, 2019,* 281, https://read.oecd-ilibrary.org/education/education-at-a-glance-2019_f8d7880d-en#page282.

than those districts where property values are low. Within the same state, for example, the average amount of money spent per child in one district may be more than three times the amount spent in a nearby district. Such spending differentials result in great educational disparities, as measured by pupil–teacher ratios, training and experience of staff, and availability of facilities, equipment, and counseling services.

11-3c SCHOOL FINANCE REFORM AND THE COURTS

As a result of numerous court decisions, efforts to equalize the disparities in funding within states have shifted some of the responsibility for funding from local school districts to the state level. A 1971 class action suit, *Serrano* v. *Priest,* charged that California's school-financing scheme was unconstitutional. The Supreme Court of California supported the parents' claim that the quality of a child's education must not be a function of wealth other than the wealth of the state as a whole. The court also held that the California system of financing schools on the basis of local property taxes violated the Fourteenth Amendment to the U.S. Constitution, which provides equal protection of the law for all citizens.

In 1973, however, the Supreme Court of the United States, by a five-to-four vote, reversed a similar decision (known as the *Rodriguez* case) involving the school finance system of the state of Texas. The court found that the U.S. Constitution was not violated because the right to an education is not guaranteed explicitly or implicitly by the Constitution. Although *federal* law had not been violated, the court did indicate that the finding should not be interpreted as a victory for the status quo. In effect, issues of inequity in school finance were returned to the province of the state courts and legislatures. Many state constitutions, unlike the U.S. Constitution, contain equal protection clauses that can be interpreted to include education as a protected right.

Since the *Rodriguez* case, other state courts have ruled that their school financing systems violate their state constitutions. In those states where the finance system has been ruled unconstitutional, the issue has centered on inadequacies in the level of educational opportunities offered to children in the poorer school districts. The courts in those states considered whether the poor children were receiving a sufficient education as required by the state constitution and as measured by contemporary education standards or by comparisons with the best or highest-spending districts. In contrast, in states where the system of school finance was upheld, the courts usually interpreted their state constitutions as guaranteeing only a basic minimum level of funding.[11] As a result of court challenges, more than 20 states have reformed their school finance laws since 1973, and some states continue to grapple with the issue. In the last few years, state courts seem to be backing away from making decisions about increasing K–12 funding, stating that education funding is a political question for the legislature, not the courts, to decide.

Educators, parents, and public officials are greatly concerned that the quality of a child's education should not depend on whether the child lives in a school district with high property values. Many of these concerned citizens are urging that state governments take responsibility for raising educational revenue and distributing all funding for local schools to the school districts. The school districts would continue to be in charge of the operation of the local schools but would no longer carry the burden of raising the money needed to do so.

As the popularity of charter schools has grown, some parents and members of the public have expressed concern regarding charter schools draining money from regular public schools. This issue will continue to be examined in years to come. For more on charter schools, see Chapter 12, "How Should Education Be Reformed?"

▶❚❚ TeachSource Video Case

© 2016 Cengage Learning®

Charter Schools Meeting Student Needs

Watch the video clips, study the artifacts in the case, and reflect on the following questions:

1. What are the major arguments *for* charter schools, and what are the major arguments *against* them?

2. Would you like to teach in a charter school? Why or why not?

Pause *and* Reflect

1. Of the various methods of school financing discussed in this chapter (local property taxes, state financing through statewide taxes, and state-run lotteries), which do you believe is most equitable? Why?
2. Do you believe state governments should redistribute money from rich to poor school districts through state taxing power? Why or why not?

11-3d FEDERAL FUNDING

Although the federal government typically provides much less money for public schools than do state or local governments, federal funds are strategically important and have a far greater impact than their proportion of school funding would suggest.

Funding in the Past

Much of federal aid to education traditionally has taken the form of **categorical grants**—that is, money that must be spent for designated purposes (or categories) stated generally in the legislation and more precisely by the federal agency administering the funds. As a result, the federal government has been able to influence school districts and institutions that have accepted or sought its aid.

In contrast to categorical grants, **block grants** are grants given to the states by the federal government that allow more discretion to the states as to how the money will be spent. For example, the **Every Student Succeeds Act**, the federal government's primary legislation to fund America's public schools, contains a block grant under Title IV for each state. Known as Student Support and Academic Enrichment grants, they are designed to address three areas of need: (1) providing students with well-rounded education; (2) supporting safe and healthy students; and (3) supporting the effective use of technology. States have considerable discretion as to how the funds can be used to address these three needs.

Compensatory Education and Title I

Although the federal government provides money for a variety of educational programs, its most significant efforts have sought to address the needs of children from high-poverty areas who are at risk for educational failure. **Compensatory education** is an approach to creating more equal educational opportunities for disadvantaged children.

Compensatory education was formalized in a section of the original **Elementary and Secondary Education Act (ESEA)** of 1965, known as **Title I**. Congress continues to strongly support Title I because the money reaches almost every school district and thus provides jobs and services in every congressional district. Few members of Congress will vote against providing these benefits to their districts. In fiscal year 2020, public schools received $16.18 billion for Title I.

Title I, Part A (Title I) of the Elementary and Secondary Education Act, as amended by the Every Student Succeeds Act (ESSA), provides financial assistance to local educational agencies (LEAs) and schools with high numbers or high percentages of children from low-income families to help ensure that all children meet challenging state academic standards. Schools in which children from low-income families make up at least 40 percent of enrollment are eligible to use Title I funds to operate schoolwide programs that serve all children in the school in order to raise the achievement of the lowest-achieving students.

To qualify for Title I funds, states have to demonstrate that they adopted college and career-ready standards and assessments, implemented school accountability systems that focused on the lowest-performing schools and those with the largest achievement gaps, and ensured that districts were implementing teacher and principal evaluation and support systems.

In fiscal year 2016, this program distributed about $14 billion on behalf of more than 26 million children in almost 56,000 schools.[12]

Compensatory programs come in many forms. Some are preventive approaches, targeting children who are "at risk" for later school failure during their preschool or infant years. Such programs may help parents learn how to interact more effectively

Early intervention programs, such as Head Start, target children who are at risk of school failure by intervening in their early years to improve skills.

David Grossman/Alamy Stock Photo

with their babies and young children in the areas of cognitive and psychosocial development. The most famous preschool initiative is **Head Start**.

Head Start

Head Start is a federal program that aims to improve the learning skills, social skills, and health status of preschool-age, poor children so that they can begin schooling on an equal basis with their more advantaged peers. Since its inception in 1965, Head Start has served more than 36 million children in total, and it currently supports just over 1 million children.[13]

Although Head Start is almost 50 years old, the program is not without its critics and, like other sectors of public education, is the target of reform. For the 2020 fiscal year, the federal government budgeted $10.6 billion for Head Start programs.

Effectiveness of Compensatory Programs

Some compensatory programs are designed to intervene with even younger children, from birth to age 3, for example. Some programs target children with developmental delays, whereas others target older children and focus on basic skill instruction, tutoring, or remediation in a variety of academic areas. Success for All, described in the "Up Close" box on page 356, is an example of a program that is implemented in elementary schools. Dropout prevention programs, job training, and adult literacy instruction are all attempts to help older individuals improve the quality of their lives through education and to help prevent the cycle of educational disadvantage from being passed down through generations.

Evaluations of Title I and other compensatory education programs, such as Head Start, have yielded mixed results. A recent evaluation of Head Start showed that children improved in both English receptive and expressive vocabulary, letter-word knowledge, and early math, but did not make gains in early writing skills relative to

Many things can wait; children cannot. Today, their bones are being formed, their blood is being made, their senses are being developed. To them, we cannot say 'tomorrow.' Their name is today.

—GABRIELA MISTRAL,
Nobel laureate in literature (1945)

same-age children in the general population. On average, teachers report improvement in aspects of children's social-emotional skills during the Head Start program year. Children demonstrate better social skills on average by the spring of the Head Start year than in the fall and more positive approaches to learning.[14]

One researcher states that although children in Head Start make learning gains, they are "well behind middle-class kids" when they start the program, and that "making modest improvements doesn't close the gap in a major way."[15]

By contrast, long-range studies that have followed students from preschool to age 27, like the study of students in the very successful Perry Preschool Program in Ypsilanti, Michigan, provide other indicators of program success. Effective early childhood programs may result in fewer special education placements, more high school graduations, lower teen pregnancy rates, increased

Up CLOSE

Success for All

One compensatory education program that has proved quite successful is the Success for All program developed by the Center for Research on Effective Schooling for Disadvantaged Students at Johns Hopkins University. The Success for All program restructures the elementary school with one goal in mind: to ensure that all students perform at grade level in reading, writing, and mathematics by the end of third grade.

Success for All schools start early, offering a half day of preschool and a full day of kindergarten, both focused on providing a developmentally appropriate learning experience for children. The curriculum emphasizes the development and use of language and balances academic readiness with music, art, and movement activities.

The program also makes use of the center's research findings to implement one-to-one tutoring, regrouping for reading, family support teams, frequent assessments of learning with immediate help on problems, and an effective reading program. Two social workers and one parent liaison work full time in the schools to provide parenting education and to encourage parents to support their children's efforts. The program also includes tutors for children in grades K–3. Each tutor is a certified, experienced teacher or paraprofessional who works one-on-one with 11 students per day. First-graders get priority for tutoring.

The Success for All program includes 90 minutes of uninterrupted reading instruction each day, during which teachers are asked to follow a fast-paced script written by the Success for All researchers. In spite of its success in teaching students to read, many teachers dislike the reading program, because

it tells them exactly what to do throughout their lessons. For some teachers, this process seems contrary to their beliefs about the importance of paying attention to the learning issues of each child and varying their instruction accordingly.

Overall, evaluation results for students enrolled in Success for All have been outstanding—much higher than for any other intervention strategy ever tried with at-risk students. Starting with one Baltimore school in 1987, the Success for All program had spread to more than 1,000 schools in 48 states, working with 50,000 educators, and it has produced dramatic gains in students' reading proficiency. Almost all Success for All programs are in high-poverty, Title I schools, and the costs of implementing the program are about the same as the costs for supporting students in other Title I schools.

The primary lesson learned, according to the major developer of Success for All, Robert Slavin and his colleagues, is that disadvantaged children can routinely achieve substantially greater success in schools that are neither exceptional nor extraordinary. Rather than having to depend on the availability of an outstanding principal or charismatic teacher to ensure success, every child, regardless of background, has an excellent opportunity to succeed in school.

Source: Robert Slavin, "Success for All," in *Encyclopedia of Education*, James W. Guthrie, ed., 2nd ed. (New York: Macmillan Reference, 2003); Robert E. Slavin and Nancy A. Madden, eds., *Success for All: Research and Reform in Elementary Education* (Mahwah, NJ: Lawrence Erlbaum Associates, 2001); Success for All Foundation, http://successforall. com/about/index.htm; Debra Viadero, "In Whole School Reform, Staying True to Model Matters," *Education Week* (May 16, 2007): 12–13.

employment and earnings, fewer crimes committed, and greater commitment to marriage.[16] *Early intervention*—beginning the program early in the child's life—may provide the key to success in compensatory education programs.

Critics of Title I see little point in strengthening programs that they believe have failed to meet their original goals. Proponents of Title I argue that, considering the enormity of the problem, the expenditures devoted to such programs are a mere drop in the bucket. In spite of what seems like an enormous amount of money, only about 50 percent of all eligible children receive services from Title I funds. Because Title I has never been funded at a high enough level to meet the needs of low-income schools and because its resources are widely dispersed, even the recent funding increases have not checked the growing educational crisis in low-income areas.

Proponents can also point to recent gains in achievement. A 2007 national assessment of Title I showed that students whom Title I is intended to benefit (including low-income students, racial/ethnic minorities, English language learners, migrant students, and students with disabilities) have made modest gains in meeting proficiency levels on state assessments in reading and mathematics, as well as on the National Assessment of Educational Progress (NAEP) tests in reading and mathematics (see Chapter 5, "What Is Taught?," for more on NAEP). Although the performance of students in high-poverty schools is improving, they continue to lag behind their higher-income peers in meeting basic standards of performance in both reading and mathematics.[17] As the centerpiece of the ESSA law, Title I will likely continue to receive funding increases in the years to come.

Both sides acknowledge that not all programs are equally effective. The best programs achieve desired results, whereas the less effective programs do not seem to have lasting effects on student performance. Likewise, both sides can agree that, in addition to education efforts, a simultaneous attack should be made on external factors that contribute to low achievement, such as poor housing, family instability, health and nutrition, and low income.

OUR FINAL WORD

What does the future hold in terms of school governance and financing? The federal government, through the ESSA law, assumed a major role in education in the United States, much more than it played in the past. The ESSA has moved away from a strong federal presence and accountability requirements to more state-controlled educational reform. In the future, we are likely to continue to see this see-sawing back and forth between the states and the federal government for control and influence of public education in America.

WHY TEACH? YOUR FINAL WORD

1. What role, if any, do you think the federal government should play in compensating for educational disadvantages that result from living in poverty?

2. Do you believe you would like to become a school principal or local superintendent someday? Why or why not?

3. The National Education Association and the National Association of Secondary School Principals make this statement about successful secondary schools: "In good secondary schools, the principal and teachers develop and maintain a variety of cooperative links with the community. Family and community involvement and support complement the efforts of the school." Describe some of the cooperative links you would suggest at either the elementary or secondary level.

KEY TERMS

block grants (354)
categorical grants (354)
chief state school officer (338)
compensatory education (354)
Elementary and Secondary Education Act (ESEA) (354)
Every Student Succeeds Act (354)
Head Start (355)

local school board (339)
parent–teacher organization (PTO) (344)
privatization (347)
state board of education (338)
state department of education (339)
superintendent of schools (340)
Title I (354)

FOR FURTHER INFORMATION

Web Resources

National Education Association

The NEA website offers many resources, including an annual report (called "Rankings of States and Estimates of School Statistics") that features many statistics on the states, including average teacher salaries, per-pupil expenditures by state, per capita expenditures on education, and many other interesting statistics. To find the report, go to the Search function and enter "Rankings and Estimates."

U.S. Department of Education

This home page will keep you abreast of educational initiatives developed by the federal government. Entering National Center for Education Statistics in the search will give you access to many government publications and statistics on education.

Print Resources

Vern Brimley, Jr., Deborah A. Verstegen, and Robert C. Knoeppel, *Financing Education in a Climate of Change*, 13th ed. (New York City, N.Y.: Pearson, 2019).

This comprehensive text examines how schools are financed in the United States, the role of the federal government, and significant court cases affecting school finance.

Michael W. Kirst and Frederick M. Wirt, *The Political Dynamics of American Education*, 4th ed. (Berkeley, CA: McCutchan, 2009).

This text presents an analysis of the politics of education by two leaders in the field.

Theodore J. Kowalski, *The School Superintendent: Theory, Practice, and Cases*, 3rd ed. (Thousand Oaks, CA: Sage Publications, 2013).

A comprehensive examination of the school superintendency.

How Should Education Be Reformed?

iStock.com/Christopher Futcher

LEARNING OBJECTIVES

12-1 Identify two prominent elements of school reform over the last 30 years.

12-2 Name at least two positive and two negative elements of the Every Student Succeeds Act legislation.

12-3 Name four common emphases of state educational reform efforts.

12-4 Describe the differences among these forms of school choice: magnet schools, charter schools, and voucher plans.

12-5 Explain which of the school reform efforts advocated by the authors appeals most to you, and why.

Truth OR Fiction?

T F   Approximately 2 million students in the United States are educated at home.

T F   Research shows that charter schools are academically superior to regular public schools.

T F   School voucher plans have become widespread through most of the United States.

This chapter takes a concentrated look at the educational reform movement. For more than 30 years, politicians and educators have been working vigorously to alter the course of American elementary and secondary education. Although the results of their efforts have been mixed to date, certain patterns and key educational ideas are evident.

It has been said that trying to change or reform our schools is like trying to change a flat tire on a speeding car—something that needs to be done but is nearly impossible to achieve. For nearly 100 years, attempts have been made to bring about change in American schools, with mixed results. Many of these reform efforts have been fueled by philosophical debates as to what the purpose of schools should be (see Chapter 2, "What Is a School and What Is It For?").

For example, in the early 1900s, with the development of factories, which were seen as a more efficient way of producing goods, some people argued that students could be more efficiently educated if schools looked and functioned like factories. They also thought that students would become better adult workers if their schools resembled factory assembly lines. Opponents of this view (including John Dewey, who is profiled in Chapter 9, "What Are the Philosophical Foundations of American Education?") thought that schools should educate students to be good thinkers and citizens who, as adults, would work to bring about a better, more equitable society. Thus our schools became more democratic.

The most recent movement to bring about change in U.S. schools grew out of an influential 1983 report by the National Commission on Excellence in Education, entitled *A Nation at Risk*. In clear and forceful language, the commission described what it called a "rising tide of mediocrity" in the schools. The report demanded that this tide be stemmed through a greater focus on the academic achievement of students.

In the 30 years since this report was released, some progress has been made toward reforming schools. How much more can or must be made remains open to debate. Some educators and politicians argue that much more needs to be done to improve U.S. schools, given that the reforms implemented to date have not led to significant gains in academic achievement. Others disagree, stating that U.S. schools are a great social achievement, educating more children to higher levels than the schools supported by any other society in the world.

Skeptics believe that the schools—and particularly the public schools—are "broken" and incapable of being reformed. Other observers argue that schools, as institutions, are deeply resistant to change and that, unlike corporations, whose effectiveness can be judged by bottom-line profits or losses, the effectiveness of schools is all but impossible to measure, in part because their purposes remain vague and multiple. Without a single, clear definition of a well-educated person, schools cannot agree on how to reform themselves.

Pause *and* Reflect

1. Based on your own personal school experiences, do you believe our schools need to be reformed and changed in any major ways? Why or why not?
2. What do you believe are the most compelling reasons to reform U.S. schools?

12-1 Recent Reform Initiatives

The United States has historically been an education-oriented society. As a society, we have been proud of our schools and their accomplishments of providing an achievement ladder for anyone who took advantage of them. In recent decades, this faith has eroded, and more and more evidence piles up, first, about the achievement gap between our students and those of many nations, and, second, about the failure of so many schools to adequately serve children from poverty backgrounds and students of color.

Although the issue of school reform has been on the national agenda with health care and the environment, it emerged to new prominence in 2010. Major television networks devoted time and resources to exploring what was wrong with our schools and what should be done. Independently and within months of one another, filmmakers released four powerful documentaries—*Waiting for "Superman," Race to Nowhere: The Dark Side of America's Achievement Culture, The Lottery*, and *The Cartel*—all of which are highly critical of our educational system. This intense media attention focused in particular on our urban schools and how they are educating African American and Latino students and newly arrived immigrants.

Two themes that have come to prominence both in the education literature and in the popular media are high-stakes testing and school choice. Testing, which 20 years ago was seen as the spearhead of the school reform movement, is increasingly being seen as overused and sucking the air out of what should be the joy of learning. The theme of parental choice of schools is hardly new but has gained in intensity as many parents seek educational alternatives for their children. These themes and the others to which we now turn have been intensified by the current economic demands and the realizations that our national future depends so on the quality of the education we are providing our children today.

Again, though, most educators agree that the modern reform effort started with the 1983 federal report *A Nation at Risk*. This strongly worded document declared that the United States was in serious danger because its schools had left the nation vulnerable to its military and economic competitors. The report called for longer school days, more homework and effort on the part of students, tougher grading policies, more testing, and more demanding textbooks. It arrived at a time of particularly widespread dissatisfaction with the public schools. The remainder of the 1980s saw a blizzard of national and state reports, most hitting many of the same themes and all calling for massive change.

The 1990s was a period of intense development of curricular, programmatic, and pedagogic initiatives aimed at bringing about change in schools and better student performance. Several different groups at the national, state, and local levels created proposals for reform. So what have been the results?

12-2 National-Level Reform Efforts

Since the publication of *A Nation at Risk* in 1983, education has had a prime place in every presidential candidate's platform. After President Reagan, President George H. W. Bush launched an aggressive educational reform effort called **National Education Goals (Goals 2000)**. With the support and cooperation of the

50 state governors, this program committed the nation to achieve six educational milestones by the arrival of the new millennium. The next president, Bill Clinton, added two more goals and recommitted the nation to achieve these goals by 2000.[1] Although well intentioned, in retrospect the National Education Goals for 2000 effort seems somewhat naïve, promising more than the schools could reasonably deliver.

12-2a NO CHILD LEFT BEHIND ACT (NCLB)

The next major educational reform effort was the No Child Left Behind Act, which President George W. Bush signed into law in 2002. This bill revised the Elementary and Secondary Education Act (ESEA; originally passed in 1965) and greatly increased the federal role in education by putting into place requirements that reached into virtually every public school in the United States.[2]

The main goal of NCLB was to close the "achievement gap" between students who perform well in schools and those who perform poorly. To do so, NCLB required that all teachers be "highly qualified" and that every student be "proficient" in reading and mathematics. The law also put pressure on school districts to turn around low-performing schools, with a series of negative consequences for schools that persistently fail to demonstrate "adequate yearly progress" toward having all students meet state standards. NCLB changed the federal government's role in K–12 education by asking U.S. schools to describe their success in terms of what each student accomplished.

As a result of considerable dissatisfaction with NCLB, in 2012, then-U.S. Secretary of Education Arne Duncan began issuing waivers to states that exempted them from some of the most onerous provisions of the law: by the end of 2013, 34 states had received waivers.[3]

12-2b EVERY STUDENT SUCCEEDS ACT

Building upon and replacing No Child Left Behind is the Every Student Succeeds Act (ESSA), a law passed in 2015. The federal government's largest K–12 education investment, ESSA emphasizes each school's responsibility to prepare "all students for success in college and career." A key provision of ESSA requires each state to develop its own student performance targets that focus on college and career readiness; this is to include students taking standardized exams for reading/language arts and mathematics each year from grades three through eight, and once more in high school. Students must also take standardized exams for science once between grades three and five, another exam between grades six and nine, and another exam between grades ten and twelve.

Through ESSA the federal government provides what it calls "guardrails." However, schools and teachers are ultimately accountable to their state governments for the success of their students. This means that states are required to develop their own accountability system—ways of identifying and supporting low performing schools—and publicly report the academic outcomes of all schools and groups of students.[4]

12-2c RACE TO THE TOP

In 2010, President Obama and Secretary of Education Arne Duncan presented what has been described as a "stick-and-carrot" program to jump-start what they consider to be exemplary educational ideas and practice, in hopes that other states will adopt similar practices. Called Race to the Top, the program's goals are to reward school reform efforts and provide educational exemplars to the nation's educational community. Using $4.35 billion of stimulus monies as awards (i.e., "carrots") and attaching various conditions (i.e., "sticks"), such as eliminating legal barriers to charter schools, the administration hoped to bring about specific changes.[5]

The prize money for Race to the Top was awarded to 18 states and the District of Columbia. A recent report evaluating the Race to the Top initiative concluded that the program is limited in what it can accomplish, given the amount of money available, and that the winning states overpromised what they could achieve. Further, the report concluded, the Race to the Top program did not address some of the most important reasons for low student achievement, including factors outside the school and school funding inequities.[6]

12-2d NATIONAL STANDARDS

Under NCLB, each state was required to develop standards of learning and to test children annually in English language arts and mathematics. Some states developed high standards and rigorous assessments, whereas other states' standards and assessments were less rigorous. Because of the great variability from state to state, the National Governors Association and the Council of Chief State School Officers initiated the Common Core State Standards project to develop common standards in English language arts and mathematics. In 2020, 41 states, the District of Columbia, four territories, and the Department of Defense Education Activity had adopted the standards.[7] In addition, several science organizations have developed the Next Generation Science Standards for K–12 schooling. (See Chapter 5, "What Is Taught?," for more on these national standards efforts.)

Since the adoption of the Common Core State Standards by the vast majority of states, significant opposition to the standards and assessments has arisen. As a condition for getting waivers from NCLB, the U.S. Department of Education required states to adopt the Common Core State Standards, which conservatives protested on the basis of federal intrusion into states' rights. Some liberals also objected to the standards, arguing that they have not been field-tested and that the whole standards movement in the United States has failed to improve academic performance in a significant manner.

Although most other countries have national education standards, the issue in the United States remains a highly controversial topic.

12-2e A NATIONAL CURRICULUM

There is a difference between standards and curriculum. Standards are statements of agreed-upon expectations of what students are expected to know and be able to do in certain subjects and at certain grade levels—in other words, outcomes. A curriculum consists of the approaches and materials that teachers use to help students meet the standards. Although the United States seems to be moving closer to a set of national standards, at least in certain subjects, the notion of a national curriculum at present is far off.

One advocate for a national curriculum, however, is E. D. Hirsch, Jr., who popularized the concept of "cultural literacy." He presents the equality argument, insisting that a national curriculum is needed because so many students move around from state to state and from school to school. With a national curriculum, relocated students would be able to integrate easily into their new school environment, with no time lost academically. Hirsch points to facts such as these: one-fifth of all Americans relocate every year; one-sixth of all third graders attend at least three different schools between first and third grades; and a typical inner-city school has a 50 percent student turnover between September and May.[8]

Others make the quality argument by citing the educational excellence attained by France, Germany, and Japan—all countries with national curricula, national standards, and national exams. These proponents insist that a national curriculum will ensure that all students in the United States receive a high-quality education, no matter where they attend school.

Other educators strongly oppose national standards and an accompanying curriculum and testing program, fearing an educational power grab by the federal government. In their view, the idea of Washington bureaucrats, instead of locally accountable individuals answering the questions "What should our children know?" and "How well should they know it?" seems both educationally flawed and politically dangerous. Opponents also believe that in a large nation with so many racial, religious, and ethnic groups and so many regional traditions, a national curriculum would trample on cultural diversity and promote a bland sterility. Further, many are convinced that a national curriculum would put disadvantaged students at an even greater disadvantage. It would appear that the current Common Core State Standards movement represents a compromise: national standards, but on a voluntary basis.

12-2f NATIONAL VOLUNTARY NETWORKS

One of the most interesting educational developments is the appearance of networks of schools and school districts. Among these loose, voluntary alliances are:

- the Coalition of Essential Schools begun by the late Theodore Sizer;
- the network of schools modeled after James Comer's New Haven School Development Program;
- John Goodlad's National Network for Educational Renewal;
- Robert Slavin's Success for All schools;
- Henry Levin's Accelerated Schools; and
- Schools of Character, formed by the Character Education Partnership.

Schools in these networks commit themselves to a common educational ideal or set of ideals rather than a prescribed course of study or approach to teaching and learning.

12-2g HIGH SCHOOL REFORM

Most of the reforms of the previous two decades, successful and otherwise, took place in elementary schools and, to a lesser extent, middle schools. However, in 2005, a long-overdue campaign to reform U.S. high schools was launched. The initiators of this transformational project are a coalition of state governors, foundation directors, and business leaders, including Microsoft's Bill Gates, himself a rather successful college dropout.

The group believes that the current American high school is an "obsolete" institution, out of touch with the global world of work and the demands of higher education. Its members are concerned that our trading partners around the world have more rigorous and productive high schools than those of the United States. In response to these concerns, they are dedicated to implementing several of the changes recommended in this chapter, especially higher academic standards accompanied by a more rigorous curriculum and a better testing and accountability system that measures students' readiness for work and for college.

Armed with strong financial support from businesses and foundations, plus fresh, compelling evidence of the inadequacies of many high school graduates, this coalition is seeking wider support to transform U.S. high schools. It launched the American Diploma Project Network, by which governors, state education

Up CLOSE

The Partnership for 21st-Century Skills

In many ways, the reform of American education is too important to be left to educators alone. Everyone has a stake, particularly now as the health of the nation's economy and position in the world has been so clearly related to the quality of our schools. The Partnership for 21st Century Skills (P21) is a national organization that has not only called attention to the need for K–12 educational reform, but also for its members to provide tools and resources to help schools, teachers, and pupils get ready for the demands of the twenty-first century.

Essentially, P21 is a catalyst organization, a partnership among leaders from education, business, the foundation world, and government, that calls attention to the profound gap between the knowledge and skills most students learn in school and the knowledge and skills they need in typical twenty-first-century communities and workplaces. More than that, P21 is attempting to get our schools to take a fresh look at what and how they are teaching. To do this, P21 has created a well-developed

model, one involving fusing the classic "three R's" and what it calls "the four C's "(critical thinking and problem solving, communication, collaboration, and creativity and innovation). (These "four C's" are quite similar to "the Tools for Learning" we describe in the "Up Close" feature on page 384.)

Although the three R's are necessary to master the core subjects (English, history, the arts, mathematics, science, foreign languages, geography, economics, civics, and government), P21 insists that students need to move beyond basic mastery of these subjects. They must master them at a higher level, enabling them to weave them into what P21 calls **twenty-first-century interdisciplinary themes,** such as global awareness; financial, economic, business, and entrepreneurial literacy; civic literacy; health literacy; and, finally, environmental literacy.

P21 presents educators with a fresh and challenging vision of our work that we can only touch on here. We urge you to follow up and check out the P21 website at www.p21.org/index.php.

officials, postsecondary leaders, and business executives work together to improve postsecondary preparation by aligning high school standards, graduation requirements, and assessment and accountability systems with the demands of college and careers. The network has grown to 35 states, educating 85 percent of all public school students.[9] Whether this unique partnership of businessmen, foundation directors, and governors has the energy and leverage to change U.S. high schools in fundamental ways remains to be seen.

12-2h IMPLICATIONS OF NATIONAL-LEVEL REFORM EFFORTS

Overall, two things are clear about educational reforms at the national level. First, we are in the middle of a strong push toward national influence on education. Second, there has been a robust response from the states to improve their content standards and to hold local school districts accountable for these standards by imposing statewide testing with high-stakes consequences (graduation-dependent testing). The days of strong local control over schools in the United States appear to be waning.

12-3 State Educational Reform

As education evolved into more of a national issue, reform also became a hot political topic on levels from the state house to the mayor's office. Statewide task forces were formed by governors, state legislatures, and state boards of education, and a large number were formed by citizens' groups and foundations. Some states had several task forces operating on the same issues at the same time. Numerous local school districts established their own blue-ribbon commissions to respond to what was increasingly called *the school crisis*. There was, however, one common theme: the call for excellence.

Throughout both American industry and education, mediocrity was the dominant criticism of the existing educational system, and excellence became the rallying cry of the reformers. Many of these state and local task force reports have *excellence* or *quality* in their titles. Because these task forces and reports were sponsored by state governmental agencies or well-connected citizens' groups or educational foundations, their recommendations were quickly turned into legislative proposals for school reform.

12-3a COMMON ELEMENTS IN STATE REFORM

At the state level, the "call for excellence" came down to specific proposals for change. The most widely adopted state reforms are described next.

An Increase in Graduation Requirements

Instead of mandating that students take only one or two years of English and history, states began requiring three and four years in core subjects. To be awarded academic high school diplomas, science and advanced mathematics courses were required. The idea of "social promotion" (i.e., moving students through the grades so that they could stay with their own age groups independently of their performance) came under great pressure and has been eliminated in many places, especially with the advent of mandated tests for graduation.

Spurred on by the United States' mediocre performance on recent international studies of math and science proficiency, the majority of states have increased the number of academic credits needed for graduations, with particular increases in the number of years of science and mathematics.[10]

More Academic Learning Time

Research has shown that *quality* instruction time, rather than time merely spent in class, is the key to quality schooling. Nevertheless, in the minds of many educators, the short school day and the long, academically fallow period between June and September are major causes of the poor performance of U.S. students. More time in school overall, they suggest, improves the chances of having more high-quality time.

In response to this notion, school days, which in many locales were only five and a half to six hours, were lengthened to six and a half to seven hours. The school year, which in many states was between 170 and 175 days or fewer, has been lengthened to an average of 180 days, although states still vary from between 160 days (Colorado) and 190 days (New York) of school per year.[11] Though many of the reform reports recommended that U.S. schools follow the example of Japan (240 days) and Germany (216 to 240 days), no states and relatively few school districts have taken such a major step in lengthening the school year. One reason is that lengthening the amount of schooling is extremely costly.

In some states, the idea of **year-round education** has attracted the attention of educators. In most year-round schools, students go to school the same number of days as in traditional schools, but the school days are more evenly distributed throughout the school year. The most popular schedule is referred to as "45–15." Students attend school for 45 days, and then have 15 days of vacation. In the summer, students have six weeks of vacation instead of the usual 8 to 10 weeks. As of 2019, almost 3,200 public schools as well as many private schools in the United States had adopted some kind of a year-round schedule.[12]

Critics of year-round education cite the strain such a schedule places on school finances when upgrades such as air conditioning are needed. They are also concerned about disrupting established family life patterns and summer opportunities for teachers' professional development. On the other hand, proponents insist that the long 10-week summer vacation is hardest on poor children, for whom camps and pricy recreational and enrichment programs are out of reach. They argue that the academic ground lost over the summer is a significant contributor to the achievement gap that separates high- and low-income children. President Obama, citing the fact that students in many other countries yearly spend at least a month longer in school than our students, urged that American students have a longer school year.[13]

Higher Expectations for Teachers

One of the major state-driven reform efforts of the 1980s and 1990s was the move to improve the quality of the U.S. teaching force. Two initiatives were particularly notable in this regard: teacher competency testing and career ladder programs.

The first initiative, **teacher competency testing**, was not new, though it emerged with a vengeance during the last two decades of the twentieth century. Almost all states have some form of teacher testing, which typically takes place when candidates are leaving their teacher education programs or before they receive state licensure.

One vexing issue that has plagued the movement for teacher competency testing has been the definition of an appropriate and valid standard to which all teacher candidates should be held. In some states, cutoff scores have been set so low as to make them meaningless. In effect, teachers are supposed to demonstrate their proficiency by jumping over a hurdle, but the hurdle has been so low that anyone

Increased graduation requirements and calls for more testing are part of many states' educational reforms.

©luminaimages/Shutterstock.com

could jump it. In other states, the standard is considered too arbitrary, dissuading teachers from seeking licensure in those states. There is also variation regarding which competencies are being tested, such as general English and math proficiency, along with content knowledge. In some states, efforts are being made to test competencies beyond mere paper-and-pencil tests and to observe for competence in actual classrooms. The second teacher-related initiative involved **career ladders**. Critics have long complained about the "flatness" of the career structure in teaching. The criticism goes something like this: "Beginners have too much responsibility at the start of their careers and too little opportunity to make the most of their abilities once they really learn to teach. The only way to get promoted in education has been to be promoted *away from students*, by becoming a department chair, curriculum coordinator, or administrator." With the encouragement of state legislatures, a variety of teacher specialty programs, such as master teacher programs, differentiated staffing, and mentoring programs for new teachers, have now appeared on the scene. Typically, these programs give experienced teachers new roles, new responsibilities, and usually new rewards. Although these innovations have had limited adoption, the assumption that "a teacher is a teacher is a teacher" has been dispelled, and new roles, such as mentor teacher, lead teacher, and team leader, have been opened to teachers who not only want new challenges but also want to stay in the classroom, close to students.

Higher Salaries for Teachers

A key problem revealed by the blizzard of reports published in the 1980s and 1990s was the weak rewards system for teachers. Career ladders and other schemes that expand and enrich the teacher's role represented one way to reward teachers, but more was needed if teaching was to become an attractive professional option for talented students. Salaries were an obvious target. During the 1980s, the average teacher salary increased at a rate twice that of inflation. Since then, average salaries have generally kept pace with inflation.

Closely linked to this change has been a significant move to make teaching more attractive by increasing the starting salaries of teachers. In the late 1980s, beginning teachers earned $12,000 to $13,000. By the 2018–2019 school year, the national average for beginning teachers was $40,154 .[14] (See Chapter 13, "What Are Your Job Options in Education?," for more information on current salary trends.) Meanwhile, various commissions and commentators continue to press for higher salaries both for teachers entering the field and for experienced teachers. All across the United States, the lock-step pay scale under which teachers were rewarded only for years of service and number of courses taken or degrees earned has been altered to allow for **performance pay (pay for performance)**, a form of recognition and reward for acquiring new knowledge or skills, or for increasing student achievement. In 2007, 28 nationally recognized, award-winning teachers came together and issued a widely hailed report, "Performance Pay for Teachers: Designing a System that Students Deserve," which forcefully calls for changes in the way the United States recognizes excellence in teaching.[15] Also, the Obama administration made pay for performance a strong plank in its Race to the Top school improvement plan. In 2010, however, supporters of merit pay plans, such as pay for performance, received a setback with the release of a study by the National Center on Performance Incentives. This large-scale study concluded that students of teachers receiving performance pay achieved no better on tests than those taught by teachers not receiving such financial bonuses.[16] However, we doubt that this is the end of efforts to provide pay incentives to outstanding teachers.

12-4 School Choice

As we stated at the beginning of this chapter, school choice (along with testing) is a major theme in efforts to provide better education for American children. Implemented on both the local and state levels, the school choice reform aims to offer families more options about where their children will attend school. Technically, all parents have a choice as to where they wish to have their children educated. If they do not like the public, state-supported school to which their children are assigned, they can send them to a private or religious school (if one is available in their locale), or they can move to another community where the schools are more to their liking. Another increasingly popular option has been for parents to teach their own children at home. This "option" became a reality in the spring of 2020 when the COVID-19 pandemic forced school closings across the country and the number of American students being schooled at home suddenly shot up from 3 percent to 100 percent overnight!

Once the schools opened the following fall, the case for home schooling and other forms of choice (i.e., private and religious schools) were affected by the Supreme Court decision in *Espinoza* v. *Montana*. This ruling found unconstitutional state laws prohibiting using tax monies for non-public schools and has cleared the way for potential support of school choice. State legislatures could be offered dozens of new measures to promote the tax support of private schools, religious schools, and home schools.

While the 2020 COVID-19 school lockdown increased the interest of many parents in home schooling, may more came to realize it was not for them. Anecdotally, it has been reported that American parents have a new and greater appreciation of the work of their children's teachers. Nevertheless, for the large percentage of parents without the time and ability to conduct home schooling or the resources to pay tuition at private or religious schools, there has been a new interest in **school choice** as an

Up CLOSE

Home Schooling

Hilary Tucker is a mother of four children who lives in Auburn, Alabama. She is one of a growing number of parents who have decided to educate their children themselves, most often in their home. It is estimated that over 2 million children are home-schooled in this country. Reasons cited for home schooling range from concerns about the moral climate in public schools, to religious objections or the curriculum, and to the absence of particular courses of study. In all cases, however, parents strongly believe that they can provide a better education for their children than the public schools can.

Ⓣ F
Approximately 2 million students in the United States are educated at home.

Regulations for home schooling vary from state to state. In some states, parents have to submit an educational plan for their home-schooled children; in other states, they merely inform the school and/or the state education agency of their intention to home-school their children.

Home schooling these days offers every child an opportunity for a world-class education. It doesn't have to cost a great deal, and it is adaptable to many circumstances and individuals.

In recent years, the opportunities for co-op classes, tutoring, and online courses have exploded. Home-schooling parents no longer have to do it all themselves. My 13-year-old takes Latin, theology, and humanities with an online academy. She also takes Spanish and biology in local home-school classes, but she is most impassioned about the

(Continued)

ideas presented in her online classes and reading assignments. Ten eager elementary students come to study Latin and Roman history with us on Wednesday mornings, providing the classroom experience of more formal schooling, tests, and competition. A friend with teaching experience teaches them English grammar, and the older students meet with a math tutor, who teaches them individually.

By having personally tailored curricula and individual attention, home-schooled students' time is rarely wasted. My children have their formal lessons during the morning hours, but in some way, the schooling never stops. There are many hours in the week for both directed and leisure reading, and the TV rarely comes on in this house. My preschooler is working through reading lessons, memorizing poetry, and otherwise engaging in creative activities.

During the afternoons, once the assignments are done, the kids follow their own interests. The older children practice piano and violin and are involved in sports, dance, and other programs. The hobbies are fruitful too. At age 7, my daughter charted the birds that came to our yard. She's learned how to knit and sew (thanks to an obliging friend), has started her own blog, and is teaching herself web design. During their younger years, my children spent many an afternoon climbing trees and examining bugs. And they played. They worked out elaborate fantasies about knights and princesses, formed pioneer families, and discovered elves. They built forts and pressed flowers.

For home-schooling parents, offering each child (not just the brightest) the opportunity to become passionate about ideas is worth the sacrifice of having their children under their supervision for most of the day. Students develop the habit of learning, so they don't always have to depend on an instructor. They come to know what it means to master bodies of knowledge and how to reason. They can progress at their own rate. The advanced student is not held back and made to repeat exercises she has already learned. The slower student does not miss out on building foundational skills because other students are ready to move on. Where the student has weaknesses, he receives extra help. Where there are strengths, he has the opportunity to soar. As a teacher, I am able to teach my children a time-tested curriculum so the child is spared trendy new subjects that may not be around in 10 years.

Perhaps understandably, parents of home-schooled kids are often asked, "What about socialization?" It is true that home-schooled children do not spend their days in a classroom filled with 22 peers and are deprived of this particular group experience. Yet this freedom from the bustling crowd can be an advantage. The children learn to cooperate with other children of all ages, primarily and significantly their siblings, but friends and peers in the neighborhood and in community sports leagues and other activities too.

Home schooling is not an insular experience for the children I know. Support networks are well developed and surprisingly diversified. Most days, tennis, music lessons, dance classes, and trips to the library get this family out of the house. The kids have played in city sports leagues and been in local theater programs. They also have more time with grandparents and neighbors. And, of course, their friends come over to play. With all this, the children divide their time between other children and the adult world. This is one reason why home-schooled students are so strikingly comfortable around people of all ages.

I believe I, and many other parents, can serve my children and society best by educating them in our home. And, besides the progress they are making, I am enjoying it immensely.

important aspect of access and educational opportunity. Many argue, too, that poor parents should have a choice in the schools their children attend, just as wealthier parents do. Accordingly, being able to choose the school your children attend is, first, the right of parents, and second, an important way to ensure access to educational opportunity. If the neighborhood public school isn't doing an adequate job, shouldn't parents have alternative choices of schools?

The advocates of school choice see the current system as monopolistic. The United States, they note, is recognized around the world as a consumer's paradise. Whether it is soft drinks in the supermarket, jeans in a clothing store, or sports cars at the auto dealer, the principle of choice rules—except in K–12 schooling. School choice advocates want to redesign the way we organize education, shifting the decision of where a child must go to school from the school system to the child's parents. In essence, they want *market forces* to regulate the schools, instead of the educational monopoly that they claim currently operates.

Parents as Educational Consumers

Advocates for school choice say that the current public schools have no real incentive to better serve students because educators' salaries and benefits are unaffected by either good or poor student results. Teachers who work 16 hours a day and give heart and soul to the school are on the same salary scale as teachers who are the first ones out of the parking lot at 2:30 p.m. According to school choice advocates, if parents can act as consumers, schools will have real incentives to improve. Free-market principles suggest that "more choice equals more competition equals better products at lower prices." Here, the phrase "better products" means better-educated students. Supporters of school choice also suggest that the group getting the worst public education today—urban minorities—stands to benefit the most under such a plan.

The choice concept appears to be gaining support across the United States. In addition to home schooling, at least three kinds of school choice exist. The least controversial kind, **within-district choice**, allows parents to choose from among the various public schools that a school district or state operates. Many school districts have created a variety of schools with different goals and purposes, and allow parents to select the one they want their child to attend. A more controversial and popular kind of school choice is the *charter school* concept, and the most controversial kind is *school voucher plans*. The major political parties have staked out positions on the choice issue, with Democrats typically favoring choice within the current public school system and Republicans tending to support voucher plans. Although the teachers' unions usually give only token support to charter schools, they typically draw support from both Republicans and Democrats.

Public School Choice

Increasingly, public school systems are offering parents and students options, in addition to the traditional neighborhood school, as to which schools students attend. Some schools have a particular specialty such as mathematics or science. Others are "alternative" schools designed for youth who don't seem to fit well within traditional schools.

Several varieties of public school choice exist, most of which are fairly non-controversial. Districtwide (intradistrict) choice allows parents to select among the schools within their home district. These school choice options are offered in numerous school districts, including Boston, Seattle, Minneapolis/St. Paul, and District 4 in New York City. Statewide (interdistrict) choice allows students to attend public schools outside their home school district.

Charter Schools

Over 40 years ago, a number of American cities adopted an early form of school choice, called **magnet schools**. These elementary, middle, and high schools specialized in a specific academic area, such as science or the arts, and in basic skills. Magnet schools were originally designed to stop white flight from urban schools and to attract (like a magnet) white students back to inner cities. Although still in existence in many cities, enthusiasm for magnet schools has been displaced by what has become the darling of choice advocates: charter schools.

Charter schools are public schools with special privileges. Recent years have brought a rapid growth in charter schools. By 2020, there were 7,400 charter schools in the country, serving over 3 million children.[17] Teachers, administrators, parents, and community representatives who wish to open a charter school in a district negotiate an agreement with the school district or other agency authorized to grant charters. As long as they meet the specifications of their charters, these schools are free to control their own budgets, hire their own consultants, design their own curriculum, and infuse the school with their own educational flavor. These schools are, in effect, *independent public schools*. Typically, students are chosen randomly from those who apply to attend the particular charter school.

Because they are independent, charter schools usually have a strong element of **site-based decision making** (also known as *site-based management* or *school-based management*), in which participatory decision making is the mode of operation. In theory, the charter school's site-based decision making provides everyone—teachers, parents, and students alike—with more say about what goes on in their school and with a great degree of ownership of and commitment to the decisions that are made. An example of a network of for-profit charter schools, the Knowledge Is Power Program (KIPP) schools, is shown in the "Up Close: The KIPP Schools" feature.

Charter schools are judged on how well they meet the student achievement goals established by their charter, or contract, and how well they manage their fiscal and operational responsibilities. Although charters generally allow schools to be run with substantial autonomy, the schools must operate lawfully and responsibly with the highest regard for equity and excellence, or their charters will be taken away. In the two decades charter schools have been around, many have failed due to financial mismanagement and occasionally because of embezzlement.

Even more disappointing to charter advocates has been recent research that indicates overall rather mediocre achievement gains by students in charter schools. In 2010, the U.S. Department of Education issued a report in which 36 charter middle schools across 15 states were studied. The report concluded that, on average, charter middle schools are neither more nor less successful than traditional public schools in improving student achievement, behavior, and school progress.[18]

> T (F)
> Research shows that charter schools are academically superior to regular public schools.

Up CLOSE

The KIPP Schools

One of the most successful of the new breed of alternative schools are the Knowledge Is Power Program schools or, as they are commonly referred to, the KIPP schools. Begun in 1994 by two teachers, in 2018 there were 200 KIPP schools in 20 states, serving 50,000 students.[19] All of the KIPP schools are grade 5 to 8 middle schools, and the great bulk of them are charter schools serving a largely minority student body.

With a few exceptions, these schools are public schools under contract with their communities to provide educational service. Although initially supported heavily by foundations and donors, KIPP schools survive on budgets similar to their neighboring "regular" public middle schools. The similarities after that are few.

KIPP schools are called "no-excuses" schools because of their commitment to students' development of self-discipline and good behavior.

And these qualities are seen as the keys to their impressive record of achievement. Over 90 percent of KIPP middle schoolers attended college prep high schools, and over 85 percent have gone on to college. This from a population of students of whom 95 percent are either Latino or African American.

The schools' achievement is based on a fierce commitment to excellence, which in turn rests on KIPP's five pillars:

- *High expectations.* KIPP schools have clearly defined and measurable high expectations for academic achievement and conduct that make no excuses based on the students' backgrounds. Students, parents, teachers, and staff create and reinforce a culture of achievement and support through a range of formal and informal rewards and consequences for academic performance and behavior.

(Continued)

- *Choice and commitment.* Students, their parents, and the faculty of each KIPP school choose to participate in the program. No one is assigned or forced to attend a KIPP school. Everyone must make and uphold a commitment to the school and to each other to put in the time and effort required to achieve success.

- *More time.* KIPP schools know that there are no shortcuts when it comes to success in academics and life. With an extended school day, week, and year, students have more time in the classroom to acquire the academic knowledge and skills that will prepare them for competitive high schools and colleges, as well as more opportunities to engage in diverse extracurricular experiences.

- *Power to lead.* The principals of KIPP schools are effective academic and organizational leaders who understand that great schools require great school leaders. They have control over their school budget and personnel. They are free to swiftly move dollars or make staffing changes, allowing them maximum effectiveness in helping students learn.

- *Focus on results.* KIPP schools relentlessly focus on high student performance on standardized tests and other objective measures. Just as there are no shortcuts, there are no excuses. Students are expected to achieve a level of academic performance that will enable them to succeed at the nation's best high schools and colleges.[20]

Although KIPP schools have many of the advantages of charter schools, such as parents' selecting into the school and the capacity to expel poor-performing or uncooperative students, they still have many features that are seen as quite compatible with regular schools. This capacity to provide inspiration and competition is one of the major contributions of the school choice movement.

On the other hand, there are studies that show low-income and low-performing charter school students perform better in mathematics than students in traditional public schools, and charter school students are more likely to graduate from high school and attend college.[21]

Often, however, evaluations have been carried out by individuals with vested interests in either proving the effectiveness of charter schools or showing that they are ineffective and lack accountability. More time will be needed to see whether charter schools will revolutionize public education or remain just a boutique innovation.

States vary greatly in the ease with which charter schools may be created and in the number of restrictions and amount of autonomy these schools are granted.

Many supporters see charter schools as a way to encourage innovation, provide parents with school choice, and still be supportive of the public school system. Opponents wonder why the charter schools should be exempt from regulations, whereas the rest of the public schools must abide by them. They also see charter schools as a form of "voucher lite"—that is, a foot in the door toward the creation of school vouchers, to which we now turn.

Vouchers

More controversial than charter schools are school **voucher plans**. In their typical form, vouchers give the parent-consumer the widest array of choices. In effect, this type of plan gives parents a piece of paper, a voucher worth a certain dollar amount, that they can use to help pay the costs for their child to attend the public or private school of their choice. The school collects a voucher from each student who chooses that school and then turns in its vouchers to the state government for real dollars with which to run the school.

The voucher idea came to public attention 1955 when Nobel Laureate economist Milton Friedman wrote an article entitled "The Role of Government in Education," based on well-known free-market principles, in hopes that increased competition would lead to student achievement gains and lower costs.[22] Friedman strongly questioned the appropriateness in a democracy of the government (national, state, and local) dictating what is taught in school. According to Friedman, in a "pure choice" system, all schools would be public schools, the way all department stores are public stores. Advocates of the voucher system believe it would release an enormous amount of competition-driven creativity in our schools. Teachers and administrators would join together to provide high-quality, unique educational programs that would attract students and parents. Educational institutions would be like most other American enterprises, competing to put out the best possible product—namely, students. Those that succeeded would prosper, attracting many students (and therefore voucher dollars). Those schools and teachers who failed to attract or hold "customers" would "go out of business," perhaps to start again with a better educational idea.

> **T (F)**
> School voucher plans have become widespread through most of the United States.

By 2019, 18 states and the District of Columbia have voucher programs, with nearly 190,000 students using vouchers.[23] Of those, eight states offer vouchers to special needs students, four states plus the District of Columbia offer them to low-income students or students from failing schools, and two offer them to certain rural students. Louisiana and Ohio have programs for both low-income and special needs students.[24]

Some public education critics see the voucher concept as the savior of education in the United States. Others see it as a plot to undermine both the public schools and their interpretation of the meaning of the separation of church and state. Many politicians who support charter schools oppose voucher plans. They see charter schools as providing choice opportunities to parents and encouraging school reform efforts while staying within the public education system, but view voucher plans as draining money from the public schools and delivering those funds to private and religious schools. Vouchers reduce

Voucher programs that allow students to use public funding to attend private schools are quite controversial.

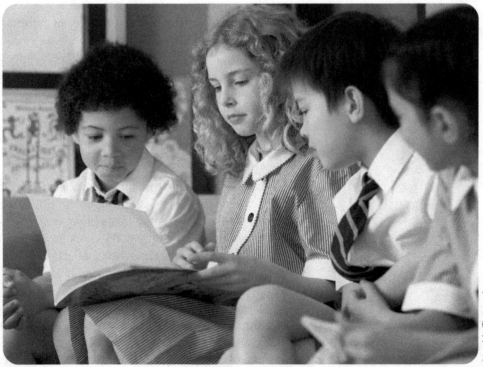

sirtravelalot/Shutterstock.com

funding indirectly by decreasing public school enrollment, which is one of the factors on which governments base their allocations of money to public schools. (Learn more about school finance in Chapter 11, "How Are Schools Governed, Influenced, and Financed?")

Opponents of voucher plans have voiced several other objections and concerns to these ventures:

- They argue that voucher plans bring false hopes of school choice because the private schools, not the parents, do the choosing through admissions decisions, and a private school is under no obligation to accept students with vouchers.

- In some proposals, the vouchers are worth only $1,000 to $2,500 per student, seriously limiting the choices of schools for which these amounts would pay the actual costs of tuition. On the other hand, in Washington, DC, eligible, low income parents can receive vouchers for amounts ranging from $8,000 for elementary school to $12,000 for high school to pay for their children's private school education.[25]

- Citing the fact that vouchers are being used to educate children in religious schools and in spite of the recent Supreme Court ruling, many still see this use of vouchers as breaching the wall of church–state separation.

- Many voucher opponents, including the two largest teacher unions, suggest that if voucher plans become widespread, the public schools will lose much-needed revenue and be forced to educate children with great needs, whom the private schools would not accept, while lacking the resources to do a good job.

- Voucher opponents contend that applying market forces to educational institutions doesn't make sense, arguing instead that schools should be driven by the need to serve the public good, not the desire of individuals and corporations to earn profits.

Those who support voucher plans offer counterarguments to many of these objections. For example, although funding private and religious schools with public money is very controversial in the United States, it is a less contentious issue in many other countries. The United States is one of the few developed nations with such strict limits on parental choice of schools. Many other Western democracies fund private or religious schools with public money, although if these schools accept public money, they usually have to meet certain conditions required by the government.

Voucher supporters also point out that although many people believe U.S. tax dollars fund only public schools, private and religious schools already benefit from public money. The major breakthrough for private and religious schools was the passage of the Elementary and Secondary Education Act of 1965, which funneled millions of dollars into private schools through federal Title I programs to support the education of poor children. In addition, private schools in many states have received public assistance ranging from pupil transportation, textbooks, health services, and general auxiliary services to salary supplements for teachers. In general, state assistance in areas other than transportation, milk, school lunch programs, and textbooks has been attacked in the courts. On the other hand, both federal and state monies have been used to provide scholarship aid to students attending religious universities and colleges.

Another argument cited in support of voucher plans notes that the private schools, which provide education for more than 5 million students each year, lighten the burden of the public schools. If, for example, the cash-strapped Catholic school system collapsed, about 2 million new students would enroll in the public schools, creating a massive shortage of space, teachers, and money. Advocates of private school aid argue that by partially subsidizing private schools to keep them in operation, the public schools can avoid a deluge of students whom they would be unable to assimilate readily. If a substantial number of these schools were to shut down, the public schools would incur a substantial portion of these costs.

As is the case for charter schools, research on the success or failure of various voucher plans is limited and, in the eyes of many, driven by ideological issues. The issue of school choice is likely to remain a contentious one for some time to come.

12-4a FOR-PROFIT SCHOOLS

A small but growing element of the school choice picture is **for-profit schools**, also known as *educational maintenance organizations* (EMOs—modeled on health maintenance organizations [HMOs]). These financially driven businesses typically contract with a community or school district to provide educational services. Although school districts have long hired private companies to provide food services, transportation, and technological support, only recently have districts contracted for a total educational package: curriculum, teachers, administrators, buildings. Four of the best-known EMOs are K12 Inc. (which focuses on online education), Edison Learning Schools, Advantage Schools, and KIPP (Knowledge Is Power Program, described earlier).

Although many people criticize the underlying business model of EMOs (i.e., making a profit from educating children), proponents of these schools believe that the imagination, drive, and rigor that has made U.S. business the envy of the world is just what has been lacking in our schools. If nothing else, the advent of these for-profit schools is testimony of the American public's hunger for quality education.

Pause *and* Reflect

1. Which form of school choice appeals most to you? Why?
2. Do you support the use of school vouchers for students to attend private or parochial schools? Why or why not?

Diane Ravitch, an educational historian, attacks the notion of privatization, writing, ". . . the transfer of public funds to private management and the creation of thousands of deregulated, unsupervised, and unaccountable schools have opened the public coffers to profiteering, fraud, and exploitation by large and small entrepreneurs."[26]

Like many of the other choice plans and alternatives, EMOs have generated a great deal of interest and criticism, but rigorous evaluations of their effectiveness have yet to appear. We will have to wait to see whether an educational Starbucks, Walmart, or Staples emerges on the scene soon.

12-4b LOCAL-LEVEL SCHOOL REFORM

Former Speaker of the U.S. House of Representatives, the late Tip O'Neill, was fond of saying, "All politics are local." The same is true of education. Children are educated at their local schools, not at the state capitol or in Washington, DC. Although some

Up CLOSE

Steve Jobs on Educational Reform

Not long before he died in 2011, Steve Jobs, the legendary co-founder of Apple and creator of the Mac, the iPhone, the iPod, the iPad, and many more electronic devices, spoke to President Barack Obama about the need to reform our schools. In a one-to-one meeting, he spoke passionately about the need for teachers to be treated as professionals and not as industrial assembly-line workers. Further, school principals should be empowered to control the hiring and firing process to ensure the quality of teaching and learning in their schools. Jobs also urged that the president champion an effort to extend the school day until 6:00 P.M. and the school year for a full 11 months. He ridiculed the current system where teachers stand at blackboards and students rely on textbooks. He pressed for the whole process—textbooks, materials, and assessment—to be digital and interactive in a system tailored to individual students.

The president was open to Jobs's ideas and suggested that Jobs pull together a dinner meeting between the president and a half dozen of Silicon Valley's business titans. The evening had no shortage of suggestions, particularly those centering on reviving American industry and making it more competitive. When it was Jobs's turn, he spoke about America's failure to educate and produce the engineers that were crucial to our economic viability. At the time, Apple had several factories in China, employing 700,000 workers. He explained that the reason these factories were in China and not in the United States was due to the fact that these workers had to be supported by 30,000 engineers, and he simply could not find them in the United States. Jobs's answer was for the nation to mount a major effort to train American students in basic engineering skills for manufacturing. That meant more tech schools, community colleges, and trade schools. He ended by telling the president, "If you could educate these engineers, we could move more manufacturing plants here."

Source: Walter Isaacson, *Steve Jobs* (Simon and Schuster, 2011), 544–546.

school reform efforts, such as the Coalition of Essential Schools Project, are national in scope, even those programs are implemented in local schools under the supervision of a school district.

At present, the great majority of changes being made in schools are coming at the direction of the various states' departments of education, and educational funds are often linked to how faithfully and quickly a school district implements the desired reform mandates. Locally initiated reform efforts, although in no way stopped, have slowed down, partly because of a shortage of local funds. Growing competition for fixed amounts of municipal tax dollars—from police and fire departments to agencies serving the poor and the elderly—and competing thoughts on the primary purpose of public education have made it difficult to secure monies for new, locally supported reform efforts. What we are witnessing is a classic shift in power, with the statehouse and the White House increasingly dictating to the localities not just *what* should be taught but *how* it should be taught.

Although the center of gravity may be elsewhere, the local school district is, nevertheless, deeply involved in the current reform movement. Furthermore, the overwhelming majority of reform ideas that have made their way onto the agendas of national and state reform groups first emerged at the local level. Put simply, they became statewide or national because they succeeded first at the local level. Even more innovative ideas, such as block scheduling, year-round education, service-learning requirements, single-sex schools, school uniforms, and site-based decision making, will undoubtedly continue to bubble up from our local schools in the future.

12-5 What Ought to Be the Elements of Educational Reform?

We believe firmly that the most important players in educational reform are the teachers. Overwhelmingly, the changes and improvements in schooling have come from classroom teachers who were seeking a better way to serve students. Although millionaires, politicians, and foundations provide resources and support for educational change, it begins—and ends—with the teachers. It is essential, therefore, for teachers to see themselves as fundamental to the reform process. But every change agent needs goals, or what we call "educational oughts," that is, a menu of ideas to support and develop. Besides supporting higher and better academic standards and more carefully targeted accountability systems, we offer the following candidates for reforming our schools.

We must put greater knowledge directly in the hands of teachers and seek accountability that will focus attention on "doing the right things" rather than on "doing things right.

—LINDA DARLING-HAMMOND,
Stanford University professor of education

12-5a AUTHENTIC ASSESSMENT

Many educators and parents have expressed grave concerns about what they perceive as an overemphasis on high-stakes testing. Measuring school excellence by administering standardized tests poses a danger, which arises because of the limited and simplistic

▶❚❚ **TeachSource** Video Case

© 2016 Cengage Learning®

Performance Assessment: Student Presentations in a High School English Class

Watch the video clips, study the artifacts in the case, and reflect on the following questions:

1. The teacher notes that students seem to be more engaged in their learning when they know they will be expected to demonstrate their knowledge via a performance assessment. How might teachers increase students' interest levels for materials that are included on required standardized tests?

2. Do you agree with the teacher that a key goal or benefit of assessment should be to provide students with "ways to feel successful"? How do the various forms of assessment described in this section contribute to or detract from that goal?

"Who would've thought Ms. Kent was following our tweets?"

Campbell, Martha/CSL, CartoonStock Ltd

nature of the tests. Evaluation experts warn that relying on tests developed by external sources can be unduly limiting if schools organize their curricula solely to conform to the content of the tests. When they adopt that perspective, schools may fail to teach what is difficult to test. In some instances, the content and actual form of tests have become the curriculum itself, with weeks of classroom drill being based on previous versions of tests. Some educators and parents see a connection between the dramatic rise in student obesity and the emphasis on high-stakes testing, because recess and physical education are often eliminated or cut back to provide more time for test drilling.

Not long ago, educators and the business community began calling for schools to emphasize higher-order thinking skills, such as critical thinking and problem-solving abilities. These qualities are difficult to measure through multiple-choice and other objective tests, so some educators called for a different type of assessment—one that would directly measure real student performance on important tasks. For example, if we want to know how well students can write, we can examine samples of their writing. If we want to know how well students understand scientific concepts and can carry out scientific processes, we can ask them to conduct an actual experiment. In other words, the assessment would actually measure what we wanted students to be able to do rather than relying on them to choose the correct response on a multiple-choice test item. This type of assessment is known as **authentic assessment**, or **performance assessment**. Advocates claim that authentic assessment involves performance tests that get closer to how students *apply* knowledge rather than how they *store* it in their minds. The Video Case, *Performance Assessment: Student Presentations in a High School English Class,* shows an extended example of how one teacher goes about assessing her students' creative performance. In the Video Case, *Assessment in the Elementary Grades: Formal and Informal Literacy Assessment*, watch how one second-grade teacher administers several of the forms of assessment discussed in this chapter.

One method of authentic assessment involves having students collect their work over time and assemble it to create **portfolios**. See the Video Case, *Portfolio Assessment: Elementary Classroom,* for details on this method of assessment. These portfolios might showcase students' best work, much like an artist's portfolio. In other instances, the work in the portfolio is representative of work done throughout the semester, demonstrating students' growth over time. In either case, students and teachers can evaluate these portfolios to determine learning progress. In many parts of the country, in fact, student teachers assemble portfolios of their own work to show their professional skills when they apply for employment. (See Chapter 13, "What Are Your Job Options in Education?," for more on teaching portfolios.)

Authentic assessment is not without its critics and unresolved issues. The ability of performance assessments to satisfy both the validity requirement ("Is this a true measure of what I want to assess?") and the reliability requirement ("Will this test yield a similar result when administered at different times and under different circumstances?") has yet to be determined. Cost is also a major concern. Evaluating writing samples or

▶❙❙ **TeachSource** Video Case

© 2016 Cengage Learning®

Assessment in the Elementary Grades: Formal and Informal Literacy Assessment

Watch the video clips, study the artifacts in the case, and reflect on the following questions:

1. What are the benefits to teachers, students, parents, and the school of each of the various types of assessment: standardized tests, informal assessments, performance assessments, and portfolio assessments?

2. Which kinds of useful information can an informal assessment, such as the running record in the bonus videos, add to that provided by standardized test scores?

3. What are the benefits and challenges for these same groups of developing a complete assessment program featuring multiple types of assessments?

judging students' success in conducting a scientific experiment is much more time-consuming and therefore more costly than machine-scoring a multiple-choice exam. Standards of judgment present another difficulty. Even if testers use **rubrics** that specify criteria and standards of assessment, the subjectivity of the human evaluator is an important consideration. In addition, questions remain about how to judge excellence, originality, and creativity in art and writing, let alone math or science.

Evaluation, where it be quizzes, final exams, the grading of projects or written themes, is rarely popular with both teachers and students. During the 2020 COVID-19 pandemic, students across the country were taught online. However, when it came to evaluations, the teachers unions of several major cities—in the interest of fairness to students whose schooling had been dramatically interrupted—lobbied for giving all students As or pass/fail grades. That said, evaluation is a fundamental building block of education. Any educational reform needs to include some way of knowing if students are actually meeting the standards set and becoming the well-educated individuals that society wants. Therefore, a major item on the school reform agenda is to broaden the means by which we measure student learning.

12-5b ACTIVE LEARNING: THE CONSTRUCTIVIST'S APPROACH

There is an old saying that all teachers know well: "You can lead a horse to water, but you can't make it drink." Similarly, you can have a child in a classroom, but you cannot make him or her learn. Pouring information into students or forcing them to do workbooks or problem sheets won't always do it. Nor will the great majority of students learn if simply allowed to wander through a library or laboratory on their own. Something must happen *inside* learners before they learn. Curiosity? A problem that they want or need to solve? And then, with the direct or indirect help of a teacher, students "construct" knowledge from the information available to them.

Constructivism is a theory of knowledge acquisition built on the idea that learners interact with new information to "construct" meaning from it. (See Chapter 7, "What Should Teachers Know about Technology and Its Impact on Teaching and Learning?" and Chapter 9, "What Are the Philosophical Foundations of American Education?," for more on constructivism.) Constructivism provides a frame of reference for organizing classroom practices so that students learn in all content areas. Unlike educational practices in which learners passively receive information, the constructivist approach requires that learners actively interact with the information, building on their prior knowledge, attitudes, and values. The Video Case, *Elementary School Language Arts: Inquiry Learning,* shows a lesson that takes the constructivist's approach and, as the teacher states, "put[s] students in charge of their own learning." As learners encounter new information or experiences, they ask themselves, "What makes sense here? What happens when I do this or change that?" In this **active learning** process, learners build and add to their understanding of concepts, rules, and strategies through direct, hands-on experimentation.

Although the focus is on the students in theory, teachers play a key role in constructivist classrooms.

▶❚❚ **TeachSource** Video Case

© 2016 Cengage Learning®

Portfolio Assessment: Elementary Classroom

Watch the video clips, study the artifacts in the case, and reflect on the following questions:

1. In one of the bonus videos, the teacher mentions the time pressure felt by many teachers. How can teachers who are pressed for time avoid the temptation to "teach to the test"?

2. Can teachers effectively use portfolios to help them meet or cope with demands to teach students the material that will be tested on their standardized assessments? How?

3. What information would standardized test scores add—for a teacher, for parents, and for students—to the information gained from portfolio reflections?

Through a technique called scaffolding, teachers use clues, questions, and hints to extend students' understanding. (See Chapter 6, "What Makes a Teacher Effective?," for additional discussion of scaffolding.) In this way, teachers help students construct a scaffold by linking in prior knowledge to make sense of the new information.

How does constructivism advance the goals of educational reform? First, the primary ingredients of the constructivist approach are learners who take responsibility for their own learning. Teachers and the school play important supporting roles in this effort, but the initiative of the learners is essential. In short, students can achieve excellence only if they take responsibility for their learning. Ideally, constructivist classrooms foster experiential, inquiry-based learning in an atmosphere of *intellectual play*. Constructivism incorporates many of the ideas that have been written about in this text, including inductive teaching, student–teacher interaction, cooperative learning, multidisciplinary and interdisciplinary teaching, and extensive use of new technologies.

Although constructivism has many virtues, it is merely one theory of learning, one way of thinking about how knowledge and understanding are formed. It is certainly not the only way. Indeed, critics of this approach are quick to point out that students can "construct" incorrect answers. Further, critics remind us it is a formidable task to regularly put constructivism into practice, to translate this theory of learning into a theory of teaching.[27]

Nevertheless, we believe constructivism can be a valuable corrective to much of classroom life. It can bridge the gap between teacher-centered drill or rote learning on the one hand, and excessively abstract learning on the other hand. An ancient Chinese proverb captures well the essence of constructivism: "Tell me and I forget. Show me and I will remember. Make me do it and I learn."

▶❚❚ TeachSource Video Case

© 2016 Cengage Learning®

Elementary School Language Arts: Inquiry Learning

Watch the video clips, study the artifacts in the case, and reflect on the following questions:

1. How has this teacher prepared the lesson to allow students to take an active role in their learning, as described in this chapter? How might she have prepared differently if she did not take a constructivist view?

2. What are the benefits and the challenges for the teacher who takes a constructivist approach? What are the benefits and the challenges for students?

12-5c A SENSE OF COMMUNITY

The past few years have brought a growing realization that the largest of our schools, although more resource rich, efficient, and cost-effective, can have some destructive side effects. To some students, such large schools have an aura of impersonality that results in disengagement. It is common to hear such statements as "I'm lost here," "No one really knows me and no one cares," or "I'm just a name in someone's gradebook." Although these criticisms are directed most often at high schools, they hold for many junior high and middle schools and even some elementary schools. Clearly, the larger our schools get, and the greater the number of classmates and adults with whom students must interact, the more students disengage—and disengaged students cannot achieve excellence.

Some studies have found not only a decline in student engagement and therefore in academic achievement in large schools, but also a decline in faculty morale and an increase in faculty absenteeism in these facilities.[28] Large schools are often equally overwhelming for parents, who then tend to remain at a distance and uninvolved in their children's school lives.

School-as-community advocates believe that any school whose principal does not know the names of all the students is too big. Reformers such as James Comer, of New Haven's School Development Project, and the late Theodore Sizer, founder of the Coalition of Essential

Constructivist principles stress the importance of learners taking an active role in creating their own knowledge.

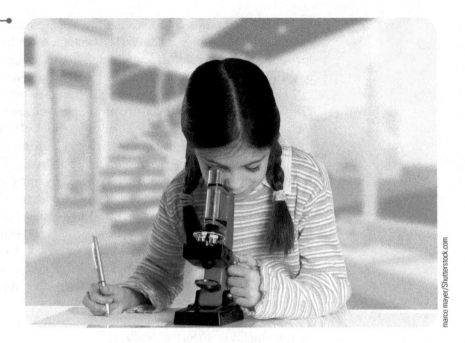

marco mayer/Shutterstock.com

Pause *and* Reflect

1. Reflecting back on your own recent schooling, did the schools you attended have this sense of community? Your elementary school? Your high school?
2. Does the college or university you are attending have this sense of community? What could be done to give it more of a sense of community?

Schools, argue that a sense of community is essential to the development of an academic environment. In these reform projects, new schools are purposely kept small, and existing large schools are broken up into "houses" of 100 to 400 students. The number of teachers with whom the students interact is similarly reduced, such that these houses function as **schools-within-schools**. Because students and teachers stay in the same house for several years, they are able to establish stronger and deeper relationships. Each student is a *known* person rather than a name on a class roster.

One obvious advantage of the house plan is that it allows teachers to plan together and to bring to bear their different perceptions of a child who is having difficulties or who has special strengths. In addition, these smaller, more intimate school environments provide a more stable emotional climate for students. Faculty advisers have better knowledge of and more exposure to students, and can offer them more help in dealing with students' problems or challenges. In this smaller setting, advocates argue, students are much more likely to achieve the standards of excellence set for them.

To date, the federal government has devoted close to $100 million to its Smaller Learning Communities Project. The Gates Foundation has given *$2 billion* to create small stand-alone schools and help break up large high schools into several smaller schools-within-schools. Although research suggests these changes are bringing about a better social climate, the hoped-for academic achievement results have not yet appeared. In fact, the unimpressive achievement test scores have caused the Gates Foundation to abandon its support of restructuring schools into smaller units.[29] Whether or not this was a wise move will take years of research to ferret out. The overriding idea of establishing in a school and a classroom a strong sense of community and bonds of trust and warmth among students and between teachers and students must be a priority of true educational reform.

12-5d LIFELONG LEARNING

In our global, rapidly evolving social and economic environment, people need more than a high school or college education. We must also be capable of continuous learning. Ten years from now, the jobs and tasks we perform will likely be quite different from the jobs and tasks we perform today. For this reason, schools must attend to the habits of mind and the skills that will keep people learning throughout their lives, making them **lifelong learners**. Not only must students become good learners, but they must also be enthusiastic learners. In other words, students must know *how* to learn, and they must *want* to learn.

Tools for Learning

The human brain is a glorious instrument capable of enormous feats of creativity, from writing symphonies to making scientific breakthroughs. The average brain can store and manipulate more information, by several hundred times, than the largest computers. Unfortunately, the brain has some drawbacks too. It loses or "misfiles" information. Numerous and assorted messages enter it through the eyes, ears, and other senses and somehow get lost. When we want to remember an idea, it often is simply "not there." Sometimes the information received gets modified so that when we take the exam, we are sure without a doubt that there are two quarts in a gallon and four pints in a quart. Thus, although the brain is humankind's treasure, it is hardly perfect.

In any event, to work well, the brain must be trained and well maintained. By *trained*, we mean we have to teach people how to manage and use their brains effectively. Most likely the majority of our readers have been urged a time or two by parents and teachers to "Use your brain!" Our meaning is both an extension of that request and a more specialized suggestion. We are urging that we give our brains more power through the use of new tools. In the same manner that reading extends the power of the brain by giving it access to vast amounts of important information, other tools can make the brain more efficient and better able to take in, interpret, process, store, and retrieve information. *Well maintained* means we continue to make use of these important tools long after we have left the hallowed hallways of schools.

A fresh focus on the skills of learning can and ought to be a major part of school reform. Of course, we must attend to the three R's; we are not suggesting that we give a lower priority to subject matter. Rather, to make knowledge (i.e., **intellectual capital**) more useful, students need to learn how to learn. As teachers, we must give our students the necessary **tools for learning**: advanced reading, remembering, recording, researching, test taking, analyzing, and creating. These tools can help students excel not just in school but also later in the workplace and in life in general. (See the feature "Up Close: A Sample of the Tools for Learning.")

12-5e RECLAIMING CHARACTER EDUCATION

Reminding us that education is not merely about the acquisition of knowledge, Socrates (featured in Chapter 9, "What are the Philosophical Foundations of American Education?") said, "The purpose of education is to make people both smart and good." The excellence in education is not limited to just academic achievement. Many reformers have also been concerned about excellence of character. Much of the dissatisfaction with schools that has fueled recent educational reform efforts comes from parents and community leaders who believe the schools have not done enough to shape the character and ethical values of students in positive ways. Many reformers are equally convinced that a failure to address these needs of students lies at the heart of the schools' problems.

A "good student" has come to mean someone who does well on tests and achieves academically rather than someone who is a good person and who demonstrates characteristics such as responsibility, consideration for others, self-discipline, and the ability to work hard. To achieve excellence in student achievement, according to these critics, serious school reform must address the issue of **character education**, which we define as the effort to help the young acquire a *moral compass*—that is, a sense of right and wrong and also the enduring habits necessary to live a good life. Character education, then, involves helping children *to know the good, love the good, and do the good.*[30]

Up CLOSE

A Sample of the Tools for Learning

Here is a list of some skills, which we call *tools for learning*, that we believe ought to be taught to all students:

- *Various methods for remembering important information.* This skill largely involves teaching people how not to forget—how to move information from the fleeting short-term memory to the more enduring long-term memory.

- *Two or three methods of taking notes and saving important information.* Definite skills are associated with capturing what another person is saying, and students should systematically learn these skills.

- *Study reading.* People practice "study reading" when the material is complex and contains information they want to remember later. This technique is quite different from reading a novel or reading a telephone book. This set of skills lies at the heart of academic success, as well as success in many jobs.

- *Preparing for different kinds of tests.* Schools should teach students how to study for different types of tests, such as objective and essay tests, and how to deal with test anxiety in various situations. Because examinations and tests do not end with graduation, schools should teach students how to cope with and master these challenges.

- *Doing research.* Students need to learn how to get answers to questions by using libraries, the Internet, expert sources, and data-gathering resources of all kinds. In essence, these skills focus on finding and accessing different data sources and using the information to solve a problem.

- *Thinking through a problem in a systematic way.* Instead of jumping to conclusions or relying on how they feel about an issue, students should learn how to think critically.

- *Generating creative ideas.* Much of life—in and out of school—requires new solutions or imaginative resolutions. Students need to learn techniques for generating novel and creative ideas individually, as well as group-oriented techniques such as collaborative brainstorming.

- *Getting the academic job done.* Students need to know how to set goals, develop a work plan, monitor their own behavior, bring a task to successful closure, and gradually become more successful at academic learning. This ability is important not simply to succeed in school but also because the modern workplace demands these same skills.

TeachSource Digital Download

Character is like a tree and reputation like its shadow. The shadow is what we think of it; the tree is the real thing.

—ABRAHAM LINCOLN (1809–1865),
16th president of the United States

Arguments Pro and Con

Some people argue that the public school has no role in character development and moral education because both are rooted in deeply held religious worldviews. As such, they are deemed "out of bounds" to public schools, which should concentrate primarily on cognitive skills such as reading, writing, and application of the scientific method.[31] According to proponents of this view, if parents want attention paid to moral values, they should put their children in private or religious schools.

Others question character education by asking, "*Whose* values should the public schools teach?" In a nation of diverse cultural backgrounds, a nation committed to freedom of thought and expression, can any one set of values be taught without infringing on someone's deeply cherished beliefs? One solution to this dilemma would have the tax-supported public schools teach the civic virtues that are necessary for life in a democratic society, such as respect for the rights of others, courage, tolerance, kindness, and concern for the underdog. Another way to seek an answer to this question is first to take a mental trip around the school described in the following paragraph and then to answer the question "Should schools stick simply to academics and skills?"

A counselor is calling a student's home about apparently excused absences, only to find that the parent's letters have been forged. A young boy is in the principal's office for threatening his teacher with a knife. Three students are separated from their class after hurling racial epithets at a fourth. A girl is complaining that her locker has been broken into and all her belongings stolen. A small group of boys are huddling in a corner, shielding an exchange of money for drug packets. Female students complain that they are being rudely groped when their teacher leaves the room. In the playground, two girls grab a third and punch her in the stomach for flirting with the wrong boy.[32]

Schools that tolerate such behavior not only are failing to address the character education needs of their students but also have become places where the intellectual goals of schooling are seriously impaired. In addition, such schools win little support from the general public, the people who pay for public education.

We believe that most educators know it is impossible to educate students in a moral vacuum. The process of schooling necessarily affects the way children think about issues of right and wrong and affects the ways they behave. Further, the overwhelming majority of Americans, regardless of religion, class, or racial background, support certain moral values such as respect, a thirst for justice, honesty, responsibility in our dealings with one another, consideration, compassion, persistence at hard tasks, and courage in the face of adversity. For many years, we believed that teaching these moral values effectively would have the indirect and important result of helping students become more academically successful. Recent research has borne out this linkage.[33]

Further, we believe that most people would wholeheartedly support schools' vigorous advocacy of these virtues. Teachers and schools can positively influence the development of desirable habits and character formation in numerous ways, but two in particular are worthy of note: using the curriculum and involving students in service activities.

Character in the Curriculum

One major approach is to use the curriculum that already exists in most schools to teach more directly and more vigorously the positive moral values that are embedded in our culture. Our history and literature are permeated with value issues and moral lessons from the past. Instead of simply having students study the facts of a historical period or read a story to build vocabulary or appreciate prose style, a teacher can confront them with ethical issues and moral lessons that are integral to the subject matter. Instead of merely teaching scientific methodologies and findings, the teacher can have students examine the real-world implications of applied science, such as genetic manipulation. Through such explorations, students will see that the use of science and technologies, such as cloning, fossil fuel–based energies, and genetic manipulation, is not neutral; rather, how we use science has ethical implications. As teachers, we must see the content of our curriculum as the carrier of our moral heritage and work to engage our students in that moral heritage. Since many of these issues are controversial, it is imperative that they be examined in an even-handed, non-ideological manner.

> *Character cannot be developed in ease and quiet. Only through experience of trial and suffering can the soul be strengthened, ambition inspired, and success achieved.*
>
> —HELEN KELLER (1880–1968), author

Service Learning

Knowing about virtues, such as justice, compassion, and courage, is one thing. Making them a part of one's life and practicing them diligently is another. If students are to make these virtues part of their character, they need real opportunities to practice them. As many reformers realize, schools can create opportunities for students, beginning in the early grades and continuing throughout the entirety of their education, to help one another and the adults in the school building. As students get older, they can be given more responsibility for working with and caring for younger students. In the later stages of high school, groups of students can take on projects in the larger community, such as helping a parent whose child has a disability or assisting at a senior citizens' center helping people with technology skills. Likewise, individual students can provide companionship to elderly shut-ins or peer counseling to troubled youngsters. The emphasis in such programs is not merely on the study of virtues but also on virtues in action.

Service-learning programs are widespread in U.S. schools. For example, in Montgomery County, Maryland, high school students opt to learn about waste management and then volunteer to educate residents on recycling, waste reduction, buying recycled materials, and composting. Since the program's inception in 2001, they have provided over 17,500 hours of service and have helped the county come closer to its goal of recycling 50 percent of the waste it generates.[34]

Although Maryland is the only state to make service a requirement for high school graduation, 18 other states permit community service or service-learning activities to be applied toward high school graduation requirements.[35]

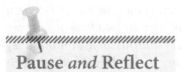

Pause *and* Reflect

1. Which of the elements of school reform described to this point do you most favor? About which do you have doubts? If we made you czar of American education, are there any mentioned reforms you would make, and why?

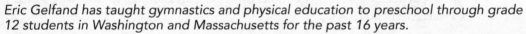

VOICES from the Classroom

Building Character Education into the PE Curriculum

Eric Gelfand has taught gymnastics and physical education to preschool through grade 12 students in Washington and Massachusetts for the past 16 years.

I can remember one of the members of my gymnastics team getting very upset about not winning. Tyler was 11 years old, and anything less than first place resulted in distress, inability to concentrate, and a feeling of failure. His reaction was stronger than others, but many on our team shared the sentiment: Self-esteem and success depended on winning. I decided to initiate a discussion of our definitions of winning with the entire team.

In this discussion, we discovered that our definition of winning was based on beating others and factors over which we had no control, like the score that the judge would give us. The new definition of winning that we developed focused on giving our best effort in each moment. We also decided to concentrate only on factors that we could control, such as improving our focus and technique, supporting each other, learning from our competitors, and regulating our thoughts and emotions. We decided if we did these things, then we had each won.

Tyler's feelings of self-esteem and success slowly began to change, but not the first time we talked about it, or the 10th time I reminded him to refocus on our new goals, or even on the 50th time that he made himself feel good by remembering that he had done his best. Through the efforts of the entire team over a period of three to four years, Tyler arrived at a place where winning meant something very personal and attainable at all times. This evolution meant valuing respect, persistence, temperance, and compassion for ourselves and others above all else. These virtues slowly became habits, which slowly became a part of our character and who we are today. It is incredibly hard to keep ourselves focused on this goal when our society values a very different definition of winning.

In reading this chapter, you will learn that school reform depends on the efforts of individual teachers to help our children become good workers and citizens. What do you think the definition of "winning" is in academics? If the current definition is not attainable by all of your students, how can you change the system or work within it to make every child successful? I believe that the key is to value the building of character as much as achievement within a discipline. It's simple; it just takes a few years of relentless hard work and compassion.

OUR FINAL WORD

Teachers must be at the center of educational change. Behind the somewhat head-spinning array of school reform ideas and programs, one fact is clearly discernible: The quality of our schools ultimately depends on our teachers. Educational reform is meaningless if it keeps teachers from inspiring the minds, imaginations, and characters of students on a one-on-one basis. Given the de facto connection between students and teach-

ers, the final decisions about educational reform are, by necessity, made by teachers. Although it is discouraging (and even threatening) to know that we have not yet achieved our goal of reforming our schools, Americans are often at our best when challenged. Clearly, school reform is part of the unfinished business of the United States and American teachers. A job of critical importance to all of us awaits you.

WHY TEACH? YOUR FINAL WORD

1. Which three of the various reform efforts described in this chapter do you believe are most important for the improvement of American education? Why?
2. What do you believe are the most serious barriers or hindrances to the reform of U.S. schools?

3. Were any of the reform efforts described in this chapter evident in your schooling?

KEY TERMS

active learning (380)
authentic (performance) assessment (379)
career ladders (368)
character education (383)
charter schools (371)
for-profit schools (376)
intellectual capital (383)
lifelong learners (383)
magnet school (371)
National Education Goals (Goals 2000) (361)
performance pay (pay-for-performance) (368)

portfolios (379)
rubrics (380)
school choice (369)
schools-within-schools (382)
site-based decision making (372)
teacher competency testing (367)
tools for learning (383)
twenty-first-century interdisciplinary themes (365)
voucher plans (373)
within-district choice (371)
year-round education (366)

FOR FURTHER INFORMATION

Web Resources

American Diploma Project

Sponsored by Achieve, Inc., this nonprofit organization, created by the nation's governors and business leaders, is "working to help states raise academic standards, improve assessments, and strengthen accountability in our high schools."

ASCD SmartBriefs

SmartBriefs is a free educational news service that can be received through email. It contains news, commentary, and educational resources.

Center for Educational Reform

This think tank is a pro–school choice center and clearinghouse for research and information on various efforts to offer parents and educators more educational choices.

The Educational Gadfly

For a conservative slant on educational news and policy developments, you can sign up for *The Gadfly*, a weekly bulletin of policy news, book reviews, and lively commentary by Chester E. Finn.

The National Education Association's Issues and Action

For a liberal slant on an educational reform agenda, see the website of NEA, the nation's largest teacher's union. The NEA has definite positions on many of the issues discussed in this chapter, from school choice to performance pay.

Print Resources

Frederick M. Hess, *Letters to a Young Education Reformer* (Educational Innovations Series, 2017.)

This book is the fruits of 25 years of research and teaching by one of the country's leading educational reformers.

John Merrow, *Below C Level: How American Education Encourages Mediocrity and What We Can Do about It* (John Merrow, 2010).

This wide-ranging collection of essays covers many of the reform topics discussed in this chapter. Merrow is a former teacher and currently is the senior educational reporter for the PBS *News Hour*.

Jal Mehta, Robert B. Schwartz, and Frederick M. Hess, *The Futures of School Reform* (Cambridge, MA: Harvard Education Press, 2012).

The culminating work of education scholars that maps out a variety of bold visions that go beyond our current thinking on school reform.

13

What Are Your Job Options in Education?

Alexander Raths/Shutterstock.com

LEARNING OBJECTIVES

13-1 Identify major factors that influence the availability of teaching jobs in the United States.

13-2 Identify the major criteria that determine teacher salary schedules in public schools.

13-3 Describe at least four strategies that will increase your chances for obtaining a teaching position.

13-4 Provide definitions for the following terms: *licensure; alternative licensure; certification.*

13-5 Identify some skills learned in teacher preparation programs that would transfer to careers related to teaching.

Truth OR Fiction?

T F   Of new teachers, 30 to 40 percent leave the classroom within five years.

T F   Only 20 percent of American teachers are from minority groups.

T F   Salaries for private school teachers are about the same as those of public school teachers.

This chapter provides you with information about the availability of teaching positions in elementary, middle, and secondary schools, both within the United States and overseas. In addition, teaching opportunities in private schools, as well as public schools, are addressed. It also explores other career opportunities, both within and outside the educational field. Study the information carefully and discuss it with your instructors and your career planning and placement office. Your program of study may offer more job options than you have realized.

This fictitious ad contains many messages about the roles that teachers play. It also highlights the fact that there is a serious need for skilled new teachers in U.S. schools. As you have thought about teaching as a career, you have probably wondered whether you will be able to obtain a teaching position when you graduate. Although we would like to answer this question for you personally, we obviously cannot. For example, certain subject matter fields have shortages of qualified teachers, while other fields have surpluses. Providing you with this kind of information may help you increase your chances of obtaining the kind of teaching position you are seeking.

13-1 Will There Be Job Openings in Education?

Teaching is a large occupation, with 3.7 million elementary and secondary teachers, representing 4 percent of the entire civilian workforce in the United States. There are more K–12 teachers than registered nurses, three times as many teachers as lawyers, and twice as many teachers as engineers in this country.[1] Given the vast size of the teaching workforce, many jobs exist. The demand for teachers appears to show a slow, but steady, increase over the next decade. The employment market continues to be challenging in many areas of the country, and teaching candidates must work hard to secure these teaching openings. Figure 13.1 shows past, current, and projected numbers of classroom teachers in the United States.

Up CLOSE

Wanted

Men and women with the wisdom of Solomon, the patience of Job, and the nerves of David before Goliath; need to prepare the next generation for productive citizenship in the twenty-first century, often under adverse conditions. Applicants must be willing to fill in gaps left by unfit, absent, or working parents; satisfy demands of local bureaucrats and state politicians; impart healthy self-esteem; and, oh, by the way, teach content!

Hours: 50 to 60 hours per week
Pay: Growing respectable
Reward: The luxury of always knowing that you are doing something significant with your life

FIGURE 13.1 Classroom Teachers in Public and Private Schools (in thousands)

Source: William J. Hussar and Tabitha M. Bailey, *Projections of Education Statistics to 2027* (Washington, DC: National Center for Education Statistics, 2019), Table 8, p. 50, https://nces.ed.gov/pubs2019/2019001.pdf.

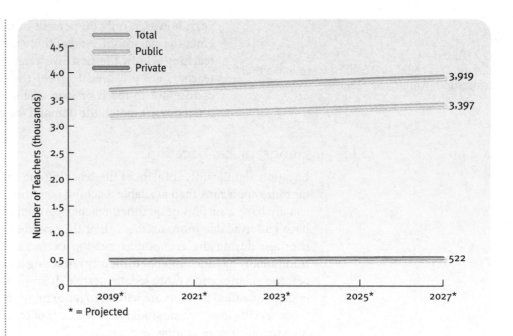

* = Projected

13-1a FACTORS INFLUENCING TEACHER SUPPLY AND DEMAND

Many variables influence the supply and demand for teachers in the United States. The following sections discuss a number of these factors.

Student Enrollment in Schools

Obviously, when more students are enrolled in schools, more teachers are needed. The good news is that enrollment in public and private schools reached 56.6 million students in 2019, and is projected to increase to 58.4 million in 2027, an increase of almost 2 million students. In the United States, enrollments in secondary schools will increase by about 2 percent through 2027, while enrollments in elementary schools will increase by just under 3 percent. The number of classroom teachers is expected to increase by 244,000 from 2019 to 2027, from 3.7 million in 2019 to 3.9 million by 2027.[2]

Class Sizes

During the 1980s and 1990s, the demand for new teachers was boosted by declining class sizes, especially in California, where the legislature tried to reduce class sizes in K–3 classrooms to around 20 students.

Nationally, current class sizes now hover around 21 students in public elementary schools and have reached over 27 students per teacher in public secondary schools. Class sizes in private schools are slightly smaller than those in public schools, averaging slightly less than 20 students per class for both elementary and secondary schools. Private schools averaged 12.5 students per teacher, compared with an average of 15.4 students per teacher in public schools.[3] However, the changes in class sizes during the next few years are expected to be small, and they are not likely to affect the demand for new teachers in any significant fashion.

Enrollment in Teacher Education Programs

Enrollments in teacher education programs have declined by more than a third since 2010. Across the United States, approximately 160,000 teachers are prepared each year; however, only 60 percent of those prepared to teach actually enter the classroom. And of these individuals, 30 to 40 percent leave teaching within the first five years.[4] Thus, an adequate number of teachers are prepared to meet the demand, but because so many choose not to teach or stop teaching after a few years, the supply often doesn't match the demand for new teachers.

Ⓣ F

Of new teachers, 30 to 40 percent leave the classroom within five years.

Geographical Location

Location significantly influences the teaching job market. Some communities have far more applicants than available teaching positions. University towns, for example, usually have a surplus of qualified teachers. Although large urban areas historically have had available more teachers than they needed, they experienced a significant shortage during the economic recession between 2007 and 2009. Rural America traditionally has encountered difficulty attracting and holding onto teachers because of lower salaries and a more sedate lifestyle than what many young teachers seek. Not enough qualified teachers are willing to teach in urban and rural schools, particularly those serving low-income students or students of color. These schools also experience high turnover rates among teachers.

Student enrollments in different geographical regions of the country are following different patterns as well, which influences teaching opportunities. Enrollments—and consequently teaching opportunities—are increasing in the western and southern parts of the United States and declining in the northeastern states.

Teachers tend to be more "place bound" than many other professionals. That is, because of family commitments or the importance of geographical location, many teachers seeking jobs are reluctant to stray far from home. Even though teaching jobs may be available in other parts of the country, teachers from the Northeast, for example, may not want to relocate to California.

Subject Matter and Grade Levels Taught

Teachers are not interchangeable units. They are prepared for different specialties (e.g., special education, elementary education, art, or secondary social studies), and the job market in each of these subfields is different. Moreover, the job market for specific subfields may change often. It is unwise, therefore, to decide whether to become an English teacher because you have heard that today there is generally either a surplus or a shortage of such teachers. There have been and continue to be chronic national teacher shortages in certain subjects, including computer science, science, mathematics, special education, English-language learning, hearing and visually impaired, Chinese, Japanese, and reading diagnostician. There is some surplus of teachers in pre-K and elementary education, English/language arts, and social studies.[5]

In addition to looking for teachers in the subjects just listed, schools are seeking greater numbers of minorities and males. Because 77 percent of all teachers are female, schools want to increase the number of males in the teaching force, especially at the elementary school level, where only 11 percent of the nation's 1.9 million elementary public school teachers are men.[6]

Retiring Teachers, Teacher Turnover, and Returning Teachers

There is no national database on annual teacher retirements, but estimates indicate that between 2 and 3 percent of teachers retire each year. The United States is experiencing record teacher retirements as the teaching force continues to age. One

There is a demand for male teachers at the elementary school level, where they account for only 11 percent of the teaching force.

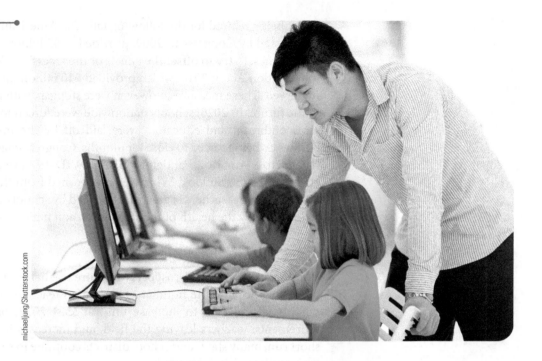

michaeljung/Shutterstock.com

report estimated that from 2010 to 2018, 1.5 million more teachers retired.[7] One factor that bodes well for the long-term job outlook is that teachers, like much of the rest of the American workforce, are getting older. More than 30 percent of teachers are at least 50 years old.[8]

Another factor influencing job availability relates to the percentage of eligible teachers who elect not to teach or those who leave teaching after a few years. As mentioned earlier, 40 percent of those prepared to teach decide not to enter teaching, and of the 60 percent who do teach, 30 to 40 percent leave teaching within the first five years. Sadly, the brightest novice teachers, as measured by their college-entrance exams, are the most likely to leave. Teachers who leave because of dissatisfaction cite testing and accountability pressures, student discipline problems, poor working conditions, lack of support from the school administration, poor student motivation, and lack of teacher influence over schoolwide and classroom decision making as major reasons.[9]

What is difficult to estimate is the number of licensed teachers, currently not teaching, who might reenter the teaching force if jobs are readily available. When teacher shortages have been predicted in the past, these returning teachers have filled the anticipated shortages. Whether this pattern will continue remains to be seen. Teachers licensed through alternative routes (like those discussed later in this chapter) are estimated to account for approximately one-third of the new teachers hired in this country.[10]

Teaching was the hardest work I had ever done, and it remains the hardest work I have done to date.

—ANN RICHARDS,
former governor of Texas

Economic Conditions

In spite of the positive long-term outlook for the teaching job market, in times of economic hardship, school districts may find it necessary to reduce the size of their teaching forces to balance budgets. During the severe 2007–2009 recession, many school districts in most states found it necessary to reduce their teaching forces for lack of money. As state and local government revenues dropped dramatically, school districts' budgets were also reduced. Many school districts were forced to issue reduction-in-force (RIF) notices to teachers, informing them that they were in danger of not being rehired for the following fall. The American Recovery and Reinvestment Act, passed by Congress in 2009, provided $785 billion dollars, much of which went to the states, to try to offset the effects of the recession. As a result of this act, and the Job Creation Act of 2010, which provided $10 billion more, many teachers' jobs were preserved. These measures, however, were stopgap, with no guarantee of continuation in the future. In 2020, schools nationwide were forced to close due to the COVID-19 virus outbreak, and educators were laid off by the millions. As a result of many businesses being forced to close for months, Congress enacted laws to provide financial relief across America. Pandemics like COVID-19 have an unexpected but dramatic effect on the job outlook. What we have learned from these painful recessions is that the demand for teachers is greatly influenced by school district budgets, which in turn are affected by the health of the state, local, and national economies.

Summing Up the Job Outlook

What, then, are the job prospects for future teachers? In the long run, the situation is promising because the number of classroom teachers in elementary and secondary schools is projected to increase until at least 2027, primarily because of teacher retirements, teachers leaving the field, and increases in student enrollments. In the short run, many states and school districts continue to suffer financially, which affects their ability to hire new teachers.

Keep in mind too that demographic projections and supply-and-demand forecasts are not just hard to apply but are also very inexact and short-lived. Although their task is difficult, forecasters try to take into account the various factors we have discussed, such as retirement rates, number of former teachers reentering the field, and programs that may attract individuals from nonteaching fields into the profession. Given the fluctuating effects of these forces, what seems to be true now for a particular geographic area, a particular teaching field, or a particular year may soon be "out of date."

For all these reasons, you should make every effort to get the most up-to-the-minute information possible about teacher supply and demand. Consider such information carefully before you make a choice about pursuing a career in education and, in particular, about entering a specific subfield within education. This is especially true for people who are unable to wait for openings in their areas of teaching interest or who are unable or unwilling to relocate. Sources of data with which to begin your search include your school's career counseling office, the department chairperson's or dean's office, and your state department of education. Also see the listing of useful references at the end of this chapter.

The bottom line is that demand for teachers will increase in the coming years. Remember too that there has never been a surplus of good teachers in any field.

13-1b THE SEVERE SHORTAGE OF MINORITY TEACHERS

One of the greatest teacher supply-and-demand problems concerns minority teachers. At a time when the minority school-age population is increasing rapidly, the number of minority teachers is decreasing. This shortage is severe now and appears likely to become worse in the future.

As discussed in Chapter 3, "Who Are Today's Students in a Diverse Society?," enrollments of students from minority groups are increasing; these children currently account for about 52 percent of all students in public schools. Teaching staffs, by contrast, are overwhelmingly white. Of public school teachers, 80 percent are white, 7 percent are African American, 9 percent are Hispanic, and only 4 percent come from other minority groups, including Asian American or Pacific

Ⓣ **F**
Only 20 percent of American teachers are from minority groups.

The shortage of minority teachers deprives both white and minority students of positive role models.

iStock.com/Christopher Futcher

> [Emma Belle Sweet] taught me many things. . . . But nothing could be so important to me and of such enduring quality as her simple, human act of figuratively leading me gently by the hand to a sense of self-respect, dignity, and worth.

—RALPH BUNCHE,
first African American
Nobel Peace Prize winner (1950)

Islander, and Native American or Native Alaskan.[11] Most minority teachers are located in central cities rather than in suburban or rural areas. Although minority enrollment in teacher education has been increasing in recent years, the need for such teachers is still acute.

This shortage of minority teachers is problematic for several reasons. First, minority children deserve to have positive minority role models who can help guide them in a world still plagued by racism. Second, white children need to have minority teachers as positive role models to help them overcome the effects of stereotyping and racism. Third, it is important for the United States' well-being to have a teaching staff that reflects the diversity of racial and ethnic backgrounds in its population. Fourth, minority teachers are needed to serve as "cultural brokers" who can help all students navigate their school environment and culture.

A number of reasons explain the shortage of minority teachers. Before desegregation efforts, nearly one-half of African American professional workers were teachers. When schools desegregated in the 1960s and 1970s, resulting in the consolidation of formerly all-black and all-white schools, thousands of African American teachers were dismissed. Today, other professions that pay more and have higher status are actively recruiting minority college students. Another causal factor has been the increasing use of competency tests at either the beginning or the end of teacher education programs. Many minority teaching candidates are either having difficulties with these tests or are being discouraged from even considering teaching as a career.

What can be done to address this problem? Teaching salaries must continue to improve if teaching is to compete with other professions for well-qualified candidates. Assistance programs to help minority candidates perform well on competency tests have been effective in a number of universities and should be expanded to more colleges. Active recruitment programs for minority candidates must be developed and implemented, and they must reach down into the middle and high schools to encourage minority students to consider teaching as a career long before they enter college. As will

LEADERS in Education

Jaime Escalante (1930–2010)

David Mercado/Reuters

It is early in the fall term at Garfield High School in East Los Angeles, once a crime-ridden school filled with low-achieving Mexican American students. It is the morning after the second game of the World Series, and as he enters the class, the teacher, known as *el professor*, shouts out his first question: "Who won the game?" After a pause, the students begin to chant enthusiastically, "Dodgers! Dodgers!" Having captured their attention, Jaime Escalante moves to the math lesson. Slapping a baseball into his mitt, he says, "As x approaches a, f of x [f(x)] is the trajectory. Could be a curve ball." And they are off—teacher and 59 students—on a journey into the mysteries of calculus.

Jaime Escalante, the son of an elementary school teacher, was born in La Paz, Bolivia, and began his own teaching career before age 20. Although he was a high school math and physics teacher, his students began to accumulate prizes, and he soon gained national recognition. Still in his 20s, he organized the first Bolivian national symposium of physics and math teachers. In 1963, amid growing social strife in Bolivia, Escalante and his family decided to move to the United States.

The next 10 years were years of adjustment and struggle, during which Escalante learned English, went back to college, and worked as a busboy and a cook. When he finally graduated, he took a job in the fast-growing computer industry and studied for the California teaching license in his free time. Soon the news came that he had passed the test and would be assigned to a rundown, troubled high school in the barrio—and Escalante turned his back on his substantially larger paycheck from the high-tech world and headed for Garfield High School.

When the school's accreditation was threatened because of its students' low academic performance and high dropout rate, Escalante made his move. Supported by reform-minded administrators, he began setting high standards and making serious demands on students. They were not allowed into his class unless they proved that they had done their homework. He skillfully used the time-honored carrot-and-stick approach to cajole his pupils into reaching greater heights. In this case, the "carrot" was college and the world of opportunities higher education opened up for his students. The "stick" was his constant challenging of them: "You *burros* have math in your blood! Our Mayan ancestors were the first to develop the concept of zero!"

In 1982, his largest class of students took and passed an advanced placement test in calculus. Some of the students' test scores were invalidated by the testing company because it believed that the students had cheated since no one expected Hispanic students from an economically disadvantaged school to do so well. Despite Escalante's protests, the students had to retake the exam several months later. Once again, they did well, exceeding expectations and proving that they knew the material and that the company was wrong.

Jaime Escalante, the subject of the Academy Award–nominated film *Stand and Deliver*, later taught at Hiram Johnson High School in Sacramento, California. He hosted the PBS series, *FUTURES with Jaime Escalante*, produced by the Foundation for Advancements in Science and Education. In addition, he received numerous awards, including the prestigious U.S. Presidential Medal for Excellence in Education and induction into the National Teachers Hall of Fame. Escalante was more than the man who has helped hundreds of Mexican American children discover self-discipline and learning and the enormous self-pride that comes with those accomplishments—he was a tide turner. He set an idea in motion, the idea that poor and immigrant children are capable of great intellectual feats. He showed how remedial, slowed-down education can be replaced by demanding, accelerated education. "My skills are really to motivate these kids, to make them learn, to give them *ganas*—the desire to do something—to make them believe they can learn." Escalante has always been clear about why he taught: his love of young people and his love of his subject.

Until his death in March 2010, Escalante remained a clear and forceful spokesman for quality education, especially for minority children. He took a strong position against extensive bilingual education, believing it handicaps rather than helps Latino students. Instead, he urged a demanding education that will give minority students the knowledge and skills they need to compete in a demanding world. His educational views are captured in his famous motto: "Determination + Discipline + Hard Work = Way to Success."

be described later in the chapter, alternative licensure programs have been successful in recruiting minority teachers and should be continued. Scholarship and loan-forgiveness programs are needed for students who want to teach but cannot afford to pay for college. Finally, the American public must communicate in a variety of ways that it values teachers and the work they do. See the "Leaders in Education" feature for a biographical sketch of one of America's most outstanding minority teachers, Jaime Escalante.

13-1c EMPLOYERS BESIDES THE PUBLIC SCHOOLS

Although much of the data presented in this chapter refer to public elementary and secondary schools, teachers can work in a variety of other school settings. Federal government schools and private schools are two major alternatives to teaching in a local public school.

U.S. Government

A large employer of teachers is the U.S. government. The Department of Defense operates 163 elementary and secondary schools in seven states, Puerto Rico, Guam, and 11 countries around the world. These schools enroll more than 70,000 students and employ about 8,700 teachers. Salaries are comparable to those in the United States, but preference is given to applicants who have at least one year of successful full-time employment as a professional educator.[12]

Private Schools

Private education is a highly significant part of the American educational system. The 32,460 private schools in the United States have an enrollment of about 4 million elementary and secondary school students and employ approximately 482,000 full-time equivalent teachers. About 10 percent of all U.S. children in elementary or secondary schools attend a private school, with the overwhelming majority attending religion-affiliated schools.[13] (See Figure 13.2 for the percentage of students attending private schools affiliated with various religious denominations.)

Private schools employ approximately 6.6 percent of all elementary and secondary teachers in the United States, and 35,000 more teachers will be needed in 2027 than in 2019.[14]. Thus, private schools offer a growing employment opportunity for new teachers. Helpful references for finding teaching jobs in nonpublic schools are provided at the end of this chapter.

FIGURE 13.2 Percentage of Students Attending Various Kinds of Private Schools

Source: Stephen P. Broughman, Brian Kincel, and Jennifer Peterson, *Characteristics of Private Schools in the United States: Results from the 2017–2018 Private School Universe Survey: First Look* (Washington, DC: National Center for Education Statistics, 2019), https://nces.ed.gov/pubs2019/2019071.pdf.

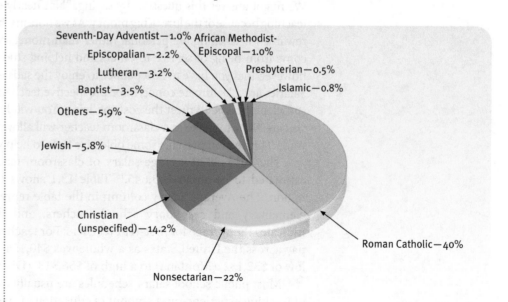

Seventh-Day Adventist—1.0%
African Methodist-Episcopal—1.0%
Episcopalian—2.2%
Presbyterian—0.5%
Lutheran—3.2%
Islamic—0.8%
Baptist—3.5%
Others—5.9%
Jewish—5.8%
Christian (unspecified)—14.2%
Roman Catholic—40%
Nonsectarian—22%

If you are considering a position at a private school, you should reflect on the relative importance of the various rewards of the job from your personal perspective. Many teachers who work in religion-affiliated schools do so because of religious motives. These teachers are often willing to work for less money than their public school counterparts; as a result, the average teacher salary in private schools is about 25 percent lower than that in public schools. In many cases, lower salaries tend to be offset by favorable working conditions. Compared with public schools, private schools have fewer classroom control problems, stricter discipline, smaller classes, fewer students using drugs, students who are absent less often, parents who are more supportive, a higher percentage of colleagues who share the school's mission, and a more supportive administration. Although private school teachers tend to work about two more hours a week than their public school counterparts, they believe they have greater influence over important school policies.[15] Thus, for many individuals, teaching in a private school represents an attractive alternative to teaching in the public schools. The "Voices from the Classroom" feature presents one teacher's comparison of the experience of working in public and private schools.

> T (F)
> Salaries for private school teachers are about the same as those of public school teachers.

Pause *and* Reflect

1. What are the present and projected teacher supplies in the field that currently interests you? In the geographic area you desire?
2. Are you willing to leave your current location to find a teaching position? Are you willing to teach in an urban school? A rural school? A private school?

13-2 What Are Teachers Paid?

We might answer this question by saying, "Not nearly enough." No one ever went into teaching because of the lure of big money. As we note in Chapter 1, "Why Teach?," the major rewards for teaching are personal rather than monetary. Most of teachers' satisfactions come from being of service to others and helping students learn. That does not mean, however, that you have to be a pauper to enjoy the satisfactions that come from teaching. Salaries are a legitimate concern for prospective teachers—after all, everyone must have sufficient income to meet the costs of living. You will have to decide whether the salary you are likely to make as a classroom teacher will allow you to establish the lifestyle you want. This section presents some objective facts to help you make your decision.

The 2019–2020 average salary of classroom teachers in the United States was estimated to be about $63,645.[16] Table 13.1 shows how salaries vary by state and region. The Average Salary column in the table represents the average for *all* public elementary and secondary school teachers, and the Beginning Salary column indicates the average for *first-year* teachers. For teachers in their first year, the average pay across the United States as a whole was $40,154 in 2018–2019, ranging from a low of $32,132 (Montana) to a high of $56,313 (District of Columbia).[17]

Most public school salary schedules are usually determined by two factors: years of teaching experience and amount of education, usually expressed in terms of college credit hours or advanced degrees. Thus, the longer you teach and the more college education you receive, the more money you will make. In addition, some states and school districts have used various forms of merit or performance pay (pay-for-performance) plans to reward teachers for exceptional teaching, acquiring new skills needed by the school, achieving national board certification, raising student test scores, or assuming more professional responsibilities. (See Chapter 15, "What Does It Mean to Be a Professional?," for more on national board certification.) Many politicians support performance pay plans as a way to reward those teachers who are deemed most effective. Such plans, they say, ensure that effective teachers' efforts are recognized, and should lead to fewer good teachers leaving the profession. Most teachers unions have opposed performance pay plans, maintaining that fair and equitable means for determining the salary increases under these schemes are elusive. (See Chapter 12, "How Should Education Be Reformed?," for more on performance pay plans.)

As Table 13.1 shows, salaries vary considerably from state to state. Each school district determines what it will pay its teachers, with many states setting a minimum base salary below which the school district cannot go. Generally, the large and middle-size school districts pay better than the small ones, and urban and suburban school districts pay better than rural ones. Many school districts offer extra pay for special duties such as directing the band or coaching athletic teams. Some offer summer teaching or curriculum development jobs. Most states and school districts provide public school teachers with

VOICES from the Classroom

Teaching in Public versus Private Schools

Karen Irving has taught chemistry and other science disciplines at the secondary and college levels, including six years of public high school teaching and six years of private high school teaching.

I loved the pulse of my urban high school, with its creative and energetic faculty. With three other chemistry teachers in our school of just under 2,000 students, we never lacked ideas or opinions about how to best help our students succeed. Sometimes we struggled to match our equipment availability to our classroom plans, but we always benefited from the sharing of experiences and expertise.

In addition to a large and diverse faculty, my urban high school boasted a large and diverse student population. However, with just three to four hours of planning time per week and 130 to 150 students in five sections, as well as science fair projects, science teams, and other extracurricular responsibilities, little time remained in my schedule to offer extra help to my students.

After six years of public high school teaching, I accepted a science teaching position at an independent, college preparatory girls' school. Because my teaching assignment at the private school included 60 to 65 students in four sections, the amount of time during the school day to plan lessons and work with students (eight hours a week) doubled from what I was used to

in the public setting. In addition, because the weekly school schedule included time for faculty meetings and student clubs during the school day, teachers and students shared free time before and after school for help sessions, makeup work, and additional student enrichment. Other conditions were different too. More parents returned teacher telephone calls, provided necessary home support for learning, made arrangements for students to attend help sessions, attended school functions, and generally worked together with school personnel to ensure that their children received a quality education.

If I had the chance to create an ideal high school environment, I would blend elements of both public and private schools. Ideal High would boast a diverse, creative, and energetic faculty and student population with small classes and sufficient time for teachers to plan and deliver quality lessons. Each student would have the opportunity to reach his or her full potential. Parents, administrators, teachers, and students at Ideal High would share a common vision of an educational community of disciplined effort and academic achievement.

TABLE 13.1	Estimated Average and Beginning Teacher Salaries, by State and Region					

State	Average Salary ($) 2019–2020	Beginning Salary ($) 2018–2019	State	Average Salary ($) 2019–2020	Beginning Salary ($) 2018–2019
New England			**Great Plains**		
Massachusetts	$83,622	$46,737	Iowa	$58,917	$37,406
Connecticut	$78,247	$46,407	Minnesota	$58,663	$39,554
Rhode Island	$67,323	$43,092	Nebraska	$55,267	$35,116
Vermont	$61,108	$39,567	Kansas	$52,554	$36,781
New Hampshire	$60,003	$38,305	North Dakota	$52,328	$39,748
			Missouri	$50,817	$32,600
Maine	$54,967	$35,477	South Dakota	$49,220	$38,819
Mid-East			**Southwest**		
New York	$87,543	$46,426	Texas	$57,091	$42,418
District of Columbia	$79,350	$56,313	New Mexico	$54,256	$36,405
			Oklahoma	$54,038	$37,014
New Jersey	$76,376	$52,854	Arizona	$50,381	$36,400
Maryland	$73,444	$45,685	**Rocky Mountains**		
Pennsylvania	$70,258	$44,404			
Delaware	$64,853	$42,412	Wyoming	$59,014	$45,814
Great Lakes			Colorado	$57,269	$34,229
Illinois	$68,305	$39,817	Idaho	$52,875	$36,370
Michigan	$62,185	$37,111	Utah	$52,819	$40,569
Ohio	$59,713	$36,709	Montana	$52,135	$32,132
Wisconsin	$59,176	$38,538	**Far West**		
Indiana	$51,508	$36,498	California	$84,659	$48,207
Southeast			Washington	$72,965	$47,416
Georgia	$60,578	$35,656	Alaska	$70,877	$48,047
North Carolina	$54,682	$37,739	Oregon	$67,685	$37,181
Alabama	$54,095	$39,479	Hawaii	$65,409	$48,428
Virginia	$53,933	$41,077	Nevada	$56,672	$40,190
Kentucky	$53,907	$36,932	**U.S. Average**	$63,645	$40,154
Tennessee	$51,862	$37,951			
South Carolina	$51,485	$34,471			
West Virginia	$50,238	$35,767			
Louisiana	$50,217	$40,400			
Arkansas	$49,822	$34,724			
Florida	$48,800	$37,932			
Mississippi	$45,192	$35,067			

Source: Average Public School Teacher Salaries: Rankings and Estimates 2019–2020 (Washington, DC: National Education Association, 2020), Figure E-7, 47.

a number of fringe benefits, including sick leave, health and life insurance programs, and retirement benefits. When applying for a teaching position, be sure to ask about these benefits; they are a major advantage for public school teachers over employees in the private sector, especially as many private employers are cutting back on such benefits.

Pause *and* Reflect

1. Are the average teacher salaries reported in this chapter about what you expected? How do the salaries in your geographic area compare with the national average? What might account for any differences that you note?
2. Judging from the salary information here, what do you estimate your salary as a teacher would be? Are you confident that this salary would meet your expenses?

13-3 How Do You Obtain a Teaching Position?

The job market may be encouraging for beginning teachers, but regardless of how great the demand for teachers is or how effective you may be as a teacher, school district personnel are not likely to walk up to you and offer you a job unless you have taken the steps outlined in this section. Here we suggest several courses of action that will greatly increase your chances of finding the best teaching job for you.

13-3a CAMPAIGN ACTIVELY

First, you must be determined to campaign actively for a teaching position. Draw up a plan, in writing, stating how you will proceed. Don't wait for happenstance. You might get lucky and land a job on your first try, but why take a passive attitude when you can do much more to increase your chances of obtaining satisfying employment? For example, try attending job fairs sponsored by various colleges, universities, and school districts.

Job seekers often make two common mistakes.[18] First, they try one strategy, wait for results (positive or negative), and then try something else. What you should do instead is to pursue many avenues or strategies simultaneously. Second, job seekers block themselves out at the wrong stage in the process. Some teachers halfheartedly write for information or never complete the application form; others withdraw their applications prematurely. Remember, you can always say "no" to a job offered to you, but you can never say "yes" to one that has not been offered. Keep your options open.

> *I'm a great believer in luck, and I find the harder I work, the more I have of it.*
>
> —THOMAS JEFFERSON (1743–1826),
> third president of the United States

13-3b PREPARE MATERIALS

Next, you need to get certain materials ready—namely, your résumé, cover letter, credentials, and transcripts. Your résumé allows you to present yourself the way you want to be presented to prospective employers. Its purpose is to help you get an interview with school district officials. You should make several copies of your résumé and bring extras with you to any interview.

Many sources are available to help you write your résumé. The office of career planning and placement at your college or university is a good place to start. These offices often run workshops on résumé and cover letter writing and frequently have samples of well-written résumés and cover letters available for you to examine. The American Association for Employment in Education (AAEE)'s annual *Job Search Handbook for Educators,* which is listed in the "For Further Information" section at the end of the chapter, is also an excellent source on how to write résumés and on other job search strategies.

Another set of materials that an increasing number of teachers are using to help them obtain jobs is called a **teaching portfolio**. Just as artists, actors, architects, and journalists use portfolios to display the products of their work, so can teachers. A teaching portfolio can include an organized collection of such items as research papers, letters of commendation or recommendation, videos of student performances, essays, pupil evaluations, teaching units, and digital recordings of lessons you have taught. There is no set format; you are limited only by your common sense and your own imagination. Remember, the purpose of the portfolio is to market yourself effectively, so don't be modest. A properly constructed portfolio will say much more about you than your résumé ever can.

Many beginning teachers are constructing electronic portfolios and making them available to potential employers either as websites or on DVDs. The advantage of an electronic portfolio is that it is easily accessible by potential employers and can be changed or enhanced as needed. Electronic teaching portfolios are also being used to demonstrate that prospective teachers have achieved standards—such as the edTPA portfolio, discussed later in the chapter. The National Board for Professional Teaching Standards (discussed in Chapter 15, "What Does It Mean to Be a Professional?") has advocated teaching portfolios as a means of assessing a teacher's work for national certification.

Almost all school districts require credentials, or the whole package from your college, recommending you for licensure. Check with the career planning and placement office about how to establish your **credential file** and what should go into it. Typically this file includes letters of recommendation, a copy of your transcript, and a résumé. Career planning and placement office personnel will help you assemble this file, and they will send copies of your file to school districts on your request. You should start working on this file early in your program so that you will have plenty of time to accumulate the required materials. Letters of recommendation should be recent, and they should come from those who are familiar with your teaching, academic knowledge, and character. Be certain to include letters from your university supervisor and your cooperating teacher in whose classroom you did your student or internship teaching. Be familiar with the Family Educational Rights and Privacy Act, also known as the Buckley amendment (discussed more fully in Chapter 8, "What Are the Ethical and Legal Issues Facing Teachers?"), which affords you certain kinds of legal protection regarding what goes into your file.*

Many applications require that job seekers submit transcripts as well. Because colleges charge several dollars per transcript, you can save money by reproducing the transcript yourself. Most school districts will accept such unofficial transcripts (i.e., transcripts sent from you rather than directly from the college) for the initial screening process. If you receive a job offer, you will then have to provide the school district with an official copy.

When you send your résumé, transcripts, and other materials to prospective school districts, the package should include a cover letter. The cover letters you write should be addressed individually. The letters may all have the same or similar content, but the recipients should not feel they are receiving a standard letter. And be sure to ask for an interview at the end of the letter—that's why you are writing it!

Review your personal Facebook and other social media accounts to be certain that they don't negatively affect your consideration for teaching positions. Check your privacy settings and delete any pictures, videos, or web links that could be perceived as inappropriate by potential employers, such as images or links showing you using alcohol or tobacco, or being inappropriately dressed.

*A copy of this law appears in *Federal Register* 53, no. 69 (April 11,1998): 11942–11949. It can also be obtained by writing the U.S. Government Printing Office, Washington, DC 20402.

Up **CLOSE**

Typical Questions Asked during Job Interviews

Most interviews follow a simple question-and-answer routine. Your ability to communicate effectively with a stranger in this undoubtedly stressful situation is critical to being offered the job. Being prepared is the best way to avoid a disorganized answer. Sometimes the interviewer may play "devil's advocate," disagreeing with a position you articulate to see whether you will back down from it in deference to an authority figure. You should be aware of this possibility: Be prepared to assess your position straightforwardly, and then stand behind it. Avoid "waffling." Your success in interviewing depends on how convincingly you can convey your ability to teach.

Interviews are often subjective, so your enthusiasm, self-confidence, eagerness, and believability will affect the outcome of your interview. Be sincere and mean what you say. Look the interviewer in the eye. First impressions are important, so dress conservatively. Remove visible body piercings and cover up tattoos!

At the conclusion of the interview, restate any important points you want to emphasize. Ask the interviewer for a business card, and ask when the selection decision will be made. Send the interviewer a thank-you note—courtesy can make a difference.

Questions you may be asked include the following:

Motivation/Experience/Education

- Tell us about yourself.
- Why do you want to teach?
- Why do you want to work in our school district?
- Which grade levels or subjects are you most interested in teaching?
- What do you consider to be your strongest attributes as a teacher? Weaknesses?
- What was your biggest problem in student teaching? How did you resolve it?
- How would you work with students who perform below grade level, especially those from poverty backgrounds?

Teaching Skills

- What is your philosophy of education?
- What are the most important learning outcomes you want your students to achieve?
- What skills and experience do you have in employing cooperative learning strategies or computers for instructional purposes?
- How can you motivate unmotivated learners?

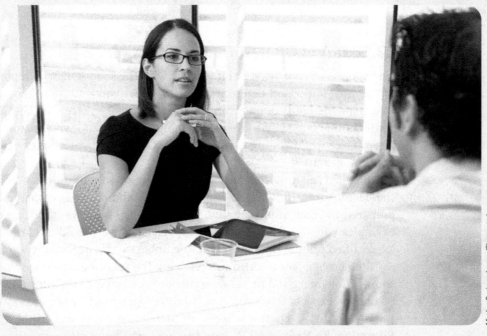

Monkey Business Images/Shutterstock.com

(Continued)

- How would you involve parents to help students learn?
- Describe how you have differentiated a lesson to accommodate specific students' needs.
- What is your grading philosophy?
- How have you incorporated curriculum standards into your lesson plans and units?

Classroom Management

- What ideas do you have about maintaining classroom control?
- Which rules for students would you establish in your classroom?
- How would you enforce these rules?
- Describe the most difficult student discipline situation you have faced and explain how you handled it.

Professional Responsibilities

- How do you plan to keep growing as a professional?
- Which professional journals do you read?
- Which added school responsibilities are you willing to accept?

Hypothetical Questions

- What would you do if you caught a student cheating?

- If money were unlimited, how would you improve education?
- How would you handle a student who refused to do the work you assigned?

During a job interview, you will answer many questions. But to gain the information that will help you choose among the jobs offered to you, you will also need to *ask* questions. Remember, you are interviewing the prospective employer too. Before you accept a position, you will need to know about the following:

Instructional Assignment

- Characteristics of the school district and student population
- Curriculum and resources available
- Typical class size
- Salary and benefits (medical and dental coverage and retirement)
- District's expectations and reimbursement policies for professional development
- Orientation or support services available for beginning teachers

These are just a few suggestions. For additional information on interview questions, see "Commonly Asked Interview Questions," in *2020 Job Search Handbook for Educators* (Columbus, OH: American Association for Employment in Education, 2020).)

13-3c DEVELOP INTERVIEW SKILLS

The success of your personal interview with the school district representative is one of the most important determinants of whether you get hired, so be prepared. Try to anticipate the kinds of questions that might be asked (see the "Up Close" feature for some sample questions). Try role-playing with a friend who assumes the role of the interviewer while you play the candidate. Audiotape your "interview" so the two of you can criticize it.

One survey indicated that the major factor school officials consider as part of the decision-making process is whether the candidate has empathy for children. Be prepared to show your empathy, not by saying you have it, but rather through the examples you give from your own experience. You should also ask those who write letters of recommendation for you to emphasize this aspect of your character.

Remember, *you* are also interviewing the school district or specific school. You should look for a good fit between you and your style of teaching and what the school or district expects from you. Don't be so eager to get any position that you ignore the issue of fit. As charter schools continue to emerge (see Chapter 12, "How Should Education Be Reformed?"), new teachers will have more options to choose from in terms of work climate, educational philosophy, and learning goals. In addition, consider whether you will have access to an induction program and a mentor teacher.

Research shows that having a good mentor teacher increases the likelihood of your success as a teacher. Secondary school teachers should also ask whether the number of class preparations is reduced for beginning teachers. Having only one or two types of classes to prepare for makes the first year of teaching much easier than having to complete three or four preparations for different courses.

13-3d DETERMINE JOB AVAILABILITY

Your next major task is to find out which jobs are available and where. You can use many different strategies to obtain this information. Your college's career planning and placement office receives hundreds of notifications of position vacancies, so contact that office often to see whether there are any vacancies that might interest you. Be on the lookout for job fairs, where school districts and potential teachers come together at one site to explore job opportunities. Your college or university may also sponsor such a job fair. Another source of information may be the teacher employment office operated by the state department of education. Approximately one-third of the states run such offices, and you can register with them for free or for a small charge. These offices send registered candidates a listing of openings in their specialty area for both state and out-of-state vacancies.

In addition, some private and professional organizations keep current nationwide teacher vacancy lists and will try to match your qualifications with those vacancies either for little or no cost. ASCD (formerly the Association of Supervision and Curriculum Development) has created a website called Job Ramp, which allows teachers to post résumés, scan job openings, and receive help in locating a teaching position free of charge. Another such organization is Teachers-Teachers.com, which is offered for free to prospective teachers and allows job seekers to post their résumés online; these documents can then be accessed by thousands of schools seeking teachers. (See the "For Further Information" section at the end of the chapter for more information on this website.)

Personal contacts are often very effective in securing a position as well. Don't hesitate to call friends and acquaintances who might be able to help you obtain interviews. They probably cannot get you a job, but they may be aware of vacancies and know whom you should contact.

Contacting specific school districts directly is another way to determine which positions are available. Call, write, or visit the personnel offices of the school districts in which you are interested in obtaining current information directly from the school district. Alternatively, you can use the Internet to check the home pages of the school districts that interest you to see which job openings are listed.

13-3e GAIN EXPERIENCE BY WORKING WITH CHILDREN

Many education students develop valuable experience, earn some money, and "get a foot in the door" at a school district by serving as substitute teachers. Some universities even offer course work in becoming an effective substitute. Besides giving you the opportunity to

© Cengage 2016

▶II TeachSource Video Case

The First Year of Teaching: One Colleague's Story

Watch the video clips, study the artifacts in the case, and reflect on the following questions:

1. View the bonus video, where Mr. Starner reflects on his first year of teaching. Do his observations surprise you in any way? If so, how?

2. Does this teacher offer any new information about the first year of teaching?

3. What is the most important advice or information you think this teacher conveyed to you?

refine your teaching skills, substitute teaching can provide a competitive advantage in the job market. Some school districts are apt to hire full-time teachers from their substitute ranks if the substitutes have done a good job. After all, school officials would rather hire a known teacher in whom they have confidence than take a chance on a new teacher they don't know. If you're interested in being a substitute teacher, visit the district personnel office to find out the requirements and attend substitute-teacher training sessions if they are offered.

You can also gain experience working with children by tutoring or doing volunteer work with children at Boys and Girls Clubs, after-school programs, and various sports leagues. Getting to know children, how they behave, and how to interact with them will serve you well when you begin your teaching.

The Video Case, *The First Year of Teaching: One Colleague's Story,* depicts a fourth-grade teacher who speaks candidly about his first year of teaching.

Pause *and* Reflect

1. Which strategies might you use to increase your chances of being hired when you are ready to teach?
2. Which of the interview questions in the "Typical Questions Asked during Job Interviews" feature do you believe you would find most difficult to answer? Which would you find easiest?

13-4 How Do You Become Licensed?

All 50 states and the District of Columbia require public elementary and secondary school teachers to be licensed to teach by the department of education in the state in which they work. The terms *licensure* and *certification* are often confused or misused. **Licensure** is the official recognition by a state governmental agency that an individual meets state requirements, whereas **certification** is the process by which the profession grants special recognition to an individual who has met certain qualifications specified by the profession. Often, the term *certification*—as in, "I'm going to get my certification to teach"—is used when *licensure* is meant. This usage is a carryover from earlier times. Today, some states continue to use *certification* as a synonym for *licensure,* but in this book we have tried to distinguish between the two terms.

13-4a TRADITIONAL LICENSURE PROGRAMS

Traditionally, to qualify for licensure, a teacher has had to complete an approved teacher education program. Besides conferring a bachelor's or master's degree, which provides the necessary liberal arts background, teacher education programs fulfill the state requirement that prospective teachers take certain education courses or demonstrate certain competencies.

Since the mid-1980s, the overwhelming majority of states have increased the requirements for licensure, adding test requirements such as the PRAXIS examinations (teacher competency exams developed by the Educational Testing Service) or, in some cases, state-developed competency tests of basic skills. Currently, 18 states and over 600 teacher preparation institutions now require prospective teachers to develop an edTPA portfolio. **edTPA** is a standards-based assessment used to measure and support the knowledge and skills teachers need. To complete an edTPA portfolio, teacher candidates produce and analyze artifacts that demonstrate their teaching knowledge in three areas: (1) Planning for Instruction and Assessment; (2) Instructing and Engaging Students in Learning; and (3) Assessing Student Learning. edTPA is subject-specific, meaning that requirements differ depending on what you're applying to teach.

If the school district in which you are interested requires the edTPA, the higher the score you make on the assessment, the more competitive you will be as a candidate. In some states, further requirements for licensure include U.S. citizenship, criminal background checks, an oath of allegiance, and a health certificate.

Because the requirements for licensure differ from state to state, you should become aware of the requirements for the state in which you will seek employment. A teaching license is valid only in the state for which it is issued, and licensure and testing requirements are never static. However, a number of states have reciprocal agreements to accept one another's licenses as valid. If you move from one state to another, you may want to check whether your teaching license is accepted by the state to which you are moving. To check on the licensure requirements for the state in which you are interested, you should consult the following website: **https://www .teachercertificationdegrees.com/certification**. This website has links to each state's licensure requirements.

Besides the basic licenses for teaching at the elementary and secondary levels, many states require different licenses, or *endorsements*, for such specialization areas as special education, bilingual education, and kindergarten. If, as you gain experience, you want to move out of teaching into a supervisory, administrative, or counseling position, you will need a special license to make that transition as well.

You would be wise to become licensed or endorsed in more than one teaching area, if possible. Adding a second field of licensure will make you more attractive to prospective employers, particularly in smaller school districts, which have less flexibility to hire specialists who teach in only one area. If you plan to become an elementary school teacher, having an additional license or endorsement in reading, special education, early childhood education, or bilingual education would be very worthwhile. Another way to increase your appeal to prospective employers is to major or minor in mathematics, one of the sciences, or instructional technology. Elementary school teachers with expertise in these areas are in short supply. If you plan to teach at the secondary level, you can broaden your appeal by becoming licensed to teach in two or more subject fields. For example, if you are a Spanish major, minor in French; if you are a chemistry major, minor in physics or mathematics. Any doubling up of teaching fields will work to your advantage.

In summary, individual states use licensure requirements to assure the public that the teachers who are educating the youth of our society have been adequately prepared. Licensure requirements should present you with little difficulty as long as the teacher education institution you attend meets the general regulations of the state department of education and as long as you maintain contact with the college official responsible for coordinating the education program with the state licensure requirements.

> *Keeping young teachers in our schools is of immense importance, but keeping them there with spirits strong and souls intact is more important still. If we lose this, we lose everything.*
>
> —JONATHAN KOZOL,
> American educational author

13-4b ALTERNATIVE LICENSURE

In many states, the traditional route to licensure—graduation from an approved teacher education program—is no longer the sole route to gaining a teaching license. **Alternative licensure** programs have been developed as a response to (1) teacher shortages and (2) the perception on the part of some lawmakers that courses in education contribute little to a teacher's effectiveness. Generally, those licensed through alternative means hold a bachelor's degree in the subject area they will teach but have taken fewer credit hours in professional education courses than are normally required for teaching licensure. Often these candidates are required to have at least a B college grade average and to have passed a basic skills test and a test in a subject or specialty area. As mentioned above, many states also require graduates of alternative licensure programs to prepare a portfolio à la edTPA requirements.

One alternative program that has attracted considerable attention is Teach for America. This program recruits motivated undergraduate students with arts and science majors from selected colleges and universities to teach for two years in rural or urban areas that have had difficulty recruiting teachers. Although the program has been successful in attracting significant numbers of minority teachers, its dropout rate is high. Also, the number of teachers produced through the Teach for America program is very small compared with the number graduated through approved teacher education programs.

How successful are these alternative licensure programs? All 50 states have some form of alternative licensure option, with approximately 18 percent of licensed teachers having gone through one of these alternative licensure routes, and 676,000 individuals having been issued teaching licenses through an alternative route in the 2015–2016 school year.[19] Few formal evaluation studies of alternative licensure programs have been carried out, however, and those that have taken place have sometimes been conducted by people with vested interests in the outcomes. To date, a synthesis of what research has been done concludes: "Research on teacher outcomes indicates quite clearly that traditional programs are more effective than alternative programs. Traditional teacher preparation consistently yields better instructional knowledge, self-efficacy, and teacher retention than alternative preparation across all levels of schooling, except kindergarten."[20] One analysis of a national sample of teachers who entered teaching through alternative licensure routes concluded that they tended to have lower academic qualifications than those who entered through other routes, and were less likely to stay in teaching.[21] On the positive side, compared with graduates of traditional teacher education programs, those entering teaching through alternative licensure programs tend to be older, have more work experience in occupations other than education, are more likely to be males, are more likely to be teaching in inner-city schools serving more economically disadvantaged students, and are more likely to be people of color.[22]

Supporters of alternative licensure programs argue that the ability to attract men and minorities into teaching speaks to the need for these types of programs. The federal government provides millions of dollars to help mid-career professionals and retiring military personnel become licensed as teachers.

Nevertheless, tensions exist between those who want to break college-based teacher education's monopoly and professional educators who believe that completion of an approved teacher education program is the public's best guarantee that a teacher is "safe to practice." The variety of alternative licensure programs operating across the various states is testimony to the differing views on how teachers should be prepared. The real issue is not whether traditional programs are better than alternative licensure programs, but rather what the most important elements constituting effective teacher preparation are and whether that preparation occurs through a traditional or alternative program. edTPA requirements for licensure will provide data on how well graduates of traditional versus alternative licensure programs compare. One thing seems certain: Alternative licensure programs will continue to expand to meet the projected need for teachers.

Pause *and* Reflect

1. Do you have any opinions about the alternative licensure programs currently offered in most states? What do you see as their strengths? Their drawbacks?
2. Are you clear about the difference between "certification" and "licensure"?

13-5 If You Don't Teach, What Then?

For many different reasons, a substantial number of teachers each year find themselves looking for jobs outside education. Has your preparation equipped you with skills that are in demand in fields outside education?

13-5a TRANSFERABLE SKILLS

Many noneducational employers are eager to employ teachers and people who have gone through teacher preparation programs, because they have skills that many college graduates lack. Which generic or transferable skills—that is, skills that are needed in most businesses and professions—are you likely to have developed in your preparation as a teacher? Among the skills and abilities that teachers acquire are the following:

- Planning and decision making
- Working under pressure
- Conducting performance evaluations
- Keeping records and organizing materials
- Using technology
- Establishing and maintaining good interpersonal relations
- Communicating effectively in oral and written form
- Managing groups of people

In short, many of the skills required of teachers are required for other types of work as well. Naturally, additional training may be necessary, depending on the exact type of work. Now let's examine some alternative careers.

13-5b OTHER JOBS

In addition to teaching, schools and school districts offer a number of other educational occupations, including librarian, counselor, supervisor, administrator, and school psychologist. Although these roles don't involve full-time teaching of children, they may require some minimum teaching experience and additional licensure. All these roles are important in the educational enterprise. If you decide that you are interested in education but not necessarily in long-term elementary or secondary school teaching, one of these other occupations may be right for you.

There are many alternative careers for people who are prepared as teachers but who elect not to teach in schools.

You might also investigate employment in early childhood education and day care centers. Because early childhood education is a growing field, numerous new occupations are developing within it, such as reading specialists to help diagnose learning abilities and curriculum specialists to help plan the studies. State, local, and federal government agencies need researchers, planners, evaluators, and others to administer the growing number of early childhood projects they fund.

Another area that requires teaching skills is in the field of adult education, which attempts to provide basic education and literacy skills for the many adults who lack such competencies and therefore have difficulty finding work in a technologically oriented society. Adult education occurs in many venues, including public schools, community colleges, and public service organizations.

Large businesses also conduct extensive training programs for their employees, and they require the services of people who can design and implement such programs. Many people who have been trained as teachers find their way into such jobs. Several hundreds of thousands of people are employed (full- and part-time) in training and development in the United States.*

The field of recreation and leisure activities attracts many people trained as teachers. Workers in this field plan, organize, and direct individual and group activities that help people enjoy their leisure hours. They work with people of various ages and socioeconomic groups, the sick and the well, and those with emotional and physical disabilities. Employment settings range from wilderness to rural, to suburban and urban. Examples of recreation program jobs include playground leaders; program specialists in dance, drama, karate, tennis, the arts, and other physical activities; recreation center directors; therapeutic recreation specialists; camp counselors and wilderness leaders; senior citizen program leaders; civilian special services directors in the armed forces; and industrial recreation directors. Recreation workers held about 408,000 jobs in 2019, and that figure is expected to increase in the future.[23] The majority worked in local, public, tax-supported agencies, such as municipal and county park and recreation departments.

*The American Society of Training and Development, 1640 King Street, Box 1443, Alexandria, VA 22313, can provide more information about corporate career opportunities for teachers.

The publishing industry affords numerous job opportunities for education-oriented writers, technology experts, editors, and salespeople. If you have good writing and analytic skills, you might be interested in helping develop or edit textbooks for use in elementary and secondary schools and in colleges. If you enjoy meeting people and traveling, being a textbook sales representative might appeal to you. Another growing area is the development of computer software related to education. Individuals who combine computer skills, including web design, with an understanding of classroom instruction will have a distinct advantage in this job market.

Preparation as a teacher is also important for work related to professional organizations such as the National Education Association (NEA), American Federation of Teachers (AFT), Phi Delta Kappa, Kappa Delta Pi, National Council of Teachers of Mathematics, and National Council for the Social Studies. These organizations and others like them hire people for fieldwork, writing, research, and other staff positions.

OUR FINAL WORD

Many indicators point to a strong demand for teachers in the coming years, once the country emerges from COVID-19 recession hangover. Impending retirements in the current teaching force and increased school enrollments are encouraging signs for prospective teachers, though some former teachers might reenter the job market to compete with recently graduated teachers for these job openings. Successful job searches may require special steps such as relocating to another area or state to secure a teaching position in your field.

There has never been a surplus of good teachers. If you and your credentials are good and you are willing to go where the jobs are, you can find a teaching job.

Preparing yourself well for school districts' needs, especially by gaining expertise in more than one teaching field, can expand your job options and make you more attractive to prospective employers.

The United States has become an education-oriented society. As a nation, we now realize that reaching our individual and national goals depends on achieving high levels of education. Doing so requires being committed to more and better education, and to lifelong learning in and out of schools. Almost 100 years ago, President Calvin Coolidge said, "The business of America is business." Today and into the future, the business of America is education. Teaching is where the action is and will continue to be!

WHY TEACH? YOUR FINAL WORD

1. Describe your "ideal" teaching job. Which elements of that job are most important to you?
2. Now that you have surveyed the educational job market, what do you see as the pluses and minuses of preparing yourself to teach?
3. Which grade level and/or subject matter do you want to teach? How will you go about determining whether your current choice is right for you?

KEY TERMS

alternative licensure (408)
certification (406)
credential file (402)

edTPA (407)
licensure (406)
teaching portfolio (402)

FOR FURTHER INFORMATION

Web Resources

Preparing a Teaching Portfolio: A Guidebook, produced by the Center for Teaching Effectiveness at the University of Texas–Austin

This online resource provides detailed instructions on how to prepare a teaching portfolio.

Teachers-Teachers.com

Sponsored by several educational organizations, this website allows schools to contact prospective teachers who have posted their résumés on the site. There is no fee for teachers.

Print Resources

American Association for Employment in Education, *Job Search Handbook for Educators* (Columbus, OH: Author).

This annual publication is designed to assist both new and experienced educators in their job searches and is the single most important reference on this topic. *The Handbook* is usually distributed through career planning and placement offices in colleges and universities, but it may also be obtained from the AAEE office at 3040 Riverside Drive, Suite 117, Columbus, OH 43221–2550 or by calling (614) 485-1111. AAEE's website also provides links to public school systems and educational organizations.

Richard Nelson Bolles, *What Color Is Your Parachute? 2020: A Practical Manual for Job-Hunters and Career Changers* (Berkeley, CA: Ten Speed Press, 2020).

This best-selling practical manual for job hunters and career changers is updated yearly.

Jay Mathews, *Escalante: The Best Teacher in America* (New York: Holt, 1990).

This is the biography of Jaime Escalante, who is profiled in this chapter and is the subject of the film *Stand and Deliver.* Escalante wins over his students, largely urban Hispanics, with a combination of challenges to pride, demands of dedicated hard work, and demonstrated love.

REFERENCES FOR LOCATING JOB OPPORTUNITIES

GENERAL INFORMATION

Education Week. Available at www.edweek.org

Education Week is an independent newspaper published 40 times a year. For a subscription, write to Education Week, 4301 Connecticut Avenue, NW, Suite 250, Washington, DC 20008.

Education America Network

This career site for education professionals assists them in finding jobs.

PRIVATE SCHOOLS

National Association of Independent Schools (NAIS)

This organization represents more than 1,600 independent schools nationwide and abroad. Contact the Associate Director of Academic Services, National Association of Independent Schools, 1129 20th Street NW, Suite 800 Washington, DC 20036-3425, (202) 973-9700. Also visit the website for information on how to secure a teaching job at one of its schools.

TEACHING OPPORTUNITIES ABROAD

U.S. Department of Defense Education Activity

Teachers in these American schools are U.S. government employees. Contact Department of Defense Education Activity from its website.

Council on International Educational Exchange

The council offers paid overseas teaching experiences in seven countries—Chile, China, Dominican Republic, South Korea, Spain, Thailand, and Vietnam—for university graduates to teach English.

International Schools Services (ISS)

This resource contains names, addresses, and other information on nearly 500 international elementary and secondary schools. Ask for the *ISS Directory of International Schools.* Contact ISS, 15 Roszel Road, P.O. Box 5910, Princeton, NJ 08543, (609) 452-0990.

What Can the New Teacher Expect?

InTASC Standards 9 and 10

LEARNING OBJECTIVES

14-1 Analyze why many teachers are deeply shocked by what they find in their new school.

14-2 Describe the complex role of school administrators and their relationships with new teachers.

14-3 Explain the complexities of new teachers' relationships with older, experienced colleagues.

14-4 Discuss why the act of instructing students can be a stumbling block of new teachers.

14-5 Identify the complicating factors in new teachers' dealings with students.

14-6 Explain why new teachers often have difficulties with parents who should be their natural allies.

14-7 Summarize the chief strategies that can contribute to a successful first year of teaching.

Truth OR Fiction?

T F One of the benefits of being a student for so many years is that the first year of teaching holds few surprises for new teachers.

T F It is important for new teachers to work to eliminate the traditional social distance between themselves and students.

T F In general, it is good advice to hold your students' parents at "arm's length."

Starting their career is for most people one of the most exciting and energizing periods of their lives. For most young people, it represents their unofficial entrance into the adult world. They are often in a new environment with new people and challenges, and they have real responsibilities. This is especially true for new teachers.

For many, the transition into full-time teaching is relatively easy and satisfying. For others, however, the first year is a struggle. Some new teachers are shocked and disappointed by their initial experience of being a teacher. For most, however, the first year of teaching is a mixed bag of highs and lows. In this chapter, we try to help prospective teachers anticipate some of the problems that lie ahead. All of the material comes directly from the experiences of beginning teachers.

We have good news and bad news for you. First, the good news: Forecasters predict that as a result of teacher retirement and student enrollment growth, the number of teachers in the U.S. will grow from 3.67 million in 2019 to 3.92 in 2027, and increase of 244,000.[1]

As we describe in Chapter 13, "What Are Your Job Options in Education?," people entering the teaching profession in the third decade of the twenty-first century typically will have a rich variety of options and opportunities from which to choose. So much for the good news.

Now the bad news: The first year of teaching can be a rough one—too rough for many beginners. Each year, many new teachers walk into their classrooms with energy, high hopes, and rose-colored glasses, only to face unexpected problems that cause them to give up on teaching or radically lower their perceptions of their capabilities as teachers. The tips in the "Voices from the Classroom" feature give you an idea of what you might expect the first year.

Rather than ignoring or—even worse—sugarcoating these problems, we focus on them, even at the risk of frightening some readers. We do so because we believe "forewarned is forearmed," and many of the problems discussed in this chapter can be either prevented or radically reduced in intensity. Further, new teachers can actually find satisfaction in solving their problems and in succeeding as professionals.

Surprise is a big part of the first year too. New teachers often report their astonishment at this or that experience or event. The first year is intense because of the unexpected demands and the startling events that lurk in what was thought to be a familiar world: the classroom. These surprises often come wrapped in everyday boxes; some contain sweet treasures, and others hold booby traps. We have categorized these surprises and organized them in the following way:

- The school milieu: the shock of the familiar
- Administrators: mixed bag, as well as many hats and pressures
- Colleagues: a mixed blessing
- Instruction: so much to learn
- Students: friends or fiends?
- Parents: natural allies with different agendas

In this chapter, we look at each of these categories and try to take some of the surprises out of the first year of teaching. Our larger intention, however, is to help you mobilize yourself by preparing for the problems, developing your strengths, and shoring up your weaknesses.

VOICES from the Classroom

Tips for Your First Year

Lauren Manganiello has been an English teacher at Boston Collegiate Charter School in Dorchester, Massachusetts, and has recently been promoted to director of instruction.

The most valuable tip I can give to a prospective first-year teacher is that you should expect to work *very hard*, and sometimes *very late*, every night. The summer before I started teaching, I worked diligently at preparing units and lessons; still, I had no idea how much work I had coming to me. Granted, the amount of work you'll need to do will depend on your school and your curriculum; I have total control over what I teach, which translates to a lot of work for me. I spend between one and two hours correcting on weeknights and even more on weekends; I spend most afternoons securing the next day's lessons.

Next, expect to do a lot of learning in your first year. Most new teachers are fresh out of college or graduate school and know their specific subject matter very well; however, knowing material and knowing how to teach material are two completely different concepts! Making the switch from higher education back to high school or even elementary school education is a challenge.

Finally, expect to:

- Struggle—practice makes perfect, and if you push yourself too hard at the beginning of your career, you might burn out before your time (think of teaching as a marathon).

- Be overwhelmed with paperwork—there's a letter or form for *everything*.

- Meet amazing students who will keep you coming back to your job.

- Have responsibilities outside of your classroom, such as corridor duty, study halls, or, my favorite, bathroom duty.

- Be shocked by the sometimes cynical conversation in the teachers' lunchroom.

- Find some amazing teachers in your department and school who can be your best resources and best allies.

- Be surprised—what you worry about now will seem ridiculous once you're finally in the classroom, and what you've never even given a thought to will suddenly become your everyday amusement, pleasure, or headache!

Parents are not always the teacher's ally.

14-1 The School Milieu: The Shock of the Familiar

One of the oddest occurrences related to becoming a teacher is the new teacher's sense of strangeness in what is, after all, a very familiar setting. People who become securities analysts, astronauts, or psychiatric social workers know they are moving into a strange environment, and they expect these new work worlds to present them with very different experiences from those they had as students. New teachers, however, are reentering a familiar setting, even if their schools are not the same ones in which they were taught. Nevertheless, beginning teachers are often overwhelmed by their initial exposure to school.

The new teacher's very familiarity with life in schools is a problem in that it lulls many into a false sense of understanding of what is happening around them—and thus a false sense of security. "School" is a very complicated network of people, structures, and interactions.

However, having "studied" school from the perspective of a student is hardly the same as understanding it from the perspective of a teacher. Being 1 of 25 students learning from a teacher is quite different from being in front of 25 young people and having responsibility for their learning. Also, new teachers not only have to learn a new set of school routines for their particular school, but also must understand how to administer those routines. They have to learn their way around a new building and find out how to requisition the supplies they need. They have to get acquainted with their administrators' policies, their fellow teachers, and especially their students. On top of everything else, first-year teachers often have to develop lesson plans from scratch. They must build complete units, design bulletin boards, devise an evaluation system, and make up and grade short- and long-term tests of students' understanding. And they have to learn the many skills that make up the craft of teaching, such as passing out papers or taking attendance without taking up precious minutes or causing minor chaos. The sheer volume of all this "newness" puts enormous pressure and strain on beginners.

T (**F**)

One of the benefits of being a student for so many years is that the first year of teaching holds few surprises for new teachers.

> " *But how do I feel at the end of each day? I feel proud of my students. I feel more knowledgeable about living, teaching, and learning. I feel lucky to be a teacher. I feel…full of sparks.*
>
> **—IRASEMA ORTEGA-CRAWFORD,**
> biology teacher

14-1a CULTURE SHOCK

Beginning teachers' disorientation with what they thought would be the familiar turf of school often shows up in visible signs of mental and physical stress. In the early months of the school year, many new teachers experience depression and self-doubt, outbursts of crying, physical exhaustion, insomnia, crankiness, inability to control temper, and even fits of vomiting before going to school in the morning.

The stresses and strains many new teachers experience are similar to the phenomenon known as culture shock. **Culture shock** is the feeling of dislocation that people experience when they initially live in a foreign country.[2] Peace Corps volunteers, overseas aid workers, exchange students, tourists, and newly arrived immigrants often report that when they are first thrust into the strange life patterns of a foreign culture, they feel numbingly disoriented, forced to assimilate too much too soon, and afraid they have made a drastic mistake by going to this strange country. It is easy to explain the culture shock experienced by Peace Corps volunteers and immigrants, but why teachers? Haven't we just said that teachers, as ex-students, are accustomed to the culture of school?

The following account by a new second-grade teacher speaks to the kinds of culture shock problems related to the large amounts of "newness" many first-year teachers experience.*

Pause *and* Reflect

1. Think of a time when you may have experienced culture shock, and try to remember, in as much detail as possible, how it made you feel.
2. Did you experience any sense of disorientation or depression during your initial months at college? Which strategies did you find helpful in getting oriented?
3. Have you ever been in a class with a teacher you thought might be experiencing culture shock?

PRESERVICE to PRACTICE

Charlotte Tucker: Second Grade

The next time I hear someone say, "Teaching is an easy job," I think I'm going to slap his or her face . . . or cry! I can't believe how tired I am. I've been teaching for five weeks, and it seems as if it has been five months. I never realized that life on the teacher's side of the desk could be so different, so tiring. I remember seeing the movies set in high schools and thinking they were exaggerated. My kids are younger and don't have the kinds of problems those high school kids in the movie had, but they still have problems, and they are so demanding! They all want my attention, and they all seem to want it at the same time. "Miss Tucker, someone took my pencil! Did you do it?" "Miss Tucker, Ralph and Maxine put gum in my hair." "Miss Tucker, my father doesn't think we're doing enough arithmetic in this class and says I can tell the kids to shut up if you won't." "Miss Tucker, I need to see the nurse. I have a terrible nosebleed coming on!" And on and on.

And the forms! They never end. Forms for shots. For lockers. For parent volunteers. For books. And we have an attendance procedure here that must have been designed by a sadist! It consumes hours of time. The principal's office continually wants information. I keep filling out forms and sending them in, only to be greeted with more forms. I can't imagine what they do with all the information.

On top of all this, I'm supposed to teach! I leave school in the afternoon—always the last one out of the building—and I'm numb from the hairline down. On some nights, I can hardly unwrap a microwavable dinner. And I spend what little free time I do have staring at my TV set and having imaginary arguments with Sandra's know-it-all father (whom I have yet to meet) about why we actually are, in fact, doing just the right amount of arithmetic. What is most discouraging is that Sandra's father wins the arguments.

Clearly, this has been the most frustrating five weeks of my life. I feel as if I've been swimming in molasses. Student teaching was a breeze compared with this!

Pause *and* Reflect

1. Do you remember ever being in the class of an inexperienced teacher as frustrated as Charlotte Tucker? What was it like?
2. What specific advice would you give her to escape her downward spiral?

*All cases in this chapter that are not accompanied by specific citations are slightly altered or fictionalized accounts of situations and problems experienced by the authors or by beginning teachers with whom the authors have worked. The names have been changed to save us all from embarrassment.

But many of the surprises of school life are very pleasant ones. There can be much love and human warmth in the classroom. Some of the aspects of school life that you may have dreaded never materialize. The content about which you feel uncertain could turn out to be your strength. Also, within the four walls of the classroom, some people find a new self they didn't know existed. Such is the case of the once-shy Margaret Julia Gomez.

PRESERVICE to PRACTICE

Margaret Julia Gomez: High School Mathematics

All through elementary and high school, I was bashful. In my high school graduating class, I won the "Most Shy" award. I dreaded being called on, even when I knew I had the right answer! Part of it is that I blush so easily, so my approach was to be like the furniture or the wallpaper and hope that the teacher wouldn't see me. Still, I liked school and always liked my teachers, even the ones who had fun with my blushing. When I decided to become a math teacher, I knew my shyness was going to be a problem, but I figured that I could pass my blushing off as a permanent sunburn.

Something happened, though, when I became a teacher. I began to notice a change when I was student teaching, and once I had my own class, it was quite clear: I'm a different person in my class. I feel very outgoing, almost to the point of being aggressive. Also, I've discovered that I'm a ham actor. And what a stage my classroom is! I love it. My students seem to love it, too. It seems so odd that after all these years of trying to be invisible, now I'm discovering a whole new side of myself.

Pause *and* Reflect

1. Which personal quality of yours do you feel might be a drawback or a problem as a teacher?
2. Can you think of a time when you discovered a whole new side of your personality?

14-2 Administrators: Mixed Bag and Many Hats

As elementary and secondary school students, most of us had pretty simplistic notions of administrators. The superintendent, if we ever saw one at all, was a vague presence we occasionally glimpsed in the hall talking to one of the staff or in front of a microphone on ceremonial occasions. The principal was much more a part of our school lives, existing as someone beloved or feared, and occasionally both. Even though the principal was near at hand, our student's-eye view was rather one-dimensional: The principal represented AUTHORITY. In all but the rarest instances, the principal stood metaphorically directly behind the teacher, supporting the teacher and the system (or so we thought!). When, as students, we went to the principal's office, it almost always meant we were in trouble. Now it could mean so many things!

14-2a THE MULTIPLE ROLES OF THE PRINCIPAL

New teachers' relationships with their principals are hardly one-dimensional. School principals loom quite large in the lives of beginning teachers, and the teacher–principal relationship (as well as relationships with vice principals, department heads, and master teachers) has many facets. Most importantly, the principal is now a *colleague*, a fellow educator joined with you in the common task of bringing civilization to unformed youth. You are both professionals. You are both part of a common tradition. You probably share common goals (such as improving the educational opportunities of children) and attitudes (e.g., that people engaged in the important work of educating the young need more support from the public than they receive). But there is more to this relationship.

Principals are the *official leaders* in the school. They make decisions or act as the funnel for the decisions of higher authorities. Decisions made by teachers or students are normally checked with principals. Principals speak for the school community to the superintendent, the press, and the local citizens. Nothing is ever quite "official" unless the principal has been involved.

Principals are *helpers*. They can dispense information and materials, and, as experienced teachers, they are sources of tips, shortcuts, and helpful suggestions. Principals also visit classrooms and hold conferences with teachers, especially new teachers. They stand ready to aid beginning teachers who are encountering difficulties and confusion.

Principals are *policy makers*. A school system is a bureaucracy whose long arm extends from the state commissioner of education to the local district superintendent of schools to the individual school principal. That "long arm" is, in fact, educational policy—the ideas that are supposed to direct what happens in a school and, more specifically, in your classroom. Principals act on behalf of the school district's bureaucracy by introducing teachers to the policies and monitoring the policies' implementation. In addition, they often set their own policies unique to their school building, such as discipline and dress codes, assembly activities, and a character education program.

Principals are *crisis managers*. When something happens that a teacher cannot handle, the principal's office is where he or she naturally turns for help. A principal needs to be fully briefed about crises, real or potential, to deal with them effectively.

Principals are *facilitators*. Schools run on things: pencils, books, paper, heat, hot lunches, sanitary toilets, lights, construction paper, petty cash, computers, and keys. It is the principal's job to keep teachers supplied so that they, in turn, can carry out the aims of the school.

Principals are *reward dispensers*. They assign classes to teachers, deciding which kind of children they will teach and whether those children will be at the level or in the subject for which particular teachers are prepared. Principals also assign teachers to extracurricular duties and activities. In addition, they can give or withhold compliments on teacher performance.

Principals are *judges*. A principal makes the decision about a new teacher's qualifications to teach in the school, and later decides whether the teacher's performance merits rehiring him or her. After all, first-year teachers are neither permanent members of the faculty nor permanently licensed members of the teaching profession. Principals can write recommendations for or against teachers, thereby enhancing or destroying individuals' reputations as teachers. This role of judge is one that new teachers often don't appreciate until it is too late.

Principals act as *buffers* between teachers and angry parents (or, occasionally, angry students). Teachers can be quite vulnerable to public attack. Parents hear tales from their children or from other parents and, if they have a question or a complaint to make against a teacher, often go directly to the principal, bypassing the teacher. The principal is the official "complaint department." This delicate position requires the principal to be open and responsive to complaints and, at the same time, to support the position of the teacher involved. Such situations call for the skills of high diplomacy.

Finally, principals are *sacrificial lambs*. If the community, the teachers, or the school board become dissatisfied with what is happening in a particular school, the school's principal is vulnerable. If a school fails to make adequate yearly progress on some state or federal policy or program, the principal may be replaced. No one suggests replacing the students or the parents! Tenured staff cannot be dismissed (except under very special circumstances), so the principal, who may or may not be responsible for the reported problem, is likely to pay the penalty. The ease with which a principal can be dismissed is, incidentally, a characteristic shared with beginning teachers because principals rarely have tenure as principals.

The need to wear all these hats makes for a complicated existence. Today's school principal has a most difficult job, and doing the job well requires the strengths of a field general, a philosopher, a psychiatrist, and a saint. A recent study reports how in just the last few years, a principal's job has become much more complex and demanding.[3] Given that the strengths required of a principal are in short supply, it is not surprising that new teachers sometimes find themselves in conflict with their principals. Principals have to make many quick and difficult decisions, often with insufficient information or time, and they are sometimes wrong.

When principals observe in teachers' classrooms, they may appear to be there as helpers, but they cannot put aside their role as *judges*. At some point, they must make recommendations about "their" teachers to their superiors, and they obviously are influenced by what they have seen during their "helping" observations. For this reason, confusion and potential conflict between the administrator and a new teacher are possible. In addition, beginning teachers often do not know how to work in a bureaucracy (i.e., how to make the organization work for their ends), and they sometimes are antibureaucratic, or overly critical and complaining. This behavior can put them into direct conflict with their administrators, whose job it is to train beginners in bureaucratic procedures and whose primary responsibility is to ensure

Up **CLOSE**

You Know You're in Trouble When...

- You have threatened that if there is one more sound in the classroom, you will personally call every parent to complain—and then you hear a sound.

- The principal asks you what you plan to be doing next year.

- You have your students correct their own tests and the lowest mark in the class is 96 percent. And they are smirking.

- It is 10:15 A.M., and the class has ripped through three-quarters of the work you have prepared for the day.

- It feels like February, and it's only late September.

- The teacher across the hall comes in and offers to show your kids how to behave.

- The parents of 11 of your students ask to see the principal, and you are not invited.

- Unsolicited, your principal offers to write a recommendation for your placement file.

- You are convinced you have finally come up with challenging and interesting work for your class, and when you present it, they chorus, "We did that last year."

- After sitting in your class for five minutes, your supervisor starts to look at the clock.

- You walk into your usually noisy classroom, and immediately all the students get in their seats and smile at you.

- You return after being sick for three days, and the students chant, "We want the substitute!"

that the school, as a totality, runs smoothly and that students learn what is expected of them. Perhaps not surprisingly, given the many roles the administrator plays, slippage and breakdown can occur.

An error of first impressions can also work the other way: The administrator who seems severe and distant can turn out to be warm and supportive. Principals (and others who have supervisory responsibility over beginning teachers, such as lead teachers and department- and grade-level chairpeople) can be a crucial source of professional expertise and moral support. In addition, research shows that supportive administrators actually help teachers to become reflective and solve their own problems.[4]

Nevertheless, new teachers need to be proactive and not wait for the help to come to them. Administrators or supervisors may potentially be able to provide the following kinds of assistance:

- They may have valuable advice on dealing with specialized problems, such as an extremely reticent student.
- They can put you in contact with specialists in your building or elsewhere in the school district to help you on a range of issues, from curricular matters to dealing with disruptive students.
- They may be able to do demonstration lessons or special presentations in your class.
- They may be able to come to your classroom, observe you in action, and provide focused feedback on your early efforts to carry out a strategy such as cooperative learning.

Although we suggest you seek help from administrators and supervisors, we also urge prudence. Consult them honestly, directly, and somewhat sparingly. Consider the case of earnest Peter James.

PRESERVICE to PRACTICE

Peter James: Middle School Science

During the special orientation meeting for new teachers, the principal told us all that whenever we have a problem, we should come and see him. He didn't expect us to be perfect, and he told us that he felt his major job was to help new teachers. Later that week, he stopped me in the hall and warmly repeated his offer of help. I really took him at his word. So in early October, when I started having trouble planning and finding materials, I just went to see the principal. He was very cordial and, although he talked a lot about himself, he did give me some fairly helpful advice. I went to see him for three short visits. Just talking the problems out seemed to help. I started finding good materials, and my classes really improved. I felt I was really doing well, and I couldn't wait to get to school in the morning.

Then, in early December, I started getting treated in an odd way by some of the senior teachers. They were always asking me whether they could help, and if they could get me a glass of water (sort of like I had some incurable disease). It was weird. Finally, I asked two of them in the lunchroom, "Why all the

concern?" Well, it came out that the principal had told them that I was having "big trouble," and he had told a number of the senior teachers to do what they could for me. He had not been in to observe me once.

Later in the year, the principal came in for two brief observations (to conform to minimum standards in our district), and he never had time for a conference. He did, however, write up supervisor conference reports. They were lukewarm and had no specifics. He did mention in both reports that I was improving and overcoming early problems. What improvement? What problems? All he had to go by was what I told him. I got so mad that I wrote him a note to the effect that my self-reported problems had cleared up some time ago and that I felt my teaching was better than his report had indicated. I could see the writing on the wall, though. I started looking for another position and got one without too much trouble. I liked the kids in my first school and many of the teachers. Somehow, though, early on, I had put myself in a box for the principal, and he wasn't going to let me out.

Pause *and* Reflect

1. What mistakes in judgment were made in this case?
2. Asking for help is often a two-edged sword. How would you have handled this situation?

14-3 Colleagues: A Mixed Blessing

New teachers are vulnerable to many outside forces as well as to their own insecurities. If a supportive administrator can turn a potentially disastrous year into a year of growth, a beginning teacher's professional peers can be even more influential in the process of learning how to teach and how to survive in the classroom. Mary Lopez is a case in point.

PRESERVICE to PRACTICE

Mary Lopez: Sixth Grade

I had a hard time finding a teaching job. I had hoped to teach in my hometown, but there were just no jobs at the level I wanted to teach. The best job was on the other side of the state, and when it became clear that there were no jobs on the local horizon, I took it. I was very excited about teaching; I really felt that I was starting out on an adventure. I was, however, also moving away from my parents. Being so far away from home meant that there were lots of things that were going to be new to me. I had to get a car, find an apartment, establish a bank account, and take care of lots of other things—all at once. It was literally like a crash course in being an adult. And that's what I felt like right from the beginning: an adult. It was so different from college and even student teaching. At my school, people treated me like an adult, and they expected me to act like one. For the first months I felt as if I was playacting at being a grown-up. Well, now I guess the role is comfortable, or maybe I just have my act down pat.

Although I made friends with a few people in my apartment building, I was really very lonely at first. I don't think I would have made it without Joan Silver. Joan teaches in the classroom next to mine. She's been, as she says, "in the trenches" for 18 years, but she's got more ideas and energy and dedication than any of us fresh troops. Joan was a lifesaver for me. She took me under her wing even before school started. She has been a source of ideas, great

materials, and inspiration, and she has never made me feel like a taker or a leech. *I* actually taught *her* some things! That's one of the reasons I admired her so much. She really wanted to know about the new ideas I had learned in my education courses, and she put a lot of them to work in her class.

I guess we talked every day after school. A lot of the time, we just spent the hour after school laughing. A couple of times the janitor came in thinking there was something wrong, but what he found was the two of us broken up with laughter. And about once a month, she would drag me home for dinner. Joan always seemed to know when I was a little low, and that's when she'd insist that I come home with her and have dinner with her family.

There's so much to learn in the first year, and not just about subject matter. Some important things—like how to get information from the school secretary and how to stay on the right side of the janitor—you never learn in education courses. Joan was my guide on everything from how to fill out my planbook to which memos from the front office I had to pay attention to and which I could put in what she called the "circular file."

It seems funny to say this, given the fact that Joan is 20 years older than I am, but I really think she's my best friend. She certainly has made this year a terrific one for me. I hope that during my career, I can mentor other new teachers in the same way.

Pause *and* Reflect

1. Do you anticipate that you will search actively for a mentor-teacher? Why or why not?
2. How might your new teaching peers be "mixed blessings"?

Although there is increasing cooperation among teachers and greater access to specialists, mentors, and aides, teachers work independently in their own classrooms and with their own students for the most part. When they are engaged in their professional work, they typically are isolated from one another. Although administrators are the official source of support and help for beginners, fellow teachers serve as a much more accessible and less threatening source of assistance. As the preceding case illustrates, a teacher's colleagues can be a powerful influence, especially in the beginning. They can be an ever-ready source of ideas and teaching tips and can initiate newcomers into the customs of the school and lead to their desire to stay in teaching.[5] Like Joan Silver, a peer can be an inspiration and show by example what the phrase "teacher as professional" means.

Sometimes, however, teachers can have a negative influence, undermining beginning teachers' idealism, lowering their standards, and offering no help at all. The teachers' lunchroom may be the venue for serious disillusionment. Many teachers use the lounge to "unwind" by delivering harsh criticism of students, mocking administrators, and offering negative pronouncements about the teaching profession. Although not especially different from similar "off-camera" remarks in hospitals and businesses, such comments in the teachers' lounge can blunt a new teacher's idealism and enthusiasm. The lounge is a source of much learning for beginners, but in some cases the private side of colleagues can be a rude awakening for them.

Although we strongly believe that the teaching profession has a larger percentage of dedicated, selfless people than any other profession (except, perhaps, the clergy), it also has its share of rogues and fools. Therefore beginners should pick their way carefully among this field of new colleagues.

14-4 Instruction: So Much to Learn

Ultimately, a teacher's only real problem is his or her students' failure to learn and to develop. All other conflicts, triumphs, and defeats pale in significance if the children are learning and developing their human potential. The degree of the children's success as learners is the best measure of a teacher's success or failure. Many pay-for-performance plans give bonuses to teachers whose students exceed expectations on the state-mandated examinations. Although the link between a teacher's instruction and a student's learning is often overstated and difficult to measure, this relationship is crucial. Teacher effectiveness is an area in which there are few naturals, and first-year teachers generally have much to learn in this area of instruction.

One major difficulty is the sheer newness of the role of teacher. After a little student teaching, you suddenly find yourself totally immersed in all the responsibilities that go with managing a classroom. You are in charge of your own class and responsible for taking it from the first day of school to the last. One particularly vexing problem for beginning teachers is the search for effective curricular materials, as the case of Grace Joyce illustrates.

PRESERVICE to PRACTICE

Grace Joyce: Third Grade

The overriding question of this year has been "What works?" I'm in a constant search for materials. It is never ending. My kids aren't especially brilliant, but they devour material and look at me as if to say, "Well, what's next?" Our school's curriculum guide is only five years old, but it is terribly dated. The students know a lot of the stuff already. They learned it in lower grades or just picked it up. They are bored by a good bit of the rest, too. I'm constantly squeezing ideas and tips from the other third-grade teachers. They are helpful, but they are in the same boat I am. Sometimes I get a big buildup on a particular workbook or special unit by a teacher who had fabulous success with it. I try it, and I fall on my face with it.

Then there are the kids. They are so fickle! A couple of times, I took their suggestions on things they wanted to study and work on. After much work and many late hours, I'd get these classes prepared and the very same kids who were so anxious to make the suggestions didn't care at all.

My school district has curriculum specialists. Some of them are very good, too—particularly the math specialist. He would give me *too* much material. I'd spend hours deciding which approach to use to teach 10 minutes' worth of material. The language arts specialist was a sweet lady but very rarely available, and most of her ideas were really out to lunch; I was on my own there. When you get right down to it, you have to make the curriculum and the materials *yours* before they are any good to you. Someone else's great materials are nothing until you have made them your own. This is hard to do the first year.

Pause *and* Reflect

1. What are the major insights about teaching that Grace recounts here?
2. How comfortable are you asking for help and advice? What are the "upsides and downsides"?

Although the curricular and instructional aspect of teaching can be a thicket of difficulty for many beginners, it is very exciting and inspiring for others. Take a look at the world through the eyes of Nicholas Briggs.

PRESERVICE to PRACTICE

Nicholas Briggs: Middle School Social Studies

School has always been hard for me. But then again, if the truth be known, I've always worked hard. In high school, I really got turned on to history, and I think it was then that I decided to become a teacher. In college, I took every history course I could. I was way over the required number of history courses for certification. And I was lucky to teach at a very

academic high school as a student teacher. I think I did well, too. At least that's what everyone said.

I was really disappointed when I couldn't find any openings as a history teacher. I was getting very discouraged until I was finally offered a middle school job in the same school district where I had done my student teaching. My first thought was to

(Continued)

let it go and wait for a "real" history job. What they wanted me to teach was social studies. There was some history involved, but there was also a lot of other social science material to teach. What I really wanted to teach were modern European history and the rise and fall of totalitarianism, and what they wanted was what seemed to me pretty low-level stuff. I was ready to hang it up. I could possibly work for the company my dad works for, or I could go back to school. Well, anyway, I decided I'd give middle school teaching a chance.

The great surprise of teaching for me was not the kids or anything like that. It was, on the one hand, how little I knew about my strength—history—and,

on the other hand, how intellectually exciting teaching in general can be. I had taken tons of history courses and considered myself a super buff, but I had missed the essential meaning of history. That's what I have been learning these first two years, and it has been as stimulating as anything in my life. Now I feel I'm just beginning to understand the purpose of history and what should be taught. I came to teach and probably ended up learning more than my students.

Incidentally, I was offered the position I thought I really wanted, a position on the high school history faculty. I turned it down. I couldn't be happier than I am here.

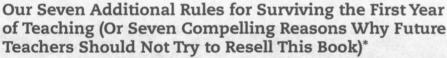

Pause *and* Reflect

1. Which aspect of teaching or the instruction process do you believe will be most challenging? How sure are you?
2. Which part of teaching are you most confident about?

Up CLOSE

Our Seven Additional Rules for Surviving the First Year of Teaching (Or Seven Compelling Reasons Why Future Teachers Should Not Try to Resell This Book)*

1. *When in doubt, think.* Instead of simply fretting about problems or panicking, use your best tool—your mind. Reflect. Problem-solve. Try to identify the problem and possible solutions; think about the resources that are available to you; and then act and judge whether that option helped the situation.

2. *Don't look for love in the classroom.* You should definitely demand respect, but not necessarily love. Even expecting appreciation may lead to disappointment. Among many members of the "Entitled Generation," appreciation is an elusive trait. If you need love, buy a puppy.

3. *Deal with your authority problems before you enter the classroom.* Come to terms with the fact that you will be responsible for maintaining

an orderly, civil, and safe environment, and think hard about how you will accomplish this feat.

4. *If you are not organized, get organized.* Coping with the planbooks, student papers, office memos, attendance records, grades, report cards, and so on requires much more organization than many beginning teachers have practiced to this point. If you are "challenged" by organization, consider getting one of the many fine books available of this subject. *You must stay on top of the paperwork!*

5. *Love thy school secretaries and custodians.* Many beginners fail to realize how important the school secretaries and custodians are in enabling teachers to do an effective job and in the school's "informal communication network."

(Continued)

6. *Focus on learning.* Many beginners fail to concentrate on making sure their students really learn something and therefore have feelings of accomplishment. Students will put up with a great deal of "beginning teacheritis" if they sense they are learning. Remember too that they usually need to be reminded that they actually have learned something!

7. *Don't—we repeat, don't—get married two weeks before the start of your first teaching job.*

For reasons unknown to the authors, each year thousands of new college graduates decide to simultaneously jump into two of life's most difficult undertakings: beginning a career and starting what they hope will be a lifelong relationship.

*The authors promise that if you follow these seven rules faithfully, you will survive the first year of teaching. You may even like it! If you do not survive the year, return the unused portion of this book to your instructor for a refund.

14-5 Students: Friends or Fiends?

And now we come to the main event: students. Becoming comfortable and sensing that they are effective with children is a major concern for new teachers, as it well should be—students are the main event! They make the good days good and the bad days bad. The relationship between teacher and students is multifaceted. An important aspect of the relationship is based on how well the students are achieving the goal of learning.

Although students are the primary source of a teacher's success, they can also be a source of failure. Three areas in particular cause problems: discipline, social distance, and sex. Behind each of these areas of difficulty is an inaccurate set of expectations teachers hold about students.

In the classroom, words of encouragement go a long way.

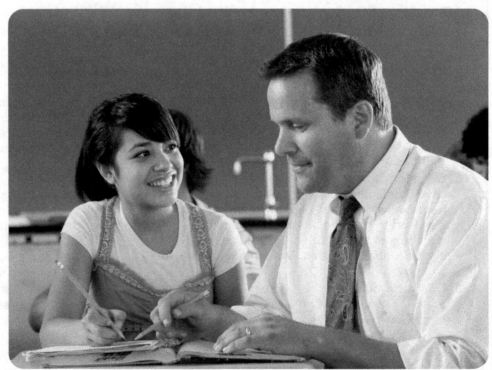

Denise Andersen/Shutterstock.com

Pause *and* **Reflect**

1. What are some of your hypotheses about why beginning teachers' attitudes change in this way?
2. Can you recall experiencing a new teacher's swing in attitude toward your class? What accounted for it?

It's not what the teacher does that's important. It's what the teacher gets the children to do.

—PHIL SCHECHTY,
educational reformer

One indication of these out-of-line expectations is the sharp change in attitudes people experience as they go through teacher education and then begin their first years of classroom teaching. Studies have shown that the longer college students stay in teacher education programs, the more positive and warm their attitudes toward students become.[6] Conversely, among beginning teachers, positive attitudes toward students drop sharply. In fact, beginning teachers score significantly lower on attitude inventories than students just entering teacher education. Before going on, take a moment to consider the experience of Catherine Foley.

14-5a SOURCES OF A DISTORTED VIEW

Our experience in working with college students (for more years than we care to report) has convinced us that most students who are preparing to become teachers have high ideals in general and become particularly idealistic about children and education during their preparation. They believe that as teachers, they should have positive and warm relations with students, and they want to make the classroom more relaxed and more responsive to the needs of students than the traditional classroom in which they were educated. As college students take more education courses and observe in classrooms, their views of children become even more idealistic and, as a result, more positive. By graduation, the rose-colored glasses are firmly affixed.

Also, college students have managed to shut out many less positive memories of their own childhood and adolescence. They forget things like the time they joined with the other seventh-graders to put four tacks on Miss Derriere's chair. They blot out all the juicy stories other students have told about the young physical education teacher, even though they knew most were untrue. They forget about how they enjoyed reading (or writing) obscenities about their math teacher on the lavatory wall. They forget how cruel kids can be to kids. Somehow the dark side of human nature recedes from view during teacher education. But fear not—it reappears in the beginning teacher's classroom. New teachers rediscover human

PRESERVICE to PRACTICE

Catherine Foley: Fifth Grade

I have enjoyed my students this year, probably more than I should have. The only real down moment I had come right toward the end of the year, when something one of the sixth-grade teachers said really shook my confidence. She made some comment at lunch about how much fun and games was going on in my class. All of a sudden I began thinking that although I was having a great time, maybe the kids were having a great time and not really learning anything. I tried to think of what I had taught them that was really important, and my mind was blank. I tried to think of particular students who I thought had really shown a lot of progress, and I couldn't think of anyone specific. I went around that way for a couple of days, and I got sort of panicky.

Finally, almost by accident, I came across one of the student's notebooks, which had all of his work from September, even his diagnostic tests. It was really enlightening. I could almost see the change from week to week in what he knew. The problems became more difficult, but he could master them. His compositions became more interesting, and the mechanics became sounder. His handwriting looked so much more mature. I figured, though, that maybe that was just one student. I asked to look at a few other students' notebooks, and there it was. They had changed. They were different. Not just different but *better*. And I was an important part of that change.

The class clown! Almost every classroom has one.

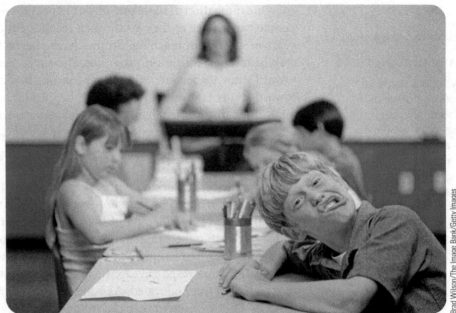

Brad Wilson/The Image Bank/Getty Images

▶❚❚ TeachSource Video Case

Elementary Classroom Management: Basic Strategies

Watch the video clips, study the artifacts in the case, and reflect on the following questions:

1. This teacher mentions the importance of starting the day off well, which she accomplishes with a morning meeting. In this chapter, the authors offer seven tips for starting the school year off well. Based on your own educational experiences, what, if any, "don'ts" would you suggest for the beginning of the day or the school year?

2. Which of the administrator's roles, described earlier in this chapter, seems to best describe the principal shown in this case? How can the tone set by administrators make it easier or more difficult for a new teacher to maintain classroom discipline?

frailty and fallibility in their students and in themselves. All too often the sad result is that their positive attitudes toward children plummets. (The Video Case, *Elementary Classroom Management: Basic Strategies*, shows how two teachers at different levels keep things flowing smoothly in their classes.)

Normally, teachers' positive attitudes make a comeback, although they rarely regain the heights they reached during the latter stages of teacher preparation. Nevertheless, beginners' unrealistic expectations are a great source of their problems in the classroom. Although problems of this kind abound, here we look at just the three areas mentioned earlier: discipline, social distance, and sex.

14-5b CLASSROOM MANAGEMENT

Classroom management, classroom control, or discipline (pick your euphemism label) is one of those problems that shouldn't exist. After all, school is an opportunity for children. The teacher works hard to help them. It's simple: The teacher is there to teach, and the students are there to learn. Unfortunately, things do not always work out that way.

The great majority of schools, whether kindergartens or high schools, are organized with the expectation that the teacher will be "in charge" of the class. You may not like this structure, but there are things you can do about it. (For example, zero-tolerance policies in many schools regarding weapons or illegal substances take some of the burden of enforcement off teachers.) But being in charge is still what is generally expected of a teacher by the administration, your teacher-peers, and, yes, the children.

(We return to this matter of expectations in the section on social distance later in this chapter.) Few (and lucky) are the teachers who do not have to come to grips with their role as disciplinarian.

Unaccustomed to Being in Charge

A discipline problem occurs when someone violates the expected orderly pattern of classroom behavior. In most cases, the breach of discipline is an overt act by one or more students that distracts attention from or interrupts the performance of the task at hand. Few teacher education students of traditional college age have had much opportunity to be "in charge," give orders, coordinate the activities of a group of people, or say such things as "Quiet down!" or "Stay in your seat!" Students, by contrast, are accustomed to being taught by experienced teachers who know how to manage and control them, usually rather effortlessly.

> *I am not a teacher, but an awakener.*
>
> —ROBERT FROST (1874–1963), poet

Students can sense uncertainty and hesitancy in a new teacher's behavior. Moreover, school is not fun and games for children, who can get restless and bored in the classroom. (Remember how long the school day was when you were in elementary and secondary school, how long you had to sit still at a stretch, and how much you had to do that didn't interest you?) These conditions, plus the potential for friction that always exists in any group containing so many people, make it almost inevitable that first-year teachers will have some trouble establishing the kind of productive relationship with students that they seek. (In the Video Case, *Secondary Classroom Management: Basic Strategies*, a teacher discusses maintaining a consistent social distance, as well as other aspects of classroom management.)

As we have implied, many new teachers start out with a rather idealized picture of children as victims. They assume that misbehavior is a result of some condition external to the child, such as a disruptive home life or poverty. Often the suggestion is made that something in the teacher's class provokes or brings forth the problem. If only the teacher would "establish the right environment" or "reach out to the child in just the right way," the problem would be solved. This idea is a subset of the larger view that people are not capable of evil, only social arrangements are capable of evil—an idea that had many adherents in education at one time and still has some advocates today. This idea that all children are innately good, combined with the first-year teacher's insecurities and search for approval, makes it difficult for many new teachers to deal confidently with their role as disciplinarian. (See Chapter 6 for a more in-depth discussion of classroom management.)

© Cengage 2016

TeachSource Video Case

Secondary Classroom Management: Basic Strategies

Watch the video clips, study the artifacts in the case, and reflect on the following questions:

1. This teacher echoes the point made in this chapter that teachers should maintain a consistent social distance, either relaxed or strict. How does his teaching demonstrate this point?

2. How does this teacher demonstrate that he is "in charge," as described in this chapter?

3. What is the most important piece of advice this case offered for you, as a preservice teacher?

14-5c SOCIAL DISTANCE

The term "social distance" became famous during the COVID-19 outbreak. We're talking about the relationships between teachers and their students. Establishing the right social distance was once confined to face-to-face contact with students in the classroom or with a student who has a crush on you and insists on walking with you to the parking lot. Now social distance is wrapped up with social media and students using Facebook, Twitter, Instagram, or email, often revealing personal matters or asking their new teacher intimate questions. Increasingly, school districts are establishing policies and guidelines regarding social media. If your district hasn't yet developed rules, make your own. Use common sense and follow the principle that all your electronic communications with students, and also other teachers, should be able to stand the potential scrutiny of your administrators, parents, the public, and even the courts. Nevertheless, establishing an appropriate **social distance** from students occupies a good deal of a beginning teacher's attention and energy. Like disciplinary techniques, the ability to establish the correct social distance does not come with a teaching license or one's first job. The accompanying Preservice to Practice feature provides some advice on how beginning teachers can begin developing the appropriate distance on the very first day of school.

Up **CLOSE**

Our Guide to the First Day of School

In many areas of life, from job interviews to dating, first impressions are powerful. The same is true at the beginning of the school year—students' first impressions set the tone for how the rest of the school year will proceed. With that in mind, we offer a few tips we have picked up along the way.

1. *Teach your very best lesson.* Often teachers use the first day for filling out forms, assigning lockers, and handling essential but boring "administrivia." Such a day can set a tone for students that this year will be just like all the other years, like all the other classes. Students, by contrast, will be fresh from the summer at this point, carrying renewed expectations that this year may be different. Capitalizing on this attitude with a really interesting lesson will create important momentum for your class. You can catch up on the forms and other items later in the week.

2. *Establish class rules and procedures.* Although a good lesson is most important on the first day, setting the stage for good classroom management cannot be stressed too much. Let your students know you plan to maintain an orderly classroom with rules that foster respect and a healthy work environment. You need not take a "lay-down-the-law" stance, but you should let your students know that your classroom will have clear rules to enhance the chances of everyone succeeding.

3. *Start learning and using students' names.* As soon as you receive your class lists or rosters, start familiarizing yourself with the students' names. Once you meet your students, start matching names with faces and, whenever possible, use their names. Nothing signals your interest in them and your capacity for being on top of the situation like using their names on Day One.

4. *Be friendly but businesslike.* Often the insecurities of new teachers get the best of them. They vacillate between being Mr. or Ms. Nice Guy and Attila the Disciplinarian. A beginning teacher's early commitment to a friendly but task-oriented atmosphere is the key to its realization.

5. *Share with students your vision for the year ahead.* Students want to succeed. Even the ones with a history of difficulty with other teachers want the new school year to be better. Don't tell students how hard they are going to work; tell them how much they are going to know at the end of the year and what they can do with this new knowledge.

6. *Establish procedures for communicating with parents.* You need parental support, and students want to know whether you'll contact parents about both good and bad events. Let them know that you plan to establish communication with their parents and that you see parents as your partners, as your co-teachers.

PRESERVICE to PRACTICE

Carole Foster: Fourth Grade

I was convinced that a good class was a happy class and that I wasn't going to be like those grouchy teachers I remember from my own elementary school. So in the first part of the year, I let a lot of small infractions go unnoticed: talking during silent reading period, lateness on assignments, yelling out the window to students on the playground, and the like. It was a little hard on my nerves, but I thought I was establishing an open and creative environment. It soon became clear that it was open, but not particularly creative. In fact, I first discovered reality when a friendly parent suggested that the room was too noisy and disorderly for the children to get their work done. I tried to "tighten up," but the students were already used to my "open and creative" environment. I just couldn't get them to settle down.

Finally, the straw that broke the camel's back—and almost broke mine—was when the principal came in to observe. The kids behaved horribly. I felt as if they were trying to make me look bad. Whatever their intentions, the situation was not lost on the principal. During the follow-up conference, he was very frank with me, telling me that if I couldn't maintain better discipline, he might have to "relieve" me. One thing I particularly remember him saying was, "Carole, if you can't *keep* school, you can't *teach* school." Then he gave me some specific suggestions. Even with those good suggestions, I had a very difficult time working my way back in charge and establishing a more civil and orderly classroom. Next year things will be different!

Beginning teachers often take refuge in one of the two extremes of behavior. Many hide their insecurities by acting harshly and maintaining a strict and extremely businesslike manner, sometimes bordering on hostility. Others attempt to be completely "natural," rejecting the "stiff" or aloof teacher" image and seeking to break down all barriers between themselves and their students. The first extreme, the overly strict teacher, can give rise to long-term difficulties, whereas the "natural" teacher usually has short-term but rather severe problems.

"Please remind your mom and dad that it's a parent–teacher conference, not a parent–teacher–attorney conference."

The problem with playing the role of the overly strict, aloof teacher is that it may become a permanent habit. Acting like a Prussian general may appeal to a hidden need to make others submissive. Also, one may begin to believe that slogan "a quiet class is a good class."

Pause *and* Reflect

1. Do you remember having an inexperienced teacher like Carole who was always "running hot and cold"?
2. What problems, if any, do you anticipate with relating to students?

The problem confronting overly "natural" teachers is that their view of natural behavior often clashes with students' expectations. Students expect teachers to interact with them in certain recognizable ways; that is, they expect a certain degree of social distance. They are confused or put off when a teacher acts like "one of the gang."

T Ⓕ

It is important for new teachers to work to eliminate the traditional social distance between themselves and students.

The crux of the problem, then, is that beginning teachers often want to be a friend or a pal, whereas students expect and want teachers to be adults. Because they are uncertain and striving to be adults themselves, students seek strength and maturity in their teachers. Often they interpret a beginning teacher's efforts at naturalness and informality as weakness.

PRESERVICE to PRACTICE

Monica Lew: High School Math

Most of my year was spent alternating between being Wanda the Witch and sweet little Miss Muffet. I started out determined to be different from all those cold teachers I had growing up. I was going to be everyone's sweet "big sister." I really was surprised when this plan didn't work. The children didn't respond; if anything, they seemed to be confused. Some of them actually started treating me like their big sister, and I found myself getting annoyed. They became very familiar and started asking me both in and out of class all sorts of embarrassing questions such as "Are you going on a date this weekend?" or "Did you ever do drugs in college?" The final straw came when one of my boys—one of my favorites too—came up to me in the hall while I was talking to a senior teacher. Smiling, he patted me on the back and said, "How's it going, Miss Candis?" I was mortified.

After that little incident, I became tough. I was all business. If anyone got close to being familiar, I cut him or her off at the knees. I really said some nasty things. I was just so uptight that I overreacted. I guess I was hurt that my big sister routine didn't work. Later. I realized that one reason behind my wanting to be big sister was simply that I wanted to be liked, at any cost. I guess my insecurities led me to seek approval from my students. Anyway, I spent most of the year going back and forth on this issue—one week being Wanda and the next being Miss Muffet. It was really a strain for both the kids and me. Finally, toward the end of the year, I got my sea legs and I stopped playing a role. The class settled into a serious work routine. It was much more fun that way. I think everyone was relieved.

Pause *and* Reflect

1. Have you considered the issue of social distance between teachers and students? How much social distance do you believe is appropriate for you?
2. What are your ideas about how to establish effective discipline in a classroom?
3. Do you anticipate that classroom control will be a strength or weakness for you?

Sex

Sexual attraction and romance between students, and even between teachers, is alive and well in American schools—and most people recognize this fact. Nevertheless, the idea of sexual attraction or romance between students and teachers generally remains a taboo subject (except, of course, on TV and in the movies!). In fact, there is no surer way to end your career quickly and unhappily than to become, or even appear to become, romantically involved with a student.

Beginning teachers are more likely than experienced ones to confront this problem. For one thing, many of them are nearer in age to their students than they are to the majority of teachers in their building. For another, they are often single, new to the community, and lonely. The strain of a new job may increase their need for affection, and this need may find expression in their relationships with students.

In much the same way, students often become attracted to their teachers. They sometimes get what is best described as a "crush" on their teachers, becoming emotionally attached to them, greeting them eagerly in the morning, sending them personal emails and text messages, and walking them to their cars after school. This can be a very awkward situation in that the student wants to be treated as special and to feel that the affection is reciprocated. If a teacher rejects or embarrasses the student, the student can be hurt deeply.

Besides the platonic attachments teachers can form to young children, a 22-year-old teacher quite conceivably can find a 16-year-old student sexually attractive. Thus, as the above account indicates, high school teachers are particularly vulnerable to sexual attraction or manipulation. Our only advice in this area is an emphatic *don't*.

Up CLOSE

Protecting against Accusations of Sexual Misconduct

In recent years, heightened sensitivity toward sexual behavior in our schools has emerged. Because of their age, new teachers are particularly vulnerable to accusations of sexual misconduct. Being new to a particular school environment and lacking a reputation, a first-year teacher can be a victim of damaging rumors or even false charges. Here are five practical steps you can take to limit false accusations of sexual misconduct:

1. Avoid being in a private space alone with a student. If a student wants to have a private conversation with you, take him or her to a public space, such as a hallway, and speak in a low voice.

(Continued)

2. Do not give students your home phone number. If you have to call a student at home, be sure that a parent is on the phone during the conversation.

3. Avoid being in a car alone with a student. If it is necessary to transport a student, have another adult in the car. Also, notify your administrator and the student's parents before doing so.

4. If anything of a sexual nature occurs in your classroom (such as suggestive remarks, leering, sexual drawings or notes), take careful notes or keep a computer log of the event. If the number of such events increases, share the issue with your administrator. Don't try to resolve the situation on your own.

5. Be exceedingly careful about speaking about sexual topics or using language that might have sexual connotations in front of students. If this happens inadvertently and an "innocent" comment is left open to misinterpretation, document the situation.

Even though these rules may appear excessively fussy, we urge you to follow them. A little caution may save you a messy "he said/she said" confrontation— or worse.

Source: Adapted from "Protect Yourself," written by LaRae G. Munk, director of legal services for the Association of American Educators. Reprinted by permission of the Association of American Educators and the author.

PRESERVICE to PRACTICE

Gary Cornog: High School English

In one class, there dwelt a fair young creature who found me to be an easily flustered appreciator of her many charms. She was a coquette and, to my way of thinking, a dangerous one. She had me at a great disadvantage. Although she could liltingly ask special favors of me (such as my continued toleration of her misbehavior in class), I could not cope with her in anything like a spontaneous way. Unless I was in a phenomenally commanding mood, I could expect to hear such daily entreaties as "Oh, Mr. Cornog! Mr. Cornog! Could you come here and help me?" or "Mr. Cornog, I just don't understand!" (All this spoken in a voice of tender urgency.) She would have her left arm raised, her right arm aiding it, and would be leaning forward and upward from her desk so that (I thought) I would not fail to notice her finer endowments (I didn't).

"What is it, Julie?" I would reply, hoping the fear in my heart would not be evident in my voice. It nearly always was.

"Mr. Cornog, there's something here I don't understand. Could you come here and look at it?"

"*Don't,*" I tell myself. "*Don't.*"

"Read it to me and I'll explain it." (*From here,* I almost added, but that would be too obvious.) No. She's getting up.

"I'll bring it up there."

She approaches. She arrives at my left side. I note a scent of lemony perfume, an attempt at makeup about the eyes. She leans over to place the book in front of me, and some of her long dark hair grazes my shoulder. By this time, I feel thoroughly unwilling to answer any question regarding syntax. *What about private tutoring?* I hear my lecherous innards suggesting. Heaven forbid! My frustration causes me to blurt a response to her query, hoping that she'll return to her seat. The class, by this time, has observed me melting into a limpid pool behind the desk. She must be smiling triumphantly above me, her glory reflected in my devastation.

If only she had been as innocent of malice in her manipulations as I had been tender in my innocence, then all would have been well. Alas, she was not. She thought it great sport to exercise her arts for the benefit of her friends, and I could think of no way to break the spell. I could not ignore her, because then the class would notice my attempt and think that she had really gotten to me. I could not allow her to continue to dominate me, for then the respect I sought would never appear. Who could respect a henpecked English teacher? The befuddled teacher doing battle with the temptress every day—what a tableau! What a cliché. It pained me to see myself in such a humiliating posture. It was so absurd.[7]

Source: Gary Cornog, "To Care or Not to Care," in Kevin Ryan, ed., *Don't Smile until Christmas: Accounts of the First Year of Teaching* (Chicago: University of Chicago Press, 1970), pp. 18–19. Copyright © 1970. Reprinted by permission of Kevin Ryan.

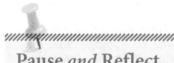

Pause *and* Reflect

1. What are your thoughts about keeping proper social distance between yourself and students?
2. How should Gary have handled this situation?

A final comment on your relations with students: Some first-year teachers become terribly discouraged by their relationships with students. Most of us teach because we like young people and want to work with them. When we are rejected or fail in some aspect of teaching, it is painful. The German philosopher, Friedrich Nietzsche, could have been speaking to new teachers when he wrote, "That which doesn't destroy you, makes you stronger." Remember, you will be better and stronger next year.

Developing satisfying relationships with students usually involves some initial uncertainty. Most problems with students are a result of inexperience, and the majority of second-year teachers find that most of their first-year problems disappear and they feel very much at ease with their students. Experience with young people before beginning teaching—as a parent, camp counselor, or tutor—can also help you learn about how you relate best to them and ease the transition.

14-6 Parents: Natural Allies with Different Agendas

Parents and teachers are natural partners. Both are working to help children become more fully developed people, and both want the children to be happy, sensitive, intelligent, and well balanced. Therefore, it is crucial for teachers to establish and maintain effective channels of communication with parents. Sometimes, though, the relationship between a teacher and parents runs amok, and the natural allies become antagonists. Instead of devoting their energies toward understanding and aiding a child, they waste them on conflict with each other.

T (F)
In general, it is good advice to hold your students' parents at "arm's length."

The great majority of parent–teacher conferences are cordial, constructive, and characterized by mutual respect. Although problems of perception or communication may arise initially, the parents' and teachers' shared interest in the children is typically enough to overcome these minor blocks. At other times, more persistent problems develop—and they are not always the fault of the parents.

The sources of teacher–parent problems are the same as those involved in any human relationship, but these encounters are more highly charged than in most relationships. This intensity is natural, because children and their future are at issue. With that in mind, consider Walter Connor's self-inflicted wound.

PRESERVICE to PRACTICE

Walter Connor: High School History

In the late winter, we had our annual parents' night. All the teachers were to work with students on displays and projects. And, of course, we had to get lots of students' work up on the board. The drab old school building looked like the Rose Bowl Parade by the big night.

We met the parents in our rooms and gave them an overview of what we were doing for the year. I thought I would be nervous, but somehow

I wasn't. I was so distracted and fascinated by their faces. I never suspected that they would look so much like their kids! Or rather, vice versa.

When I finished my talk, I handed out folders of the children's work and told the parents I would be happy to talk with them individually. Most of my students had been doing fairly well, so most of the evening went well. The parents of my two prize ding-a-lings didn't show, an event I greeted with mixed emotions.

(Continued)

One set of parents hung back. I hadn't met them yet, but I knew immediately who they were. They were Bill Russell's parents. Bill is a great big happy kid. He is not bright, and he struck me as being quite lazy. All he likes to do is play his guitar, which he is pretty good with. The only time I have gotten any work from him was during a unit on the Civil War. I persuaded him to look up the folk songs and marching chants of the Civil War. He gave a "singing and strumming" report to the class. But after that—nothing! (Bill was carrying something between a D and an F at that time.) Well, the Russells asked a lot of questions, and I stayed with the straight-facts-no-sugar-coating approach, which I was convinced was the right approach. Then Mr. Russell glanced anxiously at his wife, looked over his shoulder to see that none of the other parents was within earshot, and said, "Tell me, Mr. Connor. We're both college men. My son, Bill . . . is he, you know, college material?"

I didn't know what to say, so I said, "What do you mean?"

"We just want to know if we should be saving to send him to college. Is he, you know, college material?"

All I thought of was that here was a guy who really wanted a straight answer, so I said, "Well, no. I don't think so." Then I looked at Mrs. Russell. I should have looked at her before answering because I saw tears beginning to run down her cheeks. But after the tears came the hostility. "How dare you prejudge my boy! Bill was right! Admit it, you don't like Bill. You are trying to ruin his chances. We work hard to raise our only son, and then some young know-it-all teacher ruins everything!"

Underneath the hysteria, which subsided in about five long minutes, she was right. I was way off base. I had no right to make that judgment. I had known their son for a half year in one course that clearly didn't interest him much. I didn't have enough data. Well, I made another appointment with them. During that meeting, I saw the frightening intensity of their desire to get my class's number-one guitar player into college. Some good things came out of this conference. Bill's work picked up. He actually ended the year with a C. I was the one who learned a good lesson, though. Wanting to be honest doesn't mean arrogantly abandoning good judgment.

Pause *and* Reflect

1. What was Walter's first mistake? His second?
2. What sorts of complexities do you see in teacher–parent relationships?
3. What direct steps can teachers take to establish good relationships with parents?

14-6a REASONS FOR PARENT–TEACHER PROBLEMS

The Walter Connor case study you just read illustrates a few reasons that parents and teachers may have a difficult relationship with each other or even fall into direct conflict. But to get a fuller picture, consider all seven of the following factors:

1. *Varied perceptions.* Teachers and parents are quite likely to perceive the same phenomenon in very different ways. A hassled teacher may perceive a particular child as a wild, undisciplined, troublemaker, whereas the parents may see their child as energetic, spontaneous, and sociable. Or an apparently quiet, shy child may turn out to be a chatterbox in the security of home.

2. *Judgments on students.* Evaluation is another area of difficulty. It is part of the teacher's job to make judgments about a child's performance, a process that can touch on some deep insecurities. It can dash the parents' hopes and put brakes on their aspirations, particularly in this age of anxiety when parents see education as their children's royal road to success. In our competitive society, being average is taken by some as failure. For these reasons, teachers need to be especially sensitive when dealing with issues of evaluation and would do well to stay away from judgments such as students being "above average" or "below

average" or comparing certain children with other students. (Remember what happened to Walter Connor.)

3. *Differences of social class and experiences.* Issues of social distance have been at the hub of much parent–teacher antagonism in recent years. Because most teachers are middle class or aspiring to the middle class, they normally have relatively few problems communicating with middle-class people. By contrast, when they deal with parents from a lower or higher socioeconomic class or a different ethnic group, or both, the potential for communication difficulties heightens. Upper-class parents may look down on public schools and treat teachers condescendingly. Poor parents may personally have had unfortunate and unpleasant experiences with schools and, as a result, regard teachers and schools with fear or suspicion. Often, these parents speak a different language or dialect than the teacher. What teachers see as a humble classroom is to some parents a strange, uncomfortable part of a huge, impersonal bureaucracy. In many urban areas, this impression of the school as a cold, unfriendly, and impersonal institution is supported by the evidence: The school doors are locked, and parents have to pass by police officers and assorted hall guards before receiving a pass to see the head secretary and obtain permission to see a teacher. The fact that many lower-class parents, as children, encountered prejudice in schools and found going to school more discouraging than helpful makes communication even more difficult.

4. *Overburdened parents.* Another factor, as noted in Chapter 4, "How Do Social Issues Affect Students?" is the changes that are occurring in the American family. Now most mothers—who in an earlier era stayed home, kept house, and guided their children through school—have full-time jobs. Usually, it is very difficult for working parents to leave work so as to meet with their children's teachers or attend parent–teacher organization (PTO) meetings and after-school functions that would put them in closer contact with teachers. For teachers these events are part of the job, but for some parents they are unwelcome chores in an already stressful life.

5. *The pain of change.* Going to school changes children. School, in fact, exists to help children change in specified ways: to read, to solve problems, to speak a new language, and to learn how to get along with others. And students do change. They master things. They acquire confidence—or they lose confidence. They become increasingly independent of their parents. Some parents rejoice at their child's growing freedom from them. For others, the process in which their child's independence grows is painful. Hearing her little girl talk about how much she loves her teacher may arouse jealousy in a mother and cause her to act in a hostile manner when the mother meets the teacher. When a high school student comes home from school with political, social, or hostile religious views that conflict with those of his parents, resentment and confusion can result. When faced with these sometimes unsettling changes, parents often approach a conference with a teacher with a sincere mixture of appreciation and hostility.

6. *Special problems.* Not all homes are traditional and peaceful. Many children come from chaotic households filled with anger and frustrations, which can spill over into a parent–teacher conference. Conferences with separated or divorced parents can be particularly tricky and quickly lead to "the blame game" ("I thought you promised to monitor his TV watching!"). If anger flares up in a conference, don't try to be a marriage counselor. Gently, but firmly end the session. In military parlance, "Terminate engagement and withdraw!"

7. *Privilege and responsibility.* It is often the parents who give new teachers the sense of what a privilege *and* a responsibility it is to be a teacher, as reported by a new teacher in New Mexico.

PRESERVICE to PRACTICE

Scott D. Niemann: Third and Fourth Grades

When the bell rang at 8:15 A.M. on August 28, a new reality entered my mind. Parents stopped by the classroom to familiarize themselves with the new third- and fourth-grade teacher in the village. Some of the concerned looks I spied on the parents' faces as they left their children were heartfelt. Breaking out in a cold sweat, I realized the amount of trust the parents were handing over to me. There was one term that entered my mind: *in loco parentis*, a legal term meaning "in place of the parents." I was taking on the responsibility of a parent!

Following the first day, I expressed my concern to a fellow teacher and he replied, *Encargada!* He explained how parents in Mexico often use this Spanish term when they are putting their child's life in a teacher's hands. It means, "We are handing our child over to you and now you are in charge." Wow! What a responsibility.

Pause *and* Reflect

1. How did your own parents feel about your schools and your teachers? Were their attitudes different when you were in the earlier grades than when you were in later grades? If so, why did their attitudes change?
2. Which of these seven potential problem areas do you believe represents the greatest threat to you? What are you going to do about it...now?

14-7 Surviving the First Year of Teaching

When one of the authors was about to begin his first year of teaching, his battle-scarred department chairman cryptically commented to him, "Promise yourself today that you will teach a second year." At the time, the meaning behind the remark was unclear. However, after the emotional yo-yo ride of that initial year had taken a few swoops and plunges, the chairman's message came into sharp focus. A person's first year of teaching is too unusual, too filled with extremes and emotional highs and lows to provide a sound basis for deciding whether teaching is the work on which one wants to spend one's life. Nevertheless, fully one-third of all new teachers leave the profession by the end of their third year.[8]

But these kinds of statistics need not determine your personal fate. Many of the problems and issues that cause teachers to leave the field are preventable through planning and a few resolutions. Most importantly, be aware that a single—and nontypical—year is rarely the basis for a sound career decision.

14-7a BEGIN NOW

Start now to prepare for the predictable events and problems of the initial year. Make a systematic study of your strengths and weaknesses, with an eye toward *using* your strengths in the classroom and gradually eliminating your trouble areas. With both problematic areas and your strengths, seek the advice and help of trusted friends,

Not only students find delight in learning.

Tyler Olson/Shutterstock.com

family, and teachers. For instance, if you have an especially good reading voice, plan to capitalize on it as a teacher. Students from preschool through college love to be read to.

If you are painfully self-conscious and shy, develop a plan to overcome this shortcoming. Don't try to defeat your shyness with big, dramatic gestures, such as trying out for the lead in the college play. Take an incremental approach, using small steps. Plan to speak to someone standing in line next to you whom you don't know; volunteer answers in class. Realize that your shyness may never completely go away, but you will gradually feel more and more comfortable speaking and working with people if you push yourself to make small advances regularly, such as making direct eye contact with people. You may surprise yourself.

14-7b KEEP A TEACHING JOURNAL

A **teaching journal** can be any notebook that is large enough to hold your teaching thoughts and suggestions. If you prefer working at a keyboard, a computer file can serve the same purpose. Some teachers started such books in grade school when they first decided to become a teacher. However, the beginning of one's formal preparation as a teacher is a very good time to begin a teaching journal.

You can use your teaching journal to record all the useful ideas and helpful strategies you discover, saving them for the time when you are actually teaching. This material can include teaching skills learned in lectures or observed in the field, such as how to grade papers effectively or how to give students evaluative feedback on in-class presentations. In addition, it could include methods of disciplining in different situations, easy and efficient ways to take attendance, ways to present particularly difficult concepts, things to do when students get restless or overexcited, and sources of good curricular materials. We urge, however, that your teaching journal be private, a place for your reflection, and not Facebook entries or a blog.

Having such a journal serves two functions: First, the teaching journal serves as a constant reminder that you are preparing to actually be in charge of your own classroom (a fact that often is not in sharp focus for preservice teachers). Second, the journal can be a lifesaver when you are struggling during the first year. A typical journal entry might look like this:

Tuesday, October 7
Ninth-grade English

Began the introductory lesson on Shakespeare and the Globe Theatre today. The biographical info went over only minimally well. Brian and Mark loudly wanted to know why they needed to know when he was born and died and what difference it made. Some of the other kids looked bored as I went into my spiel, and I realized I was probably lecturing too much.

Next time, I should review the information that I present and figure out what's important for them to know and what's extraneous. Just because I'm fascinated with it doesn't mean that it's all appropriate or necessary for a ninth-grader's introduction to Shakespeare. Also, maybe some sort of question–answer sheet about Shakespeare would work better and get more involvement from the kids.

On the bright side, they all seemed to love the Globe Theatre model. They really liked the way it opened, showing the cross-section with all the various stage areas. Brian and Mark were among the most interested in the model. The kids also seemed to be able to follow along on their photocopied drawing of the Globe. Jon and Elizabeth (who usually aren't impressed with anything) told me that it was "pretty cool." The next time, maybe I'll start with the theater and allow more time for them to explore it.

Besides offering professional advantages, the teaching journal can serve as a valuable personal record. One 20-year teaching veteran in Massachusetts has kept a journal about his teaching experiences throughout his career. He finds that it has "captured the moment," recording what he was thinking and experiencing as he taught throughout the years.

An alternative form of this idea is a card file of "teaching tips," utilizing either index cards or in a similar computerized format. This file of tips can provide quick, easy reference for planning or problem solving.

Keeping a journal is one of the chief characteristics of *reflective practitioners*, a goal and ideal we have stressed throughout this book.

14-7c MAINTAIN THE PROPER FRAME OF MIND

It is important to maintain the right frame of mind during your first year of teaching—that is, to realize that you are someone who is untested and who has a great deal to learn. Humility is a virtue that has been all but drowned out in our modern, "We're Number One" culture. Zen masters and teachers of the spiritual life urge beginners to assume an attitude of submissiveness before what is to be learned—showing not weakness, but openness to learning and humility. Many new teachers strive hard to *avoid* humiliation, not realizing that a humble person cannot be humiliated. Instead of assuming a false confidence, acknowledge that you have much to learn and open yourself up to that learning.

Making use of this suggestion is somewhat tricky. The humble frame of mind we urge you to adopt is one of alertness and quiet observation of your new context, expecting difficulties of some sort but being quietly confident that solutions will come. By all means, it does *not* mean becoming a *doormat*. In a way, new teachers should be like good apprentices: working hard, keeping eyes open, asking questions, and being eager to learn everything possible about the craft.

One key aspect of having a proper frame of mind is understanding the social and economic context within which your new school exists. Schools vary immensely, depending on their social, ethical, religious, and economic makeup. (You will find background information in Chapter 2, "What Is a School and What Is It For?," and Chapter 11, "How Are Schools Governed, Influenced, and Financed?") Study your new community and ask questions, so you are not blindsided by attitudes and behaviors that you may be encountering for the first time.

14-7d FIND A MENTOR

First-year teachers can have no greater gift than a good **mentor**, an experienced teacher who is willing to act as a guide and confidant through the first year. Besides all of the information and tips that a mentor can give you, a good mentor is an interpreter-guide on what is essentially foreign turf. A mentor can tell you which pieces of paper from the principal's office must be responded to immediately, who has the formal power and who has the real power, what administrators emphasize most in teacher evaluations, and which teachers are most willing to share ideas and which ones are not. Perhaps even more important, a mentor is a friend. (Remember Mary Lopez and Joan Silver.)

A growing body of research provides solid support for the benefits of mentoring programs. In one study, beginning teachers who had no mentor were three times more likely to leave the profession than those who had mentors.[9] Sixty-seven percent of teachers who have been mentored claim that the experience significantly improved their teaching. Another study of beginning teachers in New York City schools found that the more hours mentors spent with their teachers, the higher the teacher's own students' scored on both reading and math achievement tests. Also, the researcher found that the mentor's years of teaching in a particular school positively affected new teacher retention.[10] In other words, being close to someone who "knows the ropes" leads to being rehired and staying on at a particular school.

In recent years, many school districts have developed special arrangements to help beginning teachers. Some offer special induction programs, some support mentor programs, and some have both. In 2018, thirty-one states required induction and/or mentoring support for new teachers. Ten states required induction and/or mentoring for one year, 10 states required induction and/or mentoring for two years and seven states required induction and/or mentoring for three years or no more than three years.[11] In situations where there is no induction program or a mentor is not assigned, we nevertheless urge you to make finding a mentor a high priority.

14-7e MAKE YOUR STUDENTS' PARENTS YOUR ALLIES

We suggest that all teachers—but particularly new teachers—take a very proactive, positive approach toward parents. Instead of having parents get to know you indirectly through the often distorting eyes and mouths of their children ("My new teacher, Miss Sniddly, hates me. And besides, she can't teach. How come I got stuck with a new teacher?"), help them get to know you and engage them with what you will be doing with their children this school year. Here are some practical suggestions for how to do so.

First, prepare a short statement to be carried home, signed, and returned, introducing yourself to parents and outlining your major goals for the year. Stress that you and they are in a partnership to help their child have a productive year.

Let them know how to get in touch with you. Tell them the date for Back-to-School Night and that you are looking forward to meeting them. One new first-grade teacher we know sent a letter with an insert photo of herself to her first-graders and their parents once she received her class list in the summer. She wrote a little about herself, told them some of the things they would do during the coming school year, and (for the parents) explained her approach to teaching. Besides being exciting for the students, this technique helped the new teacher start the year (and, more importantly, finish the year) with her students' parents as strong allies.

Second, once you have established disciplinary and homework policies, send a copy of those policies home for parental sign-off and return.

Third, on the first day, get the home, work, and cell telephone numbers of each student's parents or guardians. The fact that you possess these valuable bits of information will not go unnoticed by your students, particularly those who might be inclined to push the disciplinary envelope.

Fourth, it is a good idea to call all parents early in the fall. In particular, call the parent(s) as soon as a student appears to be falling behind, tuning out, or misbehaving: "Mrs. Tate, this is Philip's teacher. Philip's performance has begun to slip. What can we do to get him back on track?" "Mr. Coleman, this is Joan's teacher. Joan just won't stop talking in class. It is interfering with other students and keeping her from doing the work she is capable of. What can we do to make this the good year we all want for Joan?" The key word in dealing with parents is *we*, as in "What can *we* do?" Phone calls should be made and brief notes sent home for positive reasons as well. Such a "good news" call can make a parent's month!

Finally, if problems persist, insist on a parent visit. (Conversations that include messages such as "We need to work together to get little Adolph involved in his schoolwork" are helpful for everyone involved.) There is no surer way to get children's attention than to have them realize they are the reason their parents had to leave work early to come to school. Although this is an upsetting bother for many parents, the extra effort is usually worth it because of the positive effect it can have on their child's school experience.

14-7f TAKE EVALUATION SERIOUSLY

The news that they are to be evaluated by their principal or some other administrator often comes as a surprise to novice teachers. Even more shocking is the revelation that the related evaluation reports are sometimes the cause of not being rehired.

Typically, it is a major job responsibility of principals and other district administrative personnel to visit systematically and evaluate the performance of new teachers. Depending on the district and the conscientiousness of the administrator, this type of observation and evaluation can take place anywhere from once to a dozen times during the first year. Usually, the administrator makes three or four evaluative visits, which are followed up closely by feedback conferences during which the administrator goes over his or her observations of the individual's teaching. Together, these evaluative visits play an important part in the school district's decision to rehire a teacher or terminate his or her employment.

It is important, then, for new teachers to understand thoroughly how their work will be evaluated. Before you accept a teaching position, be clear about how and when your work will be evaluated. Most school districts have an official evaluation and feedback form, and you should get to know this form well. Check out the department of education's website in your state to see how new teachers are evaluated. If the school or district's evaluator gives you advance notification of a visit, prepare for the occasion. Find out from your mentor teacher what the administrator really stresses in teaching. And do your best. If the evaluator raises issues or makes suggestions for improvement, take them very seriously. You do not necessarily have to agree, but you should not casually ignore the issues. In most cases, the comments are legitimate, and the new teacher should strive to repair or strengthen the area that was criticized.

14-7g TAKE CARE OF YOURSELF

One of the greatest surprises of full-time, fully responsible teaching (as opposed to student teaching) is initially how tiring it is. Teaching is physically, mentally, and emotionally draining, particularly until one gets conditioned to it—that is, until one gets into "teaching shape." This is true for many jobs. The stress and strain of new employment wear newcomers down and sets them up for colds, flu, and other mild ailments. This problem is compounded in teaching because it is such an "in your face" occupation (referring to all those coughing, sniffling, and wheezing faces you encounter every day). A classroom is a magnificent germ factory, with viruses claiming new victims daily. Teachers who are exhausted, run down, and regularly staying up late reworking lesson plans and correcting papers are prime targets for whatever is circulating in the environment.

The stress and strain of a new teaching position also can cause mild depression. In their first year, few teachers live up to their own expectations. Often, new teachers are separated from their regular support system of family and friends. Having not yet established realistic standards, they really don't know whether they are succeeding or failing. A difficult class or even a single resistant or disrespectful student can emotionally unseat them. To counter this vulnerability to sickness of body and spirit, new teachers need to give special attention to their health. When you feel yourself becoming overstressed or burned out, take deliberate steps to rectify the situation. Reduce stress directly by trying to solve key problems that are bothering you, and look for ways to relieve stress indirectly as well. Plan a weekend away, take vitamins, get a yoga DVD, or join an aerobics class. Instead of getting overtired and run down, beginners need to take special pains to get enough rest, eat well, and get adequate exercise.

Physical education is not what it used to be!

Pete Saloutos/Shutterstock.com

OUR FINAL WORD

Much of this chapter has dealt with the trials and tribulations of being a new teacher. Nevertheless, most new teachers have a great sense of accomplishment and are proud of themselves at the end of their first year. They have learned an enormous amount in 9 or 10 months. Along with the undoubtedly difficult challenges, teaching has its pleasures and bright moments, making it a rewarding and fulfilling occupation for most. English novelist Joyce Cary has written that human joy comes not from the great events but from the little, everyday things, like a good cup of tea.* The joys and satisfactions of teaching can lie in mundane happenings and small surprises. As a teacher, you may find joy in the following:

- Experiencing those electric moments when you can *feel* the students thinking and *see* those new connections being made
- Watching two lonely kids whom you brought together walk down the hall side by side, now friends
- Getting your planbook back from your supervisor with the comment, "These are *excellent* lessons"
- Finding in your box, on a rainy Friday afternoon, a note written in a childish scrawl: "You are my most favorite teacher. Guess who?"

- Shopping at the mall and meeting one of your students, who proudly introduces you to her mother as "my teacher," and being able to tell by the mother's response that you are respected in their household
- Having a former student call to tell you that he has a "nonschool" problem and needs your advice
- Chaperoning a dance and having what you thought was your most hostile student happily introduce his girlfriend to you
- Hearing in the teachers' lunchroom that your supervisor called you "a real professional"
- Being observed by the principal and having your students make you look terrific
- Surviving until June, being bone-tired but proud of what you and your kids have been able to do
- Cleaning out your desk on the last day of school after the kids have been dismissed and finding a box of candy with a card signed by the whole class
- Realizing—be it daily, weekly, or monthly—that what you are doing with your life *really does make a difference*

*Translated into U.S. speak, that means joy comes from a good cuppa coffee.

WHY TEACH? YOUR FINAL WORD

1. Can you remember any new teachers you have had who fit the scenarios described in this chapter? Did they encounter any situations similar to those described in this chapter?
2. What do you expect to be your major problems as a beginning teacher? What steps can you take now to prevent those problems?
3. Make a list of your potential teaching strengths. How can you sharpen them and use them effectively in your teaching?

KEY TERMS

culture shock (416)
mentor (441)

social distance (430)
teaching journal (439)

FOR FURTHER INFORMATION

Web Resources

Teach.com/blog

This excellent website has many fine resources for teachers. For instance, it has valuable advice on how to establish good relationships with parents, how to stay fit, and a host of other topics.

About Teaching and the First Year

The U.S. Department of Education has a special website to support first-year teachers. Comprehensive and current, it can provide you with many answers to everyday questions.

New Teacher Center

New Teacher Center (NTC) is a national nonprofit dedicated to improving the effectiveness of new teachers and, thus, the learning of students. This site is also the gateway to many services and material aimed to help beginning teachers.

EZSchool

This website is a treasure of resources for new teachers. It is filled with good ideas, teaching plans for a range of subject matter, and worksheets. EZSchool provides free printable worksheets, online games, study tools, tutorials, and stories for grades K–12.

TeachersFirst

This website is a reservoir of information, good ideas, lesson plans, and even humor. It is well organized and easy to search for the topic or need of choice.

Print Resources

Parker J. Palmer, *The Courage to Teach: Exploring the Inner Landscape of a Teacher's Life,* 10th Anniversary Edition (Jossey-Bass, 2007).

This classic book, available as a hardcopy, an eBook, and an audible book, is for teachers who have good days and bad days but who refuse to harden their hearts, because they love learners, learning, and the teaching life.

Stephen D. Rogers, *My First Year in the Classroom: 50 Stories That Celebrate the Good, the Bad, and the Most Unforgettable Moments* (Avon, MA: Adams Media Corporation, 2009).

In this collection, 50 teachers share their ups and downs, their good days and bad days. Much of this is funny, some sad, but there is much for new teachers to learn from these vivid and honest tales of the first year on the job.

Ron Clark, *End the Molasses Classes* (Touchstone, 2012). (Available on Audible.com)

This exuberant teacher explains how to make education exciting, interesting, and anything but "slow." Clark describes in this 10 hour-plus audiobook how he keeps his classes alive and moving and, yes, learning.

Esme Raji Codell. *Educating Esme: Diary of a Teacher's First Year.* Algonquin Books, 2001.

This book is an account of a new fifth-grade teacher in a Chicago inner-city school. Hip, imaginative, and irreverent, the book takes readers through the teacher's triumphs and travails with students and a particularly dense administrator.

Harry K. Wong and Rosemary T. Wong, *The First Days of School: How to Be an Effective Teacher* (Sunview, CA: Harry Wong, Paperback, 2009).

This highly acclaimed handbook abounds with tips and strategies to help new teachers get a strong start through motivation and minimizing discipline and the other problems that plague new teachers.

What Does It Mean to Be a Professional?

LEARNING OBJECTIVES

15-1 Evaluate the current status of the teaching profession.

15-2 Compare different levels of professionalism.

15-3 Describe the work of the National Board of Professional Teaching Standards.

15-4 Discuss the role of the Interstate Teacher Assessment and Support Consortium.

15-5 Assess the contributions of professional associations.

15-6 Analyze and summarize your own professional development.

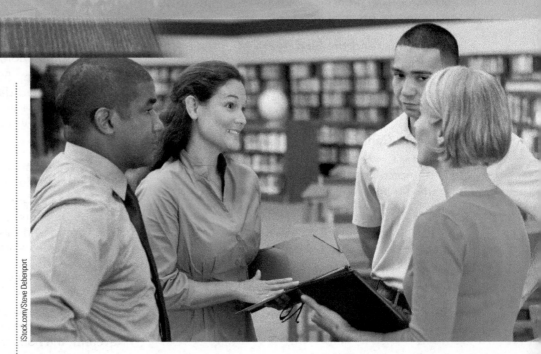

iStock.com/Steve Debenport

Truth OR Fiction?

T F   There is little debate that teaching is and always has been not just a career, but a profession.

T F   Neither the National Education Association nor the American Federation of Teachers, professional organizations that represent the majority of the nation's teachers, take positions on political issues or endorse individuals running for office.

T F   The term *professional development* refers to moving through and up the ranks in the educational hierarchy.

In this chapter, we focus particularly on teachers as professionals—that is, as members of an occupational group. We will see how this rather abstract concept of *professionalism* affects the daily life of classroom teachers. In effect, we examine the role of individual teachers within the larger context of being members of a profession.

The essence of a career in teaching is close, hands-on work with the young. When people think about becoming teachers, their thoughts and musings usually revolve around working with students. Rarely do they bother with hypothetical issues beyond the scope of the classroom. This narrow focus is both natural and appropriate because a teacher's success or failure depends on his or her effectiveness with students. Nevertheless, there is much more to being a teacher. Teachers work within a system that exposes them to pressures from many quarters. Prospective teachers are often somewhat naive about these pressures and forces, and that naiveté can be dangerous, both in making a career decision and in making a successful career.

To help you see this point, we would like you to indulge in a set of thought experiments for a few moments. We will offer you a few brief scenarios, and after reading each one, you should reflect on how you might react. As you read each scenario, imagine yourself as a first-year teacher in that ideal classroom you carry around in your head. Assume that you appear to be doing a fine job. You are really enjoying your teaching experience. Your students are making nice progress, and they seem to be interested in their work. A few "helicopter" parents have indicated that although they were initially worried that their precious children were to have a new (in other words, *untested*) teacher, they are pleased with their children's progress in your class. So, things are going very well, until . . .

- **Scenario One:** You get a special-delivery letter from a group called Parents Action Party (PAP). You have heard they are very active in your area and are especially interested in schools. Their letter informs you that their lawyer is preparing a case against you for using books on their disapproved list. (You didn't know there was such a list, but sure enough, there is, and you have been using books from it!) They claim they have evidence that you are "waging a subtle but nevertheless vicious war against the cause of justice and liberty and have succeeded in temporarily deflecting the minds of some of your students from the truth." Furthermore, they want to know why you display the United Nations flag and why there are no pictures of past presidents on your classroom walls. Finally, you are said to have "racial preferences that manifest themselves in your treatment of students." This is the first you have heard of these charges or even of the PAP's interest in you. You think of yourself as a loyal citizen and bias-free, and are shocked by the letter. They have requested that you respond in writing by next week or they will begin legal proceedings.

- **Scenario Two:** In late January, the principal, who holds a conference with each new teacher, told you she thought you were doing a fine job and that she wanted you to return next year. In passing, she remarked that she would be getting a contract to you in the spring. Toward the end of April, you got a little nervous and called her office. You spoke to her executive secretary, who said not to worry, that you were on the list and that a contract would be coming before long. You stopped worrying. Today is the last day of school, and you find a very nice personal note from the principal in your school mailbox. She thanks you for your fine work during the year and says she is sorry you will not be back next year. You call the principal's office. She is "in conference," and her executive secretary says they are not renewing your contract. She cannot remember speaking to you in April. She knows nothing about the case. She does know, however, that the board of education has put on a lot of pressure for cuts in next year's personnel budget. She ends by telling you, "you must be very disappointed, dear. I know how you must feel." Wrong. No, she has no clue

- **Scenario Three:** One lunch hour, you noticed something peculiar when you sat down at the faculty dining table. Conversations stopped, and you had the distinct impression your colleagues had been talking about you. A few days later, an older teacher stopped you in the hall after school and said, "I don't want to butt in, but you really are upsetting Mrs. Hilary and Mr. Alexander." Mrs. H. and Mr. A. have the classrooms on either side of yours. Apparently, they claim your class makes so much noise that they "can't get anything done." Both are very traditional in their approach to education, whereas you believe in a more activity-oriented approach. Although your class is rather noisy occasionally, it is never chaotic, and its noise is usually a by-product of students' involvement in a task. Twice Mr. Alexander has sent messengers with notes asking that your class be quieter. You have always complied. You hardly know either teacher. You have never really talked to Mr. Alexander except to say hello. Mrs. Hilary, with whom you've chatted, prides herself on being a strict disciplinarian. What she means, you have inferred, is that she is able to keep the children quiet. You know Mr. Alexander is chummy with Mrs. Hilary. You go to the vice principal, who seems to know all about the case, but only from the Hilary–Alexander angle. Inexplicably, the vice principal gets quite hostile and claims that until you came along, the faculty got along beautifully, and that, furthermore, you are being very unprofessional in making complaints against experienced teachers. You feel as if you are trapped in a bad dream.

These horror stories, of course, are not everyday occurrences. Also, keep in mind that entrance into any profession has its trials and booby traps. These accounts are intended to help you realize that you can be an effective teacher and still have trouble keeping your job. What is the common theme running through each of these anecdotes? You, the teacher, were succeeding in your work with children, but forces outside your classroom began to impinge on you. PAP wanted to make a target case of you. The school system bureaucracy was ready to put you on the unemployed rolls. Two of your colleagues damaged your reputation with the faculty and administration. You are feeling abandoned and vulnerable.

Although you may feel confident that you could handle some of these situations, it is doubtful that you could cope with all such cases that might arise. In some instances, you would be powerless to respond effectively to your adversaries, and you might end up a helpless victim of circumstance. Fortunately, a teacher is not alone. Like people in many other occupational groups, teachers have organizations whose job it is to protect them from such indignities and injustices. These organizations function on several levels, from the local to the national, and usually their very existence keeps situations like those described from occurring. When they do occur, these organizations are there to support the teachers. At least, that is the way they should work.

In becoming a teacher, you are not just committing yourself to work with children. You are joining an occupational group composed of other individuals with similar responsibilities, concerns, and pressures whose help you may need and who, in turn, will need your help.

Pause *and* Reflect

1. Were any of the issues described in the scenarios ones you had considered? Describe one you considered and one that somewhat took you by surprise.
2. Other than protecting you, what other reasons can you think of for joining a professional association?

Correcting papers and discovering what your students *haven't learned* can be deeply frustrating.

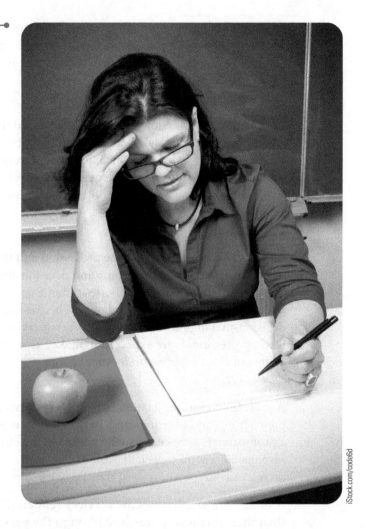

iStock.com/code6d

15-1 The Status of Teaching: A Profession or Not?

The question "Is teaching a profession?" probably arouses deep yawns in many of our readers. Most people thinking about a career in teaching are more interested in whether it will be a personally rewarding way to spend their time than in whether it is a "true profession." Will teaching bring me personal satisfactions? Will it provide an outlet for my talents and energies? Will I be effective with kids? These questions are, we suspect, closer to your heart. Nevertheless, the question of professionalism and the related issues are important to teachers and influence the quality of education teachers provide for children. They will also affect the quality of your life as a teacher.

So what is a profession? A **profession** is more than a group of individuals all engaged in the same line of work. Professions have a more or less recognizable set of characteristics that distinguish them from nonprofessions.[1]

As you read the following list of characteristics, check whether you think teaching qualifies on each premise:

1. A profession renders a unique, definite, and essential service to society. Only the people in the particular profession render the service; for instance, only lawyers practice law. The service rendered must be considered so important that it is available to all the people in a society.
   ☐ yes ☐ no

2. A profession relies on intellectual skills in the performance of its service. This does not mean that physical actions and skills are not needed; rather, the emphasis in carrying on the work is on intellectual skills and techniques.
   ☐ yes ☐ no

3. A profession entails a long period of specialized training. Because professional work requires special intellectual skills, it requires specialized intellectual training. General education such as that represented by a bachelor's degree is valued but is not considered adequate. The specialized training must cover a substantial period and not be obtained in cram courses or correspondence schools.
   ☐ yes ☐ no

4. Both individual members of the profession and the professional group enjoy a considerable degree of autonomy and decision-making authority. Professional groups regulate their own activities rather than having outsiders set policies and enforce adherence to standards. Whereas factory workers have very limited decision-making power and are closely supervised in the performance of their work, professionals are expected to make the most of their own decisions and be free of close supervision by supervisors.
   ☐ yes ☐ no

5. A profession requires its members to accept personal responsibility for their actions and decisions and, in general, for their performance. Because a professional's service is usually related to the client's human welfare, this responsibility is an especially serious one.
   ☐ yes ☐ no

6. A profession emphasizes the services rendered by its practitioners more than their financial rewards. Although the personal motives of any individual professional are not necessarily any higher than any other worker's, the professional group's public emphasis is on service. The "Leaders in Education" feature provides one example of the teaching field's emphasis on service.
   ☐ yes ☐ no

7. A profession is self-governing and responsible for policing its own ranks. As a consequence, professional groups perform a number of activities aimed at keeping the quality of their services high and looking out for the social and economic well-being of the professional members. Also, these self-governing organizations set standards of admission and exclusion for the profession.
   ☐ yes ☐ no

8. A profession has a code of ethics that sets out the acceptable standards of conduct for its members.
   ☐ yes ☐ no

These characteristics, then, are the major requirements of a profession. Although few professions satisfy all of them fully, this list does serve as a benchmark against which occupational groups can measure themselves and direct their development if they wish to enjoy professional status. With these criteria in mind, let's look at some of the arguments that people have made for and against teaching as a profession.

15-1a THE CASE *AGAINST* TEACHING AS A PROFESSION

The roots of teaching as an occupation go back to ancient Greece, where slaves called *paidagogos,* or pedagogues, taught children to read and write and helped them memorize passages of poetic history. Despite this long history, a careful look at current practices reveals that sadly teaching does not qualify as a profession.

Child's Many Teachers

If education is a teacher's unique function, a teacher certainly has a great deal of competition. Children today learn a tremendous amount from media offerings, including *Sesame Street,* the History Channel, YouTube.com, and Ted Talks. The *non-*teacher-educators include parents, ministers, older friends, neighbors, employers, best friends, coaches, scout leaders, camp counselors, and grandparents. The world is bursting with teachers, and those who hold forth in school buildings have only a small piece of the action.

Limited Training

Most professions and certainly the skilled trades have an extensive period of apprenticeship where individuals learn the "tools of the trade" in an up close and personal way. Although teaching has intellectual and theoretical foundations, it nevertheless requires a rather short period of specialized training. Also, entrance into the occupation is not especially competitive, particularly on intellectual grounds. If teaching is a profession, it is one composed of college graduates with a sweeping span of academic abilities, varying levels of commitment, and a wide range of motivations for becoming teachers.

Constraints on Autonomy

Although a good deal of talk touts teachers' autonomy and decision-making power (and teachers have, indeed, come a long way since the early days of the United States, as described in the "Up Close: Rules and Duties for Teachers in the Nineteenth Century" feature), teachers in today's classrooms still have a very low level of autonomy and decision-making power. Teachers are at the second rung from the bottom (above only students) of the "school hierarchy," which is ultimately commanded by the local board of education and increasingly by state and federal initiates. Unlike lawyers and doctors, who can reject clients, teachers have students assigned to them. They also have supervisors: their principal, lead teacher, department head, and others farther up the chain of command. They teach a curriculum and are responsible for their students' meeting content standards that others have chosen or developed.

Unlike in other professions, teachers do not formally evaluate other teachers; instead, administrators do this. Moreover, most of the important decisions that affect teachers' daily lives—even those that bear directly on the standards of their own profession—are made by nonteachers (administrators and citizen school board members). Although teachers are beginning to get more involved in teacher preparation programs and are acquiring some influence in the licensing and certification of teachers, laypeople and bureaucrats still wield a great deal of the decision-making power. Some teachers, like factory workers, even have to punch a time clock (or, put more genteelly, they "sign in" and "sign out"). In sum, they have very little to say about what goes on in their "shop."

LEADERS in Education

Robert Parris Moses (b. 1935)

Bob Moses is most famous as a lifelong social activist and civil rights pioneer, but he is also a visionary educator. Born in 1935 in New York City and raised in a Harlem housing project, he attended public schools. Identified as an able student, he was admitted into one of the city's academic elite schools, Stuyvesant High School. From there he received a full scholarship to Hamilton College, earning his BA in 1956. Next, Moses moved to Harvard University to study philosophy, and just one year later received his MA. Working toward his doctorate, he was forced to leave graduate school because of the death of his mother and the hospitalization of his father. He returned to New York City, taking up a position as a math teacher at the prestigious Horace Mann School.

During this period of academic study and teaching, he gradually and then increasingly became involved in the nascent black protest movement. In the early 1960s, he became a member of the Student Nonviolent Coordinating Committee (SNCC), one of the earliest and most action-oriented civil rights groups. His calm leadership style contributed to his fast rise within the organization. In 1964, he was made director of the Freedom Summer project, which had as its goal to end racial disfranchisement. The means toward that goal was to recruit white college students to work with local blacks to educate and register voters in Mississippi. The state's 1890 constitution included requirements for voter registration, such as poll taxes, residency requirements, and literacy tests, which made it nearly impossible for blacks to register and vote. Moses's larger goal was to develop self-reliant organizations and leaders who could continue the struggle after organizers had departed.

Missing for two weeks, the bodies of three of his recruits were discovered decomposing in a landfill. Hearing the news of their colleagues' murders, the rest of the group was frozen on the spot and in fear for their lives. Witnesses have told of how this quietly charismatic man called his recruits together and said that, given their situations, it was completely understandable if they felt they should leave. And further, that no one in the movement, particularly him, would be critical of their returning home. No one moved. No one left. They all continued their work.

Bob apparently was growing more and more at odds with the escalating tactics of SNCC and he gradually withdrew from the movement. First, he went to Canada and then in 1969, he and his wife went to Tanzania to teach mathematics. Six years later, he returned to Harvard to further his study of philosophy. He also began teaching math at the local Cambridge high school.

In 1982, Bob became one of the earliest recipients of the famed MacArthur Foundation's "Genius" Awards. Around that time his daughter was experiencing difficulties in math. Convinced that algebra was the gateway to mathematics and, that in turn, mathematics was the key to academic success and upward mobility, he used the substantial MacArthur prize money to start work on what has become the Algebra Project [Available at: https://algebra.org/wp/].

Project Algebra is not built around a new breakthrough mathematical theory or an innovative instructional technique. Rather the project has used algebra as an organizing tool to raise the conscientiousness of students, parents, and educators regarding how mathematics is the key to quality education and future success. Instead of reinventing the wheel, Project Algebra uses the best educational research in the development of curricular materials and teacher training programs. Reminiscent of the Freedom Summer project, a major part of the work of Project Algebra is recruiting, training, and deploying black and white high school and college students. These "math literacy workers" work with and teach their younger peers, not just in algebra, but a variety of math learning issues. Project Algebra has documented that the project's participating schools have substantial increased student enrollment in college preparatory mathematics classes and increased numbers of students going on to higher education.

With his Algebra Project, Bob Moses has brought together his two lifelong passions: education and individual civil rights. In recent years, this modest man has been the recipient of numerous civil rights and educational prizes and awards. He has many classrooms around the nation. Most recently, in 2012, he was teaching a course in the African American Studies program at Princeton University. His widely hailed project now serves 10,000 students in 28 cities in 11 states. At an age when most men are long-retired and playing golf, Bob Moses is still teaching and guiding the Algebra Project.

Steve Schapiro/Black Star/NEWSCOM

It is important to remember that parents are your students' first teachers.

Ephraim Ben-Shimon/Spirit/Corbis

Responsibility for Their Profession

Although things are beginning to change, it is a rare event, indeed, when a teacher loses his or her job because Johnnie cannot read or Samantha failed calculus. After a teacher achieves tenure, it takes some form of gross negligence, clear incompetence, or serious sexual offense for him or her to be fired. As professionals, teachers do very little policing of their own ranks. Their professional organizations are just like other self-serving organizations, whether composed of teamsters or office workers—that is, the primary energies of teacher associations and unions and professional associations are devoted to their own survival and growth. Secondarily, they attempt to protect their members, increase their salaries, and expand their benefits. Their students are rarely the direct beneficiaries of their policies.

Most teachers, however, are only minimally involved in the major professional associations and their activities. Except when the organization calls a strike—a rare but still somewhat contradictory activity for a "profession" supposedly dedicated to serving children—teachers generally just pay their dues. Most teachers claim they are too busy to take an active role in professional affairs. This lack of fully engaged involvement in professional activities may stem from the fact that so many teachers supplement their incomes with second jobs in the after-school labor market. And, many, too, have child care and homemaking responsibilities that eat up their discretionary time. Still others avoid union involvement due to disagreement with the organization's political stances.

Job Security and Salary

Teachers work in circumstances very different from those encountered by other professionals. Like other public servants, they are hired, rather than operating as independent agents. They are on a fixed salary schedule and are protected by tenure laws rather than independently having to find a market for their services. In effect, teaching is a low-paying, relatively high-security job rather than a high-paying, low-security profession. Seniority as a teacher appears to be more important than competence. Talk about "being a professional" may be personally satisfying to teachers, but it does not conform to the reality of the teacher's occupational life.

Up CLOSE

Rules and Duties for Teachers in the Nineteenth Century

- Teachers will fill the lamps and clean the chimney each day.
- Each teacher will bring a bucket of water and a scuttle of coal for the day's session.
- Make your pens carefully. You may whittle nibs to the individual tastes of the pupils.
- Men teachers may take one evening each week for courting purposes, or two evenings a week if they go to church regularly.
- Women teachers who marry or engage in improper conduct will be dismissed.
- Every teacher should lay aside from each day's pay a goodly sum of his earnings. He should use his savings during his retirement years so that he will not be a burden to society.
- Any teacher who smokes, uses liquor in any form, visits pool halls or public halls, or gets shaved at a barber shop will give good reasons for people to suspect his worth, intentions, and honesty.
- The teacher who performs his labor faithfully and without fault for five years will be given an increase of twenty-five cents per week in his pay.

Source: From the rules and duties for teachers teaching in an 1872 Missouri school district.

15-1b THE CASE *FOR* TEACHING AS A PROFESSION

The evidence for the status of teaching as a profession is witnessed and attested to by the very nature and nobility of the teacher's work. Society has entrusted teachers with its most important responsibility: the education of its young. Throughout history, many great thinkers have acknowledged how crucial the work of the teacher is to the fulfillment of personal and national goals. As this realization has spread in recent years, opportunities and rewards for teachers have continued to improve.

Teachers' Commitment to Service

Service to others lies at the very heart of what it means to be a professional. Teachers make large material sacrifices to serve children. The overwhelming percentages of people who teach could find work that, at least in material terms, is much more rewarding. Many could command large salaries in business or more lucrative professions. A recent study found that teachers surveyed said they spent that school year an average of $479 of their own money on school supplies and an additional $538 on instructional materials—a total of $1,017—for their classrooms.[2]

This is truly service above and beyond the call of duty!

Teachers' Unique Skills

Although children learn from many people—from parents to television personalities—teachers are the specialists who pass on to the young the key skills they need to participate effectively in the culture. They aid the young in acquiring the most difficult, if not the most important, skills—those that involve thinking and manipulating ideas. Neither reading nor geometry is often learned on the street. Teachers are the indispensable midwives of the "knowledge society." Although teachers do not undergo a particularly lengthy period of specialized training, they are in a sense continually educating themselves. Further, teachers are expected (and, in most states, required by law) to upgrade their teaching skills and content knowledge periodically. It should be noted, however, that ever since the COVID-19 pandemic hit the world in 2020, many parents, having sheltered-in-place with their school aged children, have a new respect for the skills required to teach well!

> *What office is there which involves more responsibility, which requires more qualifications, and which ought, therefore, to be more honorable than that of teaching?*
>
> **—HARRIET MARTINEAU (1802–1876),**
> nineteenth-century feminist and abolitionist

Teachers' Autonomy

Teachers have an immense span of personal control. They normally determine the method of instruction. They decide which aspects of the curriculum they will highlight and which they will cover quickly. The limits on their creativity in the classroom are few, if any. After the initial few years of teaching, they are seldom observed and evaluated. Teachers' classrooms are their castles. If teachers believe they do not have enough autonomy or do not agree with their administrators, they are free to move to another school.

A teacher's autonomy is accompanied by a responsibility to teach effectively. Like other professionals, teachers must be able to justify the manner in which they render their social services, whether through grading or disciplinary actions. Teachers take responsibility for their actions and, like other professionals, are open to criticisms of their performance.

Pause *and* Reflect

1. To you, what are the best arguments for and against the professional status of teaching?
2. Where do you stand on the question, "Is teaching a profession?" Is the designation "a profession" important to you?

15-1c A THIRD POSSIBILITY: AN EVOLVING PROFESSION

Like most other complex questions, our query about whether teaching is a profession cannot be answered satisfactorily with simple pro and con arguments such as those just offered. Also, the conditions under which teachers work differ so dramatically, and teachers possess such varying degrees of knowledge, commitment, and expertise, that it is difficult to come up with a definitive, one-size-fits-all answer. In most schools, teachers fulfill many of the criteria of professionals. In other schools, they seem to function somewhat as clerks and technicians.

In certain ways, teaching clearly is eligible for professional status; in other ways, it deviates sharply from accepted canons of professionalism. On the one hand, teachers provide an intellectual service to the community. They undergo specialized training to master the theoretical basis of their work. Ethical standards guide their work with students. On the other hand, they too often function like many other lower-level white-collar workers and civil servants. Too often, seniority and job security are the rules that guide their work-lives path rather than excellence and independence. Like many other occupational groups that are considered professional, at this moment in history, teachers only partially qualify for this sobriquet. For these reasons, some educators call teaching a "semiprofession," a label we reject as pejorative and demeaning.

Another way to look at the issue (and one we favor) is to think of teaching as an *evolving profession*—that is, it is in the process of becoming a full profession. Today, great efforts are being made to increase the professionalism of teaching. What will determine whether teaching actually becomes a full-fledged

T (F)
There is little debate that teaching is and always has been not just a career, but a profession.

profession during your lifetime? Among the key factors are the trends toward greater self-determination, better preparation, and recognizing excellence in teaching.

Greater Self-Determination

Perhaps teachers do lack the autonomy of, say, small-town lawyers. Yet every profession has limits on its autonomy. For example, an increasing number of doctors and dentists are now employed by health maintenance organizations (HMOs) and are forming unions to protect their rights against their HMO managers. The crucial point for teachers, though, is the direction in which teaching is moving.

In the same way that the United States is committed to civilian control of the military, Americans are committed to civilian (i.e., parents, community leaders, and school boards) control of their schools. Control over the teaching profession is a different matter, however, and should be largely in the hands of teachers. In particular, to make teaching a full profession, teachers must assume a larger role in the governing of their career affairs. Up to now, the great majority of teachers have taken the attitude "Let someone else do it," allowing others to make the major decisions about who should teach, how teachers should be trained, and under what conditions they should render their services. This situation will not substantially change until teachers take the lead in making it change.

Better Preparation

To make teaching a full profession, teachers must also demand better preparation requirements. As long as the public believes that any college graduate with a smattering of education courses can walk in off the street and do a teacher's job, people will tend not to treat teachers as professionals. As described in Chapter 13, "What Are Your Job Options in Education?," this dangerous perception may even worsen if, owing to teacher shortages, states issue alternative licenses to individuals without any professional training at all! We are definitely not suggesting that teachers should adopt artificial trappings, like a doctor's smock or a general's braided uniform, so that they will appear more distinctive and impressive. Rather, teachers must appear better because they *are* better. Like architects and surgeons, teachers must know their work, and their vocation must be imbued with a sense of high purpose. When that happens, the public will decide affirmatively that teachers should be treated and respected as full professionals.

Recognizing Excellence in Teaching

Not all of the nearly 4 million people working in U.S. schools are interested in and, in some cases, capable of measuring up to the standards of professionalism discussed earlier. At present, what we are calling (and will continue to call) the *teaching profession* is a mixed bag, with a great many transients "just passing through," a great many rather uncommitted teachers, and a great many truly excellent, dedicated career teachers.

Over 50 years ago, an educator captured what we believe to be the essence of the professional teacher in the following statement:

> Let us define a career teacher as one who plans to, and actually does, make a life occupation of teaching; one who is philosophically, emotionally, and spiritually committed, who is never satisfied with what he does and how well he's doing it, and who fully intends to keep on growing for the rest of his life.[3]

Until the great majority of teachers satisfy this educator's definition or until there is a qualitative regrouping of those presently identified as "teachers," the designation of teaching as a full-fledged profession will be in doubt.

15-2 Levels of Professionalism

What people (yourself included) think of the professional status of teaching is clearly important. Even so, this issue is dwarfed in importance by how you will live out your professional life and how you *will be* as a teacher. One way to think about this point is to conceive of teaching as having three levels, or three ways that teachers go about their work:

- Level one is the *imitative-maintenance* teacher;
- Level two is the *meditative* teacher; and
- Level three is the generative-creative teacher.[4]

15-2a LEVEL ONE TEACHERS

Individuals functioning at level one are essentially going through the motions prescribed by someone else in a rather mechanical fashion. They tend to be preoccupied with classroom discipline and keeping students busy. Such teachers may be successful at getting students *through* their lessons and examinations, but they are somewhat robotic in narrowly following preset patterns—namely, patterns set out in curriculum guides or textbooks. Level one teachers find security in *teaching to the test* and in what are pejoratively called *teacher-proof materials,* rigid instructional materials that offer step-by-step guidance for teachers' actions. Many new teachers, before they get their "sea legs," operate for a time at this level.

Although not in itself a problem, the imitative-maintenance approach doesn't allow teachers to respond to the unique needs of students or to the special circumstances that continually arise in a classroom. Level one teachers don't know how to respond to the interesting, off-the-wall question or what to do when something unexpected happens. Instead, they let the "teachable moment" float by. This kind of unimaginative teaching makes teaching more of a technical occupation than a profession.

15-2b LEVEL TWO TEACHERS

As the label "meditative" implies, teachers at level two mentally reflect on what they are doing in a classroom, but their reflection lies within a narrow range. They have an awareness of the uniqueness of their classroom and their students, and they go beyond their curricular guides and materials, but their adaptations are few and seem more like tinkering around the instructional edge. They may, for example, deviate from the prescribed teaching guide, but not very far. Level two teachers may vary their instructional patterns to fit certain classroom events—that is, the obvious boredom of students—or they may bring in supplemental materials. However, they are hardly innovative.

15-2c LEVEL THREE TEACHERS

There is a large jump to the generative-creative level. These teachers focus on their individual students, and they take a wide view of knowledge. They attend to their curricular guides and the prescribed materials, but those materials serve as launching pads rather than being the sole targets of their instruction. These teachers' classrooms are characterized by a wide variety of instructional approaches and problem-centered materials. Level three teachers play off the interests and talents of their students, but not in a casual or pandering way. Their expectations for students are high and transcend required tests and examinations. They approach instruction as diagnosticians, seeking the best ways to engage students in their own mental growth. They do not simply transmit knowledge, but rather create: They create in students a desire to learn and they create classroom environments where individual students become self-directed learners.

Technology often stimulates interest in science.

David Grossman/Alamy Stock Photo

Few new teachers burst on the educational scene as level three generative-creative teachers. Many start at level two or attain this status quickly. As a beginning teacher, you will need to have an understanding of your current behavior and to work toward this highest level. The very embracing of the goal of striving for higher levels of proficiency will put you on the road to full professionalism. This concept of levels of teaching, besides offering a path to excellence, points to a particularly challenging professional opportunity, an opportunity to which we now turn.

The habits of continually probing and examining your reasons for teaching and of routinely reflecting on what you have done in the classroom will make you a true professional, one like the teacher in the following poem.

What Teachers Make

by Taylor Mali (www.taylormali.com)

He says the problem with teachers is
What's a kid going to learn
from someone who decided his best option in life
was to become a teacher?
He reminds the other dinner guests that it's true
what they say about teachers:
Those who can, do; those who can't, teach.

I decide to bite my tongue instead of his
and resist the temptation to remind the dinner guests
that it's also true what they say about lawyers.

Because we're eating, after all, and this is polite company.
I mean, you're a teacher, Taylor.
Be honest. What do you make?

And I wish he hadn't done that—
asked me to be honest—
because, you see, I have this policy:
if you ask for it, then I have to let you have it.

You want to know what I make?

I make kids work harder than they ever thought they could.
I can make a C+ feel like a Congressional Medal of Honor
and an A— feel like a slap in the face.
Don't waste my time with anything less
than your very best.

I make kids sit through 40 minutes of study hall
in absolute silence.

I make parents tremble in fear when I call home.
I make parents see their children for who they are
and what they can be.

You want to know what I make?

I make kids wonder,
I make them question.
I make them criticize.
I make them apologize and mean it.
I make them write, write, write.

I make them read.
I make them spell *definitely beautiful, definitely beautiful, defi-*
nitely beautiful
over and over and over again until they will never misspell either
one of those words again.
I make them show all their work in math
and hide it on their final drafts in English.
I make them understand that if you've got *this*,
then you follow *this*,
and if someone ever tries to judge you
by what you make, you give them *this*.

Here, let me say it simply, so you know what I say is true:
Teachers make a difference! Now what about you?

15-3 National Board for Professional Teaching Standards

Since it began in 1987, the **National Board for Professional Teaching Standards (NBPTS)** has been working to recognize and provide greater support to superior (or level three) teachers. In the process, this organization attempts to strengthen the claim of professionalism for the career of teaching and to play a leading role in this effort.

Over the years, the lack of recognizable high standards has discouraged some potentially outstanding people from entering teaching and has lowered the level of aspiration of others. High standards tend to focus people's attention and harness their energies. For example, in long-distance running, the four-minute mile was long considered an unbreakable barrier. For many years, sports commentators pontificated that it was beyond the capacities of humans to run a mile in four minutes or less. Then, in 1957, Roger Bannister, a relatively obscure British medical student, broke the magic barrier. A new standard was set, and runners reset their sights. The following year, *37* runners broke that "unbreakable barrier." Today, breaking the four-minute barrier is commonplace, simply because a new standard has been set and people have risen to it in great numbers. The NBPTS is trying to perform a similar function for the teaching profession.

The NBPTS has established standards for teaching practice and has developed a series of board certification assessments based on these standards. As of 2020, approximately 125,000 teachers, from all 50 states and the District of Columbia, had achieved board certification.[5] Board advocates believe these standards allow teachers to gain a highly regarded, professional credential like that available to physicians, accountants, architects, and other professionals. So far, however, although 90 percent of all U.S. physicians and 30 percent of U.S. architects are board certified, about 4 percent of U.S. teachers have achieved that feat.[6]

15-3a CORE PROPOSITIONS AND CHARACTERISTICS

The NBPTS is dedicated to and directed by five core propositions:

1. Teachers know the subjects they teach and how to teach these subjects to students.
2. Teachers are committed to their students and their learning.
3. Teachers are responsible for managing and monitoring student learning.
4. Teachers think systematically about their practice and learn from experience.
5. Teachers are members of a learning community.[7]

In addition, the organization has five distinguishing characteristics:

1. The NBPTS supports experienced teachers—that is, teachers with a baccalaureate or an advanced degree who have graduated from an accredited college or university and have at least three years of teaching experience.
2. "Taking the boards" is completely voluntary. It is not intended to be a condition of work, like state licensure, but rather an achievement testifying to an individual teacher's attainment of a high level of professionalism.
3. "Taking the boards" involves submitting oneself to a set of examinations and assessments in particular areas or subject matters such as early childhood, English language arts, and physical education and health. Currently, board certification is offered in 25 different teaching fields. The standards are updated every seven to ten years to stay current. The National Board convenes the experts and facilitates the process by which those experts write the standards that define accomplished practice in their field. A standards committee of practicing classroom teachers and other relevant experts such as researchers, teacher educators, and subject-matter specialists guide that work, although teachers are a majority of the committees. In addition, the assessments are updated every 10 years to measure the content of the updated standards.
4. These assessments are not typical paper-and-pencil tests. Teaching, by its very nature, is a mixture of thought and action and is not measured well

I ask for philosophy from my union and it gives me politics, partisanship, and public relations. Teachers learn to be pragmatists or they don't survive. Underneath their veneer of practicality, they are dreamers. Truck drivers and longshoremen might not need a philosophical guiding light from their union leaders, but teachers do. Teachers yearn for commitment, for caring, and for conscience.

—SUSAN OHANIAN,
author and educational commentator

by traditional "sit-down" testing. Among the means of assessment are videotapes of the individual's teaching and an evaluation of his or her professional portfolio. Such a portfolio might include examples of students' work, sample lesson plans, and other items that teachers believe will support their candidacy. Candidates do, however, take examinations to assure depth of knowledge in their field. They are also asked to respond to and justify their responses to classroom circumstances.

5. The primary control of the NBPTS is in the hands of a 27-person board of directors. Although administrators, teacher-educators, and the general public are represented on the NBPTS, two-thirds of the board members are teachers—a further step toward achieving professionalism in teaching.

15-3b ADVANTAGES OF BOARD CERTIFICATION

In recent years, NBPTS certification has meant a salary bonus for those teachers so designated. However, in 2019, the amounts of these awards, which can reach a $10,000 annual stipend,[8] have been reduced, victims of recession-driven budget cuts. The states remain committed to NBPTS certification, as is the federal Department of Education. The National Board received an Investing in Innovation grant from the U.S. Department of Education to integrate the videos of National Board-certified teachers in teacher education programs for use with preservice teachers: resulting in the Accomplished Teaching, Learning and Schools® (ATLAS) "library of authentic video cases showing National Board Certified Teachers at work in the classroom."[9]

Board certification also means that school boards have a recognizable basis on which to award merit pay or pay for performance other than arbitrary and impressionistic criteria, such as "Her children do well on tests" or "He seems to work long hours and is popular with the brightest students."

Besides raising salaries, board certification offers a number of other advantages for teachers. Teachers who have achieved NBPTS certification are professionally more portable, meaning that they can move more freely across state lines. Also, this effort should stimulate research on what constitutes superior teaching. Likewise, it should trigger more attention to this research-based knowledge within teacher education and throughout the teaching force. Most of all, it should contribute to the essential but difficult mission of creating a system of recognition for highly skilled and dedicated professionals.

15-3c CRITICISMS OF THE NBPTS

The NBPTS is not without critics. Some educators claim that there is no solid knowledge base in teaching (as opposed to medicine or architecture) on which to ground the board's assessments. Others see the NBPTS as a public relations move to enhance the status and salaries of teachers with artificial trappings ("Yep, Eloise got herself board certified, but we all know she couldn't teach a stone to drop!"). Still others, suspicious that the NBPTS is controlled by its majority of teacher members, see it becoming a vehicle by which to serve the economic interests of teachers and to insulate them further from their "clients" (the students and their parents). Finally, some critics dismiss the NBPTS as just another organization promoting a failed "progressive ideology" (i.e., self-esteem, multiculturalism, and cultural relativity) rather than focusing on content knowledge and whether students are *actually* learning.[10]

For two decades, critics of board certification for teachers were uncertain that the process was sound and that it really made a difference, particularly in the classroom where the educational rubber meets the road. Recent research has confirmed that National Board certification has a positive impact on student achievement, teacher retention, and professional development. In particular, the research showed that board-certified teachers brought about more higher-level thinking, or more of the "deep thinking" needed by a competitive twenty-first-century workforce.[11]

15-4 What Every New and Old Teacher Should Possess: The InTASC Answer

In the same year that the NBPTS began its work, the Council of Chief State School Officers (CCSSO) began parallel work that focuses on what prospective teachers ought to know and be able to do to attain initial teaching licenses in their states. Called the Interstate New Teacher Assessment and Support Consortium, the effort sought to lay out standards for a common core of teaching skills and knowledge for all beginning teachers at all grade levels and subject areas. Recently, the CCSSO has shifted its focus from standards for beginning teachers to all teachers, new and old. In the process, the name was changed, dropping the "new," now to be called the Interstate Teacher Assessment and Support Consortium (InTASC). Together with the NBPTS, it is working to create model standards for "board-compatible" teacher licensing. Although their focuses are different, they are, however, complementary. The InTASC standards are seen as core standards that apply across grade levels and subject matter for all teachers, whereas the NBPTS has developed standards that apply across a grade-level range and are subject specific.

Although all this talk of NBPTS, CCSSO, and InTASC may seem like so much alphabet soup, the educators behind these letters are working hard to develop clear and practical standards. The purpose behind these standards is not only to have teachers across the country possess a common core of professional abilities, but also to lay the foundation for a seamless transition to acquiring the board certification later on. The InTASC standards are, in effect, the "first tier" of skills and knowledge that all new teachers should possess.

Currently, 34 states have developed and implemented teacher-licensing standards that are based on 10 core principles developed by InTASC.[12] These 10 InTASC standards for all beginning teachers are listed on the inside covers of your book. Find more information on InTASC and the standards at the website that accompanies this book.

Pause *and* Reflect

1. What are you doing now to ensure that you meet the InTASC standards as a beginning teacher? Who can you ask about this?
2. Does the idea of working toward board certification appeal to you? Why or why not?

15-5 Professional Associations

Like other occupational groups, such as doctors and teamsters, teachers have associations whose function is to protect their interests and attempt to improve their lot in life. For example, teacher salaries (which are the major cost of schooling) and other educational expenses come out of taxpayers' pockets. Tax revenues are used for many purposes, and intense competition occurs among groups that rely on tax money to support their efforts to fight crime and delinquency, increase aid to the elderly and to the poor, and so on. In the rough-and-tumble world of a democracy, teachers need someone or something to look out for their interests and the interests of the recipients of their services: children. This is the avowed function of many teachers' associations. Protection of teachers' rights and improvement in their rewards and working conditions will not just happen. There is an old saying: "Nobody gives you nothin' for nothing." The advances teachers make will occur largely as a result of their hard work and their willingness to stand up for what they believe.

Our primary focus in this section is on the large "umbrella organizations" of teachers, the **National Education Association (NEA)** and the **American Federation of Teachers (AFT)**. These two groups have the most immediate and sustaining effects on the lives of teachers. Although private-sector unionism fervor has waned in recent decades, the NEA and AFT have emerged as major forces in U.S. education and in the labor movement itself. NEA membership numbers 3 million; while, the AFT reports a membership of 1.6 million.[13] Both associations claim to represent teachers to the federal, state, and local governments; to educational authorities at the state and local levels; and, finally, to the general public. Both organizations also come to the aid of teachers, like those in the vignettes on pages 447 and 448, whose legal rights are being violated or who are being treated shoddily or unethically. On the other hand, many educators and members of the public have recently become critical of the policies and political stances of the two organizations. One administrator of an urban charter school recently complained, "They have more than a billion dollars a year of combined budget. Goodness knows how much of that is channeled into buying influence."[14]

It is important to know something about the NEA and the AFT because if you become a teacher, they will claim to be speaking for *you* and influencing your professional life. Many new teachers report being asked to join a professional association their first day on the job. Until recently, teachers in nearly half of the states were required, whether they supported their school's union or not, to contribute dues to it, but in 2018, the Supreme Court ruled in favor of a public employee who challenged this legal requirement (*Janus* v. *AFSCME*). However, two years later, over half the country's teachers were unaware that they were required to pay dues, the life blood of the two major unions.[15] Many observers believe the ruling in *Janus* will have a profound effect on organizations representing the teaching profession.

As you read the following pages, be aware that the NEA and the AFT are and have been engaged in a struggle for the hearts, minds, and, yes, the membership dues of teachers for decades. Further, each is concerned with advancing its cause and gaining the support of future teachers. In addition, there is a short feature about one of the newer, smaller professional associations, the **Association of American Educators (AAE)**, which is taking a very different approach to supporting teachers than the major professional organizations of teachers.

15-5a THE NATIONAL EDUCATION ASSOCIATION

Founded in 1857, the NEA today is a complex institution that operates on the national, state, and local school district levels and serves a diverse clientele of rural, suburban, and urban teachers. The bulk of its 3 million members are classroom teachers. However, that figure includes teacher aides, administrators, professors, retired educators, and college students preparing to become teachers. The NEA has some 14,000 local affiliate chapters in approximately 80 percent of the nation's school districts.[16]

Services to Members

The NEA offers its members a wide range of services, from an extensive array of publications, to research on issues such as comparative salary scales and the attitudes of teachers on various topics. In addition, its UniServ program has some 1,800 professionals in the field working with teachers, ready to give local teachers help in such specialized areas as collective bargaining.[17] A number of special services are available to members as well, such as travel programs, insurance policies, mutual fund programs, and book club programs.

The NEA and Political Issues

Since the NEA's inception, its goal has been "to elevate the character and advance the interests of the profession of teaching and to promote the cause of education in the United States." In advancing this goal, it has come out against issues such as competency testing of teachers. Despite this stance, since 1987, the NEA has supported the NBPTS, and it has long been a champion of small class sizes and special programs for linguistic and ethnic groups within schools.[18] Further, it has taken forceful positions on other issues. It has, for example, been a vigorous opponent of various voucher plans that call for using public tax monies for religious and other private schools. Also, the organization has given only lukewarm and qualified support for charter schools.[19]

T (F)
Neither the National Education Association nor the American Federation of Teachers, professional organizations that represent the majority of the nation's teachers, take positions on political issues or endorse individuals running for office.

When it was started a century and a half ago, the NEA tried to speak for all public educators, including both teachers and administrators alike. That all changed about 50 years ago, when two things happened: first, the work of the organization became more concentrated on improving the lot of public school teachers; and, second, it started to flex its muscles in the political arena. In 1976, the NEA for the first time formally backed a presidential candidate (Jimmy Carter). Since then, it has consistently backed mostly democratic candidates for national and most state offices with active support and dollars.

The NEA has become a strong political player for various reasons. At the time, one political commentator referred to teachers as "bright, articulate, and reasonably well informed, making them naturals for political activism."[20] What was true then is even truer now. Today, the NEA is big and rich. NEA gets its money from mandatory dues. The average dues for local, state and national membership in can be approximately $600, but can also be as high as $1,200 in one state.[21]

Its sheer size, money, and presence in many congressional districts are huge assets to any candidate or party it would care to support. And, in turn, the recipient politicians have been supportive of the organization's agenda. Based on federally required filings, the Center for Responsive Politics has estimated that between 1990 and 2020, 80 percent of the NEA's substantial political contributions went to Democratic party candidates and 95 percent of contributions went to Democrats in

2020.[22] However, the NEA's one-sided support of the Democratic party has caused many to question the wisdom of putting all these human and financial "eggs" into one political basket. In addition, many members are at odds with the NEA's support of various social and political causes, such as Jesse Jackson's rainbow PUSH coalition, the Gay and Lesbian Alliance Against Defamation, plus the organization's continued support of pro-abortion groups.[23] This is particularly so since the nation's teachers individually tend politically to split evenly. In a recent study of the political leanings of educators, 43 percent reported being "moderate," 29 percent "liberal" or "very liberal" and 27 percent "conservative" or "very conservative."[24]

15-5b THE AMERICAN FEDERATION OF TEACHERS

The AFT's membership is approximately one-half the size of the NEA's, but this organization represents teachers in key urban areas across the country. Currently, it bargains for teachers in New York City, Chicago, Philadelphia, Cleveland, Pittsburgh, Kansas City, St. Louis, Detroit, Boston, Houston, Dallas, Atlanta, and Washington, DC.

The AFT's leadership is very clear about placing the organization squarely within the American labor movement. The organization itself is affiliated with the American Federation of Labor and Congress of Industrial Organizations (AFL-CIO), which has a membership of more than 14 million. The AFT alone has more than 1.6 million members, with 43 state affiliates and 3,000 local affiliates nationwide.[25] Much of the AFT's growth in the past five decades has resulted from its success in introducing the collective bargaining process into the annual salary negotiations of teachers. Its aggressive techniques, which include strikes and the threat of strikes, are credited with achieving substantial salary increases for teachers and with forcing the NEA to adopt more militant tactics. On the downside, the shrinking student enrollments in some major cities, which are the AFT's real power base, have preoccupied the organization and sapped its energies. In 2012, it was reported that nationally this shrinkage has cost the AFT 40,000 members.[26]

The AFT's Stance on Issues

Although the AFT is noted for its hard bargaining on bread-and-butter issues such as salaries and benefits, it has also been a defender of academic freedom and greater participation in decision making by teachers. In spite of the fact that the AFT opposes many of the same issues as the NEA, such as vouchers, and shares with it only qualified support for charter schools, the AFT has a more progressive reputation, owing largely to the efforts of its long-time leader Albert Shanker, who died in 1997. Once seen by many as the champion of raw "teacher power" and as concerned only with the good of teachers, Shanker became a strong advocate of educational reform in his later years. He lobbied both his own organization and the public in support of many reform efforts, such as the NBPTS, certain kinds of merit pay, higher minimum standards for teachers, and longer and more intense teacher education. In contrast, the NEA has only recently come to support many of these reform efforts.

A Possible Merger?

For more than 30 years, the leaders of both the NEA and the AFT (along with many members of the press) have been discussing the possibility of merging the two groups into one organization that would represent the entire teaching force. Although there have been many conversations over the years, the two organizations appear to want to remain separate and independent, but come together to lobby for common causes.

> *Don't even slack off. If ever we needed you, we need you today.*
>
> **—CHARLES SWINDOLL,**
> pastor and radio broadcaster

15-5c REFORMERS IN THE RANKS: THE ASSOCIATION OF AMERICAN EDUCATORS

Established in 1994, the Association of American Educators (AAE) represents a fresh approach for teachers who are dissatisfied with the two major labor unions. Since its inception, AAE has become the largest national, nonunion teacher association in the United States. As such, it offers educators an alternative to the nation's teacher unions. Currently, AAE helps to lead a coalition of over 350,000 teachers in all 50 states, teachers whom it claims are focused on professionalism and putting the needs of our children first. Although not antiunion, AAE is opposed to many of the stands taken by the NEA and the AFT, such as teacher strikes, forced unionism, and opposition to education reforms like performance pay, school vouchers, weakening of teacher tenure, and many accountability reforms.

AAE has the following key goals:

1. To encourage and support teachers who embrace certain views on education in the United States, such as the view that schools should aim to improve a young person's character as well as his or her intellect.

2. To keep the governance of the organization in the hands of practicing teachers. Currently, more than half the AAE's board of directors comprises classroom teachers who have won national Teacher of the Year awards.

3. To keep the focus on educational issues and to stay out of partisan politics. In contrast to the $500 to $1,200 combined annual local, state, and national dues charged by the labor unions, AAE dues are a mere $180, and much of that goes for liability insurance.

This lean organization does not collectively bargain, or engage in partisan political activity. It does, however, offer an alternative for those who are tired of paying hefty dues and who disagree particularly with the political stands and social views of the larger organizations.[27]

Pause *and* Reflect

1. Once you are established as a teacher, does the idea of becoming active in one of these two professional organizations or unions appeal to you personally? If so, what is the attraction?
2. What questions or concerns, if any, do you have about joining one of the two major teacher organizations?

15-5d OTHER PROFESSIONAL ASSOCIATIONS

In addition to the NEA and AFT, many other educational organizations exist. Each supports certain constituents and serves their special interests. Table 15.1 offers a sample of these groups. The ones listed under the heading "Specialized Associations of Teachers" are primarily for teachers of a particular subject matter or area within the life of the school. Under the second heading, "Nationwide Special-Interest Groups in Education," are more broad-based organizations that typically include members of the public, administrators, people from higher education, and teachers. The third heading, "Nationwide Groups Supporting Teacher Education," identifies an organization

TABLE 15.1 **Nationwide Organizations of Interest to Teachers**

Specialized Associations of Teachers

Council for Exceptional Children

National Science Teachers Association

National Council of Teachers of English

National Council for the Social Studies

National Association for Music Education

National Association for the Education of Young Children

Association for Career and Technical Education

International Reading Association

National Council of Teachers of Mathematics

American Council on the Teaching of Foreign Language

National Art Education Association

American Alliance for Health, Physical Education, Recreation and Dance

Association for Education Communications and Technology

National Association for Gifted Children

Nationwide Special-Interest Groups in Education

National School Boards Association

American Association of School Administrators

ASCD (Association for Supervision and Curriculum Development)

American Educational Research Association

Council of Chief State School Officers

Nationwide Groups Supporting Teacher Education

Association of Teacher Educators

involved in teacher education. Through journals, in-service training, or professional development institutes, as well as conferences and conventions, such organizations play a vital role in keeping teachers informed about research and developments in their fields. It is here where much of the teacher's professional activity goes on. We urge you to consider joining those associations closest to your interests.

There are also professional associations dedicated specifically to future teachers. The largest of these is the NEA's Aspiring Educators Program, which consists of over 60,000 members across more than 1,000 college/university campus chapters and 50 state programs.[28] As a branch of the NEA, the SNEA offers many of the benefits of NEA membership, such as liability insurance when members student-teach, access to the NEA's research files, and subscriptions to its regular publications, *The NEA Handbook* and *Today's Education*.

Three other professional groups that are open to prospective teachers include the honor societies of Pi Lambda Theta, Phi Delta Kappa, and Kappa Delta Pi. These associations are international in scope but typically organize around chapters on university or college campuses. They hold regular meetings to discuss recent developments in the field, such as constructivist approaches to learning, brain research, and character education. These organizations provide an excellent opportunity for students to meet other education students in a nonclassroom setting and particularly to meet practicing teachers and administrators in a professional yet informal setting.

If membership in such honorary associations interests you, we suggest that you check out their websites; speak to one of your education professors about which, if any, of the organizations are on your campus and how you can learn about them; and call, write, or email the headquarters of these organizations to obtain general information and to learn whether there are chapters on your campus. It is not unheard of for beginning education students to initiate new chapters on their campuses.

15-5e WANTED: A NEW PROFESSIONALISM

The era of aggressive trade unionism in the U.S. private sector of the economy has receded in recent years. In its place, a new cooperative spirit has brought about a revival of many of our industries. By putting slogans such as "excellence" and "reengineering" into practice, workers and management have altered the economic landscape. Many see a similar pattern being followed by members of public school teachers' public-sector unions. Serious, prolonged teacher strikes are becoming a rarity. Also, we have witnessed the beginnings of a revival similar to that seen in U.S. industry in the guise of the "educational excellence" movement and the "restructuring" efforts currently sweeping through our schools. In our view, the issue of teacher professionalism is very much wrapped up in these broader school renewal efforts. Whether teachers are treated as professionals will depend on the bottom line: the performance of our schools. To promote that performance, teachers must begin, both individually and collectively, with a personal commitment to excellence. If *professionalism* is to mean anything, first and foremost it means looking out for the concerns of one's clients, who in this case are our children.

15-6 Your Own Professional Development

Think back over your education and the teachers you have had. Were any of them sincere souls but deadly dull? People of good will, whose classes were unfortunately morgue-like? Teachers who seemed to have a magic touch enabling them to stretch an hour into a week? If you haven't had one of these mind-numbing teachers, consider yourself among the fortunate.

Once upon a time, these teachers most likely were filled with energy, ideas, and idealism, but something happened—or something didn't happen. They probably survived their first years of teaching and then quietly settled into routines. Then with the passage of time, those routines became mindless. Now, when they enter the classroom, these teachers unknowingly switch over to autopilot. These autopilot teachers undoubtedly went to all of the in-service days, did graduate work after school or during the summers, and probably hold advanced degrees. But something *didn't* happen, because they failed to take personal control of their **professional development**.

15-6a WHAT IS PROFESSIONAL DEVELOPMENT, ANYWAY?

Professional development is a large term encompassing the efforts both by a school (or school district) and by individual teachers primarily to improve their skills and competencies as teachers. In this final chapter, we focus on the professional development efforts of new teachers. Teaching, and particularly "sage on the stage" teaching (where the teacher is the center of attention and information), can be draining, both intellectually and emotionally. Without recharging one's batteries through professional development and learning new theories,

T (F)
The term *professional development* refers to moving through and up the ranks in the educational hierarchy.

methods, and skills, many of the embedded joys and satisfactions of teaching go flat over time. In the 1990s, the U.S. Army had a motto: "Be all you can be! Join the Army." The essence of the professional development activities described here is that they offer ways and means for you as a teacher to "be all you can be."

15-6b THE NEW IMPERATIVE: YOUR OWN PROFESSIONAL DEVELOPMENT

As we have stressed throughout this text, schooling in the United States is changing. Where once schools could be satisfied with teaching basic skills and conveying preset bodies of information, today the shifting societal and economic landscapes are demanding change. We are increasingly becoming a "knowledge society" in which the demands on our students, who face the challenge of surviving and thriving in a global economy, increase yearly. A dramatic example can be seen in the rising interest in technological literacy: As American society has become increasingly dependent on electronic information services, the needs and advantages of being comfortable and competent with computers, the Internet, networking, and the latest technologies have become more evident. Of course, the demands on today's students go much further than that.

The field of education has a great deal to learn in this regard from U.S. industry. For two decades, successful businesses and corporations have made a major commitment to "reengineering" or "reinventing" themselves. A good example of this continual growth and development is Apple, the organization developed by the late Steve Jobs, which has introduced a stream of novel electronic products, from the Mac to the iPod, and the iPhone to the iPad. Another is Tesla, a company that is currently accelerating the world's transition to sustainable energy with electric cars, solar panels, and integrated renewable energy solutions for homes and industries. Creatively oriented firms such as Apple and Tesla make a major investment in their employees; those individuals, in turn, know they must grow as employees.

Similarly, our schools must become **learning organizations**, where the goals and priorities are driven by questions such as "What does this student need to get past his or her individual learning barrier?" and "How can I find the right material or right question to ignite this student's mind?" At the same time, classical educational questions such as "What is most worth knowing?" and "Are students *really* understanding this material?" must be continually revisited and augmented by a new priority for student learning.

This shift in the ground beneath our feet has profound implications for teachers. Rather than a skills trainer or an information dispenser, a new teacher must be a "learning professional." In today's world, that means becoming a continuous learner, committed to one's growth both as a person and as a professional. It means knowing the most current information in one's field *and* knowing how to share it with students. It means being part of a community of learning with other teachers, both giving and taking knowledge.

Not many decades ago, it was considered adequate for a teacher to obtain an undergraduate education and a teaching license and then have no further training. Today, most states have legislated continuing education for teachers. In fact, in more than half of the states, it is no longer possible to gain permanent licensure. An increasing number of states are requiring teachers to keep up with developments in their fields or specific areas of education.

Although we have known a few of what might be called "born teachers" or "naturals," the overwhelming majority of teachers have to learn our craft. In addition, because this "craft" is continually evolving, we need to be *continuous learners*. The broad, operational vehicle for becoming a continuous learner is professional development. This term refers to a whole range of activities available to help teachers "stay alive" professionally.

One of the great stumbling blocks to professional development is time. When does a teacher have the time? The National Staff Development Council found that teachers in the United States are given significantly less time and support for high-quality professional learning than their counterparts in other developed nations. The study compared U.S. teachers' average of 1,080 hours per year in classroom teaching time with that of teachers from European and Asian counties, where primary school teachers teach 803 hours per year and secondary teachers only 664 hours per year.[29] The report states, "A significant number of schools in high-achieving countries schedule time into teachers' work day or week for professional development, prominently including forms of collaborative work on instructional issues."[30] As this report strongly suggests, more time for professional development should become a major educational priority.

15-6c PROFESSIONAL DEVELOPMENT OPPORTUNITIES

Teachers have two broad categories of professional development available to them: programs offered by institutions and self-initiated activities.

Most schools and their districts sponsor professional development in the form of **in-service programs,** such as courses, workshops, or short retreats. These professional development programs often focus on some particular problem or issue such as communication with parents, or target some new area such as environmental education. (The Video Case, *Parent–Teacher Conference,* shows two teachers role-playing how the conversation between parent and teacher might go at conference time.) Or, for instance, if students in a particular school are getting unsatisfactory grades on standardized mathematics achievement tests, the district may choose to provide special training for the faculty, or the district may decide to switch to a new, supposedly better mathematics program, a change that will also require special training for the faculty.

This type of collaboration among teachers is an example of positive *social capital.* This term refers to the quality of the relationships within a group, and it is used to measure the value added to the collective work of a group. Researchers at Stanford have applied this concept to schools, focusing on the quality of the relationships and professional sharing among faculty members. An indicator of positive social capital would be where a teacher with a discipline problem, instead of consulting the principal or an expert, consults another teacher or asks for help in a teachers' meeting. The researchers found that this type of social capital in a school is positively related to student achievement.[31] On the other hand, some schools abound with *negative* social capital, such as teachers hording materials from one another and socializing in cliques, and faculty meetings that are rare and unpleasant.

© Cengage 2016

▶❚❚ TeachSource Video Case

Parent–Teacher Conference

Watch the video clips, study the artifacts in the case, and reflect on the following questions:

1. Several types of continuous learning opportunities are described in this chapter. Which are depicted in this case?

2. Earlier in the chapter, the authors described several aspects of teaching that either contributed to the case *for* teaching as a profession or contributed to the case *against* teaching as a profession. Do you believe that conducting parent–teacher conferences is a responsibility that can be used as evidence either for or against teaching as a profession? Explain your opinion.

Working with colleagues can be one of the greatest joys of teaching.

Monkey Business Images/Vetta/Getty Images

Supervision

Another form of professional development comes through supervision. During a teacher's early years in the profession, school districts provide professional advice that amounts to one-on-one help. For instance, if you are a new high school teacher, your department head may observe your classes regularly and discuss the observations with you; if you are an elementary school teacher, your building principal or lead teacher may make regular visits and follow them up with feedback sessions. Although supervision can sometimes be quite threatening, particularly to nontenured teachers, it offers an opportunity to obtain valuable insight and information about your teaching techniques and skills.

Mentoring

In recent years, many school districts have instituted mentoring programs whereby more experienced teachers are assigned to assist beginners. The same study cited previously found that three out of four new teachers were participating in special induction programs, and four out of five had been assigned mentors. Regrettably, these supports were available for a significantly lower percentage of teachers in high-poverty, high-minority schools.[32] (Mentoring is discussed in more detail in Chapter 14, "What Can the New Teacher Expect?") Along with special training, these mentors may receive a reduction in teaching responsibilities, a salary increase, or both. Mentoring programs formalize and make more systematic the time-honored process in which experienced teachers take a rookie under their wing. Serving as non-judgmental colleagues, they help the beginners make the necessary theory-into-practice transitions.

Group Study

Group study is yet another common form of continuous learning for teachers. It often takes the form of committee work. When a problem arises in the school, for which there is no apparent solution, a group of people takes upon itself the task of exploring the problem, with a view toward recommending an enlightened course of action. In recent years, to obtain opinions from outside the school, teachers and administrators have begun inviting community residents to these study groups. Typical issues these groups might address include curricular alternatives, dealing with bullying on the playground, an analysis of the unused education resources in the community, a program of writing across the curriculum, and the potential benefits and costs of using support professionals in a high school.

Graduate Study

A popular form of self-initiated professional development, and a way for you to continue to learn, is to take courses or to work toward an advanced degree. It is the rare area that does not have a college and university offering courses suitable for and interesting to teachers. Special and regular courses are offered in the evening, on weekends, and during the summer vacation. More and more universities are now offering online or computer-based distance-learning courses, which enable teachers (and others) to do advanced study without leaving their homes. These courses and degree programs not only allow teachers to gain a deeper understanding of their work but also make it possible for some teachers to train for other jobs in education, such as guidance counseling, administration, or college teaching. One of the side benefits of "going back to school" for teachers is that they again experience being "on the other side of the desk." This, in turn, helps them empathize with their students struggling to learn.

> *It is better to know some of the questions than all of the answers.*
>
> —JAMES THURBER (1894–1961),
> American author and humorist

Independent Study

One aim of education is to develop the ability to engage in independent study. Independent study is jargon for being able to "go it alone." Although this approach is much discussed among educators, students seem to get little actual practice in choosing and systematically investigating their own areas of interest. Nevertheless, self-initiated independent study is one of the most important means for continual self-renewal available to you as a teacher. Teachers are confronted daily with things they do not understand about children, and about human learning:

- Is there anything in this talk about learning preferences, and how I can apply it in my classroom?
- What does the new brain research suggest about teaching topic A and subject B?
- What are the fundamental skills of composition that children should know?
- How can I help my students use history for their own benefit?

Such questions are daily grist for teachers' independent study mill. Answering them—that is, engaging in this kind of independent study—used to mean traipsing off to a library and haunting the stacks for information. Today, online search engines, such as Google and Bing, bring a flood of information, theory, and advice with a few keyboard clicks. Even if you cannot find teachers in your own building who are interested in a particular question or issue, you don't have to go on this quest alone. The Internet has come to the rescue! Google, for example, has established the Google Teachers Center, a portal to all sorts of useful resources and materials. One of these resources is Google for Educators Discussion Groups, where you can join a "virtual group" centered on a particular topic, or start your own group.

Of course, your study should not be confined to professional problems. Your own personal interests may lead you into such areas as organic gardening, physical fitness, classic movies, the politics of colonial America, the humanizing of the corporate state, or harnessing the media. "The teacher doth not live by professional problems of teaching and learning alone!"

Systematic Reflection on Practice

As we said at the beginning of this book, of all the approaches to professional development mentioned here, *the most important* is developing the habit of reflecting on one's practice. If teachers, whether new or old, are to improve, they need to make systematic reflection on what is happening in their classrooms a regular part of their professional lives. In the "spaces" in their lives—the time between classes, driving home, working out at the gym, or cooking dinner—they need to ask themselves questions like these:

- What went right in class today?
- What didn't work?
- Which students am I not reaching, and what should I do about it?
- What can I do to get my uninvolved students more engaged?
- Are there other ways of presenting this material that will connect with students who have different learning styles?
- The next time I teach this material I'm going to keep X and change Y.

Becoming a reflective practitioner—that is, developing the habit of systematic reflection on your work—is *the royal road* to excellence in teaching!

Professional Learning Communities

One of the most promising school improvement innovations in recent years has been the professional learning communities (PLCs) movement. Many names and labels in education don't speak directly to what they are about and can be confusing.

> *Teachers are the first learners.*
> —LUCIANNE BOND CARMICHAEL,
> educator and author

PLCs are the exception. The aim of PLCs is to form the teachers and administrators in a particular school into a group that is working together to grow and improve as professionals. Some have called PLCs *communities of continuous inquiry and improvement,* and see them as potent instruments for changing a school's climate and learning outcomes. In PLC schools, structured time is provided for teachers to observe one another's classrooms, and have time for giving one another feedback. Time, too, is available for teachers and administrators to study new instructional and curricular ideas, and plan together how to implement them in their particular setting. Many of the forms of professional development outlined previously—such as mentoring, group study, and supervision—come together in a coordinated way in the promising method of helping teachers and administrators become truly continuous learners.[33]

15-6d TAKING CONTROL OF YOUR OWN PROFESSIONAL DEVELOPMENT

Educational reform expert Michael Fullan suggests that teachers seeking to improve themselves are characterized by four attitudes: (1) They accept that it is possible to improve; (2) they are ready to be self-critical; (3) they recognize better practice than their own; and, (4) most importantly, they are willing to learn what they have to learn to do what needs to be done.[34] In our view, teachers who are not engaged in learning activities because of lack of opportunity or lack of personal incentive are stunting their own career and are barriers to the educational reform we need. In the "Voices from the Classroom" feature, one teacher describes the moment she first realized how deeply the commitment to lifelong learning can run among teachers.

VOICES from the Classroom

Professionalism

Theresa Madison taught 10th-grade language arts at Brighton High School in Brighton, Massachusetts.

Before I began teaching, I had a certain vision of what the world of teachers would be like. I prepared myself for hearing a lot of "when you've been around as long as I have" and "when you get to be my age, you'll understand." I felt a sort of preembarrassment for all the mistakes I would probably make before I "got it." To me, the profession presented itself as a kind of hierarchy where the big cheese of the school would offer condescending advice and rolled eyes at my rookie mishaps.

Now, only six months into the experience, I am happy to say that my fears were quite wrong. Not too long ago, I went to visit a colleague of mine, Jane, in her classroom during one of her planning periods. She's been a teacher for about six or seven years and at our school for only three. About a minute or two into our conversation, I noticed that the door that adjoined her room with Mrs. Conner's room was open and students were moving between the two. Soon Mrs. Conner herself came bustling in and out of Jane's room, looking for glue sticks and getting a clarification about some graphic organizer.

After asking what was going on, I made a concerted effort to hide my surprise. Jane was asked to take on a smaller class load this year and to spend the remaining time as a literacy coach. She told me that the job included sitting in on classes for a week or so and then working one-on-one with that particular teacher to experiment with different instructional practices and techniques. But Mrs. Conner? She had been teaching for 30 years. This was a woman who had a way with students, parents, and other teachers that I wished I could bottle and sell. It was one thing to smile and nod at staff meetings when younger teachers spoke, but to invite a teacher with far fewer years on the job into your classroom was quite a different scenario.

I could only describe the feeling as humbling. Nobody, it seemed, was out to get me or laugh at my naiveté. The more I began to look around, the more I noticed that many of my colleagues were "age blind." The task at hand was to educate students, and if someone had a better way of doing things or if some workshop came along that could benefit a teacher's practice, then many of these educators were up for another learning experience. I had always heard that teachers were learners for life, but I wasn't sure how many of them bought that old cliché. As it turns out, seeking more for our students and our own practice is not considered a sign of weakness or a stigma by all of those scary veterans; it's simply part of being a professional.

Question You Should Ask about Professional Development Opportunities

When you are considering taking a teaching position, you should investigate the school district's policies about professional development. In particular, you should find answers to the following questions:

1. Are the schools conceived of as **Professional Learning Communities (PLCs),** in which everyone—adults and children alike—are always learning?

2. Does the school to which you are being assigned have an atmosphere of relational trust and positive social capital?

3. Do teachers, specialists, and administrators see their continuing educational growth as an integral part of their workday?

4. Does the district's definition of "professional development" take into account whatever contributes to making an educator more effective?

5. What professional development costs are to be borne by you or by the school district or the state?

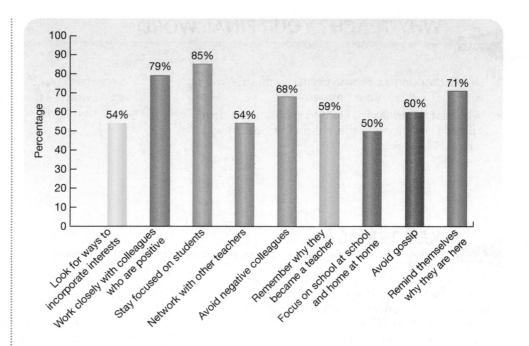

FIGURE 15.1 What Teachers Do to Stay Happy

Source: Beth Hurst, Kathleen B. Scoles and Kayla Lewis. "Happy Teachers: Resolve to Find Joy" in *Education Matters*, May, 2013, p. 2.

Professional Development, Happiness, and You

Although the school district that employs you will have a substantial impact on your growth and development as a teacher, ultimately the task of professional development is yours. In order not to become the dull, burnt-out teacher we described at the beginning of this section, you have to act. As much as possible, you have to be in control of your own professional development. Doing so will not only make you a better teacher, but it will also bring you happiness.

A study on teacher happiness that we discussed in Chapter 1, "Why Teach?," asked over a thousand teachers, "What contributes to teacher happiness?" These top two factors were selected: "Making a difference in students' lives" and "Watching students learn." Ninety-one percent of the teachers selected these factors, which are both the benefits and end products of good teaching. Along with other factors (see Figure 15.1), such as "Learning with students" (71%), "Bringing their own interests into teaching" (66%), and "Collaborating with other teachers" (63%), they point to outcomes that define professional success and individual happiness.[35]

OUR FINAL WORD

Becoming a teacher may be compared with sculpting a work of art from a piece of stone. The difference is that the teacher is both the sculptor and the stone. The teacher begins with a vision of what he or she wants to be and then sets to work transforming the vision into a reality. The process requires an understanding of the material with which one is working—the self—and of the tools one can use. It also requires a vision of the teacher one desires to become. Finally, like a good sculptor, you should expect to spend long hours of chipping away and then polishing the surfaces. To be a teacher, particularly a teacher who is continuously moving forward, is a lifelong commitment to be an artist. For you, the reader, the process has begun.

WHY TEACH? YOUR FINAL WORD

1. Do you aspire to become board certified? Why or why not? Explain your answer.

2. Which of the ideas for lifelong professional development described in this chapter appeal to you most? Why?

3. Do teachers need a professional organization? Ideally, which essential functions should such a group perform?

KEY TERMS

American Federation of Teachers (AFT) (463)
Association of American Educators (AEE) (463)
in-service programs (470)
learning organizations (469)
National Board for Professional Teaching Standards (NBPTS) (459)

National Education Association (NEA) (463)
profession (449)
Professional Learning Communities (PLCs) (474)
professional development (468)

FOR FURTHER INFORMATION

Web Resources

American Federation of Teachers www.aft.org

The AFT's website provides information on the organization and its programs, commentary on current issues, and links to other interesting web pages.

National Board for Professional Teacher Standards www.nbpts.org

This website has extensive information on the organization and the standards as well as extensive resources of interest to teachers.

National Education Association www.nea.org

This website offers a great deal of information about the NEA and its programs. Also, it has extensive information on NEA programs, conferences, and special interest groups for teachers and lays out the various benefits to member teachers.

Association of American Educators www.aaeteachers.org

The AAE's website explains this organization's unique mission as a non-union professorial organization and the various benefits for teachers, such as liability insurance, available legal representation, and its monthly publication, *Education Matters*.

Print Resources

Ken Robinson, *Out of Our Minds* (New York: Wiley, 2011).

This book is a passionate and powerful call for a radically different approach to teaching and the professional development of teachers. The message is geared to meet the new demands of twenty-first-century students.

Sylvia Martinez and Gary S. Stager, *Invent to Learn: Making, Tinkering, and Engineering in the Classroom* (On Demand Publishing, LLC-Create Space, 2013).

This practical guide describes ways to open up a classroom to new and interesting experiences and experiments providing students with direct encounters with an assortment of high- and low-tech materials.

Tina H. Boogren, *180 Days of Self-Care for Busy Educators: A 36-Week Plan of Low-Cost Self-Care for Teachers and Educators*, (Solution Tree Press, Publication date unavailable).

This teacher self-help book aims to help teachers lead a happier, healthier, more fulfilled life inside and outside of the classroom. It provides 36 weeks of daily self-care strategies and techniques, each corresponding with a week of the school year.

... Let's return to our first question, "Why teach?" Why should you select a career in the teaching profession from the myriad of occupational choices open to you? Although only you can answer these questions, we would like to offer a few final thoughts to help you grapple with them further. First, however, we need to acknowledge up front that we are biased. We have loved being a teacher. Also, the people we like and admire most in the world are teachers. And the individuals whose lives have inspired us most throughout our lives have been our teachers.

But we have worked hard in *Those Who Can, Teach* to present an honest, warts-and-all picture of the teaching profession. Like every occupation, it has its pluses and minuses. Teaching is special, however; it affects people in a deeply personal way. Think again about some of the details we reported in the first chapter, "Why Teach?"

- An incredible 96 percent of new teachers said they teach because it "is the work they *love* to do"! Surely there isn't another occupation that generates such enthusiasm.

- In a survey of school administrators, these school leaders are enormously enthusiastic about the new generation of teachers entering their schools. *Ninety-eight percent* described their new teachers as "motivated" and "energetic."

- In another study, high school graduates were asked about who they believe has most influenced them, and *three out of five* said that person was a teacher.

- The general public, too, holds teachers in extremely high regard. When asked to rate which of eight professions (including physician, lawyer, nurse, and journalist) provided the greatest benefit to society, 62 percent selected teachers. Teachers were cited *four times more* than the second choice, physicians.

This is compelling evidence that teaching is a deeply satisfying and much appreciated occupation. But here are some other points we think you should consider:

- Unless you are independently wealthy, you will have to work. Whether you are a worker in a Dilbert-like office cubicle or a forest ranger in a national park, some questions will regularly occur to you, such as, "Is what I'm doing, what I'm spending my life on, *really* significant? Is what I'm doing with my life making a difference or simply putting bread on my table and clothes on my back?" One of the greatest benefits of being a teacher is that you never have to worry about these kinds of questions. You will always be aware that you are doing profoundly important work. As a teacher, you will be changing people. You will always know that you are making *marks* on students' minds and characters. After a few years of teaching, it will be a regular occurrence to get calls and letters from former students thanking you for what you have done for them.

- You will be working with high-minded, dedicated individuals. Of course, there will be the occasional person who rushes into school in the morning unprepared and almost runs over students in her race to get out of the building at three o'clock. But they are rare. Individuals who select careers in education represent a socially crucial subgroup of people who are deeply concerned about the next generation. They want children to get a good start in life, to gain the knowledge that will give them real access to a good life. They are concerned that young people forge the habits that constitute good character. In surveys stretching over 30 years and more, *seven out of ten* practicing teachers report that their primary reason for originally selecting teaching is their *"desire to work with young people."* Their second reason is their conviction about the importance of education to society. These are the kinds of people you will be working with and be surrounded by as a teacher. Not a bad team to be on!

- It is a truism that no one goes into teaching for the big money. On the other hand, there are important quality-of-life issues to consider. We quipped earlier in the book about the three best reasons to be a teacher: June, July, and August. But summer vacations, along with winter and spring breaks, are not to be dismissed. Only having to show up for work about half the days in the year gives teachers a great deal of control over their own lives. Although much of this so-called free time is spent in study and professional development, the great majority of it is at your own disposal.

- All work, whether as a plumber or a lawyer, falls after a while into a pattern. You have done it before . . . and before that. The work becomes routine. And, yes, teaching has its patterns and its routines. Still we know of no other career where there are more elements that fight against the work becoming routine or boring. Each student is different, with different talents and learning characteristics and different learning barriers or problems. Each class has its own personality. The content you teach, whether as a second-grade teacher or a high school social studies teacher, has built-in mysteries and challenges. You will never know all there is to know about your content or about the various ways to teach it. The work of teaching is endlessly fascinating.

The Habit of Reflection

The "Why teach?" question is one theme of this book. The other is reflection, the practice of getting the full richness of the meaning out of your experiences. A teacher without this habit is like the golfer who plays regularly but never really thinks about what he is doing. In essence, he is *practicing his mistakes*. An unreflective teacher, too, makes the same mistakes over and over. Before you lay aside this book, we urge you—one last time—to stop and reflect on some important issues. In this exercise, we ask you to think about four main questions:

1. What have you learned about yourself?
2. Why will you make a successful teacher?
3. What have you learned about teaching and education, and aspects of teaching?
4. What more do you still want to know about education?

(1) What are the three most important things you have learned about yourself during this course?

a. _____

b. _____

c. _____

(2) List at least five qualities you have that will make you a successful teacher.

a. _____

b. _____

c. _____

d. _____

e. _____

(3) What are the three most important things you have learned about teaching and education, things that you did not know before the course began?

a. _____

b. _____

c. _____

(4) What aspects of teaching and education do you want to know more about? Questions you still want to have answered? Concerns you still have? List at least three questions or concerns.

a. _____

b. _____

c. _____

The habits of continually probing and examining your reasons for teaching and of routinely reflecting on what you have done in the classroom will make you a true professional. Make it your life habit!

And One Final, Final Word

You may have been wondering about the rather odd title we gave to this book: *Those Who Can, Teach.* When we were racking our brains for a title for this book, someone reminded us of the nasty comment George Bernard Shaw, the late-nineteenth-century Irish playwright, made about teachers: "Those who can, do. Those who can't, teach." Although possibly true then (which we doubt), it certainly is false now. In recent decades, the importance of education for the well-being of individuals *and* society has become more and more clear. Much of America's power and prosperity has resulted from our deep commitment to education. And teachers have been the keys to our educational achievements. In Shaw's day, many people with few skills and nothing better to do drifted into teaching. Now society takes the preparation and screening of teachers seriously. One thing is crystal clear to thoughtful observers: We need even better schools and better teachers, and people are answering the call. Shaw was dead wrong. Those who can, teach!

Endnotes

Chapter 1

1. Joel, "Fifty Reasons to Love Teaching," *Teaching Community: Where Teachers Meet and Learn,* http://teaching.monster.com/benefits/articles/9628-50-reasons-to-love-teaching.

2. Sharon Feiman-Nemser and Robert E. Floden, "The Culture of Teaching," in *The Handbook of Research on Teaching,* ed. Merlin C. Witrock (New York: Macmillan, 1986), 510–511.

3. Jordan Weissmann, "Are Teachers Paid Too Much? How 4 Studies Answered 1 Big Question," *The Atlantic,* November 4. 2011, http://www.theatlantic.com/business/archive/2011/11/are-teachers-paid-too-much-how-4-studies-answered-1-big-question/247872/.

4. David Haselkorn and Louis Harris, *The Essential Profession: A National Survey of Public Attitudes toward Teaching, Educational Opportunity and School Reform* (Belmont, MA: Recruiting New Teachers, Inc., 1998), 2. A report from the 44th annual Phi Delta Kappa/Gallup Poll of the Public's Attitudes toward the Public Schools, *Phi Delta Kappan* 94 (Sept. 2012): 15.

5. Dan Lortie, *Schoolteacher* (Chicago: University of Chicago Press, 1975), 102.

6. David Haselkorn and Louis Harris, *The Essential Profession: A National Survey of Public Attitudes toward Teaching, Educational Opportunity and School Reform* (Belmont, MA: Recruiting New Teachers, Inc., 1998), 2.

7. David Leonhardt, "The Case for $320,000 Kindergarten Teachers," *The New York Times,* July 27, 2010, http://www.nytimes.com/2010/07/28/business/economy/28leonhardt.html. Now that is true "teacher power!"

8. Mihaly Csikszentmihalyi and Jane McCormack, "The Influence of Teachers," *Phi Delta Kappan* 67, no. 6 (February 1986): 415–419.

9. *A Man for All Seasons,* directed by Fred Zinneman (1966; Highland Films Company), DVD.

10. John Goodlad, *A Place Called School* (New York: McGraw-Hill, 1984); Judith W. Little, "The Persistence of Privacy," *Teachers College Record* (Summer 1990): 509–536.

11. Carol Ann Tomlinson, "Goals of Differentiation," *Educational Leadership* (2008): 26–30.

12. Leslie A. Swetnam, "Media Distortion of the Teacher Image," *The Clearing House* (September/October 1992): 30–32.

13. The Public Agenda, *A Sense of Calling: Who Teaches and Why* (New York: Public Agenda, 2000).

14. Ibid.

15. Ibid., 36.

16. Ibid., 10.

17. Ibid.

18. Ibid., 12.

19. Ibid.

20. *The MetLife Survey of the American Teacher: Collaborating for Student Success,* April 2010, 45, http://www.metlife.com/assets/cao/contributions/foundation/american-teacher/MetLife_Teacher_Survey_2009.pdf.

21. *The Met Life Survey of the American Teacher: Challenges for School Leadership,* February 2013, 45–46, https://www.metlife.com/assets/cao/foundation/MetLife-Teacher-Survey-2012.pdf.

22. The Public Agenda, *A Sense of Calling: Who Teaches and Why* (New York: Public Agenda, 2000), 11.

23. The Public Agenda, *Attitudes about Teaching* (New York: Public Agenda, 2003), 14.

Chapter 2

1. Mike Rose, *Possible Lives* (New York: Penguin, 1995).

2. James Shaver and William Strong, *Facing Value Decisions: Rationale Building for Teachers* (Belmont, CA: Wadsworth, 1976).

3. Among the leading spokesmen for this position are Michael Apple and Henry Giroux. See Michael Apple, *Education and Power,* 2nd ed. (New York: Routledge, 1995); Henry Giroux, "Critical Pedagogy: Cultural Politics and the Discourse of Experience," *Journal of Education* 67, no. 2 (1987), 23–41.

4. Paulo Freire, *The Pedagogy of the Oppressed* (New York: Herder and Herder, 1970).

5. Jacques Barzun, *Begin Here: The Forgotten Conditions of Teaching and Learning* (Chicago: University of Chicago Press, 1991), 4, 14.

6. International Baccalaureate: Country Information for the United States, http://www.ibo.org/country/US/index.cfm.

7. Donald Kagan, "Democracy Requires a Patriotic Education," *The Wall Street Journal,* Sept 26, 2014, https://www.wsj.com/articles/donald-kagan-democracy-requires-a-patriotic-education-1411770193?mod=trending_now.

8. Personal communication with Cory Callahan of the University of North Carolina at Wilmington.

9. Eric A. Hanushek, *Education Quality and Economic Growth in the 4% Solution: Unleashing the Economic Growth America Needs* (New York: Crown Business, 2012), 226.

10. Linda Darling-Hammond, "The Flat Earth and Education: How America's Commitment to Equity Will Determine Our Future" [Third Annual Brown Lecture in Education Research], *Educational Researcher,* 36, no. 6 (2007): 331, 318–319.

11. Philip W. Jackson, *Life in Classrooms* (New York: Teachers College Press, 1990).

12. Ibid., 16.

13. E. J. Susman & A. Rogel, "Puberty and Psychological Development," in *Handbook of Adolescent Psychology,* 2nd ed., R. M. Lerner & L. D. Steinberg, eds. (New York: Wiley, 2004), 15–44.

14. X. Ge, I. J. Kim, G. Brody, R. D. Conger, R. L. Simons, F. X. Gibbons, et al. "It's about Timing and Change: Pubertal Transition Effects on Symptoms of Major Depression among African American Youths," *Developmental Psychology* 39 (2003): 430–439.

15. D. P. Keating, "Cognitive and Brain Development," in *Handbook of Adolescent Psychology,* 2nd ed., R. M. Lerner & L. D. Steinberg, eds. (New York: Wiley, 2004), 45–84.

16. Benjamin S. Bloom, *Taxonomy of Educational Objectives* (Boston, MA: Allyn and Bacon, 1956). Copyright (c) 1984 by Pearson Education.

17. Ibid.

18. J. E. Marcia, "Ego Identity Development," in *Handbook of Adolescent Psychology,* J. Adelson, ed. (New York: Wiley, 1980), 159–187.

19. C. Yecke, *The War on Excellence: The Rising Tide of Mediocrity in America's Middle Schools* (Westport, CT: Praeger, 2003).

20. Ibid.

21. Hayes Mizell, Keynote speech, 2004 Conference of the National School Boards Association's Council of Urban Boards of Education.

22. Elissa Gootman, "Trying to Find Solutions in Chaotic Middle Schools," *The New York Times,* January 3, 2007.

23. Jaana Juvonen, Vi-Nhuan Le, Tessa Kaganoff, Catherine Augustine, and Louay Constant, *Focus on the Wonder Years: Challenges Facing the American Middle School* (Santa Monica, CA: RAND, 2004), http://www.rand.org/publications/MG/MG139/.

24. Mizell, op. cit.

25. Jonah Rockoff and Benjamin B. Lockwood, "Stuck in the Middle: How and Why Middle School Harm Student Achievement." *Education Next* 10, no. 4 (Fall 2010), http://educationnext.org/stuck-in-the-middle/.

26. Grace Chen, "Should Sixth Grade Be in Elementary School or Middle School?" *Public School Review*, March 30, 2008, http://www.publicschoolreview.com/articles/13.

27. Peter D. Hart Research Associates/Public Opinion Strategies, *Rising to the Challenge: Are High School Graduates Prepared for College and Work? A Study of Recent High School Graduates, College Instructors, and Employers* (Washington, DC: Achieve Inc., February 2005).

28. Robert Balfanz, Testimony for the U.S. House of Representatives, Committee on Education and the Workforce, Washington, DC, February 16, 2012, http://www.gpo.gov/fdsys/pkg/CHRG-112hhrg72814/html/CHRG-112hhrg72814.htm.

29. "High School Dropout Crisis Threatens U.S. Economic Growth and Competitiveness," Witnesses Tell House Panel, May 12, 2009, http://edlabor.house.gov/newsroom/2009/05/high-school-dropout-crisis-thr.shtml.

30. Bill Gates, untitled speech, Governors' National Education Summit on High Schools, February 26, 2005, http://www.gatesfoundation.org/media-center/speeches/2005/02/bill-gates-2005-national-education-summit.

31. Arthur G. Powell, Eleanor Farrar, and David K. Cohen, *The Shopping Mall High School: Winners and Losers in the Educational Marketplace* (Boston: Houghton Mifflin, 1985).

32. Theodore Sizer, *Horace's Compromise: The Dilemma of the American High School* (Boston: Houghton Mifflin, 1984).

33. "About the International Baccalaureate," http://www.ibo.org/general/who.cfm.

34. "Find an IB World School," http://www.ibo.org/school/search/index.cfm?programmes=&country=US&region=&find_schools=Find.

35. James J. Kemple, *Career Academies: Long-Term Impacts on Work, Education, and Transitions to Adulthood, Publications* (MDRC, 2008), http://www.mdrc.org/publication/career-academies-long-term-impacts-work-education-and-transitions-adulthood.

36. In preparing this section, we have drawn on the following studies: W. B. Brookover, *Effective Secondary Schools* (Philadelphia: Research for Better Schools, 1981); R. Edmonds, "Effective Schools for the Urban Poor," *Educational Leadership* 32 (1979), 15–17; M. Rutter et al., *Fifteen Thousand Hours* (Cambridge, MA: Harvard University Press, 1979); J. Stallings and G. Mohlman, *School Policy, Leadership Style, Teacher Change and Student Behavior in Eight Secondary Schools* (Mountain View, CA: Stalling Teaching and Learning Institute for the National Institute of Education, 1981); R. Blum, *Effective Schooling Practices: A Research Synthesis* (Portland, OR: Northwest Regional Education Laboratory, April 1984); H. J. Walberg, "Productive Teaching and Instruction: Assessing the Knowledge Base," *Phi Delta Kappan* 71 (February 1990), 470–478; T. Toch, *In the Name of Excellence* (New York: Oxford University Press, 1991); Richard J. Murname and Frank Levy, "What General Motors Can Teach U.S. Schools about the Proper Role of Markets in Education Reform," *Phi Delta Kappan* 78 (October 1996), 113–116; P. J. Kannapel and S. K. Clements with D. Taylor and T. Hibpshman, *Inside the Black Box of High-Performing High-Poverty Schools* (Lexington, KY: Prichard Committee for Academic Excellence, 2005), http://books.google.com/books/about/Inside_the_Black_Box_of_High_performing.html?id=1uE3HAAACAAJ.

37. David C. Berliner, "Effective Classroom Teaching: The Necessary but Not Sufficient Condition for Developing Exemplary Schools," in *Research on Exemplary Schools,* ed. Gilbert R. Austin and Herbert Garber (Orlando, FL: Academic Press, 1985), 127–154.

38. Peabody-Vanderbilt University website, retrieved August 18, 2010, from http://peabody.vanderbilt.edu/x12192.xml.

39. Anthony S. Bryk and Barbara Schneider, "Trust in Schools: A Core Resource for School Reform," *Educational Leadership* 60, no. 6 (March 2003), 40–45, http://www.ascd.org/publications/educational-leadership/mar03/vol60/num06/Trust-in-Schools@-A-Core-Resource-for-School-Reform.aspx.

Chapter 3

1. Anthony Cilluffo and D'Vera Cohn, "Six Demographic Trends Shaping the U.S. and the World in 2019," https://www.pewresearch.org/fact-tank/2019/04/11/6-demographic-trends-shaping-the-u-s-and-the-world-in-2019/.

2. Jonathan Vespa, Lauren Medina, David Armstrong, "Demographic Turning Points: Population Projections for the United States: 2020–2060. U.S. Census Bureau," https://www.census.gov/content/dam/Census/newsroom/press-kits/2018/jsm/jsm-presentation-pop-projections.pdf.

3. "Overview of Race and Hispanic Origin: 2010," U.S. Census brief, http://www.census.gov/prod/cen2010/briefs/c2010br-02.pdf.

4. James A. Banks and Cherry A. McGee Banks, *Multicultural Education: Issues and Perspectives*, 6th ed. (Somerset, NJ: John Wiley & Sons, 2007), 1.

5. Carl A. Grant and Christine E. Sleeter, "Race, Class, Gender, and Disability in the Classroom," in *Multicultural Education: Issues and Perspectives*, James A. Banks and Cherry A. McGee Banks, eds., 6th ed. (Somerset, NJ: John Wiley & Sons, 2007), 66–73.

6. Geneva Gay, *Culturally Responsive Teaching: Theory, Research, and Practice* (New York: Teachers College Press, 2000); and Gloria Ladson-Billings, *Crossing Over to Canaan: The Journey of New Teachers in Diverse Classrooms* (San Francisco: Jossey-Bass, 2001).

7. Leonard Davidman and Patricia T. Davidman, *Teaching with a Multicultural Perspective: A Practical Guide* (New York: Addison-Wesley, 2001), 76–80.

8. National Center for Education Statistics, "English Language Learners in Public Schools 2019," https://nces.ed.gov/programs/coe/indicator_cgf.asp.

9. Migration Policy Institute, "U.S. Immigrant Families (By Age Group and State, 1990 versus 2018," https://www.migrationpolicy.org/programs/data-hub/charts/children-immigrant-families.

10. "Fiscal Year 2012 Refugee Arrivals," U.S. Department of Health & Human Services, http://www.acf.hhs.gov/programs/orr/resource/fiscal-year-2012-refugee-arrivals.

11. Lauv. Nichols,414 U.S. 56, http://www.nabe.org/Resources/Documents/Advocacy%20page/LauvNichols.pdf.

12. Russell Gersten and John Woodward, "A Case for Structured Immersion," *Educational Leadership* 43 (September 1985): 75.

13. U.S. Department of Education, "Title III, Language Instruction for English Learners and Immigrant Students," https://www2.ed.gov/spolicy/elsec/leg/essa/legislation/title-iii.html.

14. Wayne P. Thomas and Virginia P. Collier, "The Astounding Effectiveness of Dual Language Education for All," *NABE Journal of Research and Practice* 2, no. 1, http://njrp.tamu.edu/2004/PDFs/Collier.pdf.

15. Mary Ann Zehr, "Bilingual Ed., Immersion Found to Work Equally Well," *Education Week* (April 9, 2010), www.edweek.org/ew/articles/2010/04/09/29bilingual_ep.h29.html?qs=bilingual+education+effectiveness.

16. Enright, K. A., "Making It Matter: Relevant Instruction for New Mainstream Students," *Kappa Delta Pi Record* 48 (2012): 67–71.

17. Howard Gardner, *Frames of Mind* (New York: Basic Books, 1985); and Howard Gardner, *Multiple Intelligences: The Theory in Practice* (New York: Basic Books, 1993).

18. Seana Moran, Mindy Kornhaber, and Howard Gardner, "Orchestrating Multiple Intelligences," *Educational Leadership* 64 (September 2006): 22–27.

19. Howard Gardner, *Five Minds for the Future: Cultivating Thinking Skills* (Boston, MA: Harvard Business School Press, 2006).

20. Jay Mathews, "21 Years Later, 'Multiple Intelligences' Still Debated," *Washington Post* (September 7, 2004): A9.

21. Valerie Strauss, "Howard Gardner: 'Multiple Intelligences' Are Not Learning Styles," *Washington Post*, http://www.washingtonpost.com/blogs/answer-sheet/wp/2013/10/16/howard-gardner-multiple-intelligences-are-not-learning-styles/.

22. Council for Exceptional Children, "State of the Special Education Profession Survey Report," 2019.

23. "Special Education and the Individuals with Disabilities Education Act," National Education Association, http://nces.ed.gov/programs/digest/d11/ch_2.asp.

24. Ronald M. Hager and Diane Smith, *The Public School's Special Education System as an Assistive Technology Funding Source: The Cutting Edge* (Buffalo, NY: National Assistive Technology Advocacy Project, Neighborhood Legal Services, Inc., 2003).

25. The Appalachia Educational Laboratory, *The Link* 14, no. 1 (Spring/Summer 1995): 21.

26. Digest of Education Statistics, 2009 (Washington, DC: National Center for Education Statistics, 2010), Tables 53 and 54, http://nces.ed.gov/pubsearch/pubsinfo.asp?pubid=2010013.

27. David Sadker and Karen Zittleman, "Gender Bias: From Colonial America to Today's Classrooms," in *Multicultural Education: Issues and Perspectives*, James A. Banks and Cherry A. McGee Banks, eds., 6th ed. (Somerset, NJ: John Wiley & Sons, 2007), 149.

28. National Center for Education Statistics, "Fast Facts: Degrees Conferred by Sex and Race," http://nces.ed.gov/fastfacts/display.asp?id=72.

29. Michelle Galley, "Boys to Men," *Education Week* (January 23, 2002): 26–29.

30. Jay P. Greene and Marcus A. Winters, "Leaving Boys Behind: Public High School Graduation Rates," *Civic Report*, 48 (April 2006) (New York, NY: Manhattan Institute for Policy Research), www.manhattan-institute.org/html/cr_48.htm.

31. Tim King, "Tim King Explains Why There's No Secret Recipe for a Successful School," *Chicago Sun-Times*, April 5, 2013, http://www.suntimes.com/19278797-761/tim-king-explains-why-theres-no-secret-recipe-for-a-successful-school.html.

32. The Trevor Project, "The Trevor Project's Second Annual Survey Reveals Urgent Need for Mental Health Care and Support Systems for LGBTQ Youth," https://www.thetrevorproject.org/trvr_press/the-trevor-projects-second-annual-national-survey-reveals-urgent-need-for-mental-health-care-and-support-systems-for-lgbtq-youth/.

33. National Center for Education Statistics, "Characteristics of Public School Teachers," https://nces.ed.gov/programs/coe/indicator_clr.asp.

Chapter 4

1. Lisbeth Bamberger Schorr, "Effective Programs for Children Growing Up in Concentrated Poverty," in *Children in Poverty*, ed. A. C. Huston (Cambridge, UK: University of Cambridge Press, 1991), 261–262.

2. Ibid.

3. Pew Research, *As U.S. Marriage Rate Hovers at 50%, Education Gap in Marital Status Widens*, 2017, https://www.pewresearch.org/fact-tank/2017/09/14/as-u-s-marriage-rate-hovers-at-50-education-gap-in-marital-status-widens/.

4. Annie E. Casey Foundation, *2019 State Trends in Child Well Being*, https://www.aecf.org/resources/2019-kids-count-data-book/.

5. Ibid., 21.

6. US Census Bureau, *How the US Census Measures Poverty*; US Census Bureau, *Income, Poverty, and Health Insurance Coverage in the United States: 2019* (p. 18–19).

7. Kids Count, *2013 Data Book: State Trends in Child Well-Being*, http://datacenter.kidscount.org/files/2013KIDSCOUNTDataBook.pdf, 24.

8. CLASP, "Child Poverty in the U.S.," p. 2, http://www.clasp.org/admin/site/publications/files/9.18.13-CensusPovertyData_FactSheet.pdf.

9. National Center on Family Homelessness, www.familyhomelessness.org/facts.php?p=sm.

10. National Association for the Education of Homeless Children and Youth, "Facts and Resources about the Education of Children and Youth Experiencing Homelessness?," http://www.naehcy.org/sites/default/files/dl/homeless-ed-101.pdf.

11. Education for Homeless Children and Youth Program, "Title VII-B of the McKinney–Vento Homeless Assistance Act (as Amended by the No Child Left Behind Act of 2001), Non-Regulatory Guidance" (Washington, DC: U.S. Department of Education, 2004), www.ed.gov/programs/homeless/guidance.pdf.

12. Centers for Disease Control and Prevention, "About Teen Pregnancy," http://www.cdc.gov/teenpregnancy/aboutteenpreg.htm.

13. Centers for Disease Control and Prevention, "NCHS Data Brief," http://www.cdc.gov/nchs/data/databriefs/db89.htm.

14. Centers for Disease Control and Prevention *Reproductive Health: Teen Pregnancy*, https://www.cdc.gov/teenpregnancy/about/index.htm.

15. Rebecca A. Maynard, "The Study, the Context, and the Findings in Brief," *Kids Having Kids*, http://www.urban.org/pubs/khk/summary.html.

16. *Child Maltreatment 2011* (Washington, DC: U.S. Department of Health and Human Services, Administration for Children and Families), http://www.acf.hhs.gov/sites/default/files/cb/cm11.pdf#page=11.

17. U.S. Department of Health & Human Services, *A Picture of Adolescent Health*, https://www.hhs.gov/ash/oah/facts-and-stats/picture-of-adolescent-health/index.html.

18. Child Trends, *Illicit Drug Use*, https://www.childtrends.org/indicators/illicit-drug-use-2.

19. NIDA, *Vaping Popular Among Teens: Opioid Misuse at Historic Lows*, June 4, 2020, https://www.drugabuse.gov/news-events/news-releases/2017/12/vaping-popular-among-teens-opioid-misuse-at-historic-lows.

20. J. M. Twenge, A. B. Cooper, T. E. Joiner, M. E. Duffy, S. G. Binau, "Age, Period, and Cohort Trends in Mood Disorder Indicators and Suicide-Related Outcomes in a Nationally Representative Dataset, 2005–2017," *J Abnorm Psychol.* 128(3) (2019):185–199. doi:10.1037/abn0000410

21. See http://neatoday.org/2018/09/13/mental-health-in-schools/.

22. See https://www.nasponline.org/resources-and-publications/resources-and-podcasts/mental-health/school-psychology-and-mental-health/school-based-mental-health-services.

23. United Health Foundation, *America's Health Rankings Analysis of CDC WONDER Online Database, Underlying Cause of Death, Multiple Cause of Death Files*, AmericasHealthRankings.org,

24. See https://www.mentalhealth.gov/talk/educators.

25. See https://nces.ed.gov/fastfacts/display.asp?id=49.

26. National Gang Center, "National Youth Gang Survey Analysis: Measuring the Extent of Gang Problems," http://www.nationalgangcenter.gov/Survey-Analysis/Measuring-the-Extent-of-Gang-Problems.

27. Centers for Disease Control and Prevention, *School Associated Violent Death Study*, https://www.cdc.gov/violenceprevention/youthviolence/schoolviolence/SAVD.html.

28. See https://www.stopbullying.gov/resources/facts.

29. Susan M. Swearer, Dorothy L. Espelage, Tracy Vaillancourt, and Shelley Hymel, "What Can Be Done about School Bullying? Linking Research to Educational Practice," *Educational Researcher* 39 (January/February 2010): 42.

30. National Center for Education Statistics, "Indicators of School Crime and Safety, 2012," http://nces.ed.gov/programs/crimeindicators/crimeindicators2012/index.asp.

31. Josephson Institute Center for Youth Ethics, "The Ethics of American Youth," http://charactercounts.org/programs/reportcard/2010/index.html.

32. J. McFarland, J. Cui, J. Holmes, and X. Wang., *Trends in High School Dropout and Completion Rates in the United States: 2019* (NCES 2020-117) (U.S. Department of Education. Washington, DC: National Center for Education Statistics, 2019), https://nces.ed.gov/pubsearch.

33. J. Cui, A. Rathnurn, and J. Holmes. *Trends in High School Dropout and Completeion Rates: 2018* (Washington, DC: National Center for Education Statistics, 2018), https://nces.ed.gov/pubs2019/2019117.pdf

34. Ibid.

Chapter 5

1. Catherine Cornbleth, "Hidden Curriculum," in James W. Guthrie, ed., *Encyclopedia of Education,* 2nd ed. (New York: Macmillan Reference USA, 2003), 537–539.

2. Elliot W. Eisner, *The Educational Imagination,* 3rd ed. (Upper Saddle River, NJ: Prentice Hall, 2001), 87–97.

3. Karin Chenoweth, "Reading Wars, Take 2," *The Washington Post Magazine* (May 16, 1999): 17.

4. Tricia Underwood, "Recent Trends in Literacy and Reading Instruction," *Reading Horizons* (August 16, 2012), http://www.readinghorizons.com/blog/post/2012/08/16/new-approaches-to-reading-literacy.aspx.

5. Steve Leinwand and Steve Fleischman, "Teaching Mathematics Right the First Time," *Educational Leadership* 62 (September 2004): 86.

6. Arthur W. Foshay, "Knowledge and the Structure of the Disciplines," in William A. Jenkins, ed., *The Nature of Knowledge: Implications for the Education of Teachers* (Milwaukee: University of Wisconsin Press, 1961).

7. National Council for the Social Studies, *Expectations of Excellence: Curriculum Standards for Social Studies* (Washington, DC: Author, 1994).

8. American Councils, *The National K-16 Foreign Language Enrollment Survey Report, 2017,* https://www.americancouncils.org/sites/default/files/FLE-report.pdf.

9. "What Is Career and Technical Education, Anyway?" *Education Week* (July 31, 2018), https://www.edweek.org/ew/issues/career-technical-education/index.html.

10. Dian Schaffhauser, "Feds to Pump $1.2 Billion into CTE Next Year," *The Journal* (August 20, 2018), https://thejournal.com/articles/2018/08/20/feds-to-pump-1.2-billion-into-cte.aspx.

11. NAEP, Reading Assessment 2019, *The Nation's Report Card,* http://nces.ed.gov/nationsreportcard.

12. NAEP, U.S. History 2010, *The Nation's Report Card,* http://nces.ed.gov/nationsreportcard.

13. *The Nation's Report Card,* http://nces.ed.gov/nationsreportcard.

14. TIMMS and PIRLS International Study Center, Boston College, Lynch School of Education, https://timssandpirls.bc.edu/.

15. PISA 2018 U.S. Results (Washington, DC, National Center for Education Statistics), https://nces.ed.gov/surveys/pisa/pisa2018/index.asp#/.

16. National Science Board, "Science and Engineering Indicators 2018," https://nsf.gov/statistics/2018/nsb20181/report/sections/elementary-and-secondary-mathematics-and-science-education/high-school-coursetaking-in-mathematics-and-science.

17. William Schmidt, "Are There Surprises in the TIMSS Twelfth Grade Results?" in *TIMSS United States, Report No. 8* (East Lansing, MI: United States National Research Center [TIMSS], April 1998), 4.

18. National Education Commission, *Prisoners of Time: A Report of the National Education Commission on Time and Learning* (Washington, DC: U.S. Government Printing Office, 1994), 23.

19. Jason Tomassini, "Educators Weigh E-Textbook Cost Comparisons," *Education Week* (May 9, 2012): 1, 18–19.

20. Larry Cuban, *How Teachers Taught: Constancy and Change in American Classrooms, 1890–1980* (New York: Longman, 1984).

21. Robert E. Slavin, *Cooperative Learning,* 2nd ed. (Boston: Allyn and Bacon, 1995), 3–4.

22. Ibid., 14–70.

23. Scott Willis and Larry Mann, "Differentiating Instruction," *Curriculum Update,* Association for Supervision and Curriculum Development (Winter 2000): 2.

24. Mortimer Adler, *The Paideia Proposal* (New York: Macmillan, 1982).

25. E. D. Hirsch, Jr., *Cultural Literacy* (Boston: Houghton Mifflin, 1987). Also see the Core Knowledge Foundation's website at www.coreknowledge.org.

26. Core Knowledge Foundation, "Learn about Core Knowledge Schools," http://www.coreknowledge.org/about-core-knowledge-schools.

27. Debra Viadero, "On the Wrong Track," *Teacher Magazine* (January 1999): 22–23.

28. Dominic Brewer, Daniel Rees, and Laura Argys, "Detracking America's Schools: The Reform without Cost?" *Phi Delta Kappan* 77 (November 1995): 212–215.

29. Ian Quillen, "More Top Scores Found in Tracked Schools," *Education Week* (December 16, 2009): 4.

Chapter 6

1. J. W. Getzels and P. W. Jackson, "The Teacher's Personality and Characteristics," in *Handbook of Research on Teaching,* N. L. Gage, ed. (Chicago: Rand McNally, 1963), 574.

2. Thomas L. Good and Jere E. Brophy, *Looking in Classrooms,* 10th ed. (Boston: Allyn and Bacon, 2008), 49–51.

3. Lee S. Shulman, "Knowledge and Teaching: Foundations of the New Reform," *Harvard Educational Review* 57 (February 1987): 8.

4. Chris Argyris and Donald A. Schon, *Theory in Practice: Increasing Professional Effectiveness* (San Francisco: Jossey-Bass, 1974), 3–19.

5. B. O. Smith et al., *Teachers for the Real World* (Washington, DC: American Association of Colleges for Teacher Education, 1969), 44.

6. Richard Kindsvatter, William Wilen, and Margaret Ishler, *Dynamics of Effective Teaching* (White Plains, NY: Longman, 1996), 2–3.

7. Carol Weinstein and Wilford A. Weber, "Classroom Management," in James M. Cooper, ed., *Classroom Teaching* Skills, 10th ed. (Belmont, CA: Wadsworth, Cengage Learning, 2014), 240.

8. David C. Berliner, "Effective Classroom Teaching: The Necessary but Not Sufficient Condition for Developing Exemplary Schools," in *Research on Exemplary Schools,* Gilbert R. Austin and Herbert Garber, eds. (Orlando, FL: Academic Press, 1985), 136–138; Gary D. Borich, *Effective Teaching Methods,* 6th ed. (Upper Saddle River, NJ: Pearson Education, 2007), 14–15.

9. Carol Weinstein and Wilford A. Weber, "Classroom Management," in *Classroom Teaching Skills,* 10th ed., James M. Cooper (ed.) (Belmont, CA: Wadsworth, Cengage Learning, 2014), 247–248.

10. Ibid., 249.

11. Ibid.

12. Ibid., 249–254.

13. Ibid., 254–257.

14. Good and Brophy, *Looking in Classrooms,* 94.

15. Alfie Kohn, "Beyond Discipline," *Education Week* (November 20, 1996): 37, 48.

16. Good and Brophy, *Looking in Classrooms,* 55–56, 320–322.

17. Ibid., 320–322.

18. Ibid., 317–320; William W. Wilen and Ambrose A. Clegg, Jr., "Effective Questions and Questioning: A Research Review," *Theory and Research in Social Education* (Spring 1986): 153–161.

19. Greta Morine-Dershimer, "Instructional Planning," in *Classroom Teaching Skills,* 10th ed., J. M. Cooper, ed. (Belmont, CA: Wadsworth, Cengage Learning, 2014), 56.

20. Ibid.

21. Mardell Raney, "*Technos* Interview with Jonathan Kozol," *Technos* 7, no. 3 (Fall 1998): 10.

Chapter 7

1. David A. Dockterman, "A Teacher's Tools," *Instructor* 100 (January 1991): 58–61.

2. Gene White, "From Magic Lanterns to Microcomputers: The Evolution of the Visual Aid in the English Classroom," *English Journal,* 73 (March 1984): 59.

3. Paul Saettler, *The Evolution of American Educational Technology* (Englewood, CO: Libraries Unlimited, 1990), 98.

4. Ruben R. Puentedura, "SAMR: A Brief Introduction." (October 2015) hippasus.com/rrpweblog/archives/2015/10/SAMR_ABriefIntro.pdf.

5. Mark Hofer, Robb Ponton, and Kathleen Swan, "Reinventing Power-Point: A New Look at an Old Tool," *Social Studies Research and Practice* 1 (Winter 2006): 457–464.

6. Lee Rainie, "Cell Phone Ownership Hits 91% of Adults," Pew Research Center, http://www.pewresearch.org/fact-tank/2013/06/06/cell-phone-ownership-hits-91-of-adults/.

7. Ibid.

8. Jamie Condliff, "The Average American Spends 24 Hours a Week Online," *MIT Technology Review* (January 23, 2018), https://www.technologyreview.com/2018/01/23/146069/the-average-american-spends-24-hours-a-week-online/.

9. J. Clement, "Daily Number of E-mails Worldwide 2023," *Statista* (August 9, 2019), https://www.statista.com/statistics/456500/daily-number-of-e-mails-worldwide/.

10. "Screen Time and Children," *American Academy of Child and Adolescent Psychiatry* (February 2020), https://www.aacap.org/AACAP/Families_and_Youth/Facts_for_Families/FFF-Guide/Children-And-Watching-TV-054.aspx.

11. Zeynep Tufekci, *Technosociology: Our Tools, Ourselves* (blog), http://technosociology.org/?p=832.

12. Howard Gardner and Katie Davis, *The App Generation: How Today's Youth Navigate Identity, Intimacy, and Imagination in a Digital World* (New Haven, CT: Yale University Press, 2016).

13. "Youth Statistics: Internet & Social Media," *ACT for Youth* (2018), http://actforyouth.net/adolescence/demographics/internet.cfm.

14. M. Anderson and J. Jiang, "Teens, Social Media & Technology 2018," Pew Research Center: Internet, Science & Tech (May 2018), https://www.pewresearch.org/internet/2018/05/31/teens-social-media-technology-2018/.

15. "Educator Confidence Report," *2019 Educator Confidence Report* (Houghton Mifflin Harcourt, 2019), https://www.hmhco.com/educator-confidence-report.

16. Office of Educational Technology, *National Education Technology Plan*, 2010, p. ix.

17. L. S. Shulman, "Those Who Understand: Knowledge Growth in Teaching," *Educational Researcher* 15, no. 2 (1986): 4–14.

18. M. J. Koehler and P. Mishra, "What Is Technological Pedagogical Content Knowledge?" *Contemporary Issues in Technology and Teacher Education* 9, no. 1 (2009): 60–70.

19. David H. Jonassen, *Modeling with Technology: Mindtools for Contemporary Change*, 3rd ed. (Englewood Cliffs, NJ: Prentice Hall, 2005), 3. The concept of a computer application as a cognitive tool follows from the idea that "learning is a consequence of thinking"; see David Perkins, *Smart Schools: Better Thinking and Learning for Every Child* (New York: Free Press, 1992), 8.

20. Beaumie Kim and Thomas C. Reeves, "Reframing Research on Learning with Technology: In Search of the Meaning of Cognitive Tools," *Instructional Science* 35 (January 2007): 207–256.

21. Cleborne D. Maddux, D. LaMont Johnson, and Jerry W. Willis, *Educational Computing: Learning with Tomorrow's Technologies*, 3rd ed. (Boston: Allyn and Bacon, 2001), 204–205.

22. Diane Schaffhauser, "Teacher Confidence in Ed Tech on the Rise, But Not Feelings About the Profession," *THE Journal* (January 2019), https://thejournal.com/articles/2019/01/22/teacher-confidence-in-ed-tech-on-the-rise-but-not-feelings-about-the-profession.aspx.

23. Kristen Purcell, Judy Buchanan, Linda Friedrich, "The Impact of Digital Tools on Student Writing and How Writing is Taught in Schools," National Writing Project (July 16, 2013), http://www.nwp.org/afnews/PIP_NWP_Writing_and_Tech.pdf.

24. Matthew Maurer, "Supporting Language and Literacy Development with Technology," in *Leadership in Instructional Technology*, Matthew Maurer and George Steven Davidson, eds. (Upper Saddle River, NJ: Merrill, 1998), 79.

25. Andrew Trotter, "Teaching the Basics: Beyond Drill and Practice," *Technology Counts '98, in Education Week* (October 1, 1998): 25–27.

26. Dale Hubert, M.Ed, "Flat Stanley Project" (1995), http://www.flatstanleyproject.com/.

27. Randy L. Bell, John C. Park, and Doug Toti, "Digital Images in the Science Classroom," *Learning and Leading with Technology* 31 (May 2004): 26–28.

28. Candy Beal and Cheryl Mason, "Virtual Field Tripping: No Permission Notes Needed. Creating a Middle School Classroom Without Walls," *Meridian* 2 (January 1999), www.ncsu.edu/meridian/jan99/vfieldtrip/index.html.

29. Jeffrey Hovermill Shamatha, Dominic Peressini, and Kirsten Meymaris, "Technology-Supported Mathematics Activities Situated within an Effective Learning Environment Theoretical Framework," *Contemporary Issues in Technology and Teacher Education* 3, (2004): 362–381.

30. National Council of Teachers of Mathematics, *Principles and Standards for School Mathematics* (Reston, VA: The National Council of Teachers of Mathematics, 2000), 24, www.nctm.org/standards.

31. Kelsey J. Sinclair, Carl E. Renshawa, and Holly A. Taylor, "Improving Computer-Assisted Instruction in Teaching," *Computers & Education* 42 (2004): 169–180.

32. Robyn Pierce and Kaye Stacey, "Monitoring Progress in Algebra in a CAS Active Context: Symbol Sense, Algebraic Insight and Algebraic Expectation," *The International Journal of Computer Algebra in Mathematics Education* 11 (2004): 3–11.

33. Ann M. Farrell, "Teaching and Learning Behaviors in Technology-Oriented Precalculus Classrooms," PhD dissertation, Ohio State University, *Dissertation Abstracts International* 51 (1990): 100A.

34. Lori Langer de Ramirez, *Empower English Language Learners with Tools from the Web* (Thousand Oaks, CA. Corwin, 2010).

35. International Association for K-12 Online Learning, "Key K-12 Online Learning Stats," *Fast Facts about Online Learning*, http://www.inacol.org/cms/wp-content/uploads/2013/11/iNACOL-Fast-Facts-About-Online-Learning-October-2013.pdf.

36. Alex Molnar, "Virtual Schools in the U.S. 2019" *National Education Policy Center* (May 2019), http://nepc.colorado.edu/sites/default/files/publications/Virtual%20Schools%202019.pdf.

37. Patricia Hutinger, Carol Bell, Gary Daytner, and Joyce Johanson, *Disseminating and Replicating an Effective Emerging Literacy Technology Curriculum: A Final Report* (Washington, DC: U.S. Office of Special Education Programs, July 2005), 6–7.

38. Mary Seegers, "Special Technological Possibilities for Students with Special Needs," *Learning and Leading with Technology* 29 (November 2001): 32–39.

39. National Educational Technology Standards for Students, http://cnets.iste.org/.

40. Sara Dexter, Aaron Doering, and Eric S. Riedel, "Content Area Specific Technology Integration: A Model for Educating Teachers," *Journal of Technology and Teacher Education* 14 (April 2006).

41. Thomas C. Reeves, "Technology in Teacher Education: From Electronic Tutor to Cognitive Tool," *Action in Teacher Education* 17 (1996): 74.

42. David Jonassen, Jane Howland, Rose M. Marra, and David Crismond, *Meaningful Learning with Technology*, 3rd ed. (Upper Saddle River, NJ: Pearson, 2008).

43. Henry Jay Becker and Jason Ravitz, "The Influence of Computer and Internet Use on Teachers' Pedagogical Practices and Perceptions," *Journal of Research on Computing in Education* 31 (Summer 1999): 356–384. See also Laura M. O'Dwyer, Michael Russell, and Damian J. Bebell, "Identifying Teacher, School and District Characteristics Associated with Elementary Teachers' Use of Technology: A Multilevel Perspective," *Education Policy Analysis Archives* 12 (September 2004): 1–31; and Peter E. Doolittle and David Hicks, "Constructivism as a Theoretical Foundation for the Use of Technology in Social Studies," *Theory and Research in Social Education* 31 (2003): 72–104.

44. William R. Johnston and Tiffany Berglund, "The Prevalence of Collaboration Among American Teachers: National Findings from the American Teacher Panel" (2018), https://www.rand.org/pubs/research_reports/RR2217.html.

45. Reenay R. H. Rodgers and Vivian H. Wright, *You've Got Mail: Using Technology to Communicate with Parents.* Paper presented June 25, 2007, at the National Educational Computing Conference, Atlanta, GA.

46. Andres Jauregui, "Laraine Cook, High School Coach, Fired over Facebook Photo that Shows Fiancé Holding Her Breast," http://www.huffingtonpost.com/2013/11/07/laraine-cook-fired-facebook-photo-breast_n_4234128.html; see also Ian Shapira, "When Young Teachers Go Wild on the Web," http://www.washingtonpost.com/wp-dyn/content/article/2008/04/27/AR2008042702213.html.

47. Facebook, "Family Safety Center," https://www.facebook.com/help/safety.

48. Joe Garafolo, Glen Bull, Randy Bell, and Stephanie van Hover, "Interactive Whole-Class Display Systems," *Learning and Leading with Technology* 32 (October 2004): 28–31.

49. "Apple iPad Sales to Schools Jump 32%, Selling 1M Tablets in Fiscal Q3 2017," *Edsurge* (August 2017), https://www.edsurge.com/news/2017-08-02-apple-ipad-sales-to-schools-jump-32-selling-1m-tablets-in-fiscal-q3-2017.

50. Natasha Singer, "How Google Took Over The Classroom" *New York Times* (May 13, 2017), https://www.nytimes.com/2017/05/13/technology/google-education-chromebooks-schools.html.

51. Collier, Sunya, Molly H. Weinburgh, and Mark Rivera, "Infusing Technology Skills into a Teacher Education Program: Change in Students' Knowledge about and Use of Technology," *Journal of Technology and Teacher Education* 12, no. 3 (2004): 447–468.

52. "2019 BROADBAND DEPLOYMENT REPORT" *Federal Communications Commission* (May 29, 2019), https://docs.fcc.gov/public/attachments/FCC-19-44A1.pdf.

53. Kathryn Zickuhr and Aaron Smith, "Home Broadband 2013," http://www.pewinternet.org/Reports/2013/Broadband/Findings/Further-reading.aspx.

54. Paul Attewell, "The First and Second Digital Divides," *Sociology of Education,* 74(3) (2001): 252–259.

55. Stephen Noonoo, "Equity Isn't Just About Technology. It's About Supporting Students and Families," *EdSurge* (March 2020), https://www.edsurge.com/news/2020-03-26-equity-isn-t-just-about-technology-it-s-about-supporting-students-and-families.

56. Juan Vasquez, "Forget Rap and the NFL, This Watts Teen Has iPhone Apps in Mind," *Huffington Post* (2013), https://www.huffpost.com/entry/forget-rap-and-the-nfl-th_b_3984885.

57. Kathryn Zickuhr and Aaron Smith, "Digital Differences," Pew Research Internet Project, http://pewinternet.org/Reports/2012/Digital-differences/Overview.aspx.

58. Sarah Chase Webber, "The Library's Role in Bridging the Digital Divide," *Urban Libraries Council* (March 2019), https://www.urbanlibraries.org/blog/the-librarys-role-in-bridging-the-digital-divide.

59. Cornelia Brunner, Dorothy Bennett, and Margaret Honey, "Technology, Gender, and Education: Defining the Problem," paper prepared for the AAUW Commission on Gender, Technology, and Teacher Education, October 1998.

60. Cornelia Brunner, "Opening Technology to Girls," *Electronic Learning* 16 (February 1997): 55.

61. Amanda Lenhart and Mary Madden, "Teen Content Creators and Consumers" (2005), https://www.pewresearch.org/internet/2005/11/02/teen-content-creators-and-consumers/.

62. Jill Casner-Lotto and Linda Barrington, *Are They Really Ready to Work? Employers' Perspectives on the Basic Knowledge and Applied Skills of New Entrants to the 21st Century U.S. Workforce* (New York, 2006), www.21stcenturyskills.org/documents/FINAL_REPORT_PDF9-29-06.pdf.

63. Larry Cuban, "Techno-Reformers and Classroom Teachers," *Education Week* 16 (October 9, 1996).

64. "Digital Citizenship Curriculum," *Common Sense Media,* https://www.commonsense.org/education/digital-citizenship/curriculum.

65. Judi Harris, *Virtual Architecture: Designing and Directing Curriculum-Based Telecomputing* (Eugene, OR: International Society for Technology in Education, 1998).

Chapter 8

1. From Kenneth R. Howe, "A Conceptual Basis for Ethics in Teacher Education," *Journal of Teacher Education* 37 (May–June 1986): 6. Reprinted with permission.

2. Ibid.

3. Ibid, 6.

4. See https://www.aaeteachers.org/index.php/about-us/aae-code-of-ethics.

5. See https://education.alaska.gov/teachercertification/20aac10.

6. Steven Tigner, *Educator's Affirmation* (Boston and Toledo, OH: Boston University and University of Toledo, 1989). Reprinted by permission of Steven Tigner.

7. Kern Alexander and M. David Alexander, "Due Process Rights of Teachers," in *American Public School Law,* 7th ed. (Belmont, CA: Thomson West, 2009), 887–919.

8. *U.S.L. Week 4223,* March 24, 1970, quoted in Louis Fischer and David Schimmel, *The Rights of Students and Teachers* (New York: Harper and Row, 1982), 323. Much of this chapter is drawn from the material presented in this excellent and highly readable book, and also from Louis Fischer, David Schimmel, and Cynthia Kelly, *Teachers and the Law,* 4th ed. (1995), 5th ed. (1998), and 6th ed. (2002) (New York: Addison-Wesley Longman).

9. Fischer, Schimmel, and Kelly, *Teachers and the Law,* 5th ed., 20.

10. *Smith v. School District of the Township of Darby,* quoted in Fischer, Schimmel, and Kelly, *Teachers and the Law,* 5th ed., 31.

11. Perry A. Zirkel, "Teacher Tenure Is Not the Real Problem," *Phi Delta Kappan* (September 2010): 76–77.

12. Adrienne Lu, "North Carolina Ends Teacher Tenure," *Pew Stateline,* July 29, 2013.

13. *Smith v. School District of the Township of Darby,* p. 38.

14. Ibid., 47.

15. Edwin Darden, "Firing a Teacher is Getting Easier," *Phi Delta Kappan* (December 2012): 68–69.

16. Ibid., 76–77.

17. Ibid., 101.

18. *Pickering v. Board of Education,* 225 N.E. 2d 1 (1967); 391 U.S. 563 (1968).

19. Alexander and Alexander, "Due Process Rights of Teachers," 555–556.

20. Perry Zirkel, "You Can't Touch Me!" *Phi Delta Kappan* (May 2011): 76–77.

21. Ibid., 640–641.

22. *Scoville v. Board of Education,* 425 F. 2d 10 (7th Cir. 1970).

23. *Anderson v. Evans,* 660 F. 2d 153 (6th Cir. 1981).

24. *Stroman v. Colleton County School District,* 981 F. 2d 152 (4th Cir. 1992).

25. Fischer, Schimmel, and Kelly, *Teachers and the Law,* 5th ed., 166.

26. Perry A. Zirkel, "MySpace?" *Phi Delta Kappan* 90 (January 2009): 388–389.

27. Mark G. Yudof, David L. Kirp, Betsy Levin, and Rachel F. Moran, *Educational Policy and the Law,* 4th ed. (Belmont, CA: West/Thomson Learning), 255–256.

28. Ibid., 256.

29. Ibid., 257.

30. Fischer, Schimmel, and Kelly, *Teachers and the Law,* 5th ed., 169.

31. Ibid., 169.

32. Thomas R. McDaniel, "The Teacher's Ten Commandments: School Law in the Classroom," *Phi Delta Kappan*, 60, no. 10 (June 1979): 707.

33. Fischer, Schimmel, and Kelly, *Teachers and the Law*, 5th ed., 451.

34. Ibid., 324.

35. Ibid., 297–298.

36. Ibid., 307.

37. Stuart Biegel, *The Right to Be Out: Sexual Orientation and Gender Identity in America's Public Schools* (University of Minnesota Press, 2010).

38. Fischer, Schimmel, and Kelly, *Teachers and the Law*, 5th ed., 306.

39. Bill Mears, "Court Dismisses Pledge Case," CNN.com, www.cnn.com/2004/LAW/06/14/scotus.pledge/.

40. *Lee* v. *Weisman* (90-104) 505 U.S. 577 (1992).

41. *Santa Fe Independent School District* v. *Department of Education* (99-62) 168 F. 3d 806.

42. Benjamin Senor, "Even After the Supreme Court Ruling, We're Still in the Dark about Religion Clubs at School," *American School Board Journal* 173 (August 1986): 17.

43. Cheryl D. Mills, "Important Education-Related U.S. Supreme Court Decisions," in *Challenges and Achievements of American Education*, Cordon Cawalti, ed. (Alexandria, VA: Association for Supervision and Curriculum Development, 1993), 192.

44. Caroline Hendrie, "Teacher May Lead Bible Lessons at Her Own School, Court Rules," *Education Week* (September 9, 2002).

45. Stephen Arons, "Separation of School and State," *Education Week* (November 17, 1984): 24.

46. Thomas J. Flygare, "Supreme Court Strikes Down Louisiana Creationism Act," *Phi Delta Kappan* 69 (September 1987): 77–79.

47. Rebecca Klein, "Kansas' New Science Standards Make Evolution and Climate Change Key Part of Curriculum," Huffington Post: Politics (June 14, 2013).

48. *Mozert* v. *Hawkins County Board of Education*, U.S. Dist. Ct. (E.D. Tenn.) 647 F Supp. 1194 (1987).

49. *Smith* v. *Board of School Commissioners of Mobile County*, no. 87-7216 (11th Cir., 26 September 1987).

50. Thomas R. McDaniel, "The Teacher's Ten Commandments: School Law in the Classroom," *Phi Delta Kappan* 60 (June 1979): 703. Reprinted with permission of the author.

51. Richard Riley, Secretary of Education, and Walter Dellinger, Assistant Attorney General, White House press release, July 12, 1995, pp. 2–4.

52. *Tinker* v. *Des Moines Independent Community School District*, 393 U.S. 503 (1969).

53. Fischer, Schimmel, and Kelly, *Teachers and the Law*, 5th ed., 271.

54. Nelda Cambron-McCabe, Martha McCarthy, and Stephen Thomas, *Public School Law: Teachers' and Students' Rights*, 5th ed. (Boston: Allyn & Bacon, 2004).

55. U.S. Department of Education, *Early Warning, Timely Response: A Guide to Safe Schools*, http://www2.ed.gov/about/offices/list/osers/osep/gtss.html.

56. *Goss* v. *Lopez*, 95 S. Ct. 729 (1975).

57. *Honig* v. *Doe*, 108 S. Ct. 592, 605 (1988).

58. Perry A. Zirkel, "Balancing Students' Rights," *Phi Delta Kappan* (April 2010): 77–78.

59. *Fuller* v. *Decatur Public School Board of Education School District 61*, 78 F. Supp. 2d 812 (C.D. Ill. 2000).

60. Yudof, Kirp, Levin, and Moran, *Educational Policy and the Law*, p. 525.

61. Darcia Harris Bowman, "District Dress Code Attracts Nationwide Attention," *Education Week* (October 15, 2003): 10.

62. "Fashion Dictates," *Education Week*, Teacher Blogs, http://blogs.edweek.org/teachers/webwatch/2006/09/fashion_dicates.html.

63. The Center for Effective Discipline, "Discipline at School," www.stophitting.com/index.php?page=statesbanning.

64. See https://www.edweek.org/ew/articles/2016/08/23/corporal-punishment-use-found-in-schools-in.html.

65. Fischer, Schimmel, and Kelly, *Teachers and the Law*, 5th ed., 268.

66. Ibid., 279.

67. *New Jersey* v. *T.L.O.*, 105 S. Ct. 733 (1985).

68. Perry A. Zirkel, "Turning the Tide," *Phi Delta Kappan* (September 2009): 76–77.

69. *Vernonia School District 47J* v. *Acton*, 115 S. Ct. 2386 (1995), as reported in Yudof, Kirp, Levin, and Moran, *Educational Policy and the Law*, pp. 317–320.

70. Quoted on the Monterey County Chapter of the ACLU, http://www.aclumontereycounty.org/contest2008/contest2008_essay_m2.html.

71. *Tinker* v. *Des Moines Independent Community School District*.

72. *Bethel School District no. 403* v. *Fraser*, 106 S. Ct. 3159 (1986).

73. Linda Greenhouse, "Vote against Banner Shows Divide on Speech in Schools," *New York Times Online* (June 26, 2007), www.nytimes.com/2007/06/26/washington/26speech.html?_r=1&adxnnl=1&oref=slogin&adxnnlx=1182860348-+JKe2p4I+8N5fnutayh8Lw.

74. *Hazelwood School District* v. *Kuhlmeier*, 56 U.S.L.W. 4079, 4082 (January 12, 1988).

75. Ibid.

76. American Association of University Women, *Hostile Hallways: The AAUW Survey on Sexual Harassment in America's Schools* (New York: Louis Harris Associations, 1993), 6.

77. *Davis* v. *Monroe County Board of Education*, 119 S. Ct. 1661 (1999).

78. Ibid.

79. *Owasso Independent School District* v. *Falvo*, 534 S. Ct. 00–1073.

Chapter 9

1. Aristotle, *Politics*. Translated by T. A. Sinclair (Middlesex, England: Penguin, 1978).

2. Richard M. Felder and Barbara A. Soloman, "Learning Styles and Strategies," www4.ncsu.edu/unity/lockers/users/f/felder/public/ILSdir/styles.htm.

3. "Can Character Be Taught?" Transcription of the Aspen Institute Ideas Festival 2012. Colorado: Aspen Institute, July 1, 2012; and Caralee J. Adams, "Character Education Seen as Student-Achievement Tool," *Education Week* (February 27, 2013).

4. Personal communication from Christine Erland, Director, School Programs, Core Knowledge Foundation.

5. For more information on establishing progressive-oriented classroom, consult the work of Walter Parker of the University of Washington and Diana Hess of the University of Wisconsin. Key books for each are W. Parker, "Feel Free to Change Your Mind. A Response to 'The Potential for Deliberative Democratic Civic Education,'" *Democracy and Education*, 19, no. 2 (2011): Article 9; and Diana Hess, *Controversy in the Classroom: The Democratic Power of Discussion* (Oxford, UK: Routledge, 2009).

6. See John R. Hollingsworth and Sylvia E. Ybarra, *Explicit Direct Instruction (EDI): The Power of the Well-Crafted, Well-Taught Lesson* (Corwin Press, 2017); S. Engelmann, W. C. Becker, D. Carnine, & R. Gersten, "The Direct Instruction Follow Through Model: Design and Outcomes," *Education and Treatment of Children* (1988), 303–317.

7. Bob Kizlik, "Assertive Discipline Information," June 28, 2007, www.adprima.com/assertive.htm.

8. North Central Regional Educational Laboratory, "Scaffolding," www.ncrel.org/sdrs/areas/issues/students/learning/lr1scaf.htm.

9. Parker J. Palmer, *The Courage to Teach: Exploring the Inner Landscape of a Teacher's Life* (San Francisco: Jossey-Bass, 1998).

10. Cited by David T. Hansen in a speech at Teachers College, Columbia University, Winter 2007, http://quicktime.tc.columbia.edu/users/dls2141/hansenOrig-0001.mp3.

11. David T. Hansen, *Ethical Visions of Education* (New York: Teachers College Press, 2007), Preface.

Chapter 10

1. Marvin Lazerson, "Access, Outcomes, and Educational Opportunity," *Education Week* (January 27, 1999), 46.

2. Willystine Goodsell, *Pioneers of Women's Education in the United States* (New York: AMS Press, 1970/1931), 5.

3. R. Freeman Butts and Lawrence A. Cremin, *A History of Education in American Culture* (New York: Holt, 1953), 245.

4. Ibid, 408.

5. John D. Pulliam, *History of Education in America*, 3rd ed. (Columbus, OH: Merrill, 1982), 157–159.

6. Butts and Cremin, *A History of Education in American Culture*, 260.

7. Merle Curti, *The Social Ideas of American Educators*, 2nd ed. (Totowa, NJ: Littlefield, Adams, 1959), 183.

8. Butts and Cremin, *A History of Education in American Culture*, 443.

9. Thomas D. Snyder, *120 Years of American Education: A Statistical Portrait* (Washington, DC: U.S. Department of Education, National Center for Education Statistics, 1993), 36–37; *Projections of Education Statistics to 2018* (Washington, DC: National Center for Education Statistics, 2010), Table 1, http://nces.ed.gov/programs/projections/projections2018/tables/table_01.asp?referrer=list.

10. William T. Gruhn and Harl R. Douglass, *The Modern Junior High School*, 3rd ed. (New York: Ronald Press, 1971), 46–53.

11. Jaana Juvonen, Vi-Nhuan Le, Tessa Kaganoff, Catherine Augustine, and Louay Constant, *Focus on the Wonder Years: Challenges Facing the American Middle School* (Santa Monica, CA: RAND Corporation, 2004), www.rand.org/pubs/monographs/2004/RAND_MG139.pdf.

12. Ibid.

13. National Catholic Educational Association, *United States Catholic Elementary and Secondary Schools 2012-2013: The Annual Statistical Report on Schools, Enrollment and Staffing*, http://www.ncea.org/data-information/catholic-school-data.

14. Stephen P. Broughman and Nancy L. Swain, *Characteristics of Private Schools in the United States: Results from the 2011–2012 Private School Universe Survey, First Look.* (Washington, DC: National Center for Education Statistics, July 2013), http://nces.ed.gov/pubs2013/2013316.pdf.

15. Ibid.

16. Herbert M. Kliebard, *Religion and Education in America: A Documentary History* (Scranton, PA: International Textbook, 1969), 119.

17. Religious Freedom, http://religiousfreedom.lib.virginia.edu.

18. Earle H. West, *The Black American and Education* (Columbus, OH: Merrill, 1972), 7–8.

19. Eric Lincoln and Milton Meltzer, *A Pictorial History of the Negro in America*, 3rd ed. (New York: Crown, 1968), 108–109.

20. *Historical Statistics of the United States, Colonial Times to 1970*, vol. I, Table Series H 433–441 (Washington, DC: U.S. Government Printing Office, 1975), 370.

21. Franklin Frazier, *The Negro in the United States*, rev. ed. (New York: Macmillan, 1957), 427, 432–436, 438.

22. Gary Orfield, Susan E. Eaton, and the Harvard Project on School Desegregation, *Dismantling Desegregation* (New York: New Press, 1996), 105–106; Jomills Henry Braddock II, Robert L. Crain, and James M. McPartland, "A Long-Term View of School Desegregation: Some Recent Studies of Graduates as Adults," *Phi Delta Kappan* 66 (December 1984): 259–264.

23. Anthony Lukas, *Common Ground* (New York: Knopf, 1985).

24. Howard Ozmon and Sam Craver, *Busing: A Moral Issue* (Bloomington, IN: Phi Delta Kappa Educational Foundation, 1972), 33–34.

25. *Digest of Education Statistics 2011*, Table 95 (Washington, DC: National Center for Education Statistics, 2012), http://nces.ed.gov/programs/digest/d11/tables/dt11_095.asp.

26. Gary Orfield, John Kucsera, Genevieve Siegel-Hawley, *E Pluribus . . . Separation: Deepening Double Segregation for More Students*, a report of the Civil Rights Project, September 19, 2012, http://civilrightsproject.ucla.edu/research/k-12-education/integration-and-diversity/mlk-national/e-pluribus...separation-deepening-double-segregation-for-more-students.

27. Richard M. Merelman, "Disintegrating American Public Schools," *Education Week* (February 6, 2002): 37.

28. R. Freeman Butts, *The Education of the West: A Formative Chapter in the History of Civilization* (New York: McGraw-Hill, 1973), 279.

29. Bureau of Indian Education, www.bie.edu/Schools/index.htm.

30. *Status and Trends in the Education of American Indians and Alaskan Natives: 2008* (Washington, DC: NCES, 2008), http://nces.ed.gov/pubs2008/nativetrends/index.asp.

31. Susan Aud, Mary Ann Fox, and Angelina KewalRamani, *Status and Trends in the Education of Racial and Ethnic Groups* (Washington, DC: NCES, 2010), 46, http://nces.ed.gov/pubsearch/pubsinfo.asp?pubid=2010015.

32. American Patrol Report, "Plyler vs. Doe, 1982: A Summary," http://www.americanpatrol.com/REFERENCE/PlylerVDoeSummary.html.

33. Aud, Fox, and KewalRamani, *Status and Trends in the Education of Racial and Ethnic*, 140.

34. Ibid.

35. "Asians Fastest-Growing Ethnic Group in 2012, Census Bureau Reports," U.S. Census Bureau Reports, June 13, 2013, http://www.census.gov/newsroom/releases/archives/population/cb13-112.html.

36. "Asian American/Pacific Islander Profile," The Office of Minority Health, U.S. Department of Health and Human Services, September 17, 2012, http://minorityhealth.hhs.gov/templates/content.aspx?ID=3005.

Chapter 11

1. *Today's School Boards & Their Priorities for Tomorrow*, (Alexandria, VA; National School Boards Association and K12 Insight, 2018), https://www.nsba.org/-/media/NSBA/File/nsba-todays-school-boards-and-their-priorities-for-tomorrow-2018-survey.pdf?la=en&hash=EB89E228906C828B7879BEF38AF77697B9126B09.

2. Larry Cuban, "Conflict and Leadership in the Superintendency," *Phi Delta Kappan* 67 (September 1985), 8. See also Arthur Blumberg with Phyllis Blumberg, *The School Superintendent: Living with Conflict* (New York: Teachers College Press, 1985), 32; and Susan Moore Johnson, *Leading to Change: The Challenge of the New Superintendency* (San Francisco: Jossey-Bass, 1996), 77–78.

3. *The State of the American School Superintendency: A Mid-Decade Study* (Alexandria, VA: American Association of School Administrators, 2007).

4. *The MetLife Survey of the American Teacher: Challenges for School Leadership*, February 2013, 12, https://www.metlife.com/assets/cao/foundation/MetLife-Teacher-Survey-2012.pdf.

5. Anup Shah, "Children as Consumers," in Global Issues, http://www.globalissues.org/article/237/children-as-consumers.

6. "Trump Seeks to Slash Education Budget, Combine 29 Programs Into Block Grants," *Education Week* (March 18, 2020), p. 1.

7. *Rankings and Estimates: Estimates of School Statistics 2019–2020* (Washington, DC: National Education Association, 2020), 9.

8. Ibid., 53.

9. Ibid., 57.

10. Rob Greenwald, Larry V. Hedges, and Richard D. Laine, "The Effect of School Resources on Student Achievement," *Review of Education Research* (Fall 1996): 361–396; Eric A. Hanushek, "Spending on Schools," in Terry Moe, ed., *A Primer on American Education* (Palo Alto, CA: Hoover Press, 2001), 69–88.

11. Deborah A. Verstegen, "Financing the New Adequacy: Towards New Models of State Education Finance Systems That Support Standards Based Reform," *Journal of Education Finance* 27 (Winter 2002): 749–782.

12. U.S. Department of Education, "Improving Basic Programs Operated by Local Education Agencies (Title 1, Part A)," https://www2.ed.gov/programs/titleiparta/index.html.

13. U.S. Department of Health and Human Services, Administration for Children and Families, Early Childhood Learning and Knowledge Center, "Head Start Program Facts: Fiscal Year 2018," https://eclkc.ohs.acf.hhs.gov/sites/default/files/pdf/no-search/hs-program-fact-sheet-2018.pdf.

14. "Children and Family Outcomes During the Head Start Year: FACES 2014–2015 Data Tables and Study Design," *OPRE Report 2017-100* (December 2017), https://www.acf.hhs.gov/sites/default/files/opre/faces_2014_2015_spring_child_family_data_tables_final_clean_toacf.pdf.

15. Linda Jacobson, "Research Offers Competing Data on Effectiveness," *Education Week* (April 25, 2007): 30.

16. Social Programs That Work Review, "Evidence Summary for the Preschool Perry Project" (November 2017), https://evidencebasedprograms.org/document/perry-preschool-project-evidence-summary/.

17. *National Assessment of Title I, Final Report, Executive Summary* (Washington, DC: National Center for Education Evaluation and Regional Assistance, 2007).

Chapter 12

1. Goals 2000: Educate America Act (March 31, 1994); *The National Education Goals* (Washington, DC: U.S. Department of Education, 1994).

2. No Child Left Behind, *Education Week*, September 19, 2011, http://www.edweek.org/ew/issues/no-child-left-behind/.

3. "States Granted Waivers from No Child Left Behind Allowed to Reapply for Renewal for 2014 and 2015 School Years," press release by U.S. Department of Education, August 29, 2013, http://www.ed.gov/news/press-releases/states-granted-waivers-no-child-left-behind-allowed-reapply-renewal-2014-and-201.

4. The Every Student Succeeds Act—Report (Washington, DC: U.S. Department of Education, 2016), https://www.ed.gov/essa?src=rn.

5. *Race to the Top Executive Summary*, http://www2.ed.gov/programs/racetothetop/executive-summary.pdf.

6. Valerie Strauss, "Report: Race to the Top Isn't Delivering Big Results," *The Washington Post*, September 12, 2013, http://www.washingtonpost.com/blogs/answer-sheet/wp/2013/09/12/report-race-to-the-top-isnt-delivering-big-results/.

7. See http://www.corestandards.org/standards-in-your-state/.

8. E. D. Hirsch, Jr., as quoted by Sara Mosle, *The New York Times Book Review*, September 29, 1996, p. 15.

9. Achieve, "ADP Network," http://www.achieve.org/adp-network.

10. *The Nation's Report Card, High School Transcript Study*, 2009, http://nationsreportcard.gov/hsts_2009/course_credits.aspx?tab_id=tab3&subtab_id=Tab_1#chart.

11. Marga Mikulecky, *School Calendar, Length of School Year* (Denver, CO: Education Commission of the States, 2013), http://www.ecs.org/clearinghouse/01/06/68/10668.pdf.

12. StatisticBrain, "Year-Round School Statistics," April 28, 2013, http://www.statisticbrain.com/year-round-school-statistics/; see also https://www.ace.edu/blog/post/2019/07/17/the-pros-cons-of-year-round-school.

13. McClatchyDC, "Obama Urges Longer School Hours, Extended School Year," March 10, 2009, http://www.mcclatchydc.com/2009/03/10/63663/obama-urges-longer-school-hours.html.

14. National Education Association, http://www.nea.org/home/2017-2018-average-starting-teacher-salary.html.

15. Center for Teacher Quality, "Performance-Pay for Teachers: Designing a System that Students Deserve," http://www.policyarchive.org/handle/10207/96445.

16. Melanie Moran, "Teacher Performance Pay Alone Does Not Raise Student Test Scores," *Vanderbilt News*, http://news.vanderbilt.edu/2010/09/teacher-performance-pay/.

17. See https://nces.ed.gov/programs/digest/d17/tables/dt17_216.20.asp?current=yes.

18. The National Center for Education Evaluation and Regional Assistance, see https://ies.ed.gov/ncee/pubs/20104029/pdf/20104029.pdf.

19. KIPP, "KIPP Schools," http://www.kipp.org/schools; see also https://ies.ed.gov/ncee/wwc/Docs/InterventionReports/wwc_kipp_012318.pdf.

20. Ibid

21. See https://www.ncsl.org/documents/educ/CharterSchoolStudentAchievement.pdf.

22. National Conference of State Legislatures, "School Vouchers," http://www.ncsl.org/research/education/school-choice-vouchers.aspx.

23. See https://www.greatschools.org/gk/articles/school-vouchers/.

24. See https://www.ncsl.org/research/education/school-choice-vouchers.aspx#What%20the%20research%20Says.

25. See https://www.greatschools.org/gk/articles/school-vouchers/.

26. T. Rees Shapiro, "Countering America's School-Reform Drive," a review of *Reign of Error: The Hoax of the Privatization Movement and the Danger to America's Public Schools*, by Diane Ravitch, *The Washington Post*, October 20, 2013, p. B6.

27. There are several good websites dealing with constructivism in education. Among them are Funderstanding (available at http://www.funderstanding.com/?s=constructivism) and Concept to Classroom (available at www.thirteen.org/edonline/concept2class/constructivism/index.html). For a critical perspective, see A. MacKinnon and C. Scarff-Seatter, "Constructivism: Contradictions and Confusion in Teacher Education," in V. Richardson, ed., *Constructivist Teacher Education: Building New Understandings* (Washington, DC: Falmer Press, 1997).

28. Anthony Bryk and Yeow Meng Thum, "The Effects of High School Organization on Dropping Out," unpublished paper (University of Chicago, 1988), 54–68. See also Anthony Bryk and Mary Erina Driscoll, "An Empirical Investigation of a School as a Community," unpublished paper (University of Chicago, 1988), 54–63.

29. Thomas Toch, "Small Is Still Beautiful," *Washington Monthly*, July/August 2010.

30. Kevin Ryan and Karen Bohlin, *Building Character in Schools: Practical Ways to Bring Moral Instruction to Life* (Jossey Bass, 1999), 5.

31. Ibid, 14–17.

32. William Damon, quoted by Amitai Etzione, *The Spirit of Community* (New York: Crown, 1993), 100–191.

33. J. S. Benniga, M. W. Berkowitz, P. Kuehn, and K. Smith, "The Relationship between Character Education and Academic Achievement in Elementary Schools," *Journal of Research on Character Education* 1, no. 1 (March 2003): 17–30.

34. Environmental Protection Agency, "Service-Learning: Learning by Doing," http://www.epa.gov/osw/education/pdfs/svclearn.pdf.

35. Molly Ryan, *Service-Learning After Learn and Serve America: How Five States Are Moving Forward* (Denver, CO; Education Commission of the States, June 2012), http://www.nylc.org/sites/nylc.org/files/09-ECS%20NCLC%20Report%20-%20Service-Learning%20After%20LSA.pdf.

Chapter 13

1. *Occupational Outlook Handbook, 2018–2019 Edition* (Washington, DC: Department of Labor, 2019), www.bls.gov/oco/.

2. William J. Hussar and Tabitha M. Bailey, *Projections of Education Statistics to 2027* (Washington, DC: National Center for Education Statistics, 2019), Table 2, https://nces.ed.gov/pubs2019/2019001.pdf.

3. Grace Chen, "Public School vs. Private School," *Public School Review*, April 5, 2019, https://www.publicschoolreview.com/blog/public-school-vs-private-school.

4. Erling E. Boe, Lynne H. Cook, and Robert J. Sunderland, "Teacher Turnover: Examining Exit Attrition, Teaching Area Transfer, and School Migration," *Exceptional Children*, 75, no. 1 (September 2008): 7–31; and C. Emily Feistritzer, *The Context of Teaching in the U.S.*, www.teach-now.org.

5. "Characteristics of Public School Teachers," *The Condition of Education* (Washington, D.C.: National Center for Education Statistics, 2019), https://nces.ed.gov/programs/coe/indicator_clr.asp.

6. Ibid.

7. Thomas G. Carroll and Elizabeth Foster, *Who Will Teach? Experience Matters,* (Washington, DC: National Commission on Teaching and America's Future, 2010), 3–4.

8. *Characteristics of Public and Private Elementary and Secondary School Teachers in the United States,* Table 2.

9. Desiree Carver-Thomas and Linda Darling-Hammond, *Teacher Turnover: Why It Matters and What We Can Do About It* (Palo Alto, CA: Learning Policy Institute, 2017), https://learningpolicyinstitute.org/product/teacher-turnover.

10. C. Emily Feistritzer, "The Impact of Alternative Routes," *Education Week* (November 19, 2009): 26, 32.

11. Maya Riser-Kositsky, "Education Statistics: Facts About American Schools," *Education* Week, December 31, 2019.

12. *Department of Defense Education Activity*, https://www.dodea.edu/.

13. Stephen P. Broughman, Brian Kincel, and Jennifer Peterson, *Characteristics of Private Schools in the United States: Results from the 2017–2018 Private School Universe Survey: First Look* (Washington, DC: National Center for Education Statistics, 2019), https://nces.ed.gov/pubs2019/2019071.pdf.

14. *Projections of Education Statistics to 2027*, Table 8, p. 50, http://nces.ed.gov/programs/projections/projections2021/tables/table_16.asp.

15. Council for American Private Education, "Why Teach in a Private School?" www.capenet.org/teach.html.

16. *Rankings and Estimates* (Washington, DC: National Education Association, 2020), 47.

17. National Education Association, (2018–2019) National Average Starting Teacher Salaries by State, https://www.nea.org/your-rights-workplace/fair-pay-benefits/professional-pay.

18. Most of the ideas in this section are taken from John William Zehring, "How to Get Another Teaching Job and What to Do If you Can't," *Learning*, 6 (February 1978): 44, 46–51.

19. "Characteristics of Public School Teachers Who Completed Alternative Routes to Certification Programs," *Condition of Education* (2019), https://nces.ed.gov/programs/coe/indicator_tlc.asp.

20. Sung Tae Jung and Aaron S. Horn, "The Relative Effectiveness of Traditional and Alternative Teacher Preparation Programs: A Review of Recent Research," *MHEC Research Brief* (March 2017), https://www.mhec.org/sites/default/files/resources/teacherprep2_20170301_1.pdf.

21. "Characteristics of Public School Teachers…" (2019).

22. C. Emily Feistritzer, *The Context of Teaching in the U.S.*, www.teach-now.org.

23. Bureau of Labor Statistics, *Occupational Outlook Handbook, 2018–19 Edition, Recreation Workers* (Washington, DC: U.S. Department of Labor, 2019), http://www.bls.gov/ooh/personal-care-and-service/recreation-workers.htm.

Chapter 14

1. Emma García and Elaine Weiss, *The Teacher Shortage Is Real, Large and Growing, and Worse Than We Thought: The First Report in "The Perfect Storm in the Teacher Labor Market" Series* (Economic Policy Institute, 2019), https://www.epi.org/publication/the-teacher-shortage-is-real-large-and-growing-and-worse-than-we-thought-the-first-report-in-the-perfect-storm-in-the-teacher-labor-market-series/.

2. John Macionis and Linda Gerber, "Chapter 3: Culture," *Sociology*, 7th ed. (Toronto, ON: Pearson Canada Inc., 2010), 54.

3. The MetLife Foundation, "The MetLife Survey of the American Teacher: Challenges for School Leadership," 2012, www.metlife.com/assets/cao/foundation/MetLife-Teacher-Survey-2012.pdf.

4. S. M. Kardos, S. M. Johnson, H. G. Peske, D. Kauffman, and E. Liu, E, "Counting on Colleagues: New Teachers Encounter the Professional Cultures of Their Schools," *Educational Administration Quarterly* 37, no. 2 (2001): 250–290.

5. T. M. Smith and R. M. Ingalsoll, "What Are the Effects of Induction and Mentoring Programs on Beginning Teacher Turnover?" *American Educational Research Journal* 41, no. 3 (2004): 682.

6. R. Fessler, "Dynamics of Teacher Career Stages," in *Professional Development in Education: New Paradigms and Practices*, T. Guskey and M. Huberman, eds. (New York: Teachers College Press, 1995).

7. Gary Cornog, "To Care or Not to Care," in *Don't Smile until Christmas: Accounts of the First Year of Teaching*, Kevin Ryan, ed. (Chicago: University of Chicago Press, 1970), 18–19. Copyright © 1970. Reprinted by permission of Kevin Ryan.

8. National Commission on Teaching and America's Future, "No Dream Denied: A Pledge to the American Children," www.NCTAF.org.

9. Y. Gold, "Beginning Teacher Support," in *Handbook of Research in Teacher Education*, 2nd ed., J. Sikula, T. Buttery, and E. Guyton, eds. (New York: MacMillan, 1999), 458–594.

10. Jonah Rockoff, "Does Mentoring Reduce Turnover and Improve Skills of New Employees? Evidence from Teachers in New York City" (New York: Columbia Business School, February 2008), http://www0.gsb.columbia.edu/faculty/jrockoff/rockoff_mentoring_february_08.pdf.

11. Educational Commission of the States, http://ecs.force.com/mbdata/MBQuest2rtanw?Rep=TRR1916.

Chapter 15

1. Myron Lieberman, *Education as a Profession* (Englewood Cliffs, NJ: Prentice Hall, 1956).

2. Canan Tasci, "Teachers Still Spending Their Own Money on Classroom Supplies," *Redlands Daily Facts* September 20, 2010; and Madeline Will, "The Average Teacher Spends $479 a Year on Classroom Supplies, National Data Show," *Education Week* 2018, https://www.edweek.org/ew/articles/2018/05/15/the-average-teacher-spends-479-a-year.html.

3. Walter Boggs, quoted at 1963–1964 Convention of the National Commission on Teacher Education, by Myron Brenton, "What's Happened to Teachers?" (New York: Coward-McCann, 1970), p. 242.

4. D. Tanner and L. N. Tanner, *Curriculum Development: Theory into Practice*, 3rd ed. (New York: Macmillan, 1995).

5. See https://www.nbpts.org.

6. Based on recent figures extrapolated from data reported by the NBPTS, *55,000 Reasons to Believe* (Arlington, VA: Author, 2007), 4.

7. Ibid., 3.

8. See. https://www.nbpts.org/wp-content/uploads/state_incentive_chart.pdf.

9. Ibid; Personal communication from Patrick Ledesma of the National Board for Professional Teaching Standards, Arlington, VA, July 23, 2013.

10. National Board for Professional Teaching Standards, "edTPA Partners to Join National Board Effort to Improve Teacher Training in Math and Science," Arlington, VA, November 16, 2012.

11. Chester Finn and Danielle Wilcox, "Board Games: Failure of the National Board for Professional Teaching Standards to Accomplish Objective of Improving Quality of Teaching in the US; Business Backs a Losing Educational Strategy," *National Review*, August 9, 1999; and Frederick M. Hess, *Common Sense School Reform* (New York: Palgrave Macmillan, 2004).

12. National Board for Professional Teaching Standards, "New Report Affirms Positive Impact on Student Achievement and Learning," June 11, 2008, www.nbpts.org/about_us/news_media/press_releases?ID=422.

13. Telephone conversation with staff of the Council of Chief State School Officers.

14. American Federation of Teachers, www.nea.org and www.aft.org.

15. Whitney Tilson, quoted in Diana Goldstein's *The Education Wars. The American Prospect,* March 20, 2009, http://spectator.org/search?search_api_views_fulltext=March+20%2C+2009.

16. Teacher Freedom Organization, "One Year After Janus, What Do Teachers Think?" https://teacherfreedom.org/janus-anniversary-teacher-poll/.

17. National Education Association website, https://www.nea.org./home/2580.htm?cpssessionid=SID-71221E18-E21C391E.

18. NEA Handbook: Program and Administration, www.nea.org.

19. See www.nea.org/home/12584.htm.

20. "Charter Schools," National Education Association website, www.nea.org/home/16332.htm.

21. Steven Chaufmann, "The NEA Seizes Power: The Teachers' Coup," *The New Republic* October 11, 1980, pp. 9–11.

22. Personal communications from Alexandra Freeze, Director of Communications & Advocacy for the Association of American Educators, July 15, 2013.

23. OpenSecrets, Center for Responsive Politics, National Education Association, https://www.opensecrets.org/orgs//summary?id=d000000064.

24. John Berthoud, "NEA: 30 Years of Lobbying Democrats," *Human Events Magazine* January 23, 2006; Charlie Butts, "Pro-life Teachers Protest Pro-Abortion Leaders at NEA Convention," One New Now, July 2, 2013.

25. The 2017 study by Education Week's Research Center, https://www.edweek.org/media/educator-political-perceptions-education-week-12-12-2017.pdf.

26. See https://www.aft.org/about.

27. UnionFacts.com, http://www.unionfacts.com/union/American_Federation_of_Teachers.

28. Alexandra Freeze, Director of Communications & Advocacy, Association of American Educators, 115 S. Union Street, Suite 250, Alexandria, VA.

29. National Education Association, www.nea.org/sudentprogram.

30. Anthony Rebora, "Report: U.S. Lagging in Teacher Learning," *Education Week*, March 16, 2009, www.edweek.org/tsb/articles/2009/03/16/02nsdc.h02.html.

31. Ibid.

32. Carrie R. Leana, "The Missing Link in School Reform," *Stanford Social Innovation* Fall 2011, http://www.ssireview.org/articles/entry/the_missing_link_in_school_reform/.

33. "Double Take: Research Alert," *Educational Leadership*, vol. 68, no. 4 (December 2010), p. 8.

34. Richard DuFour, "What Is a Professional Learning Community?" *Educational Leadership*, May 2004.

35. Quoted by Mark Edwards in "Turbo-Charging Professional Development," *The School Administrator*, December 9, 1998, p. 36.

36. Beth Hurst, Kathleen B. Scales, and Kala Lewis, "Happy Teachers: Resolve to Find Joy," *School and Community* (Winter, 2013): 24.

1890 institutions Colleges and universities created for African Americans as a result of the second Morrill Act passed by Congress in 1890.

academic engaged time The time a student spends on academically relevant activities or materials while experiencing a high rate of success.

academic freedom The freedom of teachers to teach about an issue or to use a source in teaching without fear of penalty, reprisal, or harassment.

academy A type of secondary school during the early national period that tried to combine the best of the Latin and English grammar schools. During the nineteenth century, it took on a college preparation orientation.

acceleration A method of teaching gifted and talented students in which they do the same work as other students but at a faster pace.

acceptable use policy A statement of rules governing student use of school computers, especially regarding access to the Internet.

active learning Learning in which the student takes control of or is positively involved in the process of his or her education; strongly associated with constructivism.

aesthetics A branch of philosophy that examines the perception of beauty and distinguishes beauty from that which is moral or useful.

alternative licensure A procedure offered by many states to license teachers who have not graduated from a state-approved teacher education program.

American Federation of Teachers (AFT) The nation's second largest teachers' association or union. Founded in 1916, it is affiliated with the AFL-CIO, the nation's largest union.

American Recovery and Reinvestment Act A 2009 act of Congress designed to create jobs, spur economic activity, and foster accountability and transparency in government spending.

app An abbreviation for an application that runs on mobile devices such as tablets or cell phones.

assimilation The absorption of an individual or a group into the cultural tradition of a population or another group.

assistive technology The array of devices and services that help people with disabilities to perform better in their daily lives. Such devices include motorized chairs, remote control units that turn appliances on and off, computers, and speech synthesizers.

Association of American Educators (AEE) Established in 1994, the Association of American Educators is the nation's largest nonunion professional organization of teachers.

at-risk students See *students at risk*.

authentic (performance) assessment A recent trend in student evaluation that attempts to measure real student performance on significant tasks; the focus is on what we want the student to be able to do. Also called *performance assessment*.

axiology The philosophical study of values, especially how they are formed ethically, aesthetically, and religiously.

behaviorism A psychological theory asserting that all behavior is shaped by environmental events or conditions.

bilingual education A variety of approaches to educating students who speak a primary language other than English.

blog (web log) A website that the user updates frequently. Most are used like a journal or as a place to share personal opinions and information.

breach of contract A failure to fulfill the requirements of a legal agreement.

Brown* v. *Board of Education of Topeka U.S. Supreme Court ruling in 1954 holding that segregated schools are inherently unequal.

Buckley Amendment Shorthand name for the Family Educational Rights and Privacy Act, which outlines who may and may not have access to a student's records.

call to excellence An educational slogan pointing students to high standards.

career ladder A series of steps in an occupation. Usually the higher steps ("rungs" on the ladder) bring new tasks, more responsibility, increased status, and enhanced rewards.

categorical grants Federal aid to education that must be spent for purposes that are specified in the legislation and by the federal agency administering the funds.

certification Recognition by a profession that one of its practitioners has met certain standards. Often used as a synonym for *licensure,* which is governmental approval to perform certain work, such as teaching.

character education Efforts by the home, the school, the religious community, and individual students to help students know the good, love the good, and do the good and, in the process, to forge good qualities such as courage, respect, and responsibility.

charter schools Public schools in which the educators, often joined by members of the local community, have made a special contract, or charter, with the chartering agency. Usually the charter allows the school a great deal of independence in its operation.

chief state school officer The executive officer of a state's board of education who is usually responsible for the administration of that state's public education. This person is also the head of that state's department of education. Also called *superintendent of education, commissioner of education,* and *superintendent of public instruction.*

civic learning (civic education) A part of social studies that emphasizes preparing students to be good citizens by becoming aware of our common heritage and engaging issues related to character and values. Students learn to apply principles of democracy to everyday concerns they will face and/or already face as citizens.

classroom management The set of teacher behaviors that create and maintain conditions in the classroom, thus permitting instruction to take place efficiently and effectively.

cognitive tools Computer applications that are used to engage and enhance thinking.

Common Core State Standards An initiative that lays out learning standards in mathematics and English language arts, and which will develop assessments to measure student achievement of the standards. As of 2019, 35 states have adopted these standards.

common schools Public elementary schools that are open to children of all classes. During the nineteenth century, the common school became the embodiment of universal education.

compensatory education Educational support to provide a more equal opportunity for disadvantaged students through activities such as remedial instruction and early learning.

comprehensive high school The most common form of high school in the United States, designed to offer a range of preparation programs, including college preparation and vocational education.

computing An approach to the use of technology where each student has access to a mobile computing device to use inside the classroom, in the field, and at home.

constructivism A theory, based on research from cognitive psychology, that people learn by constructing their own knowledge through an active learning process rather than by simply absorbing knowledge directly from some other source.

content standards Statements of the subject-specific knowledge and skills that schools are expected to teach and students are expected to learn.

continuing contract An agreement between a school district and a teacher outlining the conditions and terms of work.

contract A binding agreement between two or more parties.

cooperative learning An instructional approach in which students work together in groups to achieve learning goals. A variety of cooperative learning strategies exist.

core curriculum A common course of study for all students, often called for by essentialist reforms in the 1980s.

core knowledge See *cultural literacy*.

credential file A file established by college students—typically with the school's career planning and placement office—that contains materials important for securing a teaching job, for example, letters of recommendation, a transcript, and a résumé.

critical thinking The intent to help students evaluate the worth of ideas, opinions, or evidence before making a decision or judgment.

cultural literacy Being aware of the central ideas, stories, scientific knowledge, events, and personalities of a culture; also known as *core knowledge*.

cultural pluralism An approach to diversity of individuals that calls for understanding and appreciating cultural differences.

culturally responsive teaching A method of embracing students' cultural backgrounds by modifying classroom conditions or activities to include elements that relate to the students' culture.

culture A group that shares beliefs about what is right and wrong, and what is good and bad; it also includes the dominant ideas, stories and myths, artistic works, social habits, organizations, and language of the group.

culture shock The feeling of disorientation experienced by individuals when initially immersed in a society with different values, customs, and mores.

curriculum All the organized and intended experiences of the student for which the school accepts responsibility.

cyberbullying Bullying through information and communication technologies, such as mobile phone text messages, e-mail messages, Internet chat rooms, and social networking websites such as MySpace, Facebook, and Bebo.

dame school A school run by a housewife during early colonial days.

deductive reasoning A type of reasoning from the general to the particular, reasoning in which the conclusion follows from the premise stated.

de facto school segregation Segregation in the schools resulting primarily from residential patterns.

de jure school segregation Segregation in the schools that occurs by law.

democratic reconstructionists Subscribers to an educational perspective that focuses on developing students who are prepared to make positive changes in a democracy.

differentiated instruction A variety of techniques used to adapt instruction to the individual ability levels and learning styles of each student in the classroom.

digital storytelling An instructional approach in which students use images, often digital photos, accompanied by their own written and recorded narrative to create a story that is stored digitally.

district school The type of school that succeeded the town school and moving school in New England. A township was divided into districts, each with its own school, its own schoolmaster, and funding from the town treasury.

drill-and-practice In educational technology, software programs that give students a series of tasks to reinforce a concept or to initially diagnose a student's level. These programs monitor progress, provide feedback, and present tasks accordingly.

due process The deliberative process that protects a person's constitutional right to receive fair and equal protection under the law.

economic reconstructionists Subscribers to an educational perspective or motivation that focuses on developing students who take a critical stance toward the dominant social and economic status quo.

edTPA portfolio A standards-based assessment to measure a teacher's knowledge and skills. Many states and teacher education programs require prospective teachers to take the assessment to become licensed.

education The process by which humans develop their minds, their skills, and their character. It is a lifelong process marked by continual development and change.

effective schools Schools that provide a significantly better education (usually measured by student test scores) for a much larger percentage of their students than do other schools serving similar student populations.

Elementary and Secondary Education Act (ESEA) The federal government's single largest investment in elementary and secondary education, including Title I. Originally passed in 1965 and periodically reauthorized by Congress, most recently in 2015 as the Every Student Succeeds Act.

English grammar school A form of secondary education in the latter half of the colonial period that provided a practical alternative education for students who were not interested in college.

English language learners (ELLs) Students whose native language is not English.

enrichment A method of teaching gifted and talented students in which they are allowed or assigned to do additional work to make regular class assignments more challenging or meaningful to them.

epistemology A branch of philosophy that examines the nature of knowledge, its origins, its foundations, its limits, and its validity.

equality of educational opportunity A concept that students from less advantaged backgrounds should have equal opportunities to experience success in school. Disagreement exists on whether this implies simply providing equal resources or ensuring equal success compared to more privileged students.

essentialism An educational philosophy that emphasizes a core body of knowledge and skills necessary for effective participation in society. Proponents believe that an educated person must have this core of knowledge and skills, and that all children should be taught it.

ethics A branch of philosophy that examines the right and wrong of human conduct. The term can also refer to a particular moral code or system.

Every Student Succeeds Act See *Elementary and Secondary Education Act (ESEA)*.

extrinsic rewards Rewards to an individual that are external to the activity itself, such as grades, gold stars, and prizes.

fair use A legal principle defining specific, limited ways in which copyrighted material can be used without permission from the author.

flipped classroom The flipped classroom inverts traditional teaching methods, delivering online instruction outside the class and moving homework into the classroom.

for-profit schools Financially driven businesses that typically contract with a community or school district to provide educational services.

generational poverty Families living in poverty for two generations or longer.

grievance A formal complaint about working conditions. Procedures for filing grievances are often part of teachers' employment contracts.

Head Start A federally funded compensatory education program, in existence since the mid-1960s, that provides additional educational services to young children suffering the effects of poverty.

human capital The stock of valuable knowledge, abilities, and other things possessed by an individual.

inclusion The commitment to educate each child, to the maximum extent appropriate, in the regular school and classroom rather than moving children with disabilities to separate classes or institutions.

individualized education program (IEP) A management tool required for every student covered by the provisions of the Individuals with Disabilities Education Act. It must indicate a student's current level of performance, short- and long-term instructional objectives, services to be provided, and criteria and schedules for evaluation of progress.

individualized family services plan (IFSP) Similar to an individualized education program for school-age children, the IFSP specifies the services to be provided to children with developmental delays from birth through age 2. The IFSP is authorized by PL 99–457, the Education of the Handicapped Act Amendments.

inductive reasoning A type of reasoning, from the particular to the general, in which one can make a general conclusion based on a number of facts.

in loco parentis The responsibility of the teacher to function "in the place of the parent" when a student is in school.

in-service program The efforts by a school or school district to improve the professional skills and competencies of its professional staff. Also called *professional development* or *staff development*.

integrated curriculum See *interdisciplinary curriculum*.

intellectual capital Another term for knowledge.

intellectual property A product of the intellect that has commercial value, including copyrighted property such as literary or artistic works, and ideational property, such as patents, appellations of origin, business methods, and industrial processes.

intelligent design theory A theory about the origins of life that suggests that the complexity of life is too great to be accounted for by standard evolutionary theories and that "an intelligence" either created or somehow guided its development.

interdisciplinary curriculum A curriculum that integrates the subject matter from two or more disciplines, such as English and history, often using themes such as inventions, discoveries, or health as overlays to the study of the different subjects. Also known as *integrated curriculum*.

intrinsic rewards Rewards to an individual that come from within, such as personal satisfaction or happiness.

junior high school A separate kind of school created typically for grades 7, 8, and 9. The first junior highs were founded in 1909–1910. In recent years, they have been gradually replaced by middle schools.

Kalamazoo case The 1874 U.S. Supreme Court decision (*Stuart and Others v. School District No. 1 of the Village of Kalamazoo and Others*) that upheld the right of states to tax citizens to create public high schools.

kindergarten A division of school for children below the first grade, usually for children between ages 4 and 6; the concept, which means "garden of children" was imported into the United States from Germany during the nineteenth century.

Latin grammar school First type of secondary school in the American colonies. Its main purpose was to prepare students for college.

law The system of rules that governs the general conduct of a particular community's citizens.

learning communities Organizations in which all members are engaged in continuous learning and improvement efforts.

learning organization An organization that systematically learns from its experience what works and what does not work, with the goal to increase innovation, effectiveness, and performance.

least restrictive environment (LRE) A requirement of the Education for All Handicapped Children Act that students with disabilities should participate in regular education programs to the greatest extent appropriate.

lesbian, gay, bisexual, transgendered, and queer (LGBTQ) An initialism intended to emphasize a diversity of sexuality-based and gender identity–based cultures.

liability A legal obligation.

licensure The approval given to an individual by a governmental agency, usually the state, to perform a particular work, such as teaching.

lifelong learners People who continue throughout their lives to learn new things after they leave school.

local school board The policymaking body of a school district; it represents the citizens of the district in setting up a school program, hiring school personnel, and generally determining local policy related to public education.

logic A branch of philosophy that involves the study of reasoning or of sound argument. In a more specific sense, logic is the study of deductive inference.

looping An educational practice of multiyear teaching in which a teacher follows students to the next grade level and stays with the group for several years.

magnet school An alternative school that provides instruction in specified areas such as the fine arts, for specific groups such as the gifted and talented, or for using specific teaching styles such as open classrooms. In many cases, magnet schools are established as a method of promoting voluntary desegregation in schools.

mainstreaming The practice of placing special education students in general education classes for at least part of the school day while also providing additional services, programs, or classes as needed.

McGuffey Readers A six-volume series of readers developed by William Holmes McGuffey that sold more than 100 million copies between 1836 and 1906. The readers served to create a common curriculum for many students.

mentor A person who gives both personal and professional guidance to a novice.

metaphysics A branch of philosophy devoted to exploring the nature of the existence of reality as a whole rather than to studying particular parts of reality as the natural sciences do. Metaphysicians try to answer questions about reality without referring to religion or revelation.

middle school A school that bridges the grades between elementary school and high school, usually grades 6 to 8. It differs from a junior high school because it is specifically designed for young adolescents, with a strong emphasis on personal growth and development, rather than mimicking the high school's emphasis on academics and sports, as junior high schools often did.

Morrill Act Federal legislation passed in 1862 that granted each state federal land to establish colleges for the study of agriculture and mechanical arts. A second Morrill Act, passed in 1890, provided similar federal support to create "separate but equal" colleges for African Americans.

moving school A school of the colonial period wherein a teacher moved from village to village, spending several months in each town.

multicultural curriculum Several approaches to multicultural curriculum exist, but in essence, it promotes an understanding of and appreciation for cultural pluralism. It attempts to address issues of social injustice related to racism, sexism, and economic inequality by reducing prejudice and fostering tolerance through the formal curriculum.

multicultural education An approach to education that recognizes cultural diversity and fosters cultural enrichment of all children and youth.

multiple intelligences A theory of intelligence put forth by Howard Gardner that identifies at least eight dimensions of intellectual capacities that people use to approach problems and create products.

National Board for Professional Teaching Standards (NBPTS) The professional agency that sets voluntary standards for what experienced teachers should know and be able to do in 25 different teaching areas.

National Education Association (NEA) The nation's largest teachers' association, founded in 1857 and having a membership of over 3 million educators.

National Education Goals (Goals 2000) Goals for U.S. education, established by the president and the 50 state governors and legislated by Congress, that were intended to be reached by the year 2000.

The New England Primer The basic text used in schools during the eighteenth century. It was an illustrated book composed of religious texts and other readings.

No Child Left Behind Act (NCLB) The name of the 2001 reauthorization of the Elementary and Secondary Education Act. It was replaced in 2015 by the Every Student Succeeds Act (ESSA).

Northwest Ordinances Passed by Congress in 1785 and 1787, these ordinances were concerned with the sale of public lands in the Northwest Territory (from present-day Ohio to Minnesota). Every township was divided into 36 sections, one of which was set aside for the maintenance of public schools. The 1787 ordinance reaffirmed that religion, morality, and knowledge were necessary to good government.

Old Deluder Satan Act A Massachusetts law passed in 1647 that strengthened an earlier law requiring parents to educate their children. It required every town of 50 or more families to pay a teacher to teach the children reading and writing so they could read the Bible and thwart Satan, who would assuredly try to keep people from understanding the scriptures.

parent–teacher organization (PTO) A local organization, usually centered around each school, that consists of both parents and teachers at that school. Its purpose is to serve as a communication mechanism between the school and the parents of the school's students.

pedagogical content knowledge Teachers' knowledge that bridges content knowledge and pedagogy with an understanding of how particular topics can best be presented for instruction, given the diverse interests and abilities of learners.

perennialism A particular view of philosophy that sees human nature as constant, with few changes over time. Perennialism in education promotes the advancement of the intellect as the central purpose of schools. The educational process stresses academic rigor and discipline.

performance pay (pay for performance) A financial reward given to teachers, based on the special quality of their work.

personal practical knowledge The set of understandings teachers have of the practical circumstances in which they work.

philosophy The love or search for wisdom; the quest for basic principles to understand the meaning of life. Western philosophy traditionally contains five branches of philosophy: metaphysics, ethics, aesthetics, epistemology, and logic.

phonics An approach to reading that teaches readers to decode words by sounding out letters and combinations of letters.

Plessy v. Ferguson A Supreme Court decision in 1896 that upheld the constitutionality of separate but equal accommodations for African Americans. The ruling was quickly applied to schools.

portfolio A collection of a person's work. For students, portfolios are used as a relatively new form of authentic assessment. They can contain a great range of work, from pencil-and-paper drawings to sculpture.

private venture school A type of school in the middle states during colonial times, licensed by the civil government but not protected or financed by it.

privatization A movement to contract with private organizations, often for profit, to operate particular public schools whose students have been performing poorly on academic tests, or to provide specific educational services to public schools. The Edison Schools and Sylvan Learning Centers are examples of such providers.

probationary period Time, often lasting three years, for the school district to ensure that a nontenured teacher can teach well enough to be granted permanent faculty status.

problem solving The process of either presenting students with a problem or helping them to identify a problem and then observing and helping them become aware of the conditions, procedures, or steps needed to solve the problem.

productivity tools Applications, such as word processors, email programs, and spreadsheets, that let people accomplish tasks more efficiently than if they had to use a typewriter, a calculator, or postal mail.

profession An occupation or occupational group that fulfills certain criteria. Among other things, it must require training and knowledge, perform a social service, have a code of ethics, and have a sense of autonomy and personal responsibility.

professional development The efforts by a school or school district to improve the professional skills and competencies of its professional staff. Also called *in-service training* in education, and *staff development*.

professional learning communities (PLCs) Teams of teachers and administrators in a particular school who form groups that work together to grow and improve as professionals.

Program for International Student Assessment (PISA) An international assessment of 15-year-old students in mathematics, science, and reading, administered every three years.

progressivism A form of educational philosophy that sees nature as ever-changing. Because the world is always changing and new situations require new solutions to problems, learners must develop as problem solvers.

project approach An instructional method through which students engage in an in-depth investigation of a real-world topic worthy of their attention and effort. The process often includes field trips or expert guests and a culminating event through which children present the results of their research.

project method A method of education in which students work in groups on a topic of interest to them. Developed by William Heard Kilpatrick, who believed that because students learn only what is of interest to them, they should be the ones to determine topics of study.

psychic reward Mental and spiritual benefits. Teaching has many.

public comprehensive high school The predominant form of secondary education in America in the twentieth century. It provides both preparation for college and a vocational education for students not going on to college.

real encounters Face-to-face experiences that are powerful sources of learning.

reduction in force (RIF) The elimination of teaching positions in a school system because of declining student population or funding.

reflection Conscious and analytical thought by an individual about what he or she is doing and how the action affects others.

reflective practitioner An individual who has established the habit of reviewing his or her performance to continually improve practice.

reflective teaching A teacher's habit of examining and evaluating his or her teaching on a regular basis.

relational trust A network of trust among people that is built on four factors: respect for the other, competence, personal regard for the other, and integrity.

resegregation Schools returning to a pattern of more racial segregation after a period of progress toward desegregation.

Response to Intervention (RTI) A method of academic intervention used in the United States that is designed to provide early, effective assistance to children who are having difficulty learning. RTI seeks to prevent academic failure through early intervention, frequent progress measurement, and increasingly intensive research-based instructional interventions for children who continue to have difficulty.

romanticism A child-centered philosophy of education that condemns the influences of society and suggests instead that a child's natural curiosity and the natural world should be used to teach.

rubric A scoring tool that lists the criteria for a piece of work or "what counts" toward a grade.

scaffolding Providing assistance—some structure, clues, help with remembering certain steps or procedures, or encouragement to try—when a learner is on the verge of solving a problem but cannot complete it independently.

school choice Allowing parents to select alternative educational programs for their children, either within a given school or among different schools.

school culture The prevailing mores, values, and rituals that permeate a school.

school vouchers See *voucher plans*.

schooling Formal instruction typically conducted in an institution, adhering to standardized practices.

schools-within-schools In large schools, the establishment of "houses" of teachers and 100 to 400 students.

self-fulfilling prophecy Students' behavior that comes about as a result of teachers' expectations that the students will behave in a certain way. Teachers expect students to behave in a certain way and communicate those expectations by both overt and subtle means, and students respond by behaving in the way expected.

sexual harassment Unwanted and unwelcome sexual attention that interferes with one's life.

simulation A technique for learning or practicing skills that involves dealing with a realistic but artificial problem or situation. Typically, it provides an opportunity for safe practice with feedback on performance.

site-based decision making A school reform effort to decentralize, allowing decisions to be made and budgets to be established at the school-building level, where most of the changes need to occur. Usually teachers become involved in the decision-making process. Also known as *site-based management, school-based management,* or *school-based decision making*.

social distance The psychological relationships between individuals, ranging from the formal to the familiar.

social media Media that features content created by nonprofessionals; examples include postings by bloggers and digital photos posted at online photo-sharing sites.

social reconstructionists Proponents of the theory of education that schools and teachers need to engage in the restructuring and reforming of society to eradicate its ills and shortcomings.

socialization The general process of social learning whereby children learn the many things they must know to become acceptable members of society.

society A grouping of individuals bound together by a variety of connections, such as shared geographic space, similar racial features, or a shared culture.

socioeconomic status (SES) A system for measuring the economic conditions of people using the family's occupational status, income, and educational attainment as measures of status.

special education Educational programming provided by schools to meet the needs of students with disabilities.

spreadsheet An interactive software program allowing users to perform multiple calculations and view more than one answer at a time.

state board of education The state's primary education policymaking body for elementary and secondary education.

state department of education The state bureaucracy, operating under the direction of the state board of education, whose responsibilities typically include administering and distributing state and federal funds, licensing teachers and other educational personnel, providing educational data and analyses, and approving college and university educational licensure programs.

STEM (science, technology, engineering, and mathematics) An acronym referring to educational programs in science, technology, engineering, and mathematics.

students at risk Students judged to be in serious jeopardy of not completing school or not succeeding in school.

subject-matter curriculum A curriculum that focuses on bodies of content or subject matter, usually the traditional subject disciplines.

superintendent of schools Typically, a professional educator selected by the local school board to act as its executive officer and as the educational leader and chief administrator of the local school district.

teacher competency testing Examinations given to teachers to assess their professional knowledge and skills.

teaching journal A professional record of reflections, instructional ideas, and observations by a teacher or future teacher.

teaching portfolio Collection of items such as research papers, pupil evaluations, teaching units, and video clips of lessons to reflect the quality of a teacher's teaching. Portfolios can be used to illustrate to employers the teacher's experience or to obtain national board certification.

tenure A legal right that confers permanent employment on teachers, protecting them from dismissal without adequate cause.

Title I The section of the 1965 Elementary and Secondary Education Act (now the ESSA) that delivers federal funds to local school districts and schools for the education of students from low-income families, and supplements the educational services provided to low-achieving students in those districts.

tools for learning Cognitive skills that make independent learning possible. They include advanced reading, remembering, recording, researching, test taking, analyzing, and creating.

town school A New England elementary school during the early colonial period, required in every town of 50 or more families.

tracking The homogeneous grouping of students for learning tasks on the basis of some measure(s) of their abilities.

Trends in International Mathematics and Science Study (TIMSS) An international assessment of 4th-, 8th-, and 12th-graders in mathematics and science.

tutorials A software application designed to provide initial instruction in a given topic, check for understanding throughout the process, and evaluate learners' grasp of the topic once the program is completed.

universal education Schooling for everyone.

vicarious experiences Learnings gained not through direct experiences, but through observations or readings.

virtual field trip Computer software that simulates the experience of an actual field trip with the use of digital images and multimedia tools.

virtual schools Institutions that offer classes for K–12 students in an online learning environment.

vocation A spiritual calling to do certain kinds of work. For many, teaching is more than a job; it's a vocation.

voucher plans A type of educational choice plan that gives parents a receipt or written statement that they can exchange for the schooling they believe is most desirable for their child. The school, in turn, can cash in the received vouchers for the money to pay teachers and buy resources. Also called *school vouchers*.

wait-time The time a teacher spends waiting for an answer after posing a question. Research indicates that good questioning practices involve giving students sufficient time to think about and respond to each question.

WebQuest An inquiry-based learning activity that directs learners in using information from the Web.

webs Graphical representations of a story or concept.

whole language approach A teaching approach emphasizing the integration of language arts skills and knowledge across the curriculum. It stresses the provision of a literate environment and functional uses of language.

wiki A website developed collaboratively by a community of users, allowing any user to add and edit content.

within-district choice Allows parents to choose from among the various public schools that a school district or state operates.

writing across the curriculum An instructional approach using writing as a tool for learning in all subject areas.

year-round education An educational reform, adopted in some states, where students go to school the same number of days as in traditional schools, but the school days are more evenly distributed throughout the school year.

zero-tolerance policies School policies calling for automatic suspension or expulsion of students who bring forbidden items, such as drugs or weapons, to school or who engage in undesired behavior.

zone of proximal development A range of tasks that a person cannot yet do alone but can accomplish with assistance. This zone is the point at which instruction can succeed and real learning is possible.

Index

Note: Page numbers followed by "f" and "t" represent figures and tables respectively.